A HISTORY OF AUSTRALIA

VOLUME III

Select Documents in Australian History, 1788–1850

Settlers and Convicts: or recollections of sixteen years' labour in the Australian backwoods by An Emigrant Mechanic

Select Documents in Australian History, 1851–1900

Sources of Australian History

Meeting Soviet Man

A History of Australia I: from the earliest times to the age of Macquarie

A History of Australia II: New South Wales and Van Diemen's Land 1822–1838

A Short History of Australia

Disquiet and Other Stories

TWO AUSTRALIANS

Charles Harpur

Portrait by an unknown artist, Mitchell Library, Sydney

Jackey Jackey

Drawing by Charles Rodius, Mitchell Library, Sydney

C. M. H. CLARK

A HISTORY OF AUSTRALIA

III

THE BEGINNING OF AN
AUSTRALIAN CIVILIZATION
1824-1851

MELBOURNE UNIVERSITY PRESS

First published 1973

Printed in Australia by
Wilke and Co. Ltd, Clayton, Victoria 3168, for
Melbourne University Press, Carlton, Victoria 3053
U.S.A. and Canada: ISBS Inc., Portland, Oregon 97208

Registered in Australia for transmission by post as a book

ISBN 0 522 84054 X
Dewey Decimal Classification Number 994

For
my two friends
Don Baker and David Campbell

The mighty Bush with iron rails
Is tethered to the world.

Henry Lawson, 'The Roaring Days'

. . . it's not only the things that we've inherited from our fathers and mothers that live on in us, but all sorts of old dead ideas and old dead beliefs . . . there must be ghosts all over the country—as countless as grains of sand. And we are, all of us, so pitifully afraid of the light.

Mrs Alving in H. Ibsen, Ghosts, Act 2

PREFACE

THIS VOLUME attempts to tell the story of how we began to acquire an identity and a conscience. It attempts to show how the experience of planting a civilization in a harsh and uncouth land caused men to doubt whether God or man ever could make their life different from the one they knew. It attempts to show how men who grew up in barbarism and solitude developed their own comforters of mateship and sardonic humour. It also tells how in the struggle over free institutions and the use of convicts, the bourgeoisie won a victory not only over squatterdom, but a victory for British philistines over bush barbarians, and a victory for the survival of the British connection and influence against those who wanted a republic for the people of Australia.

The material for this volume was collected in London, Edinburgh, Cambridge, Dublin, and in the public libraries of Australia. Perhaps I may be permitted to say that visits to the sites of where those 'ghosts' in our past first appeared were often more rewarding than anxious hours poring over books, newspapers, manuscripts and archival material. After the year 1842 the story of Australia is not presented as that of the history of four separate colonies, but of Australia as a whole. I can only hope that starting it so early has not unduly suppressed the idiosyncratic features in the histories of the various colonies. My debt is especially great to the National, the Mitchell and LaTrobe Libraries and the State Archives of Tasmania.

It was my good fortune to have the help of three excellent research assistants—Deidre Morris, Susan Eade and Beverley Hooper. Pat Romans typed a difficult manuscript with great skill and Paddy Maughan was just as efficient with the footnotes. Many gave generously of what they had or what they knew. Three students in Perth—Colin Pols, Ros and Bill Lensky—gave up their time to show me Albany and Cape Leeuwin. In 1953 when she was bearing in her breast 'starry thoughts that threw a magic light' on part of our past, Margaret Kiddle gave me a copy of the letters of Niel Black and the letters of J. D. Lang to the *British Banner*. Neither of us knew then what vision was locked inside the other.

I would like to thank the ones who did not indulge in what Coleridge called 'the head-dimming, heart-damping principle' but who gave the encouragement and the strength to endure to the end. I am thinking of all those men and women to whom I owe a debt no man can repay—Keith Hancock, Don Baker, David Campbell, Lyndall Ryan, Glen Tomasetti, Alec Hope, Ian Turner, Patrick White, Michael and Margot Roe, Bede Nairn, John Ryan, James McAuley, Kathleen Fitzpatrick, Malcolm and Mary McRae, Bruce Grant, Ken Inglis, Alison Clark, Geoffrey Serle, Geoffrey Stilwell, Douglas

Stewart, Judah Waten, Shirley Bradley, Macmahon Ball, Mick Williams, Geoffrey Fairbairn, John and Max Crawford, Geoffrey Dutton, John Legge, Arch and Nancy Gray, Hope Ingamells, Robert Hope, John Molony, and Fin and Helen Crisp.

On my wife's help, words are all too inadequate. She was given that gift of tongues which smoothed some of the rough passages in the manuscript. She was given other things, without which these three volumes would never have appeared. Then there are the six children who had to put up with the experience of living close to someone mad enough to try to write a history of Australia. There were also the students whom it was my great privilege to teach. Through those golden three years in Melbourne after the war, and the twenty-three years here in Canberra they were the ones who made me feel that one should go on trying to tell that story of why we are as we are.

It was also my good fortune in Canberra to be taught by students whom I was supposed to be teaching. They all went on to publish valuable books on aspects of the period covered in this volume. I am thinking of Ruth Knight's *Illiberal Liberal*, Michael Roe's *Quest for Authority in Eastern Australia*, John Molony's *The Roman Mould of the Australian Catholic Church*, John Barrett's *That Better Country*, and Tim Suttor's *Hierarchy and Democracy in Australia*. Who could possibly write on this period without acknowledging their debt to Marnie Bassett on the Hentys, to Alexandra Hasluck and Frank Crowley on Western Australia, to John West and Kathleen Fitzpatrick on Tasmania, and Paul Hasluck and Eddie Foxcroft on the history of the aborigines? Like all other general historians, I found much food for thought and much to be grateful for in the works on South Australia by Grenfell Price and Douglas Pike.

Then there were the generous people who belonged to Old Australia—people such as Doug and Cynthia Gardiner at Coleraine, and the local people of Wapengo, such as Phyllis Hunter, Joe Smith and Jim Griffin who knew something about the land and that very vast sea on which Captain Cook rode on that day when he knew the country was inhabited. They reminded me of an Australia Annie West and 'Plugger' Bennell had shown me a long time ago on Phillip Island. At this posting place on the long journey through our past, where the method used must be changed, one can only hope that one was not sent a great delusion so that one could believe in a lie about the great story. Like the other two volumes, this one should be read as a putting into words of what one man saw when he opened a window on our past. As Thomas Hardy puts it, a man 'should watch that pattern among general things which his idiosyncrasy moves him to observe'. A man gives what he has.

M. C.

ACKNOWLEDGEMENTS

THE AUTHOR wishes to acknowledge the help and co-operation of the following people and institutions: H. Hennig of the Bureau of Mineral Resources in Canberra, who again drew the maps; Mrs A. V. R. Bunbury of Busselton for permission to reproduce the miniature of Georgiana Molloy; E. Beale of Wollongong for permission to reproduce the self-portrait of Edmund Kennedy; the clerk of the House of Assembly in Adelaide for permission to reproduce the portrait of E. J. Eyre; the trustees of La Trobe Cottage for permission to reproduce the portrait of Charles La Trobe; the trustees of the Mitchell Library for permission to reproduce the drawing of Jackey Jackey, the portraits of Charles Harpur, James Stirling, Ludwig Leichhardt and William Charles Wentworth, the engraving of George Grey, the drawings of Ben Boyd, *King Teapot and His Two Gins*, aborigines in Sydney in 1849, Henry Parkes, and the *Bushman's Night Camp*; V. W. Hodgman, the keeper of the Tasmanian Museum and Art Gallery, Hobart, for permission to reproduce the portraits of the aborigines by Thomas Bock, the portrait of John West and the drawing of the aborigines on Flinders Island by F. G. de Wesselow; F. Ellis, the director of the Queen Victoria Museum, Launceston, for permission to reproduce the portrait of Jane Franklin; the La Trobe Library for permission to publish the copy of the likeness of John Batman, and the drawing of an Attack on a Store Dray; the Castlemaine Art Gallery and Historical Museum for permission to publish the photo of Edward Stone Parker; the National Portrait Gallery, London, for permission to publish the portrait of John Franklin; and the Lord Abbot of the Benedictine Monastery at New Norcia for permission to publish the portrait of Rosendo Salvado. The author also warmly thanks Geoffrey Dutton for permission to use the Dutton Papers at Anlaby, and Peter Spillett for organizing the visit to Melville Island and Port Essington.

Similar versions of part of this volume have also appeared, or are about to appear, in *Overland, Papers and Proceedings of the Tasmanian Historical Research Association* and *Southerly*.

CONTENTS

ILLUSTRATIONS

PLATES

MAPS

ABBREVIATIONS

BATTYE L.	Battye Library, Perth
C.O.	Colonial Office
Col. Sec.	Colonial Secretary
encl.	enclosure
H.R.A.	*Historical Records of Australia*
Hist. Studies	*Historical Studies, Australia and New Zealand*
LA TROBE L.	La Trobe Library, Melbourne
M.L.	Mitchell Library, Sydney
MS.	manuscript
N.S.W.S.A.	New South Wales State Archives
NAT. L.	National Library of Australia, Canberra
P.D.	*Parliamentary Debates*
P.P.	*Parliamentary Papers*
R.A.H.S., *J. & P.*	Royal Australian Historical Society, *Journal and Proceedings*
S.A.S.A.	South Australian State Archives
S.M.H.	*Sydney Morning Herald*
T.S.A.	Tasmanian State Archives
V. & P. (L.C.N.S.W.)	*Votes and Proceedings* of the Legislative Council of New South Wales
V. & P. (L.C.S.A.)	*Votes and Proceedings* of the Legislative Council of South Australia
V. & P. (L.C.V.D.L.)	*Votes and Proceedings* of the Legislative Council of Van Diemen's Land
V.S.A.	Victorian State Archives
W.A.H.S., *J. & P.*	Western Australian Historical Society, *Journal and Proceedings*

I

THE IRON-AGE MEN OF NEW HOLLAND

IN THE BEGINNING of this period chance and circumstance seemed
to produce a brazen race of men in the outlying settlements of New
Holland and New South Wales. The environment seemed appropriate as
a backdrop to some savage, elemental human drama played out by men who
loved deeds of violence and were hard of heart, till death seized them and
snatched them out of the bright light of the sun. The Dutch sailors in the
seventeenth century had recoiled in horror from an 'arid, barren and wild
land'. At the *Swaenerevier* (Swan River) in 1696–7 Willem de Vlamingh had
seen a species of black swans. It had seemed to him that in New Holland the
natural order of things had been turned upside down, since even the swan had
lost its splendour and its majesty by wearing this mantle of sombre black.[1]

One hundred years later the English navigator, George Vancouver, had
come to the same melancholy conclusion about New Holland. He had served
for seven years with Cook in the Pacific before being promoted to the rank of
commander and being appointed to lead an expedition to the South Seas. By
nature a harsh and difficult man, and said by some to err on that side of
severity which was first cousin to cruelty, he was not lacking in grandeur of
vision. He shared the enthusiasm of his day that the Great Disposer had
reserved for Englishmen the glorious task of passing the arts and sciences
to the farthermost corners of the earth, for the instruction and happiness of the
most lowly children of nature. He shared, too, the hopes that his voyage might
establish new and lucrative branches of commerce.

He sailed from England in April 1791 with two ships, the sloop *Discovery*
and the armed tender *Chatham*. By the end of September as he moved along
the south coast east of Cape Leeuwin he noted the naked bases of the cliffs as
evidence of how excessively they were beaten by a turbulent ocean. He
noted, too, how the country consisted of a range of dreary hills, producing
little grass. He entered a spacious sound on 29 September on which he graci-

---

[1] Based on those parts of Hesiod which are relevant to the themes developed in this
chapter. See H. G. Evelyn-White (ed.), *The Homeric Hymns and Homerica* (London,
1954). For the letter on the journeys of Willem de Vlamingh see J. E. Heeres, *The Part
Borne by the Dutch in the Discovery of Australia 1606-1765* (London, 1899), p. 84; for
an amusing seventeenth-century conceit on the significance of black swans at the
Antipodes, see Ann Haaker and Richard Brome (eds), *The Antipodes* (London, 1967).
There the people rule the magistrates, the women overrule the men, parents obey their
children and their servants, the men do all the tittle-tattle duties, the swans are black, the
ravens white, and parrots teach their mistresses to talk. Ibid., I, vi, lines 117-60.

ously conferred the name of King George the Third's Sound, and called the harbour Princess Royal Harbour. But like his predecessors, the Dutch, he sensed the paradox of a majestic sea pounding away since the beginning of time on the shores of such a dreary country. To his dismay he saw a country of naked rocks and a milk-white barren sand, beyond which boundary the surface of the ground seemed covered by a 'deadly green herbage, with here and there a few grovelling shrubs or dwarf trees scattered at a great distance from each other'. He found the climate delightful, and prophesied that one day the excellent harbour of King George the Third's Sound would be important to navigation.[2]

Eleven years later in January 1802 Matthew Flinders entered the Sound in the *Investigator* at the beginning of his voyage to chart the coast of the whole continent. By temperament and disposition he was as different from Vancouver as frost from fire, for Flinders saw no reason to believe that the imagination of man's heart was evil from the start nor that the melancholy aspect of the coasts of New Holland was evidence of some malevolence towards mankind in the heart of the Great Disposer. He was a man to delight in the banquet of life. After the august splendours of the Sound in high summer he sailed due east along a coast where 'not a blade of grass, nor a square yard of soil from which the seed delivered to it could be expected back, was perceivable by the eye'. For a moment that sweet and lovely gentleman grew quite sad as his eye roved from the 'spacious world' of the sea to those desolate, melancholy shores.[3]

Fourteen years later in April 1816 William Charles Wentworth, a colonial Ishmael, a wild man whose hand would be raised all his life against every man because he would go on believing that every man's hand was raised against him, sailed into that majestic Sound on the brig *Emu* en route from Sydney to London. What he saw there confirmed his view that man's role was to emerge unscathed from nature's never-ending war without caring for the fate of the weak. For his part he disbelieved men came into the world with any innate feeling whatever. Conscience was acquired as all other habits were from long association. Because the aboriginal savages had been bred in a state of ferocious and solitary independence, they possessed no ideas of the nature of society or its obligations. Because the ties uniting them to one another had nothing to do with social feelings, the answer to their conduct against the white man was simple: they must be subdued by fear. In 1819 Barron Field, a judge in Sydney, offered a theological explanation for the existence of such a dreary, forbidding and inhospitable country. Australia was not conceived of in the beginning when God blessed his work and saw that it was good, but

[2] *A Voyage of Discovery to the North Pacific Ocean and Round the World . . . in the Years 1790, 1791, 1792, 1793, 1794 and 1795 . . . under the Command of Captain George Vancouver* (3 vols, London, 1798), vol. 1, pp. 34-6, 45-50; J. E. Heeres, op. cit., p. 51; *A Voyage of Discovery . . .* , vol. 1, pp. 141, 159-69.
[3] M. Flinders, *A Voyage to Terra Australis* (2 vols, London, 1814), vol. 1, p. 81; W. Shakespeare, *King Richard III* (Oxford, 1928), I, ii, line 247.

emerged at the first sinning, when the ground was therefore curst, and hence this barren wood.[4]

In the meantime in London some men went on entertaining hopes for New Holland as a place not just for the punishment and reformation of British criminals but also for the profit of merchants interested in the riches of the East. Ever since the loss of Java to the Dutch in the treaty that ended the Napoleonic Wars the Eastern trade lobby in London had been pressing government to explore how to recapture the rich trade of the Spice Islands. In 1817 the British Government decided to find out whether it was possible to use a port on the north coast of New Holland as an Eastern emporium. They appointed Phillip Parker King to command such an expedition. Like Lord Bathurst, King was an evangelical, a man who was bothered all his life as to why the Sabbath was devoted by one part of mankind to religion and by another part to sensual gratification. All his life he was said to be a 'great gazer beyond the stars' and a great yearner for that world in which there would be 'no more sea', a great pleader to heaven for pardon for his sins, and in general 'very busy with his God'. He had close associations with New South Wales. He was born in Norfolk Island on 13 December 1791 and was the son of a governor of New South Wales. He also knew the ways of the sea, having served in the navy from 1807 to the end of the Napoleonic Wars, after which he had taken up hydrography. Some found him the very 'beau ideal of a captain', and some said he was a rather 'trashy observer of nature', one of those men of inadequate consciousness who remained all his life a stranger to those epiphanies, those moments of majesty that Cook and Flinders had known on first sensing the spirit of New Holland. But King was by birth an Australian for whom the inhospitable coasts, the dryness, the glare, the barren plains, and the weird animals were not sights to arouse horror, loathing or fear, but part of those things from eternity which could not and indeed should not be changed.

Between 1817 and 1822 he made four journeys in northern waters. On 16 April 1818 at the north-west point of Arnhem Land he named Raffles Bay as a compliment to Sir Thomas Stanford Raffles, a distinguished servant of government in the Malay States. Two days later the ship entered to the west of Raffles Bay a magnificent sheet of water well stocked with fish. He named it 'Port Essington' as a tribute to his late lamented friend Vice-Admiral Sir William Essington, K.C.B. He found it equal to any harbour he had ever seen and believed that because of its proximity to the Moluccas and New Guinea and because it was in the direct line of communication between Port Jackson and India, and in a commanding situation with respect to the passage through Torres Strait, it must become a place of great trade.[5]

---

[4] W. C. Wentworth to D'Arcy Wentworth, 16 August 1816 (Wentworth Papers, Letters from W. C. Wentworth, MS. in M.L.); see John Keats, 'Epistle to John Hamilton Reynolds', lines 94-7; for the story behind the poem see Aileen Ward, *John Keats* (London, 1963), pp. 171-2; Barron Field, *First Fruits of Australian Poetry* (Sydney, 1819), p. 7.
[5] Bathurst to Macquarie, 8 February 1817, H.R.A., I. ix. 207-8; Macquarie to Goul-

He put this idea to Lord Bathurst shortly after he returned to London in April 1823. While he also discussed with John Macarthur junior and others a plan for an Australian agricultural company to colonize the waste lands of New South Wales by using cheap convict labour to grow wool, Bathurst decided in February 1824 to form a British settlement on the north-west coast of New Holland. He selected Captain James John Gordon Bremer to take command of a warship and proceed without loss of time to the said north-west coast and take formal possession of it between the west coast of Bathurst Island and the eastern side of the Cobourg Peninsula. On arrival in Sydney Governor Brisbane was to furnish Bremer with a small detachment of troops and allow settlers to join the expedition as well as any merchants of respectability.[6]

Bremer, who was born in that decisive year of 1786 when Lord Sydney decided to plant a colony of thieves at Botany Bay, was one of those officers with a distinguished record in naval engagements but with none of the qualities to lay the foundations of an emporium of trade in the mangrove swamps of northern Australia. While the newspapers in Sydney painted pictures of Malays, Chinese and others hastening to place themselves under the milder government of British law, Bremer set out in August 1824 from Sydney with the *Tamar* and two other ships, one captain, one subaltern, a sergeant, twenty-seven rank and file and some marines—fifty in all—to begin a new Britannia in the tropics. After passing through Torres Strait the ships entered Port Essington, but the majesty and splendours of that bay roused no response in the breast of Bremer. Stout captain that he was, he decided to look for a better site and believed he had found one on the shores of Melville Island. There on 26 September 1824 he took formal possession in the name of His Most Britannic Majesty of the area defined in his instructions.[7]

The choice was not a happy one, being off the main shipping track of Malay and Bugis seamen and hazardous of access to sailing ships. There in the glare of the tropics, amongst the pandanus and the paperbark trees with white cockatoos screeching overhead, and watched at a distance by the Tiwi aborigines, the soldiers and four women set to work to build their fort, sink their well and dig their moat while they waited for their settlement to blossom into an entrepôt depot in an area where all their predecessors had concluded there was little good to be done. In November Bremer sailed off to Burma for more of that warfare in which he was more at home than in the work of forcing men

burn, 24 September 1817, ibid., 488-9; *S.M.H.*, 28 February, 3 March 1856; W. B. Clarke, *The Dead Which Are Blessed: a sermon preached in the Church of St. Thomas, Willoughby, N.S.W. on Sunday, 2nd March, 1856, the day after the funeral of the late Rear-Admiral Philip Parker King. M.C.* (Private Circulation, Sydney, 1856); Macquarie to Bathurst, 10 December 1817, op. cit., 543-4; Macquarie to Goulburn, 21 December 1817, op. cit., 747; R. L. King to P. P. and Mrs H. King, 3 June 1842 (King Papers); P. P. King, *Narrative of a Survey of the Intertropical and Western Coasts of Australia: performed between the years 1818 and 1822* (2 vols, London, 1827), vol. 1, pp. 83-92.
   [6] For the origins of the Australian Agricultural Company see ibid., vol. 2, pp. 63-4; Bathurst to Brisbane, 17 February 1824, *H.R.A.*, I. xi. 227-9.
   [7] Brisbane to Bathurst, 12 August 1824, *H.R.A.*, I. xi. 338; *Australian*, 10 March 1825.

used to the sights and sounds of civilization to leave their mark on a site where land, sea and sky seemed to mock all human endeavour as vain. Fever, dysentery and rheumatism reminded the few with an eye for such things that man's life was brutish and short, for the island soon became a hospital for some and a cemetery for others. Those left standing often converted the fort into one general scene of riot, tumult and intemperance. The aborigines so molested them as to be quickly deemed more worthy of bullets than instruction in Christ's redeeming love for all men. Captain H. R. Hartley, Bremer's successor, soon came to the conclusion that divine providence, common sense, and the counsels of enlightened humanity alike proclaimed the unfitness of the European to conduct an enterprise in tropical climates. Far away in London, Lord Bathurst, strengthened as ever by the divine assurance that God had made man to dwell on all the face of the earth, decided that Bremer's only error had been in his choice of site, and selected yet another naval captain on half-pay to choose a more suitable site.[8]

By then Bathurst was also looking for a site for a new penal settlement on the north coast of New South Wales. As long ago as June 1822 Mr Commissioner Bigge had proposed the establishment of one or more penal settlements on the north coast of New South Wales for convicts deemed least useful to their masters, for those of irredeemable character and for future convicts who had committed crimes of cruelty and depravity. In September Bathurst instructed Governor Brisbane to lose no time in despatching the Surveyor-General, John Oxley, to report on the suitability of Port Bowen, Port Curtis and Moreton Bay as sites for penal settlements where convicts might regain that dread of exile and some of those terrors unhappily lost by the progress of colonization in Sydney. In October 1823 Oxley explored all three sites and reported in favour of Moreton Bay because of its great natural beauty, its fine soil, its abundant timber, and its noble river on which he had conferred the name of Brisbane. It had been first seen and named by Cook in May 1770 who had tried to call it Morton Bay, but later the first editor of his journal, Dr John Hawkesworth, slipped in an 'e'. It had been seen again by Flinders in July 1799 and July 1802.[9]

In September 1824 another Waterloo veteran, Captain Miller, and a party of five soldiers and forty-five convicts camped at Redcliffe Point on Moreton Bay, but were so discomfited by the ferocity of both the blacks and the mosquitoes

[8] Visit to Melville Island, 31 May 1969. Outside the school at the Garden Point Settlement is a statue of the virgin and child; H. R. Hartley to Col. Sec. of New South Wales, 8 September 1828, *H.R.A.*, III. vi. 757-61; Bathurst to Darling, 7 April 1826, *H.R.A.*, I. xii. 224.

[9] J. T. Bigge, *The Colony of New South Wales*, pp. 163-4. For the background to this recommendation see vol. 1, ch. 16 of this history; see also J. D. Ritchie, *Punishment and Profit* (Melbourne, 1970); Bathurst to Brisbane, 9 September 1822, *H.R.A.*, I. x. 791-2. In this despatch Bathurst spelt Port Curtis as Port Curteis; J. Oxley to Goulburn, 10 January 1824, encl. in Brisbane to Bathurst, 3 February 1824, *H.R.A.*, I. xi. 215-25; Cook named it after Lord Morton, President of the Royal Society. For Hawkesworth's addition of the 'e' to Morton see J. C. Beaglehole (ed.), *The Voyage of the Endeavour 1768-1771* (Cambridge, 1955), p. 318; M. Flinders, *A Voyage to Terra Australis* (2 vols, London, 1814), vol. 1, pp. 198-201, 204, vol. 2, pp. 5-7.

that Miller recommended that a better site be found. In December Governor
Brisbane, John Macarthur, the man with a great dream of a plantation society
worked by convict labour, and Chief Justice Forbes, that liberal 'cheery soul'
with such a blindness for atmosphere that he had wanted to call the place
Edenglassie, visited Moreton Bay. They recommended that the settlement be
moved to the present site of the city of Brisbane, adding that a penal depot
was the best means of paving the way for the introduction of a free population.[10]

Delighted to find a site from which convicts could not escape and where
their labour could quickly provide their subsistence, Brisbane despatched a
steady stream of convicts to the settlement. By March 1826 there were two
hundred engaged in growing maize on the river flats working with shovels,
mattocks and other hand implements from sun-up to sun-down and dossing
down at night in the barracks at Eagle Farm. In that month Captain Patrick
Logan arrived to take over as commandant from Captain Bishop who had
succeeded Captain Miller. Logan was a deeply divided man. Born in either
1792 or 1796 into a Scottish family which traced its ancestry back into the
fourteenth century, he served bravely in the Peninsular Wars, in the United
States and at Quebec, before being released on half-pay when the blood-bath
ended. He repurchased his commission in 1819 to serve in Ireland where he
married Letitia Ann O'Beirne of Sligo, possibly in 1823. It was said that he
was no more moved by the sufferings of the Irish than he had been by the
weeping mothers and wailing infants on the battlefield of Vittoria. In 1824 he
sailed with his regiment for Sydney arriving there on 22 April 1825. Early in
1826 Governor Darling asked him to take over the command at Moreton Bay.
All his life he impressed his superiors by the ardour of his character, and his
devotion to the public service. Their one regret was his seeming reluctance to
write more fully about the behaviour of the prisoners, the state and prospect of
the crops, the progress of the public works, and his own suggestions for the
future arrangements of the settlement. He had a love for and success in
extending the botanical and geographical knowledge of the areas in which he
served.[11]

By contrast his inferiors found that wherever Captain Logan held office all
hell was let loose on them. There was much in Captain Logan of that power
to charm the ladies of the Government House group while being indifferent
to all appeals for mercy from the victims of his severe punishments. To his
inferiors he showed the soul of a martinet; to his superiors he showed the
soul of a lackey. On principle he punished small offences with the maximum
number of lashes. Soon there were terrible scenes of human degradation at
Moreton Bay. One man prayed each night 'to the throne of Heaven' for a safe
deliverance from so dreadful a scene. The convicts began to talk of a 'reign

[10] Brisbane to Bathurst, 21 May 1825, *H.R.A.*, I. xi. 603-5.

[11] L. R. Cranfield, 'Life of Captain Patrick Logan', *Journal of Royal Historical Society
of Queensland*, vol. 6, pp. 302-5; C. Bateson, *Patrick Logan: tyrant of Brisbane Town*
(Sydney, 1966); Col. Sec. of New South Wales to Logan, 3 April 1828 (Col. Sec. Papers,
copies of letters to Moreton Bay, 27 August 1824 to 30 December 1831, N.S.W.S.A).

of terror'. Others began to write of Moreton Bay as a place worthy to be the abode of the damned, of Logan as a monster in human form, and of atrocities which found a parallel only in the conduct of the Spaniards in Mexico and Peru. Treated like beasts of burden, the men behaved towards each other like savages. In January 1829 two prisoners, Thomas Matthews and Thomas Allan, knocked down a possible informer with a spade and then split his head in two with a mattock. Before being hanged in Sydney, Thomas Mathews explained to the assembled crowd that Logan's tyranny at Moreton Bay drove him and his unfortunate companions to extremities to free themselves from a state of suffering worse than death.[12]

In the meantime Logan devoted his energies to what interested him most deeply—endeavouring to ascertain as accurately as possible every particular connected with Moreton Bay and the adjacent country, and preserving friendly terms with the natives who were beginning to make themselves useful by apprehending and bringing in runaways. For this he rewarded them with a supply of blankets and tomahawks which they valued very highly. He also put sufficient ground under crop to feed the settlement. When the Colonial Secretary of New South Wales, A. McLeay, asked him whether hard labour would not be preferable to flogging as a punishment, he agreed to build a treadmill as a more humane method of deterring evil-doers. His superiors in Sydney were so delighted with his achievements that they sent a steady stream of incorrigibles. In May 1826 there were forty-three males and two females. A year later there were 195 Crown prisoners in the employ of government, guarded by one captain, two subalterns, three sergeants and eighty-one rank and file. By April 1830 752 convicts were being maintained there by government.[13]

All that time Logan stuck to what he conceived to be the path of duty. He hoped fervently, as he put it in February 1829, that he would never again have the painful duty of reporting abandoned crimes such as one man killing another with a mattock. He was solicitous for the sick. He welcomed the arrival of the Reverend J. Vincent in June of that year, believing that the fear of God might help as much as the lash to persuade the abandoned and the incorrigible to turn from their wickedness. In April 1829 he was pleased to hear

[12] J. J. Knight, *In the Early Days: history and incident of pioneer Queensland* (Brisbane, 1895) pp. 22-3; Col. Sec. to P. Logan, 20 March 1827 (Col. Sec. Papers, copies of letters to Moreton Bay, 27 August 1824 to 30 December 1831, N.S.W.S.A); see, for example, P. Logan to A. McLeay, 9 February 1827 (Logan Papers); William R——s, *The Fell Tyrant, or the Suffering Convict, Showing the Horrid and Dreadful Suffering of the Convicts of Norfolk Island, and Moreton Bay, Our Two Penal Settlements in New South Wales* (London, 1836), pp. 19-20; (attributed to E. S. Hall) to Goderich, 9 February 1832 (Miscellaneous letters re N.S.W., 1832. MS. in M.L.); report of trial of Thomas Mathews and Thomas Allan for wilful murder, *Sydney Gazette*, 18 April 1829; *Sydney Gazette*, 21 April 1829.

[13] Logan to McLeay, 9 February, 24 May, 24, 27, 28 July, 1 November, 20 December 1827, 2, 28 January, 6 March, 20 May, 20 July, 20 October, 9 December 1828, 2 January, 6, 22, 24 February, 3 April, 5, 22 May 1829 (copies in Oxley Library); MS. sub-encl. A in Darling to Bathurst, 22 May 1826, *H.R.A.*, I. xii. 318; encl. in Darling to Bathurst, 15 May 1827, *H.R.A.*, I. xiii. 305; encl. no. 3 in Darling to Murray, 2 April 1830, *H.R.A.*, I. xv. 386.

of the impending arrival of more female convicts, for he thought they might be instruments of God's purposes. In the meantime Logan showed no signs that he was aware of the terrible hell he had roused in the hearts of the prisoners under his command. He had mentioned casually that relations with the aborigines had deteriorated, but it never occurred to him that convicts running away from his 'excessive tyranny' might persuade the aborigines that he was the cause of the sufferings they had endured since the white man arrived at Brisbane Water.[14]

On 9 October 1830 Logan, his servant Private Collison, five prisoners (all reputed to be good bushmen) and two pack-bullocks set out from Brisbane to chart the windings of the Brisbane River between Pine Ridge, Lockyer's Creek and the Brisbane Range, and afterwards to proceed to the Glass-House Mountains and thence back to the settlement. When they reached the ford over the Brisbane River on 11 October two hundred blacks assembled and began to show a hostile feeling. But Logan, fearless as ever, went on with his journey while the blacks ominously hid behind trees and in the long grass. Having finished the first part of his mission he set out alone on 17 November for Mt Irwin. That night the members of his party believed they heard cooees, but Logan did not return to camp. Eleven days later a search party found the body of 'poor Captain Logan' in a shallow grave, the back of his head having been much beaten by waddies, and his feet exposed by the digging of the native dogs.[15]

The civil and military officers of Brisbane and Sydney paid fulsome tributes to the character, the zeal and the chivalrous and undaunted spirit of this man to whom they had always been 'well disposed'. Up at Brisbane Water the convicts began to fashion a different memorial for Logan. They started the story that bolters from 'Logan's yoke' had persuaded the aborigines to murder him in retribution for his crimes against humanity. Soon they were singing to a melancholy Irish air a song which summed up what they had suffered at Logan's hands:

A Convict's Lament on the Death of Captain Logan

Anonymous

> I am a native of the land of Erin,
> And lately banished from that lovely shore;
> I left behind my aged parents
> And the girl I did adore.
> In transient storms as I set sailing,
> Like mariner bold my course did steer;
> Sydney Harbour was my destination—
> That cursed place at length drew near.

[14] Logan to McLeay, 22, 24 February, 2 January 1828 (date corrected from 1829 to 1828 in copy in Oxley Library), 3 April 1829; Logan to J. Vincent, 28 May, 15 June 1829 (copies in Oxley Library).

[15] G. Edwards to Lieutenant-Colonel Allen Commanding 57th Regiment, Sydney, 8 November 1830 (copy in Oxley Library); Government Order, 16 July 1827 (copy in Oxley Library).

I then joined banquet in congratulation
On my safe arrival from the briny sea;
But, alas, alas! I was mistaken—
Twelve years transportation to Moreton Bay.
Early one morning as I carelessly wandered,
By the Brisbane waters I chanced to stray;
I saw a prisoner sadly bewailing,
Whilst on the sunlit banks he lay.

He said, 'I've been a prisoner at Port Macquarie,
At Norfolk Island, and Emu Plains;
At Castle Hill and cursed Toongabbie—
At all those places I've worked in chains,
But of all the places of condemnation,
In each penal station of New South Wales,
Moreton Bay I found no equal,
For excessive tyranny each day prevails.

Early in the morning, as the day is dawning,
To trace from heaven the morning dew,
Up we started at a moment's warning
Our daily labour to renew.
Our overseers and superintendents—
These tyrants' orders we must obey,
Or else at the triangles our flesh is mangled—
Such are our wages at Moreton Bay!

For three long years I've been beastly treated;
Heavy irons each day I wore;
My poor back from flogging has been lacerated,
And oft-times painted with crimson gore.
Like the Egyptians and ancient Hebrews,
We were sorely oppressed by Logan's yoke,
Till kind Providence came to our assistance,
And gave this tyrant his fatal stroke.

Yes, he was hurried from that place of bondage
Where he thought he would gain renown;
But a native black, who lay in ambush,
Gave this monster his fatal wound.
Fellow prisoners be exhilarated;
Your former sufferings you will not mind,
For it's when from bondage you are extricated
You'll leave such tyrants far behind!'

So the treadmill tower, the commissariat store, the soldiers' barracks, the
commandant's house, and that song about the days of the convicts' great
anguish, survived as memorials of that period when the labour and sufferings

of convicts paved the way for the beginning of civilization at Moreton Bay, Ipswich and the Darling Downs.[16]

Just one month after the convicts at Moreton Bay began to experience Logan's 'reign of terror' Lord Bathurst instructed a naval officer to take command of H.M.S. *Success* and search for another site for an emporium for trade to the eastward of Melville Island. He offered the command of the ship to Captain James Stirling, one of those many officers on half-pay who after the victory over revolution and a world conqueror found the days of peace lacking in excitement, glory and hard cash. He was then thirty-five. He was born in Lanarkshire, Scotland, in 1791, the eighth child in a family with a record of careers in the great world. The mother was much given to telling her children that she was the daughter of an admiral and the sister of a baronet and to saying she wanted to be known as the mother rather than the daughter of a man of renown. War seemed to offer James Stirling such an opportunity. He entered the navy as a first-class volunteer, served in all the seas in which the British were engaged—in South America, the West Indies, the Gulf of Mexico, Hudson Bay, St Lawrence and the North Sea—during which he climbed steadily the ladder of preferment in which, like Lachlan Macquarie, he found the rungs much farther apart for one of the lesser gentry of Scotland than for a man enjoying the patronage of a great house in the south of England. By 7 December 1818 he was a post-captain on half-pay.

Stirling was a most lovable man, with a handsome face and charming manners to match. Some said that behind the gay exterior there was a man given to dreaming of castles in Spain, or even wild visionary projects. Luck seemed to be on his side. In September 1823 he stood before the altar at Guildford and swore before Almighty God that he, the man in whom a huge fire was always kindling, would love, honour and cherish one Ellen Mangles to the exclusion of all others until death did them part. Marriage united him to a family which plucked sleeves in the corridors of Westminster, and had some possibility of being heeded. His father-in-law, John Mangles, was a member of parliament and a director of that East India Company which had persuaded Bathurst to pick a suitable naval officer to select a site east of Melville Island. Mangles persuaded them that Stirling was their man. So Stirling found his way to Sydney in 1826 in H.M.S. *Success*. As he waited there for the end of the rainy season on the northern coasts, he surprised the phlegmatic Governor Darling by suggesting to him that he should examine the western coast of New Holland near Swan River at 32° S. for a site for a

---

[16] Darling to Murray, 31 January 1831, *H.R.A.*, I. xvi. 56-7; Government Order, 17 November 1830, ibid., 57-8; *Sydney Gazette*, 25 November 1830; *Australian*, 19 November 1830; C. Bateson, *Patrick Logan*, pp. 169-71; 'A Convict's Lament on the Death of Captain Logan', in D. Stewart and N. Keesing (eds), *Old Bush Songs* (Sydney, 1957), pp. 24-5; J. G. Steele, *Explorers of the Moreton Bay District* (Brisbane 1973); A. Cunningham, Moreton Bay Journals (N.S.W.S.A); W. H. Traill, *A Queenly Colony* (Brisbane, 1901); C. C. Petrie, *Tom Petrie's Reminiscences of Early Queensland* (Brisbane, 1904); H. S. Russell, *The Genesis of Queensland* (Sydney, 1888); visit to treadmill tower, commandant's house site, soldiers' barracks and Redcliffe, 6 May 1971.

naval, military and commercial station, which would forestall the French and the Americans and provide a place for the China ships to touch at.[17]

On 17 January 1827 the *Success* finally set sail for northern waters via King George's Sound and Cape Leeuwin. In March when he and the botanist Charles Fraser, another man of 'universal benevolence', took a small boat up the Swan he was overwhelmed by the beauty of the lofty trees on the banks of the river, and the bright green pendulous foliage. As sun and earth and sky seemed to beckon them to yet more delights he enthused wantonly to Darling about the delicious weather and the abundance of everything, especially the cheerfulness the place lit up in his heart. 'It appears', he wrote, 'to hold out every attraction that a Country in a State of nature can possess'. It had commercial potential, it could play a role in the China and India trade, it could produce crops, fatten beasts and provide minerals, and it had advantages as a naval and military station. To forestall the French, he urged that the site be immediately possessed by the Crown. He also recommended that it be called 'Hesperia', or land looking to the setting sun, sensing as he did that there the sun fashioned the spirit of the place.[18]

As soon as he got back to Sydney in May 1827, after a cursory search for a site on the north coast, he asked Bathurst to give him the 'Superintendence and Government' of any settlement formed at Swan River. But Stirling had to bide his time, for Bathurst was still hoping that access to the riches of the East depended on the choice of a favourable site on the north coast of New Holland rather than the heady ideas of Stirling on the prospects at Swan River. Besides, he had just chosen a new commandant, Captain Collet Barker, one of those upright evangelicals, to take command of the new northern site. Barker arrived at Fort Wellington, Raffles Bay, on 13 September 1828 with a detachment of the 39th Regiment and twelve convicts. But fate was not to be kind to this man of virtue. Just as the health of his men began to improve under his regime, and traders from Macassar began to bring gold and nutmeg and cinnamon to the settlement, that remark by Captain Hartley that the very physiology of the European disqualified him from braving the ardours of equatorial heat reached London. So orders went out from London in November 1828 that Barker was to transfer his men to a new settlement which had been founded in 1826 at that King George's Sound where Captain Vancouver had found the sea to be so majestic and the coast so barren and dreary.[19]

---

[17] Bathurst to Darling, 7 April 1826, *H.R.A.*, I. xii. 224; Bathurst to Darling, 30 May 1826, ibid., 339; Alexandra Hasluck, *James Stirling* (Melbourne, 1963); J. Stirling to Darling, 14 December 1826, encl. no. 2 in Darling to Bathurst, 18 December 1826, *H.R.A.*, I. xii. 777-80.

[18] J. Stirling to Darling, 18 April 1827, *H.R.A.*, III. vi. 551-78; and encl. no. 1 in Darling to Bathurst, 18 December 1826, *H.R.A.*, I. xii. 775-7.

[19] J. Stirling to Bathurst, 15 May 1827, encl. in Darling to Hay, 15 May 1827, *H.R.A.*, I. xiii. 307; C. Sturt, *Two Expeditions into the Interior of Southern Australia, during the Years 1828, 1829, 1830 and 1831* (2 vols, London, 1833), vol. 2, p. 243; Journal of Captain Collet Barker at Raffles Bay, 13 September 1828 to 29 August 1829 (MS. in N.S.W.S.A.); Murray to Darling, 1 November 1828, *H.R.A.*, I. xiv. 410-11.

All through 1825 and the early part of 1826 press and pulpit in Sydney and Hobart Town urged government to clean out the nests of sealers wallowing in beastly sensuality in coves along the south coast between Wilson's Promontory and King George's Sound. These settlements on Cape Barren Island in the Furneaux Group, King Island in Bass Strait, Wilson's Promontory, Phillip Island, Port Fairy, Portland Bay, Kangaroo Island and King George's Sound were composed of bolters from the convict settlements, some native women, and children from their union. Early in 1826 there were upwards of two hundred on Kangaroo Island who were about to elect their own king and pass their own laws. At all these sealing settlements convict bolters compelled their women to hunt and fish while they sat on the beach and smoked and drank. They often flogged their women, finding that fun, too, and from time to time exchanged their seal skins for food, grog and tobacco with parties from any trading vessel prepared to risk a visit to such desperadoes. At Kent Bay on Cape Barren Island, American whalers and Port Jackson desperadoes used each other in a most cruel manner. In 1804 American sailors tied ex-convicts from Sydney to a tree and flogged them as long as there was a breath of life in them. Sometimes the Americans used natives from the Sandwich Islands to club their Port Jackson rivals into insensibility. All the respectable people of Sydney and Hobart Town feared that these men would so debase human nature that the infection would spread until the whole of human society in New Holland degenerated into that godless anarchy of the cities of the plain before God sent his cleansing fire. They pestered government to despatch an armed cutter to annihilate these plague spots and establish military outposts, one at Western Port and one at King George's Sound which would prevent any recurrence.[20]

The presence of a French discovery ship in southern waters in the spring of 1826 strengthened this demand. In October Captain M. J. Dumont D'Urville anchored his ship *L'Astrolabe* at Kangaroo Island. Unlike the censorious colonial evangelicals he found there much to delight him and little to cause him to frown. He thought the aboriginal women found life with European men more pleasing than with the men of their own race because the Europeans had much more respect for them. A month later in Western Port he found much in the scenery and the life of the sealers that pleased him. Nor was the prospect of a French or a Russian colony somewhere on the coasts of Australia a cause of alarm to the people of Sydney. Some thought it might force the English to give them a constitution to their liking or, better still, make the English think the colonists of greater consequence.[21]

[20] See letter by W. H. Skelton in *Australian*, 9 March 1826; see also articles on sealers on Kangaroo Island and runaways in Bass Strait in *Hobart Town Gazette*, 20 May, 10 June 1826. A. Delano, *A Narrative of Voyages and Travels in the Northern and Southern Hemisphere* (Boston, 1817), pp. 464-6; extract from a letter by J. Murrell, encl. no. 2 in King to Hobart, 20 December 1804, *H.R.A.*, I. v. 173-6; J. S. Cumpston, *The Furneaux Group* (Canberra, 1972), pp. 26-7.

[21] *Voyage de la Corvette L'Astrolabe Exécuté par Ordre du Roi, pendant les Anées 1826-1827-1828-1829, sous le commandement de M. J. Dumont D'Urville* (5 vols, Paris, 1830), vol. 1, pp. 197-8, 125-37.

In March 1826 Darling was ordered to forestall the French by establishing settlements at Shark Bay on the west coast of New Holland, and at Western Port which had been discovered by George Bass in 1798. Influenced by the reputation of the former as the land which sheltered the 'miserablest people in the world', Darling instructed Major Edmund Lockyer to take fifty convicts and a party of soldiers to start a settlement at King George's Sound. He also instructed Captain Samuel Wright to take twenty convicts and eighteen soldiers to start another settlement at Western Port. On 9 October His Majesty's brig *Amity*, bound for King George's Sound, and the brig *Dragon* and the sloop *Fly*, bound for Western Port, sailed out of that majestic harbour and turned south into huge seas whipped up by spring gales which buffeted them till they emerged from the swing of that sea and took refuge in a cove at the north-eastern end of Phillip Island. Wright was instructed to employ the convicts to clear the ground for future settlers, and to make every effort to live at peace with the aborigines. The men cleared a piece of ground which they called 'Fort Dumaresq'. There Michael Kain, a soldier and sailor by profession but, like the aborigines, very fond of 'bolting', was flogged three times for taking to the bush. When sentenced to a fourth session at the triangles, he cut his throat, which was sewn up so that Kain could live on to face his tormentors who in April 1828 sent him to Moreton Bay where he fell into the hands of Captain Logan. Logan gave him more of the same medicine till death snatched him away from his tormentors. Well before then Wright's successor, F. A. Wetherall, came to the conclusion that the sterile, swampy and impenetrable nature of the country surrounding Western Port did not possess sufficient capabilities for colonization on a large scale. Deciding there was no disposition on the part of the inhabitants of New South Wales to settle that part of the country, Darling issued instructions on 23 January 1828 to abandon the settlement, disperse some of the cattle, take the remainder of the stock to Port Dalrymple in Van Diemen's Land and bring the troops, convicts and other stores back to Sydney.[22]

In the meantime Major Lockyer and his party were braving the peril of the mighty deep to plant European civilization on the shores of that dreary country at King George's Sound. On Christmas Day 1826, to the unspeakable relief of all on board, the *Amity* came off the green swell and sailed down the majestic waters of the Sound. Major Lockyer was a stern man, much given to rushes of blood to the head when people behaved in ways displeasing to him.

[22] Report on Western Port, encl. in F. A. Wetherall to Darling, 24 January 1827, *H.R.A.*, III. v. 835-50; Darling to Goderich, 24 December 1827, *H.R.A.*, I. xiii. 667; Goderich to Darling, 19 July 1827, *H.R.A.*, ibid., 450-1; Darling to Hay, 14 May 1827, ibid., 304; S. Wright to Col. Sec. of New South Wales, 26 January 1827, *H.R.A.*, III. v. 850-4; W. H. Hovell to Darling, 27 March 1827, ibid., 854-60; Quarterly Return of Crown Prisoners in the Employ of Government and at the Penal Settlements, 1 April 1827, encl. in Darling to Bathurst, 15 May 1827, *H.R.A.*, I. xiii. 305. At Rhyll, Phillip Island, there is a monument built in 1921 to commemorate the visit of G. Bass in January 1789, J. Grant in March 1801, N. Baudin in April 1802, Dumont D'Urville in November 1826, and the building of Fort Dumaresq in December 1826; personal visit to the site 19 May 1967. K. Bowden, *The Western Port Settlement and Its Leading Personalities* (Melbourne, 1970).

Born in Devon in 1784, he had entered the army in 1803 and come to Sydney as a major with a detachment of the 57th Regiment in April 1825. In August of that year he had inspected the settlement at Moreton Bay and also engaged in some exploration of the hinterland. In appearance he bore himself like a Roman, even down to the fringe of hair on the forehead, the head thrown back and the lips held tight. He had the air of a man who looked as though he were born to be the giver rather than the receiver of punishment.

On 26 December he and his party landed at the head of Princess Royal Harbour and began to build their store huts. Lockyer was filled with dismay. Like his predecessors, to him the splendour of the harbour was mocked by the dreary, inhospitable coast with its seemingly endless stretches of sand and stone. The day after they landed the natives stuck three spears into the body of one of his party as he stood in the shallows repairing a small boat. Lockyer cursed them and railed against them as treacherous savages. But that evening he heard some aborigines caterwauling on Michaelmas Island in the Sound. When they were rescued they told Lockyer that sealers had left them there to die. Overwhelmed with a remorse that clamoured for some gesture of expiation, he gave the next native who risked a visit to their site a tomahawk and a biscuit, which so delighted the native that he ran off up the hill having a chop at everything standing. A few weeks later a native woman showed Lockyer the effect on her arm of the many blows she had received from the sealers. Again Lockyer was overwhelmed with a sense of evil for, as he put it in his diary, 'I think I never saw so miserable an object in the shape of a Female'.[23]

Life with the convicts was just as elemental. Early in the New Year Lockyer detected a disposition to disobey and set at defiance all authority. One Sunday the overseer reported that the convicts refused to rise at six. That day one John Ryan refused to accept his ration of meat and when Lockyer ordered him to do so, replied in a most insolent manner. Lockyer ordered Ryan to be punished on the spot, but the overseer refused to inflict the punishment and a prisoner said he would not do it. So Lockyer, determined not to allow a ruffian to get the upper hand, seized the cat-o'-nine-tails himself and laid on sixteen lashes after which Ryan promised to obey. As Lockyer put it in his journal, this appeared to have the effect of putting down the spirit of mutiny. Just as an extra precaution he made a journey to Seal Island and thought it would be an excellent place for solitary confinement since there was not even a seal left on it, a few birds being the only residents. Each Sunday, weather permitting, Lockyer mustered convicts and soldiers to hear him read prayers,

[23] E. Lockyer to Col. Sec. of New South Wales, 22 January 1827, *H.R.A.*, III. vi. 460 (ms. is in nat. l.); copy of portrait of Major Edmund Lockyer, Patrick Taylor House, Albany, personal visit 6 June 1970; cairn to 'Major Edmund Lockyer of the 56th Regiment who landed here from the Brig *Amity* on the 26th December to found the first British settlement on the western side of Australia', erected in March 1936 on the shores of Princess Royal Harbour, Albany; Journal of E. Lockyer, entries for 25 December 1826 to 1 January 1827, 13 January 1827, *H.R.A.*, III. vi. 463-70; rough copy of Journal of E. Lockyer, 2 March 1827, ibid., 497.

and all united in uttering that petition 'Thy kingdom come. Thy will be done in earth . . .' No one there left a memorial of what went on in his heart as those words dropped into the silence, nor of how he or any other member of the party felt on those days when Lockyer, mindful of that mission of planting civilization in a sea of barbarism, unfurled the Union flag on a mast-head. Lockyer left on 3 April 1827 to return to Sydney where he sold his commission and took up land, settling near Marulan in 1837. He also took up land at the junction of the Murrumbidgee and the Goodradigbee on a site of great natural beauty. For there was an artist in Lockyer. In his days at Albany he had done water-colours of some distinction. He lived on to see iron ore from his estate used for the construction of the first railway in New South Wales in that era when the mighty bush was tethered to the world.[24]

By the end of 1831 there were fifty souls in the settlement, of whom twenty-four were convicts, sixteen soldiers, four children, three women, one a surgeon and two others officials. By then men had responded in all sorts of ways to the great ordeal. The surgeon, I. S. Nind, had become so misanthropic he told a sergeant he would sooner see the back of a man than his face. One day he seized the hand of the commandant, G. Sleeman, and in a fit of tears began to talk incoherently about his past misdeeds. In the early hours of the following morning he went to the soldiers' barracks and babbled on about his private affairs. Another man, on whom history cannot even confer a name, climbed each Sunday to the summit of Mt Clarence to recite the rosary after which he turned towards the west and prayed fervently to Almighty God that he would not always be left in such isolation.[25] Nind and the anonymous petitioner to the throne of Almighty God were not to know then that relief was at hand. In January 1828 the Colonial Office hinted that withdrawal of the convicts and soldiers was imminent. In December 1829 Captain Barker, fresh from Raffles Bay, took over the command. In January 1831 Governor Darling announced his plans for the relief of the military and the withdrawal of the convicts and took the liberty of predicting that free settlers would not be disposed to go there.

In April 1831 Barker set out from the Sound for Sydney where he hoped to meet again those fellow-soldiers of God who were fighting for the victory of God's purposes against the men who loved deeds of violence and were hard of heart. On the way he landed at Gulf St Vincent to examine the country between that gulf and Lake Alexandrina. In that season, between summer and autumn, of halcyon windless days calculated to fill the soul of a Barker with a great gladness and an abiding faith in a higher purpose for man in such a country, he and his companions were quite delighted with the bold

[24] Rough copy of Journal of E. Lockyer, 28 January 1827, *H.R.A.*, III. vi. 492-3; 'The First Camp', King George's Sound, and 'The Settlement', King George's Sound, water-colours by E. Lockyer in collection of Western Australian Art Gallery.

[25] J. Hoop to G. Sleeman, 10 May 1829, encl. 15 in G. Sleeman to Col. Sec. of New South Wales, 14 May 1829, *H.R.A.*, III. vi. 535; G. Sleeman to Col. Sec. of New South Wales, 7 October 1829, ibid., 545-7; P. F. Moran, *History of the Catholic Church in Australasia* (2 vols, Sydney, 1896), vol. 2, p. 554.

and romantic scenery and the natural meadows. But while walking on the sand-hills at Lake Alexandrina some natives plunged innumerable spears into his body, influenced by no other motive than curiosity to ascertain whether they had power to kill a white man. They threw his body into deep water, and the sea-tide carried it away. The mild, affable and attentive Barker, who had been so zealous in the discharge of his public duties and honourable and just in his private life, was seen no more.

What Barker stood for was to live on. His fellow-believers erected a plaque in St James's Church, Sydney, to the memory of a man who had been treacherously murdered by aboriginal natives. They went on to testify their esteem for his singular worth and their affectionate remembrance of the many virtues of this upright man. Another man of like mind was to give him possibly a more lasting memorial. In 1832 Captain Charles Sturt had arrived in London. The acclaim and preferment he had been awarded for his heroic journey down the Murray in 1829–30 had not come up to his expectations. The Barker report of a rich country near the mouth of the Murray gave him the chance to endow his journey with the glory he craved. In his book on the *Two Expeditions into the Interior of Southern Australia*, published in London in 1833, he wrote with pride of this spot on the south coast of New Holland to which the colonist might venture with every prospect of success, and in whose valleys the exile might hope to build for himself and for his family a peaceful and prosperous home. He reminded his readers that there were advantages in establishing a colony rather than a penal settlement. By then the cheerful Captain Stirling had also had his victory, because government had given him the superintendence of a settlement at Swan River. The iron-age men of New Holland were about to be overrun by a new race of British philistines.[26]

[26] Huskisson to Darling, 30 January 1828, *H.R.A.*, I. xiii. 741-2; C. Barker to Col. Sec. of New South Wales, 23 October 1829, *H.R.A.*, III. vi. 840-4; G. Sleeman to Col. Sec. of New South Wales, 20 December 1829, ibid., 547-8; Darling to Murray, 31 January 1831, *H.R.A.*, I. xvi. 55-6; plaque to Captain Collet Barker, St James's Church, Sydney; C. Sturt, *Two Expeditions into the Interior of Southern Australia* (2 vols, London, 1833), vol. 2, pp. 232-48.

2

ANOTHER PROVINCE FOR BRITAIN'S GENTRY

BY 1829 Captain James Stirling had worked a great marvel in London. He had convinced His Majesty's Government that a huge area of New Holland which had previously enjoyed the unenviable reputation of being so barren that it had produced 'the miserablest people in the world'—a people who, setting aside their human shape, differed but little from the brutes—could become a new province for Britain's gentry by establishing a colony at Swan River with himself as Lieutenant-Governor. It took him two years to convince the men in black in Whitehall that this 'very large tract of land' offered opportunities for what he called 'famous fun' for the members of his class. When he extravagantly praised the soil, the climate, the commercial and naval advantages, and the need to anticipate the French, the heart dampeners replied that His Majesty's Government had no intention to comply with his wishes in the manner to which he had alluded.[1] Once again luck was on his side. In mid-1828 George Murray took over the colonial department, and Horace Twiss replaced the young Edward Stanley, that man with the taste for putting awkward questions to men who were all heart and little head. Both were close friends of the Stirling and Mangles families. So Stirling again presented to the colonial department his puff on the 'eligibility of a certain portion of the western coast of New Holland' as a British settlement and coyly begged to disclaim 'any indirect view to his own employment in such service'. When government showed some interest, but again jibbed at the expense, Stirling asked whether there would be any objection to the unsupported employment of private capital and enterprise in the occupation and improvement of that territory and whether he and his supporters could form an association to obtain a proprietary charter upon principles similar to those adopted in the settlement of Pennsylvania and Georgia.[2]

[1] J. Stirling to his brother, 23 August 1828 (Letters of James Stirling, MS. in M.L.); William Dampier, *A New Voyage Round the World* (3rd ed., 2 vols, London, 1698), vol. I, pp. 463-4; J. Stirling to Bathurst, 15 May 1827, encl. in Darling to Hay, 15 May 1827, *H.R.A.*, I. xiii. 307; Stanley to Stirling, 29 November 1827, *H.R.A.*, III. vi. 584; Huskisson to Darling, 28 January 1828, *H.R.A.*, I. xiii. 739-40; E. G. Stanley to Stirling, 29 November 1827, *H.R.A.*, III. vi. 584; Court of Directors of East India Company to Hay, 1 August 1828, C.O. 18/1; intending players in the motives game should start with the excellent review of motives in F. K. Crowley, *Australia's Western Third* (London, 1960), pp. 3-4, and J. S. Battye, *Western Australia* (Oxford, 1924), pp. 71-3; Stirling to Hay, 30 July 1828, C.O. 18/1.
[2] Stirling to Hay, 30 July 1828, C.O. 18/1, and *H.R.A.*, III. vi. 585-6; Stirling and Major Moody to Hay, 21 August 1828, *H.R.A.*, III. vi. 586-7, Moody was a brigade major in the Royal Engineers; B. Fitzpatrick, *British Imperialism and Australia 1783-1833* (London, 1939), pp. 282-4.

This time government asked Stirling how many were interested in the proposal for a settlement on the Swan River and what their 'prospects' were. Stirling mentioned the name of one Thomas Peel, a man driven by circumstances and some flaw in his clay to cut a figure on the stage of life quite different from the role he longed to play. Born in 1793 as a younger son in a family of considerable affluence, he was endowed with all the inner drives and absence of restraints to cast him as prodigal son. He was surrounded in childhood and youth by relatives who had climbed with ease the ladder of preferment. His elder brother had sought preferment in the church. His cousin, Robert, had distinguished himself at Harrow School by showing that industry when allied to talent took a man to the top. Spurning a career in the family business, Thomas Peel decided that the one stage on which he could cut a figure was in the New World. He thought first of New South Wales but, after a conversation with Captain Stirling, came to the conclusion that at the Swan River a man with capital might become a proprietor of any-thing up to a quarter of a million acres.[3]

So, like that other second son, he asked his father for his inheritance. Armed with this he put to the Colonial Office a plan for colonization near Swan River believing he had a scheme that might not be deemed wholly unworthy of notice and consideration by those men who had that one gift he lacked, the gift to succeed in the battle of life. All his life, he was to suffer that terrible humiliation of the erratic behaviour of a passionate man being judged by men who despised such excesses. When the two representatives of Mr Money Bags—Edward Schenley and Sir Francis Vincent—pulled out, he lived for a while in that state of panic known to a man of his temperament, terrified lest his wife and the whole host of respectable people who insisted on him giving them an honest account of his affairs should find out that he had sinned against his father by squandering a large part of his inheritance on the gambling tables rather than founding a family dynasty in the wilds of Australia.

Then one day in January 1829 Solomon Levey called on him in London. Levey had been transported to Sydney in 1815, but by 1825, in partnership with another ex-convict, Daniel Cooper, had become one of the wealthiest merchants in Sydney. Like Peel, he was haunted by a feeling that the whole of his outward wealth and display was mocked by a worm of failure in the heart. He had overcome the handicaps of being a Jew and an ex-convict, only to find that a surrender to one of the great follies of the human heart—the thirst for revenge against those who despitefully used him—cheated him forever of man's regard. After his young wife had asked him on her death-bed to forgive her for being unfaithful to him, Levey had published an account of the scene in the *Sydney Gazette*. He was playing for sympathy. Others took it as one of those decisive moments of self-exposure which showed what manner of man he was.

So two desperate men confronted each other that raw winter day in

---

[3] Alexandra Hasluck, *Thomas Peel of Swan River* (Melbourne, 1965), ch. 1; T. Peel to the Colonial Office, 6 November 1828, C.O. 18/1.

London in January 1829. On the surface it looked as though they comple-
mented each other. Peel had status, but no cash; Levey had cash, but no status.
Levey undertook to obtain credit for £20 000 to be used for the charter of
vessels and to purchase requisites for the settlers. Peel was to receive £2000 as
an advance on his salary of £1500 per annum as manager of the scheme.
Finally Levey was to advance a further sum of £50 000 for supplies and stock.
So great was Levey's need that he was not able to read on Peel's face the mind
of a man who lacked the temper and knowledge for such a concern. So great
was Peel's need that he did not pause to ask whether the men who had hooked
him into the scheme, Solomon Levey, and his partner Daniel Cooper, were
not 'the greatest rogues under heaven'.

With the madness of that bitch-goddess success stirring in his blood, Peel,
who had spent most of his adult life lolling in a London Club, feverishly
worked on a plan to transplant some four hundred gentry, including their
dependants, their servants, their stock, their seed and all their worldly goods
to an unspecified site near where Captain Stirling and Charles Fraser had
known that moment of 'cheerfulness'. The Colonial Office undertook to grant
him priority of choice of 250 000 acres on the south bank of the Swan and
Canning Rivers, and an additional 250 000 acres after he had landed four
hundred settlers. After twenty-one years a further 500 000 acres was to be
granted if he met certain conditions on improvement on the two original
grants. He formed an association which undertook to grant two hundred acres
to every person who brought out one male and one female. Individuals who
paid their own passages were to receive one hundred acres each. The association proposed to select artisans and labourers and send them to Swan
River. They also undertook to provide stores, agricultural implements, seed
and stock which could be purchased by the settlers. Levey himself had undertaken to arrange for sufficient supplies from Sydney to reach Swan River to
sustain them until such time as they produced their own goods. Adult
common-class passengers could pay their own way at £25 per person, £13 2s 6d
for children. Cabin class was £60 for each adult and £30 for each child. The
association undertook to pay common labourers 3s for a nine-hour day and
5s for a ten-hour day to skilled workers. They also undertook to grant fifty
acres to every labourer indentured to the association for five years, and free
him from his indenture after three years of service. So with the London
cartoonists lampooning him as 'A Job For My Country Cousin' or 'Cousin
Thomas, or The Swan River Job', with his wife threatening not to accompany him, and the Colonial Office men telling Stirling that after their experience of a few Peel tantrums they had decided the man could not possibly
hold any public office in the new settlement. Peel feverishly tried to enrol
enough capitalists and labourers to make sure ships reached Swan River
before 1 November so that the condition for the extra quarter million acres
would be fulfilled.[4]

[4] Twiss to Peel, 28 January 1829, *H.R.A.*, III. vi. 611-12; handbill issued by the
Thomas Peel Association, 1829, reproduced in Alexandra Hasluck, op. cit., p. 55; ibid.,
chs 2-5; *Sydney Gazette*, 5 February 1824.

On 30 December 1828 Sir George Murray, the ministerial head of the Colonial Office, informed Stirling of the decision of His Majesty's Government to form a settlement at the mouth of the Swan River. Stirling was to assume the title of Lieutenant-Governor, to determine the most convenient site for a town to be erected as the future seat of government, to make all necessary locations of land in accordance with instructions, reserving a due proportion for the Crown, the maintenance of the clergy, and the support of establishments for the purposes of religion, and the education of youth, to invite settlers to locate themselves south of the Swan River, and to recommend by his counsels and example the habitual observance of Sunday as a day of rest and public worship. On 1 January 1829 he was granted permission to select 100 000 acres for himself on the island of Bauche and on land situated nearest to Cape Naturaliste in Geographe Bay. On 13 January 1829 government published its regulations for the guidance of those proposing to embark as settlers. It reaffirmed its intention not to incur any expense in conveying settlers to the new colony or in supplying them with necessaries after their arrival there. Persons who arrived in the settlement before the end of 1830 would receive in the order of their arrival grants of land free of quitrent in proportion to the capital invested, in the proportion of forty acres for every £3 invested provided they produced proof of same to the Lieutenant-Governor or other officer administering the government. Those who incurred the expense of transport for every labouring person (including women and children over ten years) would be entitled to two hundred acres per person. The full title to such land would not be granted until proof was shown to the Lieutenant-Governor or officer administering the government that the grantee had spent at least 1s 6d per acre on the cultivation of the land or on solid improvements such as buildings, roads or other works. So Stirling got his colonial governorship, a hundred thousand acres of land, the adoration of a wife, and the admiration and goodwill of the men in Downing Street—all those things Thomas Peel was grasping for but never got.[5]

Stirling had also at long last persuaded the British Government to take possession of that part of New Holland west of the degree of longitude named in the instructions to Governor Phillip. Heeding Stirling's warnings about a possible French settlement on the west coast of New Holland, on 5 November 1828 the Secretary of State for the Colonies ordered the officer commanding the naval forces at the Cape of Good Hope to despatch a ship to the west coast of New Holland and take formal possession of it. That officer in turn instructed Captain Charles Howe Fremantle to sail in the frigate *Challenger* to Swan River. On 2 May 1829 at the mouth of the Swan River the Captain in the name of His Britannic Majesty took possession of the whole of New

---

[5] Regulations for the Guidance of Those who may Propose to Embark, as Settlers, for the New Settlement on the Western Coast of New Holland, 13 January 1829, reissued on 3 February 1829 with minor amendments, *H.R.A.*, III. vi. 606-8. See also Murray to Stirling, 22 January 1829, *H.R.A.*, III. vi. 609-10. In this despatch Stirling was instructed to guard against settlers capriciously abandoning their land and to grant land to civil servants on the same principles on which it was granted to other persons.

Holland not included in the territory of New South Wales: one third of the continent, one million square miles of land and 4300 miles of coastline. Unlike Cook, he was instructed to ask the aborigines whether they consented to the act of possession. He was told to be on the alert to prevent surprise from the natives, and especially to be 'very guarded with respect to the women'. In international law there was not so much as an inch of Australia or Van Diemen's Land left for the French, Spaniards, Dutch, Russians, Americans, or the aborigines of New Holland.[6]

In the meantime Stirling pushed on with preparations for departure. Peter Brown was appointed Colonial Secretary; John Morgan was appointed store-keeper; John Septimus Roe, who had travelled with Phillip Parker King in the expeditions of 1818-22, was appointed Surveyor-General; and Captain F. C. Irwin was appointed to command the detachment of the 63rd Regiment, consisting of one other officer and sixty-six men, charged with the task of protecting the colonists against a foreign invader, the natives and civil commotion. Irwin, who had been born in 1788, the son of a Protestant Irish clergyman and schoolmaster, was a man whose face laughter and gaiety were rarely seen. Stern and uncompromising in regard to all matters of private and public morality, a strict follower of that branch of Irish Protestant puritanism which seemed to promise glory to those who were tight of lip and hard of heart, he was merciful to the penitent, and just to all who did not share his solemn, cheerless view of the divine economy.[7]

The rush to depart was so hectic that there was not even time to appoint a colonial chaplain. It was not until July 1829 that John Burdett Wittenoom accepted the position on a salary of £250 a year and the promise of a house and a glebe. He had been born in Nottinghamshire in 1789 and educated at Winchester School and Brasenose College, Oxford. Unlike Irwin, Wittenoom belonged to the High Church party, and identified religion with music and literature, seeing it as a hymn of joy to life rather than a protestation of human unworthiness. The methods of the evangelicals he viewed with a lofty disdain as the manifestation of some vulgar enthusiasm quite alien to the spirit of delight with which he addressed his God. Posterity was to remember him as a man 'under whose ministry amidst the struggles and privations of an infant colony a scion of the Church of England was planted in a remote wilderness'.[8]

On 6 February the *Parmelia* with Stirling, his wife, who was expecting to be delivered of a child at any moment, and Alexander Collie, a surgeon who was hoping that the delightful climate would avert what he called the fatal defect of his 'old wind-pipe', and some prospective settlers and artisans on

---

[6] Stirling to Twiss, 22 October 1828, C.O. 18/1; Admiralty to Twiss, 7 November 1828, C.O. 18/1; Lord Cottesloe (ed.), *Diary and Letters of Admiral C. H. Fremantle* (London, 1928), pp. 15, 18-21; *Sydney Gazette*, 6 December 1826; J. S. Battye, *Western Australia*, pp. 70-2; F. K. Crowley, *Australia's Western Third*, pp. 4-5.

[7] F. C. Irwin, *The State and Position of Western Australia* (London, 1835).

[8] R. E. Cranfield, *The Wittenoom Family in Western Australia* (Perth, 1962); plaque to John Burdett Wittenoom in St George's Cathedral, Perth.

board, weighed anchor at Spithead and made its way down the Channel to
Plymouth where on 9 February it joined H.M.S. *Sulphur* with Captain Irwin
and his soldiers for the long voyage to the Australian wilderness. As the two
ships were being tossed and buffeted by the huge swell from the south in that
vast stretch of sea between Cape Town and Leeuwin, the royal assent was being
given to an Act to provide for the government of 'divers of His Majesty's
Subjects [who] have . . . effected a Settlement upon certain wild and unoccupied Lands on the Western Coast of *New Holland* and the Islands adjacent,
which Settlements had received and are known by the Name of *Western
Australia*'. This Act empowered His Majesty with the advice of the Privy
Council to appoint three or more persons resident in that colony to make
laws, institutions, and ordinances for the peace, order, and good government
of His Majesty's subjects. So while Dr Collie was delivering Mrs Stirling of a
child on board the *Parmelia*, the colony of Western Australia received a
constitution. Two years later Viscount Goderich explained to Stirling that the
Governor, Senior Military Officer, Colonial Secretary, Surveyor-General and
Advocate-General were to discharge the several functions of both a Legislative
Council and an Executive Council.[9]

At the end of May the men on the *Challenger* sighted the *Parmelia* trying
to work a passage between Garden Island and the mainland. They signalled
frantically to desist, but Stirling, carried away by the excitement of the
moment, ignored the warning and drove the ship straight onto the rocks.
The passengers were taken to the small island where they spent four miserable days lashed by wind and rain. Women and children housed in the
Challenger sobbed and wailed and turned Fremantle's cabin into a 'perfect
pigsty'. In the confusion Stirling reproached himself for his over-confidence
and told his wife his career was ended and his ship doomed. The next day he
got the *Parmelia* off the rocks. He was lucky enough not to have a similar
ordeal with the *Sulphur* whose captain almost repeated his own error when the
ship moved into Cockburn Sound. His wife roughed it with the others. The
officers and men were prepared to do anything for her because nature had
been so very kind to her, giving her 'an exceeding nice foot and arm', a pretty
face and a loving heart.[10]

After the landing on 1 June husbands and wives huddled together on the
beach among the pianos, chairs, beds and stores wondering where Stirling's
promised Garden of Eden could be. Labourers found to their mortification
that here, as in the United Kingdom, hard work would be an indispensable
preliminary to meat and drink. Children asked their parents why the trees of
Western Australia grew in snow. Their parents, after explaining lugubriously

---

[9] An Act to Provide, until the Thirty-first Day of *December* One thousand eight
hundred and thirty-four, for the Government of His Majesty's Settlement in Western
Australia, on the Western Coast of New Holland, 10 Geo. IV, c. 122, 14 May 1829,
Statutes at Large, vol. 11; Order in Council, 1 November 1830, encl. in Goderich to
Stirling, 28 April 1831, C.O. 18/9; Marnie Bassett, *The Hentys* (London, 1954), pp. 88-9.

[10] Lord Cottesloe (ed.), *Diary and Letters of Admiral C. H. Fremantle*, pp. 24-5;
Marnie Bassett, op. cit., pp. 130-1.

that it was not snow they were seeing but sand, wondered when the rain would cease and they would enjoy the promised 'light of the sun'. Almost three weeks later on 18 June Stirling proclaimed to all and sundry that His Majesty had been pleased to command that a settlement should forth-with be formed within the territory of Western Australia. He requested them duly to regulate their conduct as good and loyal subjects ought to do, and to obey all legal commands and regulations. He went on to say that if any person or persons were convicted of behaving in a fraudulent, cruel or felonious manner towards the aborigines, such persons would be tried for that offence as though the same had been committed against any other of His Majesty's subjects. All men between the ages of fifteen and fifty were to enrol themselves in the muster-roll for military service in the event of the territory being invaded or attacked by hostile native tribes. All persons who wished to take up land were to appear at the office of the Colonial Secretary and make application for permission to reside in the settlement. All persons who intended to leave the settlement must also apply for leave to do so. The white man had come to Western Australia.

Stirling was not appalled despite problems 'enough to appal the stoutest hearts', nor was he overwhelmed with the difficulty of making a success with men whose habits had been formed in other modes of life 'as wide from this as Earth from Heaven'. He built a port at the mouth of the Swan on which later he conferred the name of Fremantle. He took a party up river to that basin which had so delighted him in 1827, and decided that it would be the site for his capital. On 12 August he again took a party to the basin of the Swan, where a Mrs Dance gave one blow to a large tree with an axe, chivalrously guided by Captain Stirling, and christened the site Perth in honour of the native town of the Secretary of State for the Colonies.[11]

After the arrival of three more ships there were two hundred settlers, thirty-five horses, seventeen cows, three bulls, twenty-five draught oxen, ten calves, two hundred sheep, one hundred pigs and hogs, a large stock of poultry, and some garden ground already producing vegetables. The officers of the *Sulphur* and the other ships had begun to amuse themselves with dinners, dancing, music, cards and drinking. On 29 August Stirling published the regulations governing grants of Crown lands. On 1 October he declared land on the banks of the Swan open for settlement. A month later he declared the land open for selection between the coast and the Darling Range to the south. But still the demands exceeded what was available and those who had searched spread rumours that apart from the river banks the land was not what they had been led to expect. When Mrs Currie's dearest returned from a search for land, he gave a very gloomy account of what he had seen.

In the meantime prospective settlers hanging round the shanty towns of

[11] Proclamation by His Excellency James Stirling . . . Lieutenant-Governor of His Majesty's Settlement in Western Australia, 18 June 1829, appendix 2 in J. S. Battye, *Western Australia*, pp. 456-8; J. Stirling to W. Stirling, 7 September 1829 (Stirling Letters, typescript in M.L.); Marnie Bassett, op. cit., pp. 92-5.

Fremantle and Perth grumbled at government for gobbling the best land or granting it to their 'cronies' in the 'men-of-war' so wantonly that men with a capital entitling them to fifty thousand acres had been put off with a measly five hundred. Gentlemen's sons were standing behind improvised counters selling tea and sugar to kill time, while women, still tent-dwellers rather than mistresses of manor houses in the Australian bush, gossiped outside their tents. Had they come all that way to be 'just roasted' by the sun by day and tormented at night by the shouts and laughter of drunken soldiers and the 'quantities of mosquitoes and fleas in their tents'? Had they come to a land where a fierce sun turned the green shoots of their crops into the sickly dry yellow of death? What manner of men would survive and prosper in such a land?[12]

Chance or the mysterious powers controlling the universe ordained that Thomas Peel and his party of ninety adults and seventy-nine children should arrive on the *Gilmore* in the midst of this 'slough of despond' on 15 December 1829. As usual everything had gone wrong for Peel. He had not met the deadline of 1 November set by the Colonial Office. The stores promised by Levey and Cooper had not arrived. His wife had stayed in London, saying she did not want her children to be eaten by black savages. Stirling had been warned about Peel's 'impetuosity and indiscretion'. On the day he first spoke to Stirling in Perth, the temperature was soaring well over the century as Stirling told him land of the magnitude he was seeking was as rare as hen's teeth.

Impulsive as ever he accepted a site at Woodman's Point on the coast some seven miles south of Fremantle, where all those who came after him would ask: Who would want to settle there? Ill luck or those great gusts of anger continued to stand between him and his dream of cutting a figure in the New World. On 13 February 1830 the *Hooghly* arrived with 173 on board, mostly mechanics and labourers who made their way down to the Woodman's Point settlement just in time to see the charred ruins from the bushfire that had swept through a few days before. By then the workmen were beginning to desert Peel because of the paroxysms of rage with which he responded to opposition or ill fortune. Again luck and what came up from inside the man seemed to be conspiring for his destruction, for in May 1830 the *Rockingham* which had arrived with more settlers for the Peel estate ran aground at Garden Island. After the *Rockingham* episode the ebullience and optimism of the early days left him never to return. He stayed on the estate, but there being no one to work the land, he whiled away the time gambling. Some said he was the victim of the laws of political economy, and some said the fault lay in himself. By one of those unkind turns of the screw a stern judge of human

---

[12] J. Stirling to W. Stirling, 7 September 1829 (Stirling Letters, typescript in M.L.); Diary of M. J. Currie, 10 July, 21 November 1829; copy of Government Notice made Public on the 28th day of August 1829 Relative to Crown Lands, C.O. 18/3; Stirling to Colonial Office, 20 January 1831, C.O. 18/3; Diary of Mary Ann Friend, 2, 7-9 February, 8 March 1830, W.A.H.S., *J. & P.*, vol. 1, 1931, pt 5.

folly was there to witness his failure. In November 1829 the ship *Success* struck a reef off Fremantle. Passengers and crew were marooned in Perth for months. One of these was Thomas Hobbes Scott, first archdeacon of New South Wales, who was returning to England. By June 1830 he was writing to England about Peel's '*total failure*' and how 'the greatest disorder and confusion, pillage & plunder' prevailed at his settlement, where the workers were 'idle, lazy, drunken, profligate & insolent'. The cause of all this lay, he believed, in Peel's 'temper' and 'lack of knowledge', since he was a man without a system or 'the slightest idea of an ultimate object'.[13]

Not only those on whom the hand of the potter seemed to have faltered had to admit defeat. On 12 October 1829 James Henty and his party had reached Fremantle on the *Caroline*. Like the other members of the gentry migrating to Swan River, he hoped that he and his family could plant an English village in the Australian wilderness, complete with squire, parson, tenant farmers and agricultural labourers. He had left England because he and his family were threatened with a descent of many steps in the social ladder which their 'feeling could ill stand'. At first he had planned to go to New South Wales where they would all be placed in 'the first Rank in Society'. A few months later Captain Stirling persuaded the Henty family that they could have all their hearts' desires—the social standing, the amusements and the huge income—at the intended Swan River colony.

So James chartered the *Caroline* and signed on four personal servants, and twenty-nine indentured servants, all of whom undertook to remain dutiful servants in return for a free passage, £20 a year, and fuel and lodgings. He also loaded the ship with blood stock, seed, trees, farm utensils, a telescope, a bugle, ten pounds of shaving soap, thirty silver spoons, pens, ink, paper and one hundred books. The rest of the family were to follow later. On arrival in Perth he joined the army of settlers searching for suitable land. He inspected sites at Leschenault Inlet, at King George's Sound and at York, but found nothing on which to risk his seed and stock. By then he had had more than enough of summer heat, flies, fleas, mosquitoes, 'country life in the raw', and that plague of every settler—the clamour of the indentured servants for houses, food and clothing, and higher wages. He began to find less and less comfort in the claim that society on the Swan was 'above reproach' simply because it was free of those vulgar upstarts, the successful ex-convicts who set the social tone in Sydney. In January 1832 he decided to try his fortunes in Van Diemen's Land.[14]

They were not the only ones to know the bitterness of disappointed hopes. On 14 February 1830 Elizabeth and William Shaw arrived at the settlement expecting favourable land and the delights of a country gentleman's life. The

[13] Based on Alexandra Hasluck, *Thomas Peel of Swan River*, ch. 6; evidence of E. G. Wakefield to Select Committee on Disposal of Lands in British Colonies, *P.P.*, 1836, XI, 512; T. H. Scott to R. Norman, 2 June 1830 (Norman Papers, Kent Archives Office, Canterbury); Diary of M. J. Currie, 12 October 1829.

[14] James Henty to William Henty, August 1828, quoted in Marnie Bassett, *The Hentys*, pp. 34-6; ibid., pp. 128-32, 202-3.

first exchange with Stirling about land left Shaw with such disappointment written on his brow that his wife decided the man who put out those stories in 1827 about good land deserved hanging nine times over. He and his wife concluded that all the arable land near the Swan had been grabbed by 'Jews, Stock Brokers, Men of Wars [sic]' and that out of the 1800 then in the colony there were only a dozen who knew what to do. As for Swan River as a province where gentry could recoup their fortunes, she would like to tell the people in Old England that here gentlemen had been reduced to the way of life of the gypsies. Ladies, gentlemen, children and working people, many without shoes or stockings, went about their lives of gardening, carting water, cooking, washing or nursing their babies. The Governor sometimes received guests without his shoes or stockings on, and was to be seen wearing a dressing-gown *en plein jour*. Mrs Stirling was sometimes to be seen at the bath-tub. The man-servants were drunken and the women dirty, idle, saucy and sluttish. Stockbrokers and Jews got the good land while gentlemen who once rode in carriages were now soiling their hands weighing out tea and sugar. The only hotel was a tent under which people ate meals often without knives, forks or plates. Both she and her husband pined for Old England, for there the world belonged to men of good family, but here the world was beginning to belong to the strong—men with the faces of vulgar louts who had neither opinions nor ideas and were proud of such emptiness and mindlessness.[15]

As the same time others, fashioned of sterner clay, and beneficiaries rather than victims of the throws of chance, went about their daily business quite determined not to allow that fierce sun, or those insects, or that inhospitable soil, or their drunken unruly servants, or those miserablest people in the world, the aborigines, to level all distinctions between man and man or reduce men to a sense of their own impotence. One of these was George Fletcher Moore who arrived on the *Cleopatra* in October 1830. Born in County Tyrone, Ireland, in 1798 a member of the minor gentry, he had studied law at Trinity College, Dublin, and had hoped to obtain a position in the new administration at Swan River. Before leaving England he had gone down on his knees to ask the 'Heavenly giver of all Good' to strengthen and support him in the days when he would be without the friendly hand of a dear parent, and fraternal love, for there was about Moore more than a hint of a woman's sadness, more than a hint that he was more dependent on God than on man for the strength to endure to the end. He took with him a part of his property and sufficient assigned servants to give him a right to choose twelve thousand acres of land. He also took with him a letter to the Lieutenant-Governor recommending him as a lawyer with the qualifications and disposition to serve in government.[16]

[15] Elizabeth Shaw to Mrs Waghorn, 10 March 1830 (Letters of Elizabeth and William Shaw, MS. in M.L.).

[16] G. F. Moore, *Diary of Ten Years Eventful Life of an Early Settler in Western Australia* (London, 1884), pp. iv-vi; see also Letters and Journals of G. F. Moore (MS. in BATTYE L.).

Luck was with him from the start. He was able to obtain land on the Swan above Guildford because the first grantee had just surrendered it. There where the pastures were lush and the soil fertile he built a hut and planted crops. Very soon there was order and discipline in his life. He loved sowing beds of carrots, turnips, cabbages, radishes and peas. He loved the climate. He loved joining with those of like mind and heart every Sunday in a hymn of praise to the author and giver of such good things. He was not altogether happy about his servants. If he was absent from his land none of his servants did any work, and if Moore dared to speak to them there was an 'exit in rage'. One night after he had composed himself for rest he was aroused by the moans of a drunken servant in a nearby ditch. He knew Saint Paul's warning that no drunkard could enter into the kingdom of heaven, but he knew also the divine command 'Judge not'. Heeding the latter would keep his servant, so he did not let his heart be troubled. By September of 1831 he was scribbling verses to express his delight:

> With care and experience, I'm sure 'twill be found
> Two crops in the year we may get from the ground;
> There's good wood and good water, good flesh and good fish,
> Good soil and good clime, and what more could you wish.
> > Then let every one earnestly strive, Sirs
> > Do his best, be alert and alive, Sirs,
> > We'll soon see our colony thrive, Sirs,
> > > So *Western Australia* for me.

True, the aborigines were stirring up 'anxious throbbings' in his 'emigrant's heart'. No one knew how many there were. No one was quite certain how in fact white men could hold the land if the blackfellows learnt how to combine and use fire-arms. But for himself he was inclined to think they were not such a despicable race as was at first supposed. He looked forward to the day when the natives became the bottle-washers, kitchen boys, stable hands and plough-boys of the white man's civilization, for he liked to believe that the black man was not innately incapable of making the leap from savagery to civilization. Those words he recited every Sunday telling how Almighty God had made all manner of men to dwell on the face of the earth reassured him a day would come when the aborigine, too, looked as though he had been made in the image of God.'[17]

Others enraged by the sight of aborigines murdering white men or disgusted by the sight of black men beating their women, decided they were not human beings but monkeys on two legs. Had not these 'black barbarians' resisted all exertions to teach them habits of industry, and did they not refuse to cover their nakedness? As they entertained no system of religion they must belong to the animal rather than the human kingdom. One son of a gentle-

[17] Based on G. F. Moore, op. cit., pp. 1-64.

man deeply shocked another man of genteel birth by saying that he had been out hunting all one morning and had only shot one black. The lower orders, too, were said to hold the life of a native of no value.[18]

The aborigines were not the only ones to lack the strength with which to survive the coming of the white man without degradation. By September 1831 one man was keeping his head in a sack because he did not want the members of his own class to see what months of drunken dissipation in Fremantle and Perth had done to his appearance. By contrast that same September Stirling and his wife gave a ball in Government House for the members of those eighty or ninety families, the civil and military officers and their wives, who had survived the great ordeal of the first two years without loss of self-respect. The rooms were so brilliantly illuminated and the women so well dressed that those present believed the show would not have disgraced one of the finest assemblies in Europe. There were quadrilles, Spanish dances, gallopades and waltzes for those familiar with the latest dancing fashions in London, while for plain country gentry the master of ceremonies called for sets. During the evening that handsome popular couple Governor Stirling and his wife danced a special waltz to show they were as competent on the dance floor as in the labours of the pioneer. Champagne flowed. Toasts were drunk to the ladies. G. F. Moore by special request sang his song 'Western Australia for me'. The ladies withdrew while the men settled down to the brandy, but even after the ladies rejoined them there were 'no marks of excess' on any face, no lewd gestures, no ruffling of ladies' dresses. In a rough stone house some two hundred white men and women were showing that 'home', the 'throne' and 'gentility' could live on in their hearts in the wilds of Australia.[19]

All along the coast between Perth and the Leeuwin by the end of 1831 there were tiny settlements of gentlemen, their families and their servants. One of these was Captain John Molloy and his wife Georgiana. They had been married in August 1829 and had gone to a special service in London where the famous preacher Edward Irving prayed that they might be like Abraham and Sarah in the land God had allotted them and that they might also reach that 'other shore' which had been ordained for them by God. Molloy was a Waterloo veteran who had been left for dead on that day which prepared the way for the spread of British civilization in the New World. Georgiana, a young woman with a distaste for the vanities of London and for any addic-

[18] A. Collie to G. Collie, 4 August 1831 (Collie Letters); F. C. Irwin to Stirling, 18 May 1830, encl. in Stirling to Colonial Office, 18 October 1830, C.O. 18/7; report by A. Collie to Stirling, 24 January 1832, C.O. 18/10; J. Morgan to R. W. Hay, 18 March 1830, C.O. 18/7; J. Hanson, *A Voyage from Madras to Swan River, King George's Sound and Van Diemen's Land* (Guildford, 1833), pp. 7-10; A. Collie to Stirling, 24 January 1832, C.O. 18/10.

[19] Diary of Mary Ann Friend, W.A.H.S., *J. & P.*, vol. 1, 1931, pp. 1-11; T. H. Scott to W. Macarthur, 27 January 1830 (Macarthur Papers, vol. 59); G. F. Moore, *Diary of Ten Years Eventful Life*, pp. 63-5; Marnie Bassett, 'Eliza Shaw and the Perth Ball', *Hist. Studies*, vol. 4, November 1949, pp. 48-58.

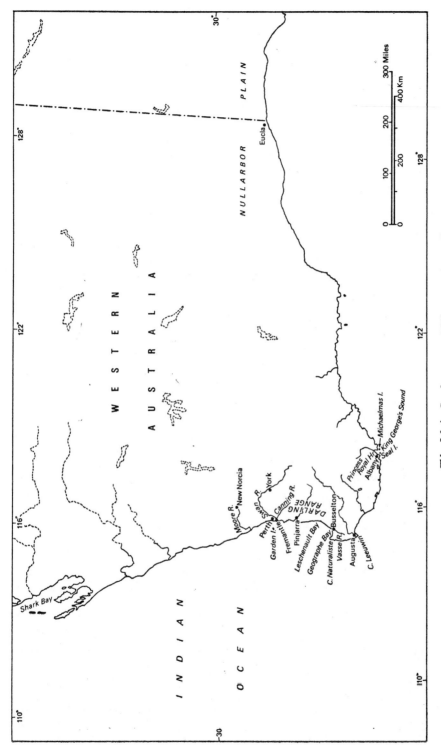

I   *The Main Settlements of Western Australia*

tion to 'dreadful vice and search after unsatisfactory things', belonged to the gentry of Cumberland. At the suggestion of his friend, the very persuasive James Stirling, Molloy had offered her the life of a country gentlewoman in the wilds of Western Australia. On 21 October 1829 they and their servants, their horses, their pigs, sheep and cattle had sailed from Spithead on the *Warrior* which finally arrived at Cockburn Sound on 11 March 1830, only to hear that all the good land on the Swan and the Canning had been taken up. So Molloy felt it wise to accept the advice of Stirling that the promised land lay at Cape Leeuwin. On 1 May the Molloys, the Bussels, the Turners and a Dr Green landed and began the task of planting a society of English gentlemen where hitherto only savages had roamed the woods. They called the site Augusta.

Within a week Mrs Molloy lay in a leaking tent with a servant holding an umbrella as she gave birth to her first child. Soon after, the baby died in her arms in that dreary land and there was no one there to comfort her except her husband. She turned to her God for comfort, for He had shown Himself to both of them in 'many wonderful instances'. For a while she tormented herself for not making proper use of this affliction her God had designed for her, and accused herself of wickedness for not witnessing to others her belief in the life of the world to come. In the years that followed, that afflicting, inscrutable but all-wise Providence punished her again by taking away her 'darling infant and only son'. She sadly missed a female of her own rank to speak to. From time to time the aborigines threatened to do violence to her and her children. But she did not give way to despair. She had her faith to sustain her through the nights of doubt and sorrow and to restrain her even from succumbing to the venial temptation of writing letters on a Sunday. Thanks to her garden, her piano, and the natural beauty she uncovered in what to others was a wilderness, she likened her life to the Garden of Eden before Eve was expelled from Paradise. She discovered that the most uninhabited parts of the earth were just as much loaded with God's bounties as the inhabited parts. After she moved to the Vasse in 1839 she was again reminded of Paradise till rheumatism numbered her days, and in great agony she sent off a message to the women she had loved in Scotland. She sang to the end a hymn of praise to all the beauty she had discovered in that part of God's world. Death took her in April 1843.[20]

[20] W. G. Pickering, 'The Letters of Georgiana Molloy', W.A.H.S., *J. & P.*, vol. 1, 1927-31, pp. 30-6; Marnie Bassett, *The Hentys*, pp. 263-78. Cairn in Augusta erected in 1930 to commemorate the centenary of the settlement, 'On this site stood the home of Captain John Molloy . . .'; personal visit to site 7 June 1970. In 1932 the government of Western Australia erected another cairn 'In memory of the pioneers of Augusta, 1830'. Mrs G. Molloy to Mrs Storey, 1 October 1833 [sic], W. G. Pickering, op. cit., p. 27; Mrs G. Molloy to Mrs Besley, 7 November 1832, ibid.; Mrs G. Molloy to Miss M. Dunlop, 18 January 1832, ibid.; Mrs G. Molloy to Captain Mangles, 21 March 1837, 25 January, 1 November 1838; extracts from letters of Mrs G. Molloy to Captain Mangles from Fairlawn on the Vasse between June 1840 and 1843, printed in W. G. Pickering, op. cit.; for the accounts of the Molloy story see Marnie Bassett, *The Hentys*, pp. 263-78 and Alexandra Hasluck, *Portrait with Background: a Life of Georgiana Molloy* (Melbourne, 1955); John Milton, *Paradise Lost*, Book XI, lines 286-92.

After the withdrawal of the military garrison and the convicts from King George's Sound in 1831, some settlers quickly descended on it to build a nest of gentlefolk in that place where Vancouver had seen a few grovelling shrubs or dwarf trees scattered at a great distance from each other on the face of the ground. In 1831 A. Collie was appointed the first government resident at Albany. But two years later when the bracing climate failed to repair the damage in his 'old wind-pipe' he withdrew. He was replaced in 1833 by Captain Sir Richard Spencer, one-time captain in Her Majesty's navy and knight of the Hanoverian Order, who had accepted the position together with the pittance of £100 a year in the hope that a substantial grant of land might keep his family at least in the ranks of the colonial gentry. He arrived in the Sound in the *Buffalo* on 13 September 1833 with his wife, nine children, twenty-two servants and agricultural labourers, sheep, pigs, poultry, seed, plants, farm implements and tools, doors, window frames, flooring and English blue slates with which to build a house appropriate to his concept of his station in life. He was then fifty-one and his wife thirty-eight. He used the aborigines of the Sound to cut down trees and clear the land in return for rations of flour and suet, and an occasional gift of a frying pan. He also handed out Bibles to the natives, for he hoped to win them for Christ so that they, too, like the white men, could put their trust 'in the merits of Him' who sat at the right hand of God interceding for all transgressors. One aborigine who worked as a house servant always attended the family prayers each day and church on Sunday. True, all the aborigines had the chronic habit of pilfering potatoes, but within a year he had taught them to flog any member of their people who broke God's commandment, 'Thou shalt not steal.' For him the aborigines were the agricultural labourers on his seigniory; he was the steward whom God required to be faithful.[21]

Spencer planted a willow tree from cuttings taken from the soil surrounding Napoleon's grave in St Helena, for as a man who had fought with distinction for his country he tried to put down in his adopted country lasting memorials to those victories and keep the flag of loyalty flying in the Southern Seas. He built the Old Farm on what he called 'Strawberry Hill', with a majestic view of Princess Royal Harbour and the Sound, hoping that within those walls the cause of culture and true religion would so flourish and abound that others, too, would see those good works and glorify their Father in Heaven. In 1835 he presided over one of 'the gayest of the gay scenes' at Strawberry Hill when he and his wife, a woman of 'startling beauty', acted as hosts at a ball for Governor Stirling and his lovely lady with the pretty foot. Sir Richard wore proudly on his heart the ribbons of a Companion of the Bath and his membership of the Hanoverian Order. Sir Richard and Lady Spencer viewed the pleasures of the evening as one of those earthly pleasures God showered on those whom he took into His keeping. Yet the people at the Sound seemed bent on thwarting God's purposes. The aborigines, after a

21 H. S. Spencer to ———, 18 January 1837 (Spencer Letters, MS. at the Old Farm, Strawberry Hill, Albany, typescript in BATTYE L.).

beginning of much promise, deserted him. A Mr Cheyne persecuted him in the most extraordinary manner from the first moment of his landing in the colony. The handsome grant of land which he confidently expected his Gracious Sovereign to confer on him for his courage and devotion during the Napoleonic Wars never materialized. Not even for Sir Richard Spencer, a hero of the British navy, was His Majesty's Government prepared to waive the decision of 1831 that the policy of making grants of land was to cease. On the evening of 24 July 1839 as he was laughing with his family, death snatched him away.

The house and the grave survived as memorials of his dream of planting a society of landed gentry distinguished for their loyalty to the throne. For over his grave, in accord with his own wishes, his wife erected a flagstaff on which from time to time that flag under which he had fought and bled almost to death might fly. She also put in writing a reminder to posterity of her husband's faith that he had now left a 'world of care and trouble for one of endless bliss and joy'. That same year a boat carrying Lady Spencer's eldest son capsized in Princess Royal Harbour and her 'poor boy sank to rise no more except as lifeless clay'. By that year there were some thirty to forty small white-washed cottages and a few small gardens in addition to the Spencer manor against a backdrop of sandy soil, coarse vegetation and a forest of stunted trees, which looked as though it would remain in a state of nature for generations to come. One visitor wrote in his diary that he never wished to walk again in so uninviting a country, for after seeing Europe, the Americas and the Pacific he had never visited one place so very dull and uninteresting as King George's Sound. Another visitor, with an eye for what went on in the hearts of men, concluded the great dryness and desolation of the country surrounding the Sound were God's special punishment for the drunkards, fornicators and liars of Western Australia.[22]

In the meantime responsible men in Perth were predicting that they might soon preside at the death of all the white man's settlements in Western Australia and hand back the land to the aborigines. The labouring classes for want of steady employment were already becoming, like the aborigines, vagabonds and scavengers on the face of the earth. The settlers were suffering from scarcity of labour, and absence of services such as roads and public transport with which to bring their goods to markets. In 1832 an angry and anxious babble of voices began to be heard on the Swan, at York and down at the

---

[22] R. Spencer to M. Liddon, 12 December 1835, Anne Spencer to Philip and Henry Mules, 14 August 1839, Anne Spencer to Jonathon Baundrett, 14 August 1839, Anne Spencer to Captain McCrea, 21 September 1840, R. Spencer to Collector of Colonial Revenue, 18 March 1834 (Spencer Letters); Letter of R. Spencer to *The Times*, 3 October 1798; portraits of Sir Richard and Lady Spencer, Old Farm, Strawberry Hill, Albany; grave of Sir Richard Spencer, Albany; plaque in memory of Captain Sir Richard Spencer, Government Resident and pioneer of Albany, Church of England, Albany; personal visit to these sites, 6 June 1970; Charles Darwin, *The Voyage of the Beagle* (Everyman ed., London, 1959), pp. 432-3; W. B. Marshall to Martha Marsden, 1 January 1835 (Marsden Papers, vol. 1, p. 569). Book of Haggai, 1: 4-11.

A MADONNA OF THE AUSTRALIAN BUSH
Georgiana Molloy

Miniature by an unknown artist, in the possession of Mrs A. V. R. Bunbury, Busselton

AN ENLARGER AND A
STRAITENER

James Stirling
*Portrait by an unknown artist, Mitchell
Library, Sydney*

George Grey
*Engraving by W. W. Alais, Mitchell
Library, Sydney*

Vasse, Augusta and Albany. Some said the facility of acquiring land in the first three years of settlement had caused that dispersion of settlement which so increased the cost of essential services such as roads, postal services and police that government lacked the revenue with which to provide them. Some said the introduction of sales of Crown land at a minimum upset price of 5s per acre had checked the tide of immigration, and suggested that Western Australia by virtue of its size and the scarcity of its population should be excepted from the new policy. Some said far too many people had turned to that 'miserable comforter' the 'shrine of Bacchus', some said the use of convicts was the best means to save the colony from a 'sickly and long childhood', and some said there was quite enough depravity already without importing convicts. In July 1832 the tradesmen, mechanics and artisans of Perth petitioned Stirling to rescue them from starvation. In the same month the settlers petitioned him for government assistance in building roads and bridges, and for the right of the agricultural and mercantile interest to elect their own representatives to the Legislative Council.

Since the colonial government lacked the means to come to the aid of either the artisans or the settlers, various circumstances connected with the state and future progress of the settlement induced Stirling to decide on making a voyage to England. He sailed on 12 August 1832, and turned up at the Colonial Office early in the following year only to find the men at the top speaking a language to which he was a stranger. Instead of promises of relief or assistance he was lectured on the folly of unsystematic colonization and making huge grants of land to capitalists. Government was not prepared to exempt Western Australia from the system of sales of Crown land at a minimum upset price. Government was prepared to empower the Lieutenant-Governor to nominate two to four members of the Legislative Council from the men engaged in commercial and agricultural pursuits, but election must wait until such time as the colonial government could pay its way. As for the artisans, they should be told it was the fate of the members of their class to earn their bread by the sweat of their brows.

In the meantime in Perth as the months rolled by without any signs of the thousands of young ladies Stirling had rashly promised to send out, or those tens of thousands of rich immigrants, the settlers again became faint of heart. One man prophesied that they would all be 'home in a trice' and the fine new houses they had built would be left to the natives. Another man warned the gentry that if they lost faith in their capacity to plant English villages in the Australian wilderness, the 'scum and refuse' of society would set the tone. Believing that chaplains, missionaries, and schoolmasters might strengthen the fibre of settlers and artisans, the administrator, F. C. Irwin, also set off for London for a shipload of such moral improvers. Succumbing quickly to the strain, his deputy, Captain R. Daniell, babbled away like a little child in Perth, while Georgiana Molloy at Augusta drew from her garden and her faith the strength to go on, Sir Richard Spencer at Albany meditated on the duty, fear and love he owed to God above, and G. F. Moore watched his crops grow and sang 'Western Australia for me' to people who needed such reassurance while they waited for Stirling to return as their deliverer.[23]

By contrast some in high places began to behave like men who were looking for scapegoats on whom to take vengeance for all they had gone through. In April 1833 the cry went up for vengeance against the aborigines for disturbing the public peace in Fremantle. On instructions from the Executive Council the police seized an aboriginal leader, paraded him in front of Perth Gaol and then shot him dead. Overwhelmed with remorse for what they had done, they captured the victim's son and offered him the gift of being a member of the white man's society, only to find to their mortification that the boy spurned such a gift from his father's murderer.[24]

On 21 June 1834 Stirling at long last reached King George's Sound after a journey of thirty-two weeks. Although he had not managed to persuade the government in London to make any considerable outlay of public money on the advancement of Western Australia or to make any exception to the 5s minimum upset price for Crown land, he was as cheerful as ever and told them that if he was sure of anything he was sure Western Australia would prosper. But when he arrived at Perth at the end of the month he found to his dismay that a great change had come over the attitude of the white men to the aborigines. Fewer and fewer shared the faith of G. F. Moore and other high-minded men that a day would come when all the aborigines in the settled district wore European clothes, spoke English and sang hymns of praise every Sunday to the white man's god. A disgust and nausea at the habits of the aborigines was replacing the earlier benevolence and pity. 'I do not know', wrote one observer, 'a more disgusting, or to a European more extra-ordinary, sight than that of a woman suckling her child (which is suspended in her bag or "cotto" on her back) by throwing her long flabby breast over her shoulder to it, where the wretched dirty infant, with its eyes and nose half closed with filth and flies, sucks out of a thing more resembling the hose of a fire engine than a woman's breast.' The aborigines, it was being said, were very revengeful and never forgave an injury. Alarmists were even prophesying that such a warlike people would exterminate the white man if ever the white man was foolish enough to give him the means to do so. At the same time some aborigines had come to the conclusion that the white man would in time reduce all the aboriginal women to harlots and helots and kill all the men who tried to resist the invasion of their tribal lands.[25]

[23] J. Hanson, *A Voyage from Madras to Swan River*, pp. 60-1; F. C. Irwin, *The State and Position of Western Australia*, pp. 43-7, 53-4; J. Mangles to Goderich, 17 January 1831, C.O. 18/9; A. Collie to G. Collie, 5 May 1832 (Collie Letters), Memorial of Trades-men, Mechanics, and Artizans to Stirling, 3 July 1832, C.O. 18/10; Memorial of Settlers to Stirling, 3 July 1832, C.O. 18/10; Stirling to Arthur, 10 August 1832 (Arthur Papers, vol. 49); Goderich to Stirling, 8 March 1833, C.O. 397/2; for the correspondence of Stirling with the Colonial Office during his London visit see C.O. 18/12; A. Collie to G. Collie, 7 April 1834 (Collie Letters).
[24] Irwin to Goderich, 10 April, 1 June 1833, C.O. 18/12.
[25] Stirling to Arthur, 24 June 1834 (Arthur Papers, vol. 49); Stirling to Stanley, 21 September 1834, C.O. 18/14; W. St P. Bunbury and W. P. Morrell (eds), *Early Days*

When Stirling heard in October 1834 that a tribe of natives in the Murray district had grown so bold, after murdering four or five white persons, that they were threatening to spear all the inhabitants in that area, he decided to deal effectually with the guilty tribe. Mustering a party of twenty-five, consisting of some senior civil officers, Captain Ellis, five mounted police and nine soldiers, he set out from Perth to scour the countryside round the estuary of the Murray in search of natives. At Pinjarra they opened fire on a group, killing some fifteen to twenty at the expense of the life of that gallant officer, Captain Ellis. Stirling hoped the punishment, distressing though it was to the private feelings of individuals, would stop the career of mischief by aborigines. Lord Glenelg, the Secretary of State for the Colonies, rebuked him and instructed him to remind the settlers that government was determined to punish any act of injustice or violence on the natives with the utmost severity. But by then Stirling believed that if at any time the natives overcame their material weakness and their chronic inability to combine they would exterminate the invader. The one way for two thousand white people in those scattered settlements to prevent fifty thousand aborigines waging a bloody war of attrition with their primitive spears, boomerangs and waddies was for the white man to display and make use of his superior fire power until such time as he outnumbered the aborigines.[26]

In colonial language, that was the whole bloody trouble! The population of the white man did not increase. When Stirling left for London in 1832 there were 1497 people in the settlement. In June 1837 there were only 2032 white people, of whom 590 were in Perth, 387 in Fremantle, 524 in the Swan River district, 41 on the Canning, 65 at York, 170 at Plantagenet, 17 on the Murray, 32 at Augusta, 21 at the Vasse, and 185 members of the military community. The Stirling and Irwin missions to London had produced neither settlers nor effective moral improvers. A Dr Giustiniani arrived in September 1836 to preach the gospel to the aborigines and attend to the spiritual needs of the white settlers. The man's whole spiritual life had been one uninterrupted uproar during which he had been a Jesuit, a Lutheran and a Methodist. His relations with his fellow-men were characterized by such violence that he became a laughing stock, while in his private life his long-suffering wife was often obliged to seek protection from her neighbours against his rages. He taught the aborigines to sing psalms and hymns of praise to the Omnipotent Deity but made no attempt to teach them how to grow crops, make clothing or manufacture goods.

in Western Australia (London, 1930), pp. 27-8, 191; Irwin to Goderich, 10 April, 1 June 1833, C.O. 18/12.

[26] G. F. Moore, *Diary of Ten Years Eventful Life*, p. 236; Alexandra Hasluck, *Thomas Peel of Swan River*, ch. 9; Stirling to Arthur, 2 December 1834 (Arthur Papers, vol. 49), F. C. Irwin, *The State and Position of Western Australia*, pp. 26-7; P. Hasluck, *Black Australians* (Melbourne, 1942), ch. 3; *Western Australian Government Gazette*, 30 July 1836; Government Notice, Col. Sec.'s Office, Perth, 21 July 1837, encl. in Stirling to Glenelg, 29 December 1837, C.O. 18/18; Stirling to Glenelg, 29 August, 3 November 1836, C.O. 18/16; F. Lancaster Jones, *The Structure and Growth of Australia's Aboriginal Population* (Canberra, 1970), p. 4.

Life in Perth remained lamentably dull, the one source of excitement and distraction being the abusing and slandering of neighbours. As for the settlers, it was said that by 1836 scarcely a property was free from mortgage. Their methods of farming were said to have the slovenly character of men who had lost hope. Deeply wedded to the old established English or Scottish farming methods, they were reluctant to make any changes to suit the climate or soil. Their wives, acquainted as they were with the elegant accomplishments appropriate in a gentlewoman's drawing- or music-room, were inclined to think of the essential occupations of the cow-yards as reserved for the more vulgar and coarse members of society. With ruin staring them in the face, their property mortgaged and themselves without a sixpence, they went on giving dinner parties, buying the finest clothes that came to the colony, and living in general as though they were well off. The cause of their financial difficulties was the high price of labour, and the high price of the necessaries of life. Those who used the laws of political economy to explain the distribution of prizes in the human lottery pointed out that they were all the victims of the 5s minimum upset price for Crown land introduced in 1832. No settler would pay 5s per acre to settle in a colony where labour was dear when for 5s he could obtain land and cheap convict labour in the penal colonies of New South Wales and Van Diemen's Land. But that 5s minimum upset price was but a symptom of one of those great upheavals in Europe, the effects of which were felt even at the Antipodes. Western Australia had been started by men whose grand conception of an aristocratic society, fresh from a victory over its mighty opposite, was becoming an unreality. Within a year of the foundation of Western Australia in 1829 men took over the seals of office in London who were looking for a solution to the problem of the redundant population of the British Isles rather than for spoils for the heroes of the Peninsular Campaign. Those men of high courage and a capacity for breaking bounds, such as Sir James Stirling, Thomas Peel, Sir Richard Spencer and Captain Molloy, touched as they were by some of the daring of a Byron, were about to be swept off the stage of human history and replaced by the men of the middle class. The British Isles which had housed men with 'largeness of vision' were about to come under the sway of the 'straighteners'.[27]

The two thousand-odd victims of that turn of fortune's wheel in Western Australia snarled at each other like wild dogs. Men who had admired the courage and responded to the warmth of heart Stirling had displayed in the early days began to whisper that his energies were erratic, his enthusiasms unstable, and that not the least reliance was to be placed on his word since

[27] Statistical Report upon the Colony of Western Australia, Drawn up at the Conclusion of the Quarter Ending June 1837, encl. in Stirling to Glenelg, 15 October 1837, C.O. 22/14; based on Stirling to Spring Rice, 4 May 1835, C.O. 18/15; Stirling to Glenelg, 12 July 1836, C.O. 18/16; minutes of Legislative Council, 22 March 1836, C.O. 18/16; Stirling to Hay, 10 March 1835, C.O. 18/15; W. St P. Bunbury and W. P. Morrell (eds), *Early Days in Western Australia*, pp. xx, 30, 63-4, 113, 140-1; for the general idea advanced in this section see 'Heinrich Heine' in Matthew Arnold, *Essays in Criticism* (London, 1964); Job, 'He enlargeth a nation, and straineteth it again'.

he was notorious for changing his mind and his measures at least ten times a day. The trifling affairs of two thousand-odd people puddling and indeed seeming to glory in their own dullness were quite insufficient to engross his attention and he passed his time still building those 'castles in Spain'. In 1827 his 'castle' had been Swan River as an emporium for trade with the East. Now in 1836–7 when the settlers were clamouring for cheaper land, cheaper labour and cheaper goods, Stirling came up with yet another of his 'wild visionary projects'—growing cotton in the tropical parts of Western Australia to free the British manufacturers from their dependence on the slave-grown cotton of the United States of America.

By the beginning of 1838 the newly founded *Swan River Guardian* wrote of him as a man who had been corrupted by the flattery of the Government House clique, those adulterers and coveters of their neighbours' wives who had so debauched the minds of the settlers that the killing of an aborigine was held to be no different from the shooting of a bronze-winged pigeon or a cockatoo. At the same time the settlers mouthed the old colonial platitude about no taxation without representation. But how could two thousand-odd white people assume the responsibility for the defence of a coastline of thousands of miles? How could a tiny band of two thousand civilize one-third of Australia? The Stirling dream of Swan River as a province for some of Britain's gentry was fading away. Stirling had tendered his resignation in October 1837 and had waited patiently till almost the end of 1838 to hear of its acceptance. On the eve of his departure in January 1839 the settlers, artisans, and mechanics thanked him for his contribution to the foundation of a 'scion of the best and greatest nation upon earth', for having introduced into the wilderness the religious and civil institutions of the parent country and for having opened to the savage tribes of a vast region access to the incalculable blessings of Christianity. G. F. Moore tried to revive their faith with a performance of his 'Western Australia for me'. Stirling spoke of his pride in having annexed so vast a region to the British Empire with so small a body of adventurers. And off he sailed on 5 January 1839 for London to serve again the Empire he adored and to die on 22 April 1865 at Guildford surrounded by those nests of gentlefolk he had dreamed of erecting in the Australian wilderness.[28]

If anyone doubted that the days of the 'enlargers' were numbered and the days of the 'straiteners' about to begin, Stirling's successor soon stripped away the remnants of that delusion with which they had sustained themselves for the first ten years. It was not just that difference between a man who was all head and no heart, and a man of a lively if erratic heart and little head. Stirling was one of those adventurers of the gentry who were living on the

[28] *Swan River Guardian*, 11, 18 January, 1 February 1838; Stirling to Glenelg, 2 October 1837, C.O. 18/18; Glenelg to Stirling, 16 April 1838, C.O. 397/5; *Perth Gazette and Western Australian Journal*, 5 January 1834; for the career of Sir James Stirling after his departure from Fremantle see F. K. Crowley, 'James Stirling' in D. Pike (ed.), *Australian Dictionary of Biography*, vol. 2 (Melbourne, 1967); *Western Australian Government Gazette*, 5 January 1839.

borrowed time won for their class by Wellington and his gallant men at Waterloo. His successor, John Hutt, belonged to the great English middle class. Alike only in the number of their years—for in 1839 they were both in their forty-sixth year—Stirling had made his career in the navy while Hutt had made his in the civil service. Stirling was a married man; Hutt was a confirmed bachelor. Stirling greeted people with a hand squeeze of greater warmth than ceremony required; Hutt's handshake was as cold as that of the proverbial fish. Stirling was open and generous; Hutt was of an austere turn of mind which seemed to cause the kindlier feelings to shrivel up in him. Stirling's dream had been to plant English villages of squires, parsons, tenant farmers and agricultural labourers; Hutt was one of those 'calculators', one of those 'economists' who believed systematic colonization was a solution to the problem of redundant population in the British Isles as well as to the problems created by the 'extreme facility of acquiring land' during the first three years in Western Australia. Within ten days of his arrival he announced that all land grants that had not met the improvement conditions prescribed in the regulation of 1829 must be surrendered forthwith. On 22 April he announced that Her Majesty's Government had conferred on him the responsibility of deciding whether the minimum upset price of Crown land should be raised from 5s to 12s an acre.[29]

By an odd irony of fate the day before Hutt let the settlers see that what mattered most to them could never be, a miserable object of a man walked into a hut in the northern outskirts of Perth and told the inhabitants about the land beyond the limits of settlement. His name was George Grey. His father had been a lieutenant-colonel in the British army. His mother was one of those 'gentle spirits' who belonged by birth to the genteel poor—the clergy. The news of her husband's death at Badajoz early in April 1812 led to the premature birth of her only son George on 14 April in Lisbon. Smothered in childhood by her love, he walked onto the stage of life driven by hopes of worldly glory but deprived of the precious gift of liking or being liked by other human beings. Debarred from going to Oxford or Cambridge by his weakness in Latin and Greek, he strove all the harder for his mother's approval in the profession his father had followed—the army. In 1830 while a young ensign in Ireland he shrank in horror from the cruelty practised by the English to preserve their domination over poverty-stricken, superstition-ridden, ignorant, filthy and degraded Irish peasants. He began to turn his eyes towards the New World as a place where the absence of such ancient wrongs might prevent the defilement of mankind. He thought of migrating to the United States, but was not prepared to serve under any other flag than that under which his father had served. So he submitted to the Secretary of State for the Colonies a plan for the exploration of the north-west coast of New Holland. On 2 December 1837 he and his party of eleven reached Hanover Bay.[30]

[29] Based on the Diary of W. Cowan, 22 May 1841 (MS. in BATTYE L.).
[30] *Perth Gazette*, 27 April 1839, 11 January 1840.

After landing they made their way south to the Glenelg River, where Grey had the satisfaction of seeing a stretch of country as verdant and fertile as the eye of man ever rested on. He believed that within a few years a British population, rich in civilization and the means of transforming an unoccupied country to one teeming with inhabitants and produce, would soon follow in his steps. Like all the other men who followed the advice of the early Dutch navigators that he who would know this country must first walk over it, he was struck with the sudden changes from barrenness and sterility to richness and splendour. He also wondered why so fair a land should only be the abode of savages and thought it was anomalous that savages should roam over unused riches. He wondered how long these things were to be and how long it would be before providence arranged for the white man to extend his dominion over these areas of barbarism. He had other things on his mind. He was prostrated by the great heat. He was racked with pain from a wound inflicted on his hip by an aborigine who resented the white man's invasion of his hunting ground, and by rheumatic pains brought on partly by diet and partly by that temperament which left him, like Job, 'never quiet'. When he returned to Hanover Bay on 15 April 1838 he had come to the conclusion that under proper treatment the aborigines might easily be raised very considerably in the scale of civilization. The religion he had learned on his mother's knee taught him that all men were made in the image of God. The flaw in his being had made communion with most white men like participation in a vaudeville of devils. But he could be warm and loving with aborigines because they did not threaten his career.[31]

All his experiences during his second journey in the Shark Bay district between February and April 1839 strengthened his conviction that the aborigines of New Holland were in a depressed condition because they were the victims of the white man's prejudice which placed them on the scale of creation nearly on a level with the brutes. He came back to Perth believing he knew how to rescue the aborigine from the fate of disappearing before the advance of civilization or being treated permanently as an inferior race. He had come to the conclusion that the laws of the aborigines, rather than their lack of intelligence, or difference of appetite or passion from the white man, prevented them from rising above barbarism. So long as they were allowed to execute their barbarous laws and customs upon one another, so long would they remain hopelessly immersed in their state of barbarism. His remedy was to make them subject forthwith to British laws, because it was a contradiction to suppose that individuals subject to savage and barbarous laws could rise into a state of civilization which those laws had a manifest tendency to destroy and overturn. The other main causes retarding the civi-

[31] George Grey, *Journals of Two Expeditions of Discovery in North-West and Western Australia, During the years 1837, 38, and 39* (2 vols, London, 1841), vol. 1, pp. 94-7; J. Rutherford, *Sir George Grey* (London, 1961), pp. 3-13; George Grey, op. cit., vol. 1, chs 5-10; for Grey on the aborigines in district between Hanover Bay and the Glenelg River see George Grey, op. cit., vol. 1, ch. 11, esp. p. 253.

lization of the aborigine were the uncertain demand for their labour, the white man's practice of only employing them in the lowest order of manual labour which was so badly paid as to offer no inducement to abandon a nomadic bush life. He suggested that the way to overcome this was to reward each settler who civilized an aborigine with money or a grant of land. He suggested that natives who could produce a marriage certificate should receive a small reward as should natives who registered the birth of a child. In these ways the work of the civilization of the aborigines would at once start on a great scale.[32]

After being appointed Resident Commissioner at King George's Sound in August 1839 in place of the late Sir Richard Spencer he pushed on with his study of the aborigines with such zeal that within four months he was ready to publish his *Vocabulary of the Dialects Spoken by the Aboriginal Races of S.W. Australia*. In the late spring of that year he fell in love with 'a very fascinating girl'—Eliza Lucy Spencer—and married her in November and was very happy for a while. He was not to know then that a day would soon come when his idea of heaven was to be a place where he could no longer hear his wife talking, and she would know that terrible moment when she discovered that this gifted, high-minded, handsome young army captain only had room in his heart for his career and his mother.

After he returned to London in September 1840 he met in Downing Street men who wanted to hear how the natives of New Holland could be saved from being wiped off the face of the earth by the expansion of the white man's society. He communed with James Stephen, Permanent Under-Secretary in the Colonial Office, who shared his view that prayer and meditation on God's holy word, rather than railways, steam-engines, and spinning jennys were the 'inexhaustible unfathomable source of all pure consolation and spiritual strength'. Now it happened that Stephen and other senior men in the Colonial Office were looking for the sort of man they believed they saw in Grey to take over the government of yet another province in Australia which was having trouble with those early steps by which 'Providence has ordered that nations should advance from barbarism to civilization'. For those who pray together are apt to be weak at reading the mind's construction in the face of each other. So Captain George Grey, and his wife Eliza, big with his child, were 'bound for South Australia' where the 'straiteners' of mankind were in the ascendancy. In the meantime the would-be 'enlargers' in Western Australia were surrounded with the wrecks and remnants of their hopes. The body of Sir Richard Spencer was rotting in the grave at King George's Sound. Down at the Vasse, Georgiana Molloy already had intimations that her days in God's world were numbered. At Peel's Inlet Thomas Peel was living in a miserable hut built of stone and covered with rushes. The clay floors, the handsome plate, the curtains for doors, the pianoforte, the windows

---

[32] Based on George Grey, op. cit., vol. 2, ch. 18; George Grey, Report upon the Best Means of Promoting the Civilization of the Aboriginal Inhabitants of Australia, 4 June 1840 (Aborigines Papers, MS. in M.L.).

without glass, and a whole pig hanging in the verandah showed what he was: a 'broken-down gentleman'. What Grey had to do was to prove once and for all that it was not necessary for men to practise 'such a dreadful waste of God's bountiful gifts' in Australia.[33]

[33] G. F. Moore, *Diary of Ten Years Eventful Life*, p. 401; Vivian Stuart, *The Beloved Little Admiral* (London, 1967), pp. 196-7; J. Rutherford, *Sir George Grey*, pp. 17-20; G. Grey to Lord John Russell, 4 June 1840, in G. Grey, *Journal of Two Expeditions of Discovery*, vol. 2, pp. 372-88; James Stephen to H. Venn, 3 April 1839 (Stephen Papers, MS. in Library of Trinity College, Cambridge); E. G. Wakefield to the colonization commissioners for South Australia, 2 June 1835, appendix to Second Report from Select Committee on South Australia, *P.P.*, 1841, IV, 394; A. Burton and P. V. Henn (eds), *Wollaston's Picton Journal 1841-1844* (Perth, 1948), pp. 60-1.

3

A BRITISH PROVINCE
WITH A LAUDABLE PURPOSE

BY 1835 two methods of planting European civilization in Australia had been tried and both had been found wanting. The method using convicts in New South Wales and Van Diemen's Land had been found to be attended with the grave moral evils of slavery and to create the germs of nations said to be most depraved in their vicious propensities. The penal colonies had created wealth, it was said, on a moral dunghill. The method used in Western Australia of making land grants to men of capital had not been attended with moral evils but with economic stagnation. Members of illustrious families in England had been quickly reduced to a way of life indistinguishable from that of the barbarian. The problem was to find a method of transplanting civilization to a wilderness without the moral evils of using slave labour or causing civilized people to fall back into a primitive way of life. On 21 August 1829, under the heading 'Australia', the *Morning Chronicle* in London began to publish a series of letters by an anonymous writer who claimed to have the answer to the problem. On 2 September the letters were given that sub-heading by which they were to be known to posterity, for on that day they were called 'A Letter from Sydney'.

The author argued that colonies went to utter ruin either because an extreme facility in acquiring land caused dispersion of settlement or because of the evils of using slave or semi-slave labour. With dispersion of settlement the people of Australia would lapse into barbarism; with slave labour they would become rotten before they were ripe. They could avoid either fate by a simple remedy. Instead of granting land to capitalists the waste lands of the Australian colonies should be sold at a 'sufficient price', by which he meant a price sufficiently high to prevent labourers from becoming landowners too soon, and sufficiently low to attract men to invest capital. The money raised from the sale of such lands should be used to pay the passages of migrants who should be selected in equal numbers from both sexes to put a stop to the era of the 'roaring lions' in the Australian colonies. The transportation of convicts should be abolished and free institutions introduced. The author wanted colonization to be conducted 'systematically', for he had the gift of dropping the memorable word. He also wanted men to enjoy the sun in Sydney, for running through all the letters was this note of a prophet of political economy who wanted men to live life more abundantly.[1]

[1] *Mechanics Magazine*, 15 November 1823 (copy sighted in Papers of Francis Place, MS. in British Museum); E. G. Wakefield to F. Place, 7 January 1825, ibid.; *Mechanics*

At the end of 1829 the twelve letters were published as a pamphlet, *A Letter from Sydney, the Principal Town of Australia*, edited by Robert Gouger, who was already known as the author of *Sketch of a Proposal for Colonizing Australasia*, first published in the *Morning Chronicle* on 27 August and 1 September 1829. Gouger was born on 26 June 1802 of French ancestry. He was a man of quite extravagant benevolence and compassion for all those who were in any way afflicted or distressed in mind, body or estate. He was extravagant in his politics, extravagant in his religious observances, spending much time in prayer and communion with his God, and extravagant in his relations with other men, meeting rebuff either with excessive displays of meekness, or a fit of the sulks. He had just enough uproar and chaos in his own soul to make him an enthusiastic supporter of any scheme that promised to impose an order on the human ant heap.[2]

The man who claimed later to have written *A Letter from Sydney* was of a quite different order of being. His name was Edward Gibbon Wakefield. He was born in London in March 1796 and educated at Westminster School and Edinburgh High School, after which he entered the diplomatic service. There were at least two persons inside him. There was that 'coarse, sinister, clever fellow', that man of evil intentions and brutish impulses, that 'child-stealer' who had been imprisoned in 1827 in Newgate Gaol for abducting a ward in chancery. For this he had forfeited the right to the society of all respectable people and was condemned to exercise influence over the destinies of mankind as a backstairs intriguer. There was also inside him a compassion for the victims of human savagery. In Newgate he became interested in the convicts transported to New South Wales. This led him on to find out what happened to them in the New World, which in turn led him to the question whether a civilization could only be transplanted by the use of slave or semi-slave labour or whether the use of free labour would always end in one of those disasters which had always befallen new colonies planted in an extensive country by emigrants from a civilized state. The fruit of all this reading and thinking in Newgate was a simplistic solution to the problem of how to sail the great ship of civilization to the New World without wrecking it on the Scylla of slavery or the Charybdis of dispersion of settlement. So a sojourn in Newgate fashioned one of the great teachers of mankind on the art of colonization, just as a visit to Newgate as an observer rather than an inmate became part of the great pilgrimage of Charles Dickens

Magazine, 15 November 1823; First Report of Select Committee on Emigration from the United Kingdom, p. 3, *P.P.*, 1826, IV, 404; H. Clissold, *Prospectus of a Central National Institution of Home Colonies* (London, 1830); *View of the Present State of Pauperism in Scotland* (London, 1830); R. Alexander, *Fate of the Colonies: a letter to the proprietors and planters of the West Indies, resident in the colonies* (London, 1830); *Morning Chronicle*, 21 August to 6 October 1829.

[2] E. G. Wakefield (Robert Gouger, ed.), *A Letter from Sydney* (London, 1829); *Morning Chronicle*, 6 October 1829 under heading 'A letter from Sydney'; 'Sketch of a proposal for colonizing Australasia', *Morning Chronicle*, 27, 28 August, 1 September 1829; Edwin Hodder, *The Founding of South Australia as Recorded in the Journals of Robert Gouger, First Colonial Secretary* (London, 1898), pp. 1-37.

to find why the idea of the Madonna and the idea of Sodom lived side by side in the heart of man, and by whose strange laws that came to be.

Like most of the great teachers of mankind Wakefield was not distinguished by modesty in his claims for the significance of his work; he was inclined to lose his composure when the logicians asked him precisely what he was trying to say; he was not overscrupulous in acknowledging the sources of his ideas. He had to learn to live with the simple contradiction that great moralizer that he was, with the greatest abhorrence of persons of drunken habits, or fornicators or adulterers, he was himself despised for his swinishness and coarseness. He was to win the regard of those who did not busy themselves preparing lists for the gate-keepers at the entrance to the life of the world to come. Karl Marx was to call him 'the most noted political economist' of his period. John Stuart Mill was also to praise the quality of his mind, and Earl Grey was to single him out as the man who laid the foundation of the prosperity of the Australian colonies in the period before the discovery of gold. The tare and the wheat grew side by side so that men in the New World might reap the harvest of a teacher and a prophet on the problem of how to erect a bourgeois society in the New World free from the evils of aristocratic privilege, but capable of reproducing the full-blown civilization of the Old World and not just providing a 'belly-full' for its members.[3]

In a pamphlet in 1830 he repeated his point that a 'sufficient price' for the waste lands could win the struggle for civilization against the barbarizing tendencies of dispersion. When news reached London in the summer of 1831 of the fertile land the gallant Captain Sturt had seen between the mouth of the Murray River and Gulf St Vincent, Wakefield, just as quick in stealing ideas as in stealing a child-wife, came up with the idea that the struggle for civilization could be won on the southern coast of Australia. By 1831 there were others in the field. From 1830-1 the *Spectator* ran a series of letters on

[3] *Conspiracy and Abduction: an accurate report of the trial of Mr. Edward Gibbon Wakefield, Mr. Wm. Wakefield, and Mrs. Frances Wakefield for a conspiracy to effect the abduction of Miss Ellen Turner* (2nd ed., Liverpool, 1827); A. J. Harrop, *The Amazing Career of Edward Gibbon Wakefield* (London, 1928), pp. 33-4; *The Trial of Edward Gibbon Wakefield, William Wakefield, and Frances Wakefield* (London, 1827); G. T. Crook (ed.), *The Complete Newgate Calendar* (London, 1926), vol. 5, p. 208; Diary of Visiting Book of the Reverend H. S. Cotton, 16 May 1827 (MS. in NAT. L.); P. Bloomfield, *Edward Gibbon Wakefield: builder of the British Commonwealth* (London, 1961), p. 70; Richard Garnett, *Edward Gibbon Wakefield, the Colonization of South Australia and New Zealand* (London, 1898), pp. 50-2; James Stephen to Jane Stephen, 23 March 1840 (Stephen Papers); *Abduction; une Nouvelle Manière d'Attraper une Femme: or a Bold Stroke for a wife* (London, 1827); E. G. Wakefield, *Facts Relating to the Punishment of Death in the Metropolis* (London, 1831); E. G. Wakefield, *Householders in Danger from the Populace* (London, 1831); Charles Dickens, *Sketches by Boz* (Oxford ed., London, 1957), ch. 25, 'A visit to Newgate'; K. Marx, *Capital* (2 vols, Moscow, n.d.), vol. 1, pp. 766, 773-4; J. S. Mill, *Principles of Political Economy* (London, 1848), p. 587; Grey to H. Parkes, August 1873 (Parkes Correspondence, F-G, Parkes Papers, MS. in M.L.); E. G. Wakefield to C. Torlesse, 6 October 1840 (copies of letters from E. G. Wakefield and members of his family, 1815-53, MS. in British Museum); for an example of a writer from whom Wakefield borrowed ideas on the evils of dispersion and how they may be checked see R. Gourlay, *General Introduction to Statistical Account of Upper Canada* (London, 1822).

the colonies in which they insisted that the success of emigration depended on a 'well-arranged and well-conducted scheme of disposing of waste land'. Like Wakefield they believed that the railway and the application of machinery to the production of cotton and woollen goods was about to produce an equality of conditions in which all distinctions and privileges based on birth would disappear. The editor, R. S. Rintoul, was altogether free from 'romantic or visionary babblement'. He was a man who believed in nothing except that poor barren book-keeper theory of life, the excess of pleasure over pain, and the greatest happiness of the greatest number, a man who was upright not for the kingdom of heaven's sake but by personal preference.[4]

At the same time others were dreaming dreams of the huge fortunes to be made by starting a plantation on that part of the southern coast of Australia near Spencer Gulf. One Anthony Bacon, a Byronic character with a preference for damnation rather than James Stephen's never-ending petition for God's mighty grace, and Sir H. Taylor, one of those businessmen like Dickens's Mr Dombey who believed the world was made so that he and his fellow-businessmen might trade in it, wrote twice to the Colonial Office for permission to start a plantation, only to be asked, as Stirling had often been asked, for proof that government would not be involved in any expense. So Bacon and Taylor lost interest in the scheme. The Colonial Office was just as off-putting with Gouger and the systematic colonizers. They were told that His Majesty's Government would have nothing to do with republicans who proposed to reduce the royal power to a cipher.[5]

Then later in 1833 Gouger came up with the idea that all the people interested in the formation of a province on the southern coast of Australia should form a South Australian Association. Strengthened by the points made in Wakefield's *England and America* (published anonymously in October 1833 because of the stain on his name), and much favourable publicity in the *Spectator*, a committee of this association, with W. W. Whitmore as chairman, and men such as C. Buller, G. Grote, R. Hill, S. Mills, W. Molesworth and R. Gouger as members, put forward a proposal to found a colony in which the comforts and conveniences of an old established country should be united as far as practicable with the advantages of a new one. As the seal for South Australia they suggested a draped Britannia, a sheep and an unclothed aborigine who was about to receive the gift of civilization. They suggested a fixed uniform price per acre for Crown land, the use of the land fund to pay passages of migrants, the selection of migrants, and the division of authority

[4] E. G. Wakefield, *A Statement of the Principles and Objects of a Proposed National Society for the Prevention of Pauperism by Means of Systematic Colonization* (London, 1830), pp. 1-2; E. G. Wakefield, *Proposal to His Majesty's Government for Founding a Colony on the Southern Coast of Australia* (London, 1831), pp. 5-12; 'Letters on the colonies', no. 4, *Spectator*, 22 January 1831; 'Locomotive carriages', *Spectator*, 5 December 1829; C. G. Duffy, *Conversations with Carlyle* (London, 1892), p. 85.

[5] H. Taylor to Hay, 13 February 1831, A. Bacon to Hay, 20 February 1831, Hay to A. Bacon, 22 February 1831, A. Bacon to Goderich, 12 June 1831, A. Bacon to Elliot, 1 November 831, C.O. 13/1; see, for example, the comments by James Stephen on the proposals of a South Australian Land Company, 14 July 1832, C.O. 13/1.

between the Crown and a board of trustees appointed by the committee. Again Stephen found 'much error' in the scheme, but he, after all, had made no secret of his dislike of Wakefield and all his ideas. Others said plain practical men would be much better able to conduct the affairs of mankind than these advocates of political theories.[6]

In February 1834 Charles Sturt, the hero of the journey down the Murrumbidgee and the Murray, wrote to the Colonial Office about the role for Britannia and sheep on the rich soil, the abundant pasture, the varied forests, the constant stream of running water, the fish of all kinds, and the myriads of wild fowl at Gulf St Vincent. If nature could so succeed, how could man possibly fail? He prophesied that the men of South Australia would one day people the heart of the continent and that the Australian colonies would emulate America. He urged them to convince the aborigine that the white man was coming as a brother. He urged them, too, not to give the aborigine trifling presents but to protect him against violence and aggression until that day when as children of the same heavenly father they had all learned to look at each other with love and charity. So a voice indistinguishable from the sentiments uttered by the Society for the Propagation of the Gospel or the London Missionary Society added its part, as it were, to that chorus of political economists, adventurers and capitalists who were beefing out their hopes for a new kind of colonial society somewhere in the neighbourhood of Gulf St Vincent on the southern shores of New Holland.[7]

At the end of June over 2500 people turned up at a public meeting at Exeter Hall in London to hear what sort of society this South Australian Association proposed to create. They were told there was to be equality of opportunity, and appropriate rewards for those who worked and remained sober, there was to be no aristocratic patronage and nobody was to have a single inch of land for nothing. They were told also that in the colony the labourers would not become squatters and backwoodsmen at leisure because they must work for a time for their masters. Without either slaves or convicts, capitalists would be able to obtain as many labourers as they wished to employ. By then the association had persuaded the British Government to introduce into parliament a bill to empower His Majesty to erect South Australia into a British province or provinces and to provide for the colonization and government thereof. The preamble recited that divers of His Majesty's subjects possessing amongst them considerable property were desirous to embark for that part of Australia which lies between the meridians of 132° E. and 141° E. and between the Southern Ocean and 26° S. and all the islands adjacent thereto, and that it was highly expedient that His Majesty's said subjects should be enabled to carry their said 'laudable purpose' into effect.

[6] R. Gouger to W. W. Whitmore, 2 December 1833, C.O. 386/10; memorandum by James Stephen on the draft bill of the South Australian Association, 4 July 1834, C.O. 13/2; Papers of the South Australian Association (MS. in M.L.); *P.D.*, ser. 3, XXV, pp. 700-12; *The Times*, 22 July 1834.
[7] C. Sturt to Colonial Office, 17 February 1834, C.O. 13/2.

The bill, which became an Act on 15 August 1834, empowered His Majesty to appoint any one or more persons resident in the province to make laws for peace, order and good government within the province. It also empowered His Majesty to appoint three or more persons, to be styled 'The Colonization Commissioners for *South Australia*', who were to make orders for the sale of land, always provided that the minimum price be at least 12s an acre and provided the funds reserved as purchase money or as rent of the common pasturage of unsold portions be employed in conveying poor migrants from Great Britain and Ireland to the said province. His Majesty was to appoint a resident commissioner in the province, or commissioner of public lands who was to act under the orders of the said Board of Commissioners. Until the sale of lands the commissioners were to pay for the passages of migrants by money raised on bond, provided the sum raised did not exceed £50 000. The commissioners were also empowered to raise on the security of the land fund a sum not exceeding £200 000 to pay for the expenses of government. No person or persons convicted in any court of justice in Great Britain or Ireland or elsewhere should at any time or under any circumstances be transported as a convict to any place within the limits of the province. A constitution might be established when the population reached fifty thousand. For the purpose of providing a guarantee or security that no part of the expense of founding and governing the said colony was to fall on the mother country the commissioners were required out of the monies borrowed on the security of the South Australian Colonial Revenue Securities to invest the sum of £20 000 for the purchase of exchequer bills or other government securities. If after ten years from the passing of the Act the population of the province had not reached twenty thousand, the public lands would be liable to be disposed of by His Majesty.[8]

When the names of possible colonization commissioners were put forward it looked as though the voices of the philanthropists, evangelicals and political economists were to be drowned by the men from the counting-houses of London. There was Samuel Mills, a retired merchant with a million of money, Jacob Montefiore, a banker who had made a fortune in New South Wales, and George Palmer and John Wright, both rich merchants. There was Robert Torrens, once an officer of marines, and a convert to systematic colonization, who had the odd eccentricity for one who advocated order and system in things colonial of rarely opening letters addressed to him and certainly of never replying to them. There was also George Fife Angas, a merchant who solemnly believed that his vast wealth was a prize from God for his righteousness. Born in Newcastle-upon-Tyne on 1 May 1789 into a family with trading interests in the major cities of the United Kingdom, South America and the West Indies, he came to believe with the Psalmist that the

[8] *Morning Chronicle*, 1 July 1834; Papers of the South Australian Association; An Act to Empower His Majesty to Erect South Australia into a British Province or Provinces, and to Provide for the Colonization and Government thereof, 4 & 5 Will. IV, c. 95, 15 August 1834. *Statutes at Large*, vol. 13.

ungodly were trapped in the work of their own hands and that the righteous would flourish and the wrongdoers lick the dust. He saw the proposal to create the province of South Australia as 'something rich in both material and spiritual possibilities', for there the righteous would be rewarded and the sinners would know ruin and disgrace.[9]

When the colonization commissioners held their first meeting in May 1835 they spoke as men with a vision of creating a society of moral philistines somewhere in the Australian wilderness. They recorded their hope of performing an act of mercy for the natives of southern Australia by bringing them the gift of their great civilization and their holy faith. They also recorded their hope of rescuing the worker from his life of brutality and stupefaction in the United Kingdom and making him the member of a virtuous and enlightened society in South Australia. But between the conception and the creation fell the shadow of human behaviour. Robert Gouger, their first secretary, startled them by his sudden changes of mind: one day he would tell them he was off to China, and the next day he would tell them not to worry because he would never give South Australia up. Their chairman, Robert Torrens, moved them all very deeply when he addressed them on the solemnity of their undertaking, but drove them to distraction when they tried to get him to answer a letter.[10]

The officials appointed by the colonization commissioners seemed calculated to promote human uproar and dissension rather than virtue and enlightenment. The Resident Commissioner, James Hurtle Fisher, was a wily lawyer, much given to the hair splitting of the legal pedants rather than entertaining visions of 'better things for mankind' in the New World. In politics he saw himself as a real 'old English gentleman', a firm supporter of the Church of England, and indeed a profound believer in all those words in the Book of Common Prayer which reminded men that God alone could rescue mankind from the fruits of the madness in their hearts. The emigration agent, John Brown, was a third-generation dissenter who liked to believe the promise that in the New World the mighty amongst the gentry would be taken down from their seat. More generous than Fisher, he hoped that in the New World, without the nobility, the gentry and the clergy, men might be able to obey the Saviour's command to love one another, though he feared that there, too, there might be 'sordid selfishness everywhere'. Unlike Fisher, he had studied the literature of the 'systematic colonisers'. The Surveyor-General, Colonel William Light, was born on 22 April 1786 in Kuala Kedan to a captain in the English army and a Malay princess. By temperament he belonged to that class of soldier, artist, and pleasure-seeker which produced men of the stature of Pushkin in Russia and Byron in England. Drawing his inspiration from the Greeks rather than the Judaico-Christian prophets, Light wanted to raise

[9] Diary of John Brown, 5 May 1835 (MS. in M.L.); G. F. Angas to Tibrunting, 5 September 1831, G. F. Angas to Mr Shepherdson, 8 September 1836 (Angas Papers); Edwin Hodder, *George Fife Angas: father and founder of South Australia* (London, 1891), pp. 65-90; G. Sutherland, *The South Australian Company: a study in colonization* (London, 1898).

[10] First Annual Report of the Colonization Commissioners for South Australia, 24 June 1836, C.O. 13/4; Diary of John Brown, 13, 26 March, 5 May 1835 (MS. in M.L.).

TWO EXPLORERS

Edward John Eyre

Portrait by an unknown artist, Parliament House, Adelaide

Charles Sturt

Photograph of portrait by J. A. M. Crossland

TWO SEEKERS

Ludwig Leichhardt

Copy of portrait by William Nicholas, in Heads of the People, 16 October 1847

Edmund Kennedy

Part of self-portrait, in the possession of Edgar Beale, Wollongong

TWO MEN OF APPETITE

John Batman

*Likeness by Charles Nuttall, La Trobe
Library, Melbourne*

Ben Boyd

Drawing by an unknown artist, in Heads
of the People, *1 May 1847*

in South Australia works of those 'enlargers' of the human spirit, rather than those 'straighteners' preferred by the political economists and the evangelicals.[11]

In their choice of men charged with the responsibility for the 'peace, order and good government' of the province, the Colonial Office chose men singularly unfitted to promote that solemnity, that dignity and high-mindedness to which the colonization commissioners had committed themselves. They somewhat unwisely offered the position of Governor to one of the heroes of the Peninsular Campaign, Colonel Charles James Napier, who briefly made a ludicrous exhibition of himself until he lost patience with the halter the commissioners wanted to tie around his neck. The Colonial Office then offered the position to Captain John Hindmarsh, a naval officer who was said not to be particularly clever and a bit of a bore with his prosy stories about his heroism as a boy on the *Bellerophon*. He was inclined to rave and shout at anyone who dared to criticize his opinions. In politics he was a Tory, a great mouther of loyalty to altar and throne, by which he meant the divine right of the nobility, the gentry, the clergy and the officers of the armed forces to govern any British society whether in the Old World or the New. When they transmitted to him his commission and instructions on 15 July 1836 they told him to seek the advice of Colonel George Arthur on the appointment of the first Protector of Aborigines. The task of the last-named would be to protect the aborigine in an undisturbed enjoyment of their proprietary rights to such lands as may be occupied by them in any especial manner. He was to encourage friendly relations between the migrants and the aborigines, to induce them to labour either for themselves or the settlers, and to lead them by degrees to the advantages of civilization and religion. As his Colonial Treasurer the Colonial Office appointed Osmond Gillies, a man whose propensity to intoxication made it perfectly impossible for any gentleman to associate with him, but he was also a convinced republican who boasted that if he had his way there would be no kings in South Australia and that he cared not a 'damn for any bugger at the Colonial Office'. As Colonial Secretary the Colonial Office appointed Robert Gouger, who had some sympathy with Gillies as a republican, but none with him as a drunkard, and no sympathy at all with the old-fashioned Tory-at-heart politics of the Governor. Nor did Charles Mann, the first Advocate-General, who believed it was his mission to assist the migration of the 'burning democrats to the wilderness of nature with the bible in the one hand and the axe in the other'.[12]

They were just as divided on the question of the connection, if any, between

[11] G. C. Morphett, *Sir James Hurtle Fisher* (Adelaide, 1955); *South Australian Register*, 2 April 1850; D. H. Pike, *Paradise of Dissent* (London, 1957), pp. 105-6; based on Diary of John Brown, passim; G. Dutton, *Founder of a City* (Melbourne, 1960); M. P. Mayo, *The Life and Letters of Col. William Light* (Adelaide, 1937).

[12] *Spectator*, 20 June 1835; G. Dutton, op. cit., pp. 149-50; C. J. Napier, *Colonization; Particularly in South Australia* (London, 1835); G. Dutton, op. cit., pp. 151-3; *Gentleman's Magazine*, no. 9, 1860; Diary of John Brown, 4 October 1835; Colonial Office to Hindmarsh, 15 July 1836, C.O. 13/4; T. H. James, *Six Months in South Australia* (London, 1838), p. 65; Diary of John Brown.

government and religion. Hindmarsh, Fisher and other supporters of the High Church position wanted the appointment of a chaplain from among the clergymen of the Church of England. John Brown and other supporters of the dissenters' position demurred. Hindmarsh got warm, threatened to leave the chair and carried the day. The Colonial Office then proceeded to appoint as chaplain C. B. Howard, the son of an army officer and a relation of the Duke of Norfolk. Born in Dublin in 1807 and educated at Trinity College, he was one of those stern, solemn supporters of the Protestant ascendancy, called his horse Luther and used his pulpit to remind his congregation that republicanism was as unjustifiable in God's eyes as adultery.[13]

While these men were snapping at each other Colonel Torrens and his officers were getting on with the business of raising loans on the security of the land fund, selling land and selecting migrants. To attract men with capital the commissioners offered free passages to labourers for every £20 their employer subscribed to the land fund. Some took this to bizarre lengths. The Colonial Treasurer, Osmond Gillies, nominated his favourite hairdresser, and Hindmarsh nominated a married cook and a pastry-maker. In January 1836 the commissioners appointed emigration agents in England, Scotland and Ireland to select migrants. They were instructed to select men and women who were capable of becoming members of a virtuous and enlightened community. They were to discourage all those of a reckless or roving disposition. Above all they were to weed out any who looked as though they might be tempted to idleness and drink and select only those who were capable of frugality and industry.[14]

While these emigration agents were feverishly trying to weed out all possible sources of those moral evils which had disgraced the penal colonies, Colonel Light was getting ready to take the advance party to the coast of southern Australia to select a site for the capital city. The Deputy-Surveyor G. S. Kingston and his staff left on the *Cygnet* in March. Light and his party left on the *Rapid* on 1 May. The commissioners had instructed him to survey 1500 miles of coast, select the best site for the first settlement, survey the town site, divide 150 square miles into sections and make reservations for secondary towns. He arrived off Kangaroo Island on 17 August 1836, where he started on his mammoth task. Quickly rejecting Encounter Bay and Kangaroo Island as unsuitable, on 21 November he found on the east coast of Gulf St Vincent one of the loveliest spots a man could behold. The harbour, the river, the fine, rich-looking country and the delightful hills reminded him of the Mediterranean where men freed at last from the sense of those 'guilty stains' could pursue a life of pleasure. But before that vision could mature other boatloads of men, women and children had begun to arrive at Kangaroo Island. That July and August they landed and were swept into a frenzy of drunkenness when relieved from the terrors and tedia of a four months' journey. After

[13] Diary of John Brown, 27 January, 24 February, 7 May, 1, 19 June 1836; comment by James Stephen on G. Grey to R. Torrens, 15 December 1835, C.O. 13/3; G. H. Jose, *The Church of England in South Australia* (Adelaide, 1937).
[14] D. H. Pike, *Paradise of Dissent*, p. 150.

that evil spirit left them, in fits of remorse and shame they turned to their God for comfort and strength and swore they would try by His help not to sin again. Men tormented by the gap between their passions and God's commands began to send up their great cry of anguish as eaters of the tree of knowledge of good and evil in a land where Light had wanted them to see how grey was all the theory of the theologians and the economists and how green the tree of life.[15]

These men, women and children were an advance party who were supposed to subscribe to the Angas view that those who prospered in this world were assured of salvation in the life of the world to come. They were prospective tenants and artisans of the South Australian Company. In January 1836 the directors of the company bought 13750 acres from the colonization commissioners at 40 per cent discount, together with the right to depasture stock on 220000 acres at 10s for every 640 acres. In January Angas resigned as a colonization commissioner to take his place on the board of directors of the South Australian Company. Under his influence the company decided to 'have no connections with any persons of dissolute habits or immoral principles or whose former actions could not undergo a strict examination'.[16]

Between the conception and the creation fell the shadow of human nature. The first colonial manager appointed by the company was one of those very men whose former actions could not undergo a strict examination. He was Samuel Stephens, a twenty-eight-year-old clergyman's son, one of those 'heels' up men' who had sighed and sobbed at a glorious Wesleyan revival and fallen to the floor in agony and cried for mercy so piteously that the Holy Ghost had showered the blessing of salvation on him. Angas, who had a soft spot for men who had turned from their wickedness so that they might live, thought he was just the man to sell and lease the company's land, to civilize the aborigines and keep alive in the hearts of its tenants and servants the image of the God of their fathers. Before the departure for South Australia there was one of those lapses to which nature's tosspots are prone, but a penitent's letter from Stephens, and the future cleansing effect of the 'multitudinous seas' again convinced Angas that the old Adam in Stephens could be washed whiter than snow.[17]

Neither God nor the sea could silence the trolls in Stephens and some of his fellow-passengers on the company's ships. One of his fellow-passengers guzzled such huge quantities of wine that he saw himself surrounded by horrid phantoms who were hurrying him into the world of the damned, until death released him from his self-inflicted torment, and the sailors threw his body into the sea as one of the pious spoke those solemn words foretelling

[15] G. Dutton, *Founder of a City*, ch. 12; Captain Martin to G. F. Angas, 29 October 1836 (Angas Papers); R. Torrens to Glenelg, 22 December 1837, appendix no. 26 to Second Report from the Select Committee on South Australia, *P.P.*, 1841, IV, 394.

[16] First Prospectus of the South Australian Company, January 1836, C.O. 13/3; G. F. Angas to G. Parsons, n.d. (probably September 1836) and G. F. Angas to E. G. Wakefield, 29 September 1836 (Letter Book of G. F. Angas).

[17] Letter of Instructions of G. F. Angas to S. Stephens, 20 February 1836 (Angas Papers); G. F. Angas to S. Stephens, 22 July 1837 (Letter Book of G. F. Angas).

how on the resurrection morning the sea would give up its dead. Sailors went on gesturing lewdly at the women much as they did on other migrant ships to the Australian colonies. After the arrival of the four ships—the *Duke of York*, the *Lady Mary Pelham*, the *John Pirie* and the *Rapid*—in July and August 1836 at Kingscote, Kangaroo Island, it looked as though the Peel disaster was to be repeated, with the element of farce that adheres to a repeat performance. Ship-hands and artisans bolted to the other colonies. Stephens took to the bottle, as other men who had crossed the oceans to plough the fields of the Australian wilderness and scatter good seed on the land lay dead drunk in their huts.[18]

Again one of those periodic showers of salvation drenched Stephens. With all the hope of a man who believed his position was still reparable he wrote off to Angas to tell him his headstrong, foolish ways might be turned into a very 'profitable folly for the share-holders'. Angas told him sternly that God did not wink at a man who was not able to control his own passions. He could only hope that the sins of drunkenness and pride would lead Stephens to Christ. For its part the company had no alternative but to appoint a new colonial manager who could procure profit for the shareholders and present an example of rectitude to its tenants and artisans. He was David McLaren, one-time candidate for holy orders in the Presbyterian Church in Glasgow, who after a season with the Congregationalists found his spiritual home with the Baptists. They encouraged him to indulge in an extravaganza of the passions while denouncing the sins of others. They also gave him much licence in questions of belief. After his arrival at Kingscote in April 1837, he was soon hard at it denouncing that 'wicked and adulterous generation', shrewdly making use of all the knowledge Stephens had of livestock and cannily planning to move the headquarters of the company to the mainland where profits would be higher, and the congregations, before whom he could perform like an Old Testament prophet, larger. Some three years later Stephens was killed while riding a horse in that reckless manner which had characterized his whole life. By that time Angas had ceased wondering why God had permitted a scheme dedicated to His honour to be mocked and defiled by sinners, and was loudly praising God for providing David McLaren as an instrument of His glory in the New World as well as the future profit of the shareholders of the company.[19]

By then, too, the white man's uproar had begun on the mainland of South Australia. By the middle of 1836 the colonization commissioners had filled two ships—the *Africaine* and the *Buffalo*—with prospective land-holders, civil and military officers, and artisans. Before the *Africaine* sailed on 3 July Robert Gouger's wife went through the anguish of parting from her loving family, but Gouger found to his surprise that, serious man though he was, he did not spend his time meditating upon the sublimity of the mighty deep but rather

[18] A. Dawsey to G. F. Angas, 8 June 1836; S. Stephens to G. F. Angas, 17, 22 August 1836 (Angas Papers).

[19] C. S. Hare to E. Stephens, 2 February 1837; S. Stephens to G. F. Angas, 27 September 1836 (Angas Papers).

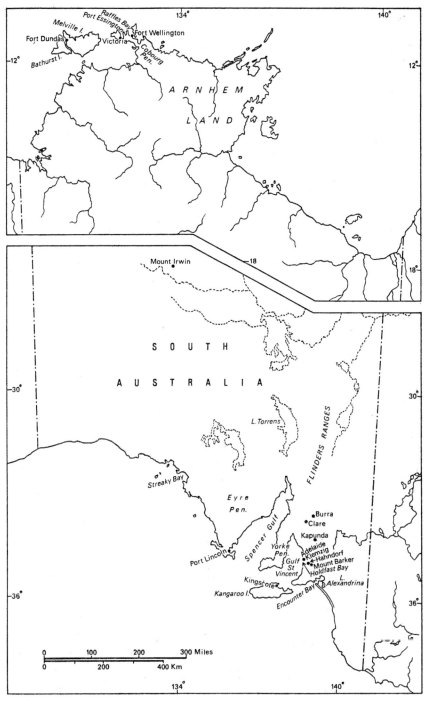

2 *The Main Settlements of northern Australia and South Australia*

in numerous discussions on the merits of pork and beef, and the diseases of
fowls, ducks and geese in overloaded coops. By contrast, John Brown, the
emigration agent, was scribbling in his diary that if God did not go with
them then the madness in the human heart would take over. Down in the
intermediate quarters of the ship Arthur Gliddon noted that one of his chums
wore a black wig and had red eye-lashes, a Mr Thomas was very hot-tempered,
Mr Everard was very nice and quiet and his wife just the contrary, another
man was very fidgety, and one of the women did not appear to be very
respectable. After calling at Cape Town they arrived at Kingscote, Kangaroo
Island, where Samuel Stephens comforted them and told them of Light's
choice of a site for a city some four or five miles inland from Holdfast Bay on
Gulf St Vincent. So they sailed again in the *Africaine* for the bay where they
landed, pitched their tents, and were so pestered by flies and mosquitoes that
some wore veils to keep them off. Gouger waited to participate in the greatest
mystery of all, the birth of a child. The aborigines showed them how to light
a fire without matches. On Christmas Day, with the thermometer standing at
100° F. twenty-four of them gathered in a rush hut to hear God's word, after
which they ate a ham, a parrot pie and a plum pudding while they waited for
the *Buffalo* to reach Holdfast Bay.[20]

While they were enjoying the freedom of the open air on the shores of
Holdfast Bay the other men charged with the responsibility of founding a
civil society were being tossed around on the *Buffalo*. They had sailed from
England late in July shortly after Fisher and Hindmarsh had once again had
one of those confrontations about who was the senior person in the colony—
the Governor or the Resident Commissioner. Hindmarsh had also fallen into
the sea and had had to be fished out by a sailor. It was just another of those
undignified events likely to happen to a man who claimed more from his
fellow-men than they were willing to concede. During the long voyage the
Reverend C. B. Howard accompanied on his violin the singing of psalms by
the emigrants, for that high solemnity and that use of religion for the taming
of the working classes were what some believed South Australia was all
about. On other evenings there was dancing and singing of songs, for with
others that was what South Australia was about—the joy and gaiety of men
who had left behind the Old World evils of poverty, class antagonism and
faction. Somewhat to the disappointment of those who thought of South
Australia as a society for the improvement of mankind Hindmarsh took no
steps on board to arrange for the education of the fifty children, and made it

[20] R. Gouger, *Some Rough Notes of a Voyage from Gravesend to South Australia*,
10, 13 July 1836 (MS. in S.A.S.A.); A. Gliddon to his brother, 18 September 1836 (MS. in
S.A.S.A.); Diary of Mary Thomas, 13 November to 25 December 1836 (MS. in S.A.S.A.); for
these and other extracts see Penelope Hope (ed.), *The Voyage of the Africaine* (Melbourne, 1968); S. Stephens to G. F. Angas, 27 September, 27 December 1836; G. F. Angas
to S. Stephens, 22 July 1837; G. F. Angas to E. J. Wheeler, 9 June 1838 (Angas Papers);
E. T. McLaren, *Dr McLaren of Manchester* (London, 1911); A. G. Price, *The Foundation and Settlement of South Australia 1829-1845* (Adelaide, 1924); *South Australian
Register*, 31 August 1837, 2 November 1839; Diary of John Brown, 26, 28, 29 June, 1, 3
July 1836.

plain that he would not support a library in South Australia: 'What good will books do our Colony?' he asked.[21]

On 28 December 1836, the day of their arrival in Holdfast Bay, some two hundred from the *Buffalo* and the *Africaine* gathered under a huge tree to hear George Stevenson, the secretary to the Governor, read the proclamation of South Australia as a province. Hindmarsh proposed a toast to 'The King', which was drunk with three times three, despite the presence of those stout republicans—Osmond Gillies and Charles Mann. Then they all joined in the singing of the National Anthem, the first line of which through long custom they sang as 'God save great George our King', which excited a smile. After the band played a rousing version of 'Rule, Britannia', Hindmarsh mounted a chair to tell them of his hopes for the colony. He called on all present to conduct themselves on all occasions with order and quietness, to respect the laws and to prove themselves worthy to be the founders of a great and free colony by their industry and their sobriety, by the strict observance of the ordinances of their religion. He went on to say that it was his intention to put the aborigines and white men under the protection of the same law and punish severely all acts of violence or injustice against the aborigines, adding that he would fulfil His Majesty's generous intentions towards them by promoting their advancement in civilization and, always under the blessing of divine providence, their conversion to the Christian faith. He ended by proposing a toast, 'May the present unanimity continue as long as South Australia exists', which made the plain ring with acclamation. But of their mission to create a society different in kind from any other Australian colony he said not a word. As darkness descended after the splendours of a hot summer's day the natives set fire to the neighbouring woods which burned brightly. The white men, their hearts overflowing with goodwill, hailed the flames as a gesture of welcome by the primitive people and not the gesture of a people who did not possess any more effective means of expressing their resentment against the invader. In the stillness of the night, the singing and shouting of celebration continued in the tents as the fires lit by the aborigines licked the blackness on the horizon, and drunken sailors tumbled and splashed in the shallows as they tried to make their way back to the *Buffalo*.[22]

Two days later Light took Hindmarsh to examine the site he had chosen some six miles inland for the city. Hindmarsh wanted a site closer to the sea. Again the Governor and the Resident Commissioner were on opposite sides. But Light quoted his instructions to choose a site, and Hindmarsh had to be content with his own instructions which were to name the place 'Adelaide'.

[21] Hindmarsh to Grey, 23 July 1836, C.O. 13/4; Journal of Young Bingham Hutchinson, 13, 23 July 1836 (MS. in S.A.S.A.); Hindmarsh to G. F. Angas, 3 July 1836 and G. F. Angas to G. Stevenson, 12 March 1837 (Angas Papers); *Portsea and Gosport Herald*, 6 August 1836; G. Stevenson, Extracts from the Journal of a Voyage in His Majesty's Ship Buffalo, from England to South Australia, 14 August, 13 September 1836.

[22] Based on Journal of Young Bingham Hutchinson, 28 December 1836; *South Australian Gazette*, 3 June 1837; Proclamation by His Excellency John Hindmarsh, 28 December 1836, C.O. 13/6; Hindmarsh to Glenelg, 6 January 1837, C.O. 13/6; Diary of Mary Thomas, 28 December 1836 (MS. in S.A.S.A.).

Then the inhabitants of those forty-odd tents and huts at Holdfast Bay began to move their goods and chattels over the plain to Adelaide. One young man used a wheelbarrow. The Fisher family put their mother on a pony with a mattress and walked beside her to Adelaide. There, as at Holdfast Bay, the white men used the aborigines by day to fetch water from the river in return for food. They could never persuade the aborigines to work after dark because of their fear of the 'Great Spirit'. There, too, as at Holdfast Bay, on moonlit nights, they heard the war whoop of the aborigines as they danced around their fires or celebrated a corroboree. The men decked their heads with emu feathers and kangaroo bones and painted their bodies with stripes of chalk and red ochre and uttered the most fearful yells and screams. Believing the aborigines might be susceptible to kindness the white man gave them blankets to replace their own primitive possum rugs. So some five hundred white men began the task of bringing the civilization of Britannia to the ten thousand natives in the province of South Australia.[23]

In the meantime the white men were beginning to display what they meant by civilization. They were deeply divided between the claims of God and Mammon. In London one J. B. Hack had often communed with his God on how to overcome the temptation to allow earthly cares to take his attention from serious reflection. He had also had much talk with J. Hutt and E. G. Wakefield on the prospects for a man of modest capital in the province with a 'laudable purpose'. He had arrived in Launceston early in 1837 where he had bought sheep, cattle and poultry, and had then set out for Adelaide hoping drink would be such a rare article in the land of virtue that the 'tipsiness' of one of his servants would be cured by lack of opportunity and encouragement. He arrived early in February feeling himself to be in the hands of Providence, which did not let him down because he was able to sell six hundred of his eight hundred sheep immediately at double the price he had paid for them. At the end of February with the thermometer registering 105° F. in the shade he took his family by bullock-dray to Adelaide and began to put up his hut. He was pleased to notice that Mrs Brown had persuaded an aboriginal chief to wear a frock, because that indicated the aborigines were becoming quite civilized.[24]

By February 1837 the man who proposed the toast to 'unanimity' on Foundation Day was describing the Reverend C. B. Howard's wife as 'an insinuating tale-bearing handsome woman of comely shapes', and the supporters of the Resident Commissioner as 'the dirty Fisher faction'. Not to be outdone,

---

[23] James Fisher, Reminiscences of 1836-7 (typescript in s.a.s.a.); R. Torrens to Glenelg, 22 December 1837, appendix no. 26 to Second Report from the Select Committee on South Australia, *P.P.* 1841, IV, 394; G. Dutton, *Founder of a City*, pp. 197-8; Journal of Young Bingham Hutchinson, passim, for January and February 1837; Recollections of Fanny Jones (typescript in s.a.s.a.); E. Stephenson to J. Orton, 17 April 1837 (Angas Papers); F. Lancaster Jones, *The Structure and Growth of Australia's Aboriginal Population* (Canberra, 1970), p. 4.

[24] Diary of J. B. Hack, 1 July, 28 August 1836, 11, 12 February, 14 April 1837 (ms. in s.a.s.a.).

Fisher countered by describing Hindmarsh as 'a man with a vulgar mind'. By August, Hindmarsh came to the conclusion that four senior officers— Mann, Fisher, Gouger and Brown—were such promoters of sedition that he wrote off yet again to London an account of his efforts to vindicate the authority of His Majesty in a remote province of the British Empire against men such as this one-time slop-seller, Gouger, and his fellow social upstarts. Nor were relations between the senior officers any more cordial. Gillies, when heated by strong drink, threatened to blow a hole in Gouger's 'b----- carcase'. By the end of August, Hindmarsh had dismissed or suspended from office Mann, Brown, Gillies and Gouger.

At the same time the press was trumpeting each week the latest moves in these faction fights to an avid reading public. When the *South Australian Gazette* began publication in Adelaide on 3 June, its editor, George Steven-son, wrote of the confidence of a young society confronting its destiny free from the disputes that had poisoned life in the Old World. His advocacy for the Hindmarsh faction was so blatant that on 31 July John Brown and Charles Mann published a manifesto in which they announced their inten-tion to publish the *Southern Australian*. Using the pen-name 'Sancho Panza', Brown also circulated a lampoon on Hindmarsh in which he accused the latter of using the office of Governor in the interests of vanity and his pocket rather than the welfare of the people of South Australia.[25]

At the same time, too, the goodwill felt in their hearts on Foundation Day towards the aborigines was giving way to disgust and resentment. Influenced as they had been by the humanitarian sentiments of the intellectual climate of London in the 1830s, and confident that the absence of convicts from their society would save them from the deeds of darkness which had characterized relations between white men and aborigines in the penal colonies, they had started off with such hope and enthusiasm that not even those nocturnal yells which broke the stillness of the night evoked either dismay or alarm. The very first report of the colonization commissioners expressed in full their hopes of the blessings the coming of civilization would confer on the aborigines. They proposed to build huts to shelter them, and to supply food and clothing to those aborigines who worked for the white man. They also had ideas on reserving land for the aborigines in which they would be taught how to grow crops and depasture stock. The colonization commissioners instructed Colonel

[25] Journal of Young Bingham Hutchinson, 15 March, 21 April, 23 May 1837; J. Brown to E. G. Wakefield, 10 April 1837 (Brown Papers, S.A.S.A.); *South Australian Gazette*, 3 June, 29 July 1837; Hindmarsh to G. F. Angas, 15 February 1837 (Hindmarsh Papers, S.A.S.A.); Diary of J. B. Hack, 16 March 1837; J. Brown to E. G. Wakefield, 10 April 1837 (Brown Papers); J. H. Fisher to G. F. Angas, 12 June 1837 (Angas Papers); Hind-marsh to Glenelg, 1 February 1837, C.O. 13/6; marginal comment by Hindmarsh in R. Gouger to Glenelg, 24 August 1837, C.O. 13/7; Journal of Young Bingham Hutchin-son, 12 August 1837; letter to *South Australian Gazette*, 29 July 1837; Hindmarsh to Glenelg, 23 August 1837, C.O. 13/7; *South Australian Gazette*, 16 September, 14 October 1837; W. Pedler, 'Recollections of early days and old colonists', *Proceedings of the Royal Geographical Society of Australasia, South Australian Branch*, vol. 6, pp. 63-5; 'Reminis-cences by Pastor Finnlayson', ibid., pp. 39-55.

Light that if he needed any wild animals for food they must be purchased from the aborigines. Both the Governor and the Resident Commissioner were instructed to display justice, kindness and forbearance in their behaviour towards the aborigines.[26] The aborigines, too, in the beginning had their own reasons for receiving the white man with awe if not with reverence. Their wise men had told them that a time would come when pale-faced men would revisit their old hunting grounds. So in the beginning, as at Sydney in 1788, there were optimistic accounts of friendliness displayed by both sides, and enthusiastic stories of the services the aborigines were rendering to the white men. In May 1837 Hindmarsh appointed Dr William Wyatt *ad interim* Protector of Aborigines and instructed him to encourage their peaceful residence with the Europeans and their instruction in the arts of civilized life. By the middle of the year disenchantment set in on both sides: white men were disgusted by the indecency of the aborigine, and by the filth; the white men began to be uneasy and squeamish about sharing water with the aborigines, and to be put off by the packs of mangy dogs around aboriginal camp sites. In the beginning a corroboree was glamorous and exciting; within six months it was just another source of irritation, along with the begging and the thieving. By the end of 1837 some were calling for acts of retaliation against the aborigine while the high-minded, such as David McLaren, were still beseeching their fellow-colonists to base their conduct towards the aborigines on the will of God and not on the standard of utility. The aborigines were administering an affront not just to the sensibilities of the white man but also to their pride. At year's end a native woman surprised the proud bearer of the gift of civilization with the retort, 'You go to England, that your country; this our country.'

By year's end, too, there were ominous signs that, despite all that 'taking thought' by the Solons of the Adelphi, they were not going to be any more successful than any other colony in planting civilization in an extensive and uninhabited country without disasters during the colony's infancy. Although the minimum upset price of 12s had been placed on waste lands partly to prevent labourers becoming landowners too soon, and so ensure both an adequate labour supply and the proper subordination of servant to master, by year's end there was a labour shortage and complaints of the subversion of good order between master and servant.[27]

The rumours of failure came as no surprise to James Stephen. He had always thought the *éminence grise*, Edward Gibbon Wakefield, to be coarse and sinister; he had always thought the ideas of the systematic colonizers to be impractical. As for the division of authority between Governor and Resi-

[26] First Report of Colonization Commissioners of South Australia, *P.P.*, 1836, XXXVI, 491; 'Reminiscences by Pastor Finlayson', op. cit.; Hindmarsh to Glenelg, 16 March 1838, C.O. 13/10; Kathleen Hassell, The Relations between the Settlers and Aborigines in South Australia, 1836-1860 (thesis in Public Library of South Australia); *South Australian Gazette*, 19 October 1837.

[27] Second Report of Colonization Commissioners of South Australia, *P.P.*, 1837-8, XXIX, 97; memorandum, James Stephen to Sir George Grey, 2 December 1837, C.O. 13/6.

dent Commissioner, that was quite fatuous. So with the colonization commissioners, the directors of the South Australian Company, and prominent
investors in the city clamouring for action he recommended that the colonization commissioners and the Colonial Office should exchange minds on the
future of South Australia. Faced with the voluminous heady correspondence in which Hindmarsh beseeched His Lordship to tell him clearly what
powers he possessed as Governor, those men in black had no hesitation in
deciding that Hindmarsh must go. Stephen promptly drafted one of those
majestic despatches befitting the high solemnity of the occasion in which
Hindmarsh was told that in such a state of feeling as existed amongst the
various local authorities it was impossible that the great undertaking in which
they were engaged should be conducted to a prosperous issue. With great
reluctance Her Majesty's Government had therefore decided to advise the
Queen to relieve him of the administration of the government of South
Australia.[28]

When this despatch reached Adelaide in May 1838 Hindmarsh clung to his
delusion to sustain him in his days of adversity. Known on every ship on
which he had sailed, in the offices of Downing Street, at the Adelphi and in
Adelaide as a wild ass of a man, he pitifully told Lord Glenelg he was not
aware of a single instance in which he had not remained calm. He solemnly
told his friends he had been the victim of those 'disciples of utopian principles'
and those republicans who taught the dangerous doctrine that nations could
be governed without authority. His friends consoled him by describing him
as a gallant and noble officer, a kind, affectionate husband and an indulgent
father who had been stabbed in the back by the members of the 'dirty Fisher
faction', and in July escorted him to the ship at that place where eighteen
months earlier in an exuberant mood he had proposed that toast to 'unanimity'. Now his enemies were openly flaunting their part in shattering that
dream by sending off to London an expression of their pleasure at the recall
of Governor Hindmarsh. All that his masters had to offer for his service in
South Australia was the governorship of Heligoland. A man who took his
stand for 'throne and altar' against the progressive forces of industrialism,
egalitarianism and liberalism thus ended his career on a weather-beaten rock
in the North Sea.[29]

In the meantime the most interesting and important event since the forma-

[28] Grey to Glenelg, 31 October 1837, C.O. 13/6; Glenelg to Hindmarsh, 21 February
1838, C.O. 396/2.
[29] Hindmarsh to Glenelg, 1 June 1838, C.O. 13/11; Hindmarsh to Sir Pulteney
Malcolm, 22 June 1838 (MS. in NAT. L.); *South Australian Gazette*, 19 May, 14, 16 July
1838; draft of a proposed address to the colonization commissioners thanking them for
the removal of Governor Hindmarsh, 23 June 1838 (Brown Papers, S.A.S.A.); exchange
of addresses between colonists and Hindmarsh on the latter's departure in the *Alligator*,
South Australian Gazette, 14 July 1838; for other opinions see A. G. Price, *The Foundation and Settlement of South Australia 1829-1845*; William Harcus (ed.), *South Australia:
its history, resources and production* (London, 1876), ch. 4; J. W. Bull, *Early Experiences
of Colonial Life in South Australia* (Adelaide, 1884), ch. 4; D. Pike, *Paradise of Dissent*,
pp. 224-8; articles on Hindmarsh in the *Australian Encyclopaedia*, vol. 4, and D. Pike
(ed.), *Australian Dictionary of Biography*, vol. 1.

tion of the colony had occurred in Adelaide. On 4 April a man in the bushman's garb of blue shirt, soiled cabbage-tree hat with broad black ribbon,
booted and spurred, with a stock-whip in the hand, and a clay pipe in the
mouth was seen in the streets of Adelaide. He was Joseph Hawdon who had
spent the previous ten weeks overlanding sheep and cattle from New South
Wales. He was the forerunner of those adventurers who would bring to South
Australia the elements of the sheep-walk society of New South Wales that
the political economists and systematic colonizers were so anxious to avoid.
By chance these cattle and sheep were lowing and bleating on the outskirts of
Adelaide while Hindmarsh was scribbling away to London about the evils of
factionalism and his stand for 'throne and altar'. As Hindmarsh was wending
his way from Adelaide to Holdfast Bay in July, another overlander, Edward
John Eyre, was telling people in Adelaide that by far the richest land he had
ever seen in New Holland lay between that town and the eastern boundaries
of the province. He was also telling a woman he admired about the loneliness
of men of his class in Australia and the absence of gentry in Adelaide.[30]

That August another overlander arrived in Adelaide as the 'shallow bab-
blers' in the faction fight went on slanging each other. He was the 'wondrous
handsome' Captain Charles Sturt. It was eight years since the gallant captain,
his cheeks caked with clay, had arrived back in Sydney to tell the world of
the verdant pastures on the plains between Gulf St Vincent and Lake
Alexandrina. Despite his claim that he always rose from a session on his
knees 'calm and confident', an anxious, haunted look had begun to appear on
that face which had once cheered his men to endure the agonies of the row
upstream on the Murray. For many things plagued and disturbed him as he
drove stock over that *'terra inhospitalis'*: the prospect of his beloved England
hastening into democracy, the ravages of what he called 'cruel and un-
relenting time', the doubt whether his wife gave him 'credit for affection',
and the fear that his Almighty Father might bereave him of his boy.

When the gentlemen honoured him in September 1838 with a public dinner
for his contribution to the foundation of South Australia he warned them not
to put their faith in steam navigation and railroads between Sydney and Adelaide, because both were utterly impracticable, but rather to put their trust in
useful roads, buildings and the Divine Blessing, and bend in grateful acknowledgement before the author of their being. No sooner had he sat down than
uproar and confusion broke out as one of the Adelaide factions proposed a
toast to the Resident Commissioner, and another to the recent Governor.
Amidst threats to throw all 'impudent monkeys' out of the window, the
chairman closed the proceedings. For a moment in that room, the forces
shaping human destiny on those sun-drenched plains had confronted each

---

[30] Alexander Tolmer, *Reminiscences of an Adventurous and Chequered Career at
Home and at the Antipodes* (2 vols, London, 1882); Joseph Hawdon, *The Journal of a
Journey from New South Wales to Adelaide* (1838; reprinted Melbourne, 1952);
J. Hawdon to Hindmarsh, 5 April 1838, encl. in Hindmarsh to Glenelg, 7 April 1838,
C.O. 13/10; *South Australian Gazette*, 7, 28 April, 14 July 1838.

other: the Sturt vision of a society of landed gentry, the McLaren vision of earthly and heavenly rewards for those qualified to enter at the 'narrow gate', the Fisher vision of the world belonging to the wily, and the vision of those unknown numbers who had sensed the significance of the arrival of the overlanders.[31]

[31] *South Australian Gazette*, 14, 16 July, 4 August, 15 September 1838; Stephen to Glenelg, 7 August 1838, C.O. 13/11; C. Sturt, Journal of 1838 Overland Journey (MS. in Rhodes House, Oxford); Napier George Sturt, *Life of Charles Sturt* (London, 1899), pp. 147, 314-15, 376; M. Langley, *Sturt of the Murray* (London, 1969), ch. 11.

4

HIGH NOON FOR MORAL IMPROVERS
IN SOUTH AUSTRALIA

BETWEEN 1838 and 1842 it looked as though moral improvers, rather than systematic colonizers or sheep-walk men, were to shape the destinies of mankind in South Australia. The new governor, Lieutenant-Colonel George Gawler, a forty-three-year-old, one-time hero of Waterloo, had been converted by reading William Paley's *Evidences of Christianity* in 1818 into believing that men should not devote their feverish activity to the accumulation of material gain but rather to the salvation of their souls. From that time he believed so passionately in 'literal veracity' and 'moral earnestness' that his lips quivered if anyone ever called them in question. Maria Cox, whom he married in 1820, was said to be as devout and earnest as Gawler himself, and that, according to the mockers, was saying quite a bit. The colonization commissioners and James Stephen were delighted to have a 'godly man' as Governor and Resident Commissioner in South Australia. G. F. Angas rejoiced that a pious man had been chosen to make South Australia into that 'happy land' promised in holy scripture to all God's faithful children.[1]

In June 1838 the Lieutenant-Colonel and his good lady boarded the ship *Pestonjee Bomanjee* bound for South Australia where they were determined with God's blessing to fight the good fight for the victory of Christian civilization over the wilderness of South Australia. Before departure Gawler's attention had also been drawn to the worldly concerns of that colony. He was told of the decision of Her Majesty's Government to combine the offices of Governor and Resident Commissioner in his person. He was told the annual expenditure of the colony was limited to £8000 a year, with a right to draw on an extra £2000: he was solemnly reminded that the colony must attempt to support itself and that except in cases of pressing emergency no public works nor any extraordinary expenditure were to be undertaken without prior authority from London. As the public debt then stood at £20 000 he was to exercise every possible economy to reduce that sum. The change in the constitution was confirmed in July 1838 in the Act to amend the South Australia Act of 1834.[2]

[1] G. H. Pitt, *The Press in South Australia* (Adelaide, 1946), p. 17; A. Heising, *Südaustralien* (Berlin, 1852), p. 6; G. F. Angas to G. Gawler, 26 September 1838; Gawler to J. Stephen, 25 April 1838, C.O. 13/11; Gawler to Glenelg, 3 May 1838, C.O. 13/11; Glenelg to Gawler, 19 May 1838, C.O. 396/2.
[2] Glenelg to Gawler, 10 May 1838, C.O. 396/2; Gawler to Glenelg, 28 May 1838, C.O. 13/11; draft reply of Colonial Office to Gawler, 7 June 1838, C.O. 13/11; An Act to

On arrival at Holdfast Bay on 13 October 1838 the Lieutenant-Colonel spoke to a small group of white men and aborigines who had gathered to welcome him. He spoke then as always as a man with more interest in what went on in the heart of a man rather than in the affairs of a counting-house. He exhorted the white men present to respect and pity their 'sable brethren' and to use them with the kindness and forbearance always shown to children, for they, too, were bone of their bone, and flesh of their flesh, and descended from one common head and saved by one common salvation. Then, turning to the aborigines, he exhorted them to be peaceful and learn to read English so that they might become acquainted with their Maker and their God. That night, at Gawler's suggestion, the Protector of Aborigines feasted the white man's 'sable brethren' on tea, sugar and biscuits. Judging by their laughter they seemed to enjoy the white man's bounty, though some tried to say they were puzzled that such kindness and generosity were suddenly being shown to them.[3]

Some changes in office boded well for what Gawler hoped to achieve. That republican babbler, Charles Mann, refused to be reinstated as Advocate-General. The new judge, Charles Cooper, was much given to court sermons on the contribution of Sunday Schools, Sabbath observance, and temperance to improving the morals of the lower orders. The Surveyor-General, William Light, a man who looked to the authors of antiquity rather than the Christian Bible for guidance on the meaning of life, had been forced to retire because of ill health. This gave Gawler the chance to offer the position temporarily to Charles Sturt, who was a great believer in bending the knee each night in grateful acknowledgement before God. Surrounded by such stout soldiers of Christ, Gawler told the respectable members of Adelaide at a public dinner early in January 1839 that he had declared war on the loose state of morals and the drinking of ardent spirits, that he hoped to bring their 'sable brethren' into a more comfortable state, and that for his part he saw South Australia as a society which would justify the faith of the Psalmist that godliness and prosperity were handmaidens of some higher purpose. Those present cheered him to the echo. Captain Sturt reminded them of God's goodness in bringing them to a country which abounded in grass for their sheep and their cattle, and fertile soil in which to grow their crops.[4]

The effect on human behaviour was striking. The irascible editor of the *South Australian Gazette*, George Stevenson, was to be seen each Sunday in his best suit and was also heard to join in the responses at church. A great boisterous cheerfulness enlivened all the social gatherings at which Presbyterians, Methodists, Baptists and Congregationalists came together for that 'most sumptuous, orderly and refreshing repast' of drinking tea. David

Amend an Act of the Fourth and Fifth Years of His Late Majesty, Empowering His Majesty to Erect South Australia into a British Province or Provinces, 1 & 2 Vic., c. 60, 31 July 1838, *Statutes at Large*, vol. 14.
    [3] *Southern Australian*, 20 October 1838; *South Australian Gazette*, 4 August 1838.
    [4] *South Australian Gazette*, 4 August, 29 September, 13 October 1839; Gawler to Glenelg, 13 October 1838, Gawler to Glenelg, 26 October 1838, Gawler to Glenelg, 26 October 1838, C.O. 13/11; *Southern Australian*, 16 January 1839.

McLaren was happy to mount the pulpit of Presbyterian, Methodist, Baptist or Congregationalist churches because in all four he had the opportunity to praise liberty of conscience and condemn cards, dancing, theatres, drinking and fornicating. He also reminded them of the excellent counsel of John Wesley to all Christians—to be serious, to avoid all lightness as they would hell-fire, to avoid trifling as they would cursing and swearing, to touch no woman, but to be loving with each other, not to curl the hair or wear gold and precious stones, but to dress in that plain simple manner befitting persons professing godliness, and to set their face against all diversions such as excessive laughter as they were surely the work of the Devil. In church and chapel men and women in Adelaide were encouraged to a licentiousness in things spiritual, and an austere discipline in their behaviour. They were exhorted to be libertarians in belief, and conformists in conduct.[5]

At the Congregational church, members of the congregation heard the word of God expounded by a man with a sense of the majesty of their task. He was Thomas Quinton Stow. He had arrived in Adelaide in October 1837 to serve the cause of truth and piety. Born in 1801 and educated in the principles of independence, he had come to the colony in the service of the Colonial Missionary Society. In December 1837 he was elected first pastor of the Congregational Church in Adelaide. From the beginning of his mission he was grateful to God for His goodness in placing him in so fair and sweet a portion of the earth. Grieved though he was to find that in South Australia human nature was already making 'fresh disclosures of its folly and degeneracy', that sottishness prevailed over the lower orders, and irreligion over the mass, that the aborigines found his religious services far too quiet and much preferred a corroboree because there at least they could make one hell of a noise, he asked God to give him 'wisdom, devotedness and strength' to communicate to his congregation his sense of their good fortune in participating in a leap forward by the human race. He told them a godless people would degrade and pollute the wilderness of Australia, but a pious people would light the way to the life of the world to come.[6]

This belief in their destiny to play a part in the victory of good over evil attracted some of the settlers to three early works by Charles Dickens—*Oliver Twist*, *The Pickwick Papers* and *Nicholas Nickleby*. A serialized version of the last-named began publication in the *South Australian Gazette* in October 1839. In these works Dickens confronted those who were filled with loving

[5] G. H. Pitt, *The Press in South Australia*, p. 17; *South Australian Gazette*, 13 July 1839; R. Southey, *The Life of Wesley* (2 vols, Oxford, 1925), vol. 2, pp. 290-3.

[6] G. C. Morphett, *Rev. Thos. Quinton Stow* (Adelaide, 1948); *Southern Australian*, 6 November 1839; *South Australian Gazette*, 12 December 1839; see also *Southern Australian*, 6 November 1839, for speech by T. Q. Stow on the contribution of the Wesleyans to civilization; *Southern Australian*, 12 December 1839; speech by Charles Cooper, *South Australian Gazette*, 4 May 1839; lecture by T. Q. Stow on 16 August 1839 to Adelaide Literary and Scientific Association, *Southern Australian*, 28 August 1839; *Redemption Interesting to Angels*, a sermon preached at the opening of the Wesleyan Chapel, Adelaide, 18 March 1838, by the Rev. Thomas Quinton Stow (Adelaide, 1838); *Patriot* (London), 3 September 1838.

kindness and benevolence in their hearts towards all men, and enjoyed life hugely (they were prepared to gloss over the obvious pleasure Mr Pickwick derived from malt liquors and to note just how much the good man loved his food and his fellow-men), with those, such as Fagin, Sikes, and Wackford Squeers, who were driven by some hell in their hearts to savage their own kind. He painted a lively picture of the battle between the innocent and evil men, and the victory of men of goodwill. He told them, through Mr Pickwick, how some men, like bats, had better eyes for the darkness than for the light. They liked to believe that in the New World men would have no trouble in seeing the light because of the absence of darkness. They liked to believe that a man of darkness, like Sir Mulberry Hawk in *Nicholas Nickleby*, ended his days thrown into jail for debt, and perishing miserably, while an innocent man like Nicholas Nickleby ended rich and prosperous, his life enlivened by children's pleasant voices and a wife who was filled with love for all about her. Some also looked into the works of Robert Burns and found there a reflection of themselves—a sentimental benevolence, a trust in the 'cup of kindness', and a belief in a society free from aristocratic privilege—a society where every man, no matter what his birth, was a man 'for a' that . . . a man's a man for a' that'.[7]

One Sunday in April 1839 while the congregations in the churches were brim full with love and charity for their neighbours, and intending to lead a new life following the commandments of God, an aborigine crept up behind William Duffield, a shepherd, and knocked him on the head with a waddy after which two other aborigines trampled on him, stabbed, stripped and robbed him and left him there to die. At a meeting in Adelaide on 7 May to discuss what should be done, angry men, disgusted by the fruits of a policy of 'amity and kindness' and 'useless charity' towards the aborigines demanded that the guilty ones be punished with death. Did this mean they were reverting to the law of the jungle where it was notorious that the strong devoured the weak? Charles Mann reassured them on this point. The white man, he said, had not come to the wilderness of South Australia to usurp or thieve the black man's property, but rather on the basis of a great law of nature. This great law of nature gave the earth and the fulness of its produce in common to all mankind until labour created that progress from communal to private property, which was concurrent with the progress from barbarism to civilization. To rebel against this change was to rebel against the creator of the universe. Since it was the will of God to introduce civilization into South Australia, it was proper to deprive the aborigine of his spears and his waddies because they might be used to impede progress. During the change from barbarism to civilization the white man should heed his Saviour's command to treat all men as brothers and provide the aborigine with the equivalent in food and clothing to what he enjoyed before the white man came. But as an

[7] *South Australian Gazette*, 12 October 1839; Charles Dickens, *The Posthumous Papers of the Pickwick Club* (Oxford ed., London, 1948), ch. 57, and *The Life & Adventures of Nicholas Nickleby* (Oxford ed., London, 1950), pp. 830-1.

instrument of that civilization it was right for the white man to claim proprietorship of the land. It was proper, too, for the white man to enforce law and order. All present agreed to request Gawler to prosecute the aborigines for murder.

On 21 May in a crowded court-room, with the overflow jostling at the windows to get a peep at the show, the Crown solemnly charged Yarr-i-cha, otherwise called George, Monich Yambena, otherwise called Acter, and Parloobookh, otherwise called Williami (sic), having forsaken God and being in league with the Devil, with feloniously murdering William Duffield, shepherd to Osmond Gillies. Judge Cooper opened the proceedings with a solemn reminder to those present that they were about to show that in a British court a fair and impartial trial was available even to the most helpless of God's creatures. Witnesses swore to speak the truth, the whole truth, calling, as ever in a British court, on God to help them to do so. Learned counsel had their say, the judge summed up, and the jury of white men retired to consider their verdict. The foreman informed the court that in the jury's opinion two of the aborigines were guilty of murder. His Honour, after dwelling at some length on the virtue of a legal code which insisted that no man, whether his complexion be fair or dark, could take the law into his own hands, went on to tell the two aborigines that they would be hanged by the neck until they were dead. Nothing he said altered the 'gloomy calmness' the aborigines wore on their faces throughout the proceedings.

On 31 May another huge crowd gathered in Adelaide to watch two terrified aborigines, seated on coffins, make the journey from the gaol to the scaffold. There the Reverend C. B. Howard and the Reverend T. Q. Stow urged them to make their peace with God, but, when the two men responded to such blandishments with the same 'gloomy calmness', the two gentlemen turned their eyes toward heaven and asked their God to forgive these two black men for breaking the divine prohibition on murder. After they were hanged tears coursed down the cheeks of their fellow-aborigines. By contrast the white man was well pleased with himself. The press congratulated their fellow-countrymen for not blotting the annals of South Australia with any stain of cruelty or oppression towards the poor savages. The punishment would only cement the good relations that happily existed between the two peoples. Gawler congratulated the officers of his government for arranging the execution 'with great propriety'. When the appointment of M. Moorhouse as Protector of Aborigines was announced a month later, Gawler instructed him to bring the aborigines into actual and beneficial contact with civilization and religion. He was also urged to labour hard to remove the prejudices and errors of the aborigines.[8]

By then the forces of the moral improvers of mankind had been greatly strengthened by the creation of two settlements of German colonists at Klemzig on the Torrens and Hahndorf near Mount Barker. Driven from the

[8] *South Australian Gazette*, 27 April, 12, 18, 25 May, 1, 8 June 1839; Sheriff to Col. Sec., 31 May 1839, encl. in Gawler to Glenelg, 31 May 1839, C.O. 13/14; *Southern Australian*, 10, 22 May, 19, 26 June 1839.

kingdom of Prussia because of their refusal to allow a secular sovereign to dictate the practices of their holy religion, their pastor Ludwig Christian Kavel had negotiated in 1838 with G. F. Angas for their migration to South Australia. By January 1839 four boatloads or 537 migrants all told, arrived at Holdfast Bay. Believing they had come not from any foolish greed for earthly treasures but out of faith in God and His holy word, they had asked God to lead them to a spot in His wide creation where they could live and proclaim His holy word in its truth and purity. Joseph Menge, a fellow-German and a servant of the South Australian Company, who delighted them at landfall by playing Lutheran hymns on a gum-leaf, tried to persuade the first two boatloads to lease land near the great bend of the Murray. David McLaren, the South Australian manager of the company, persuaded Kavel to lease land from the company at a site on the north bank of the Torrens, which they called Klemzig after their native town in Prussia.

This land which was held on lease for seven years at an annual rental of 5s an acre, was parcelled out by lot in proportion to the size of each family. By a display of virtue and industry they effaced the features of the wilderness within five months of taking up the land. They built thirty neat clean comfortable houses of *pisé*, and some humbler cottages of brushwood and thatch. By the labour of their hands the men tilled the soil, milked cows, chopped wood and carried water. Women and children, too, laboured with their hands for the common good, for there was about the settlement the air of a community that had turned its back on the Europe which was moving into the age of the steam-engine, the railway and the factory, and all those 'noisy nothings' about the rights of man and the pursuit of happiness. At Klemzig men knew that one class of men was made to lead and another to follow: men raised their hats to their superiors, and women dropped a curtsy to men.[9]

In January 1839 as the Germans who had arrived on the *Zebra* and the *Catherina* were lolling around like lost sheep at Holdfast Bay one W. H. Dutton offered to settle them on part of the four thousand acres he and his partners, J. Finniss and D. Macfarlane, had acquired in the neighbourhood of Mount Barker. He offered them one hundred acres, seed, stock, and

[9] E. Hodder, *George Fife Angas* (London, 1891), pp. 184-6; A. Lodewyckx, *Die Deutschen in Australien* (Stuttgart, 1932), pp. 42-3; 'Extracts from the reminiscences of Captain Dirk Meinertz Hahn, 1838-1839', translated from German by F. J. H. Blaess and L. A. Triebel, *South Australiana*, vol. 3, September 1964, p. 109; based on information in H. Capper *South Australia* (3rd ed. Adelaide, 1839). Estimates vary on numbers on board, as well as on departure and arrival dates; quoted in Thanksgiving Service. *125th Anniversary (1838-1963) of Landing of Lutheran Pioneers and First Lutheran Service* (Adelaide, 1963), p. 7; G. F. Angas to D. McLaren, 22 July 1837, G. F. Angas to W. Teburmann and C. G. Teithelmann, 28 May 1838 (Angas Papers); D. McLaren to G. F. Angas, 29 October 1838, Flaxman to G. F. Angas, 15 December 1838 (Angas Papers); Diary of J. C. E. Jaensch (MS. in Lutheran Church Archives, Adelaide); D. Van Abbé, 'A German eccentric in South Australia, 1836-1852', *Hist. Studies*, no. 39, November 1962; *Register*, 17 September 1901; *Southern Australian*, 2 July 1838, 18 September 1839; *Observer*, 24 February, 2, 9, 16, 23 March, 13, 27 April, 4, 11, 25 May 1844; T. Hebart, *The United Evangelical Lutheran Church in Australia* (Adelaide, 1938), p. 35; for the story of the repayment of their advance from G. F. Angas see D. H. Pike, *Paradise of Dissent* (London, 1957), pp. 209-11.

advances of salaries for their clergymen and schoolmaster, with the promise of more land at an appropriate rent at the end of the first year. After the trek from Holdfast Bay to the site, the Germans called it Hahndorf in honour of the captain of the *Zebra*. By June 1839 that great hymn of praise 'Ein feste Burg ist unser Gott' was being offered up near that place where the pious Captain Barker eight years earlier had sensed it was God's purpose for the white man to plant his civilization on the plains of South Australia.[10]

Dutton was another one of those overlanders from New South Wales. He had arrived in Sydney in 1830 and had taken up land in partnership with his brother Frederick on the Goodradigbee River, on the Monaro, and at Mullengandra near Albury. From there he had overlanded cattle to Adelaide in 1838 and taken up his special survey at Mount Barker in the following year. The country districts of South Australia were being occupied by large landed proprietors who were leasing land to frugal, industrious and virtuous tenant farmers. In the verdant district of Mount Barker respectable families on their leases of forty- to eighty-acre blocks soon created all those English or German creature comforts with which men were familiar in the Old World. They put up their stone houses, sowed crops of wheat, barley and oats, planted potatoes and maize, bred dairy cows, sheep and pigs, and cultivated luxuriant gardens and orchards. The large landed proprietor rather than the systematic colonizer was about to show that it was possible to found a society in the New World without using slave labour or lapsing back to barbarism.[11]

Just as the overlanders, capitalists, clergymen and school-teachers were winning the battle against barbarism, Edward John Eyre came back from the interior of their colony to tell them of the seas of desolation to the north and the west. Born in 1815 in England into one of those families which cherished the belief that they had belonged to the landed gentry ever since the days of William the Conqueror, Eyre had migrated to Sydney in 1833 in the hope that such a career would preserve his membership of that class. The profits from his property at Queanbeyan, and two overlanding expeditions provided the material background for his appearance in the drawing-rooms of the gentry of Adelaide. They also provided the experience essential to any man seeking the whereabouts of grass for the sheep and cattle of the would-be gentry of South Australia. When he and three other Europeans, two aborigines, sundry drays, horses, dogs and supplies for two months left Adelaide in May 1839, James Baxter was so drunk he fell from his horse. Eyre rebuked him because he believed a drunkard was not a pleasing sight to that God with whom he held a daily interview. Until they reached Clare they travelled through familiar country, but then they turned towards the Flinders Range, where he had his first sight of the glazed bed of a lake, which was surrounded by such a vast and sterile desert, that he turned east making for the great bend

---

[10] The terms of the agreement between W. H. Dutton, J. Finniss, D. Macfarlane and D. M. Hahn are summarized in 'Extracts from the Reminiscences of Captain Dirk Meinertz Hahn, 1838-1839', pp. 123-6; *Southern Australian*, 30 January 1839; Francis Dutton, *South Australia and its Mines* (London, 1946), pp. 136-7.

[11] Ibid., pp. 108-9.

in the Murray, and then back to Adelaide where Baxter remained drunk for a week while Eyre wondered why a benevolent Providence had made the womb of their country so dry and barren.[12]

On 8 July he and his party set out by ship for Port Lincoln on Spencer Gulf intending to explore the hinterland of the country Flinders had ominously described as rocky and barren. After travelling west as far as Streaky Bay he returned to Adelaide in October past the bed of the lake he had seen on his first journey, which he named in honour of Colonel Torrens. This time he told them he had not crossed a single creek, river, or chain of ponds, or seen any permanent water anywhere. The locals were sorry the results of the journey had turned out so very unfavourably to the quality of the land, but no one wondered whether they were destined to become just as flat, dreary and sterile by that huge arc of barren land to their north and their west, whether the spirit of that place would in time impose its own pattern on them. Quite undismayed Gawler honoured Eyre by calling the land west of Spencer Gulf Eyre Peninsula. Eyre and Sturt gave a ball in honour of the ladies of Adelaide. The Reverend T. Q. Stow continued to tell his flock of the glorious future for those who used God's gifts of the soil and climate of South Australia.[13]

This dryness of the interior and the taking up of the usable land by capitalists such as the Dutton brothers, J. Finniss, J. Morphett and the directors of the South Australian Company provided the setting both for a crisis in relations with the aborigines, and in the financial stability of the government of South Australia. As long as arable land was in plentiful supply there was no conflict between government policy to reserve some land for the use of the aborigines and the demands of the settlers. By the beginning of 1840 holders of land orders began to grumble about the practice of reserving land in districts for the exclusive use of the aborigines. In July 1840 David McLaren on behalf of the South Australian Company, and H. Nixon, J. Allan, R. Gouger, J. H. Fisher, J. Morphett, and F. Jones, all owners or representatives of owners of preliminary land orders, complained to Charles Sturt, Assistant Commissioner, that they had reserved certain sections of country land in various districts under the full confidence that they were entitled to make their selections in preference to all persons whatever, only to find to their regret that certain sections had been withdrawn from public choice in favour of the aborigines. They asked Sturt not to confirm the choices of land made by the Protector of Aborigines until after they had made their selections. Sturt was instructed by the Governor to inform them that he was surprised the claims of the Europeans to the lands of the province should be deemed to be preliminary to those of the aborigines. These 'natural inde-

---

[12] *Southern Australian*, 1 May, 16 October 1839; E. J. Eyre, Autobiographical Narrative (MS. in M.L.); G. Dutton, *The Hero as Murderer* (London, 1967), pp. 64-7.

[13] *South Australian Gazette*, 19 October 1839; *Southern Australian*, 23, 30 October 1839; G. Dutton, op. cit., pp. 69-71; E. J. Eyre, op. cit. and *Journals of Expeditions of Discovery into Central Australia and Overland from Adelaide to King George's Sound* (2 vols, London, 1845).

feasible rights' of the aborigines were vested in them as their birthright, and confirmed by the royal instructions to the Governor, which commanded him to protect the aborigines in the free enjoyment of their possessions, to prevent injustice and violence towards them, to take all necessary measures to advance them in civilization, and not to disturb them in possession of those lands over which they might possess proprietary rights and of which they were not disposed to make a voluntary transfer. His Excellency therefore could not perceive the justice of the settlers' proposition that the aborigines should have second choice. If the claims of the natives were not void before all, they were preliminary to all. They could not occupy a middle station.[14]

At the same time the settlers were gradually pushing the aborigines out into areas where their chances of survival from hunting and fishing diminished. On the frontiers of settlement the white men confronted tribes not touched by civilization. Both causes contributed to bloody encounters between aborigines and white men. After the brigantine *Maria* was wrecked at Encounter Bay in July 1840, the aborigines butchered the survivors and strewed human legs, arms and mutilated bodies all over the sands. Gawler, believing that to allow this band of 'most ferocious, insidious, unprovoked, and inveterate murderers and robbers' to go unpunished would defeat the ends of justice and humanity, summoned the Executive Council which recommended the execution of summary justice by 'temperate means'. He then despatched the Commissioner of Police, Thomas Shuldam O'Halloran, and a party of armed men to overawe the aborigines of Encounter Bay. On 25 August they captured two aborigines, took them to the spot where the white men had been butchered, charged them with murder, hanged them and left the bodies dangling there so that their fellow-aborigines might learn what happened to murderers. Back in Adelaide there was talk of treating the Milmenrura natives of Encounter Bay as a foreign enemy. But Gawler, determined though he was not to succumb to 'that unhealthy sentiment . . . miscalled philanthropy', which led the weak and the faint of heart to condone wanton crimes, pinned his faith to reports that the temporary resort to terror had caused the Milmenrura savages to vacate the district. He was not to know that for months they met around the decaying bodies of their fellow-countrymen and vowed to kill every white man they saw and any member of their people who was friendly to white men.[15]

By then the bourgeoisie of Adelaide and the settlers in the country districts

[14] David McLaren and others to the Assistant Commissioner, 9 July 1840, and Assistant Commissioner to David McLaren and others, 11 July 1840, *South Australian Gazette*, 25 July 1840.
[15] *South Australian Gazette*, 13 August, 5 September 1840; C. Cooper to Gawler, 12 August 1840, C.O. 13/16; encl. in Gawler to Secretary of State for the Colonies, 15 August 1840, C.O. 13/16; *Southern Australian*, 4 June 1841; marginal comment by J. Stephen on Gawler to Secretary of State for the Colonies, 19 February 1841, C.O. 13/16; protest by Aborigines Protection Society in London, March 1841, encl. in Gawler to Secretary of State, C.O. 13/16; Kathleen Hassell, The Relations between the Settlers and the Aborigines in South Australia, 1836-1860 (thesis in Public Library of South Australia).

were disturbed by the drift of events in the public life of the colony. There were complaints of intolerable delays in the Survey Department, and malicious stories that Sturt was so blind he could not even see the files in his department, let alone read what was inside them. Government revenue from the sale of land had dropped alarmingly, partly because settlement had reached the frontiers of dryness and partly because immigrants were leasing land from the South Australian Company or the lucky holders of the special surveys, rather than buying land and so contributing to government revenue. As early as 19 December 1839 there had been a public meeting in the court-house in Adelaide at which speakers such as David McLaren and John Morphett had asked for improvements in the Survey Department, and the admission of representatives of the commercial, agricultural, pastoral and general interests of the colony into the Legislative Council. Charles Mann in the *Southern Australian* at the same time had argued that every immigrant had the right to find in the colony the institutions of his native country, adding that as men they had a claim to be consulted on all that affected their own and their children's interests. Gawler would not budge, but took his stand on the simple principle that any public criticism of the officers of his government was an exercise not in liberty but in licentiousness.[16]

In January 1840 the *Southern Australian* had written of the gloomy and portentous aspect of their sky. It was rumoured that government had already spent £200 000 that year, an amount far in excess of the authorized sum, and that Gawler had no plans to reduce the indebtedness of government to the money-lenders of Adelaide except by calling on London to authorize his expenditure on public works on the grounds of pressing emergency. What if the Treasury in London refused to honour such bills? Gawler, puffed up as he was with self-congratulation for the fruits of his aboriginal policy, his encouragement to the improvers of the morals of his people, and the hum of activity in Adelaide produced by such lavish government spending, paid no heed to such demands. Instead by one of those deeds of folly men commit when preening themselves on their achievements, he spent much time in March showing 'open friendship' to Captain George Grey, one-time superin-tendent of King George's Sound, by taking him over his public works, lacking as ever the talent to read the signs in another man's face. He and Grey warmed to each other on the mission of the white man to teach English to the aborigines so that they might become acquainted with and learn to revere their Maker and their God.[17]

By April he was busying himself with the details of a bill which gave the bourgeoisie of Adelaide a chance to show whether they were to be trusted with a share in the government of South Australia. On 19 August, acting on

---

[16] *Southern Australian*, 4, 12, 26 December 1839; *Southern Australian*, 20 November, 4, 12 December 1839; *Southern Australian*, 23, 30 January 1840; Gawler to Normanby, 10 October 1839, C.O. 13/14.

[17] *Southern Australian*, 23, 30 January 1840; Gawler to Russell, 27 August 1841, C.O. 13/20.

instructions from London, his Legislative Council passed the Colonial Municipal Corporation Ordinance which provided for the election of nineteen councillors and three aldermen by adult males of six months' residence who possessed property in houses or land to the value of £20 a year and who either lived in Adelaide or within seven miles of it. Such councillors or aldermen were to be possessed of property of an annual rental of £50 or of the value of £500. After the elections on 31 October and the first meeting of the Council on 4 November, at which J. H. Fisher was elected mayor, Gawler rashly came to the conclusion that the Council was filled with men who had already displayed their liberal leanings at previous public meetings. Fearing similar liberals would be elected to a Legislative Council, he preferred to sign bills on the Treasury in London rather than conclude any pact with the men of property who in return for the right to elect their representatives to the Legislative Council would allow their property to be taxed and so hasten the coming of the day when the colony could defray the expenses of its government. He remembered that good man James Stephen telling him that the South Australian system of government was founded in total ignorance of the real business of colonial government and was an example of ignorance taking the airs of philosophy.[18]

While Gawler was comforting himself with the delusion that at least in Downing Street there was a 'shire for men who understand', the men in the Colonial Office were puzzled by the reports from South Australia and wondered what to do. In January 1840, believing that perhaps the source of the trouble was that the number of colonization commissioners was too large for efficient administration and that the Agent-General for Emigration to the other Australian colonies had too many duties, they appointed three men (T. F. Elliot, R. Torrens and E. E. Villers) to be a board of commissioners for the management of sales of land in British colonies, and for promoting a well-regulated emigration. By June it was clear that lack of funds was causing migration to dwindle. So government in July authorized the commissioners to raise £120 000 on the security of the revenues of the colony. That was used up by October. By then both the colonization commissioners and the manager of the South Australian Company were stressing to Lord John Russell the inconvenience and loss to which the purchasers of land in the colony would be subjected by the non-transmission of a further number of emigrant labourers during 1840.

In October Lord John asked the Lords of the Treasury to investigate the

---

[18] Proceedings of the Legislative Council of South Australia, 19 May 1840, reported in *South Australian Gazette*, 23 May 1840; An Ordinance to Constitute a Municipal Corporation for the City of Adelaide, no. 4, 1840, *Acts and Ordinances of South Australia from the Establishment of the Colony in 1836 to the Close of the Session of 1851* (Adelaide, 1851); T. Worsnop, *History of the City of Adelaide* (Adelaide, 1878), pp. 15-21; *South Australian Gazette*, 5, 26 September, 10, 31 October 1840; proceedings of the Municipal Council, 4 November 1840, *South Australian Gazette*, 7 November 1840; Gawler to Russell, 14 January 1841, C.O. 13/20; Gawler to J. Stephen, 3 May 1841, C.O. 13/20.

finances of the colony, and promised to bring under the consideration of
parliament, at the earliest opportunity, the whole proceedings which had led
to the embarrassments in question as a preliminary to a full revision of the
system under which the government and financial arrangements of the colony
had been conducted. On 3 November a Treasury minute was ready for
transmission to Lord John. They noted that the Governor of South Australia
had already drawn bills on the Colonization Commission in excess of the
£120000 loan the Treasury had authorized the Commission to raise in July.
The question now was, were those bills to be honoured when they reached
London, and what steps were to be taken to place revenue and expenditure
on a secure footing? The Treasury minuted that the holders of bills drawn
on the commissioners should be informed that no pledge could be given for
the acceptance or payment of them, but that the most peremptory instructions
should be addressed to the Governor to confine the public expenditure within
the limits of the revenue and that any future bills drawn without specific
authority from London would not be accepted. Deeply impressed by the
danger and distress to which the population of South Australia would be
exposed by the subversion of the credit of the local government by dishonour-
ing the bills and by the non-fulfilment of contracts by the commissioners to
parties to furnish shipping and stores for emigrants already conveyed or now
in passage to the colony, they recommended that the commissioners be
authorized to raise a further £200 000 in colonial revenue securities to liquidate
existing liabilities and such drafts drawn in the colony before the prohibition
on expenditure reached the governor. On 5 November Lord John informed
the colonization commissioners that he entirely concurred with the view the
Lords of the Treasury took of the subject.[19]

While the colonization commissioners, the Lords Commissioner of the
Treasury and the Colonial Office were feverishly exchanging ideas on how to
reduce government expenditure, they were dismayed to receive a despatch
from Gawler, written on 31 October 1839, in which he offered his resignation
unless the British Government agreed to raise his salary to £2000 a year. In
July 1840 Russell wrote off to say that if Gawler persisted in the request he
would have no alternative but to advise Her Majesty to accept the resignation,
adding his surprise and concern at the huge expenditure into which the
colony had been plunged. When that first loan was quickly mopped up by
the arrival of yet more bills from Adelaide, Russell wrote to Gawler on
26 December that in consequence of the report made to Her Majesty's Government by the colonization commissioners for South Australia respecting the
financial state of the province, and respecting the amount of the bills Gawler
had drawn on the commissioners in excess of his authority it had become his
unwelcome duty to advise Her Majesty to relieve Gawler of the offices of

---

[19] For the appointment of the colonial land and emigration commissioners see Russell
to Gipps, 31 January 1840, *H.R.A.*, I. xx. 491, 863-4; Russell to South Australian commissioners, 5 November 1840, appendix to Second Report from Select Committee on
South Australia, *P.P.*, 1841, IV, 394.

Governor and Resident Commissioner in the province of South Australia, and he had appointed Captain George Grey as his successor.[20]

In the preceding November, Grey had succeeded in convincing both the colonization commissioners and the Colonial Office that it was possible to reduce government expenditure in South Australia. He had recommended that government suspend the system of special surveys, each of which cost government at least £2500, and locked up eleven thousand acres for every four thousand taken up. He also had ideas on what to do with the public buildings in the course of construction, the imprudence of a governor living in a house too large to furnish and run on his existing income, the reduction of salaries of government officers, the abolition of certain government positions, the need to create local corporate bodies which would assume the responsibility for the formation and management of roads, the possibility of reducing the cost of the police force by employing soldiers to maintain law and order, and the importance of the governor setting an example of plainness and frugality to society at large. Russell and his advisers were so delighted that on 29 December Grey was formally commissioned Governor and Resident Commissioner, and instructed to suspend the special surveys, to encourage the creation of corporate bodies and to practise diligently the economies he had suggested in his minute.[21]

When the news reached Adelaide in February 1841, the public works programme came to a standstill. For a season gloom and fears for the future seized the hearts of people who had blithely assumed a bag of gold in this world and eternal bliss in the world to come were the rewards for those who bent the knee to their God, eschewed evil and were faithful disciples of the gospel of work. Charles Mann argued in the *Southern Australian* that the crisis was caused by entrusting to one man uncontrolled power over the lives and properties of Her Majesty's subjects. He and those of like mind called a series of public meetings at which their supporters roared away about 'no taxation without representation', but by May, Mann was beginning to wonder whether their society was suffering from 'political rabies', for not even fears for the fate of the advances made to government could rouse the bourgeoisie of Adelaide and the land-holders in the hinterland to concerted political action, let alone convince them the time had come for them to take over the government of the colony. Cheering and waving of hats and handkerchiefs at public meetings were as far as they were prepared to go.[22]

The ministers of religion, the respectable people, the participants in Methodist 'love-feasts', Lutheran spiritual extravaganzas, and Temperance tea-parties—all those who had contributed towards this high noon for moral

[20] Gawler to Normanby, 30 October 1839, C.O. 13/14; Russell to Gawler, 13 July 1839, C.O. 396/2; Russell to Gawler, 26 December 1840, C.O. 396/2.
[21] Minute by Captain Grey to Lord John Russell, encl. in Grey to Russell, 18 November 1840, C.O. 13/16; Russell to Grey, 29 December 1840, C.O. 396/2.
[22] Gawler to Russell, 22 February 1841, C.O. 13/20; the announcement in Adelaide of Gawler's recall and Grey's appointment is in *South Australian Register*, 3 April 1841; address to Governor Gawler and reply by Governor Gawler to the address, 23 March 1841, *South Australian Gazette*, 1 April 1841.

improvers in South Australia—expressed their gratitude to Gawler for what he had done. So did the aborigines of Adelaide who told him, 'he us did hide from the white man who insulted. Lament we at his absence, he at us well did look our father he did sit regarding food meat clothing he us did give, land for food us he back gave school house he for the children of us did build words to learn as white children do thus black children'. To all his well-wishers Gawler offered the hope that the Almighty would reward them with blessings in the world to come. For his faith was all he had to give him the strength to endure that dark night of the soul when on 14 May his successor George Grey, a mere boy of twenty-nine years and a junior captain in the army, took over from a hero of Waterloo.[23]

When he boarded the *Dumfries* on 22 June, Gawler was ready to devote the rest of his life to the salvation of his own soul and the souls of all men. On his arrival in England in January 1842 he was received with the greatest cordiality, offered a committee of inquiry and told that everyone in high places was confident that he would make a satisfactory defence of his policy. But worldly reputation was not the prize he coveted. He wanted to be known as the man who was not ashamed to confess faith in Christ and manfully to fight under His banner against the world, the flesh and the Devil. What did it matter if a week after he sailed on the *Dumfries* many men who had comforted him in his days of anguish were already fawning on his successor? Till his death on 7 May 1869 he never realized that he—a man who professed to love all mankind and to have compassion for 'the least of the little ones' because of the love of Christ—lived in a dream world.[24]

By contrast his successor had both the gifts and the luck to preside over the colony while government proved it could be self-supporting and society at large proved it was possible to plant a colony without establishing some sort of slavery or experiencing the disasters that usually befell new colonies planted in an extensive country. George Grey looked very much the part when he landed from the *Lord Glenelg* in May 1841. He was tall and upright in figure, his face wore a pleasing, amiable expression, and his manners were gentle, polished and agreeable. He was then only twenty-nine. His wife, who was a mere twenty, was a remarkably pretty woman with beautiful dark eyes and hair and the presence of a graceful hostess. She waited at Holdfast Bay until the time came to put her child in the baby basket, the head resting on a pillow inscribed 'Welcome, little stranger'. But the child died, giving the Governor's lady that moment of insight into the heart of her husband, for he was foolish enough to let her see that to him her agony meant little and his triumph on the stage of public life everything.

While she waited in vain for one word of sympathy and understanding

[23] Address of Protector of the Aborigines and Missionaries to Gawler, *Southern Australian*, 28 May 1841; *Southern Australian*, 14 May, 26 June 1841; C. Sturt to G. Macleay, 4 May 1841, and C. Sturt to R. Darling, 25 January 1843 (Sturt Papers).

[24] Based on C.W.N., *George Gawler, K.H. 52nd Light Infantry*, compiled under the direction of his daughter, Jane Cox Gawler (London, 1900); for Gawler in London see *Southern Australian*, 8, 15 July 1842.

from her husband, he was ingratiating himself with all the respectable people of Adelaide. He asked the members of the Legislative Council to advise him on the steps he should take to meet the expected deficit of £16000 to £18000 that quarter. They were delighted. He told the members of the Chamber of Commerce that although government could not honour immediately the bills so extravagantly issued by Gawler, he was prepared to issue an order certifying the obligation of government to pay up when its financial position improved. They were reassured. They were more than reassured when Grey introduced measures to reduce government expenditure. Positions were retrenched, salaries were slashed to bridge the gap between a revenue of £30 000 and an annual expenditure of £94 000. When he heard of these measures, James Stephen was delighted by their 'great sagacity and moral courage', and even Edward Stanley for once was prompted into words of praise for a colonial governor. Captain Sturt, who dropped £200 a year in salary and slid in rank from Assistant Commissioner to Registrar-General, complained of a breach of faith, but everyone knew he had put himself forward to be Gawler's successor. Grey found it quite pleasing to give a second twist of the screw to a man of Sturt's temperament, a motive strengthened by his knowledge that Sturt had been soft of heart on the Gawler question.[25]

No one could accuse Captain Grey of softness of heart. When the number of people dependent on government relief reached 1240, that is one in every twelve of the population of the province was living on public charity, he offered them reduced payments out of government funds, or assistance to find work with the settlers up country. When the unemployed sent a deputation in October to protest against the hardships they suffered from such economies, he docked them a day's payment. The unemployed again exhorted him to save them from the fate of slipping back into the semi-barbarism of the manufacturing districts of England and Scotland. In reply Grey reminded them that it was not the task of government to help them, that they must wait patiently till their conditions were improved by supply and demand for labour resuming their natural balance. Unlike his predecessor, he had no intention to allow government to interfere with the labour market, nor to countenance any mischievous attempt to encourage a feeling of discontent among the labouring population. Was he not himself setting an example by going without dinner at Government House five days a week?[26]

[25] *South Australian Register*, 15, 22 May 1841; Russell to Grey, 29 December 1840, C.O. 396/2; *Southern Australian*, 14 May 1841; Grey to Russell, 20 May 1841, C.O. 13/20; Mrs Jane Isabella Watts, *Memories of Early Days in South Australia* (Adelaide, 1882), pp. 66-7.
[26] Grey to Russell, 20 May 1841, and Grey to Russell, 22 May 1841, C.O. 13/20; *South Australian Register*, 12 June 1841; Grey to Russell, 5 June 1841; Grey to Russell, 7 June 1841, C.O. 13/20; *South Australian Register*, 21 August 1841; memorial of the working classes to Grey, 14 October 1841, encl. in Grey to Russell, 18 October 1841, C.O. 13/21; Grey to Russell, 4 July 1841, C.O. 13/20; minute by Stephen on above; draft reply of Stanley to Grey, 7 February 1842, C.O. 13/20; C. Sturt to W. Sturt, n.d. (written late in 1841 or early in 1842) (Sturt Papers); Diary of C. W. Davies, March 1842 (MS. in S.A.S.A.).

While Grey was skilfully presiding over the transition from extravagance to moderation in government expenditure, others were keeping alive the high-minded aspiration of the founders of the province to spread civilization over the wilderness of South Australia. On 18 June 1840 a party of men gathered at Government House for the reading of prayers and the presentation by Captain Sturt to Edward Eyre of a Union Jack, woven in silk by the ladies of Adelaide, which Sturt urged Eyre to carry to the centre of the continent and leave there as a sign to the savage that the footstep of civilized man had penetrated so far. That day Eyre, John Baxter, E. B. Scott, two aborigines, thirteen horses and forty sheep, plus stores for a three months' journey set out to discover the interior of Australia. Driven back once again by the arid country around Lake Torrens, Eyre took his party to Streaky Bay, from where he made yet another futile attempt to strike north. Undaunted he set out from Streaky Bay with Baxter, the aborigine Wylie and two other aborigines to walk to King George's Sound, which he and Wylie reached on 7 July. When Eyre got back to Adelaide by ship a year later he had a sorry story to tell of the murder of Baxter at Eucla by two treacherous aborigines. He also told them how he had passed over a barren and desolate region which was almost destitute of grass, timber and water, and covered in places with an impenetrable useless scrub. Optimistic as ever, the colonists hailed Eyre as a hero who would one day plant the emblem of civilization, the Union Jack, in the centre of their mysterious province. For them such vast stretches of barren desolate country must be part of the plans of a benevolent providence and not evidence of their misfortune in attempting to civilize an uncouth country.[27]

By then Grey was anxious to use Eyre for the other 'laudable purpose' for which the white man had come to South Australia—to prevent that 'lamentable thing' of the 'progress and prosperity of one race conducing to the downfall and decay of another'. Eyre, like Sturt, was known to cherish a special kindness towards the aborigines and to feel some sympathy with them. When he came back to Adelaide the overlanders of stock from New South Wales, who were rapidly dwarfing in significance the calculators and moral improvers of Adelaide, were reported to be having trouble with the aborigines at the big bend of the Murray. In April and May 1841 pitched battles were fought between parties of ten or eleven overlanders and three to four hundred natives. Extremists asked Grey to declare war on the aborigines as a hostile foreign power. Grey decided to follow a middle course. Justice to the aborigines, he said, as well as to the European servants of the landed

---

[27] C. Sturt to C. Campbell, 3 July 1840 (Sturt Papers); E. J. Eyre, *Journals of Expeditions of Discovery into Central Australia*, vol. 1, pp. 19-20; for the murder of Baxter see ibid., vol. 1, pp. 401-2; for Eyre's response to the murder of Baxter see ibid., vol. 2, pp. 1-2; G. Dutton, *The Hero As Murderer*, chs 6, 7, 8; there is a monument to John Baxter near Eucla on the Great Australian Bight; see also monument erected to the memory of Edward John Eyre, and to the memory of Wylie, Albany, Western Australia, (personal visit 6 June 1970); *Southern Australian*, 27, 30 July 1841; *South Australian Register*, 28 August 1841; *Sydney Herald*, 30 August 1841.

proprietors, required that the force accompanying an overland party should be so large as to overawe the former and protect the latter. But while doing everything in his power to protect the lives and properties of settlers, he would not authorize the levying of war or the exercise of belligerent rights against the aborigines of Australia. At the end of May, Grey despatched the Commissioner of Police, T. O'Halloran, to ensure a safe passage for the sheep and cattle of the overlanders. Despite the taunts of the aborigines to O'Halloran and his party at the Rufus River about 'plenty sheepy' and 'plenty jumbuk' and cries of 'cornie' (the local aboriginal word of abuse for the white man) this display of force so pacified the district that Grey was ready to ask Eyre in July to try what kindness could do to replace fear with respect.[28]

He asked Eyre to accept the position of Resident Magistrate and Protector of the Aborigines at Moorundie some twenty miles south of the great bend in the Murray at a salary of £250 a year with forage for a horse, and the assistance of twelve men and one non-commissioned officer. As evidence of amity and kindness Eyre mustered the aborigines at every full moon to hand out blankets and flour. He began to teach them the rudiments of bartering and to show them the benefits of working for wages in the hope that the adoption of the way of life of civilized people would wear away the wilder shades in their own character and so end those physical clashes with the white man which could only end in the total annihilation of the original inhabitants of the soil of South Australia. Quite unrestrained by any feelings of remorse or conscience, and looking upon the white men as their foes, the aborigines soon renewed attacks on overlanding parties. For nothing Eyre could do with blanket handouts could put an end to their habit of avenging wrongs against their people. Once again the overlanders shot down their would-be avengers, and the wails of aboriginal women and children mourning for their dead men could be heard along the high banks of the Murray from Moorundie to the Rufus.

As these stories of bloody revenge and retribution reached Adelaide, opinion hardened in favour of using bullets to deter the wildness in the black man's heart. In August 1842 a black man named Manicha was flogged in front of the gaol in Adelaide while his fellow-aborigines howled in horror and anger, and some white men were ashamed that such an obsolete punishment as flogging should be used against a simple savage. Eyre stuck to his task of trying to prevent the 'lamentable thing', the success of the white man being so fatal to the aborigine, hoping to persuade the aborigines to throw off the trammels of custom and prejudice, embrace the habits and pursuits of the white man and make an effort to rise in the scale of physical and moral improvement. Like Grey he believed the white man should stamp out the

[28] Grey to Secretary of State for the Colonies, 29 May 1841, C.O. 13/20; T. O'Halloran, Journal, 31 May to 23 June, and T. O'Halloran to Grey, 27 June 1841, reprinted in *Proceedings of the Royal Geographical Society of Australasia, South Australian Branch*, vol. 7, pp. 70-91; *South Australian Register*, 10 July, 11 September 1841; *The Times*, 18 February 1842.

cruel and degrading customs the aborigines practised on each other. He believed in stripping them of all their lethal weapons. He hoped that if aborigines were permitted to testify against each other in British law courts then inter-tribal barbarities might end. He wanted to take away from the aborigine the distinctive features of his own culture in the hope that he would then become a true son of Britain.

In 1846, when no signs from earth or heaven testified to any lasting good being accomplished, he set off to take up the position of Lieutenant-Governor of New Zealand, where he squabbled incessantly, showed a strange pre-occupation with gold braid and ceremonial and a sanctimonious preoccupation with Sabbath observance. He then went as Governor to Jamaica where his brutality in putting down a negro insurrection in 1865 caused Karl Marx to liken the beastliness of the 'true Englishmen' to the Russians, and John Stuart Mill to accuse him of murder. The hero of the Nullarbor Plain and the 'gentle spirit' of Moorundie was metamorphosed in time into a murderer in a 'nigger insurrection'. He lived in seclusion in Devon for thirty-six more years, a kindly old man of few words, looking more like the man who had had compassion on the original tenants of the desert of Australia than the hangman of Jamaica, and doing his duty, as he saw it, in that state of life in which it had pleased God to call him. His life was one of those riddles God sets the sons of men to unravel as best they can. He died on 30 November 1901.[29]

While Eyre was trying to persuade all and sundry that the only hope of preserving the 'unfortunate race of New Holland' was to educate the children to win them away from the evil influences of their own people, and let them see that British laws and customs were to supersede their own, others were bothered by quite different things. One recently arrived settler was confronted with another sisyphean problem of human behaviour in South Australia— the problem of how to get country workers out of the taverns of Adelaide. He was bothered, too, lest the great heat of summer—another part of that inscrutable plan of 'the great disposer of events' for the human race—might make the white man lazy. At the same time the proprietors of sheep and cattle were reminding His Excellency that it was of the utmost importance that the disease of scab in sheep should be eradicated. The Reverend T. Q. Stow was telling the members of his congregation that those who had the clear vision of faith would one day see heaven opened and the angels of God ascending and descending on that ladder that led from earth to heaven. The body of John Baxter who had known those moments of ecstasy and damnation at the great Australian communion rail was lying in the inhospitable soil at the head

---

[29] R. Gouger to E. J. Eyre, 1 October 1841, (s.a.s.a. 24/4/4); Grey to Russell, 30 October 1841, C.O. 13/21; Grey to Stanley, 19 March 1842, C.O. 13/25; *Southern Australian*, 5 August, 4, 7 October 1842; E. J. Eyre to Col. Sec. of South Australia, 7 March 1842, 1 February 1843, 28 February 1844 (s.a.s.a. 24/6); M. Moorhouse to Col. Sec. of South Australia, 12 January 1846 (s.a.s.a. 24/6); E. J. Eyre, *Journals of Expeditions of Discovery into Central Australia*, vol. 2, pp. 499-500; G. Dutton, *The Hero As Murderer*; E. J. Eyre, op. cit., vol. 2, pp. 499-501; J. Morris, 'Eyre: a portrait', *Encounter*, July 1970.

of the Bight. The Total Abstinence Society went on holding their tea meetings at which penitent drunks testified in the presence of their wives. Wesleyan itinerant preachers went on proving that souls saved for Christ made good civil subjects.[30]

Grey, too, was pleased that June of 1842 with the world as it was. Nothing any longer disturbed the quiet of Adelaide. The debt of the government to the South Australian Company had been paid off, the number of able-bodied labourers receiving government assistance had been reduced by seventy-one. As revenue raisers, Grey proposed a moderate excise duty on the distillation of spirits and an increase in the harbour dues. The *Register* described Grey as 'an exceedingly troublesome eyesore to the colonists of South Australia', and the people of Adelaide were summoned to a public meeting in July to protest against this move to impose taxation without representation. At this gathering the buffoons and the extremists first held the floor, with one Jemmy Crawford voicing a pale echo of the Patrick Henry cry, 'Give me liberty or give me death!' and one Nicholls, an atheist with revolutionary views on the family and private property, being shouted down so that Charles Mann could explain how they could be 'great, glorious and free' without adopting the principles of social levellers and red republicans. When the moderates asked Grey to undertake not to tax them until they had acquired the right to elect representatives to the Legislative Council he treated them facetiously: 'Gentlemen', he said, 'I shall tax you first, and you shall be represented afterwards.' Another meeting was summoned for 16 August at which they passed with acclamation the text of a petition to Her Majesty praying she would be pleased to direct that no taxes whatever should be imposed upon Her Majesty's dutiful subjects of South Australia until the Legislative Council should be extended by the introduction of colonists elected by the colonists. Once again, Grey made a joke rather than concur with the request of the petitioners. He told the mayor of Adelaide that if all taxation were prohibited until such time as elections could take place, the colony would be plunged into anarchy and confusion. He told London not to take any notice of the rantings of the turbulent.[31]

Just as the press began to accuse Grey of egotism and of possessing the bombastic literary style of a vain and proud coxcomb, news reached Adelaide of fundamental changes in the constitution of the colony and the disposal of its waste lands. Ever since the end of 1841 the men interested in public questions had scanned the English press anxiously for news of the recommendations of the select committee on South Australia. By October rumours were running around Adelaide that the committee on South Australia had recommended doing away with the humbug of the colonization commissioners and

---

[30] Diary of G. F. Dashwood, 24 November, 21, 30 December 1841, 23 January, 23, 25 February 1842 (MS. in S.A.S.A.); memorial of stock- and sheep-holders to Grey, September 1841, *South Australian Register*, 2 October 1841; *Southern Australian*, 28 October 1842.

[31] Grey to Stanley, 6 June 1842, C.O. 13/26; *Register*, 4 June 1842; *Southern Australian*, 8 July, 16, 26 August, 16 September, 4 October 1842; Grey to Stanley, 22 September 1842, C.O. 13/27.

liberating South Australia from the evil effects of the maladministration of the Adelphi Solons. In December these rumours were confirmed. The Act for the better government of South Australia, which had received the royal assent on 30 July 1842 abolished the colonization commissioners for South Australia and the office of Resident Commissioner in Adelaide. It created a Legislative Council of at least seven members. Grey was instructed to nominate three of the seven from persons holding public office, and the other four from persons not holding any public office. The Act also empowered Her Majesty to convene a general assembly elected by the freeholders of the colony; the despatch accompanying the text of the Act made it clear that such was not to happen until the colony became self-supporting. The despatch put forward proposals to liquidate the accumulated debt and to use debentures on the security of the future revenues of the government to pay outstanding debts. The Act reaffirmed that no convict was to be transported to any place within the province.[32]

It looked as though all that was left of the 'laudable purpose' of the founders was the determination not to solve the problem of planting civilization in an immense territory by 'convict pollution'. By contrast the Act for regulating the sale of land in the Australian colonies, and the despatch justifying and explaining its several clauses, still smelt to high heaven of the idea that systematic colonization could prevent the disasters of slavery and white barbarism. Both the Act and the despatch accepted the point made in the second report of the select committee on South Australia that the first principle of colonization was to maintain a due proportion between the extent of land appropriated and the extent of land occupied. Since all the evidence before the select committee and the Colonial Office had convinced them that the price of 12s per acre was not sufficiently high to prevent the appropriation of more land than could be used, and so increasing the cost of administration for police and roads, they had recommended that the Act should increase the minimum upset price to £1 an acre. Fifteen per cent of the gross proceeds was to be used for the benefit, protection and civilization of the aborigines. The remaining revenue derived from such sales was to be divided into two equal portions, one of which was to be devoted exclusively to paying the costs of migration, and the other to government expenditure.[33]

The foundations of civilization had been laid without the use of slaves or

---

[32] Second Report from the Select Committee on South Australia, *P.P.*, 1841, IV, 394; *Southern Australian*, 18 October 1842; Stanley to Grey, 6 September 1842, C.O. 396/2; An Act to Provide for the Better Government of South Australia, 5 & 6 Vic., c. 61, 30 July 1842, *Statutes at Large*, vol. 16; Additional Instructions to Our Trusty and Well-beloved George Grey, 29 August 1842. Papers Relative to South Australia, *P.P.*, 1843, XXXII, 505.

[33] Second Report from the Select Committee on South Australia, *P.P.*, 1841, IV, 394, pp. xvii-xviii; Stanley to Grey, 15 September 1842, C.O. 396/2; C. E. Trevelyan to J. Stephen, 30 August 1842, and Stanley to the colonial land and emigration commissioners, 27 August 1842, encls in Stanley to Grey, 15 September 1842, C.O. 396/2; *The Times*, 6, 20 July 1842; An Act for Regulating the Sale of Waste Land Belonging to the Crown in the *Australian Colonies*, 5 & 6 Vic., c. 36, 22 June 1842, *Statutes at Large*, vol. 34.

convicts. In their population, which reached almost 15 000 in 1842, unlike the convict colonies the men did not outnumber the women by four or three to one but were approximately equal. Unlike the convict colonies the Irish were at the most only one in fifteen and the number of Catholics so low (approximately one thousand out of fifteen thousand) that the society could give off the air of the Protestant stamp of mind: industry, frugality, sobriety, and concern for liberty which was said to distinguish such men of heroic ingredients. The tiny Catholic community kept alive embers of their faith while they waited patiently for the day when a priest would celebrate the sacraments in their colony. Unlike the convict colonies South Australia already had a high proportion of small property holders and leaseholders, men with such a stake in the country that they were not likely to allow their society to be convulsed by those upheavals which threatened to engulf the Old World.

Unlike the convict colonies they were free of convict contamination. Like the Pharisee they thanked their God for being rid of such a pestilence. All that they had seen had convinced them of the superiority of their civilization, and their privilege in being members of it. They had now seen primitive man in his rude untutored state, uninfluenced by the blessings of education and with passion undisciplined and unsubdued. They had seen how in such a state brutality, grossness of vice, insensibility and lawlessness prevailed. They had seen man unassisted by divine and heavenly succours. They had opted for civilization. Unlike the convict colonies, too, the tone of their society was set by immigrants. By 1842 there were two generations of native-born in New South Wales and one in Van Diemen's Land. The convicts of New South Wales and their families and to a lesser extent those of Van Diemen's Land were quick to shed their ties with their mother country and look on Australia as a country which belonged to them. Migrants were the men for the complex fate of living at the Antipodes while their minds were stuffed with the sentiments of the Old World. In South Australia each Christmas the migrant became nostalgic for an English, an Irish or a Scottish Christmas. At Easter he was nostalgic for that renewal of nature which was so appropriate to and congruous with the Christian looking for the resurrection of the dead. Unlike the convict colonies the tone of South Australian society came from those very zealous supervisors of morals—the clergy and the laity; those supporters of Sunday as a day on which men should neither labour nor rejoice, and even abstain from idly gazing out of windows because that exposed them to the risk of 'beholding vanities abroad'. They promoted those virtues of temperance, frugality and industry they had carried with them as part of their baggage from England on the sun-drenched plains of South Australia, where a very different society soon set up a tension between their profession of faith and what nature and their experience of life seemed to be saying to them.

There was the sameness and the dryness of the land but hope was rekindled at year's end when news reached Adelaide of the discovery of a new rich country stretching along the western banks of the Glenelg River, admirably suited for grazing or agriculture. When the Governor and his lady, the civil and military officers, the clergy and most of the respectable inhabitants of Adelaide and the country districts gathered at Government House on the night of 28 December to mark the sixth anniversary of the foundation of the colony, they were brim full with joy. For some there were the ghosts from the past. Captain Sturt was still wondering why he did not enjoy the respect of his wife or his fellow-men, and why he, the hero of the Murrumbidgee and the Murray, and the father of the province, was precisely a Registrar-General —no more and no less—while that young puppy Grey was Governor and Captain-General in and over the province of South Australia and its dependent territories. Grey and his wife danced together, great strangers though they had become to each other. That night gaiety prevailed as couples danced the mazurka, a traditional Polish dance which had only been introduced into the ballrooms of London twelve years previously. It was a dance for those who took pride in their bearing, a dance, too, which had its moments of wild ecstasy. It was as though they were dancing towards those 'better things' which they believed they could fashion out of the wilds of Australia, not sensing then in the pleasure of the dance what would happen to them when they retained their morality after they had lost their faith, or that those 'better things' were to come not from any theories of colonization but from human ingenuity, and the mineral wealth in those arid places about which they preferred not to think.[34]

[34] *Southern Australian*, 20, 30 December 1842; J. B. Polding to Mr and Mrs Phillips, 17 September 1840 (typescript in Polding Papers, Catholic Archives, St Mary's Cathedral, Sydney); T. H. James, *Six Months in South Australia* (London, 1838), pp. 39-42; *South Australian Gazette*, 6 November 1839.

5

OVERSTRAITERS, OVERLANDERS
AND OTHERS DESCEND ON PORT PHILLIP

BY 1840 the European inhabitants of the Port Phillip District also saw themselves as builders of a way of life more respectable, more virtuous and more industrious than those moral cesspools which convicts and parvenu landlords had erected in the penal colonies of New South Wales and Van Diemen's Land. Like the inhabitants of South Australia they were trapped by the contradiction of attempting to plant a British version of bourgeois civilization, with its restraints on and frowns for the crimes, follies and passions of mankind, in a land which seemed intended by its creator for some elemental, savage confrontation between men and their environment. The gentle Matthew Flinders had been so awe-struck in 1798 by the huge seas rolling through Bass Strait, pounding the south coast of New Holland and the north coast of Van Diemen's Land, that he had chosen a symbolical name for the north-west promontory of the latter: he had called it Cape Grim. In 1800 James Grant, who had given names to Portland Bay and Cape Otway, noted how the winds whipped up 'much sea' in the strait. So did all the navigators who were his contemporaries. The few Europeans who had walked over the land near the coast had used that language of horror and dismay which had characterized their response to the spirit of places in other parts of the continent of New Holland. One of the party belonging to the convict settlement at Sullivan's Cove, Port Phillip, in 1803 had described it as 'a dried up country' which 'would never be resorted to by speculative men'. At Sealers Cove on Wilson's Promontory, at Cape Woolamai on Phillip Island, at Port Fairy and at Portland Bay sealers and whalers pursued a way of life as savage and elemental as the never-ending roar of that sea, the gales that blew in the winter, and the storms that rolled over the land in the summer.[1]

The intrusion of civilization on such a land was to prove just as relentless

[1] M. Flinders, *A Voyage to Terra Australis* (2 vols, London, 1814), vol. I, pp. 113-15, 171-3; this voyage by Flinders is also described in vol. I, pp. 188-9, of this history; for Captain Cook at Cape Howe see J. C. Beaglehole (ed.), *The Voyage of the Endeavour 1768-1771* (Cambridge, 1955), p. 300; James Grant, *The Narrative of a Voyage of Discovery, Performed in His Majesty's Vessel the Lady Nelson* (London, 1803), pp. 67-78; W. S. Campbell, 'The Lady Nelson', R.A.H.S., *J. & P.*, vol. 3, 1915-17; King to Portland, 29 March 1802, *H.R.A.*, I. iii. 482-3; P. G. King to J. Banks, 16 March 1803 (Banks Papers, Brabourne Collection, vol. 7, MS. in M.L.); M. Flinders, op. cit., vol. I, pp. 115-17, 218; this voyage by Flinders is described in vol. I, pp. 174-82, of this history; for the settlement at Sullivan's Cove in 1803 see vol. I of this history, pp. 183-5; see also Collins to Hobart, 14 November 1803, *H.R.A.*, III. i. 35.

as the seas pounding the coast. In 1824 Hamilton Hume and William Hovell rescued this southern part of New Holland from the stigma of being barren and inhospitable and useless for all the purposes of civilized man. The press in Sydney and Hobart Town began to prophesy with all the insolence of men effortlessly taking over a huge inheritance that the tide of civilization was about to sweep over those rich plains where the aborigines of New Holland had floundered since time immemorial in a sea of barbarism. By 1832 settlers were pushing south from Jugiong and Gundagai to Wagga Wagga, the place of the crows, and Mullengandra. It was only a matter of time before they reached the Murray and crossed that noble stream near those majestic river gums and lush meadows.

At the same time some men in Van Diemen's Land were poised for a descent on Port Phillip. By 1832, the year in which the overlanders from New South Wales were pressing on towards the Murray, those settlers in the north of Van Diemen's Land, who aspired to a way of life such as was enjoyed by James Cox at Clarendon or Joseph Archer at Panshanger or Edward Dumaresq at Mount Ireh, knew that they must find fresh land on which to plant their manors. At the same time thousands of miles away in the United Kingdom young men of good family, but threatened by an adverse turn in fortune's wheel, men such as George Russell, Niel Black and others whom history was not destined to rescue from anonymity, were anxiously surveying the press, pamphlets, and printed books for an account of a country that promised that one thing denied them in the land of their birth—membership in the landed gentry. There were others, too, anxious simply for that belly-full the society of the Old World either could not or would not provide for them and their families, all those anonymous men and women who were persuaded they could better at least their material condition by emigration to a country where desirable situations with good wages were available, and where there was the promise of retaining their freedom. They were waiting to be shown where they could have material well-being without the taint of convictism and where they could have their belly-full without loss of virtue or respectability. They were a freak tide backing up, waiting to flood any land suitable for its own purposes, while the high-minded men in the House of Commons and in Whitehall proclaimed how deeply impressed they were with the duty of acting upon the principles of justice and humanity in the intercourse between inhabitants from the United Kingdom and the indigenous inhabitants of their colonial settlements. They were similarly impressed by the duty of white men to protect aborigines and provide an enjoyment of their civil rights, while converting them to that civilization and religion with which a benevolent providence had blessed their own nation.[2]

In 1833 the tide began to flow. In that year Thomas Henty, who had concluded that neither New South Wales, nor Western Australia, nor Van Diemen's Land would place the members of his family in that 'first rank in society' to which he believed he and they were entitled, inspected the

---

[2] For an account of the spread of settlement to Wagga Wagga, see K. Swan, *A History of Wagga Wagga* (Wagga Wagga, 1970), ch. 2; see also ch. 11 of this volume.

picturesque and beautiful land James Grant had seen in the neighbourhood of Portland Bay. He decided that here at last was the long looked-for land in New Holland capable of gratifying the ambitions he entertained for his family. In February 1834 he offered to surrender his land order for 80 000 acres at Swan River if government gave him the right to purchase 25 000 acres for himself at 5s per acre at Portland Bay and 25 000 acres for each of his sons in the neighbourhood of that bay. He offered to preserve a good understanding with the savages, for he, too, was steeped in the benevolence of the age towards primitive people. Not waiting for a reply, in October 1834 his son Edward set out from Launceston in the *Thistle*, loaded with sheep, bullocks, cows, calves, heifers, dogs, seed and plants, for Portland Bay, landing there on 19 November to pioneer a new province for Britain's gentry. For two years his men watched the sheep, thatched a roof, coopered a barrel, cooked their food, enticed aboriginal women to share their beds and other things and turned the dogs onto aborigines who pilfered their supplies. Their only excitements were those days when 'Dutton got a whale' (William Dutton had been whaling in the bay since 1829) and the days on which a ship arrived from Launceston. Just when they were ready to take that step forward from the crude improvisations of the pioneer into the splendours of squatterdom, news trickled down to the bay that other overstraiters were starting a settlement at Port Phillip. By yet another cruel turn of fortune's wheel, Thomas Henty and his sons were condemned to a life on the frontier of a new society rather than given that central position, that 'first rank in society', which had driven them to make the long journey across the oceans of the world.[3]

To add almost a note of comic irony to the news of Port Phillip the prime mover for the settlement, John Batman, belonged by birth to that convict society in New South Wales whose vulgar rise to wealth and prominence had been one of the reasons deterring Thomas Henty from trying his luck in the mother colony of Australia. His father was a convict; his mother was a convict. He himself was one of those native-born members of the convict class who made no secret of their belief that all the land of Australia, including Van Diemen's Land, belonged to them and their descendants. He was born in Sydney on 21 January 1801 and moved to Hobart in 1821 where he lived with a convict woman, Eliza Thompson (also known as Callaghan), whom he married in 1828 in St John's Church, Launceston, after he took up land grants in Kingston near Launceston. Inside Batman was a man who abandoned himself wantonly to the Dionysian frenzy and allowed no restraint to come between him and the satisfaction of his desires. He had about him, too, the air of a Promethean figure, the air of a man prepared to steal fire from heaven and defy the gods to punish him for his excesses. When

---

[3] T. Henty to G. Arthur, 17 February 1834, C.O. 280/47; Arthur to Hay, 18 April 1834, C.O. 280/47; G. Arthur to R. Bourke, 23 or 29 June 1832; Letters of Colonel George Arthur, December 1825 to October 1836 (MS. in M.L.); *A Statement of the Claims of the Messrs. Henty, upon the Colonial Government* (London, 1841); Journal kept by Edward Henty at Portland Bay, 19 November 1834 to 30 August 1836 (MS. in LA TROBE L.); Marnie Bassett, *The Hentys* (London, 1954), pp. 294-300.

drunk he terrified those near him so much that one brave man said he would gladly give away all the fleeces of New Holland rather than expose himself again to the cruelties of a drunken Batman. His appetite for women was just as huge as his thirst for drunken oblivion. Yet this man, through whom such wild gales were to blow till the end of his stay on earth, displayed such tenderness and understanding towards the aborigines of Van Diemen's Land that he won the approval of the Lieutenant-Governor, George Arthur. Though on paper he was as much a broad-acres man as Thomas Archer at Woolmers, Joseph Archer at Panshanger, or James Cox at Clarendon, those three lived in their manors in lush countryside while Batman and his family lived in a stone-and-mud hut in scruffy country at Kingston, hemmed in by the surrounding hills, and, besides, had to endure the malice and insolence of the free-born towards convicts and their descendants. Port Phillip offered a kingdom where a man, he believed, had a chance to be freed from such ghosts of his past.[4]

In 1834 he had had many discussions at Kingston with John Helder Wedge, outwardly a persevering type of man of some dryness of soul, a meticulous sober fuss-pot of a man, who found inwardly that he was a 'secret sharer' in the frenzy and uproar in the heart of Batman. They were joined by Charles Swanston, James Simpson and J. T. Gellibrand. Swanston was a one-time captain in the British army in India who had come to Hobart Town in 1829 to recuperate from the rigours of such a life, and had stayed on to become a rich man, partly through his own import and export business and partly through wool broking. Nature had endowed him with the gifts to go into the jungle of the business world and come out rich. Simpson was a one-time commissioner of the land board who, much to the surprise of those who had seen him as a man much given to godliness and quiet living, suddenly became infected with this Port Phillip mania. Gellibrand, a lawyer by profession, was well known as a man with the gift and the appetite for buying and selling land at a huge profit. In 1835 the four of them joined with nine others to form the Geelong and Dutigalla Association (later known as the Port Phillip Association), by which they committed themselves to a plan of sending John Batman to Port Phillip to negotiate with the chiefs of the aborigines for the purchase of their land by the association.[5]

Batman and the other members of the association knew that the British Government still stood by that instruction to Captain Cook that no European

[4] J. Simpson to J. Wedge, 28 April 1835 (Port Phillip Association Papers, typescript in LA TROBE L.); J. Batman to P. A. Mulgrave, 15 March 1830 (MS. in M.L.); for the number of acres tilled by Batman and his stock see Port Phillip Association Papers; the tombs of William and Mary Batman, John's father and mother, may be seen in the cemetery of St John's Church, Parramatta; the crest of Thomas Archer was a bear's paw clutching an arrow, and the motto was 'Le fin couronne l'oeuvre'; personal visit to Batman hut at Kingston on 10 April and to Woolmers on 11 April 1973.

[5] G. Arthur to R. Bourke, 14 January 1836 (Letters of Colonel George Arthur, December 1835 to October 1836), J. H. Wedge to J. Bonwick, 24 May 1856 (Port Phillip Association Papers). For further references see C. P. Billot, *Melbourne: a bibliography* (Geelong, 1970), pp. 14-45; A. S. Kenyon, 'The Port Phillip Association', *Victorian Historical Magazine*, vol. 16, 1937.

nation had a right to occupy any part of a country or settle in it without the voluntary assent of the original inhabitants. Privately the members of the association were deeply divided in their attitude to the aborigines. Swanston and Gellibrand favoured 'sitting on the blacks to eat them out, or drive them out'. The more prudent members were bothered by what the 'professors of brotherly love for the black fellow' would say to that. Simpson and Wedge wanted to colonize Port Phillip not by knocking the aborigines on the head but by buying their property and endeavouring to teach them such industrious habits as would equip them to become active members of white civilization. As for Batman, there was a great difference between Batman drunk and Batman sober. Drunk, he loathed all men, especially wives and 'black bastards' and anyone to whom he was responsible. Sober, he entertained quite a different vision of the world. He wrote to Arthur about his hopes to civilize a large portion of the aborigines of New Holland. At the same time he told all the scoffers at brotherly love for blackfellows that he was only putting it this way because that was what 'Little George' (he meant Arthur) liked to hear. Little George was no fool. While Batman was preparing for his expedition to Port Phillip, he was telling Bourke that he had not been 'gulled' by all this talk of civilizing the natives.[6]

At the end of May, Batman, his party of seven aborigines, all prospective interpreters and reassurers for their sable brethren in New Holland, and three European servants set out from Launceston on the *Rebecca* and proceeded to Indented Head near the western entrance to Port Phillip Bay. There in a moment of ecstasy Batman fingered the 10-inch-high grass on which his beasts would fatten. He then continued to the head of the bay where he found a site where ships could ride in safety at the mouth of a river which the aborigines called Yarra Yarra, or flowing water. The following day he met the chiefs of the aborigines at a place where a creek, which they called Merri, joined the Yarra Yarra.

Through his interpreters Batman explained to the chiefs that he had come to settle amongst them on friendly terms, adding that although he was a white man he was 'a countryman of theirs' and would protect them. That day he gave the men blankets, tomahawks, knives, scissors, and looking-glasses and hung around the necks of each woman and child a necklace. They appeared highly gratified and excited. The next day he explained to the chiefs that the object of his visit was to purchase a tract of their country, since he intended to settle amongst them with his wife, his seven daughters, his sheep and his cattle. He proposed, he said, to employ the people of their tribe, clothe and feed them, and pay them an annual tribute in necessaries as a compensation for the enjoyment of the land. The chiefs seemed fully to comprehend his proposals, and much delighted with the prospect of having him live amongst them. On the following day, 6 June, after the deed of purchase was read out

[6] Earl Norton, Hints Offered to the Consideration of Captain Cook (MS. in NAT. L.); memorandum by J. Simpson, 16 September 1835, J. Simpson to J. Wedge, 19 June 1835 (Port Phillip Association Papers); J. Batman to G. Arthur, 25 June 1835 (Arthur Papers, vol. 33); Papers on Port Phillip, 1833-39 (MS. in M.L.).

and carefully explained to the chiefs, the three brothers Jaga Jaga, Jaga Jaga and Jaga Jaga, and the other chiefs, Cooloolock, Bungarie, Yanyan, Moowhip and Mommarmalar, of the Dutigallar tribe in the district of Iransnoo and Geelong granted to John Batman 100 000 acres in which he could place sheep and cattle in exchange for twenty pairs of scissors, fifty handkerchiefs, twelve red shirts, four flannel jackets, four suits of clothes, fifty pounds of flour, and a yearly rent or tribute of fifty pairs of blankets, fifty knives, fifty tomahawks, fifty pairs of scissors, fifty looking-glasses, twenty suits of clothing and two tons of flour. By a similar deed of purchase he took possession of 500 000 acres in the vicinity of the Yarra Yarra. In return for a few knives, tomahawks, scissors and looking-glasses, and enough grog to put them in a mood to say 'yes' to anything and laugh about it, a few aborigines had made John Batman and the other members of the association amongst the largest landed proprietors in the world. In the mood of a man feeling like a king he wrote down in his diary a few days later, 'this will be the place for the future village'. Then on 14 June he left for Launceston.[7]

Some days after his return to Launceston he wrote to Arthur an account of his expedition to form an extensive pastoral establishment on the southern coast of New Holland with an air of quiet confidence. 'I am', he wrote, 'a native of New South Wales' and went on to assure Arthur that his object had not been possession and expulsion or, what is worse, extermination, but the civilization of a benighted but intelligent people. He told him of his plans to graze twenty thousand stock. He assured Arthur that he need not fear yet another convict Sodom and Gomorrah, because the members of his association proposed to use only married men of good character as overseers or servants. That surely should 'gull Little George'. Flushed with this sense of glory as the son of a convict entering the kingdom of the mighty men of renown, he set out for Hobart Town where he discussed with Swanston, Gellibrand, Wedge and other members of the association how they would divide up their kingdom of over half a million acres and how they would let other would-be overstraiters in Van Diemen's Land know that the Port Phillip Association had already gobbled up the best land. They also agreed to write to the Secretary of State about the happy and philanthropic results they anticipated from Batman's two deeds of purchase, and asked the Crown to confer on them the rights to that land on such principles as His Lordship might deem the case required.[8]

Little George was not deceived by all these protestations of brotherly love

[7] J. Batman to G. Arthur, 25 June 1835 (Arthur Papers, vol. 33); Diary of John Batman, 10-31 May, 8, 9, 11 June 1835 (MS. in LA TROBE L.); text of the deeds of purchase (MS. in LA TROBE L.); cairn in honour of John Batman at Indented Head, 'John Batman, Founder of Melbourne, formed a base here, Indented Head, on 29th May, 1835', personal visit to site, 19 February 1972.

[8] J. Batman to G. Arthur, 25 June 1835; Members of the Geelong and Dutigalla Association to the Principal Secretary of State for the Colonies, 27 June 1835. Copy of Indenture made by John Batman, Charles Swanston and Others for Defining the Objects of the Parties who Propose to Establish a Settlement on the Territories of Geelong and Dutigalla, 29 June 1835 (Arthur Papers, vol. 33).

for black men, or assurances that the members of the association would take care only to issue liquor to their servants for medicinal purposes. He wrote to Richard Bourke, Governor of New South Wales, early in July that Batman's pretensions were quite absurd, adding that he himself was not taken in by all this talk about civilizing aborigines. Two months later the Governor of New South Wales proclaimed to all and sundry that whereas divers of His Majesty's subjects had taken possession of vacant land of the Crown under the pretence of a treaty, bargain or contract for the purchase thereof with the aboriginal natives, every such treaty or contract was void and of no effect against the rights of the Crown, and all persons found in possession of any such lands without the licence or authority of His Majesty's Government would be considered trespassers.[9]

In the meantime with an astonishing insensitivity to the way the wind was blowing in high places in Hobart Town and Sydney, John Helder Wedge applied for leave from the Survey Department so that he and Henry Batman (John Batman's brother) and his family could return to Port Phillip as an advance party for the men, sheep and cattle that were to follow. When leave was refused, Wedge resigned, thinking the life of a country squire was preferable to that of a pen-pusher and theodolite reader in Van Diemen's Land. When they landed from the *Rebecca* at Indented Head on 7 August, Wedge found to his surprise a wild white man, William Buckley. Over a month earlier this William Buckley came walking up to the native huts at Indented Head, a most surprising sight since he was clad the same as the natives and seemed highly pleased to speak to William Todd whom Batman had left at Indented Head to warn off trespassers. Todd offered Buckley a piece of bread which he ate very heartily. He stood almost 6 feet 7 inches in his socks, this native of Cheshire and one-time convict, with his dark brown beard, his bushy eyebrows, an erect military gait, and a mermaid, a sun, a half moon, seven stars and a monkey tattooed on the upper part of his right arm, and the letters W.B. on the lower part. He had taken to the bush to escape the savagery of the white man.

After he had escaped from the settlement at Sullivan's Cove in 1803 he had lived in a cave or what he later called his sea-beach home, and ate shell-fish, pig-face and berries, and offered fervent prayers of thankfulness to God for sustaining him until, in response to great yearnings for human society he foresook his Robinson Crusoe hut and joined the aborigines, who first gazed at him with wonder and then accepted him and gave him one of their women and a possum skin rug. As the months passed Buckley forgot his mother tongue as he acquired their language and lost all the habits of the white man except the white man's God whom he thanked fervently for preserving him. In the wilderness he often prayed earnestly and fervently to the great creator of the universe for health and strength and forgiveness. Many years later some aborigines showed him a coloured cotton handkerchief fastened to the end of a spear which they had been given by strangers on a ship at Indented

---

[9] G. Arthur to R. Bourke, 4 July 1835 (Arthur Papers, vol. 33); *New South Wales Government Gazette*, 2 September 1835.

Head. Buckley wondered whether to risk giving himself up as an absconder or to remain at his 'unmistakable liberty'. The decision was made for him by aborigines who pointed him out to the white men, to whom he found he could not speak, having forgotten his native tongue. He managed to get them to understand that he was not 'native born', after which he fervently thanked God for his deliverance. Gradually he began to understand that the white men proposed to stay in the country. Within a few days he had gone over to the service of the white men and accepted their suggestion that he should try to keep alive good understanding between the two races. Buckley saw his story as that of a man who ended on that day many long years of solitude and captivity and returned to freedom.

Wedge, who had hopes that one day the aborigines would adopt the way of life of the white man, welcomed Buckley as a man who might speed up the coming of that day. Arthur, to whom he put his idea, was very obliging, for not even eleven years in Van Diemen's Land had disabused him of that great illusion. He sent off a pardon for Buckley dated 25 August 1835. Wedge proved to be no better a judge of the character of Buckley than a reader of the mind of Colonel Arthur. Those wondrous eyes of his, which Thomas Bock stressed in his portrait of Wedge, were the windows of a heart that knew only loving kindness and nothing of treachery, deceit or evil. Harsher judges of men were to see quite quickly that Buckley preferred the aboriginal way of life because it gave him two women as wives, and slaves to attend him, and that he was more at home with them because, like them, he had the body of a man and the mind of a little child.[10]

After inspecting a site on the Barwon River in the Geelong district in company with Buckley, Wedge set out for the Yarra Yarra where he found to his dismay another party of white men camped. When he told their leader that they would have to go since they were intruders on the land the association had purchased from the chiefs of the aborigines, he was told to 'take the treaty with him when next he had occasion for the use of waste paper'. Now that was not how either Wedge or Colonel Arthur thought human beings should talk to each other. On the banks of the Yarra Yarra the dream of that meticulous fuss-pot John Wedge and of the Byronic John Batman, and those greedy bankers and merchants of Hobart Town began to vanish into the mists of time. For Wedge was not to know then that just five days before he was told rather rudely to use the precious parchment on which those two treaties were written as lavatory paper the Governor of New South Wales had branded all of them—the members of the association as well as this intruder he had met on the banks of the Yarra—as illegal trespassers.[11]

The man behind that second party of white men on the banks of the Yarra, John Pascoe Fawkner, was also a member of convict society in Van

---

[10] Based on J. P. Fawkner, Reminiscences of Early Settlement at Port Phillip (MS. in LA TROBE L.); G. H. Crawford, W. F. Ellis and G. H. Stancombe (eds), *The Diaries of John Helder Wedge 1824-35* (Hobart, 1962), pp. xvii-xviii; Diary of William Todd, 6 July 1835 (MS. in LA TROBE L.).

[11] J. P. Fawkner, op. cit.

Diemen's Land. He was born at Cripplegate in London on 20 October 1792. In 1801 his father was sentenced to transportation for fourteen years for receiving stolen goods. Perhaps that was where the habit of lying about the facts of his life started, for who knows why the truth is in some men and not in others and why the great liars are often consumed with an inner loathing for their fellow-men. Who knows why the mysterious powers in charge of the universe should condemn Byronic figures such as John Batman to an early death, and leave the Fawkners of this world to live on as gad-flies to the stern-faced men who were destined to print their mark on the settlement. Was this all fated to happen, or did blind chance distribute the prizes in such a manner that those who came after discerned a pattern, even an occasion for wisdom and understanding, in those frenzied years when the Batmans and the Fawkners believed they had found a place where the past no longer weighed on them, and had founded a society in which men of their unsteady, erratic qualities could enjoy the first rank?

In Fawkner's case the lying was spiced with a vituperative wit. On the exile of his family in 1803 to the convict settlement at Port Phillip he wrote later, 'it was known to that family that they must proceed to Port Phillip to assist in colonising the wilds of New Holland'. Nor was he ever able to tell the truth about being himself sent as a convict from Hobart to the coal mines at Newcastle, or about his marriage, never an easy subject to face honestly. In real life he cohabited with and then married a convict woman in 1822. What he told the world was a charming story of how he first tried to marry a pretty migrant woman but got so beaten up that he selected the ugliest woman from a migrant ship who became a guardian angel and a true friend when trouble or pain or anguish oppressed him. Shortly before his marriage to Eliza Cobb they both moved to Launceston where Fawkner prospered as proprietor of the Cornwall Hotel. In 1828 he edited the *Launceston Advertiser*, in which he powerfully advocated the cause of the emancipist class, while his clashes with officialdom made him one of the storm-centres of Launceston. In 1829 'they' refused to renew his licence for the Cornwall Hotel on the grounds that he was not a proper person to keep a hotel! Like Batman he thought of Port Phillip as a place where he and his family might prosper without being haunted and hunted by the ghosts of their past. His advance party under John Lancey arrived in that port on 16 August 1835. Fawkner himself took up residence on the banks of the Yarra in October.

It was not long before the tiny settlement learnt what manner of man he was. Over and above the energy that allowed him to run a hotel, edit a newspaper, farm his land and speculate in the business world, the man had a taste for the exchange of insults, the capacity to revile and persecute his rivals and to endure without flinching or whining any abuse he received in exchange. Within a few days of his arrival at Port Phillip he told that little world that John Batman was an illiterate drunkard who was claiming half a million acres of land in exchange for a few toys. He denounced him as a cheat and ridiculed him as 'King John the First of Port Phillip'. He accused John Batman of bribing the natives to split open Fawkner's own head with a

tomahawk so that 'King John' could once again become the lord of all he surveyed. He denounced John Batman's brother Henry as a hopeless swiller of
gin. Yet despite these private hells in his heart he managed to save £20 000
during his first four years at Port Phillip by following the trade in which he
had first prospered in Launceston—hotel-keeping.[12]

Soon after the arrival of Fawkner, the affairs of the members of the Port
Phillip Association began to decline. After John Batman's eighth child—a son
—was drowned, he seemed to lose all faith in himself as a man and to wander
around the settlement of Bearbrass on the Yarra Yarra like a man who knew
his days were numbered. Gellibrand lost heavily when many of his sheep
were suffocated in the hold of his ship or died of thirst. He himself was so
distressed by the heat on first landing at Western Port that he developed
violent palpitations and had to lie down to recover. Wedge only lost fifty out
of his flock of eight hundred sheep, but he had other sources of disquietude.
He had hopes of converting the aborigines of Port Phillip to industrious
habits. His idea was not to coerce the natives into labour but to give all
occupations the appearance of amusement. He wanted government to reward
with a gift of land anyone who managed to civilize a native. He even had a
dream early in 1836 of a day when the natives became the fishmongers of
Port Phillip when their skill as anglers had been supplemented with the
equipment provided by the white man. When the natives murdered a settler
and some of his servants, Wedge began to wonder whether it was going to be
Van Diemen's Land all over again with the extermination of the aborigines
as the inevitable consequence of the spread of European settlement. All
through 1836 the members of the association asked the government in Sydney
to give them priority in the purchase of land as a reward for laying open and
developing the resources of such a fertile country. But the Executive Council
insisted that all the land in Port Phillip be put up for sale by auction at a
minimum upset price of 5s an acre without granting priority of purchase to
any man or association.[13]

By then these seekers after the life of the free began to think more kindly of
the virtues of civil government. As soon as the stockmen stopped handing out
presents to the aborigines a 'day of collisions' began. The aborigines speared
their sheep; the packs of dogs that followed the natives also harassed their
sheep. Vandemonian convicts were practising riot and uproar in their tiny

[12] Based on Journal of J. P. Fawkner, extracted on 27 June 1932 from original text
in possession of W. Oliver (typescript in LATROBE L.); J. P. Fawkner, Reminiscences of
Early Settlement at Port Phillip; J. P. Fawkner to another, 1839 (typescript in Port
Phillip Association Papers, MS. in LA TROBE L.).

[13] H. Anderson, *Out of the Shadow: the career of John Pascoe Fawkner* (Melbourne,
1962); J. T. Gellibrand, Memorandum of a Trip to Port Phillip, 17 January to 15 February 1836 (Arthur Papers, vol. 33); G. H. Crawford, W. F. Ellis and G. H. Stancombe
(eds), op. cit., pp. xvii-xix; copy of extract from the minute of the Executive Council of
New South Wales, 21 October 1836, copy of letter of committee of Dutigalla Association
to the Col. Sec. of New South Wales, 29 October 1836, reply of committee of Dutigalla
Association, 1 November 1836, reply by Col. Sec. of New South Wales to committee of
Dutigalla Association, 10 November 1836 (Arthur Papers, vol. 33); J. H. Wedge to
C. Swanston, 23 July 1836 (Port Phillip Association Papers).

settlement of about 170 people. On 1 June 1836 the victims of such anarchy met on the banks of the Yarra for a good old grumble about the inconveniences they suffered from a want of established authority, followed by a humble petition to the Governor of New South Wales to appoint a resident magistrate. The Governor lost no time in establishing civil authority in the District for the protection of the aborigines and the due administration of the laws. In September 1836 Sir Richard Bourke, having deemed it expedient to appoint a civil and military force for the preservation of good order, named Captain William Lonsdale to be police magistrate for the District of Port Phillip. He was to have the assistance of a member of the Survey Department who would act as a commissioner of crown lands, of an officer of customs and of a surgeon cum catechist. He was instructed to take a census of all the inhabitants of the District; he was also told that it would be one of his most important duties to protect the aboriginal natives of the District from any manner of wrong and to conciliate them by kind treatment and presents, assuring them that the government was most anxious to maintain a friendly intercourse with them, and to improve by all practical means their moral and material condition; he was also to report at an early opportunity the number of aborigines with whom he was able to communicate and the general result of his exertions for their advantage. Finally he was told that it was the desire of government to expedite the regular location of settlers in those parts.

Lonsdale arrived at Port Phillip on 29 September. He was then thirty-six years of age. An army officer by profession, he was one of those amiable, conscientious, hard-working men who was not endowed by nature with any inclination to let his mind range. His was a clear-cut soldier's view of the world. He spent his days issuing licences to establish public houses, admonishing those who were keeping disorderly houses, and assembling the convicts each Sunday to hear God's word as expressed in the Book of Common Prayer on the simple principle that the fear of the Lord was a useful supplement to the fear of the lash in deterring evil-doers. His problem, as he saw it, was how to keep law and order in a thinly peopled sheep-run and how to prevent the District from becoming a haunt for the flotsam and jetsam of New South Wales and Van Diemen's Land. The point guarding the entrance to Port Phillip was eventually named after him. His wife Martha lived on in the name of the mountain named after her.[14]

On 3 March 1837 Governor Bourke disembarked at Port Phillip from the *Rattlesnake*. A few days later in the presence of some fifty or sixty settlers and at a respectful distance from two hundred aborigines who viewed the scene with a mixture of curiosity and fear, His Excellency stood in the full

---

[14] G. Arthur to R. Bourke, 14 January 1836 (Letters of Colonel George Arthur, MS. in M.L.); J. H. Wedge to C. Wedge, 17 April 1836, J. H. Wedge to C. Swanston, 23 July 1836, J. Simpson to J. H. Wedge, 19 August 1836 (Port Phillip Association Papers); Address of the Inhabitants of Port Phillip to His Excellency Major General Sir Richard Bourke—Governor of New South Wales, 1 June 1836 (Arthur Papers, vol. 33); Bourke to Glenelg, 15 September 1836, *H.R.A.*, I. xviii. 540-2; Col. Sec. of New South Wales to W. Lonsdale, 14 September 1836; Col. Sec. In Letters to and from Port Phillip, 1836 (N.S.W.S.A., 4/2334-5).

uniform of a Lieutenant-General and had the satisfaction of 'affixing' yet another Whig name in the bush of Australia by naming the town Melbourne. Using William Buckley as his interpreter he exhorted the aborigines to good conduct and attention to the missionary, George Langhorne. He then gave four brass plates as honorary distinctions for good conduct to aborigines recommended by Captain Lonsdale. To celebrate the occasion the day closed in Bourke's tent with a dinner of kangaroo pie, 'kangaroo steamer', kangaroo steak and wild duck. The Vandemonian John Batman was there, but now only a shadow of the man who had dreamed of carving out a kingdom in that English parkland, for the man was already plagued by the fruits of his 'pleasant vices'. John Pascoe Fawkner was also there, outwardly polite but inwardly mocking at Bourke as a 'low mean Minded Man' with a 'shop-keeper spirit'.[15]

After the departure of Bourke at the end of March the surveyor Robert Hoddle and his assistant Robert Russell were left behind to draw up a site plan for the town. Some malicious individuals said Hoddle had a long history of passing off the work of his subordinates as his own. They sneered at him as a man with such a poor brain that he could scarcely spell, and such a mean soul that he was happy only when he was in chains. His supporters eulogized him as a man with such a sense of design and order that he used attendance at religious services as an occasion for expressing his gratitude to the 'Mighty Planner'. A man with geometry in his soul began to design a city like a rectangular grid with the streets so straight that there was nothing to stop the north wind converting the town into a fiery furnace in the summer, or the south wind making it shivery and sodden in winter. While Hoddle and his assistant Russell fiddled over the drawing-board with their design for a neat town, far enough away from the coast so the inhabitants could not hear the roar of that huge sea, the Wesleyan preacher J. Orton was telling the settlers each Sunday that 'consistent deportment' would help them to inherit eternal life, and appealing to them on behalf of those 'poor depraved creatures', the aborigines. The voice of bourgeois philistinism began to be heard on a site where previously the only human sounds had come from the aborigines, or the drunken cries of Batman and his party in their moments of wild delight.[16]

The coming of law and order to Port Phillip had been attracting for some

[15] Journal of Richard Bourke, 1-29 March 1837 (MS. in LA TROBE L.); W. Lonsdale to Col. Sec. of New South Wales, 30 September, 20 October, 1, 23, 24, 26 November 1836, 17 January, 3, 10 February, 11, 13 March, 3, 31 May 1837 (Chief Secretary, Letters Outwards, 20 September 1836 to 30 April 1840, V.S.A.); Last Will and Testament of John Batman, 18 December 1837 (copy in Port Phillip Association Papers, MS. in M.L.); Bourke to Glenelg, 14 June 1837, *H.R.A.*, I. xviii. 780-3; J. P. Fawkner to anon., n.d. (probably 1839), (Port Phillip Association Papers); R. Bourke to his son, 14 April 1837 (Bourke Papers, vol. 6, MS. in M.L.); statement of George Langhorne (MS. in M.L.); Hazel King, *Richard Bourke* (Melbourne, 1971), pp. 188-9.

[16] R. Hoddle, Map of Melbourne, 25 March 1837 (MS. in LA TROBE L.); I. Selby, 'The planning of Melbourne', *Victorian Historical Magazine*, vol. 13, 1928; H. S. McComb, 'Surveyor Hoddle's Field Books of Melbourne', *Victorian Historical Magazine*, vol. 16, 1937, vol. 17, 1938; memorandum by J. Orton, quoted in J. C. Symons, *Life of the Rev. Daniel James Draper* (London, 1870), p. 136.

time settlers of quite a different stamp from the Batmans, the Gellibrands and the Fawkners. There was George Russell who was born at Fife in June 1812 into a family which believed that the righteous would not be forsaken, nor would they be seen begging bread. From his mother he had learned that the Lord would punish liars, idlers and wasters according to their deserts. From his own observation he had seen that the family holding was not able to sustain him in that way of life to which he believed God had called him. So in 1830 he migrated to Van Diemen's Land, where he prospered so well that by 1835 he was looking for land for his ever-increasing flocks. Impressed by reports he had heard of 'the extensive tracts of fair country' on the shores of Port Phillip he decided in March 1836 to spy out the land. On his return to Van Diemen's Land he heard that his neighbour at Bothwell, Captain Patrick Wood, had formed the Clyde Company with six others, all of whom had invested £1200. They offered him the position of manager with an eighth share in the profits at the end of five years.

In October 1836 Russell sailed again for Port Phillip to select a site for the company. He chose an area in the valley of the Leigh River near the Barrabool Hills. In the beginning he and his five companions packed down at night under a small bell-shaped tent some ten feet in diameter. They were building a sod hut, that first source of separation of a master from his men in the bush of Australia, and putting up hurdles for the sheep when the news reached them early in 1837 that J. T. Gellibrand and a Mr Hesse had not been seen since they travelled up the Barwon looking for sites for sheep-runs, though the natives of Cape Otway were putting round a story of how two white men had wandered into a native camp in a very weak state, and one had died and the other had been killed by the blackfellows. So the first of the adventurers from Van Diemen's Land disappeared into the silence while the man with the fear of becoming a ploughboy was building a sod hut, believing his God would one day reward him with the mansion of a gentleman for frowning on liars, idlers, fornicators, drunkards and wasters.[17]

In the meantime on the mainland of New Holland the news was spreading that the Surveyor-General of New South Wales, T. L. Mitchell, had walked over flowery plains and green hills to the south of the Murray River. By one of those odd ironies in the history of the country he was a man who loathed Australia, the white men, the Whig governor, the bishop, the clergy, the judges, the usurers, the Jews, the aborigines and above all the appearance of the country, and had returned to Sydney in November of 1836 with news that he had at long last seen in New Holland a patch of country worthy of being 'English for thousands of years'. He was then forty-four years old. A veteran of the Peninsular Campaign, he had migrated to New South Wales in 1827 to take up the position of Deputy Surveyor under John Oxley at a time when promotion in the army was far too slow for a man of his restless temperament

[17] Journal of Richard Bourke, 7 March 1837; P. L. Brown (ed.), *The Narrative of George Russell of Golf Hill* (London, 1935), pp. 27-39, 49-50, 75-9, 116-25, 136-7.

and ambition. Irascible with all men and much given to denouncing his fellow-men for their folly and their stupidity, he was partial to a conversation with the ladies, for the beauty of women was one of the few pleasures he ever knew in New South Wales. It was his fate or his cross to belong to that long list of gifted and courageous Englishmen for whom Australia was a land that was cursed and its inhabitants as barren and empty as the land that surrounded them. In 1835 he attempted to trace the Darling from the point reached by Sturt in 1828 down to its junction with the Murray but gave up at Menindee and returned to Sydney raging at the 'dry and naked wilderness' and those wild men the aborigines, and raging that he, an officer and a gentleman, had been obliged to employ convicts in his exploring party.[18]

In March 1836 he was off again with a party of twenty-five to explore the Darling, Murrumbidgee and Murray river country. Again he raged against a 'vile scrub' country where a series of water-holes purported to be a river. To his companions he behaved with such inhumanity that one of them noted in his diary that anyone who wanted a foretaste of Hell should travel with the Major over the wilds of Australia, but since this accuser was often to be found drunk under a dray it is possible that he was not a reliable witness on the cause of his anger with Mitchell. By the time the party reached the present site of Cohuna on the Murray in June, he was so angry with both men and country that he was reminded of that savage passage in the Book of Isaiah about a land where fear and the snare and the bit disquieted a man. He was about to enter a country of surpassing loveliness. Travelling south-west from Cohuna he climbed to the top of a hill, which he named Pyramid Hill, from where he could see pleasing grasslands instead of that dried-up, salt-bush country out on the Darling. There was better to come. On 11 August he reached the junction of two rivers, the Wannon and the Glenelg. There, near the present town of Casterton, he was so refreshed, in the midst of such rich pasture, by what he foresaw as 'one of the finest regions upon earth' that he decided to trace the Glenelg to its mouth, hoping to find 'an outlet to the sea of proportionate magnitude', only to find, as his rival Sturt had found to his mortification at the mouth of the Murray, that the outlet was choked by the sand thrown up by the sea. So he returned to the junction of the Wannon and Glenelg to rejoin the party he had left there, and set out for Portland Bay, where on 29 August he found to his surprise that there were Englishmen living there. The Henty brothers told him they were importing sheep and cattle as fast as vessels could be found to bring them over from Launceston. He told them of the beauty of the country at the junction of the Wannon and the Glenelg.

---

[18] T. L. Mitchell, *Three Expeditions into the Interior of Eastern Australia* (2 vols, London, 1839), vol. 2, p. 333; based on H.H.P., A Few Slight Remarks on Major Mitchell's Face and his Family (MS. in M.L.); T. L. Mitchell to his mother, 28 May, September 1834 (Mitchell Papers, vol. 7); T. L. Mitchell, *Journal of an Expedition into the Interior of Tropical Australia* (London, 1848), pp. 429-30; T. L. Mitchell, *Three Expeditions*, vol. 1, p. 275, vol. 2, p. 51.

Leaving Portland early in September Mitchell travelled north-east towards the Murray. By 21 September east of Mount Abrupt (east of the present city of Hamilton) he travelled over a country quite open, slightly undulating and well covered with grass. Here at long last in New Holland he had found a land favourable for colonization. Flocks might be turned out upon its hills, or the plough at once set to work in the plains. The land, as he saw it, was open and available in its present state for all the purposes of civilized man. Having traversed in two directions the flowing plains and green hills fanned by the breezes of early spring he decided to name the region 'Australia Felix', the better to distinguish it from the parched deserts of the interior. He hoped and believed his fellow-countrymen would establish there 'a lasting monument of British power and colonization, thus to engraft a new and flourishing state, on a region now so desolate and unproductive . . . by such means as England alone can supply'.

From that moment of exaltation he and his party went on their way rejoicing past the present site of Newstead and Lake Linlithgow till they crossed a river he named the Campaspe after a woman known by Alexander the Great. He then climbed a mountain from which he looked at Port Phillip through a telescope and saw 'a mass of white objects which might have been either tents or vessels'. He named that mountain Mt Macedon after Philip of Macedon. So the man who wanted Australia Felix to be English for thousands of years took off the map the name Hamilton Hume had given to the mountain. He had named it Mt Wentworth in honour of Australia's 'great native son'. On 8 October he crossed the Goulburn at a place which came to be known as Mitchellstown, and made for the Hume and Hovell track at Violet Town which he followed through Benalla and Wangaratta, still in such a generous mood towards man and nature that he did not even take a side swipe at Hume and Hovell as explorers as he made for the Murray at Howlong. He reached the Murrumbidgee at Oura on 24 October, then continued to Jugiong, Yass, Goulburn and on to Sydney which he reached on 3 November. There he lost no time in telling all and sundry of the great dream he had conceived of as his heavy carts sank in the rich soil of Australia Felix—that British power and genius should plant there a little England clean different from the sink of degradation in the interior of New South Wales and that this 'champagne country' should be 'English for thousands of years'.[19]

[19] G. C. Stapylton, Journal of T. L. Mitchell's Expedition, 1836-7, 17 October 1836 and passim (MS. in M.L.); T. L. Mitchell, *Three Expeditions*, vol. 2, esp. pp. 155, 217-27, 239-45, 271, 276, 328-33; Edward Henty, Daily Journal at Portland Bay, 29, 30 August 1836 (MS. in LA TROBE L.); *New South Wales Government Gazette*, 5 November 1836; draft of a poem by T. L. Mitchell (Mitchell Papers, vol. 7); Lonsdale to Col. Sec. of New South Wales, 5 October 1838; Col. Sec. In Letters from Port Phillip, 1838 (N.S.W.S.A.); J. H. L. Cumpston, *Thomas Mitchell* (London, 1954), ch. 9. There are cairns for Mitchell at Pyramid Hill, Casterton, Portland Bay, Hamilton, Dunkeld, Newstead and Nagambie. Some of these were erected to mark the hundredth anniversary of the journey. About two miles from the cairn for Mitchell at Pyramid Hill a stone cairn was put up by the Pyramid Hill Historical Society in 1968 to the 'Exploration Party of Burke and Wills [who] passed this way on 1st September 1860 during the first overland crossing of Austra-

The idea caught on. The *Sydney Herald* of 10 November 1836 published Mitchell's report of 24 October from his camp on the Murrumbidgee that he had explored, under the protection of Providence, the vast resources of a region more extensive than Great Britain, equally rich in point of soil, specially prepared by the Creator for the industrious hands of Englishmen. The *Sydney Gazette* of 10 November predicted that colonization would be drawn to the southward. In 1837 Mitchell was fulfilling his earnest wish of being himself the bearer of his journals and maps to Lord Glenelg and receiving a knighthood and an honorary doctorate from the University of Oxford. In the same year Edward Henty and his party threw up their hats with a cheer when they saw the country over which Mitchell had enthused with them in August of 1836 and put their horses to the gallop for the site of a station in those rich plains at Muntham. There Edward Henty took out a licence for a run of some 77 000 acres on which within three years he was running 55 000 sheep, 8000 cattle and 500 horses and employing fifty workers, twenty shepherds, twelve hut-keepers and a blacksmith. In 1838 the tall, charming, handsome Protestant gentleman from Ireland, Samuel Pratt Winter, took out a licence for Murndal in the same district. Within a few years he was dreaming in his sod hut on the Loddon of that day in the future when he would be surrounded by liveried servants and lead the life of a grand seigneur in a country that previously had only seen the corroborees of the aborigine. In 1839 Charles Wedge and his brothers took out a licence to pasture stock at Grange Burn, the future site of Hamilton, not far from that place where Mitchell had conceived the idea of the region being open and available for all the purposes of civilized man.[20]

Within a few months of the reports of a region of 'flowery plains and green hills' appearing in the Sydney press, overlanders from the settler districts of New South Wales descended on Port Phillip. To assist them Bourke established military posts on the Murray, the Ovens River, Violet Town and Mitchellstown. Some overlanded stock for sale in the settlements of Melbourne, Geelong and Portland. Some of these then changed from their overlanders' togs of wide-brimmed hats, scarlet flannel shirts, broad belts and shaggy beards into the best clothes their money could buy, and went out 'on the spree'. Then they took to the road again, since their taste was not for a life 'fenced in with walls or gates' but rather to wander the bush of Australia 'free as an overlander'. Some, whose bodies were covered with torn and dishevelled shirts and greasy moleskins but whose hearts sheltered a picture

lia by white men from south to north.' Personal visit to Mitchell sites 17-19 February 1972. For the inquiry into Mitchell's conduct towards the aborigines on the banks of the Murray see Bourke to Glenelg, 25 January 1847, C.O. 201/379 This despatch is reproduced in *H.R.A.*, I. xviii. 656, without the enclosures. See also Bourke to Glenelg, 19 February 1837, *H.R.A.*, I. xviii. 691-2.

[20] *Sydney Herald*, 7, 10 November 1836; *Sydney Gazette*, 5, 8, 10 November 1836; cairn to Muntham on road between Coleraine and Casterton; Diary of Edward Henty, passim; Margaret Kiddle, *Men of Yesterday* (Melbourne, 1961), pp. 36, 78.

of themselves as gentlemen, were ashamed to arrive in Melbourne, Portland or Geelong looking like ragamuffins.[21]

Some moved their stock into Australia Felix as the first step in the creation of a plantation. The news of a country of 'flowery plains and green hills' planted this idea in the head of A. F. Mollison down at Uriarra on the Limestone Plains of the Canberra district. Ever since his arrival in New South Wales in 1833 he had found that suitable runs for sheep were not easy to obtain. He always saw himself as separate from and superior to the mass of mankind. In his world, as he put it, 'both the bipeds and the quadrupeds' were 'continually going wrong', and it was his 'duty and never ending care to put them all right again'. So on one of those magical days in the autumn of 1837 he and his party of thirty men, 5000 sheep, 634 head of cattle, twenty-eight working bullocks, twenty-two horses, and drays packed with stores, left his hut on the Murrumbidgee and set off down stream for Jugiong, Gundagai, Mullengandra, the Murray and Melbourne, following the route which the currency lad Hamilton Hume had followed in 1824. His men got drunk, the aborigines were frightened by the firing of guns, the sheep got sick, the rivers they had to cross were often in flood, the bullocks strayed and the men grew more lazy, careless and insolent as they moved out of the reach of magistrates and floggers. When they reached the outskirts of Melbourne in August 1837, the men remained drunk for a week and were still so befuddled by rum when Mollison finally got them out of the hotels and brothels of Melbourne that he wondered whether the solution to his problem was to teach the aborigines habits of industry, treat them kindly and protect them from the insults of their convict and emancipated servants.[22]

After selecting a run in richly grassed country suitable for conversion to an English parkland on the Coliban River near the present site of Malmsbury he and his men within a year imprinted the 'appearance of labour and industry' where previously there had been nothing. They built sod huts for the men, a shearing shed forty feet long and thirty-five broad, a store forty feet long and a house of four rooms for himself. They made five hundred hurdles for the sheep, washed and shore the sheep, ploughed and sowed twelve acres of land, fenced in some twenty-one acres with posts and rails and erected a large yard for the herd of cattle. Within the year a self-contained manor or village had been planted in the bush of Australia. The problem of how to get

---

[21] R. V. Billis and A. S. Kenyon, *Pastures New: an account of the pastoral occupation of Port Phillip* (Melbourne, 1930), pp. 46-9; T. F. Bride (ed.), *Letters from Victorian Pioneers* (Melbourne, 1898), pp. 53, 258-9; [G. Hamilton], *A Journey from Port Phillip to South Australia in 1839* (Adelaide, 1879); D. Stewart and N. Keesing (eds), *Old Bush Songs* (Sydney, 1957), pp. 132-3; L. J. Blake, 'Talking of overlanders', *Victorian Historical Magazine*, vol. 40, 1969; for other examples of overlanders who settled in the Port Phillip District see T. F. Bride (ed.), op. cit., pp. 50-4, 135-7, 168-80; A. S. Kenyon, 'The overlanders', *Victorian Historical Magazine*, vol. 10, 1924-5.

[22] A. F. Mollison to Jane Mollison, 11 October 1833, 22 October 1834, 25 April 1837 (Mollison Letters, MS. in LA TROBE L.); A. F. Mollison, Diary of a Journey made between 7 April and 6 December 1837 from Uriara [sic] on the Murrumbidgee to Port Phillip (MS. in LA TROBE L.).

a proper day's work out of his men remained; so did the problem of keeping his men off the rum. Convinced of the general worthlessness of the emancipated convicts he decided to try some immigrant Highlanders, but by the middle of 1839 he was longing for some 'old hands' to rescue him from the ineptitude of 'new chums', who also quickly acquired the 'disease' of free workers in the Australian colonies and bolted as soon as they fancied a job did not 'suit them so well'. He was bothered, too, by the dirty, disorderly and vulgar people who frequented the inns of Melbourne when he visited that town every six weeks or so. So were other overlanders and overstraiters who were anxious to separate themselves from the vulgar herd. In November of 1838 a group of them joined together to form the Melbourne Club, where the dinners were, at least in Mollison's eyes, 'more stylish than necessary' but, and this he did enjoy, at least 'great sobriety and decorum' were maintained. In this way these honourable Christian gentlemen who had once slept under mia-mias in the bush of Australia began to mark themselves off from those workers whose labour had created the wealth to enable them to put on such airs.[23]

By that time the Major Mitchell vision had reached the British Isles. He conceived of this territory as 'flowery plains and green hills' being inhabited by a powerful people speaking the English language, diffusing around them English civilization and arts and exercising a predominant influence over eastern Asia and the numerous and extensive islands in that quarter of the globe. The words of the irascible Major were being passed around: 'It has been in my power, under the protection of Divine Providence, to explore the vast natural resources of a region more extensive than Great Britain, especially rich in point of soil, and which now lies ready for the plough in many parts, as if specially prepared by the Creator for the industrious hands of Englishmen'. These words were published first in Scotland where they were seen by one Niel Black, a Scottish farmer's son who sailed from Greenock in April 1839 with £6000 in his pocket, and in his heart the conviction that all the ungodly would perish in the presence of God. He was shocked by the vulgar paganism in Sydney where the men worshipped at the altar of the golden calf, and bulky gaudy women waddled around under a load of fat and finery. So off he went by sea to Melbourne where he found to his delight a people altogether Scottish in their habits and manners, a people who prized not only material wealth but also respectability and were free from the habit of social cringing, for Black was steeped in Robert Burns as well as in Genesis, Leviticus, Numbers and the Psalms of David.[24]

From Melbourne he set out on horseback to look for a run on the plains of

[23] A. F. Mollison to Jane Mollison, 19 June 1838, 24 December 1839, 20 April 1841 (Mollison Letters); T. F. Bride (ed.), *Letters from Victorian Pioneers*, pp. 182-3; personal visit to site of Mollison run, 5 April 1973.

[24] [D. L. Waugh], *Three Years' Practical Experience of a Settler in New South Wales* (Edinburgh, 1838); Diary of Niel Black, 26, 28 October, 27 November, 1 December 1839 (MS. in LA TROBE L.); M. Kiddle, *Men of Yesterday*, pp. 43-4.

Australia Felix. Carried away by the beauty and the abundance of grass he sang a song of praise to his God for making such wondrous things as the earth, the grasses and the trees of New Holland. At Glenormiston, some twenty miles from Derrinallum, he found a man prepared to sell his run and his stock. Here with the horizon shimmering in the heat of the summer sun he thanked Almighty God for the great benefit he had just received at His hands. But between him and his men a great gulf was fixed. They laughed at him when he called on them to spend the Lord's day in the Lord's way. While he was praying at night to his God they drank liquor with such frenzy that they ended not even being able to remember that they were men. They slept with a lubra and if she offended one of them in any way she was shot dead. They told him a bullet was the only thing a blackfellow understood. On his visits to Melbourne or Geelong they tippled so wantonly that he wasted hours heaving their drunken sodden bodies onto the drays. At times he wondered whether God had been so bounteous in his gifts of grass and sun that he had forgotten to be gracious to man. Yet within a year, despite all the drinking, the beastly sexual play, and the butchery of the blackfellows, he began to prosper. He was not bothered by the source of his wealth or by any thought that the lotus flower of his own outward and visible self derived from 'moral filth'. Such a question never crossed his mind.[25]

By the end of 1839 the tide of overstraiters, overlanders, and overseas men was in full flood. In September 1836 there had been 2024 men in the whole district. By September 1838 there were approximately 3500, of whom 3000 were males and some 430 females. By then the aborigines were beginning to flee before the invader, since they lacked the material strength and the ability to combine with which to exploit the initial advantages of numbers and know-ledge of the country. There were probably just over eleven thousand aborigines in the district south of the Murray and east of the South Australian border when Batman signed his treaty. Nothing they could do could impede the spread of the white man over the plains of Australia Felix. Nor could anything prevent what was fated to be. John Batman was writhing in agony in his wheelchair as the Russells, the Blacks, the Mollisons, the Learmonths, the Armitages, the Austins, the Hentys, the Faithfuls and others made their take-over bid to plant a society that would be 'English for thousands of years', whatever other intimations men might get from that sea rolling forever through Bass Strait, or that spirit of the place which seemed to suggest a vast indifference to all human endeavour.[26]

[25] Diary of Niel Black, 1, 3, 4, 7, 9, 10, 26 December 1839, 1, 8, 9, 10, 26 January, 2, 23 February, 23 March, and all entries for April 1840.

[26] Abstract of the Number of Inhabitants of New South Wales, According to a Census taken the 2nd September 1836, *V. & P.* (L.C. N.S.W.), 1837; W. H. Archer, *Statistical Notes on the Progress of Victoria* (2nd ed., Melbourne, 1860), p. 4; F. Lancaster Jones, *The Structure and Growth of Australia's Aboriginal Population* (Canberra, 1970), p. 4.

6

ENGLAND'S ECHO IN THE ANTIPODES

DURING 1838, press, pulpit and schoolroom took up the task of teaching both the European and aboriginal inhabitants of Port Phillip how to be 'English for thousands of years'. In the first handwritten and hand-sewn issue of the *Melbourne Advertiser* on 1 January 1838 Fawkner urged 'adventurous Port Phillipians' to make their mark on the 'Chart of advancing Civilization' as 'Sons of Britain'. On Easter Sunday the Lord Bishop of Australia, William Grant Broughton, told the members of the congregation, who gathered to hear him in a small wooden building as the rain outside came down in torrents, that the Church of England was not only charged with the task of leading all men to salvation but was a stronghold for all God's people against the assaults of the Romish superstition and the abyss of unbelief. The times, he warned them, were ominous. In the storms that were to come, the Church of England, as the spiritual leader of English civilization, was the one guard against the waves on which the ark of their civilization was being tossed about.[1]

On 27 October the first issue of the *Port Phillip Gazette* appeared in Melbourne. Edited in part by a man probably only eighteen years old who was of the very stuff of Old England and claimed kinship with Shakespeare's mother, one George Arden, the paper took pride in the planting of British civilization on the southern coasts of New Holland. As Arden saw it, men of old colonial experience from Van Diemen's Land, and persons of decision, activity and energy of character had descended on the land around Melbourne which no other human beings had been able to improve. After two years the noise of the hammer and the saw could be heard where previously the woods had only echoed to the shrill cooee of the savage, or the long wild howl of native dogs. He wanted the civilization of Port Phillip to be quite different from that 'broken, cold and unnatural form of society' which had sprung up on the sheep-walks of New South Wales. With their beautiful country, their rich soil, their admirable port, and the enterprising character of their population, they should start agriculture and build a society of farmers to encourage 'the better and more kindly feelings of their natures'. A man with a picture in his mind of a land where 'daisies pied and violets blue and lady smocks all

[1] *Melbourne Advertiser*, 1 January 1838; W. G. Broughton to A. M. Campbell, 22 May 1838 (Australia, Letters Received, vol. 1, Society for the Propagation of the Gospel Archives, London); G. W. F. Hegel, *The Philosophy of History* (New York, 1956), p. 87.

silver white and cuckoo-buds of yellow hue painted the meadows with delight' wanted to make English for thousands of years a country whose wild, uncouth, harsh coastline, limitless plains, and rugged mountains spoke of man's impotence and insignificance.[2]

There was at least one huge gap between their aspirations and the implacable factors of their situation. They were aiming high: they wanted to convert the aborigines of New Holland into English gentlemen. They had some idea of the magnitude of their task, for all the attempts of their predecessors in other parts of New Holland to spread civilization among the aborigines and lead them to the beautiful and voluntary reception of the Christian religion had ended in failure. In 1837 a committee of the House of Commons on aborigines in British settlements overseas had come to the melancholy conclusion that intercourse with Europeans had cast over the aborigines of New Holland a deeper shade of wretchedness than the debasement in which they had lived before the arrival of the white man. The effects had been dreadful beyond example both in the diminution of their numbers and in their demoralization, for the aborigines appeared to be vanishing from the face of the earth. What was most appalling was that after contact for nearly half a century with a Christian people these hapless human beings still continued in their original benighted and degraded state. As the contagion of European intercourse extended itself among them they gradually lost the better properties of their own character and appeared to acquire in exchange the most objectionable and degrading qualities of the European. The committee recommended the appointment of a protector to the aborigines. They suggested that he learn the native languages, win the confidence of the aborigines with gifts, excluding liquor, and teach them an industry, reserve such land for them as might be necessary for their support, where they could hunt without molestation, appoint missionaries to educate the young, and give every assistance in their power to any scheme that promised improvement to their material or spiritual welfare.[3]

In January 1838 Glenelg informed the Governor of New South Wales that Her Majesty's Government had directed their anxious attention to the adoption of some plan for the better protection and civilization of the native tribes within the limits of his government. They had decided to appoint a chief protector of aborigines who was to fix his principal station at Port Phillip. He was to be aided by four assistant protectors who were to divide Port Phillip into four districts. Each assistant protector should attach himself closely and constantly to the aboriginal tribes in his district and accompany them in their movements from one district to another until they could be induced to assume more settled habits of life. He was to endeavour to conciliate their respect and confidence and to make them feel he was their friend.

[2] *Port Phillip Gazette*, 27 October 1838; W. Shakespeare, *Love's Labour's Lost*, V, ii, lines 890-3.

[3] Report from Select Committee on Aborigines (British Settlements), *P.P.*, 1837, vii, 425, pp. 1-6, 10-14, 82-4.

He must watch over the rights and interests of the natives, protect them from any encroachment on their property and from acts of cruelty, oppression or injustice, and faithfully represent their wants, wishes or grievances through the chief protector to the government of the colony. For that purpose each assistant protector was to be commissioned as a magistrate. If the natives could be induced to locate themselves in a particular place, each assistant protector should teach and encourage them to engage in the cultivation of the grounds, to build suitable habitations for themselves, and in whatever else that might conduce to their civilization and social improvement. The education of the children was to be regarded as a matter of primary importance. Each assistant protector was to promote the moral and religious improvement of the natives by instructing them in the elements of the Christian religion. He was to learn the language of the natives so as to be able freely and familiarly to converse with them. He was to take charge of and be accountable for any provisions or clothing placed under his care for distribution to the natives. He was to obtain as accurate information as possible of the number of natives within his district, and of all important particulars with regard to them.[4]

Glenelg also informed the Governor of New South Wales that the chief protector was to be G. A. Robinson, who was then in charge of the aboriginal establishment on Flinders Island. He was fifty years of age. He saw himself as an instrument in the hands of God to instruct the aborigines in the arts of civilization and to help them adore that Supreme Being who made all things in heaven and earth. 'O God,' he wrote in his journal on 4 November 1832, 'what is man when left to himself? Do thou preserve and protect me and never, no, never leave me. Without thee I can do nothing.' A year after he arrived at Wybalenna at the end of 1835, his catechist summed up his hopes by putting into the mouth of one of the aborigines these words in the *Aboriginal or Flinders Island Chronicle*:

> the Divine blessing to the heart and head that has been instrumental in uniting us together and providing us with Instruction and guiding us into the habits of civilised life, and the enjoyment of security from the oppression of bad men we date our history of Events from the month of October 1835 when our beloved father made his appearance among us dispelling the darkness and cheering us with a dawn of hope freedom and happiness we had been in a deplorable state . . . [a] market was established . . . to buy our provisions . . . after market we were regaled with a dinner of mutton and pudding we are learning the use of money.

Yet after three years at Wybalenna rooting out the aboriginal culture and trying to replace it with a theocentric subsistence agriculture in which the natives were taught to read and write so that they could read the Bible, to sell their products in the markets of Launceston and Hobart to get money with which to buy food, clothing and tobacco, to give up the habit of painting

[4] Glenelg to Gipps, 31 January 1838, *H.R.A.*, I. xix. 252-5.

their bodies, to give up their native names and replace them with such cultu-rally prestigious names as Constantine, Hannibal and Juliet, he wrote in his diary the melancholy truth that he must leave this place of sickness before all the black men were dead.

The aborigines began to decline in numbers. Mannalargenna, the last chief of the Portland tribe, died there on 4 December 1835. Despite all Robinson and his catechist and the convict workers had done to make the aborigines comfortable by providing stone houses, a chapel, agricultural implements and clothing, the aborigines spent much of their time sitting on top of the hill overlooking the settlement from where they gazed with tears in their eyes not at the house of God, but at their homeland of Tasmania which the white man had forced them to leave. The face of Truganini took on that look of a woman determined to endure the blows of fate without showing what was going on in her heart. That great sadness which the painter Benjamin Duterrau caught so well began to appear on Robinson's face just as it had on the face of Salvado at New Norcia as he wondered why God had created a people who did not want to hear His word or adopt the way of life of those to whom God had revealed His precious gift of salvation. Despite this awareness of likely failure, Robinson went on hoping it was possible to advance aborigines towards civilization by treating them as rational beings, because he had found in Van Diemen's Land and on Flinders Island that then their ferocious character and their hostility towards white men began to disappear. He was caught up in all the contradictions of history. He wanted to treat the aborigines as equal before the law with the white man, but shrank from the inhumanity of enforcing the law on indecent exposure or the vagrancy law against them. He knew the ultimate sanction for the law affecting the white man was force, but clung to the hope that with the aborigines he and his fellow assistant protectors would find 'moral suasion' effective. When the call came to take up his new position in Port Phillip he tried to persuade the Governor of New South Wales to allow him to take the remaining Tasmanian aborigines with him. After sounding out opinion in Sydney, Sir George permitted him to take a handful of the Vandemonians. By then Robinson was a man inspired by a great vision, but had no clear idea of how to carry it into effect.[5]

[5] Ibid., 253; for the career of G. A. Robinson in Van Diemen's Land see vol. 2, pp. 137, 143-7, 256-7, 305-6, of this history; N. J. B. Plomley (ed.), *Friendly Mission* (Hobart, 1966), pp. 275, 677, 932-4; portrait of G. A. Robinson by Benjamin Duterrau (Tasmanian Museum, Hobart); B. Bridges, 'George Augustus Robinson: chief protector of aborigines, Port Phillip, 1838-1849', *Papers and Proceedings of Tasmanian Historical Research Association*, vol. 18, 1971; N. J. B. Plomley, 'George Augustus Robinson and the Tas-manian aborigines', *Papers and Proceedings of Tasmanian Historical Research Association*, vol. 5, 1956; *Aboriginal or Flinders Island Chronicle*, 10 September 1836, copy in Museum of 'Dryazell' near Wybalenna, Flinders Island; personal visit to site, 11 April 1973; Robert Travers, *The Tasmanians: the story of a doomed race* (Melbourne, 1968); cemetery for aborigines and white people near chapel at Wybalenna. See, for example, the tombstone for Mannalargenna and the plaque erected by the Historical Association to the one hundred aborigines buried in the vicinity of Wybalenna, 1833-47; lithograph by J. S. Prout, 'The Residence of the Aborigines', Flinders Island, 1847.

Like other men in high places in Sydney, Sir George Gipps was a divided man on the question of the aborigines. During the month in which he opened the despatch from Glenelg in which he was instructed to direct his anxious attention to the adoption of some plan for the better protection and civilization of the native tribes within the limits of his government, the *Sydney Herald* was reporting yet another barbarous murder of fourteen out of fifteen white men who were driving a flock of six thousand sheep near the Broken River at Benalla in the District of Port Phillip. As usual the aborigines had scattered the sheep into the bush. The *Herald* asked Gipps to ensure that settlers should be properly armed so as to be prepared for the blacks should these savages manifest any hostile designs. They wanted strong measures taken against these 'savages of the interior'. So while his masters in London were saying firmly 'no more wanton killing of blacks', the most powerful class in the colony, the squatters of New South Wales, were sending delegations to him to teach him that these aborigines were incurable savages who, not being restrained by moral scruples, and placing as they did little value on human life, would go on perpetrating outrages because they were driven on by a natural stupidity and ferocity.[6]

Again in November Sydney was in an uproar over the aborigines. Eleven white men were on trial that week in the Supreme Court of New South Wales for the murder of thirty-one aborigines at Myall Creek in the New England district of New South Wales. Some white men snorted with rage at the very idea that men of their race should be put on trial for the murder of men little higher in the scale of creation than monkeys. Others denounced the 'maudlin sentiment' of exciting sympathy for the 'murderous cannibals of New Holland'. Others were telling Sir George how God had made all manner of men to dwell upon the face of the earth and how in the eyes of God all men were of equal significance.[7]

At the height of all this sound and fury the four assistant protectors arrived in Sydney and had an audience with the new governor of New South Wales, Sir George Gipps. The very appearance of the men and what they stood for were enough to make Sir George prickly on that day. Three of them—E. S. Parker, J. Dredge and W. Thomas—were clearly *pasteurs manqués*, high-minded schoolmasters, who held the naïve delusion that if the white man wore on his face a smile as a symbol of the love of Christ in his heart for the black man, if he used loving kindness and got the black man to read the Bible, all would be well. Sir George could see at a glance that the other man

---

[6] Report of Select Committee on the Aborigines Question, *V. & P.* (L.C. N.S.W.), 1838; W. Thomas to G. A. Robinson, 27 November 1838 (Robinson Papers, vol. 49, ms. in m.l.); Gipps to Glenelg, 10 November 1838, *H.R.A.*, I. xix. 668-9; [George Arden], *Latest Information with regard to Australia Felix* (Melbourne, 1840).

[7] *Sydney Herald*, 14, 21 May 1838; The Memorial of the Undersigned Colonists, Landholders and Proprietors of Stock to Sir George Gipps, Col. Sec. of New South Wales to the Gentlemen Signing that Memorial, 23 June 1838, encls 1 and 2 in Gipps to Glenelg, 21 July 1838, C.O. 201/274; the story of the Myall Creek massacre is told in ch. 7 of this volume.

—C. W. Sievewright, an ex-army man—was one of those types he had often come across in his own army days. He was a sponger who paid off his gambling debts by pinching his wife's allowance, a man who was delighted to take £250 a year plus allowances in return for professions of benevolence towards the aborigines of New Holland. Sir George began by reminding them forcefully that everything that had been undertaken for the aborigines had proved a failure, and went on to caution them that the settlers resented public money being spent on the vain attempts to civilize savages. Then, calming down, and remembering the tone of those despatches from his masters in London, Sir George told them that if they were to succeed it would not be by a display of fire-arms, but by the use of mild measures.[8]

Down in Melbourne everything seemed more hopeful. To inaugurate the protectorate, Lonsdale gave a dinner at which there was much cheerfulness, as all present washed down the ample helpings of roast beef and potatoes with just enough strong drink to promote benevolence and conviviality, taking care, as high-minded men generally do, not to imbibe that little bit extra which might put decorum and respectability in jeopardy. By the time James Dredge was ready to go into the field in May, it looked as though the government of New South Wales was on the side of the protectors. For in that month Gipps moved a proclamation in which he reminded all persons in charge of sheep and cattle beyond the limits of location that if they were found practising the abominable and un-Christian proceeding of detaining aboriginal women by force in their huts then their licences to depasture stock would be cancelled. He also reminded all the people of New South Wales that as human beings partaking of man's common nature, as the native possessors of the land and as subjects of the Queen, the aborigines had an equal right with people of European origin to the protection and assistance of the law of England.[9]

Dredge set out for the Goulburn River district in May. He was instructed to protect and civilize the natives, to keep a journal, to make a census of the aboriginal population, and to prepare a list of aboriginal place names and an account of the customs and habits of each tribe, especially whether their attitudes were hostile or amicable. Believing that a handout of food and clothing would persuade the aborigines that he was their friend, Dredge asked Robinson for an advance to allow him to purchase adequate supplies of both items. Robinson passed the request on to Gipps who, knowing what would happen if he put that item of expenditure into the budget of New South Wales, turned down the request. This confronted Dredge with a great dilemma. He saw clearly that as the white man spread over the country, driving the aborigines into the tribal lands of other aborigines, bloody inter-tribal wars would break out. If the aborigines mingled with the white invader then their own mythology which had sustained their people for thousands of years would

---

[8] Gipps to Glenelg, 10 November 1838, *H.R.A.*, I. xix. 668-9.
[9] *New South Wales Government Gazette*, 21 May 1839; [George Arden], *Latest Information with regard to Australia Felix*, ch. 7.

cease to have meaning for them, and something would have to be put in its place. He believed that 'something' was the Christian religion, but that would cost government money. Since government clearly had not the slightest intention of footing that bill, he resigned in June 1840 and was replaced by W. Le Soeuf, who opened a school and persuaded the natives to cultivate the land, only to find that as soon as his meagre supplies of handouts ran out the natives took to the bush and resumed their own erratic life.[10]

In the spring of 1839 Edward Stone Parker put up at Jackson's Creek (near present site of Sunbury) his 'palace of self-denial'. It was a wattle-and-daub hut with a thatched roof, earthen floors, sod chimney and screens of sacking to cover doors and windows. It was to be his headquarters for the Macedon or north-western district which was bounded on the south by the district of Geelong, on the west by the boundary of South Australia, on the east by a line running north from Mt Macedon, the northern boundary being un-defined. Like Dredge he was a great believer in the love-of-Christ smile on the face, displays of loving kindness, and reading the Bible. Nature had endowed him with a woman's gentle face. When he came to man's estate and put away childish things, he still wore on his face the innocence and purity of a child, and behaved like a man who never saw all the evil in the world, because there was no such stain on his own heart. He chased one tribe up the Loddon almost to its junction with the Murray, with that love of Christ on his face, and a Bible in his hip pocket—all to no avail. By February 1840 he came to the conclusion that the rapid occupation of the Loddon district by settlers, and the consequent deprivation of the aborigines from the natural products of their land was the root-cause of the ill-feeling of the black man for the white man. The settlers believed the possession of a squatting licence entitled them to exclude the aborigine from their runs. As he saw it, if the aborigines were to be saved from extermination, government should assert forthwith the right of the aborigine to the soil and to its indigenous productions. He did not believe for one moment that anyone in high places seriously proposed to stop the onward march of the settlers or to stop the white man slaughtering the game on which the aborigines depended for their food. He saw quite clearly that if the aborigines lost their own source of supply they would be forced to steal and destroy the white man's sheep and cattle. The other possi-bility was to reserve an area for the aborigines and teach them the arts of cultivation and the advantages of a settled mode of existence. Though he was puzzled by the nomadic habits of both old and young and bothered by their indolence and their dislike for 'constrained labor', he was happy to report that there were some cases of aborigines being successfully employed as shepherds in his district. He hoped time would prove that they were not insurmountably

[10] Diary of J. Dredge, 8 January, 15 February 1840 (MS. in LA TROBE L.); J. Dredge, *Brief Notices of the Aborigines of New South Wales, including Port Phillip* (Geelong, 1845); E. J. B. Foxcroft, *Australian Native Policy* (Melbourne, 1941), pp. 60-2; for the instructions by G. A. Robinson to the assistant protectors on 1 April 1839 see [George Arden], op. cit., pp. 91-2.

opposed to work. He hoped, too, that government would provide the assistant protectors with the means to protect the aborigines against injury, because otherwise terrible things would happen: the aborigines would be excluded from lands they regarded as their own property, they would be denied the right of humanity and classed with and treated as wild dogs, and they would be driven to more frequent depredations and exposed to more rapid and certain destruction.[11]

In the autumn of 1839 William Thomas, one-time schoolmaster from England, a Wesleyan by conviction, and a man who longed to tell the black man that Jesus was keeping a place for him in the sky, for he contained in his person childlike simplicity of manners with great goodness of heart, set out from Melbourne for Narre Warren to begin his duties as Assistant Protector in the Western Port or Melbourne district. This was bounded in the south by a line running from Point Nepean eastward, in the north by the Australian Alps, in the west by the bay of Port Phillip, and undefined to the east. By 1841 he had had at times as many as sixty aborigines working on his station at Narre Warren. Like Parker he came to the conclusion that to attach them to settlers would surely lead to the speedy extinction of their race, since they did not learn from the settlers how to bow the knee to God and did not learn a single letter of the alphabet but became drunkards instead. By joining the white man's society, the aborigines lost the status of inheritors of their native soil and became hired labourers. To attach members of a tribe to settlers would be the dawn of slavery for the aborigines of Australia and the acceleration of their speedy extinction. He wanted to teach them to cleanse their ways so that they would be worthy to receive the approbation of God. On 13 June 1841 he wrote in his diary: 'Of all the Sundays this beat all. In the morning Visitors, had to cheque several Gentlemen on their unseemly behaviour in Endeavouring to entice the Blacks to go Kangorooin—Oh sorry exempel, who need to wonder at the ill success of Christianity among them'. He was more impressed by the influence of the blacks on each other: 'with pleasure', he wrote in his journal three days later, 'have I often heard Billibellary and [word indecipherable] Tom give charge to the Young Men on going to Melbourn not to get Drunk, & tho' the Sabbath is little respected in the Bush, yet they never attempt to Corrobery on that Day, at Nerre Nerre Warren there was evidently a growing observance and increasing attention'.

On the question whether the aborigines would abandon the chase and the consequent erratic habits and adopt civilized occupations such as grubbing, fencing, splitting, mortising, boring, sawing, digging and ploughing he was not certain of the answer. They had the same capacity and powers as white men, but they lacked the white man's stability. In their present state he did not believe that any aborigine could be employed for more than two moons unless he was removed beyond the pale of his own tribe. The other weakness of the aborigine as a worker was his indolence. He preferred sleeping and saunter-

[11] E. Morrison (ed.), *Early Days in the Loddon Valley* (n.p., 1966), pp. 9-10; photo of E. S. Parker in Castlemaine Museum, personal visit, 5 April 1973.

ing about to work, unless he was asked to do something that pleased him such as riding after cattle. Those who went in search of food one day generally loafed all the next day. Their humane disposition to each other shielded the indolent since they shared the fortunes of the day with the indolent. They showed not the slightest interest in saving, let alone in storing up possessions or treasures for themselves on earth, since in their estimation everything unnecessary was a burden. Thomas hoped, like Parker, that in time they would be persuaded to live under cover, that a catechist would teach the children to read and write and that they could be taught how to handle sheep and cattle and how to grow crops. He thought wild blacks should be discouraged from visiting the station since they only seduced the men on the station back to their old erratic habits. He wanted to keep all aborigines out of towns, because there the life demoralized and unhinged them. When he found that the aborigines on his station did not or could not want the white man's civilization, he concentrated his energies on attempting to prevent their extinction. Like his two colleagues he was forced to abandon the hope of turning the aborigines into 'sons of Britain' and to concentrate on the problem of their survival.[12]

The fourth assistant protector, Charles Wightman Sievewright, exposed the protectorate to public scandal. It was said of him that he neither brought character to the colony nor gained or maintained it. In the autumn of 1839 he took up his duties as an assistant protector in the Geelong or Western district. From the start Sievewright's conduct attracted unfavourable attention. While the other three took their families into the solitary bush and perambulated doggedly in the footsteps of those great vagabonds the aborigines of New Holland, Sievewright preferred the comforts of Geelong. Where the other three conscientiously prepared a census of the aborigines in their districts and took steps to learn the local languages, Sievewright steadfastly refused to do either, much to the displeasure of the Chief Protector, G. A. Robinson.

By an odd irony he was the one Assistant Protector who seemed to have liked and admired the aborigines. He admired their quick perception and great bodily activity which, he believed, entitled them to be placed much higher in the scale of intelligent beings and useful appendages to an establishment than those specimens of ineptness that generally constituted the character of agricultural labourers. He believed they could become useful labourers through kindness, good food, clothing and the judicious distribution of such luxuries as tea, sugar, tobacco and flour. He perceived that the crux of the problem was to convert them to the mental habits and tastes of capitalist individualists and to persuade them to shed the habits of collective loyalty. Before he could put his ideas to the test, John Pascoe Fawkner mocked him as 'a man who preferred sitting at his ease on the police bench to

---

[12] W. Thomas, Information for the Committee of the Legislative Council Concerning the Employment of Aborigines, 1841 (Aborigines Papers, MS. in M.L.); Journal of W. Thomas, 13, 16 January 1841 (William Thomas Papers, MS. in M.L.).

migrating through the wilds of the bush'. So the man who tried hard to stop the appalling loss of life on the plains of Australia Felix was branded by the philistines of Melbourne as a moral leper who would contaminate respectable bourgeois society.[13]

At the same time Christian missionaries were attempting to civilize the aborigines of Port Phillip. In December 1836 Bourke appointed George Langhorne missionary to Port Phillip and instructed him to persuade as many natives as possible to settle in villages in which he and his assistants would gradually wean the blacks by proving to them experimentally the superior qualifications to be obtained in civilized life. After arriving at the Yarra site in January 1837, Langhorne create a black village in which the aboriginal children were washed, clothed, and taught fixed habits of work and residence, and adults were taught those crafts which would qualify them for employment in the white man's society. By March 1839 Langhorne was reporting that his mission was a complete failure, since the fourteen children left at the school had run away and had not been seen, while the adults were only learning the low habits and petty vices of the lower order of Europeans.[14]

Quite undaunted by his failure the Reverend Joseph Orton decided in 1838 to send missionaries to Port Phillip. Orton had arrived in Sydney in 1831 to take charge of Wesleyan missions in New Holland. He had seen the Port Phillip blacks during a visit there in 1836 and had come back to Sydney with his heart full of pity for the 'poor creatures', and a burning desire to tell them of the love of Christ. In 1838, after receiving promise of financial assistance from Sir George Gipps, he arranged for the Wesleyan Missionary Society to send two missionaries to establish a reserve at Port Phillip where they could encourage the aborigines in habits of industry and teach the children to become Christian ladies and gentlemen. In March 1838 the Reverend Francis Tuckfield and the Reverend Benjamin Hurst and their families, all of whom, on their own confession, spent their waking moments panting, hungering and thirsting after divine grace, arrived in Hobart Town on the first leg of their journey in fulfilment of their Saviour's command to go into all the world and preach the Gospel to every creature. Four months later, after crossing to Port Phillip, Tuckfield chose 640 acres as a reserve at

[13] G. A. Robinson to La Trobe, 9 July 1842, *V. & P.* (L.C. N.S.W.), 1843, p. 34; letters to Superintendent La Trobe relating to charges of immorality against Assistant Protector Sievewright, his subsequent dismissal and claims made by him to the government for sums of money (MS. in LA TROBE L.); G. A. Robinson to La Trobe, November 1847 (Robinson Papers, vol. 57A); C. W. Sievewright, answers to questionnaire on employment of aborigines, 12 June 1841 (Aborigines Papers, MS. in M.L.); FitzRoy to Grey, 14 March 1848 (transcript of missing despatches from governors of N.S.W., 1847-55, MS. in M.L.); P. Corris, *Aborigines and Europeans in Western Victoria* (Canberra, 1968), ch. 6; *Port Phillip Gazette*, 14 March 1840; *Sydney Herald*, 6 April 1840; FitzRoy to Grey, 14 March 1848 (transcript of missing despatches from governors of N.S.W., 1847-55).

[14] Memorandum by W. Burton to Governor of N.S.W. (Aborigines Papers, MS. in M.L.); Bourke to Glenelg, 14 June 1837, *H.R.A.*, I. xviii. 783; E. J. B. Foxcroft, *Australian Native Policy* (Melbourne, 1941), pp. 39-45.

'MY DEAREST LOVE'

John Franklin
*Portrait by Thomas Phillips, National
Portrait Gallery, London*

Jane Franklin
*Portrait by Thomas Bock, Queen Victoria
Museum, Launceston*

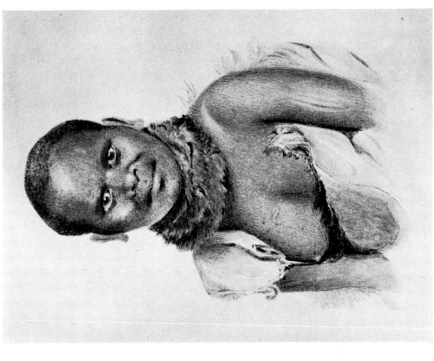

Truganini

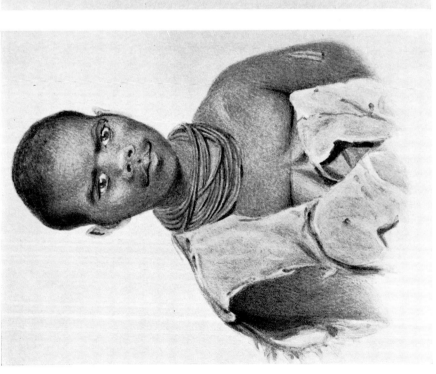

Jinny

WHEN THE ABORIGINES OF VAN DIEMEN'S LAND WERE NAKED AND NOT ASHAMED

Water-colours by Thomas Bock,
Tasmanian Museum and Art Gallery, Hobart

Birregurra some forty miles up stream on the Barwon from Geelong. Hurst decided to open his mission at Geelong, Orton having made it clear to both of them that they should not intrude on Langhorne's preserves at Melbourne and Arthur's Seat. Tuckfield called his station Bunting Dale in honour of the Reverend Jabez Bunting, a distinguished Wesleyan preacher in England.

In the beginning, like all their predecessors, both Hurst and Tuckfield found their missions full of promise. To his great delight Tuckfield found the aborigines so intelligent that he believed them capable of receiving instruction of any kind. Like all his predecessors in the field, he believed that as soon as the natives perceived the superiority of the European way of life, by which he meant a settled existence, private ownership of property, the monogamous family, and the worship of God the Father who had pronounced ten commandments for men to keep, and of Christ His Son who had only bound men to two commandments, that then they would shed that part of their way of life which prevented them from rising above barbarism. He knew that during those months in every year when their food supplies were low, they were tempted to go walkabout and abandon a fixed abode or address or to steal the white man's sheep and cattle. He hoped that the knowledge of God's plan for the human race would wean them from deeds of darkness. Yet in this, progress was painfully slow. He tried to get them to understand that God never slept, that that other person of the Godhead, the Holy Spirit, saw all man's works. In December 1839 the blacks near the mission station enticed an aboriginal girl away from the station, murdered her and ate part of her body. Tuckfield reported the crime to the Chief Protector, who not only did nothing but clearly had no idea what he ought to do.[15]

There was much in the behaviour of the aborigines that filled Tuckfield either with horror or disgust. He was not happy about the way the black men treated their wives. In fights over their women they became so noisy that he and his wife had scarcely any sleep as men, women and dogs raged, wailed and barked into the night. He was bothered, too, that although he gave the blacks extra quantities of food and a special talk on the heinous evil of Sabbath breaking, they did not take the slightest notice of him. So he prayed all the more fervently to God for help. 'May God Almighty', he wrote in his journal on Sunday 12 January 1840, 'put this law into their heads and write it upon their hearts!' When the blacks speared each other again he wrote 'That God Almighty may stop the fury of the heathen! And that we may see your face soon is the prayer and anxious desire of your brother in the Gospel'.[16]

For he had his faith that the wandering savage would eventually cling to those blessings and advantages on which civilization stood and that in the fulness of time God would raise those whom ignorance and oppression had

---

[15] G. W. Greenwood, 'Rev. Francis Tuckfield's magnificent failure at Bunting Dale', *Heritage* (Methodist Historical Society of Victoria), no. 6, 1956; Journal of Francis Tuckfield, 13, 14 October, 14 December 1839 (MS. in LA TROBE L.).
[16] Journal of Francis Tuckfield, 17 February, 17 April 1840.

debased and degraded. By the middle of 1840 he was beginning to form ideas on how the black man could be protected against the invader. As he saw it, the coming of the white man's herds and flocks had inflicted a serious loss on the aborigines without any equivalent gain. Their game had been driven away and valuable roots eaten by the white man's sheep. No wonder these hungry and indolent savages took to begging, stealing and deeds of revenge. In the latter they were humiliated by the gap between the feebleness of un-tutored barbarians and the skill and power of civilized man. In addition they were exposed to the oppression and contaminating influence of convict shep-herds and stockmen, and the outcasts of England. Believing it would be a disgrace to the British character if the white man's presence doomed the blacks to starvation, he suggested that reserves should be set aside for the aborigines where they could be protected from the white men and get their own food. There, in time, they might learn from the Gospel of a higher motive for man's existence than the chase and corroboree, for, despite the indifference of the aborigines, nothing would shake his faith that the Gospel was the only leaven that could raise nations to the rank of civilized man. All through 1841 he went on trying to protect the aborigines from corruption and death. He badgered the Chief Protector to stop C. W. Sievewright issuing fire-arms to natives, and followed in the train of his people as they travelled around the Colac district in case God's servant could help the 'least of the little ones'. He kept the Bible in his pocket and prayed each morning and each night that God would work a miracle and shed His light on these poor benighted creatures so that they would be vouchsafed a clear sense of the divine forgiveness. The glory to God in the eternal salvation of these strange creatures was the sole object of all his labours on the plains of Australia Felix.[17]

While Thomas, Dredge, Le Soeuf, Parker, Hurst, Langhorne and Tuck-field waited anxiously to see what the smile of loving kindness and the Bible could do to rescue the aborigines from their deeds of darkness and save them from extermination, settlers were saying openly that a few pleasant rounds of musketry would settle the problem of the aborigines far better than the 'nostrums of exaggerated philanthropy'. These settlers knew the aborigines as wild animals who broke the legs of their sheep and then danced a corro-boree round them as they writhed in agony on the ground, after which they left their dogs to finish off the work they had begun. The country districts of Port Phillip were reproducing the same rude and licentious form of society as the interior of New South Wales, a society of sly-grog shops, marauding bush-rangers, and murderous savages who so terrorized country districts that men were being compelled to give up their establishments and sell off their stock, since only one in twenty, it was said, could be persuaded to stay on a sheep

[17] F. Tuckfield to general secretaries, Wesleyan Mission House, London, 31 June 1840, and F. Tuckfield to J. M. Kenny, 20 May 1842 (copied in back of Journal of Francis Tuckfield); E. J. B. Foxcroft, *Australian Native Policy*, pp. 81-5.

station. When the settlers asked for adequate protection they received lectures from city philanthropists.[18]

The odd irony was that all those high and mighty men in London who felt such pity for this 'helpless race of beings' and such a desire to prepare them to receive the doctrines of Christianity and all the other advantages of civilization, had themselves sanctioned a waste lands policy which contributed to the dispersion of settlement in Port Phillip and elsewhere and proved so fatal to the aborigine. In 1839 the minimum upset price of Crown land was raised to 12s an acre and in 1840 to £1, a decision which was given the air of permanence by being written into the Sale of Waste Lands Act of 1842. The men of moderate or slender capital who flocked into Port Phillip between 1839 and 1842 to purchase land in response to those reports about a 'champagne country' were obliged to go beyond the limits of location, outside the boundaries of the counties of Bourke, Grant and Normanby, where they could depasture the stock purchased by their capital on a run for which they paid a licence fee of £10 a year.[19]

By 1840 squatters had spread west as far as Casterton on the junction of the Wannon and the Glenelg Rivers, north to the belt between Bendigo and Avoca and on to Ararat. Two or three years later they were so deep into the Loddon country that Assistant Protector Parker wondered whether the proximity of the white men would cause 'these unhappy people' to lapse back into the degradation and wickedness in which they had so long grovelled before he persuaded them to live apart from the white man. By 1842 squatters were on the southern fringe of the Wimmera. In 1835 George McKillop of Hobart Town overlanded stock from the Monaro to Omeo. He was followed by the usual band of outlaws. In February of 1839 Lachlan Macalister, a Scot with the gifts of winning the confidence and respect of the aborigines, overlanded stock from the Monaro to south of Omeo, from where he opened a road 130 miles long to Port Albert. By 1842 the occupation of the habitable parts of the lands east of Western Port was well under way.[20]

By then yet another white man's activity was bedevilling the relations with the aborigines. For the aborigines, killing a kangaroo was one way of obtaining food; for the white man a kangaroo hunt was good sport. As early as September 1839 the first hunt with trained thoroughbred hounds took to the field in Australia Felix. Eighteen horsemen, with a sprinkling of red coats and what was called at the time a 'capital show of clean limbed sound winded hacks', joined a little pack of English-bred dogs near Melton, a little to the north-east of Melbourne. It was a fine cold morning with a southerly wind and a thin frost upon the ground—a setting to put men, dogs and horses in

[18] *Sydney Herald*, 5 July 1839, 14 February, 2 March, 24 May 1840.
[19] La Trobe to Gipps, 1 February 1841, encl. in Gipps to Russell, 24 February 1841, C.O. 201/307.
[20] A. W. Greig, 'Beginnings of Gippsland', *Victorian Historical Magazine*, 1912; T. F. Bride (ed.), *Letters from Victorian Pioneers* (Melbourne, 1898), p. 199; S. H. Roberts, *The Squatting Age in Australia* (Melbourne, 1935), pp. 218-20.

high spirits. Away they went, with many a wild halloo and jolly laugh, to hunt kangaroos, believing sincerely that there 'was not so much harm to it'. That day, the kangaroo bounded away with his tail in the air at a rate that baffled the whole hunt. The white men returned to Melbourne empty-handed for their drinks. But they would be back in the field slaughtering for sport one of the aborigines' sources of survival. That was part of the grim price the aborigines had to pay if the District of Port Phillip was to remain 'English for thousands of years'.[21]

By 1839 they were boasting about their chance of sounding off an echo of Old England in their part of the New World. In December of the previous year the Colonial Secretary of New South Wales informed the settlers in the Port Phillip District of the intention of Her Majesty's Government to dis-continue the assignment of convicts south of the Murray. Soon after that Melburnians and the people at the Pivot (Geelong) were proud to tell new-comers and overlanders from the Ma Colony of New South Wales, 'Of course, as you know, here we are not on the felonry side of the colony'. That left them with a problem. If the settlers were not to use prison labour, and could not or would not use aboriginal labour, and rejected Asian or Pacific Islands labourers on the grounds that they would prefer 'men of their own colour', they must rely on migration from the United Kingdom to supply the demand for labour. Free passages were granted in the United Kingdom on nomina-tion by purchasers of land at Port Phillip to persons capable of labour and prepared to declare their intention of working for wages after their arrival.

In 1839 1036 labourers arrived from the United Kingdom, 1064 from Van Diemen's Land, 35 from South Australia and 517 from Sydney. Yet the demand for labour in the country districts still exceeded the supply. One of the reasons for this, it was argued, was that not all the money raised from the sale, leasing and licensing of Crown land was being used to pay the passages of migrants to Port Phillip. Some of it, they said in Melbourne, was being spent on migrants who took up positions in that part of New South Wales north of the Murrumbidgee. Some of the money raised in Port Phillip was being squandered on futile schemes for the civilization of the aborigine or to save them from extinction. In May 1839 in the *Port Phillip Patriot*, which had begun publication on 6 February 1839, Fawkner asked some simple questions. Why should the inhabitants of Melbourne and Port Phillip submit to petticoat government from Sydney? Why should they allow the rich men of Sydney to monopolize the profits of their valuable territory? Why should they suffer from the gross parsimony of the Legislative Council of New South Wales led by that notorious 'old woman' Richard Jones? Did not the whole body of the people in Port Phillip long for separation from New South Wales?[22]

These first salvoes for separation from the 'felonry side of the colony', this

[21] Meeting at Port Phillip, supplement to *Australian*, 1 October 1839.
[22] *Sydney Herald*, 19 February 1840; *New South Wales Government Gazette*, 12 December 1838; *Port Phillip Patriot*, 6, 13 May 1839.

proclamation of Melbourne as a city of bourgeois rectitude, were fired off just as life was fading fast from John Batman. Reduced to being wheeled around the town in a rush-work perambulator, his face rendered hideous by nasal syphilis, he was a shadow of that man who four years earlier had had his moment of ecstasy on the banks of the Yarra Yarra. In his last months he had raged against his wife and had taken mad revenge against her by leaving her only £5 in his will, and the rest to his beloved daughters. On 6 May Batman breathed his last, being then just thirty-eight years old, just as the men of moral rectitude began to set the tone of public life in Melbourne.[23]

Five months later, with the rain pouring down in torrents, the new superintendent of Port Phillip told the inhabitants of Melbourne it was not by the possession of numerous flocks and herds that a people secured enduring prosperity and happiness but by the acquisition and maintenance of sound religious and moral institutions without which no country could become truly great. Charles Joseph La Trobe was a man of such elegance and the possessor of such an effeminate giggle that local barmen summed him up as a man with the tastes and morals more suitable for looking after blackfellows than governing civilized colonials. Born in London on 30 March 1801 into a family of Huguenot descent, he grew up so surrounded by those men of the evangelical revival in England that all his life he was to speak and act like a *pasteur manque*. In the twenties he had travelled extensively in Mexico and North America, and had returned to Europe with the reputation of 'a man of a thousand occupations'—a botanist, a geologist, a hunter of beetles and butterflies, an amateur musician, a sketcher of no mean pretensions—a busy and a cheerful man. All his life he had the buoyancy and accommodating spirit of a native of the Continent. After marrying the daughter of a Swiss councillor in 1835 he had won a reputation in the Colonial Office by his reports on the measures necessary to fit the emancipated slaves in the West Indies for their freedom, and a reputation in the literary world for his evocation of the impression on the senses of tropical regions. He advocated a sober education for the negroes, 'one rather calculated to discipline the mind and to bring its opening powers into wholesome subjection, than to excite it'.

Glenelg and his advisers were so delighted with La Trobe that they decided he was the man to preside over the civilization of the blackfellows of Port Phillip and prevent their sinking into slavery. In February 1839 Glenelg notified the Governor of New South Wales of La Trobe's appointment to the office of Superintendent of the Settlement of Port Phillip within the Colony of New South Wales at a salary of £800 a year plus allowances. He arrived at Sydney on 25 July, picked up his detailed instructions from the Colonial Secretary, and then set off for Melbourne. He was told that within his district he would exercise the powers of a Lieutenant-Governor, and would stand in the same position in respect to the Governor of New South Wales as the Governor himself stood with respect to the Right Honourable the Secre-

[23] *Port Phillip Gazette*, 8 May 1839; *Port Phillip Patriot*, 13 May 1839; C. P. Billot, *Melbourne: an annotated bibliography to 1850* (Geelong, 1970), pp. 85-6.

tary of State for the Colonies. All the local officers, whose appointments were of a strictly local nature would look only to him for instructions, and all officers of the civil government would look upon him as their immediate head. He was warned not to make any expense which had not been provided for by the local legislature or expressly charged upon the land revenue and specifically authorized by the Governor. He was told that savings were to be made wherever practicable and that because a certain sum of money had been provided for any particular service it did not follow that it must necessarily be spent. In all matters of convict discipline he was to exercise the same powers as the Governor. He was not to have the powers of pardoning offenders or the remission of punishments. He was invited especially to direct his attention to the treatment of the aborigines and to prevent as far as possible collisions between them and the colonists.[24]

The man himself was a bundle of contradictions. There was that man who was inclined to decide whether to visit a house by the number of pretty girls he would meet. There was that sensitive man whose nostrils quivered compassionately when people told him of aborigines mangling the bodies of white men, or of overlanders committing abominations during one of their sprees. When told someone displeasing was to visit him he would complain of yet another pester from 'that infernal old rip', but as soon as the visitor entered he would tell him how very glad he was to see him. A vacillator, like most effeminate men, he was also much given to making jokes about his wife. Publicly he spoke the language of a universalist; privately he denounced Jews as 'scavengers of wealth' and 'murderers of Christ', denounced Roman Catholics as the correctors of Christ's work and subscribed to the great prejudice of his own 'tribe' that reason only prevailed in the affairs of men who were British by birth or by adoption. Publicly he spoke of the noble task of elevating the aborigines from barbarism to civilization; privately he let it be known that in his eyes the natives looked like a race of beings who were never intended to be swaddled at all, that they were wild animals living off an uncouth continent.[25]

Within a year of his arrival he was bewailing his fate, transported sixteen thousand miles beyond the reach of the daily means of improvement and enjoyment possessed by those who breathed the air of Europe. He saw himself as an exile in a country where nature was in its swaddling clothes, the natives wild animals, the white man's society in its infancy, and the arts and sciences

[24] H. McCrae (ed.), *Georgiana's Journal: Melbourne 1841-65* (2nd ed., Sydney 1966), pp. 71-3; Grey to La Trobe, 4 February 1839, encl. in Glenelg to Gipps, 29 January 1839, *H.R.A.*, I. xix. 786; A. Gross, *Charles Joseph La Trobe* (Melbourne, 1956); Washington Irving, *Works of Washington Irving* (10 vols, London, 1850), *A Tour on the Prairies*, vol. 3, pp. 2-3; La Trobe to J. Murray, 15 December 1840, quoted in S. Smiles, *A Publisher and his Friends* (London, 1891), p. 47; C. J. La Trobe, *The Solace of Song* (London, 1837); Col. Sec. of New South Wales to La Trobe, 10 September 1839 (N.S.W.S.A.); G. H. Courtenay to C. J. La Trobe, 9 March 1860 (C. J. La Trobe, letters to his wife, La Trobe Papers).

[25] La Trobe to the Chief Protector, 22 October 1839, and La Trobe to Col. Sec. of New South Wales, 15, 18 January 1840 (Chief Secretary, Letters Outward, 8 October 1839 to 13 November 1840, v.s.a.).

unborn. In the year of his arrival the inhabitants of Melbourne either wallowed in mud or choked in the dust. One rut in Elizabeth Street was deep enough to act as a grave for a wagon and horses. Wits advertised for stilts to help them negotiate the mud. A writer of doggerel wrote in a sardonic vein,

> Escaping from one quagmire
> There's room enough for more;
> Such a beautiful town as Melbourne,
> Was never seen before.

Some of the houses were brick, some of weatherboard, but the majority were wattle-and-daub huts roofed with sheets of bark or coarse shingle. The sight of a woman in the streets was rare. The most conspicuous white people were the squatters down from the country to sell their wool or buy stores—heavily bearded men in serge shirts, cabbage-tree hats, moleskin trousers, boots and spurs, and ample tobacco pouches buttoned to their belts amidriffs. Black people wandered about the streets half naked much to the disgust of La Trobe who asked the Chief Protector to do his best to get them out of earshot and sight of the white men. The streets resounded to their cooees, the barking of their mangy dogs, the shouts and curses of the bullock drivers, and the groans of drunks in the gutters. For most of the publicans of Melbourne accepted a 'Sticking Plaster', a money order from their employers to shearers, shepherds or itinerant workers which they plastered on the walls of the hotel as credit while they guzzled away in the bar till they lost consciousness, after which the barmen put them in the Dead House till they were ready to be chucked into the street for a groan in the gutter while they 'dried out'.[26]

For spectator sports there were the fights between the aborigines. On 15 April 1840 Niel Black, still troubled by the doubt whether a white man's life was secure on the plains of Australia Felix unless he was prepared to give the blacks a few doses of lead, was in Melbourne to pick up supplies. That afternoon hearing yells coming from the bank of the Yarra he followed the crowd running towards the source of the noise where he saw black men, under the influence of a most fearful excitement, hurling spears at each other. The white spectators cheered and urged them to greater deeds of violence till suddenly the spear throwing stopped and a great cackling noise replaced the previous savage roars as a lubra rushed into the middle of the ring and shook her whole body in a wild frenzy while the anger of participants and spectators simmered down. To Black's horror he heard black and white people gloating over the prospect of further sport of a similar kind within a day or two.[27]

Some were shocked to find that in Melbourne in its raw days even the country gentry cared so little for their appearance that the shopkeepers and

---

[26] La Trobe to the Chief Protector, 28 October 1839, ibid.; Gipps to La Trobe, 23 December 1839 (La Trobe Papers); La Trobe to J. Murray, 15 December 1840, quoted in S. Smiles, *A Publisher and his Friends*, p. 456; J. Bonwick, *Discovery and Settlement of Port Phillip* (Melbourne, 1883), pp. 115-18; R. D. Boys, *First Years at Port Phillip* (2nd ed., Melbourne, 1935), pp. 88, 99-100.

[27] Diary of Niel Black, 15 April 1840.

workers lost all respect for them. If a gentleman dared to find fault with his wine at an inn, the waiter would probably knock him down. Tradesmen and labourers were in the habit of abusing anyone who was obnoxious to them, and not, alas, accustomed to making an exception for the self-styled gentry. They used such bad language that country squires from the settled districts of New South Wales were prophesying that Melbourne would be remarkable for the turbulence of its character. In their eyes even the members of the Melbourne Club looked rough and uncouth. Many of them were dressed like ploughmen or sons of ploughboys. One in particular disregarded attention to personal appearance so much that he actually walked about with 'such a rent in his trowsers as displayed to the wondering gaze of the multitude the ample fulness of his brawny buttocks'.[28]

While some wallowed in the mud, others were working feverishly to lay the foundations of that bourgeois way of life which was to prove the greatest calmer of the wilder passions in the human heart since the days when all men roamed the earth like the beasts of the field. In 1839 James Conway Bourke opened an overland mail route from Yass to Melbourne, and banks and insurance companies opened for business. In May 1840 the Melbourne Water Works Company was formed to supply water to the town. In July G. W. Cole started business as a general merchant, and owner of a fleet of paddle-steamers which plied on the Yarra and Port Phillip. In the same month the first directors of a Port Phillip Steam Navigation Company were elected as talks took place to form a Joint Stock Company to build a bridge across the Yarra. By the end of the year there were nearly 10250 white people in the District.[29]

While traders and merchants preached the gospel of industrial progress, priests and clergy held out to their congregations the prospect of prizes in this world to the strait-laced, and the richer prize of eternal salvation in the life of the world to come. From May of 1839 the Reverend P. B. Geoghegan was urging all Catholics to live in love and charity with their neighbours if they wished to find solace here and happiness hereafter, while in the parish school the children were being tamed and trained for the quiet life. In the Anglican church the Reverend J. C. Grylls, in the Established Church of Scotland the Reverend J. Forbes and in the Independent Church the Reverend W. Waterfield held out the prospect of rewards both here and hereafter for those who were upright in their ways, and reminded their congregations that those who ploughed iniquity and sowed wickedness reaped the same. By Christmas of 1840 the publicists for the repression of those poisonous passions of revelry, riot and debauchery were pleased to note that Melbourne was already presenting those features of repose and order which distinguished the best of the English towns. Instead of the brawling and drunken revelry of previous years the working classes were now displaying a sober demeanour and a very proper distaste for the tippler's life. Improving lectures, concerts featuring

[28] Diary of T. A. Murray, 13 February 1841 (ms. in NAT. L.).
[29] J. Bonwick, op. cit., p. 115; J. C. Bourke Papers (ms. in Royal Historical Society of Victoria); R. D. Boys, op. cit., pp. 110-13.

sacred music, and the decorous dancing of a quadrille or a waltz were replacing the gross swinish pleasure of the days when John Batman and other wild men reeled drunkenly around on the banks of the Yarra.[30]

In the country districts, too, the practitioners of a life of evangelical piety were becoming as prominent as the roisterers who first pastured sheep and cattle on the grasses of Australia Felix. Early in May 1840 Anne Drysdale, a member of a family of some prominence in the public life of Scotland, left her native land believing that she must flee from Scottish dankness if she were to pursue her favourite pastime of exerting a salutary influence on her fellow-creatures. She was said to be no longer youthful, and not graced by beauty, except a great beauty of spirit which more than made up for the jest of the Creator in her appearance. In the second half of 1840 she took out a licence for a 10 000-acre run at Boronggoop near the Barwon River some four miles from Geelong. There she was joined by her friend Caroline Newcomb, a Methodist Missionary Society member who had worked in Port Phillip since 1836 as governess to the children of John Batman. She, too, was an extraordinary creature, being very ugly, very gruff, and always at the same time full of loving kindness. The two erected a thatched cottage with glazed windows, surrounded by a garden as a replica of those of their native land with which to mock and defy the surrounding barbarism. In time Caroline Newcomb became so pleasing in the eyes of Anne Drysdale that she wrote in her diary, 'Miss Newcomb who is my partner, I hope for life, is the best and most clever person I have ever met with; there seems to be magic in her touch, everything she does is done so well and so quickly.' They rose at 7 each day, said prayers presided over by Caroline Newcomb who pleased Miss Drysdale by praying extempore very beautifully. They dined at 2, took tea at 6.15, prayed again at 8, and went to bed at 10. Both of them hoped not only that the meditations of their hearts would be acceptable to their Lord and Redeemer but an example to the white and black barbarians of the Australian bush. It was said that under their influence even the horses and cattle took on a 'tameness' rarely seen in the squatting stations of the interior of New South Wales.[31]

Although the Port Phillip District was what one observer called 'a money making place' where men boasted unashamedly of their hope to become 'disgustingly rich', these prospective seigneurs of the sheep-walks of Australia Felix were dining off mutton, damper and tea three times a day. A woman was a rare sight in the bush. There were no schools and no churches. The men lived in wooden erections put up with upright posts upon which were nailed weatherboards, thin deals overlapping each other to form the walls. The roof

[30] Advertisement by P. B. Geoghegan in *Port Phillip Gazette*, 18 May 1839; R. D. Boys, op. cit., pp. 101-2, *Port Phillip Herald*, 10 July 1840; *Port Phillip Patriot*, 28 December 1840.

[31] J. D. Lang, *Phillipsland; or the Country hitherto Designated Port Phillip* (Edinburgh, 1847), pp. 110-13; extracts from the diary of Anne Drysdale, quoted in P. L. Brown (ed.), Clyde Company Papers, vol. 5, pp. 78-9; R. V. Billis and A. S. Kenyon, *Pastoral Pioneers of Port Phillip* (Melbourne, 1932), p. 54; W. Russell to G. Russell, 3 October 1839, in P. L. Brown (ed.), Clyde Company Papers, vol. 2, pp. 270-1.

was thatched with long grass, and the floor was laid with boards or, failing them, consisted of beaten clay. The huts were sparsely furnished with stretchers for beds, and a table and chairs. There was also a men's hut which doubled as a kitchen, sometimes plastered with mud, but more often the cracks between the wattle planks were not plugged. Although by 1841, out of a total population of 11 738, 3201 or about 27 per cent were employed as shepherds, stockmen, gardeners and persons in agricultural pursuits, land-holders were not prepared to spend money on improvements so long as they were only squatters on government land and liable at any time to be removed from it if a purchaser made his appearance. On this point the government of New South Wales had made it clear it proposed to leave them as tenants-at-will, fearing that if they should grant them a right of pre-emption, the squatters would become too strong a section of the community.[32]

The squatters looked more to gain than to comfort, while their men laboured in a sea of barbarism. From time to time the townspeople were reminded of the horrors of such a life. Early in April 1840 two bushrangers were sentenced to death in Melbourne for attempted murder. After their condemnation they ate and drank like wild creatures. Even on the day of execution one of them seemed to go beyond that line of demarcation between the human and the brute. He was said to have been bordering on intoxication the night before. On the day itself he walked to the scaffold with a pipe in his mouth, and not even the solemn warnings by the parson could bring the unfortunate wretch to a sense of his situation. He roared defiance so loudly that the hangman had to kick him into a sufficiently quiet state to get the rope round his neck.[33]

From the bush there came terrible accounts of human degradation and savagery. All through 1840 and 1841 there were stories in the press of white men coming upon the mangled remains of their fellow-countrymen, of men stripped naked, their faces hacked, and their flesh pecked at by birds of prey, as their wrists were speared to the ground by those inhuman monsters and butchers—the aborigines. There were stories of aborigines killing their gins to avenge some slight to their pride. There were stories, too, of the brutality of white men. Emancipated convicts, whose ideas of good and evil had been driven out of them during their bondage, put blacks to death without compunction when they could get a chance. This led to further deeds of revenge by the black men, deeds which they were finding easier to perform since they had gained access to the fire-arms of the white man. Angry white men were demanding that magistrates be empowered to sentence aborigines to a flogging for sheep or cattle stealing. They were pestering La Trobe to arrest the next murderer of a white man and hang him and were gloating over

[32] Lady Jane Franklin to Sir John Franklin, 5 April 1839 (Franklin Letters, MS. in NAT. L.); H. McCrae (ed.), *Georgiana's Journal*, p. 58; W. H. Archer, *Statistical Notes on the Progress of Victoria* (2nd ed., Melbourne, 1960), p. 14; P. L. Brown (ed.), Clyde Company Papers, vol. 2, pp. 244-50; Gipps to La Trobe, 20 February 1841 (Gipps-La Trobe Correspondence).
[33] *Port Phillip Patriot*, 13 April 1840.

the simple fact that the blacks would eventually disappear before the settlers and that every murder of white men would further thin their numbers.[34]

As reports to La Trobe poured in from almost all the eighty-odd sheep men holding squatting licences in the District of Port Phillip in the first half of 1840 that the blacks were becoming more saucy, more hostile and more treacherous every day, he feared the squatters were reaching the limits of endurance beyond which no fear of future condemnation would quell their desire for self-preservation, or retaliation for the infliction of unprovoked injury. La Trobe knew the Protector and his assistants had not achieved any moral influence over the behaviour of the aborigines. The Chief Protector said this was because of the inadequate funds at his disposal and not because his assistants were gentlemen who were not calculated by previous habits or attainments to assist in a work of whose true character they could not have the slightest conception before they arrived in the colony. La Trobe was critical of Robinson for sitting still in Melbourne when he should have been out in the field. He knew Sievewright loved liquor and women rather than the souls of black men, and could do nothing about it. As for the other three, he wondered whether they were capable of the self-denial, and that drive to perform their duties for God's sake rather than from ambition or any vague principle of philanthropy. As the natives became more and more decidedly hostile, the idea crossed his mind that forbearance was a virtue few savage nations either practised or comprehended. Then as though shocked by what that implied, he added that for his part as long as there existed a chance of achieving something by friendly and peaceable means, nothing but extreme and imperative necessity could palliate the shedding of blood.[35]

La Trobe was not the only one to understand the causes of this bloody collision between two peoples entertaining diametrically opposed views of the meaning of life and the use to which man should put the resources of the earth. The gentlemen of the press, the publicists, the missionaries, the Protector and his four assistants, indeed all men with eyes to see, knew that the aborigines were oppressed by famine because the game on which they relied for food had been driven into the interior by the rapidly increasing flocks and herds of the settlers. For that reason alone the aborigines were 'jealous of the intruders'. All men of goodwill knew that 'blood-thirsty and villainous atrocities' were also committed by men whose skins were white. But as for that 'consummation devoutly to be wished for', what the gentlemen of the press called 'the domestication of these unfortunate beings' by bringing them to 'sit down quietly in any establishment that may be founded in the interior for that purpose', their nature was too erratic and their disposition both too indolent and too wild ever to accomplish that. By the end of 1840 the angry,

---

[34] Foster Fyans, *Reminiscences* (MS. in LA TROBE L.); letter by Thomas Grant in *Sydney Gazette*, 12 June 1841; The Blacks, C.O. 201/307, pp. 98-100.

[35] F. A. Powlett to La Trobe, 18 September 1840, encl. in Gipps to Russell, 3 February 1841, C.O. 201/307; F. Fyans to La Trobe, 20 September 1840, encl. in ibid.; La Trobe to Col. Sec. of New South Wales, 15, 18 January, 31 March, 7 October 1840 (Chief Secretary, Letters Outward, 8 October 1839 to 13 November 1840, v.s.a.); La Trobe to Major Lettsom, 10 October 1840 (v.s.a.).

the loathers, the irritated, the puzzled, the love-of-Christ men and the philanthropists were all asking themselves whether anything could be done.

By that time some were saying that, insofar as the object of Great Britain in taking possession of the country was not to benefit and improve the natives but rather to open a field for the enterprise and industry of its own teeming population, that first great act of spoliation must be disastrous for the natives. He who would exploit the wealth of the country, they argued, must steel his breast to the wrongs he must commit against the aborigines of New Holland, for all such wrongs were unanswerable. Those who chose to stay in this 'money-making place', those who aspired to become 'disgustingly rich' as well as those who were content with a 'belly-full' must expect to see crows and hawks pecking at the mangled remains of white men and black men on the plains of Australia Felix. It was just seventy years since Captain Cook had looked on the aborigines as 'far more happier than we Europeans . . . and that whereas the first Parents [of the Europeans] that after they had eat of the forbidden fruit they saw themselves naked and were ashamed; these people are naked and are not asham'd . . .' In the majesty of the moment of seeing a people not affected by Adam's curse Cook had allowed himself a wee joke at the expense of Joseph Banks, the amoroso on the *Endeavour*: 'Although some of us were never very near any of their women, one gentleman excepted', now the black man languished and decayed while the Niel Blacks, the Pratt Winters, the Russells, the Learmonths, the Hentys, the Armitages and the Austins rode on to glory and sang on Sunday the words, 'Keep innocency, and take heed unto the thing that is right: for that shall bring a man peace at the last. As for the transgressors, they shall perish together'.[36]

As they saw it, it was the manifest destiny of the people of Port Phillip to take the lead over all the Australian colonies and sit among the nations as 'Empress of the Southern Seas'. They should not torment themselves with guilt or be so extreme as to mark what was being done amiss in their adopted land. Besides they had other matters of much greater moment on their minds. The question of questions still remained: Where was the squatter to get his labour? Up on the Goulburn River A. F. Mollison tried some Scottish Highlanders, only to pine again for prison labour. Down at Glenormiston in the very heart of Australia Felix Niel Black wanted at least five times the workers he could get. The natives were proving more troublesome. He believed that unless speedy action and measures were adopted by government to keep the natives in check there would be scenes of slaughter and bloodshed similar to what had happened in Van Diemen's Land. Settlers were not likely to go on quietly submitting to being robbed and murdered just because of the absence of workers and adequate protection from govern-

---

[36] *Port Phillip Patriot*, 17 February, 21 December 1840, 30 May 1842; La Trobe to Col. Sec. of New South Wales, 18 January 1840 (Chief Secretary, Letters Outward, 8 October 1839 to 13 November 1840), encl. in Gipps to Russell, 3 February 1841, C.O. 201/307; J. C. Beaglehole (ed.), *The Voyage of the Endeavour 1768-1771* (Cambridge, 1955), p. 399; J. Cook to J. Walker, 13 September 1771, ibid., pp. 508-9.

ment. Personally he had just found a remedy—'21 Horsemen Galloping full tilt after them is a Sight they Never Saw in Port Phillip nor do I think they will like to take the risk of a repetition of it'. For himself he was not very keen on hired labour. He found Vandemonians great bouncers, men with a far too 'swaggering air', strutters with 'far too much to say about themselves' and the appearance of men who believed they had no equal even though they were only paltry shopkeepers' boys. All in all Vandemonians were far too self-important and conceited for his taste. He wondered whether the solution was to import coolie labour from India or China. At his new station at Muntham, Edward Henty, who according to his mother was apt to grow excited and have an attack of nerves when things went wrong, refused to allow the 'convict polluters' on his estate. In Melbourne one woman was sorry for the effect of abolition of transportation on the 'poor convicts', for now they would be deprived of their one chance of reforming, because in the convict era a total change of scene, associates and occupation often led to happy results.[37]

By the middle of 1840 the publicists were saying that if Port Phillip was to take her rightful place as Empress of the Southern Seas then something must be done to solve this labour question. But, alas for Melbourne, as a contemporary put it, so long as Port Phillip remained a portion of New South Wales nothing would be done. The money that went from there to Sydney was keeping Melbourne poor. Some of the revenue from the District was being squandered on mad-hat schemes such as the colonization of Maori land. So, alas for Melbourne, they had no roads—the town was knee-deep in mud, or in dry weather the sun was eclipsed by the dust—and there was still no bridge over the Yarra. Melbourne was like a beggar's brat, wallowing in its own filth and choked by its own dust. The reason for this was that the Sydney government was not a giving but a receiving government. So God help Melbourne, for no one in Sydney ever would. That May of 1840 the public men of Melbourne and any up-country squatters who happened to be in town on the spree or, like Niel Black, forced to visit one tippling house after another in search of drunken bullock drivers, were once again worked into a fury by the latest news from Sydney, that the Colonial Treasury had to pay for police and gaols and the expense of establishing British authority in New Zealand. Stirred up by the evident damage done to Port Phillip from the non-appropriation of the funds derived from the sale of Crown lands to the promotion of immigration to its shores, a fully attended public meeting was held in Melbourne. Those present resolved unanimously that it was essential to the prosperity of Port Phillip that the revenue arising from the sale of the waste lands of the province should be expended in the introduction, on economical terms, of carefully selected migrants of the working classes from the mother

[37] *New South Wales Government Gazette*, 12 December 1838; *Port Phillip Patriot*, 31 October, 18 November 1839; A. F. Mollison to Jane Mollison, 10 June 1838, 25 December 1840, 20 April 1841 (Mollison Letters, MS. in LA TROBE L.); Niel Black to T. S. Gladstone, 5 August 1840 (Black Letters, MS. in LA TROBE L.); Diary of Niel Black, 4 April 1840; for the attitude of the Henty brothers to convict labour see Marnie Bassett, *The Hentys* (London, 1954), p. 439 and fn. 2; Mrs Turton to Mrs Williams, 16 July 1840, P. L. Brown (ed.), Clyde Company Papers, vol. 2, p. 355.

country, that money raised in Port Phillip should not be spent on police and gaols in New Zealand because their district was almost entirely excluded from the benefit of convict labour and had no interest whatever in the settlement of New Zealand, and that the use of their revenue for such purposes was contrary to the assurances given by three successive secretaries of state.

In June the merchants, land-holders, stock-holders and all others interested in that section of the colony of New South Wales commonly known as Australia Felix drafted a petition for separation from New South Wales. As they saw it, their situation as residents of a free province which formed part of a penal colony was attended with many evils. First, there was the inconvenience of not being governed by an officer stationed on the spot and gifted with full powers. This difficulty could never be lessened by allowing Port Phillip to elect representatives to any New South Wales legislature, because they would always be in a minority, and so long as the two communities had conflicting interests on such questions as the expenditure of land revenue, Port Phillip was bound to suffer. Second, the great evil of the union of a free colony with a penal colony was that the revenue derived from the sale of the Crown lands of Australia Felix was appropriated to support convicts labouring for the benefit of another province. The effects of this continued drainage of the funds of this new and rising province were visible in their limited and inefficient police force, a town of four thousand people with scarcely any public buildings, streets impassable in wet weather, a harbour without a lighthouse, and a country, though unsurpassed in natural resources, not able to use those resources because of the lack of labour. Finally, they called attention to the present advanced and rapidly advancing state of the district and capital of Australia Felix and pointed out what must be its future position among the Australian colonies. Melbourne possessed natural advantages far superior to any other seaport in Van Diemen's Land and New South Wales. She had as fine a harbour and as healthy a situation, with a more genial climate and a greater average of more productive soil in her immediate vicinity. Australia Felix must soon become one of the most populous provinces, if not the most populous province, in the Southern Hemisphere, more particularly because it appeared to be one of the few places in New South Wales where the soil would bear a concentrated population, while on the other hand a boundless extent of territory was ever opening up fresh fields of labour for the hand of man. The only remedies for these grievances consisted in 'an entire separation of the province from the territory of New South Wales, and the grant of a free representative government of its own'. They therefore asked for, first, responsible government entirely separate from and independent of New South Wales, and, second, a free and extended legislative representation, corresponding with the extent and population of the district and equal to the exigencies of a free state.[38]

[38] *Port Phillip Gazette*, 8, 11 May 1839; letter from Melbourne, 11 May 1840, published in *South Australian Register*, 16 October 1841; Diary of Niel Black, 18, 19 April 1840; *Port Phillip Patriot*, 7 May 1840; 'Petition of the undersigned inhabitants of Australia Felix', *Port Phillip Patriot*, 11, 15 June 1840.

Sydneysiders did not like that. Ever since 1838 there had been resentment in that city and in the settled districts of New South Wales that property holders should be taxed to provide facilities for a new district such as Port Phillip. Where, it was asked, was the equity in compelling a land-holder at Hunter River or Argyle to pay the cost of erecting a public building for a body of persons who voluntarily took themselves to a distant part of the territory in search of abundant water and rich pasturage? This resentment was fanned into hostility by the pharisaical stand of the Melburnians who not only thanked God they were not as other men in Sydney, but added the insult that Port Phillip Bay was superior to Sydney Harbour! So when the petition for separation reached Sydney it received a cool reception both in the Legislative Council and the press. When news reached Melbourne and Sydney at the end of the year that Her Majesty's Government had decided to divide New South Wales into three districts for the administration of its affairs—a northern, a central and a southern or Port Phillip district based on a line from the southern limit of the nineteen counties from Moruya to the Murrumbidgee, then following that river to the South Australian border—the Melburnians took it as the beginning of a glorious era in the history of their province, and the date on which freedom from New South Wales began. Sydneysiders spoke of a 'deep, serious wound', how they trembled for the future of Australia and how there would be even less money available to transform the wilderness into scenes of improvement and order. The more the Melburnians convinced themselves that they were wallowing in mud or choking in dust because of those 'old women' in the Legislative Council in Sydney, the more they pro-tested that they were the true sons of Britain. In their whole history they were to be cursed by this quest for the unattainable, this insistence that they had not changed their inner selves by that long journey across the seas, and cursed, too, by the conviction of the moral superiority of a society of new chums over the descendants of the thief colony at Botany Bay.[39]

The first ship from London in 1841 brought disquieting news. On 25 August 1840 that tiny insignificant-looking man Lord John Russell wrote to Gipps of the intentions of the Queen's Government 'to do justice and shew kindness to the Natives' of New Holland. There were two problems. The first was that the natives were diminishing in numbers and might finally disappear. As he saw it, the best chance of preserving the unfortunate race of New Holland lay in the means employed for training their children. Missionaries could teach them to read and write, and give them 'oral instruction in the fundamental truths of the Christian Religion'. The boys should be taught to dig and plough, and taught the trades of shoemakers, tailors, carpenters and masons; the girls should be taught to sew and cook and to wash linen and keep clean the rooms and furniture. He hoped that if they were trained early, 'the capacity of the race for the duties and employment of Civilized life would be fairly

[39] Article on Port Phillip in *Sydney Herald*, 25 June 1838; *Sydney Gazette*, 15 November 1838; *Port Phillip Patriot*, 10 September, 31 December 1840; Russell to Gipps, 31 May 1840, H.R.A., I. xx. 641-8; Gipps to La Trobe, 11 February 1841 (La Trobe Papers); V. & P. (L.C. N.S.W.), 10 December 1840; *Sydney Herald*, 12 December 1840.

developed'. The other problem was 'the vast and perhaps insuperable difficulty of the conflict carried on with little intermission between the Colonists
and the Natives'. The only effectual remedy for this lamentable evil, Lord
John believed, was an organized force adequate to keep both parties in check
and confine each to the limits assigned by government. He suggested that
15 per cent of the yearly produce from land sales be used to pay for the cost
of such a force.[40]

It was an unfortunate year in which to suggest that a slice of the public
funds should be used to pay for the civilization of savages or the maintenance
of law and order between white man and black man. By June of 1841 mercantile matters were in a most miserable state. Businessmen in Melbourne were
acting as mere onlookers and not doing a single piece of business they could
avoid. Down at Glenormiston Niel Black anxiously watched the fall in prices
of wool, runs and all primary produce, and passed on to England the rumours
that the depression was becoming worse than in Sydney. At the same time he
was very happy with the new carabine someone had sent him which, he said,
was one of the best he had even seen for a black hunt, though he hastened to
add that that was a use to which he hoped he might never have occasion to
apply it. When all his men bolted at Christmas except one, things became so
bad he decided to barter rather than sell all his stock. Money was so tight that
Gipps took occasion to remind La Trobe that George Gawler in South
Australia had been thrown overboard for extravagance, and government
might well do the same to him without scruple if he was at all prodigal.[41]

It was a society in which bizarre and extravagant characters had brief
periods of prominence. From the moment he arrived in Melbourne on
12 April 1841 to take up duty as resident judge for the District of Port Phillip,
John Walpole Willis turned his court into such 'an arena of unseemly
squabbles' that people attended to join in the fun and enjoy what was 'as good
as a play'. He scolded barristers, assailed Captain Lonsdale, poked fun at the
Superintendent, the Sydney judges and the government of New South Wales,
and browbeat solicitors into retiring from practice. He dismissed one lawyer
from his court for the trivial offence of wearing a moustache; he refused
another lawyer leave to appear because he had advertised the services of his
stallion. All his life Willis was a storm-centre. He was expelled from Charter-
house School in England, removed from his legal office in Upper Canada,
had his first marriage declared null and void, and quarrelled so obsessively
in Sydney that the Chief Justice was delighted to offload him onto the people
of Port Phillip. Yet the man himself was dedicated to the highest principles.
He usually 'leaned towards the poor as against the wealthy, and it was his
pleasure to hawk at high rather than low game'. A barrister, he believed,
should not in deference to a wealthy or powerful client, much less for the
sake of gain, undertake a cause that did not appear to be just. He should not

[40] Russell to Gipps, 25 August 1840, *H.R.A.*, I. xx. 774-6.
[41] Niel Black to T. S. Gladstone, 31 July, 16 August, 30 December 1841 (Black Letters);
Gipps to La Trobe, 11 February 1841 (La Trobe Papers).

TWO APOSTLES OF
CHRISTIAN CIVILIZATION

Edward Stone Parker
*Photograph in Castlemaine Art Gallery and
Historical Museum*

William Grant Broughton
*Copy of portrait by William Nicholas,
Mitchell Library, Sydney*

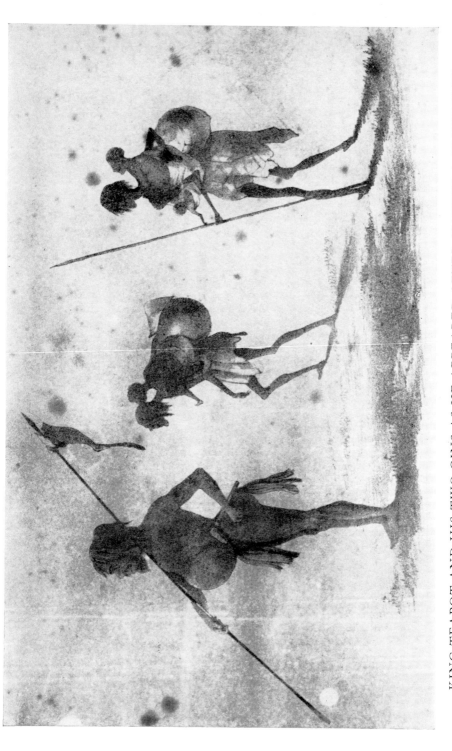

KING TEAPOT AND HIS TWO GINS AS HE APPEARED AFTER HAVING A TIGHTENER

Drawing by T.B., 1833, Mitchell Library, Sydney

use witnesses who were disposed to make free with the truth. He should never intimidate an opponent (Willis was very light on self-knowledge). All court officers should display forbearance towards each other, perseverance and that charity which strengthened them to endure all things. He believed that the justice of God and the good of mankind were laws written on the breasts of every man, and men should avoid anything, such as drunkenness, that rendered them capable of evil and depravity.

Yet he also believed that a judge should wield the power of punishment with such a black aspect and red eye that he struck terror into the hearts of the guilty. If in a moment of excitement, intensified by swallowing quantities of strong drink, a man 'passed a joke' with a female, Willis gaoled him for two years. When the aborigine Bonjon came before him in September 1841 on a charge of murder, Willis was at great pains to find out whether the accused understood the significance of his behaviour and was capable of deciding he had committed a crime. He was found not guilty. When three aboriginal women and two men came before him in December of the same year charged with the murder of two sailors at Port Fairy, Willis relished the role of the punishing judge when the time came to pass sentence on the two men whom the jury found guilty. He told the two guilty men, Bob and Jack, two Vandemonian aborigines 'God's fool' G. A. Robinson had brought with him from Flinders Island, that their pain would be greatly increased because they lacked the consoling hope of their crime being pardoned in the hereafter by means of true repentance and the mercy and forgiveness of Almighty God. The light of Christianity, the only rational piety, he said, had glimmered for a moment in their minds, but not long enough to illuminate by its calm splendour their journey through a world of misery and to direct them to a haven of eternal rest. He regretted that the civilization the white man had generously bestowed on them had not been attended with salutary consequences. But since they were not ignorant of the ordinary laws of the British people it was proper for him to pronounce that they should be hanged by the neck until they were dead.

For days before the time set for the execution Bob was very dejected, while Jack sustained the most perfect indifference. On 20 January a sobbing and moaning Bob and a placid Jack were brought to the foot of the scaffold in Melbourne before a crowd of four or five thousand laughing and merry white people who awaited the awful scene as though it were a bull fight or a prize ring. Twenty aborigines perched on the branches of the neighbouring trees. Jack never once flinched. Bob was stupefied with terror. The Reverend Mr Thomson persuaded Bob to express his conviction that he should suffer divine wrath for the murder he had committed. Jack held his tongue. The Reverend Mr Thomson prayed to God to look down with mercy on His two creatures: after all, they were part of the potter's clay. The executioner later told the gentlemen of the press, 'Jack hung beautiful'. So ended the first execution of aborigines in Port Phillip for murdering white men who, as the *Port Phillip Herald* pointed out, had 'never given them any offence'.

At the same time Judge Willis continued his warfare in court so fanatically that one observer likened him to a kangaroo perched upon the stump of a tree surrounded by a pack of yelping, biting dogs at which he used to snap and snarl in return, and when one of them would approach too near, the 'old man' would give him a claw or a hug which he would have reason to remember. Afterwards the judges in Sydney, the Attorney-General and others in high places suggested to Gipps that the joke had gone on long enough, and Gipps informed Stanley in October 1842 that the Resident Judge was afflicted with an infirmity of temper which, notwithstanding his varied requirements and acknowledged talents, went far to unfit him for the calm and dispassionate administration of justice. By then it was clear that Willis was one of those men in whom the slightest suspicion of a challenge to his authority or an outrage to his vanity was followed by a rush of blood to the head and a display of hysterical rage. G. Arden, the journalist, and Redmond Barry, the barrister, two young men of talent, had been special victims of his tendency to 'hit below the belt'.[42]

Caught as they were between two worlds—the old convict society which was crumbling all around them and the new free immigrant society which was struggling to be born—they clutched at any remedy to solve the labour shortage. In June 1841 His Excellency the Governor suggested to the Legislative Council the possibility of having recourse to the services of the aboriginal natives to supply the prevailing want of labourers in all agricultural and pastoral operations. The Council's immigration committee decided to inquire into what practical success had so far attended the employment of aborigines. They sent out a questionnaire to the employers of labour in rural districts. The replies from the Port Phillip District reflected the temper of the times. William Ogilvie of Merton told the committee that the only way to keep an aborigine as a worker was to cut off his big toes so that he could not climb the trees for possums. Physically fit aborigines only needed two hours' labour every day to collect their food. Why should they exchange that way of life for the white man's drudgery? They were not fools. They were not prepared to work as labourers for the same reason that English gentlemen were not labourers—they lived without working just as comfortably as they wished. Like Diogenes, the aborigines had nothing but contempt for the amenities of

---

[42] Gipps to Stanley, 13 October 1842, *H.R.A.*, I. xxii. 320-3; for the formal complaint against Willis from the three judges, the formal complaint against him by the Attorney-General, and a petition to the Queen from the people favourably disposed to Willis, see encls in Gipps to Stanley, 24 September 1842, C.O. 201/323; G. B. Vasey, 'John Walpole Willis', *Victorian Historical Magazine*, vol. I, 1911; Jillian Raven, John Walpole Willis in Port Phillip (thesis, Department of History, Australian National University); La Trobe to Gipps, 26 July 1842 (Gipps-La Trobe Correspondence); *Port Phillip Gazette*, 18 September 1841; Case Books of Judge Willis (Book 12, Willis Papers, Royal Historical Society of Victoria, Melbourne); Memoranda Book of Judge Willis, ibid.; speech by Judge Willis to close legal term, 9 July 1842 (Willis Papers); address by Judge Willis at close of trial of Bob and Jack (Willis Papers); *Port Phillip Herald*, 21 January 1842; Susan Adams (Weston Bate, ed.), *Liardet's Water-colours of Early Melbourne* (Melbourne, 1972), no. 14, 'The First Execution'.

life and all those trappings of civilization the white man created by his labour. They were the naked philosophers of the Australian bush and saw no reason to exchange their way of life for membership of a degraded class in the white man's society. As a sign of the edgy mood of the times, the clerk of the Legislative Council ordered that Ogilvie's replies not be included in the published proceedings of the committee on immigration.[43]

By February 1842 Niel Black was telling his friends in the United Kingdom that what with the assistant protectors, the thieving by the aborigines, the commercial depression and the low moral character of shepherds and stockmen Port Phillip was 'a land of troubles'. Men who were not restrained by Black's faith that a wise and loving God had made all manner of men to dwell on the face of the earth were mumbling that all this palaver of the assistant protectors about 'common humanity' only encouraged the blacks to commit more outrages, for they were cunning enough to see that such 'mealy-mouthed spouters of benevolence' and of texts such as 'He that hateth his brother abideth in death' were just too squeamish to practise the necessary blood-letting on the plains of Australia Felix. By the end of 1841 La Trobe had lost the little faith he had ever held in the capacity or the desire of the aborigines to become sons of Britain. He told the Colonial Secretary of New South Wales that he could detect no steady inclination in the aborigines to attach themselves to a homestead or to a reserve managed by one of the assistant protectors. In the aborigines there was some incurable malignancy which explained all the butchery of man and beast which stank in the nostrils of civilized men. In the towns of Melbourne white women lived in fear of being outraged by the aborigines. As a woman was coming to town from Heidelberg in December 1842, carrying a bundle in her hand, she was met by two lubras who attempted to snatch the bundle from her. The woman screamed for assistance, whereupon the two lubras cracked her head open with a waddy and made off. From the country there were reports of the revolting savage customs of the aborigines, how they ate the flesh of the dead, how they disembowelled the dead, how they placed a dead body of one of their people in a tree, and waited till a worm fell out of it, after which they journeyed in the direction in which the worm pointed till they met another hostile tribe one of whom was instantly sacrificed and devoured under the impression that they were responsible for the death of the deceased member of their own tribe.[44]

Confessions of failure became the order of the day. The missionaries George Langhorne and the Reverend Benjamin Hurst had lost all hope of winning the aborigines for Christ. Down at Birregurra the Reverend Francis Tuck-

[43] Replies by W. Ogilvie to questions circulated by Select Committee on Immigration, June 1841, minute by N. Macpherson on that reply (Aborigines Papers, MS. in M.L.).
[44] *Sydney Herald*, 14 February, 2 March, 24 May 1840; Niel Black to T. S. Gladstone, 9 February 1842 (Black Letters); La Trobe to Col. Sec. of New South Wales, 28 June 1841 (Chief Secretary, Letters Outward, 13 November 1840 to 1 July 1841, V.S.A.); *Port Phillip Herald*, 6 December 1842.

field saw no hope of stopping the frightful slaughter of the aborigines by the white men, and began to wonder whether it was part of God's plan that these 'least of the little ones' should disappear off the face of the earth. One golden autumn morning in May 1842, one of those days on the Barwon Downs calculated to gladden the heart of any man who believed that putting the fingers in God's soil secured a man from the evil in the human heart, he found to his dismay that there was not a single black man left on his station at Birregurra. Wondering whether he had been unworthy of God's trust or whether such failure was part of the design of an inscrutable Providence, he wrote to his brother in Christ in London, 'our present mission is a complete failure'.[45]

That same month of May Charles Joseph La Trobe finally decided something must be done about Assistant Protector C. W. Sievewright, who was in very bad odour with the settlers from Geelong to Glenormiston and even as far west as Portland. Respectable people were cutting him on all occasions and not allowing him to enter their houses. The gossips passed on the rumour that as long ago as 1838 he had seduced Mrs Parker, the wife of his fellow assistant protector. Some even hinted that the man had practised darker deeds of moral infamy—that he had copulated with his own daughter, with the aborigines and God as witnesses of his degradation. Those who did not put on such black looks when their neighbour behaved in ways that were displeasing to them accused him of supplying fire-arms to the aborigines. Robinson accused him of neglect of duty. On 3 June Gipps decided to suspend Sievewright from his position as assistant protector not just for his general inefficiency but because of reports injurious to his moral character. After six years of paper warfare, with Sievewright protesting his innocence, and Robinson and La Trobe showing neither mercy nor forgiveness, Gipps's successor, Sir Charles FitzRoy, told Earl Grey that Sievewright was 'totally unworthy of his Lordship's future notice'.[46]

When those reports that the blacks were further than ever from morality and civilization and closer than ever to extermination reached London, Lord Stanley, in language befitting the tragic grandeur of the occasion, solemnly told the Governor of New South Wales that he still hoped he would come forward with a plan that would enable both government and society to acquit themselves of the obligations they both owed to a 'helpless race of beings'. He was not prepared to admit that nothing could be done, that with respect to the aborigines of New Holland the doctrine of Christianity must be

---

[45] F. Tuckfield to J. Kenny, 20 May 1842 (copied into Journal of Francis Tuckfield, MS. in LA TROBE L.); cairn to commemorate the founding of the Buntingdale Mission by the Rev. Francis Tuckfield, August 1839, at Birregurra, personal visit to site, 19 February 1972.

[46] G. A. Robinson to La Trobe, 9 July 1842, November 1847 (Robinson Papers, vol. 57A); C. W. Sievewright, answers to questionnaire on employment of aborigines (Aborigines Papers, MS. in M.L.); *Port Phillip Gazette*, 14 March 1840; *Sydney Herald*, 6 April 1840; FitzRoy to Grey, 14 March 1848 (transcript of missing despatches from governors of New South Wales, 1847-55, MS. in M.L.); P. Corris, *Aborigines and Europeans in Western Victoria*, ch. 6.

inoperative and the advantages of civilization incommunicable. He was not prepared to admit that aborigines were innately incapable of improvement or that they would be extinguished by the advance of the white settler. For his part he was still willing and anxious to co-operate in any arrangement for their civilization that might hold out a fair prospect of success. But although those riders in God's chariot, Parker, Thomas and Le Soeuf, had not given up hope either for the victory of civilization, or the preservation of the aborigine, fewer and fewer shared their faith that the natives of Australia Felix had any inclination to abandon their own way of life and become sons of Britain.[47]

In the commercial world, matters continued as bad as ever. In the first half of 1842 several business houses closed their doors. The ceaseless attacks by the savages forced Niel Black to the conclusion that the Port Phillip squatter was 'worse off than the veriest serf in Russia', because in Russia the white men at least enjoyed the protection of government against savages while here they had to guard against a people who could never be won by deeds of kindness. In late October a public meeting was held in Melbourne to consider means of relieving the existing commercial depression. The economic crisis gave an edge to the agitation for separation from Sydney, as both in Melbourne and Portland papers such as the *Port Phillip Patriot* and the *Portland Guardian* charged those wicked men in Sydney with arbitrarily disposing of public funds for the aggrandizement of the seat of government in Sydney. But in this, too, their hopes were shattered, for despite the promising use of the title 'Lt. Governor of Port Phillip' in Lord John Russell's despatch on the aborigines at the end of 1840, Lord Stanley in September 1842 only conceded one of their two demands in the separation petition of 1840. He agreed to the right of Melbourne and the right of the District to elect members to the Legislative Council, but did not agree to their separation from New South Wales or their erection into a separate province.[48]

In grief and anger they denounced the failure of the British Government to release them from their thraldom. Some wrote that they were 'utterly disgusted with the rank injustice of the Home Government'. Others quickly made Sydneysiders the villains who had thwarted their chances of building a society that would echo faithfully their country and origin. Even here there was often a gap between desire and capacity. On 1 December on a day when the brightness of the day gave promise of good things for mankind, the

---

[47] [George Arden], *Latest Information with regard to Australia Felix* (Melbourne, 1840), pp. 97-9; Stanley to Gipps, 20 December 1842, *H.R.A.*, I. xxii. 439. This part of the story of the relations between the aborigines and white men should be written by a man or woman with the gift Rilke detected in Ibsen. See R. M. Rilke, *The Notebook of Malte Laurids Brigge* (2nd ed., London, 1950), pp. 76-9, quoted in M. Meyer's monumental third volume of his biography of Ibsen. See M. Meyer, *Henrik Ibsen, the Top of a Cold Mountain* (London, 1971), pp. 340-2.

[48] Bells and Buchanan to G. Russell, 1 February 1842, quoted in P. L. Brown (ed.), Clyde Company Papers, vol. 3, p. 174, and G. Russell to W. Cross, 10 September 1842, ibid, p. 240; Niel Black to W. Steuart, 18 June 1842, and Niel Black to T. S. Gladstone, 5 August 1842 (Black Letters); Russell to Gipps, 25 August 1840, *H.R.A.*, I. xx. 776; Stanley to Gipps, 5 September 1842, *H.R.A.*, I. xxii. 238-43.

property owners of Melbourne took part in the election of Melbourne's first municipal council. On the surface it looked like a local government election in an English provincial town. Flags waved over the polling booths, supporters of the various candidates pinned ribbons on the lapels of their coats, and candidates liberally handed out refreshments to the burgesses. After the declaration of the poll the successful candidates in the various wards were cheered and borne off to their respective residences. With nightfall the excitement subsided, leaving in the streets dilapidated fragments of electioneering placards as the only sign of the tumult and anxiety of the day. On the surface it all looked very English, but there had been ugly scenes. At an election meeting at the Adelphi Hotel a fight broke out which put an end to all decorum. Lights were turned off and pandemonium reigned. Within a few weeks colonial backbiting and character assassination reminded observers that in this first exercise of the birthright of Englishmen standards of conduct had slipped. John Pascoe Fawkner was telling his readers that one of the elected councillors, John Stephen, who was regularly to be seen walking the streets of Melbourne with a lubra on his arm in 'open and shameless disregard of the law of God and man', now associated politically with J. J. Peers, the leader of the Methodist Church Singers, and one of the main props of Methodism in Melbourne. La Trobe was so shocked to have no 'infusion of people of the higher order' as councillors that he believed the auguries for popular government were unfavourable.

At the same time Samuel Pratt Winter at Murndall, Edward Henty and his brothers and all their wives at Muntham, George Russell at Golf Hill, Niel Black at Glenormiston, Thomas Learmonth at Ballarat, and most of the other eighty-odd run-holders in the Port Phillip District struggled to erect that society of country squires and landed gentry who were tied by the nexus of the market and by sentiment to English things, not knowing that in the country that had put such a picture in their hearts the railway, the steamship, the factory, and the electric cable were dealing a death-blow to country gentry, and not foreseeing that the wool they shipped directly to Liverpool was speeding up the development of industrial civilization. For they were both the creators and grave-diggers of their own type of society. In their eyes the rolling country from Coleraine to Casterton was the Sussex Downs of the Antipodes, and the land round Koroit like those parts of Ireland in which the Protestant ascendancy had enriched English landlords. They did not sense that that huge sea, over which Batman had ridden to his damnation, and Edward Henty to his glory, and the spirit of the place were indifferent alike to both winners and losers in the human lottery, indifferent, too, to the success of the white man in putting his mark on the land, and to the terrible price the aborigines paid for their failure to resist the invader.[49]

[49] *Port Phillip Patriot*, 1, 5 December 1842, 2 January 1843; *Port Phillip Herald*, 25 November 1842; Gipps to La Trobe, 30 December 1842 (Gipps-La Trobe Correspondence); J. C. King, *Acts of Council relative to the Corporation of Melbourne and Geelong* (Melbourne, 1850).

7

A GRAND CENTRE
FOR AN AUSTRALIAN CIVILIZATION

WHILE THE INHABITANTS of Port Phillip were laying the foundations of a society they hoped would be English for thousands of years, the people in the other districts of New South Wales were also caught up in a debate on their destiny. Some accepted the Wentworth vision of 'A New Britannia in another world'. Some pointed out that just as America had received her language, her manners, her literature and the germs of her laws and political institutions from the British Isles, so too had Australia. They also predicted that just as America at length outgrew the trammels of national juvenility, so too at some far distant period would *Terra Australis* become too wealthy, too powerful and too enlightened to need the leading strings which now held her. They predicted that New South Wales would become the grand centre of a new civilization in the South Seas. By contrast, others, who were put off by the appearance of the place, predicted that since the land was cursed so were all those who were overwhelmed by its vast indifference to all man's hopes. In January 1836 the English naturalist Charles Darwin was so appalled by the 'useless sterility' of the country around Sydney, and so disenchanted by the 'extreme uniformity in the character of the vegetation' during a journey to Bathurst, by the open woodland covered with a most thin pasture, and the bark of trees hanging dead in long shreds which swung about with the wind, making the woods appear desolate and untidy, that when he left the shores of this country two months later, he said he did so 'without sorrow or regret'.[1]

Each Christmas the recent immigrants bemoaned all those 'absent things' which caused an exile to make that simple utterance of despair, 'It b'ant like home'. For here there were no palaces, no castles, no manors, no old country houses, no parsonages, no thatched cottages, no ivied ruins, no cathedrals, no abbeys, no universities, no great public schools, no Oxford, no Cambridge, no Eton, no Harrow. What single building or institution did Australia possess connected with art or science worthy of the name? Where was the

[1] Nora Barlow (ed.), *Charles Darwin's Diary of the Voyage of H.M.S. Beagle* (Cambridge, 1933), entries for 12 January, 14 March 1836; C. Darwin to J. S. Henslow, January 1836, published in Nora Barlow (ed.), *Darwin and Henslow: the growth of an idea* (London, 1967), pp. 112-14; Barron Field, 'The Kangaroo', *First Fruits of Australian Poetry* (Sydney, 1819); W. C. Wentworth, *Australasia: a poem* (London, 1823).

'counter charm' in Australian life and countryside to compensate for what had been left behind? Were the bright light and a 'belly-full' adequate substitutes for those things the absence of which was giving Australia the reputation of being a cultural desert? Was Australia to be a country like America in which there was 'no shadow, no antiquity, no mystery, no picturesque and gloomy wrong, nor anything but a commonplace prosperity in broad and simple daylight', which would produce painting, literature or music of its own?[2]

Each year on 26 January, the anniversary of that day when the aborigines had hollered in vain at the coming of those convict ships to Sydney Harbour, the native-born took the opportunity to affirm their faith in New South Wales as a future grand centre of civilization. In 1838 this day was a very special occasion, marking as it did the fiftieth anniversary. Yet for the native-born the day had its paradoxes and uncertainties. It began with the followers of the various Christian persuasions gathering at their respective churches to render thanks to Almighty God for all the benefits they had received at His hands. At St James's Church the Anglicans heard the Lord Bishop of Australia, William Grant Broughton, preach an excellent sermon. There was much about the Lord Bishop to endear him to his people. He had served them long enough (ten years) to resent any slurs on their honour. In public he could be quite genial over a glass of wine. Yet the native-born eyed him as a man who did not belong in their great river of life. They loved to have a 'hit' at the Lord Bishop for the stand he had taken against the liberal tendencies of his age. They were out of sympathy with the excessive concern he seemed to show for rank and station. Why did the man warn them to beware lest Presbyterians and dissenters made republicanism triumphant, or papists enslaved all Protestants to their spiritual and political despotism? There was something incongruous, too, in the fervour with which he sang those hymns which breathed the very essence of the Old World, something false in singing lugubriously those words

> Abide with me; fast falls the eventide;
> The darkness deepens; Lord with me abide!

in a country distinguished for its garish sunlight and inhabited by a people most of whom were strangers to the metaphysical yearnings of the Old World. When Broughton preached a very judicious sermon on anniversary morning on the present state and future prospects of Australia, he dwelt on the prevalent vices in the community and the indifference to religion, and told the congregation that only those to whom God was the Lord and for whom immorality was a reproach could be considered truly happy. The

[2] *New South Wales Register*, April 1828, no. 3, pp. 198-200; H. James, *Nathaniel Hawthorne* (Edinburgh and New York, 1967), pp. 55-6; N. Hawthorne, *The Marble Faun* (New York, 1859), preface; H. Parkes, 'My Native Land', poem in *South Australian Magazine*, January-February 1841.

Reverend Ralph Mansfield expressed similar sentiments to his congregation in the Wesleyan Church, and the Reverend John Saunders preached the virtues of respectability to a most respectable congregation in the Baptist Chapel.[3]

On the same morning the Roman Catholics gathered at the church on the hill to hear John Bede Polding, Bishop of Hiero-Caesarea *in partibus infidelium* and Vicar Apostolic of New Holland, Van Diemen's Land and the adjoining islands, tell the faithful of the prize of eternal salvation for those who kept the image of Christ alive in their hearts. Wherever he went Polding shed an aura of sanctity. His face was lit by a kindly smile and his whole being radiated sweetness and charm. His hair was silvery. The sentiments he expressed seemed to match the suggestion of spirituality, as though Agape had triumphed over Eros in him. His large and loving heart recommended peace and forbearance to all and a wide and embracing sympathy, not just for what was high and good, but especially for all those who were in any way afflicted or distressed in mind, body or estate. He spoke of Christ's love and compassion for those 'helpless creatures', those 'denizens of the forest'—the Australian aborigines. He laboured hard to divest himself of all that was imperfect and fallen in human nature to render himself like that previous being who had once walked beside the waters of Galilee. Yet although he was no stranger to the patriotic sentiments in the hearts of the native-born and indeed since 1834 had been teaching his flock to be proud of being Australians, inwardly, like Broughton, he thought of the country as 'spiritually the most destitute of the British dominions', and of its people as being 'very wicked'. The very unworldliness of the sentiments he recommended to his congregation was also in collision with the tendencies of his age. In an era of 'this-sidedness', in an age in which men equated material well-being with happiness, Polding spoke like a voice from the past rather than a man leading his people along the paths of their choice. The world and its business, he had stated in his pastoral instructions for Lent in 1837, was occupying the place in men's hearts that God alone should occupy. As a sovereign remedy against vice, blasphemy, violation of the sanctity of marriage, and that monster of drunkenness which daily sacrificed its victims to Hell, he urged people to repent, to make a perfect reconciliation with God, to meditate on the great truths of Death, Judgement, Hell and Heaven, and to deny all ungodly desires. For him sin was the great cause of all temporal and spiritual miseries, and the sacraments of the church the only means of releasing man

<hr>

[3] *Sydney Herald*, 29 January 1838; *Sydney Gazette*, 7 June 1836; G. Nichols, Notes on Bishop Broughton (MS. in M.L.); *Sydney Standard and Colonial Advocate*, 2, 9 September 1839; *Sydney Herald*, 4 January 1838; W. G. Broughton to Bourke, 29 April 1837 (Twenty Two Letters from Broughton to Bourke 1836-7, MS. in M.L.); the summary of Broughton's state of mind is based on his letter to E. Coleridge, 6 February 1838 (letter of W. G. Broughton to E. Coleridge, microfilm in NAT. L.); see also the text of his sermon preached at an ordination service in St James's Church, Sydney, 23 September 1838, in which he referred to the contribution of dissenters to the decay of faith, B. Harrison (ed.), *Sermons on the Church of England . . . by . . . William Grant Broughton* (London, 1857), pp. 168-82; *Colonist*, 31 January 1838.

from captivity and the power of iniquity. For him death was the door of life, which reunited men with those whom they had loved but saw no more. His thoughts went 'up'; the thoughts of men of his age went 'down'. An angel with a vision of God's throne was trying to lead men whose only concern was the 'here and now'.[4]

The one clergyman capable of presenting that day a picture of the future of the people of Australia was the Reverend J. Dunmore Lang, the incumbent of Scots Church in Sydney. He had returned to Sydney the preceding December confident, as he put it, that his fellow-minister McGarvie and his drunken party would be 'dead now and forever'. For God or chance had planted a destroying angel in the heart of his chosen servant. Yet Lang had ideas. By 1838 he was looking forward to the day when the people of Australia established a republican government for themselves and elected a president of the Australian states. He had no doubt that Australia's destiny was not to be tied like a child to its mother's apron strings, but always took care to add that no one of any pretensions to common sense in New South Wales ever dreamed of its speedy realization, much less desired it. For Lang, like all the other stoopers before the throne of grace, had too lofty an idea of the role of divine providence in human affairs, and too deep a conviction of man's total depravity to believe in his capacity to create 'better things'. Besides he had been long enough in Sydney for some to suspect that he had created Jehovah in his own image, that the Almighty was his own private God who justified everything the good doctor did, and punished all who thwarted his projects, sometimes with quite unpardonable cruelty.[5]

Outside the churches, with their gloomy talk of man's unworthiness and the punishments for human wickedness, the people gathered to celebrate the day in the bright light of the sun. The newspapers on that day exhorted them to take pride in the achievements of Australians. A piece of music entitled the 'Australian Jubilee Waltz' was composed by Thomas Stubbs to commemorate the occasion, and since it was the work of a native musician the press believed it would meet with the liberal encouragement of the colonial public. For in their eyes the ability of Australians and their achievements were the talking-point of the occasion. Fifty years earlier barbarism of the most wretched and degrading description desolated their land. Now, instead of savages and beasts roaming this gloomy land, there were civilized human beings. Vessels capable of cruising every ocean had replaced the frail and clumsy canoes of the aborigines in the harbours. Australia now contained the germ of a wonderful and extensive empire. The regatta at Sydney Harbour that afternoon emphasized this confidence of the people in themselves and in their future.

---

[4] Letters of H. Elliott, 10 August 1849 (Elliott Papers, MS. in M.L.); J. B. Polding, *The Pastoral Instruction for Lent* (Sydney, 1837); *Sydney Herald*, 29 January 1838; J. B. Polding to Father President of Benedictine Order, 29 January 1834, and J. B. Polding to G. Phillips, 19 July 1860 (Polding Letters, Catholic Archives, St Mary's Cathedral, Sydney); notes on life of J. B. Polding (Catholic Archives, Sydney).

[5] A. Gilchrist, (ed.), *John Dunmore Lang* (2 vols, Melbourne, 1951), vol. I, pp. 82, 226.

A party of Australians hired a ship appropriately called '*Australia*', and unfurled the flag of the native-born to deafening and enthusiastic cheering, and there was talk among the onlookers of a day, not far off, when that flag would be seen in every port of the world as the emblem of an independent and powerful empire. Significantly, a 'boisterous progeny of Watt' puffed steam into the limpid air, giving promise of their progress as a people into the age of steam, the iron rail and the electric telegraph. Surely such ardour and such patriotism were sufficient to rescue their names from ridicule and contempt. Great Britain must surely be proud of such an infant offspring.

At night crowds thronged the streets of their illuminated city. Forty gentlemen, the cream of the native-born, sat down to the traditional anniversary dinner to drink their toast to 'the land, boys, we live in'. But that night no speaker rose to the majesty of the occasion. The chairman G. R. Nichols, the son of a convict who, like Simeon Lord and Samuel Terry, Daniel Cohen and Solomon Levey, had made a fortune in New South Wales, spent his time apologizing modestly for not being able to say what the occasion demanded. W. C. Wentworth, who some fifteen years earlier had put down on paper his rallying cry to all those who had 'Australasian hearts', to all those for whom 'Dear Australasia' was their 'Mother Earth', had stopped going to anniversary dinners the previous January, a step which had caused his erstwhile cronies to hold him up to scorn as a one-time patriot who was now howling and frothing for the conservative cause like a rabid bulldog. Charles Harpur, Charles Cowper and James Martin were still too young to take their place on the stage of public life. The toasts symbolized their divided hearts. They toasted the Queen and the royal family and the land of their fathers, while the band played 'God Save the Queen', followed by 'Hearts of Oak'. They also toasted the sister colonies while the band played 'Hail Australia'. They drank to the Sons of Australia while the band played 'The Honey Moon'. Then they drank to the Sons of Saint George, Saint Andrew and Saint Patrick while the band played 'Green Grow the Rushes, O'. So the night ended without either young or old dreaming the great dream of an Australian Shakespeare or an Austral Milton soaring with the daring of an eagle in the sky, or men, like Prometheus, stealing fire from heaven and becoming 'Good, great and joyous, beautiful and free!' What touched them was the speed of their advance, that from Adam downwards there was not another single instance of such an advance.[6]

Before a month was out, on 24 February, the civil and military officers, the Chief Justice, the Bishop of Australia, the Bishop of Hiero-Caesarea, the members of the Legislative Council, Lang, Wentworth, McLeay, G. R. Nichols and others on the Government House visiting list crowded into Government House to welcome Sir George Gipps as Her Majesty's Captain-

[6] Based on *Sydney Herald*, 29 January 1838; *Colonist*, 27 January 1838; *Monitor*, 29 January 1838; *Australian*, 19, 26, 30 January 1838; for Wentworth's attitude to the anniversary dinner in January 1837 see vol. 2, pp. 245-6, of this history; concluding speech by Demogorgon in Shelley's *Prometheus Unbound*.

General and Governor-in-Chief in and over the colony of New South Wales and its dependent territories. Sir George had about him that day the air of a man who believed that intercourse with the mass of humanity was not part of his duty as an officer and a gentleman. He was tall and spare, with the stance of a self-confident man and a mask over his face to prevent his mind's construction being scanned by his fellow-men. He was then just forty-seven years of age. Born in 1791, the son of a clergyman, he had been educated at King's School, Canterbury, and the Royal Military Academy at Woolwich before taking up a career in the army. There he discovered that administration was the great passion of his life. On that day when the corn fields of Waterloo were trampled in the great fight while women prayed in Brussels and the 'dauntless English infantry' were repelling the charges of the French, Captain George Gipps was busy with his paper work at Ostend. In the next twenty years he so distinguished himself for his liberal, fair-minded, if somewhat Whiggish reports on sundry subjects that he was promoted to the rank of major, given a knighthood and the offer to succeed Sir Richard Bourke who had performed his duties with so much credit to himself and so much advantage to His Majesty's service. Soon after he arrived in Sydney he confided to a woman that he spent sermon time in church drafting despatches to London. His industry was prodigious. He rose at six and worked for the rest of the day, leaving only the briefest time for hurried meals. Though he prayed each morning and each night that no vulgar rage should disturb his calm in public life, those close to him soon learned to go in fear of that moment when Sir George savaged them for presuming to disagree with him. He took refuge in hard work, prayer and the encouragement of a wife who had a woman's insight into those humiliations of an upbringing in a family of the genteel poor which had driven the handsome Sir George into a 'close' man who could not trust anyone to handle the most trifling affair without his assistance and advice. A sensitive, vulnerable man had come to preside over a society enslaved to vulgar passions, to extravagance, violence and barbarism.[7]

Protestants wrote of the priests of the Catholic Church as 'spruce gentlemen who spent their time closetted with females'. Catholics wrote of Pro-

[7] *Sydney Gazette*, 27 February, 8 March 1838; *Sydney Herald*, 26 February 1838; *Colonial Times*, 19 December 1837; Lady Franklin to Sir John Franklin, 21, 27 May, 15 June 1839 (Franklin Letters, MS. in NAT. L.); Ruth Knight, *Illiberal Liberal: Robert Lowe in New South Wales 1840-50* (Melbourne, 1966), pp. 27-8; Diary of Lady Franklin kept on journey from Port Phillip to Sydney, 1839, 19 May 1839 (typescript in NAT. L.); S. Sidney, *The Three Colonies of Australia: New South Wales, Victoria, South Australia: their pastures, copper mines, and gold fields* (2nd ed., London, 1853), pp. 111-12; S. C. McCulloch, 'Unguarded comments on the administration of New South Wales, 1839-46', *Hist. Studies*, vol. 9, 1959, p. 42; R. Therry, *Reminiscences of Thirty Years' Residence in New South Wales and Victoria* (London, 1863), pp. 308-13; J. D. Lang, *An Historical and Statistical Account of New South Wales* (2 vols, 3rd ed., London, 1852), vol. 1, pp. 297-9; Marnie Bassett, *The Hentys* (London, 1954), pp. 495-501; for Gipps as a 'close' man and a hard worker see J. C. Blackett to J. Dobson, 6 December 1838 (Blackett Letters, Allport Collection, T.S.A.); N. D. Hill (ed.), *Our Exemplars* (London, 1860), p. 224; W. M. Thackeray, *The Works of William Makepeace Thackeray* (22 vols, London, 1869), *Vanity Fair*, vol. 1, p. 365.

testants as pharisees who went to their temples to thank their God that they were not as other men, when the only god the Protestants worshipped was Mammon. The press was filled with vulgar abuse of public men and their rivals rather than a fair-minded discussion of the issues of the day. The *Australian* accused the *Colonist* of 'gorging too voraciously its natural food of hatred and uncharitableness'. The *Colonist* retorted that their man was far too thick-skinned to be 'kill't . . . with a little dirty water squirted at him' from a printing establishment. The *Colonist* branded the *Sydney Herald* as 'that pure merino and high Tory establishment'. The *Sydney Herald* snapped back that if anyone saw a fellow comfortably tipsy in the streets of Sydney, he could set him down for a Whig at once. It was as though the press knew its reading public fed ravenously each week on mockery and malice. Scarcely a week passed without digs at the two patriots Sir John Jamison and W. C. Wentworth as fathers of bastards and drunken sots. When the gentle William Cowper appealed to the youth of Australia to take away the reproach of intemperance from their native land, the drinkers retorted that they failed to see why the ears of females should be polluted by the squeamish nonsense of 'penitent sweeps and draymen fresh from the delights of delirium tremens'. It was typical of the pompous Alexander McLeay, whose eyes were specially moistened on public occasions by the waters of loving kindness, to take the chair at a temperance meeting, because everyone in Sydney knew that if McLeay had a chance to revise the Lord's Prayer he would add the words 'Give us this day our daily clap'. Some said it was to be expected that a society built out of a 'pack of D----- convicts' and their descendants would breed public men who behaved as though they had been nurtured in a sewer.[8]

Yet when news reached Sydney in May 1838 that London was being told the people of New South Wales had taken a vast portion of God's earth and made it into a cesspool, great indignation swept over the public. A meeting was held on 25 May at which Gipps was asked to do something to remove the 'erroneous insinuations' and to persuade the British Government to use the money raised from the sale of waste lands on a more efficient system of immigration that would enable New South Wales to capture the wool market of the world and become at no distant period the most useful appendage, if not the brightest ornament, of the British Crown. For the insult to the public's honour did not fan the flames of any independence movement but rather encouraged their protestations of loyalty. It did not occur to anyone at that meeting that a stigma of inferiority was an ineluctable consequence of their colonial status. When Gipps brought the request before the Legislative Council, the landed magnificoes, dependent as they were on cheap convict labour for their opulence and their splendour, were quick to see the connection between repudiating the slur on their national honour and retaining the convict system. Bishop Broughton helped them all to feel confident in themselves. He solemnly assured them that, notwithstanding the filth with which

[8] *Sydney Herald*, 4, 25 January, 1, 3, 8 March, 21 May 1838; *Australian*, 2 February, 20 July 1838; *Colonist*, 27 January, 28 February 1838.

they were surrounded, there was a solid foundation left on which they would build a superstructure that would be an ornament to the Mother Country. Hannibal Macarthur, employer of some assigned servants, was understandably certain that this was not a degrading community. Sir John Jamison, the squire of Regentville at Penrith, who knew that the high living so dear to his heart was made possible in part by the labour of the assigned convicts on his grazing runs, naturally enough thought it a 'most judicious plan to assign convicts to settlers' and, stranger though he usually was to moralizing, added that a great reformation had already taken place in the inhabitants of the colony. Alexander Berry, the squire of Coolangatta on the Shoalhaven, an employer of some one hundred convicts on his 10 000-acre estate, had a month earlier written to England telling how a country of savages had been colonized by convicts, and that on the new roads of New South Wales travellers met hundreds of drays carting wool or stores for the landed gentry. He was a man who was proud of his part in fashioning industrious agricultural workers out of British thieves, and told them that colonists could not do without convict transportation and that convict labour was far better than the drunken persons who had been thrown into the colony by the immigration system. As he saw it, the transportation system had the advantage of a degree of control over the worker that could not be exercised over the immigrant, that great exploiter and abuser of freedom.[9]

On 17 July 1838 the Legislative Council adopted twelve resolutions on the convict system. They concurred in the opinion expressed at the public meeting —that the character of the colony, insofar as the social and moral condition of its inhabitants was concerned, had unjustly suffered by the misrepresentations put forth in certain recent publications in the Mother Country, and especially in portions of the evidence taken before a committee of the House of Commons. They went on to assert that the numerous free immigrants of character and capital, together with a rising generation of native-born subjects, constituted a body of colonists who, in the exercise of the social and moral relations of life, were not inferior to the inhabitants of any other dependency of the Crown and were sufficient to impress a character of respectability upon the colony at large. Then after pats on each other's backs for contributions to the advancement of 'Virtue and Religion', they resolved that in their opinion no system of penal discipline or secondary punishment would be found at once so cheap, so effective and so reformatory as that of well-regulated assignment, the good conduct of the convict and his continuance at labour, being so obviously the interest of the assignee, whilst partial solitude and privations incidental to a pastoral or agricultural life in the remote districts of the colony, by effectually breaking a connection with companions and habits of vice, was better calculated than any other system of punishment to produce moral reformation when accompanied by adequate

---

[9] The texts of the two petitions are printed in the *Sydney Herald*, 26 May 1838; Gipps to Glenelg, 18 July 1838, *H.R.A.*, I. xix. 504-5; *Sydney Herald*, 4 June, 11 July 1838; *Australian*, 6, 20 July 1838; A. Berry to E. Wollstonecraft, 12 April 1838 (Berry Letters, MS. in M.L.); see also Some Aspects of the Berry Papers (typescript in M.L.).

religious instruction. They also established a connection between the survival of assignment and the success of assisted immigration. If convict labour were suddenly withdrawn, the means of the colonists to purchase Crown lands would be curtailed, and consequently the supply of funds for the purposes of immigration. The produce of the labour of convicts in assignment was thus one of the principal though indirect means of bringing free persons into the colony. Obviously, therefore, the continuance of immigration in any extended form must necessarily depend upon the continuance of the assignment of convicts.

Outside the Council the *Sydney Herald* accused the landed magnificoes of New South Wales of plunging into a sea of absurdity. They suggested that those who voted for the resolutions should have the fairness to append to them a list of the convicts each possessed. The *Colonist* warned its readers that the resolutions were designed to perpetuate an aristocratic type of society of large land-holdings giving a large revenue to their proprietors in return for a small expenditure of human labour. What was needed in the colony, they said, was a virtuous middle class which would sustain religious, philanthropic and educational institutions, because otherwise Australia would become like Ireland, with a Protestant landed aristocracy and a working class of convicts enslaved in mind to Romish priests.[10]

It was such a dry year that from Australia Felix to the Riverina, the Monaro, the Bathurst Plains, Patrick's Plains and the Liverpool Plains, the growth of vegetation had almost completely stopped. It was that year of drought when those savages near Wangaratta rushed on George Faithful and party with shouts, savage yells and a shower of spears, and George used his rifle to make them bite the dust so that they might notice what sort of stuff the white man was made of. Up at Inverell whenever stockmen gathered for a yarn over a quart-pot of tea or something stronger there was talk of the need to wipe out the 'black bastards'. On 9 June, led by a 'clean skin' named John Fleming, the son of a local squatter, eleven of the 'felonry' of New South Wales arrived at the Myall Creek bush hut on Henry Dangar's squatting run and told the shepherd George Anderson, a prison worker, that they were going to tie together with a rope any aborigines they caught, take them over the hill and frighten the daylights out of them. A few minutes later Anderson heard shots. Two days later, after an unsuccessful search for more aborigines, the party of white men piled together the bodies of the men, women and children they had slaughtered on a heap of timber and threw a fire-stick on it.

Some days later when William Hobbs, Dangar's manager on the Myall Creek run, returned to the hut and saw the charred remains of twenty-eight bodies of men, women and children, he told Charles Kilmaister it would be his duty to report the crime to the police magistrate at Muswellbrook. Now Kilmaister was Irish, a succumber to the madness in the blood, only to be tormented by the dread of damnation and the great 'doom's image', while

[10] Resolutions on the Systems of Transportation and Assignment, *V. & P.* (L.C. N.S.W.), 18 July 1838; Gipps to Glenelg, 18 July 1838, *H.R.A.*, I. xix. 504-5.

Hobbs was English and not a man to be swayed by extravaganzas of fear and remorse. Kilmaister went down on his knees before him and begged him for Jesus Christ's sake not to do it, but Hobbs told him he must report the crime. So off he went on the 250-mile journey on horseback over the Liverpool Plains to Quirindi and Muswellbrook where he reported what he had seen to Captain Edward Denny Day, a magistrate of wisdom, justice and mercy, a clergyman's son from Ireland, with huge appetites for the traditional pleasures of the landed gentry, the chase and the bottle, and an affection for the lower orders provided they kept the place man and God had allotted to them. He was to live on in that early bush song 'Billy Barlow'. He decided to pass on what he had heard from Hobbs to the Colonial Secretary, Edward Deas Thomson, who in turn asked Gipps whether twelve white men should be charged with the wilful murder of twenty-eight aborigines.[11]

For days Sir George went through terrible anguish of heart and mind. Though his sympathies had not been moved by seeing the plight of those helpless people, the aborigines, for he had spent his days since his arrival 'in the closet' slaving away at *paperasserie* rather than becoming acquainted with the land and its people, he was a paragon of obedience to those in authority. The problem was that if he obeyed his superiors in London he might antagonize the landed proprietors of New South Wales. Glenelg had told his predecessor Bourke of the importance government attached to the life of a native, and also of the anxious attention of government to the better protection and civilization of the aborigines. In obedience to those instructions he had drafted in April a Government Notice to be published on the measures to be pursued in cases of the death of blacks by violence. In it he urged upon the colonists the solemn nature of their obligations towards that race by which he and they were all bound, as men and as Christians. 'As human beings, partaking of one common nature, but less enlightened than ourselves', the Notice continued,

> as the original possessors of the soil from which the wealth of the colony has been principally derived, and as subjects of the Queen, whose sovereignty extends over every part of New Holland, the natives of the whole territory have an acknowledged right to the protection of the government, and the sympathy and kindness of every separate individual . . . In disputes between aborigines and whites, both parties are equally entitled to demand the protection and assistance of the law of England. To allow either to injure or oppress the other, and still more to permit

---

[11] *Sydney Herald*, 16 July, 1 August 1838; *Australian*, 24 July 1838; *Colonist*, 21 July 1838; T. F. Bride, (ed.), *Letters from Victorian Pioneers* (Melbourne, 1898), pp. 150-4; A. Harris, *Settlers and Convicts* (London, 1847), pp. 382-400; *A Full and Particular Report of the Trial of Eleven Men* (Glasgow, 1839), copied from *Sydney Gazette*, 15 November 1838; Gipps to Glenelg, 21 July 1838, *H.R.A.*, I. xix. 508-11; B. W. Harrison, The Myall Creek Massacre and Its Significance in the Controversy over the Aborigines during Australia's Early Squatting Period (thesis, History Department, University of New England); B. W. Champion, 'Captain Edward Denny Day', R.A.H.S., *J. & P.*, 1922, pp. 345-57; Captain Day is referred to in verse 6 of 'Billy Barlow', D. Stewart and N. Keesing (eds), *Old Bush Songs* (Sydney, 1957), pp. 53-5; personal visit to Myall Creek site, 25 August 1969. Now the Faculty of Rural Science of the University of New England has a research station on the site where Kilmaister and his men were driven on by the madness in the blood. The bull-frogs still croak and the crows still continue their search for carrion.

the stronger to regard the weaker party as aliens, with whom a war can exist, and against whom they may exercise belligerent rights, is not less inconsistent with the spirit of that law, than it is at variance with the dictates of justice and humanity.

So in accordance with those principles and in obedience to Her Majesty's Government Gipps was pleased to direct that on every occasion of a violent death occurring among the aborigines wherein any white man was concerned or supposed to be concerned, an inquiry was to be held by the nearest coroner or magistrate in exactly the same manner as inquests or inquiries were held when the deceased were Europeans or white men.[12]

That was in April. By July Gipps was still refraining from publishing the notice on account of the degree to which the public mind continued to be exasperated with the blacks because of the outrages they had committed against the whites. By then the settlers outside the boundaries were asking him either to levy war against the blacks or sanction the employment of a militia for that purpose. Gipps decided to ask his Attorney-General, John Hubert Plunkett, for advice on what to do. Plunkett had just turned thirty-six. Born in Ireland into an old Catholic family he had arrived in Sydney in June 1832 with his wife and sister to take up the position of Solicitor-General. He was the first Catholic to hold a high office in Australia. In February 1836 he had succeeded to the office of Attorney-General when John Kinchela was forced to retire because of deafness. Some dismissed him smartly as 'the archetype of immaculate inanity and respectable humbug'. Others noticed that though he was decidedly liberal in his political opinions, he was somewhat diffident in the expression of them, since his eloquence was not of the first order. The possessor of a highly cultivated mind, a great honesty of purpose, and an energy and firmness which commanded respect, a great sadness descended on his face when he on the violin and his wife on the piano played Beethoven's Kreutzer Sonata, for she was barren and looked like a woman in whom the springs of life were drying up. His great passion was to introduce equality before the law and liberty of religion for all men in New South Wales. By 1838 he had been the driving force in extending such equality to emancipists. Gipps's request gave him the chance to suggest that the same equality before the law should be extended to aborigines.

As soon as Plunkett had persuaded Gipps that in disputes between aborigines and whites both parties were equally entitled to demand the protection and assistance of the law of England, Gipps ordered Captain Day to proceed from Muswellbrook to Myall Creek with a party of mounted police to inquire

[12] Glenelg to Bourke, 26 July 1837, *H.R.A.*, I. xix. 49; encl. in Gipps to Glenelg, 27 April 1838, C.O. 201/272; for the discussion of these issues by the Executive Council of New South Wales see the minutes of the Council of 25, 30 April, 22, 26 May 1838 in Col. Sec. Correspondence 4/1013 (N.S.W.S.A.); see also Statement of the Principal Outrages Committed By, or On, the Aboriginal Inhabitants of New South Wales . . . Since 26 April Last, ibid.; on 25 April Gipps minuted 'That white men are entitled to protection nobody doubts—the object of the notice is to prove that blacks are too', minute of 25 April, ibid.

into what had happened and to collect evidence in order to bring the offenders to justice. After an absence of some fifty-three days Day reported back to Gipps that he had captured eleven of the twelve persons known to have taken part in the massacre, that these eleven had all arrived in the colony as convicts and that the free man John Fleming, a native of the colony, had escaped. The squatter's son lived on; the eleven members of the convict community faced the possibility of death. The Attorney-General formally charged the eleven on four counts with the murder of an aboriginal black named 'Daddy', and on five counts for the murder of an aboriginal black name unknown.[13]

The land-holders and stockmen of New South Wales were incensed. Up on Patrick's Plains a meeting, chaired by Robert Scott, formed a Black Association to raise money to buy the best legal brains for the defence of the white men. They predicted that the blacks would become more outrageous and that great numbers of them would fall victim to the white man whose vindictiveness would be kindled by such abominations. Down in the pot-houses of Sydney people laughed at the absurdity of putting white men on trial for the murder of men little higher in the scale of creation than monkeys. The *Sydney Herald* said that white men had been driven to the extremity of murder because of the supine government in Sydney, whose 'sympathies and charities were exclusively excited by the possessors of an Ethiopian visage'. They in turn were only acting for 'the gaping idiots' and the 'old ladies' at home who in a mood of 'maudlin sympathy' had conceived the mad idea of the protectorate. Just to prove they had not completely gone overboard on the question of equality of white and black, Gipps and Plunkett passed through the Legislative Council that September a revision of the bill regulating the sale and consumption of fermented and spirituous liquors in New South Wales, which made it an offence for a publican to serve fermented liquor to an aborigine in a quantity which produced intoxication. The Act, it was hoped, would reduce those disgraceful states in which aborigines were to be seen after being supplied with intoxicating liquors. On the principle that white men could be tried for the murder of black men they stood firm.[14]

---

[13] Gipps to Glenelg, 21 July 1838, *H.R.A.*, I. xix. 508-11; D. H. Deniehy to H. Parkes, 28 November 1856 (Parkes Papers, MS. in M.L.); A. Halloran, 'Some early legal celebrities', R.A.H.S., *J. & P.*, 1924, pt 10, pp. 169-98; Gipps to Glenelg, 19 December 1838, *H.R.A.*, I. xix. 700-4; R. H. W. Reece, The Aborigines and Colonial Society in New South Wales before 1850 (thesis in library of University of Queensland); depositions before E. D. Day at Myall Creek (Muswellbrook Bench Book 1838-42, N.S.W.S.A.); depositions before E. D. Day at Newton's Station, 14, 15, 28, 30, 31 July, 2, 3, 6, 8, 14, 15, 20, 21, 22, 24, 25, 27, 30 August, 10 September 1838 (Muswellbrook Bench Book, MS. in M.L.).

[14] *Sydney Herald*, 21 June, 27 July, 10 September 1838; Gipps to Glenelg, 20 December 1838, *H.R.A.*, I. xix. 704-6; Section 49 of An Act for Consolidating and Amending the Laws Relating to the Licensing of Public Houses, and for Further Regulating the Sale and Consumption of Fermented and Spirituous Liquors in New South Wales, 2 Vic., no. 18, 26 September 1838, T. Callaghan, *Acts and Ordinances of the Governor and Council of New South Wales* (2 vols, Sydney, 1844), vol. I, pp. 183-4; *V. & P.* (L.C.N.S.W.), 3, 11, 13, 26 September 1838.

On 15 November the Chief Justice, James Dowling, and a jury of twelve accused eleven white men of being instigated by the Devil and wilfully murdering an aboriginal black named Daddy, and an aboriginal black name unknown at Myall Creek on 10 June. George Anderson, the assigned servant hut-keeper for Mr Dangar at Myall Creek, told the court what had happened on that day when the twelve white men roped the aborigines together. He told the court that the blacks cried for assistance, and moaned as a mother and children would cry, that there were 'small things' that could not walk, and that Daddy and another old man named Joey were crying. He told how he had heard two shots, how later Edward Foley, son of one of the accused, showed him a sword which was covered with blood, and how on the day after the slaughter three of them took fire-sticks out of the hut. After hearing other evidence, the Chief Justice solemnly told the jury it was quite clear that a most grievous offence had been committed; their duty was to decide whether the accused were the men who had committed that offence. He charged them to remember in their deliberations that in the eye of the law the life of a black man was as precious and valuable as that of the highest noble in the land. The gentlemen of the jury took twenty minutes to decide the accused were not guilty. The spectators in the court cheered. Within a week one member of the jury was telling his friends, 'I look on the blacks as a set of monkeys, and I think the earlier they are exterminated the better. I know well they are guilty of murder, but I, for one, would never consent to see a white man suffer for shooting a black one!' The *Sydney Herald* raved on about the prevalence of cannibals in the land, and sets of monkeys, while the *Australian* and the *Colonist* urged their readers to take a more magnanimous stand.[15]

Plunkett asked for the prisoners to be remanded so that they could be charged with murdering the women and children. He decided to lay the information of murdering an aboriginal child named Charley against seven of the prisoners (Kilmaister, Hawkins, Johnston, Foley, Oates, Parry and Russell) and give the other four (Palliser, Lamb, Toulouse and Blake) an opportunity to give evidence on behalf of the seven accused should they wish to do so. On 27 November, with the *Sydney Herald* spluttering angrily that the court should not allow white men to be put in peril of their lives for every jaw-bone, thigh-bone, finger or toe the scouts of the Attorney-General might ferret out, the seven men were charged before Judge Burton and a jury of twelve. Counsel for the defence raised legal objections whether there was sufficient certainty in the description of the aboriginal child Charley and whether men could be charged again for an offence for which they had already been acquitted (the plea of *autre fois acquit*). After the judge discussed those two pleas the trial began on 29 November and lasted till 2 a.m. the following

---

[15] *Australian*, 12, 15 January 1839; *A Full and Particular Report of the Trial of Eleven Men*; Gipps to Glenelg, 21 July 1838, *H.R.A.*, I. xix. 508-11, and Gipps to Glenelg, 19 December 1838, ibid., 700-4; *Monitor*, 19 November 1838; *Sydney Herald*, 19, 28 November 1838; *Australian*, 23 October, 20 November 1838; *Colonist*, 31 October 1838; *Sydney Gazette*, 20 November, 11 December 1838.

morning when the prisoners were found guilty of murdering the child. They were remanded again so that the court might hear counsel for the defence again on a point of law. On 5 December, when this demurrer had received the solemn consideration of the three judges of the Supreme Court and been dismissed (the repetition of the plea of *autre fois acquit*), proclamation of silence was made and Judge Burton proceeded to pass sentence.[16]

In the colony at large Burton had a reputation for excessive pride in his station, an incurable infirmity of temper, and the delusion that his judgements were God's judgements. He was also known for his conviction that the law-lessness, abominations and outrages committed by prisoners of the Crown and emancipists outside the limits of location were the fruits of godlessness. He believed himself to be called by God's providence to fill the office of a judge. He never presumed to undertake its solemn responsibilities without constantly asking from the giver of every good gift for those qualities which were necessary for its just exercise. He never sought the praise of men. He spoke that day as a man for whom religion was the leading principle of his life. This was the sentence he proclaimed to those seven frightened men:

> You have been found guilty of the murder of men, women and children, and the law of the land says, whoever is guilty of murder shall suffer death . . . This is not a law of mere human convenience which may be adopted or rejected at pleasure according to the conventional usages of society, but it is founded on the law of God, given at the earliest period of scripture history when there were only a few people on the face of the earth . . . I cannot expect that any words of mine can reach your hearts, but I hope that the grace of God may reach them, for nothing else can reach those hardened hearts which could surround that fatal pile, and slay the fathers, the mothers and the infants . . . You burnt the bodies for the purpose of concealment, but it pleased God to send a witness to the spot before they were entirely consumed . . . I feel deeply for the situation in which you are placed, whatever may have been the motives by which you were stimu-lated . . . that you had not the fear of God before your eyes but were moved and reduced by the instigations of the devil . . . I cannot but look at you with com-miseration; you were all transported to this Colony, although some of you have since become free; you were removed from a Christian country and placed in a dangerous and tempting situation; you were entirely removed from the benefit of the ordinances of religion; you were one hundred and fifty miles from the nearest Police station on which you could rely for protection . . . [and] by which you could have been controlled. I cannot but deplore that you should have been placed in such a situation . . . that such circumstances should have existed; and above all . . . that you should have committed such a crime. But this commisera-tion must not interfere with the stern duty, which, as a Judge, the law enforces on me; which is to order that you, and each of you, be removed to the place whence you came, and thence to a place of public execution, and that at such time as His Excellency the Governor shall appoint you be hanged by the neck until your bodies be dead, and may the Lord have mercy on your souls.[17]

[16] *Sydney Herald*, 26 November, 3, 7 December 1838; *Sydney Gazette*, 11 December 1838; Gipps to Glenelg, 19 December 1838, *H.R.A.*, I. xix. 702-3.

[17] *Australian*, 26 March 1839 (see esp. the letter of W. Burton to M. C. O'Connell and others of 7 March 1839, quoted in that issue); *Sydney Herald*, 7 December 1838.

On 7 December the Executive Council unanimously agreed that the sentence of the law should take effect. Three petitions for mercy were presented to Gipps. The *Sydney Herald* went on vilifying the aborigines as that most degenerate, despicable and brutal race of beings who stood to shame the whole human race. The *Sydney Gazette* wrote that very little more dependence could be placed upon the verdict of a jury than upon the tossing up of a dice, whenever political feelings or political interests were involved. On 14 December Gipps told the petitioners that he did not feel he could consistently with his public duty pay regard to them. The seven men maintained that they found it extremely hard that white men should be put to death for killing blacks. On the morning of 18 December the four Anglicans were escorted by their two chaplains and the three Catholics by their chaplain to the scaffold, where that unfortunate hot-hearted man Kilmaister seemed deeply dejected. All shook hands with the gaoler and kissed each other, resigned themselves and 'were speedily launched into eternity'. Or so the reporter in the *Colonist* hoped. The *Sydney Gazette* reminded their readers that these men had gone to meet the reward of an Almighty God, for in the mind of the sound Calvinist editor of that paper, God was unlikely to show mercy. The other four were set free early in 1839, Blake for lack of sufficient evidence, and Toulouse, Lamb and Palliser because the only aborigine who could testify against them was not sufficiently instructed in the ordinances of religion to understand the nature of an oath.[18]

The terror of black against white, and white against black, redoubled in fury. Some said Gipps and Plunkett had planted in the minds of aborigines the idea that in their deeds of retaliation they were acting with the sanction of public authorities. Down at Portland Bay a black man caught red-handed carving up a bullock, saucily told a white man, 'If you touch me, the Gubbna will hang you'. The execution of seven white men only served to make the blacks so outrageous that great numbers of them fell victims in 1839 to the vindictive spirit kindled in the hearts of white men. As the wilder blacks were incited into more and more deeds of violence to the property of settlers, the shepherds, hut-keepers and stockmen shot them with no more compunction than they shot a dog. The more ruffianly and ferocious among the whites got rid of troublesome aborigines by poison. Again the settlers raised their old cry: give us protection, or there will be a bloody war of extermination; send men with guns, because that is the only way to bring the aborigines into submission. The missionaries, such as Threlkeld, Tuckfield, Hurst, Langhorne, and Williams, redoubled their efforts to win these 'mischievously bent . . . sable creatures' for Christ and civilization, but nothing they could do could efface from the mind of the aborigine the simple fact that the white man had deprived him of his land. Why should he adopt the religion or the way of life of a people who had done him such evil?

The massacre and its aftermath were a reminder that the spread of settle-

[18] *Sydney Gazette*, 11, 18, 20, 24 December 1838; *Sydney Herald*, 8, 10 December 1838; *Australian*, 16 February 1839; *Colonist*, 19 December 1838; Gipps to Glenelg, 19 December 1838, *H.R.A.*, I. xix. 703-4.

ment was fatal to the black man, that wherever white men flourished, black men decayed or died. That forced the white man in New South Wales, just as similar events forced the white man in Western Australia and South Australia, to ask the fundamental question: had the white man usurped the right of the aborigines to the land of New Holland, and deprived them of their possessions by force? The members of the Aborigines Protection Society said they had, but they were as a voice crying in the wilderness. The decision-makers of Sydney, like Charles Mann in Adelaide, were just as sure of the white man's right to the land as they were of their own existence. As they saw it, the aborigine had bestowed no labour on the land, and so their right to the land was no more than that of the emu or the kangaroo. Only labour on the land could bestow a right of property in it. Who would dare to assert that the great continent of Australia was ever intended by the Creator to remain an unproductive wilderness? Which was basically what it would have remained but for the labour of civilized man. The British people, they argued, found a portion of the globe in a state of waste and they took possession of it under the divine authority by which men were commanded to go forth and people the land and subdue it. The title of the settlers to their respective lands was as good as that of any land-holder in England. Whatever the white man did for the protection, support and improvement of the aborigines was not part of his duty as their expropriator, oppressor or destroyer, but an act of charity. Charles Harpur wrote 'An Aboriginal Mother's Lament' about the one black woman at Myall Creek who had escaped the white man's vengeance. It described the ejaculations of the mother after watching white men slaughter her people like cattle. But the sentiments of a young man of fine conscience affected but little the attitude or behaviour of white people.[19]

It had been a dry year. Down on the Murrumbidgee at Jugiong and Gundagai, where ten years earlier the eyes of the handsome Charles Sturt had moistened with pleasure on seeing such a beautiful country, sheep and cattle were crawling to dried-up water-holes. At the suggestion of the clergy Sir George Gipps declared Sunday 2 November 1838 to be a national day of fasting and humiliation on account of the drought. On that day, before a capacity congregation at St James's Church, Broughton besought God to look down upon his unworthy servants who were suffering the chastisement of their offences, and assuage their sufferings by sending them moderate rain and showers. At Scots Church John Dunmore Lang told his congregation that national sins had provoked divine punishment. After rain fell in Sydney on 4 November, an influenza epidemic broke out. Lang then told his people that because they had not been sufficiently grateful to God for his mercy and had not sufficiently humbled themselves under His afflictive dispensation, God

[19] A. Harris, *Settlers and Convicts*, pp. 398-9; P. P. King to board of directors of Australian Agricultural Company, 10 October 1839 (Company In-Despatches 78/1/16, Australian National University Archives); *Sydney Herald*, 7 November, 26 December 1838; *Australian*, 3 January 1839; S. H. Roberts, *The Squatting Age in Australia 1835-1847* (Melbourne, 1935), p. 408; Gipps to Glenelg, 20 December 1838, *H.R.A.*, I. xix. 704-6; Charles Harpur, An Aboriginal Mother's Lament (Harpur Papers, MS. in M.L.).

3   The Main Settlements of New South Wales and Van Diemen's Land

had been pleased to 'pour with that cup of mercy a few drops from the vial of his indignation and wrath'.[20]

While Broughton and Lang were busy with their chastising God, Mr Bourke in Sussex Street, Sydney, was manufacturing a steam-engine by copying an American model. In January 1839 two shops were brilliantly lit by gaslight, a promise that the time was not far distant when the streets of Sydney, like London, Paris, New York and Vienna, would be lit up by gas-light. In January some were predicting the time was not far off when a portion of the labouring population of Great Britain would be conveyed to the ports of New South Wales in steamships which would make the journey in two months. That January there was talk of the introduction of a general system of education in the colony in which the minds of the children would not be stuffed with the absurdities and superstitions of antiquity but would be filled with knowledge to equip them for the task of building a grand new centre of civilization in the Antipodes. Australians were to be known in the portals of human fame not just as the men who built bush huts where previously there had been cannibals and possums, but as men who had made a distinctive contribution to the conversation of mankind.[21]

In 1838 and 1839 the voices of a young generation of native-born Australians began to be heard in the land. As long ago as 1823 Mr Commissioner Bigge had penned those words about the appearance and behaviour of the currency lads—how they were unusually tall in person and slender in their limbs, of fair complexion and small features, how they were capable of undergoing more fatigue and were less exhausted by labour than native Europeans, how they were active in their habits but remarkably awkward in their movements, how in their tempers they were quick and irascible but not vindictive, and how their fathers, unlike colonists in other British possessions, regarded New South Wales as their future home. Four years earlier that English exile J. H. Bent had told the Select Committee on the State of the Gaols that the convicts believed the colony belonged to them and their descendants and not to free settlers or immigrant workers from the Mother Country. By 1825 Peter Cunningham, a convict ship's surgeon, who spent two years in New South Wales, noted how the slang phrases of St Giles in London such as 'plant' and 'swag' were becoming legitimated in the colony, how the dross of the English language in London was passing off as genuine here and how the currency youths were adopting an 'unenviable peculiarity of ingrafting a London mode of pronunciation on to their own colloquial dialect of the English language'. By 1835 visitors were noting that native-born Australians could be easily recognized as different from persons born 'at home' by the

---

[20] W. G. Broughton, *A Form of Prayer with Fasting* (Sydney, 1838); Psalm 77, v. 9; for part of what was in the mind of Broughton at the end of 1838 see W. G. Broughton to E. Coleridge, 25 February 1839 (Broughton Letters, photocopy in NAT. L.); A. Gilchrist, (ed.), *John Dunmore Lang*, vol. 1, p. 232.

[21] For the new steam-engine see *Sydney Herald*, 19 November 1838; for the Australian Steam Navigation Association see *Sydney Herald*, 26 June 1838; for a general discussion on education see *Sydney Herald*, 1 March 1838.

way in which they spoke, and how very strange that speech was. Visitors were noting, too, how certain features of the climate, especially the heat of the sun and the hot winds of summer, were fashioning the currency lads and lasses into 'hard-faced, grim-visaged, dry countenanced human beings on whom the bloom of youth quickly faded'. But except for the Wentworth poem 'Australasia' in 1823 and the occasional letters in the press, the currency lads had been reluctant to give the world a view of their hearts.[22]

Between 1834 and 1838 a tiny band of young intellectuals amongst the native-born, and the adopted members of the currency lads began to show what was in their hearts. By 1836 out of a total population of 77 096 not only did at least one half belong to the convict community, and so come under the influence of the idea that Australia belonged to them and their descendants, but for the first time there was a considerable body of young men and women reaching the age of discretion who were hungry for information on the land of their birth and resentful of those men in high places who stood between them and all hope of rising to the top in their own country. Both their spleen and their pride had been played on to some effect by Horatio Wills in his paper the *Currency Lad* which began publication in 1832. He wrote in his issue of 24 November 1832,

> Look, Australians, to the high-salaried foreigners around you! Beyond those men lolling in their coaches—rioting in the sweat of your brow—while you, yes, you, the Sons of the Soil, are doomed to eternal toil—the sport and ridicule of pettifogging worldlings . . . your children shall imbibe from the breasts that suckle them the all-absorbing desire of revenge—and look, with eager expectation, to the day when their numerical strength will justify them in declaring, 'We were not made for slaves'.

A week later Horatio Wills apologized to the Europeans, as distinct from the currency lads, for his intemperate words which were composed while recovering from a powerful emetic. For that extravagance of abuse when excited by strong drink, followed by grovelling before the Englishmen, and begging his forgiveness when overwhelmed with remorse and guilt were to be a recurring pattern of behaviour with the Australian nationalists.[23]

In 1838 there were more revelations of what went on in the hearts of the native-born when James Martin published *The Australian Sketch Book*.

---

[22] J. T. Bigge, Report of the Commission of Enquiry on the State of Agriculture and Trade in the Colony of New South Wales, *P.P.*, 1823, x, 136, pp. 81-2; Evidence of J. H. Bent to the Select Committee on the State of the Gaols, *P.P.*, 1819, vii, 575, p. 125; P. Cunningham, *Two Years in New South Wales* (2 vols, London, 1827), vol. 2, pp. 52-5; J. Dixon, *Narrative of a Voyage to New South Wales and Van Dieman's Land* (London, 1822), p. 46; G. Bennett, *Wanderings in New South Wales, Batavia, Pedir Coast, Singapore and China* (2 vols, London, 1834), vol. 1, pp. 331 2; A. Harris, *Settlers and Convicts*, pp. 12-14; R. Howitt, *Impressions of Australia Felix* (London, 1845), p. 118; H. W. Haygarth, *Recollections of Bush Life in Australia* (London, 1848), p. 123.

[23] Population figures and estimates of proportions of convicts taken from R. Mansfield, *Analytical View of the Census of New South Wales for the Year 1841* (Sydney, 1841); *Currency Lad*, 24 November, 1 December 1832.

Martin was an Australian by adoption since he arrived in Sydney in 1821 before he reached the age of one. He said about his book that it was 'the first literary production that has ever emanated from the pen of an individual educated in Australia'. Unlike those mighty men of renown, those Dutch navigators of the seventeenth century, who had concluded that there was little good to be done here, and unlike most of the visitors and migrants from 1788 onward who found the landscape dreary, barren, inhospitable and forbidding, he loved Australia generally and Bondi Beach specially. He believed that Providence had destined Australia to be ranked high among the nations of the earth. He believed, too, that the sons of Australia were at some future period destined to become famous in the annals of the world and that her poets, philosophers and statesmen would become 'the Homers, Platos and Ciceros' of the Southern Hemisphere. Yet he was singularly ungenerous and lacking in charity in his comments on his Australian fellow-intellectuals. He sneered at them as men who had the infatuated presumption to imagine themselves endowed with colossal faculties and strove to put themselves upon a level with the master-spirits of mankind. He compared one of his fellow-intellectuals to 'a snarling, diminutive whelp, possessing more assurance and impudence than a mastiff, but not one tenth of its strength and dignity', one of those men who possessed 'the melancholy madness of poetry, without the inspiration'. For Martin, like the other intellectuals among the currency lads, was a victim of that Botany Bay disease which drove him to mock at his fellow-countrymen. A taste for mockery and a pleasure in fantasizing about taking the mighty down from their seat were among the unlovely fruits of colonialism—the subterranean satisfaction of putting into words what they lacked the resources or the conscience to put into deeds. In New South Wales nativism was a piling up of resentments in the heart, but it was not accompanied as it was in America by the threat, let alone the deed, of engaging in a war of extermination against the foreigner.[24]

The alcoholic boast, the aftermath of remorse, self-laceration and loathing, and that sense of impotence to destroy the sources of the inferior standing of the Australian in his own country were all deeply ingrained in Charles Harpur. He was born in Windsor on 23 January 1813, the son of a convict father and a convict mother. In his youth he entertained the hope that he would one day be hailed by his fellow-countrymen as an Australian Shelley, only to find to his dark, undying pain that when he risked 'showing his view' to the world, he was held up to ridicule as a 'pert-looking coxcomb' who had the irritating 'self-important strut' of the native-born Australian. He loved those gum-trees which Charles Darwin and other Europeans looked on as 'miserable-looking trees that cast their annual coats of bark, and presented the appearance of being actually dead'. He praised them as objects of 'incomparable beauty'. While the raw immigrant pined for civilization, he could see no reason to prefer the dingy gloom of a London street to the 'exhilarating

---

[24] J. Martin, *The Australian Sketch Book* (Sydney, 1838), pp. vii, 35, 149-50, 180; *S.M.H.*, 5, 8 November 1886; for American nativism see the article on nativism in *Galway Mercury*, 8 November 1844.

summer aspect' of Sydney. Nor was he willing to concede that Australian butter, milk, horses, sheep, cattle or women—especially women—were in any way inferior to anything elsewhere in the world. As for gin, then 'Give me Cooper's', for that, like everything else produced in Australia, was quite 'unsurpassable'. Or so he believed.

As a colonial lad who had grown up free from the Old World social constraints, Harpur was wary of systems that threatened to reduce all men to a 'dead social level' and impose 'a regimented sort of unity', emasculating them 'of all personal free will and consequently of all true moral glory'. For that reason alone he shrank from the utopian socialists with their grandiose schemes of human harmony. He also sensed that there was something in the spirit of the place which inclined a man to the view that things would always be the same as ever, out in the Never Never. This conviction of man's impotence in the presence of nature in all its might, majesty and power, and of the impotence of the native-born Australians to remove their badges of inferiority and shame, left him a fatalist and a pessimist on the human situation. Yet paradoxically he denounced the whoring, gambling and drinking that had characterized the behaviour of the previous generation which had clothed itself in a mantle of Australian patriotism. He called them a 'set of profligate scoundrels' and the 'very Solomons of immorality'. For the Australian nationalist learnt his morality from the prophets of the Old Testament rather than from those philosophers of ancient times who had handed on to mankind the advice not to put on black looks with their neighbours when they behaved in a way displeasing to them. Harpur's life ethic as a young man was to stand firm to his faith in God and to tell his contemporaries that any life-path which led a man away from God must lead him astray. For himself, he was prepared to accept God's world and to believe that in that world 'nothing wrongly supervenes/And nothing vainly tends'. At the end of 1839, unable to endure any longer the sense of being despised and rejected in Sydney, and surviving the wound to the heart inflicted by a woman's cruel gossip that he was a hopeless drunkard, he set out for the Hunter River district.[25]

By then that spirit of optimism which had persuaded papers such as the *Colonist* to allot space to articles on the importance of a national literature and to quote with approval the remark by W. E. Channing that 'it would be better to admit no books from abroad, than to make them substitutes for our own literary activity' was beginning to fade. When William à Beckett, a 'new chum' member of the Bar in Sydney, lectured on poetry that year at the School of Arts, Richard Jones, a merchant, a land-holder and a member of the Legislative Council, one of those 'sheepish men' in Australia who spent their lives 'wool gathering' and 'money gathering', casually remarked in Council that lectures on poetry were a somewhat useless expenditure of public

25 J. Normington-Rawling, *Charles Harpur, an Australian* (Sydney, 1962), pp. 64-74; P. Cunningham, *Two Years in New South Wales*, vol. 2, pp. 56-8; Holograph Letters of H. Parkes, 1844-6 (MS. in M.L.); Charles Harpur, Poems in Early Life, see esp. 'Life Ethics' and 'The Hand of God' (Harpur Papers, MS. in M.L.).

money. He called for lectures on ship-building and general mechanical subjects. À Beckett, lapsing from that charity which he asked his God to graft in
his heart each Sunday, called Jones a 'brainless bigot'. On the surface it looked
like a confrontation between a colonial philistine and an old world representative of a higher culture. But à Beckett and what he stood for were an
outward sign of a great change that was taking place in eastern Australia. The
use of convict labour to exploit the material resources and to plant the rudiments of civilization over a vast area from Inverell in the north to Portland
in the south was coming to an end. The native-born had no sooner opened
their mouths to praise their country and their fellow-countrymen than another
invasion of the ancient, barbaric land began—the invasion of British migrants
who, like their counterparts in South Australia and Port Phillip, were
strangers to all those loves and longings, and hatreds and resentments seething
away in the hearts of native-born Australians.[26]

For a season people carried on unaware of the change. The members of
'high' society, the government officers and their wives, the members of the
'ancient nobility' of New South Wales, and the colonial landed gentry
continued not to know merchants; merchants with 'stores' continued not to
know merchants who kept 'shops', and shopkeepers had their own idea of the
distances to be observed between drapers and haberdashers, butchers and
pastry-cooks; citizens who drove in carriages did not choose to mingle with
tradespeople who only had gigs. In fashionable circles etiquette was studied
more closely than in London itself. Cards were ceremoniously left by ladies
and gentlemen who made 'calls'. If a lady made a 'call' she must not repeat
it until it had been returned on pain of being voted ignorant of due form.
The clergymen fared so well with what government put into their purses,
and handsome contributions to the 'plate' from their congregations that no
one, it was said, could mistake them for men 'belonging to Pharaoh's lean
kine'. They, too, drove in their carriages or rode around the town mounted on
handsome and well-groomed horses, the well-paid and well-fed moral policemen of the bond and the free in New South Wales. Successful emancipists
continued to overtop the free and respectable immigrants in the most osten-
tatious display of their wealth, which was said to be all the more glaring
because they were driven to avenge themselves for the 'touch me not' insolence of the untainted towards all members of the convict community. The
whole convict community—those in servitude, those set free from servitude,
their wives, their children, and their children's children—continued to be
poisoned by a silent, deep-rooted hostility to the free settlers and the 'bloody
immigrants'. To the alarm and disgust of the free, the convict community
gloried in their past and boasted of it. 'Thank God I'm not a bloody immigrant', they cried. 'Thank God I came out 'onorable'.

The free continued to accuse the convict community of spreading their
'leper-like ghastliness and deformity' over the whole of society. Drunkenness
was one of those evils. There were 224 licensed taverns in Sydney in 1837 for

[26] *Colonist*, 16 April 1838; *Sydney Herald*, 20 September 1839.

a population of twenty to twenty-three thousand in addition to the sly-grog shops. In the convict quarters of the town around the Rocks there was the 'incessant noise of fiddlers, tambours, haut-boys—the drunken song—the dissolute laugh—the heavy curse—the scream'. Filthy, swollen-faced wretches haunted the doors, and the very streets reeled and staggered with drunkenness, dissoluteness and debauchery. Some said the minds of the free were being defiled by continued contact with such people, that women were not taking the vows of matrimony but living as concubines to one lover after another, and that the very foundations of society—the institution of private property, the family, and the laws of God—were being set at defiance or laughed to scorn. Vice, it was said, was being inoculated in every class of people by contact with the convict population. What else, it was asked, could be expected from children who had convicts for fathers and prostitutes for mothers? In the country districts a ruffianly barbarous race of 'low roamers' wallowed for days in 'wild riots' in 'rum shanties' or wandered over the countryside as bushrangers or degraded the aborigines by boozing with the men and poxing the women.[27]

The native-born bitterly resented that picture of what European civilization had done to New South Wales. They were angry with Father W. B. Ullathorne for telling the Transportation Committee that there was sodomy in New South Wales; they were angry with the Reverend J. Dunmore Lang for calling the land they lived in 'a dung-hill of the Empire'. But by the beginning of 1839 to argue whether the charges were true or false was to be like Lot's wife: to look back, and not forward. For a great change was coming over the society of New South Wales. In 1837 the British Government had made up its mind that the assignment of convicts was a form of slavery with all the attendant evils of slavery, since it tended more to degrade the character both of master and slave than all the rest of the evils of the system of transportation. In May of that year Glenelg warned Bourke that Her Majesty's Government was preparing to put an end to the system of assignment in New South Wales. The following year Glenelg told Gipps that immigration would very soon supply the current demand for labour in the colony and that measures were in contemplation for the discontinuance of the transportation of convicts to New South Wales. On 15 August 1838 Gipps announced that the assignment of male convicts in Sydney and other towns of the colony would cease on 1 January 1839.[28]

The patriarchs of the Legislative Council had taken their stand on that issue

---

[27] Louisa Anne Meredith, *Notes and Sketches of New South Wales* (London, 1846), p. 52; P. Cunningham, *Two Years in New South Wales*, vol. 2, pp. 119-21; J. O. Balfour, *A Sketch of New South Wales* (London, 1845), p. 114; D. Mackenzie, *The Emigrant's Guide* (London, 1845), pp. 152-3; [James Ward], *Perils, Pastimes, and Pleasures* (London, 1849), pp. 209-11; J. C. Byrne, *Twelve Years' Wanderings in the British Colonies* (2 vols, London, 1848), vol. 1, pp. 224-32, 241-3; W. B. Ullathorne, *The Catholic Mission in Australasia* (2nd ed., Liverpool, 1837), pp. 29-30; *Sydney Herald*, 11 January 1842.

[28] *Australian*, 12, 15 January 1839; *P.D.*, 3rd ser., vol. 53, col. 1283; Glenelg to Bourke, 31 May 1837, *H.R.A.*, I. xviii. 765-6; Glenelg to Gipps, 16 November 1838, *H.R.A.*, I. xix. 679; *New South Wales Government Gazette*, 22 August 1838.

in July 1838. Now the leaders of the Patriotic Association summoned a public meeting for 8 February 1839 at which Wentworth, Jamison and Bland had no difficulty in persuading those present to accept the main point made by the patriarchs at the Council, namely, that the material and moral well-being of New South Wales depended on the continuance of transportation. They were like men shouting into a great wind. Everyone in Sydney gaped at the effrontery of Sir John Jamison discoursing on the improvement of morals when his own were so desperately in need of amendment, and the brazenness of Wentworth spouting the language of the supervisors of morals after spending his adult life walking down the primrose path of pleasure with the same reckless indifference to the finger-waggers as Byron had displayed during those giddy years in Venice. As for Bland, he was dismissed in Sydney as a man who was as ineffectual in public life as he had been in private life, and that was saying a great deal, because when his first wife had eloped as long ago as 1818 she had dropped a hint that at last she would be sleeping with a man. The Patriots had that air of men who were no longer moving with the river of life, but swimming against the current as it swept forward leaving them to rage at their own impotence to direct its future course.[29]

Men might make their own history, but colonials did not make theirs. The one chance they had of making their own history was to cease being colonial and declare their independence. Wentworth, who had advocated that state in 1819, now viewed it with dread because it would lead to a Yankee-style democratic republic with its depraved taste for equality and its vulgar tyranny of the majority. The alternative was to remain a British colony, which meant accepting immigrants and not convicts as their labour force. For nothing could shake the British decision that there was to be no more slavery and no more sodomy in New South Wales. By 1839 the evidence was there for all to see. The number of convicts arriving was tapering off—from 3425 in 1837 to 3073 in 1838 and 2293 in 1839. The number of immigrants arriving increased from 4275 in 1837 to 8840 in 1838 and 13358 in 1839. By 1839 the British Government had created a system for the sale of waste lands in the Australian colonies and for using the proceeds to assist with the passages of migrants designed to end once and for all 'the leper-like ghastliness and deformity of convict society and human barbarism in the Australian bush'.[30]

Like most 'systems' or 'designs' that historians have detected in mankind's past, this system of importing migrants acquired a semblance of reason after rather than before the event. It was designed in part to rectify those evils in the old system of land grants under which favouritism, nepotism and corruption had all flourished. It was designed also to end that more monstrous evil

[29] *Sydney Herald*, 11 February 1839; W. Bland, (ed.), *Letters to Charles Buller, Junior, Esq., M.P. from the Australian Patriotic Association* (Sydney, 1849); *Sydney Gazette*, 18 September 1828.

[30] A. de Tocqueville, *De la Démocratie en Amérique* (3 vols, Paris, 1874), vol. 1, preface and pp. 50-5, 144-53; Return of Immigrants and Convicts Arrived, and of Births and Deaths, in the Colony of New South Wales, From the Year 1837 to 1840, Inclusively, *V. & P.* (L.C. N.S.W.), 1841, p. 151.

of allowing cunning, talented and ambitious ex-convicts to accumulate wealth in land and to end the bush barbarism. In 1825 a nibble had been made at the problem by introducing a combined system of sale by auction, and a land board to reduce the scope for human frailty, error and mightiness of heart. On instructions from London, the Governor of New South Wales on 5 September 1826 defined the limits within which persons would be allowed to purchase land, or receive grants on paying an annual quitrent. On 14 October 1829 Governor Darling defined the boundaries of the nineteen counties within which settlers would be permitted to select land. In 1831 the Surveyor-General, Thomas Mitchell, published a map of the nineteen counties. In a series of despatches to Governor Darling in January and February 1831 the Secretary of State mentioned haphazardly a number of reasons for introducing a change in the disposing of Crown lands: any man given the power to grant land had an inhuman and ungracious task, land grants were designed to encourage the migration of capitalists, the interests of Great Britain and the colonists could now be best served by encouraging the emigration of labourers, and land grants had led to an 'extreme facility of acquiring land' which caused dispersion of settlement and increased the cost of administration. For all these reasons government had decided to replace the land grants system with auction sale at a minimum upset price of 5s per acre, the lands not sold to be leased to the highest bidder, and to call up arrears of quitrent owed by holders of land grants.[31]

On 1 July 1831 Darling published a notice in which he announced that it had been determined by His Majesty's Government that no land should in future be disposed of in New South Wales and Van Diemen's Land otherwise than by public sale and that all the lands in the colony within the limits of location not hitherto granted, and not appropriated for public purposes would be put up for sale at a price not below 5s an acre. Portions of land would be advertised for sale for three calendar months and would then be sold to the highest bidder, who must put down a deposit of 10 per cent upon the whole of the purchase at the time of the sale, and pay the remainder within one calendar month from the day of the sale. Land would be put up for sale in lots of 640 acres, but smaller lots might under particular circumstances be purchased on making application to the Governor in writing with full explanations for the reasons. On 1 August a supplementary Government Order provided that all free persons would be eligible as purchasers of land without any limitations as to quantity; that all military and naval officers would be entitled to a remission of payment of £300 for service of twenty

[31] Instruction for our Trusty and Well-Beloved Arthur Phillip . . . the 25th Day of April 1787, *H.R.A.*, I. i. 14; J. T. Bigge, Report of the Commissioner of Inquiry on the State of Agriculture and Trade in the Colony of New South Wales, *P.P.*, 1823, x. 136, pp. 13-17; Brisbane to Bathurst, 10 April 1822, *H.R.A.*, I. x. 630; J. D. Lang, *An Historical and Statistical Account of New South Wales*, vol. 1, pp. 207-9; Goderich to Darling, 9 January 1831, *H.R.A.*, I. xvi. 19-22; Goderich to Darling, 23 January 1831, *H.R.A.*, I. xvi. 34-8; Goderich to Darling, 14 February 1831, *H.R.A.*, I. xvi. 80-3; *Sydney Gazette*, 5 September 1826, 17 October 1829.

years and upwards, £250 for fifteen years and upwards, £200 for ten years and upwards, and £150 for seven years and upwards, provided they entered into a bond for £500 that they and their families would reside in the colony for at least seven years; and that all non-commissioned officers and privates discharged from the service for the purpose of settling in the colony would be allowed free grants—200 acres for sergeants and 100 acres for corporals and private soldiers. All Crown lands within the prescribed limits could also be let by auction at a minimum rental of £1 for 640 acres. The lands so let would be open for purchase and, in the event of their being sold, must be surrendered by the lessee on one month's notice. At the expiration of the year, the lease of each lot would be again put up to auction for the year ensuing.[32]

When the auctions of freehold and leasehold began in Sydney in the following year, observers and publicists wondered who would get the land, and what would be done with the money raised from such auctions. They had not long to wait for the answer to the first question. Just over 20 000 acres were sold in 1832, just over 29 000 in 1833, over 91 000 in 1834, and nearly 272 000 in 1835. By 31 August 1836 the total receipts from land sales amounted to £202 638. Everyone knew that most of this land had been bought by wealthy landed proprietors such as T. Icely and L. Macalister who bought land bordering their original grants to prevent it from falling into the hands of rivals. As for the use to which the money was put the colonists understood as early as the preceding July that government had a scheme to use the money to supply them with an 'abundance of cheap, honest and industrious labourers'.[33]

Again the word 'scheme' implied something more than those improvisations and compromises by which the British Government introduced payment of passages to certain categories of migrants between 1831 and 1835. It began in January of 1831 with Goderich informing the Governor of New South Wales that he had been so impressed with the demand for female servants that he had decided to send females from the Foundling Hospital at Cork. Eight months later he told Bourke that in consequence of the representations he had received from various quarters of the evils resulting from the great disproportion of the male to the female population in the colony, he had been led seriously to consider what means might be adopted for supplying the deficiency of females. His inquiries had convinced him that there were in England many young women, brought up to discharge the duties of servants in the families of farmers, but unable to gain an honest livelihood, who would gladly avail themselves of an opportunity of migrating. They had been deterred by the expense and the absence of a party to whom they could apply to make the necessary arrangements. To remove the former difficulty he had asked Their Lordships at the Treasury to sanction applying part of the terri-

---

[32] *Sydney Herald*, 11 July, 8 August 1831; *H.R.A.*, I. xvi. 850-1, 864-7.
[33] C. J. King, *An Outline of Closer Settlement in New South Wales* (Sydney, 1957), pp. 42-3; 'K. Buckley, E. G. Wakefield and the alienation of Crown land in New South Wales to 1847', *Economic Record*, vol. 33, 1957, pp. 80-96; *Sydney Gazette*, 14 July 1831.

torial revenue of the Australian colonies collected from the sale of land to assist in the payment of their passages. To meet the latter difficulty he had appointed a commission of five persons charged with the duties of facilitating such emigration. Goderich was anxious not to lose a favourable opportunity for turning towards the Australian colonies some portion of the emigration which had hitherto flowed almost exclusively to the colonies of North America. As a long-term method of payment he suggested that a tax be imposed upon settlers who used convicts. He hoped to raise £20 000 by a tax of £1 per head on all male convicts in New South Wales and Van Diemen's Land. When the settlers jibbed at this, he fell back on the use of the land fund and so made himself look like a systematic colonizer, or even a reader of Wakefield.[34]

In September 1831 the commissioners of emigration began their deliberations. They turned over in their minds the possibility of loans and the possibility of including other categories than females between the ages of eighteen and thirty, while they filled up the first ship with those women whom Goderich sometimes referred to as 'female servants' and sometimes as the improvers of the morals of the people of New South Wales. In March 1832 he informed Bourke that a ship would leave in April, its passengers having been principally selected from the charitable institutions of the towns of Dublin and Cork. When that ship, the *Red Rover*, cast anchor at the Quay in Sydney on 10 August with 202 free female settlers on board they were warmly welcomed as a 'cargo . . . of the highest value to the Country'. Even the countenances of the aged bachelors, it was said, lit up as they relished the hope of being 'restored to their primary original functions'. But those who were looking for servants steeped in those 'Rules for the Guidance of Persons in humble stations in life', or for rosy-cheeked bonnet wearers whose buxomness was not entirely concealed by their pinafores, were in for a great shock. The girls from the *Red Rover* turned out to be mainly women with bonnets-a-mode, cheap vulgar pendants hanging from their ears, and the look of women who intended to sell themselves rather than their labour. So, too, did some of the women on the *Bussorah Merchant* and the *David Scott*. By the middle of 1834 employers classified the women from the *Red Rover* as 'goods, not marketable' or the 'sweepings of the streets of London and Dublin'. They feared that to a population containing a large proportion of criminality they were about to add a grievous preponderance of vice and debauchery without that check which they could exercise over convicts.[35]

---

[34] Goderich to Darling, 5 January 1831, *H.R.A.*, I. xvi. 7; Goderich to Bourke, 28 September 1831, *H.R.A.*, I. xvi. 378-80; Goderich to Bourke, 12 October 1831, *H.R.A.*, I. xvi. 408; *New South Wales Government Gazette*, 4 April 1832.

[35] Goderich to emigration commissioners, 1 July 1831, C.O. 384/27; Goderich to Bourke, 28 September 1831, *H.R.A.*, I. xvi. 378-80; Goderich to Bourke, 12 October 1831 and encls 1-4, ibid., 408-16; Goderich to Bourke, 9 March 1832, ibid., 555; *Sydney Gazette*, 11 August 1832, 30 August, 30 October 1834; *Sydney Herald*, 20 August 1832; Goderich to emigration commissioners, 4 August 1832, C.O. 384/30; R. B. Madgwick, *Immigration into Eastern Australia 1788-1851* (London, 1937), p. 100.

Between 1832 and 1835 prospective employers and the guardians of public morals continued to grumble about the types who landed from migrant ships. Despite attempts in London to widen the categories of people eligible for assistance, to increase the assistance granted so that it covered the whole fare, and to eliminate corruption, the settlers of New South Wales stuck to their point that these migrants were only supplementing those other outcasts of the United Kingdom, the convicts, and loading the colony with a disproportion of immoral people. They clamoured for an extensive introduction of free and virtuous inhabitants who would contribute towards strengthening that moral and industrious population in place of the old convict depravity and aversion to labour.[36]

In 1831 the Reverend J. Dunmore Lang, convinced that assisted migration and transportation would only flood the country with the offscourings of English parishes and popish gaols, introduced a private scheme for mechanics who could produce certificates of moral character. He raised a loan from the Colonial Office to charter and equip a ship. He personally selected the migrants from Edinburgh, Glasgow, Greenock and Ayrshire. He paid their passage money in return for a written guarantee that they would work for at least twelve months building the Australian College in Sydney while they repaid the cost of their passage. One hundred and forty sailed from Greenock in the *Stirling Castle* in June. During the voyage Lang was married to his cousin, Wilhelmina Mackie, who allowed him to be undisputed master in the house and served him as his unquestioning collaborator. Happily for him she and Lang were the only two human beings on the planet to share the unshakable belief that Lang was always right.

Three teachers for the Australian College accompanied the emigrants. One of them, Henry Carmichael, professor of classics, gave lessons and lectures during the whole voyage on various branches of useful knowledge, believing as he did that by raising them to a high level in the scale of intelligence and by giving them a taste for scientific investigation the immigrants would be more likely to withstand the temptations to which they were exposed in the colony. While the men were instructed in the virtues of industry and sober habits with such success that they formed their own branch of the Temperance Society as soon as the ship anchored in Sydney Harbour, their womenfolk were moaning about the tough and scraggy fowls, the speckled and forbidding pork, and the weevily biscuits, or denouncing their husbands as 'great gomerils' and 'muckle asses', as wives are wont to do. For months after their arrival convicts, emancipists and other sympathizers with the convict community savaged them as 'those bloody emigrants who have come out to take the country from us', sensing that these immigrants would in time create that moral and industrious working class which was destined to take over from the old convict working class. Between 1831 and 1835 James and William Macarthur, Thomas Ryder, James Atkinson and William Lawson imported

[36] Report of Select Committee on Immigration, *V. & P.* (L.C. N.S.W.), 1835, p. 17.

migrants of good moral character and domestic habits so that they would
have sufficient reliable workers to provide for the proper care of their sheep
and cattle.[37]

To increase the number of immigrants of good moral character and industrious habits Bourke proposed in October 1835 to offer to settlers who had
the means and would prefer to engage their own mechanics or agricultural
labourers a bounty equal or nearly equal to the expense of the passage of such
persons provided they were of the ages and descriptions specified in a
government notice and provided they were passed by a board appointed to
examine them on arrival. They were required to exhibit to this board testi-
monials of good character signed by clergymen and respectable inhabitants
of note in the places of their former residence, for the whole drive was to
recruit a respectable working class to blot out the 'leprous curse' of convictism.
The arrangements to be adopted to facilitate this introduction to the colony of
useful and respectable migrants were gazetted in Sydney on 28 October 1835.
Under the government and bounty schemes, the number of assisted immigrants leapt from 808 in 1836 to 2664 in 1837, 6102 in 1838 and 8416 in 1839.
Two years later, when the figures for the census of 1841 were published,
observers noted that whereas in 1836 there were not quite two free persons to
one bondsman, in 1841 there were nearly four to one. They predicted, too,
that with the promised entire stoppage of the transportation of convicts, the
swelling influx of immigration and the growing increase from colonial births
the convicts would soon become an insignificant fraction of the population.
New South Wales was to become, like South Australia and Port Phillip,
mainly a migrant society, composed of people who had migrated from the
United Kingdom on the assurance that the evils of semi-slave convict labour
would never be reintroduced. The public life of the colony was to be
dominated in the 1840s not by the old patriots, or the nativists of Harpur's
generation, but by migrants who were exiles in the flesh but not in the heart
from their native land. The question was, would the migrant wash away the
stain left by convict society in the bush as well as in the towns of Sydney,
Parrramatta, Newcastle, Camden, Scone, Muswellbrook, Goulburn, Yass,
Melbourne, Geelong and Portland?[38]

---

[37] Evidence of J. D. Lang to the Select Committee on Immigration, ibid.; Agnes Busby
(née Thomson), (Memoirs, MS. in M.L.); A. Gilchrist, (ed.), *John Dunmore Lang*, vol. I,
p. 130; J. T. Bigge, Report . . . on the State of Agriculture and Trade, pp. 81-3; evidence
of J. H. Bent to the Select Committee on the State of the Gaols, *P.P.*, 1819, vii, 575, p. 125;
evidence of W. Macarthur, T. Ryder, J. Atkinson and W. Lawson to the Select Committee on Immigration, *V. & P.* (L.C. N.S.W.), 1835.

[38] Bourke to Glenelg, 14 October 1835, *H.R.A.*, I. xviii. 161-3; Bourke to Glenelg,
10 February 1836, ibid., 290; Bourke to Glenelg, 28 February 1836, ibid., 302; Glenelg to
Bourke, 23 March 1837, ibid., 705-6; Government Notice, Col. Sec.'s Office, 28 October
1835; copies of correspondence respecting emigration, *P.P.*, 1837, xliii, 358, p. 64.
Appendixes to the Annual Reports of the Committee on Immigration, *V. & P.*
(L.C. N.S.W.), 1836-9; R. B. Madgwick, *Immigration into Eastern Australia 1788-1851*
(London, 1937), p. 223; R. Mansfield, *Analytical View of the Census of New South
Wales for the Year 1841* (Sydney, 1841), p. 17.

By 1839 migrants were warning fellow new chums to beware of the bush of Australia:

> All you on emigration bent,
> With home and England discontent,
> Come listen to this my sad lament
> About the bush of Australia
> Illawarra, Mittagong
> Parramatta, Wollongong,
> If you wouldn't become an Orang-outang,
> Don't go to the wilds of Australia.

For there was barbarism in the bush and none of the measures taken by government since 1826 had had the slightest effect on it. There were the abominations black men and white men perpetrated on each other; there were the bushrangers; there were the 'low-roamers' who arrived at the bush shanties looking like human beings, and left looking like asses; there were the small numbers of women, as low as one convict woman for every seventeen convict men, low enough for one man to observe that the sight of a woman in the bush was an event to be commented on; there were no visible signs of civilization—no court-houses, no schoolhouses, no churches, no great houses, but only sod huts, mia-mias and movable shelters for shepherds, no roads, no evidence of a substantial nature except the sheep and cattle that the white man was exploiting the natural resources of the country from Inverell to Portland Bay.[39]

Between 1826 and 1839 government had tried various methods to reduce lawlessness and disorder in the country districts. They had drawn a line on the map in 1831 beyond which settlement was not to spread, only to find that sheep and cattle men were just as much vagabonds for grass as the aborigines were for kangaroos and possums. In August 1833, believing the evils of lawlessness and dissipation and all that enlivening and dulcifying at the bush shanty by certain members of the softer sex sprang from ex-convicts and ticket-of-leave men squatting illegally on the waste lands, they had passed through the Legislative Council an Act which appointed Crown lands commissioners to protect the Crown lands of the colony against encroachment, intrusion and trespass. These commissioners had been given the innocuous power of erecting beacons and landmarks upon Crown lands so that all and sundry would know the boundaries of settlement, and were to receive the assistance of the justices of the peace for any legal actions they took against intruders or disturbers of the peace. They lacked the power or the incentive

---

[39] 'The Settler's Lament' in D. Stewart and N. Keesing (eds), *Old Bush Songs*, pp. 71-3; T. Tourle to his mother, 9, 10 December 1839 (Tourle Letters, photocopy in NAT. L.); O. Bloxsome, Journal of a Voyage to New South Wales in 1838 (photostat in NAT. L.); *Sydney Herald*, 2, 3 January, 5, 10, 12 June 1839; *Australian*, 5 March 1839.

to tame the aborigine and the bushranger or to close down the sly-grog shops.[40]

In July 1836 Bourke, believing it was a 'perverse rejection of the bounty of providence', and anyhow quite impossible, to try to stop the flock-masters grazing stock outside the boundaries of location, introduced a licence of £10 a year which authorized stock-holders to depasture cattle and other animals beyond the boundaries, it being understood that any improvement on such a run —any hut or other dwelling, stockyard, pasture improvement, or water conservation—was to be made at the risk of the licensee. This provided an incentive to the greed of the flock-masters but did not provide an incentive to introduce the rudiments of civilization. For the next three years the dens of thieves, the cattle-duffing, the gully-raking, swell coves winking the eye at the low vices of their workers, the shooting and poisoning of aborigines, the spearing of cattle, and the bushrangers making raids on settlers' houses went on undiminished.

Broughton wrung his hands in despair that over such a vast area of God's earth a new race of men was growing up strangers not only to all forms of belief but to all those habits and principles which distinguished men from the apes. Early in 1839 Gipps came up with a proposal to create a border police to maintain law and order along and outside the boundaries of location. In March he passed through the Legislative Council an Act which divided the Crown lands into districts each of which was to be under the authority of a Crown lands commissioner, who was to reside in the district, keep the peace with the aid of a border police force, determine disputes between parties, hear complaints between masters and servants, drive away and impound the stock of unlicensed persons, seize and detain stock suspected of being stolen, and impound all unlicensed stock. To defray the expenses of the salaries of the commissioners and the border police, licensees were to pay ½d per year for every ram, wether, ewe and weaned lamb on their run, 1½d per year for every bull, ox, cow, steer, heifer and calf above the age of six months, and 3d per year for every horse, gelding, mare and foal above the age of six months. A licensee grazing ten thousand sheep outside the boundaries was up for £20 a year for his stock tax and £10 for his licence, or roughly the cost per year of a station hand. On 21 May Gipps published the proclamation dividing the Crown lands adjacent to and beyond the limits of settlement into nine districts together with the names of the commissioners for each district. On the same day he proclaimed to all and sundry that persons committing felonies, illegally selling fermented or spirituous liquors, wilfully harbouring any convict, committing any malicious injury upon any aborigine or other

---

[40] An Act for Protecting the Crown Lands of this Colony from Encroachment, Intrusion and Trespass, 4 Will. IV, no. 10, 28 August 1833, T. Callaghan, *Acts and Ordinances of the Governor and Council of New South Wales*; W. Campbell, *The Crown Lands of Australia* (Glasgow, 1855); An Act to amend an Act entitled, An Act for Protecting the Crown Lands of this Colony from Encroachment, Intrusion, and Trespass, 5 Will. IV, no. 12, 5 August 1834, T. Callaghan, op. cit.

person, not keeping a sufficient number of servants or harbouring a native woman would have their licences cancelled.[41]

In the same month of May Gipps proclaimed that the strong arm of the law would be used to preserve the peace between white men and black men, that in every case wherein any aborigines came to a violent death in consequence of a collision with white men an inquest or inquiry would be conducted, and that His Excellency was determined to make no distinction in such cases whether the aggressors or parties injured were of the one or the other race or colour, but to bring all to equal and indiscriminate justice. Once again, the *Sydney Herald* accused Gipps of having the effrontery to publish yet another one of those Whiggish apologies for the murderous black cannibals of New Holland. The prolonged dry spell added an edge to the extravagance of their anger and despair. In the country districts men heard that dread kah-kah of crows circling over dead stock. For by then there was a sense of crisis in the air as men showed all the bewilderment of human beings who knew one order was coming to an end but were not certain what was to take its place.[42]

In January 1839 those who pinned their faith to immigrant labour replacing convict labour had had rather a shock. In that month Gipps published in Sydney and Melbourne the instructions he had received from London to raise the minimum upset price for Crown lands from 5s to 12s an acre. To provide the pecuniary means of assisting migration and to prevent the undue dispersion of the migrants it was necessary, Glenelg argued, to raise the price considerably. If dispersion still continued, Gipps should restrict the amount of land offered for sale. He was confident that the rise would not affect the success of free immigration in supplying the great want of labour in the colony. That was precisely what the colonists in Sydney and Melbourne thought it would do. As they saw it, in the middle of a great dry spell which had reduced the resources of land-holders to buy land, those promoters of the 'bubble province' of South Australia had seduced Glenelg into fixing a price which would end migration to New South Wales, and so destroy the colony just as surely as the Romans had once destroyed their rival Carthage.

The patriarchs of the Council, and the Patriots of the Patriotic Association clamoured all the louder for the retention of assignment, but they were shouting to a great wind sweeping over the earth, for no man could change

[41] Bourke to Glenelg, 10 October 1835, *H.R.A.*, I. xviii. 153-8; An Act to Restrain the Unauthorised Occupation of Crown Lands, 7 Will. IV, no. 4, 20 July 1836, T. Callaghan, op. cit., vol. 2; *New South Wales Government Gazette*, 5 October 1836; *Sydney Gazette*, 25 November 1837; An Act to continue and amend an Act entitled, An Act to Restrain the Unauthorised Occupation of Crown Lands, 2 Vic., no. 19, 2 October 1838, supplement to *New South Wales Government Gazette*, 24 November 1838; *V. & P.* (L.C. N.S.W.), 14 February 1839; Report from the Committee on the Crown Lands Bill, 5 March 1839, *V. & P.* (L.C. N.S.W.), 1839; An Act Further to Restrain the Unauthorised Occupation of Crown Lands, and to Provide the Means of Defraying the Expense of a Border Police, 2 Vic., no. 27, 22 March 1839, *New South Wales Government Gazette*, 22 May 1839.

[42] *Australian*, 22, 30 March, 6 April 1839; *New South Wales Government Gazette*, 22 May 1839.

the London view that assignment was a form of slavery and a promoter of sodomy. The *Sydney Herald* and the *Sydney Gazette* suggested importing coolies from India to satisfy the great want of labour, though folk feared that those fools in the Mother Country would only indulge again in more of those 'silly ravings of senseless drivellers' about slavery, like all the 'mealy mouthed drivel' about aborigines. The *Australian* deplored the suggestion that any part of the colonial population should be recruited from the followers of Islam, the devoted victims of Juggernaut, or the disciples of Confucius. This grand centre for a new civilization in the Antipodes should be reserved for the white man. Or so they thought. So did James Stephen in London who wanted Australia to be kept as a home for the poor of Britain and built up from sea to sea as a white man's country. Coolies would 'beat down the wages of the poor labouring Europeans' until the poor became entirely dependent upon the rich. Besides to make the same law apply to coolies, Hottentots and Europeans would leave the weaker classes destitute of protection, and lead to a form of slavery—an institution no longer to be tolerated in the Queen's dominions.[43] Some asserted that free immigrants had already improved the moral, physical and political condition of the colony. Others asserted that thieves and rogues had cut such an indelible mark that New South Wales never could become a society for gentlemen or men of honour and integrity and would remain for ever 'a famous place for working men, London pick pockets, cattle stealers and swindlers . . . [and] unprincipled vagabonds'.

In July 1839 one young assisted migrant who believed he was coming to the land of the free was startled to see a convict's grave. It made him wonder whether here, too, oppressors and gaolers had caused mankind to 'droop and wither'.[44] Henry Parkes was then just twenty-four years of age. Born at Stoneleigh near Coventry on 27 May 1815, in a country whose leafy, flowery meadows and skylarks delighted eye and ear each magical May time, he had gone as a boy to Birmingham where he had seen how the early factory system brutalized and degraded human beings. Sent to work for his bread at the age of ten years, he had never been cowed or defeated, or lost hope. In Birmingham he read chartist literature which held out the promise that the application of the principles of the Charter would raise the moral character of the working people and promote the true dignity of man. He also attended the chapel where he learnt of a God who claimed to be able not only to still the raging of the sea but also the madness of the people. After his marriage to Clarinda Varney on 11 July 1836 he found he was one of the many men who

---

[43] Glenelg to Gipps, 9 August 1838, *H.R.A.*, I. xix. 537-8; *Sydney Herald*, 4, 7, 14, 18 January 1839; *Australian*, 29 January, 2, 7 March, 7 May 1839; *Sydney Standard*, 25 February 1839; P. Knaplund, 'Sir James Stephen on a White Australia', *Victorian Historical Magazine*, vol. 12, 1928, pp. 240-2; P. Knaplund, *James Stephen and the British Colonial System* (Madison, Wis., 1953), pp. 23-5.

[44] Report of Select Committee on Immigration, *V. & P.* (L.C. N.S.W.), 1839; T. Tourle to his sister Emma, 9 December 1839, and T. Tourle to his mother, 10 December 1839 (Tourle Letters, photocopy in NAT. L.); H. Parkes, 'Convict's Grave' in *Stolen Moments* (Sydney, 1842).

could not obtain the means of living in their native country. He decided early in 1839 to make a better home in the wilderness of Australia. He believed that there universal suffrage, on which he had pinned his faith in his days in the Birmingham Political Union, would usher in an age in which men were no longer treated like brutes while alive, and buried like dogs when dead. He believed, as he put it in his 'Poet's Farewell' to his native land that in Australia mortals would learn to love each other with brotherly love and gentle hearts, that light, peace, innocence and bliss would be built over misery's dark abyss and that paths of peace would extend where 'wilds now trackless lie'. Early in 1839 this man with a Dionysian frenzy in his heart boarded the *Strath-fieldsaye* for Sydney, hoping to find in a strange land that which every man ought to be able to find at home—plenty.

To his dismay he found the struggle to earn his daily bread in Sydney just as fierce as in Birmingham. In Sydney he could only accommodate his family in a low, dirty, little unfurnished room without a fireplace. With 3d left in the world he kept beating about Sydney for work. Within a few months he was up-country at Penrith, his bed a sheet of bark off a box-tree and an old door laid on two cross-pieces of wood covered over with a few articles of clothing. His disenchantment with the appearance and spirit of the place was so intense that within a year he wrote nostalgically about his native land and heartily wished himself back at home:

> It may be here that Britons find
> Scenes brighter than they leave behind:
> But oh! the counter-charm for home
> Is found not yet, where'er I roam
> O'er sea or land!

The country discomforts did not last long, for by 1841 he was back in Sydney, reading widely in Adam Smith, Plutarch, Lang's history and Sturt's expeditions into Australia, and Goldsmith and Shakespeare, and enjoying it all so much that he was able to tell his sister he was 'happy now in Australia'. He was confident that he and his fellow-exiles of English blood and breed were those chosen heirs of freedom who would liberate Australia from the convict's clanking chains and allow freedom's glad voice to be heard over all her ransomed plains. He also clung to the hope that he and other poor exiles would one day return to Old England, just as at times of dread he prayed to Him who held 'the ocean in the hollow of His hand'. In his heart he carried both the hopes of the future of humanity, and the ineffaceable legacy from his chapel-going days in Birmingham, when he had imbibed all that talk about man's unworthiness and man's wickedness and how God alone could save men from their folly.[45]

---

[45] Based on a visit to Stoneleigh, Coventry and Birmingham, May 1964, and Hatton Garden, Kirby Street, London. Parkes had lived there in February and March 1839; *Charter* (London), 24, 31 March 1839; H. Parkes, *An Emigrant's Home Letters*

One other man in whom hopes for the future of humanity lived uneasily side by side with the old Judaico-Christian view of man's destiny was William Augustine Duncan. He came to the colony in 1837 to take up duty as a teacher in Catholic schools. As a youth in Scotland, where he was born in 1811, he was stuffed with the hopes of the Enlightenment and the vision of human beings liberated from the ghosts of their past. Then, after an intensive course of reading, he was received into the Catholic Church. He was widely read in Pindar, Cicero, de Tocqueville, Leopold von Ranke and François René Chateaubriand. He was passionately fond of the music of Mozart, possibly sensing in him a kindred spirit who believed in the universal brotherhood of the Masons and the Catholic teaching on the life of the world to come. The ideas of liberty and equality so lived on in him that when he began to publish his paper the *Australasian Chronicle* in Sydney on 2 August 1839 he denounced the large landlords of New South Wales with some of the revolutionary fervour with which the Girondists had denounced aristocratic privilege in France. For, although the prime aim of his paper was to explain and uphold the civil and religious principles of Catholics and to maintain their rights, he also wanted New South Wales to cease to be in the main a society of sheep men and their workers. Like Henry Parkes and other recent arrivals, he was an advocate of a society of small property owners rather than of any revolutionary change in the ownership of wealth. Like Parkes and other migrants he was too attached to the Mother Country to entertain the idea that Australians should seize the first possible opportunity for a Boston Tea Party. Such migrants became not only the instruments for the victory of a bourgeois philistinism in Australia, but helped to ensure that when society shook with those great convulsions which swept over the civilized world between 1848 and 1852 neither radicalism nor independence were to triumph in Australia.[46]

(Sydney, 1896); *Birmingham Gazette*, 29 April 1839; Charles Gavan Duffy, *Conversations with Carlyle* (London, 1892), pp. 210-11; Minute Book of Lombard Street Chapel 1829-56 (Birmingham Public Library); *Proceedings of the Working Men's Association, Birmingham* (2 vols, Birmingham, 1839-43); Psalm 65, v. 7; H. Parkes, 'A Poet's Farewell' in *Charter*, 24 March 1839.

[46] *Australasian Chronicle*, 2 August 1839; W. G. Broughton to E. Coleridge, 25 February, 13 September 1839 (Broughton Letters, microfilm in NAT. L.); W. A. Duncan, Literary Journal (MS. in M.L.).

8

BUT COLONIALS DO NOT MAKE
THEIR OWN HISTORY

B Y THE MIDDLE of 1839 it looked as though the battle between civilization and barbarism was about to begin in New South Wales. In the towns there was ignorance; in the bush there was barbarism. In Sydney in May 1838 a girl of thirteen was found who did not know what the Bible was. She belonged to that half of the children of the colony who had not come under the civilizing influences of education or religion. In the bush white men were exposed to daily sufferings from savage and bloodthirsty aborigines who were openly boasting of their intention to kill 'all white B————rs'. At the end of 1838 at a Mr Cobb's property on the Hunter River, an assigned servant found the body of his fellow-shepherd speared through the heart, his brains beaten out and his breast cut open. In March 1839 a shepherd belonging to the Australian Agricultural Company was most barbarously murdered by the blacks and his arm neatly severed from his body with a tomahawk. In June down on the Monaro some white men watched with horror the massacre of some Bega blacks by a party of Monaro blacks, who then skinned them and ate them. In all the districts outside the limits of location thievish and murderous convicts and ex-convicts pillaged the countryside while drunken policemen dallied with female convicts or ex-convicts of 'prepossessing appearance'. Bushrangers and armed groups of ruffians terrorized the countryside from the Liverpool Plains to Australia Felix, plundering houses, and robbing drays and stations at pleasure. Up in New England One-eyed Thom held the district to ransom. On the Upper Hunter, Opposum Jack, a runaway from a government gang, pursued his course of depredation for two years, while desperate characters intimidated the settlers on the Bathurst Plains, the Wellington Valley, the Monaro, the Riverina, Australia Felix and Gippsland.[1]

Some believed the solution to this ignorance and lawlessness was to find a common ground on which the children of persons of all religious persuasions might acquire the rudiments of knowledge and the habits of brotherly love, taught by teachers in schools built and financed by government. They hoped that sectarian controversies would not prove so formidable that the total

[1] *Sydney Herald*, 1 March, 21 May, 31 December 1838, 21 June, 15 July, 28 August, 18 September 1839; *Australian*, 30 March 1839; C. Wilkes, *Narrative of the United States Exploring Expedition During the Years 1838, 1839, 1840, 1841, 1842* (5 vols, Philadelphia, 1845), vol. 2, pp. 237-8.

ignorance of the rising generation was to be preferred to the risk of children lapsing into theological error. They hoped the time was past when any priest or parson would have the audacity or the insolence to assert that he would prefer the risks of utter ignorance, and all its attendant barbarism in both town and country, to the evils of disseminating popery or propagating dissent and unbelief.

That was the great hope of Sir George Gipps when he asked the Legislative Council on 27 August to adopt the four resolutions on education that he had first put to Council on 23 August. He asked them to agree, first, that all classes of the community were entitled to equal assistance from the public revenue in the establishment of schools or places of public education; second, that owing to the extreme dispersion of the population of the colony, a system of education, to be effectual, should be as comprehensive as possible; third, that a system of education should be established that would, at best, comprehend all classes of Protestants; fourth, that if the public schools of the colony were established upon principles essentially Protestant, some corresponding advantages ought to be secured for the schools of Catholics. He explained how the colony differed from every country in the world, being composed of men of all creeds. Because it was impossible and uneconomic for government to provide separate schools for the members of every sect, he had decided that a comprehensive and general system of education was the only one that could be of general advantage. He therefore proposed that all Protestants be educated in schools run on the model of the British and Foreign Bible Society and that Catholics be educated in their own schools, which would be built and financed by government. He concluded his long, eloquent and manly speech by appealing to the patriarchs of the colony not to let their opinions be biased by the plague-spot of religious discord.[2]

The Anglican bishop of Australia, William Grant Broughton, rose to his feet and in a speech lasting about three hours explained why he, who neither dreaded censure nor coveted applause, would be obliged in conscience to oppose the resolutions of His Excellency. For his part he believed as passionately as ever in the special role for which divine providence had singled out the Church of England in all British societies. In 1836 he had opposed Governor Bourke's proposals for schools because they contained that 'bane and plague spot', the prohibition on the use of the Bible in government schools. Because he believed with all Protestants that Holy Scripture contained all the things necessary to salvation, he had no alternative but opposition. Now he must oppose the resolutions of Governor Gipps, partly because they undermined the special position of the Church of England, which had been chosen by God to ensure that British people possessed truth and enjoyed liberty, and partly because institutions for teaching 'morality without religion, and religion without a creed' must in the end be hostile to all true religion. The plan would only help the dissenters and the Catholics and work towards the fulfilment of that nightmare by which he had been haunted ever since God had called

[2] *V. & P.* (L.C. N.S.W.), 11 June, 23, 27 August 1839; *Sydney Herald*, 2 September 1839, *Australian*, 27 April, 3 September 1839; *Colonist*, 31 August 1839.

him to the high office of a priest of the Church of England, the nightmare of a British society falling prey to unbelief, to the Rabelaisian 'Do what you want to do', which would bring mankind down to the pursuit of the pleasures of the goat and the monkey. Instead of resting under the shade of the monarchy and the Church, the people would live under a republic without a religion. He viewed this prospect with such horror that he appealed to his fellow-councillors that if they valued their happiness and that of their children they would not yield to His Excellency's way of thinking.[3]

The Attorney-General, J. H. Plunkett, the only Catholic layman in the Council, surprised members by saying that the comprehensive system had his support because it was a liberal one. He was afraid that if His Excellency failed in this system, there would be no education at all. He thought that the clergy and parents, not schoolmasters, were the most proper persons to inculcate religion in the minds of the young. But he was as a man speaking without authority, for his bishop, J. B. Polding, had maintained a discreet silence during the controversy. After the propagation of religion, the object Polding had most at heart was the diffusion of sound taste and a love of the arts, and the end of ignorance. But he was having his own difficulties with his Irish priests, such as Father J. J. Therry, who wanted the congregations to go on singing those vulgar Irish chants he loathed rather than the Gregorian plain-song he had loved at the Benedictine monastery at Downside. He was also disturbed by gossip in Sydney that some of his priests, like the Protestant chaplains, were laying up for themselves treasures on earth rather than treasures in that place where neither moth nor rust would corrupt, nor thieves break through and steal. So he kept a discreet silence. Richard Jones stood up in his place as a 'Goliath of Methodism to bid fierce defiance to Schools built upon the Bible'. Faced with numerous petitions from the clergy and parishioners of the Church of England all insisting that they could not admit that a sound religious education could be imparted without the direct inculcation of all the great and peculiar doctrines of the Gospel, and the Broughton reminder that over three thousand had already signed such petitions, Gipps wound up the debate by saying he had no wish to place the Church of England in danger. He wanted to get the children of New South Wales into schools, but the wealthiest members of the colony had not had the generosity or the Christian charity to see it in that light. As the feeling of the Council was against him he would withdraw his resolutions.[4]

[3] W. G. Broughton, *Religion Essential to the Security and Happiness of Nations* (Sydney, 1834); Broughton, *A Charge Delivered to the Clergy of New South Wales . . . February 13, 1834* (Sydney, 1834); Broughton, *A Speech Delivered at the General Committee of Protestants, on Wednesday, August 3, 1836* (Sydney, 1836); Broughton, *The Speech of the Lord Bishop of Australia in the Legislative Council, upon the Resolutions for Establishing a System of General Education, on Tuesday, 27 August 1839* (Sydney, 1839); *Australian*, 3 September 1839.
[4] Supplement to *Australian*, 3 September 1839; J. B. Polding, Pastoral to All our Reverend and Beloved Clergy, 9 January 1840 (Polding Papers, Catholic Archives, St Mary's Cathedral, Sydney); P. O'Farrell, *The Catholic Church in Australia* (Sydney, 1968), pp. 56-7; *V. & P.* (L.C. N.S.W.), 20, 22, 27 August 1839; *Colonist*, 7 September 1839.

Outside the Council, men saw Broughton not as the prophet who warned his people of the signs of the times, but as a bigot who placed the interests of his Church above the enlightenment of the children. The rising generation of New South Wales were to be deprived of the one means of acquiring useful knowledge because a parson objected to the particular mode in which such education was conveyed. What, it was asked, did priests and parsons know that was not in the ordinary man? What gave them more foresight and made them more learned and pious than other men? Why should rational persons submit themselves to priestly domination or give up the reins of their understanding to a fellow-mortal? Was not the behaviour of the lower class painful proof of the necessity of a moral, comprehensive and rational education? Were not multitudes of children in Sydney and in the country growing up surrounded by every species of vice and degradation, and their minds being moulded by every low and loathsome profligacy?

That man Broughton in whom the spirit of expansive love to his fellow-creatures ought to burn and glow had opposed a rational system of education unless he could make it the instrument of his own views. The man must be as cold as a statue, and too wise to feel. While Broughton saw himself as a prophet who would not let his people see the corruption of unbelief and popery, others in the community saw him as standing between them and their advance into the light. A man who was plagued at night with dreams of that fearful spectacle of multitudes growing up in New South Wales making no acknowledgement of God weakened his chance of being heeded in the great debate on how to replace the old convict society with a moral and industrious population. As he walked into that dark night, his face began to wear the look of a man who had known a great sadness: the lips became thinner and the eyes took on that lack-lustre look of a man who had pulled down the shutters on the world. He sprinkled his public utterances more and more with the language of despair and resignation. He told people how he raised a tearful eye to heaven. He called G. A. Robinson, the Chief Protector of Aborigines, 'a visionary'. He talked of some malignity in the aborigines which left them incapable of making the leap from savagery to civilization.[5]

On 25 June 1839 the Legislative Council appointed Broughton chairman of their committee on immigration which was instructed to consider the question of immigration generally, to ascertain the present and the prospective demands of the colonists for labour and how the same might be most effectually and economically met. Profound pessimist that he had become about the fruits of human endeavour, Broughton wrote in the report of the importance to the community of a continuance and enlargement of that stream of migration which was now setting towards their shores, because with transportation

[5] *Sydney Gazette*, 29 August 1839; *Sydney Herald*, 11 October 1839; *Australian*, 3 October 1839; *Australasian Chronicle*, 3 September 1839; *Colonist*, 7 September 1839; W. G. Broughton to R. Bourke, 29 April 1837 (Twenty-two letters from Archdeacon W. G. Broughton to R. Bourke, ms. in m.l.); W. G. Broughton to R. Bourke, 1, 5 June 1837, and R. Bourke to W. G. Broughton, 3 June 1837, ibid.; W. G. Broughton, *A Charge Delivered to the Clergy of New South Wales . . . February 13, 1834*, pp. 12-13; *Sydney Herald*, 22 July 1840.

about to be discontinued numerous 'hands' would be required to supply the deficiency of agricultural and mechanical labourers thereby occasioned. Now that the principal source of contagion was about to be stopped, there was a greater probability of the immigrants continuing to preserve their habits and characters unvitiated, and so be qualified to lay the foundation of a community distinguished by superior regard to moral and religious principle. Or so he and his fellow-members hoped in November as the country, drenched by rain after a long drought, began again to wear temporarily a mantle of green which gladdened the hearts of sons of Britain in a country where the dry seasons left the grass as grey and deathlike as stubble after the harvest, and the ground as hard as iron.[6]

This experience of living in a dry land, the uncouthness of the convicts and their descendants, the savagery between white man and black man, and the degradation of the black man from the life of a nomad to a loathsome creature who had adopted the vices but none of the virtues of the white man conditioned their attitude to all movements and schools of thought that held out the hope of better things for mankind. They would have nothing to do with any experiment for the renovation of human character in the wilds of Australia. When a group of men in Sydney formed a society to propagate the ideas of Robert Owen, those who were deeply steeped in pessimism and failure by experience in Australia called them deluded and urged the government of New South Wales to take steps to check the blasphemous, obscene and disorderly conduct of these socialists who were profaning the Sabbath by using that day of all days to tell their fellow-citizens about man's capacity to build a better society. The newspapers of Sydney and Melbourne fed their readers with so many examples of human depravity that they had no difficulty in believing that the human race suffered from some calamity at the beginning of time, such as was told in the Book of Genesis, which had left them cripples.[7]

When news reached Sydney early in 1840 that Alexander Maconochie, the commandant-elect at Norfolk Island, proposed to reform convicts not by the terror of punishment in this world or in the life of the world to come but by surrounding them with love and understanding and music to promote a benevolence where all previous treatment had only sown a morbid, beast-like malevolence, they were profoundly sceptical or dismissed him rudely as a no-hoper. Maconochie was a man of enlarged views and considerable accomplishments. He had been a distinguished secretary to the Royal Geographical Society in London from 1830 to 1833, a professor of geography at the University of London from 1833 to 1834, and private secretary to the Lieutenant-Governor of Van Diemen's Land from 1837 to 1839. Like other optimists who wanted to confer a dignity on mankind in place of all that depravity and

---

[6] Report of Committee on Immigration, *V. & P.* (L.C. N.S.W.), 1839; *Sydney Herald*, 9, 16 October 1839; *Sydney Gazette*, 10, 12 October 1839.

[7] *Australian*, 25 April, 4 June 1840; *Sydney Herald*, 15 July 1840; *Australasian Chronicle*, 5 May, 2, 4 July 1840; *Commercial Journal*, 24 June, 8, 15 July 1840.

vileness which the pessimists found in the human race, he was apt to shock the ladies by his anatomical frankness when lecturing on human nature. He was also not distinguished for his modesty, being much given to pompous pronouncements that the moral character of every man in the Australian colonies would be affected by his teachings. When the obscurantists and defenders of the old order in Hobart Town attacked his ideas, he likened his situation to that of Galileo.

Shortly after taking up his duties as private secretary to the Lieutenant-Governor of Van Diemen's Land in 1837, he had come to the conclusion that the island was 'a sink of wickedness' not because of man's innate depravity but because of the 'slave moorings' of that society. He decided to devote himself to the subversion of this 'vile helotism' and sent off to the English Society for the Improvement of Prison Discipline his *Report on the State of Prison Discipline in Van Diemen's Land* which was used by the Molesworth Committee as part of the case against the convict systems in the Australian colonies. For this breach of discipline Lieutenant-Governor Sir John Franklin relieved him of his duties. On being appointed superintendent of the penal settlement on Norfolk Island at the end of 1839, he submitted to Gipps a proposal for a system of convict management in which books, music and women, rather than cruelty and terror, were to strengthen both the desire and capacity of offenders to obey the laws of human society.

Captain Maconochie believed that all rational men would share his enthusiasm for his experiment. He had not been in Australia long enough to appreciate the profound scepticism with which the inhabitants greeted any system aimed at changing human behaviour. Sir George Gipps was sceptical about the outcome. He told Lord John Russell in February 1840:

> Captain Maconochie avows his opinion that the first object of all Convict Discipline should be the Reformation of the Criminal. This opinion, however agreeable it may be to the dictates of humanity, is not, I believe, the received one of Legislators, who rather require as the first object of Convict Discipline that it should be a terror to Evildoers.

The *Sydney Herald* ridiculed him as that visionary who proposed to tame the monsters of Norfolk Island by giving them 'a fiddle and a glass and a washerwoman', and called the scheme 'a perfection of fun stamped with absurdity'. This thirst for change, they predicted, would meet the fate of all schemes based on abandoning practical experience. For few in Australia had ever dreamed that the 'hard rock' of human nature could be changed into a 'standing water'. The environment and their experience of life in Australia were fashioning a sardonic race of men whose response to life was to laugh at their own misfortunes and to laugh, too, at anyone so visionary as to imagine men could ever be any different.[8]

[8] Gipps to Normanby, 23 November 1839, *H.R.A.*, I. xx. 400-3; Gipps to Russell, 24 February 1840, ibid., 525-7; Gipps to Russell, 25 February 1840, ibid., 527-30; A. Maconochie to Captain Washington, 10, 11 January 1839 (Maconochie Papers, Royal

While some looked to frugal, virtuous and industrious immigrants to win the victory for civilization over barbarism, adventurers, driven on in part by greed and in part by that dream of being giants in the land, had their moment, too, of prominence. In 1835 John Batman and his partners played for over half a million acres in the hinterland of Port Phillip and lost. Early in 1840 W. C. Wentworth and others played for no less than twenty million acres in the south island of New Zealand in return for two hundred gold sovereigns, and an undertaking to pay the same sum each year to the Maori chiefs for their lifetimes. Gipps warned him that his treaty would be null and void and offered the chiefs ten guineas each, copious cups of tea and a cold handshake, while Wentworth filled them with rum and jokes and gave them two hundred gold sovereigns. When Wentworth refused to abrogate his treaty with the Maori chiefs, Gipps asked the Legislative Council on 28 May 1840 to pass an Act declaring that treaty to be null and void. He also announced that James Macarthur and not Wentworth would replace Phillip Parker King in the Legislative Council, having decided that Wentworth by his extravagant behaviour had forfeited the claim he had to a position he otherwise had by virtue of his vast influence in the colony and his vast possessions. Wentworth asked leave to present his case at the bar of the Council. On 30 June and 1 July he spoke for some six hours using all his gifts for rhetoric to prove that the Magna Carta and the Bill of Rights were his warranty for the twenty million acres of land in New Zealand. Broughton denounced his act as 'morally shameful'. James Macarthur told the Council that such wild assertions as Wentworth had uttered during those six frenzied hours could lead to nothing but disorder. The press of Sydney taunted him for his 'exorbitant rapacity', just as on previous occasions they had hinted at his promiscuity and his convict mother. Wentworth resigned his commission as a magistrate, to separate himself, as he put it, entirely from any official connection with the government of Sir George Gipps, and waited for the moment when he could indulge that great passion of his life for persecuting those who had stood in his way. That winter of 1840 Sir George betrayed no sign of knowing the day was to come when the landed magnificoes of New South Wales would join with Wentworth to blow him into the grave.[9]

Towards the end of 1839 Paul Edmund de Strzelecki announced his intention to continue his geological researches in the area bordering the Australian

Geographical Society, London); A. Maconochie, statement with respect to his differences with Sir John Franklin, Hobart Town, 11 March 1839 (Maconochie Papers); A. Maconochie, *Report on the State of Prison Discipline in Van Diemen's Land* (London, 1838); *Sydney Herald*, 4 March, 20 April 1840; J. V. Barry, *Alexander Maconochie of Norfolk Island* (Melbourne, 1958); S. C. McCulloch, 'Sir George Gipps and Captain Alexander Maconochie', *Hist. Studies*, vol. 7, 1957.

[9] *Sydney Herald*, 25 March, 6 April, 6 May, 30 June, 13 July 1840; *V. & P.* (L.C. N.S.W.), 28 May 1840; Gipps to Glenelg, 3 April 1839, *H.R.A.*, I. xx. 81-2; Gipps to Russell, 16 August 1840, *H.R.A.*, I. xx. 761-2; John Macarthur jun. to Elizabeth Macarthur, 12 April 1825 (Macarthur Papers, vol. 15); Col. Sec. of New South Wales to Registrar of the Supreme Court, 3 November 1840 (Judicial Papers, November 1839 to December 1840, N.S.W.S.A.).

Alps. Born in Poznan in western Poland in 1797 he had travelled extensively in England, the United States, Canada, South America, and the islands of the Pacific before arriving in Sydney in April 1839. He quickly charmed the drawing-room ladies with his hand-kissings, his compliments and his moistening of the eyes. Such gestures and extravagances of language were no recommendation to those who used the rule of the book-keeper in human affairs. Gipps was cool when Strzelecki asked for financial assistance for his enterprises. Strzelecki turned to Hannibal Macarthur who was not suspicious of men who were 'all heart'. In that dry summer of 1839–40, Strzelecki put to Hannibal Macarthur his grandiose ambition of climbing the highest mountain in the 'dark continent' while other members of the party pursued the prosaic task of looking for grass for stock in that district between the Alps and Bass Strait on which Angus McMillan had just sent back such favourable reports.

Strzelecki left Sydney with a pack-horse and a convict servant on 21 December 1839 for the Snowy Mountains. After passing through Camden and Bagalon (midway between Yass and Jugiong) his party arrived at Ellerslie, Hannibal Macarthur's station some twenty miles to the south-east of Gundagai. There he was joined by James Macarthur, the son of Hannibal Macarthur, the grass-seeker, who had put up the £500 to allow Strzelecki to attempt the high mountain. On 2 March 1840 Strzelecki, James Macarthur, James Riley (a station hand at Ellerslie), two convict servants and an aboriginal pathfinder, Charlie Tarra, left Ellerslie for the Walleregang station on the upper Murray where they arrived probably on 7 March. Leaving the two convict servants and adding another aborigine, Strzelecki, Macarthur, Riley and the two aborigines set out for Western Port on 9 March, planning to make a detour via that high mountain on which Strzelecki had set his heart. Proceeding along the south bank of the Murray they probably forded it at the Bringenbrong crossing and came to the present site of Khancoban station from which Strzelecki, Macarthur and the two aborigines left to ascend the mountain. With the thermometer standing at 90° F. they made the perilous thousand-foot descent down the Geehi walls by clinging to the shrubs and saplings for support, and stood at the foot of Mt Townsend, where Macarthur's soul made no response to the grandeur of the setting. By 12 March they had climbed to the top of that mountain, where Strzelecki proved to them another was considerably higher than the one on which they stood. He told Macarthur he planned to name that higher mountain after the Polish hero Kosciusko, because the configuration as viewed from Mt Townsend reminded him of an elevated hill near Krakow which bore the same name.

Strzelecki set off to climb to the summit of Kosciusko which he reached probably between three and four that afternoon, where standing in cloud he plucked one of those lovely wild flowers that bloom on the summit in hot summers, pressed it so that he might send it later to Adyna Turno in Poland as a reminder of freedom, patriotism and love. The first white man to stand on the summit of Mt Kosciusko, his mind turned to man's struggle and woman's love and sadness rather than to measuring accurately his height above sea level or noting the exact time of day. After rejoining Macarthur and the two aborigines at the Geehi site the group made their way back to Walleregang. Leaving there at the end of March, the party of six crossed the Murray at Corryong and made for Western Port which they reached some eight weeks later, being on starvation rations for the last fortnight as they inched their way through thick tea-tree scrub in the hinterland of that bay which they reached on 12 May at the present site of Corinella. Macarthur had seen the lush pastures he was looking for. Strzelecki waited for his moment of recognition.

When Strzelecki returned to Melbourne he announced that he proposed to confer on the new and valuable country the name of Gipps Land. The *Port Phillip Herald* wrote enthusiastically of the 'brilliant prospects' he and his party had opened up for the enterprising settlers of Port Phillip. But the recognition Strzelecki craved was not to be. Melbourne did not even muster a present in his honour. Gipps wrote of the feelings of respect and honour which had been excited towards Strzelecki among the people of the colony. There it ended. For thirty-three years Strzelecki strove for more tangible recognition till death took him in 1873 while still consumed with resentment at being passed over for positions in the Australian colonies.[10]

While Strzelecki and his party were hacking their way through the tea-tree near Western Port, another adventurer, Benjamin Boyd, was turning over in his mind in London a plan to carve out an empire for himself and his family in that vast portion of the globe. He was then in the prime of life, being probably thirty-seven years old. By birth the second son of a merchant, he had the appearance of one of those god-like men in the paintings of Rubens, and an appetite for glory to match the garments of display with which he bedecked his body. He looked and behaved then as though he would one day 'top a cloud'. In 1840 he came up with the idea of founding the Royal Bank of Australia in London which would collect capital in England where the interest rate was low, and invest it in Australia where the interest rate was high. He had ideas of investing some of this capital in buying up country stations, in whaling, and in trading in the islands of the Pacific. In October of that year he decided that the best means of further developing the resources of Australia and the adjacent islands was to effect a regular communication

[10] Memoir of P. E. Strzelecki to Sir George Gipps, appendix C. in Gipps to Russell, 28 September 1840, C.O. 201/299; Strzelecki, *Physical Description of New South Wales and Van Diemen's Land* (London, 1845); Strzelecki, Letters to Adyna Turno (MS. in M.L.); W. L. Harvard, 'Sir P. E. Strzelecki', R.A.H.S., *J. & P.*, no. 26, 1940; James Macarthur, Diary (MS. in M.L.); H. P. G. Clews, *Strzelecki's Ascent of Mount Kosciusko* (Canberra 1970); H. E. M. Heney, *In a Dark Glass* (Sydney, 1961); G. Rawson, *The Count: a life of Sir Paul Edmund Strzelecki* (London, 1954); Strzelecki, *Memorandum* (London, 1861); *Port Phillip Herald*, 2 June, 12 July 1840; Barbara Flett, Benjamin Boyd (thesis, Department of History, Australian National University); see cairn for Count P. de Strzelecki, J. Macarthur and J. Riley on beach front at Corinella, personal visit to site, 8 March 1973.

between these settlements by steamships. To do this he had already despatched at his own expense a 600-ton steamship of 250 horsepower to trade in those parts. He asked Lord John Russell to allow him to select five or six places on the coast of New Holland which he could use to coal and repair his ships, and as places of refuge. In reply Lord John promised every assistance to his scheme to promote the success of steam navigation on the coasts of Australia and the adjacent seas. In this way, Ben Boyd began to 'throw signs on History'.[11]

While Ben Boyd was dreaming of building a kingdom for himself in New Holland by exploiting cheap convict labour, Her Majesty's Government decided on 22 May 1840 that as from 1 August convicts would no longer be transported to New South Wales. Gipps announced this decision to the Legislative Council on 20 October. The planters in the Council who were dependent on convict servants stuck to their traditional position that the system of transportation and assignment was the most human and reformatory punishment that had ever been devised. In general, members of Council spoke about the things that touched them most deeply. Broughton told them he was not without a share of 'patriotic feeling' on the occasion when the 'opprobrious imputation' on the native-born was at last removed. He then went on to urge the people to take care lest the evil of convictism be replaced by a greater evil, for if the predominance of members of the Catholic faith were established in Australia by assisted immigration, the toleration and freedom of their own religious worship and rights would surely be interrupted. James Macarthur, sound Anglican that he was, said he agreed with the bishop that if the Catholics soon became a preponderant group the Protestants would not be tolerated in the exercise of their religion. He must say, though, that for his part he would prefer Irish Catholics to Asiatics. That was not the point. The point was that the colony had now arrived at such a degree of wealth as to be able to populate the country with a free and virtuous people. Thanks to convicts they had been able to introduce into the wilds of Australia a civilized race of people. As a native-born Australian he was warm in his feelings about the 'stain' and the 'slur'. Some thought Australia was at the corner of the globe, but for him it was in a most central position for all the purposes of commerce. He must say as a proud Australian that he looked forward to the time when the confederation of British colonies in this hemisphere would be looked upon as one of the most brilliant constellations in the diadem of Imperial Britain. After all, both those strains lived in him. He was an English gentleman who happened to be Australian-born.[12]

Outside the Council the free working classes raised the cry of 'morality' against the renewal of the assignment system, not because they feared 'con-

[11] *The Times*, 27 June 1856; B. Boyd to Russell, 8 October 1840, minute of Colonial Office on above, and draft of reply of Russell to B. Boyd, 19 October 1840, C.O. 201/304; Francis Webb, 'A Drum for Ben Boyd' in *Collected Poems* (Sydney, 1969).

[12] Order in Council for determining places for transportation of convicts, 22 May 1840, encl. in Russell to Gipps, 6 July 1840, *H.R.A.*, I. xx. 701-3; *Sydney Herald*, 21, 26 October 1840; *Australian*, 29 October 1840.

tamination' or that their souls might experience corruption, but because convicts challenged their monopoly of labour. The *Sydney Herald* prophesied that should the British Government unload hordes of foes to liberty from Catholic Ireland on their shores, should the Irish papist be sent out at Protestant expense to New South Wales to glorify an intolerant priesthood, to depress Protestantism and to stifle liberty in its cradle, then the 'cub of the British lion in the Antipodes' might demand, and possibly even take, more than its 'bearded parent' might be disposed to grant. But few seriously believed that, or wanted it to come to that. Most believed that they and their descendants would go on for thousands of years, with one breath hailing Australia and with the other asking God to save their sovereign. They would be men with divided hearts for years to come. Besides, now that the transportation of convicts had ceased they had to meet that demand for labour which had become so pressing that settlers did not know where to turn for a supply. The *Sydney Herald* thought that there was an 'infallible inducement' to try out Indian coolies which meant that they could not only be sure the coolies would come here as servants, but that they would always continue in that condition. Alas, the same could not be said for the assisted immigrants from 'Home', those useless and unskilful creatures with their indolent and vicious habits, who came here at free cost to themselves and promptly tried to be employers rather than join the class of permanent labourers.[13]

The masters of New South Wales had groaned to high heaven about their convict servants. They had complained of their insolence, their insubordination, their bolting, their telling lies to the injury of their master's good name, their inhaling the sea breezes instead of the smoke in their master's kitchen, their threatening to shorten their master's day, their corrupting their master's wives and children, their drinking, their whoring and their poxing lubras. But in the convict period the law was an effective instrument for the subordination of the convict and the ticket-of-leave holder. The regulations governing the behaviour of ticket-of-leave holders forbade them to leave their own police district without permission. There were other restrictions on freedom of movement. The Bushranging Act of 1834 empowered the police to require every person to prove that he was not an absconder from his master's service. On paper the assignment regulations provided protection for the convict servant against a cruel or oppressive master. The interpretation of the law in the country districts was in the hands of magistrates, or justices of the peace, who were themselves masters of convict servants. So whereas the history of the country districts of Russia in the days of serfdom and of the southern states of the United States of America in the days of negro slavery were characterized by serf or negro uprisings and the lamentations of conscience-stricken landlords or slave-masters, the history of New South Wales in the convict era was only once disturbed by a convict uprising, the ill-fated

[13] J. Sidney, *A Voice from the Far Interior of Australia* (London, 1847), p. 57; *Sydney Herald*, 6, 17 October, 12 November 1840; Report of Select Committee on Transportation, *P.P.*, 1837-8, xxii, 669, pp. v-vi.

uprising at Castle Hill in 1803. Nor was convict folk culture and sentiment distinguished by a note of rebellion, or the promise of a day when they avenged the wrongs they had suffered at the hands of their masters, or the hope of being able to 'Steal away, steal away to Jesus'.

The legendary Jim Jones of Botany Bay had sounded a note of rebellion:

> And some dark night when everything is silent in the town
> I'll kill the tyrants, one and all, and shoot the floggers down:
> I'll give the Law a little shock: remember what I say,
> They'll yet regret they sent Jim Jones in chains to Botany Bay.

In their songs the convicts looked to Heaven rather than their fellow-men to liberate them from labouring with the hoe and tending sheep for the convict slave-masters of New South Wales.

> I was convicted by the laws of England's hostile crown,
> Conveyed across those swelling seas in slavery's fettered bound,
> For ever banished from that shore where love and friendship grow,
> That loss of freedom to deplore and work the labouring hoe.
>
> Despised, rejected and oppressed in tattered rags I'm clad—
> What anguish fills my aching breast and almost drives me mad
> When I hear the settler's threatening voice say, 'Arise! to labour go;
> Take scourging, convicts, for your choice or work the labouring hoe.'
>
> Growing weary from compulsive toil beneath the noontide sun
> While drops of sweat bedew the soil my task remains undone;
> I'm flogged for wilful negligence, or the tyrants call it so—
> Ah what a doleful recompense for labour with the hoe.
>
> Behold yon lofty woodbine hills where the rose in the morning shines,
> Those crystal brooks that do distil and mingle through those vines—
> There seems to me no pleasures gained, but they augment my woe
> Whilst here an outcast doomed to live and work the labouring hoe.
>
> You generous sons of Erin's isle whose heart for glory burns,
> Pity a wretched exile who his long-lost country mourns;
> Restore me, Heaven, to liberty whilst I lie here below;
> Untie that clue of bondage and release me from the hoe.

Convict folk literature in general was distinguished more for its warning to offenders than its call to the victims to extricate themselves from their bondage. They were aware of their sufferings. All romantics who dreamed of the day when they roamed free by a purling stream holding a sweet girl by the hand were solemnly warned that in the convict colonies there were twenty men to one woman. The song 'Van Diemen's Land' contained their cry of pain:

The first day that we landed upon that fatal shore
The planters came around us, there might be twenty score.
They ranked us off like horses and they sold us out by hand
And they yoked us to the plough, brave boys, to plough Van Diemen's Land.

Significantly it ended with a warning, rather than a call to arms:

> But fourteen years is a long time, that is our fatal doom
> For nothing else but poaching for that is all we done;
> You would leave off both dog and gun and poaching, every man,
> If you but knew the hardship that's in Van Diemen's Land.

The convict servant found his consolation for the sufferings of forced labour not in Christ's promises or the teaching of the Enlightenment but in a coarse and ribald humour and what contemporary moralizers called 'wallowing in a sensual sty'.[14]

The problem in the transition from a convict to a free working class was to subordinate the free servant to his master without the aid of a penal code whose savage punishments were designed to enforce obedience by terror. The foundations of authority in the Old World were absent in rural society in New South Wales. In England, Scotland and Ireland the local justice of the peace lived in an imposing mansion; in New South Wales he often lived in a sod hut. In England, Scotland and Ireland the local justice was distinguished by dress, speech and deportment from those to whom he dispensed justice; in New South Wales, bush life stripped away most of these external differences between man and man. In England, Scotland and Ireland the labour pool was a corner-stone in the building of hierarchy and authority; in New South Wales the labour shortage eroded the authority of the master and strengthened the power of the servant. In England, Scotland and Ireland the village labourer went through the cycle of birth, mating and death in his native village; in New South Wales the rural labourers often had no fixed place of abode but moved from station to station with no sense either of permanence or of belonging, or of being part of the great chain of being. In England, Scotland and Ireland the village labourers grew up surrounded by an ideology that accepted the landowners as the great oaks in God's garden which offered protection and leadership to those of lowly estate; in New South Wales, convict servants, ticket-of-leave holders, and emancipists and their slave-masters had stripped away all the ideological mumbo-jumbo with

---

[14] An Act to Facilitate the Apprehension of Transported Felons and Offenders Illegally at Large and of Persons Found with Arms and Suspected to be Robbers, 5 Will. IV, no. 9, 5 August 1834, T. Callaghan, *Acts and Ordinances of the Governor and Council of New South Wales*; 'Jim Jones at Botany Bay', 'Labouring with the Hoe', and 'Van Diemen's Land' in D. Stewart and N. Keesing (eds), *Old Bush Songs* (Sydney, 1957), pp. 13-27.

which in the Old World the exploitation of man by man was softened and concealed. This left terror as the nexus between master and servant.[15]

The problem for the master was to find a sanction over the free as effective as the lash and other punishments had been for the bond. The masters of New South Wales had been so corrupted by the power the law conferred on them to exploit the labour of convict servants that they understandably looked to the law to provide a satisfactory foundation for their authority over the free. In 1828 the Legislative Council of New South Wales had passed an Act for the better regulation of servants, labourers and work people which imposed a maximum penalty of six months' gaol for servants absenting themselves from their employment, or refusing or neglecting to work without the consent of their employer. Despite this Act, all through the 1830s the masters grumbled as much about the indiscipline of the free as about the incompetence and the degradation of the bond. While Sydney mechanics called for three groans for Hannibal Macarthur, the avowed enemy of the working classes, and sections of the press deplored the landed classes of New South Wales using the government for the oppression of their servants, the Council passed on 20 October 1840 an Act to ensure the fulfilment of engagements and to provide for the adjustment of disputes between masters and servants in New South Wales and its dependencies. This was on the very day that Sir George solemnly told the members of Council the momentous piece of news that the transportation of convicts to New South Wales was to cease.[16]

By then the landed party in Council, led by Hannibal Macarthur, James Macarthur, Alexander Berry and Sir John Jamison, had made it clear that they proposed to use the limited powers of Council for the defence of the old order rather than give a lead in the construction of the new. On 29 July Sir George tried again to draw the attention of Council to the evils in the existing system of education. He showed them that many more schools were established in their thinly scattered population than were wanted because of the attempts by the four Christian denominations to establish separate schools for their own members. He showed them that under the existing system the poorer denominations—the Catholics and Methodists—or those most in need of assistance, obtained the smallest share of it. Again he suggested, as he had suggested at budget time in 1839, that the only way in which education would be extensively advanced in the colony was to institute government schools from which no person would necessarily be excluded by reason of their religious persuasion and to exclude all other schools from any assistance from

---

[15] For a monumental account of the relations between masters and servants in New South Wales from 1788 to 1851, see F. K. Crowley, *Working Class Conditions in Australia, 1788-1851* (thesis in library, University of Melbourne).

[16] An Act for the Better Regulation of Servants, Labourers and Work People, 9 Geo. IV, no. 9, 17 July 1828, T. Callaghan, op. cit.; A. Harris, *Settlers and Convicts* (London, 1847), pp. 295-6; *Australasian Chronicle*, 30 September 1840; *Australian*, 1 October 1840; *V. & P.* (L.C. N.S.W.), 20 October 1840; An Act to Ensure the Fulfilment of Engagements and to Provide for the Adjustment of Disputes between Masters and Servants in New South Wales and its Dependencies, 4 Vic., no. 23, 20 October 1840, T. Callaghan, op. cit.

government. Again those twelve Anglicans sat as tight of lip and tight of heart as they had in the previous year.

This time the Catholics also took fright because there was to be no special grant for Catholic schools. When Bishop Polding and Vicar-General Ulla-thorne remonstrated with Gipps, he reminded them rather rudely that numerically they were not the most powerful denomination in New South Wales. The two decided to take the first possible opportunity of showing Gipps just how powerful they really were. Late in August they used the occasion of the laying of the foundation stone of St Patrick's Church to demonstrate this strength. Some twenty thousand gathered from town and country at Church Hill to watch a procession of children, one aborigine, prominent Catholic laymen, the Vicar-General, the Lord Bishop and the clergy, who marched up King Street and entered St Mary's Cathedral for a choral singing of the Halleluiah chorus from Handel's *Messiah*. Tears of joy rolled down the cheeks of members of the congregation when that reminder rang out over their town that Christ, their King, would reign for ever and ever, even over the kingdoms of this world. In November Polding and Ulla-thorne sailed for Rome to drink again at what they believed were the waters of life.[17]

At the same time the patriarchs of the Legislative Council responded to every proposal to disturb the status quo with a similar implacable and irrational opposition. In December 1840 Gipps informed the members of the Legislative Council of a decision by the British Government to divide New South Wales into three districts for the administration of the land laws—a Northern District, from the Manning River to the tip of Cape York Penin-sula, a Middle District from the Manning to the Murrumbidgee and the Murray, and a Southern or Port Phillip District south of the area traversed by those two rivers. In the Northern and Southern Districts land would be sold at a fixed price of £1 per acre, and in the Middle District land would be sold by auction at a minimum upset price of 12s an acre. On 10 December the Lord Bishop of Australia, W. G. Broughton, asked members to adopt a petition to the Queen which complained that the new regulations would lead to the separation from the central division of their colony of several exten-sive and important districts, the retention of which was essential to their prosperity and future greatness. In a very elaborate speech His Lordship prophesied that the new boundary regulations would put an end to the system of depasturing by squatters under government licence, and that the land fund now devoted to immigration would be extinguished. Squatterdom would disappear off the map of New South Wales, a prospect he viewed with dismay because, as he saw it, the 'depasturing districts of the colony had mainly called into existence a large production of wool, a large mercantile

[17] *V. & P.* (L.C. N.S.W.), 29 July 1840; *Sydney Herald*, 31 July 1840; *Australasian Chronicle*, 27 August 1840; W. B. Ullathorne, *Autobiography* (London, 1891), pp. 167-8; see also S. Leslie (ed.), *W. B. Ullathorne: from cabin-boy to archbishop* (London, 1941); *Sydney Herald*, 16, 17 November 1840; J. B. Polding to Mr and Mrs Phillips, 17 Septem-ber 1840 (typescript in Polding Papers).

body, a very large, he might say marvellous revenue, the expenditure of which had given employment to thousands of industrious families, by enabling the settlers to transform the waste desert of yesterday into districts of smiling order, comfort and productiveness'.

All broad-acres men in the Council predicted that squatterdom and the immigration fund would be annihilated by the proposed change. The *Australasian Chronicle* accused 'a clique of sheep counts' of retaining the Bishop as their advocate to thwart the purposes of a paternal government. The patriarchs were attempting to preserve their country for ever as one vast run for sheep, or a park 'for the amusement of a few parvenus lordlings'. A month later on one of those muggy days in Sydney a large crowd of people stacked into the School of Arts to barrack madly for the spokesmen of squatterdom when they told them the proposed dismemberment of the colony threatened the sheep-walk. W. A. Duncan of the *Australasian Chronicle* tried to tell them that all Lord John Russell was trying to do was to promote a more rapid system of colonization by setting bounds to the grasping propensities of those wealthy cormorants, who wanted to make the entire continent and its inhabitants tributary to their avarice and ambition. They shouted him down.[18]

At the beginning of 1841 it looked as though squatterdom and convictism were long-term features of the human scene in New South Wales. The 'Cabbage Tree Boys' greeted immigrant women with coarse jokes and lewd gestures as they clambered down the rope-ladder from their ships. The 'larkers' bumped deliberately into men and women of some distinction in dress and deportment and mocked them with the words 'all round my hat'. Convictism had bred a race of levellers, who were only happy when they were laughing cruelly at the misfortunes of others or getting a rise out of the pretentious, and sneering at all the mighty men of renown. One night in 1841 as a band of Wesleyan missionaries marched up George Street singing a hymn, all under such a mighty influence that their faces shone with glory, a Romanist mob ran an empty dray at them, one man threw a dead cat into their midst, and others chucked crackers. Convictism had also bred a race of men who were indifferent to the great creations of the human spirit. In Sydney the vaudeville theatres were crowded each week-night, but when Conrad Knowles, a native-born Australian, celebrated his return from London in 1839 by putting on a performance of *Hamlet*, the attendance was so beggarly on the second night that Knowles had to take it off and give the locals the melodrama they craved as a mirror of the wild unbridled passions they took to be part of the fate of being a man in Australia.[19]

While the streets of Sydney still reverberated by night to the clatter of convictism, in the drawing-rooms of the bourgeoisie and the parlours of the

---

[18] *Australasian Chronicle*, 8, 12, 22, 26 December 1840, Russell to Gipps, 31 May 1840, *H.R.A.*, I. xx. 641-8; *Australian*, 15, 22 December 1840; *Sydney Gazette*, 19 December 1840; *Sydney Herald*, 9, 14, 15 December 1840, 8, 11, 12 January 1841; *Colonist*, 12 December 1840.

[19] *Sydney Herald*, 5 April, 10 June 1841; F. Irwin, *Theatre Comes to Australia* (Brisbane, 1971); N. Pidgeon, *The Life, Experience & Journal of Nathaniel Pidgeon* (Sydney, 1864), pp. 47-55.

respectable working classes, groups of men were gathering around pianos to sing songs redolent of a new age of bourgeois sentiment. The bounce of a convict ballad was giving way to the life-denying yearning of 'Home, sweet home'. The Betsey Bandicoots of the 1820s, those currency lasses who used to 'swig off a pot of peach-cyder' with their currency lads and go for 'a bit of a frisk' in the saddle were about to be tamed. On 1 January 1842 the total abstainers in Sydney published the first number of the *Teetotaller and General Newspaper* to rescue men and women from the awful vice which was the cause of their commercial embarrassment, nine-tenths of their crime, and nearly all the miseries they suffered as a community. They also proposed to rescue the aborigines from rum, brandy and other spirituous liquors, the consumption of which was causing their people to disappear off the face of the earth. They proposed to teach working men to use their money to maintain their families instead of enabling publicans to ride through the streets in a carriage and pair. They proposed to persuade men to spend their leisure time improving rather than debauching their minds. They solemnly reminded their readers that the desire for alcoholic drinks was not to be confounded with the sensation of thirst. They proposed to form a musical band and to open a library to provide entertainment for the newly reformed drunkards of Sydney.

Changes in the material setting had already prepared the way for a new life. That May the Independent Chapel in Sydney was lit up by gas lighting; a colonial wit added that preparations were happily in hand for Dr Lang's Scots Church to be similarly enlightened. That June, steam communication was established between Sydney, Melbourne, Launceston, Hobart and Adelaide. Some prophesied that the time was not far off when steamships would connect Swan River with the rest of Australia, and Australia with the ports of the United Kingdom. The quantity of wool exported increased from 1 401 284 pounds in 1831 to 8 610 775 pounds in 1840. The value of the wool clip increased from £75 929 in 1831 to £566 112 in 1840. Between 1836 and 1841 the population increased from 77 096 to 130 856. There was an even more radical change in the composition of the population. In 1821 there was one convict to every free person in the colony. When the indeterminate numbers of ex-convicts, their families and their descendants were added to the numbers of the bond, they comprised over 80 per cent of the population of New South Wales. In 1821 there were approximately seven men for every woman in New South Wales. By 1841 it was being said that with the stoppage of the transportation of convicts to New South Wales in the preceding year, the swelling numbers of free immigrants and the high birth-rate in immigrant families, the bond and their descendants would soon become an insignificant proportion of the population of New South Wales.[20]

[20] R. Covell, *Australia's Music* (Melbourne, 1967), p. 18; *Sydney Herald*, 9, 12 June 1841; *Teetotaller and General Newspaper*, 8, 15, 22 January, 21 May, 11 June 1842; Return of Wool Exported from the Colony of New South Wales from 1822 to 1840, appendix to Report of Committee on Immigration, *V. & P.* (L.C. N.S.W.), 1841; R. Mansfield, *Analytical View of the Census of New South Wales for the Year 1841* (Sydney, 1841).

The census confirmed a trend at which the anti-papists had already expressed their alarm—the increase in the proportion of Catholics to Protestants.
In 1841 Catholics comprised 27.72 per cent of the population. In April Lang
warned Protestants in his pamphlet *The Question of Questions* that their
grand centre of *future* civilization was in danger of being transformed into a
'Province of Popedom'. The *Sydney Herald* also warned that the day was not
far off when the plains of New South Wales would be inundated with
Romanists who would lower the temporal prosperity of the colony as they had
permanently reduced Ireland to the standard of living of a poor-house. With
the coming of steam power, the iron rail and the universal franchise, a
Romanist majority in New South Wales might destroy the institutions of the
free and establish arbitrary power and a priest-ridden society. W. G. Broughton and his fellow-members of the Immigration Committee of 1841 felt the
same way. They, too, were disturbed at the high proportion of Catholics
arriving as assisted immigrants, and disturbed that Protestant money was
being used to undermine the Protestant ascendancy in New South Wales.
They were not in favour of importing coolies as labourers because they were
a race of different origin, colour and habits from the European and bound to
occupy permanently a station of inferiority. They still hoped it might be
possible to teach the aborigines the advantages of working regularly at fixed
wages and being placed on the same footing as Europeans. They wanted to
create a social and political state corresponding with that of their country of
origin. They wanted their new country to be a place where the English race
would spread from sea to sea without being tainted by mixing with the
people of a lower race or caste.[21]

The events of the anniversary dinner on 26 January 1842 symbolized the
new trend in society. As the two hundred guests arrived at the Royal Hotel
the band played 'Oh the Roast Beef of Old England'. The president for the
dinner was not an emancipist or the son of an emancipist, but Captain
Maurice Charles O'Connell, military secretary to his father Sir Maurice
Charles O'Connell, the commander of the forces in New South Wales and a
son-in-law of Captain William Bligh, one-time governor of New South
Wales. In proposing the first toast to that 'young and lovely Sovereign, the
Queen' the gallant young captain said that for his part he was proud, and he
knew they were proud they were essentially British; he could say without fear
of contradiction that in no part of the vast dominions of the British Empire
would the feeling of loyalty be more felt than in their own. The second toast

[21] J. D. Lang, *The Question of Questions* (Sydney, 1841); *Sydney Herald*, 14 April,
17 June 1841; Report from Committee on Immigration, 1841, *V. & P.* (L.C. N.S.W.),
1841; minute by James Stephen, 11 July 1841, C.O. 201/310; collections of the works of
Duterrau, Bock, Wainewright and Glover in the Queen Victoria Museum, Launceston,
the Tasmanian Museum and Art Gallery, Hobart, and the Allport Collection in the
Tasmanian State Library; C. Craig, *The Engravers of Van Diemen's Land* (Hobart,
1961); R. Crossland, *Wainewright in Tasmania* (Melbourne, 1954); S. Passioura, John
Glover (thesis in library, University of Melbourne); P. R. Eldershaw, 'John Glover',
Tasmanian Historical Research Association, *Papers and Proceedings*, vol. 12, 1964-5;
personal visit to grave of Glover at Deddington Chapel and Patterdale, 7 May 1973.

was proposed by the vice-president, G. R. Nichols, the son of an emancipist: 'To Eastern Australia. May prosperity continue to shine upon her, and may her Sons learn to emulate the Patriotism and Virtues of their British Fore-bears.' There was a toast to their able and upright governor. There was a toast to their colony, which was coupled with the hope that it would never again become the receptacle of slaves. There was a toast to free institutions, proposed by that talented young man James Martin, who in a moment of passion asked them to rise to their feet and drink a bumper as a testimony of their convic-tion that without free institutions there would be no real happiness or com-mercial prosperity. As Nichols put it, for himself, and he was sure he was also speaking for others, he would sooner be poor and enjoy those civil and politi-cal rights and privileges to which he was entitled by his birth as an English-man than be loaded with gold obtained at the price of slavery. Just to prove how English they were, there had been a cricket match that day between the Liverpool Club and the Victorian Club in which, it was said, the fielding of the Liverpool Club was very inferior.[22]

Jeremiahs shook their heads and warned them not to expect too much from their birthrights as Englishmen. Broughton warned them to take heed lest Almighty God chastised them with a drought or a commercial depres-sion for their sins of overweening pride and beastly sensuality. The press warned that monetary and commercial affairs were in such a depressed state that even the richest merchants were beginning to tremble. Sydney Town was beginning to look as dull and disconsolate as an Irish clergyman on a tithing day. Insolvency petitions were becoming more and more frequent. In February the brewer J. Wright and the gentleman J. Roberts filed their petitions in the bankruptcy court. There were rumours of a catastrophic decline in British investment, and prophecies of dire consequences such as more insolvencies, the end of land sales, the end of immigration, and increases in unemployment. Henry Parkes was wondering whether he would earn enough in New South Wales to ameliorate the exile's lot, for the com-mercial state of Sydney was so gloomy that there was scarcely a mercantile house in Sydney that a man could safely say was solvent a year ago, which was not now undermined by threat of bankruptcy. Despite the widespread unemployment both in town and country, the employers still wanted to inundate the colony with workers because, accustomed to having the convict's toil for nothing, they could not bring themselves to pay for a free man. Parkes asked his family to keep him posted on the fortunes of the chartists in England, those men of vision who wanted to create a society worthy of the noblest conceptions of human dignity, because he was beginning to despair of fulfilling that dream in Australia.[23]

[22] *Australian*, 27 January 1842; *Sydney Herald*, 28 January 1842.

[23] *S.M.H.*, 10 September 1842; J. D. Lang, *An Historical and Statistical Account of New South Wales* (2 vols, 3rd ed., London, 1852), vol. 1, pp. 297-304; J. H. Williams to D. Webster, 1 January 1842 (Consular Records of the U.S.A., microfilm in NAT. L.); Ruth Knight, *Illiberal Liberal: Robert Lowe in New South Wales, 1840-50* (Melbourne, 1966),

At the same time the 'sheep-walk for ever' men were quite determined that the institutions of the free should never come under the control of chartists, radicals and levellers. At a public meeting on 16 February 1842, convened to petition the British Government to confer on the inhabitants their birthrights as Englishmen, James Macarthur maintained that they could safely leave it to the British Government to work out the details of any house of assembly. Over a year earlier he had urged the men of property to allow the exclusivist-emancipist issue to die away so that they could thwart any move for a £10 suffrage. The radicals, chartists and levellers, sensing a plot by the patriarchs to keep them off any future electoral roll, clamoured to be heard. Henry Macdermott, who was said to be a bit of a Jacobin, so inflamed the conservatives by talking of the rights of man that they shouted him down as a dangerous revolutionary who wanted to hand over power in New South Wales to a 'mob of low Irishmen'! The chairman adjourned the meeting to 28 February at the Australian College.

At this second meeting, Macdermott explained that he was not a radical, but a moderate, who did not advocate universal suffrage but did advocate a more liberal franchise than what he understood the conservatives wanted. James Macarthur explained that his objection to Macdermott was not because at the previous meeting he had allowed excitement to triumph over moderation but because he based the claim of the colonists to free institutions on the hollow and unsound doctrine of the rights of man, a doctrine which might dazzle the vulgar with the semblance of liberty but was really the meteor blaze of a wild and erring ambition of the many to tyrannize over and destroy the few. The meeting proceeded to elect a constitution drafting committee composed of patriarchal men such as James Macarthur, large landowners such as Henry O'Brien of Yass, 'Old Iron Bark' Lawson of Blue Mountains fame, Dr Nicholson, T. Icely and J. R. Holden, those two spokesmen for the Patriotic Association, W. C. Wentworth and Dr Bland, and William à Beckett. This group, composed of exclusivists and emancipists, anti-transportationists and pro-transportationists, survivors from and inheritors of old family feuds, united in their determination not to allow the lower middle-class £10 suffrage men of Sydney to use the institutions of the free either to destroy the sheep-walk of New South Wales or to create a Yankee-style democratic, egalitarian republic.[24]

At the committee discussions in March and April Macarthur and Wentworth persuaded their fellow-members that no such thing as a universal franchise could exist in their society, because like all other proposals to level out differences in society it would produce not equality but inequality. Whenever the principle of property came into collision with the equality

pp. 38-9; S. J. Butlin, *Foundations of the Australian Monetary System 1788-1851* (Melbourne, 1953), pp. 321-4; H. Parkes to his sister, 23 January 1842, H. Parkes, *An Emigrant's Home Letters* (Sydney, 1896), pp. 122-3.

[24] *Sydney Herald*, 6 February 1841, 17, 21, 29 February 1842; *Australian*, 9 January 1841, 19, 22 February 1842.

principle the former must prevail. Wentworth told them he was now a firm believer in a Legislative Council that was part nominated, and part elected on a high property qualification. The man who had written in his youth of an elected assembly as the birthright of the creators of a new Britannia became an advocate for Colonial Office ideas on the institutions of New South Wales. The *Australian* denounced this headlong descent from the sublime heights of patriotism to the woeful depths of Whiggism. Wentworth's day, they said, had ended. The man who had first taught the natives of the colony what liberty was had betrayed them and lost their confidence.[25]

Up-country the sheep men applauded the Macarthur–Wentworth stand for political power to be the prerogative of men of property. On 29 July the flock-masters in the Bathurst district gathered at Mrs Black's Hotel. Speaker after speaker spoke of sheep-stations as nurseries of the growing greatness of the colony. They patted themselves on the back for civilizing the back-blocks and dragooning the blacks to an acceptance of white ownership of the land. They looked to the future legislators in Sydney to rescue them from the 'Cimmerian darkness of Downing-street', because their Almighty Creator had decreed that their country should be pastoral and not agricultural. The Solons of Sydney should ensure that the laws of man were brought into harmony with the immutable decrees of man's Almighty Creator. In all the up-country districts of New South Wales there were men who believed God and man should reward them by concentrating political power in their hands when the Mother Country conferred on New South Wales the institutions of the free.[26]

While the flock-masters of the country districts were contributing their note of rustic bluntness to the Macarthur–Wentworth scheme for confining political power to the men of landed property, crowds lined the shores of Sydney Harbour in July to watch the arrival of the adventurer and cloud-topper Ben Boyd on the yacht *Wanderer*. He had come to carve out a king-dom in the wilds of New South Wales and to write his name in the portals of fame. But the days of the 'half a million acres' men were numbered, cheap convict labour was no longer available in New South Wales, and society was in the grip of a commercial depression in which prices for wool, sheep and cattle were falling every day. Besides, the bourgeoisie of Sydney, shop-keepers, tradesmen and mechanics saw the steamship and not the plantation planter as the symbol of the future of their society.

On 20 July the bourgeoisie of Sydney Town had their first sniff of future power. At long last the Legislative Council had passed an Act to declare the town of Sydney to be a city and to incorporate the inhabitants thereof. All previous attempts to create such a corporation had foundered on those two

[25] *Australian*, 29, 31 March, 2, 5 April 1842; for the discussion of the role of Went-worth see *Australian*, 18 January 1842.

[26] *S.M.H.*, 2, 16 August, 17 September 1842. The *Sydney Herald* became the *Sydney Morning Herald* on 1 August 1842. It also increased in size to meet growing demands on its space from 'vast circles of civilized life' in Australia. It had become a daily on 1 October 1840.

jagged rocks in the public life of New South Wales—the rights of emancipists, and the property qualification for electors. Wentworth, sensing that the
councillors would neither understand nor concur with his Whiggishness, had
tried delaying tactics, but all to no avail, for the Act conferred the right to
vote on every male person of the full age of twenty-one years who for one
year had occupied a house, warehouse, counting-house or ship of the annual
value of £25.[27]

As election day approached the conservatives openly feared that the men
of good sense and reputability were about to be overmastered by the illiterate
and the vulgar. Thousands of pounds were spent by candidates in the distribution of drink. At one polling booth an infuriated drunken mob drove a
police magistrate who was endeavouring to preserve order into an enclosure
surrounded with high palings and pelted him with bricks, stones and large
pieces of paling. At another polling booth the tent was pulled down and one
of the candidates, a shipowner, was mauled by the mob. Not to be outdone,
he armed the whalers on one of his ships with harpoons and whaling knives
and swept his opponents away from the booth. After polling day on 1 November, the Tories and Whigs of Sydney took fright at the number of emancipists, carcass butchers, tanners, wine and spirit merchants, builders, publicans
and bankers who were to wear the rich robes of office in the corporation of
Sydney. Because of the low property franchise ex-convicts and chartists and
levellers such as Edward Flood and Henry Macdermott were among the first
councillors. There was worse to come. The *Herald* demanded that the mayor
be a man not only of unblemished reputation himself but also of such
respectable connections that no one could accuse him of the slightest tinge of
convictism or say that the money of a one-time convict placed the first mayor
of Sydney in his chair. Everyone in Sydney knew this referred to John
Hosking, who was the son-in-law of Samuel Terry, the wealthiest ex-convict
in Sydney. Despite this conservative bigotry and scurrility, on 9 November
the councillors elected John Hosking, an Australian by birth and a merchant
by profession, to be the first mayor of the city of Sydney. Hosking was the son
of a Wesleyan missionary. After his rise to wealth, he had joined the Church
of England and taken up a run amongst the gentry on the Limestone Plains.
But marriage with Martha Foxlowe Terry barred his entry into the drawing-
rooms of the country gentry.

On the evening of 10 November 1842 Hosking entered the dining-room of
the Royal Hotel in Sydney wearing a purple gown edged with ermine while
the band played 'Oh the Roast Beef of Old England' and then a special
number for his wife, the Robert Burns song 'John Anderson My Joe'. To
words expressing the democratic and egalitarian sentiments sweeping the
cities of the civilized world, the daughter of a convict took her bow as the first

---

[27] *Sydney Herald*, 19 July 1842; *Australian*, 24 May, 2, 7, 11, 15 June 1842; An Act to
Declare the Town of Sydney to be a City and to Incorporate the Inhabitants Thereof,
6 Vic., no. 3, 20 July 1842, T. Callaghan, op. cit.; *Sydney Gazette*, 11 August 1842;
C. H. Bertie, *The Early History of the Sydney Municipal Council* (Sydney, 1911).

lady of the city of Sydney. Once again the sentimental attachment to Britain lived side by side in their hearts with the hope of creating in the New World a society free from the blemishes of the Old World. At the dinner Hosking toasted the health of the bishop and clergy of Australia and wished them well on their pious and important labours, for these merchants, shopkeepers, publicans, barbers, levellers and chartists were not secret but open sharers of the very respectability and philistinism their opponents—the Whigs and Tories of Sydney and elsewhere—were predicting would be brought to ruin in the coming days of rabblement. Radicals who were disappointed in Hosking for copying the dress which promoted rank in society, accused him of starting a new aristocracy which would forge fetters for their children to wear.[28]

This triumph of grocerdom in the corporation of Sydney caused the conservatives to look to London for a possible saviour. The wool clip and sentiment had already laid solid foundations for Anglophil attitudes. By the end of 1842 the Queen and Her Majesty's Principal Secretary of State for the Colonies were cast in the role of defenders of squatterdom's domination in New South Wales. Edward Stanley, the eldest son of the thirteenth Earl of Derby, seemed the answer of divine providence to the conservative's prayer. He had whiled away those early days in his career lolling in the House of Commons in the posture of a vulgar Yankee at a coffee-house rather than a highly bred scion of the English aristocracy, and had spoken of Ireland like a petulant bloodhound who enjoyed savaging the Irish people. By 1842 he had left behind the giddy days of his youth and faced up to the central question for his class—how to preserve their privileges and their power against the flood of industrial civilization and egalitarianism. He believed that there was a spirit abroad in his day which threatened to tear down and destroy the foundations of society. The task of the hierarchy of rural England—the landed magnificoes, squires, parsons, farmers and agricultural labourers—was to ensure that after that destructive spirit had passed over the land there was something left behind besides 'wreck and desolation'. When reports reached London in the middle of 1842 that the colony of New South Wales was threatened with a deluge from a great flood of levellers, chartists, Jacobins and emancipists, Stanley was quick to see that the heart of the problem was the absence in the colony of a class similar to the landed grandees of the Mother Country who could keep afloat the ark of liberty, order and hierarchy.[29]

---

[28] *Australian*, 9, 11, 14 November 1842; *S.M.H.*, 12, 17, 30 November 1842; J. C. Byrne, *Twelve Years' Wanderings in the British Colonies from 1835 to 1847* (2 vols, London, 1848), vol. 1, pp. 133-4; see also speeches by Gipps, Broughton and Hosking at banquet to citizens of Sydney on 21 December, *Australian*, 23 December 1842; C. B. Mackerras, *The Hebrew Melodist* (Sydney, 1963); F. J. Woodward, *Portrait of Jane* (London, 1951), pp. 222-5.

[29] *Spectator* (London), 17 May 1834; *Atlas*, 28 December 1844; *Cork Examiner*, 30 August, 15 September 1841; H. Maxwell (ed.), *The Creevey Papers* (2 vols, London, 1903), vol. 2, pp. 40, 76, 128, 203, 219, 295; C. C. F. Greville, *Memoirs* (3 vols, London, 1875), vol. 2; R. Blake, *Disraeli* (London, 1966), pp. 286-7.

ABORIGINES ATTACK A STORE DRAY

Drawing by S. T. Gill, La Trobe Library, Melbourne

THE ASSIMILATED ABORIGINES IN SYDNEY, 1849

Drawing by unknown draftsman, Mitchell Library, Sydney

RECEIVING THEIR NURTURE, 1845

Drawing of the aborigines on Flinders Island by Francis Guillemard de Wesselow,
Tasmanian Museum and Art Gallery, Hobart

The problem was to devise political institutions to ward off the days of 'wreck and desolation'. Ever since April 1838 James Macarthur had been urging the Colonial Office to create for New South Wales a Legislative Council composed in part of nominated members who would be as strong as those oaks of Old England, the landed aristocracy, which no revolutionary wind had uprooted, and in part of elected members, it being understood that the qualification for voting would be a high property qualification. He wanted the members of the Legislative Council to represent the character, property and intelligence of the colony. How could this be done in New South Wales where the men who owned the sheep and cattle were grazing their beasts on land in which they had no security of tenure? The very precariousness of their rights to the land had put into their mouths the slogans of would-be revolutionaries rather than supporters of conservatism. During 1841 and 1842 Edward Macarthur had patiently presented to Stanley the idea of a part nominated, part elected Legislative Council to protect society against the levellers, the convicts, the chartists, and the 'low Irish mob' who threatened to drag everyone down to their dreary level of mediocrity and vulgar materialism.[30]

By then Stanley and his advisers had had the advantage of studying the ideas of Alexis de Tocqueville, whose third and final volume of his *De la Démocratie en Amérique* had been published in 1839. In this and the two preceding volumes, published in 1835, Tocqueville had suggested that man needed a new political science for a new world. As he saw it the gradual development of equality of conditions was the principal characteristic of his age. It was not wise to believe that such a movement could be stopped. It was not wise to believe that, having destroyed feudalism, democracy would recoil before the bourgeoisie. He had written his volumes under a sort of religious terror produced in him by the sight of this irresistible revolution striding over the centuries and knocking down all obstacles in its way. The future belonged to this equality. The question was, was it possible to instruct this democracy, to revive its beliefs, purify its customs, and control its movements, and gradually to replace its inexperience and its blind instincts with the knowledge of affairs, and the knowledge of its true interests? For that, man must find a means of preserving liberty in a world in which the overwhelming majority had a depraved taste for equality, and a willingness to place themselves under the tyranny of the majority, or some plebiscitary dictator, provided they themselves could gratify their own passions for material well-being. The remedies Tocqueville prescribed were: indirect election to increase the number of conservatives in the central house of assembly; local government to give men practice in and induce a taste for participation in public life; a federal consti-

---

[30] James Macarthur to Glenelg, 10 April 1838, C.O. 201/281; correspondence between Edward Macarthur and Stanley, 1841-2 (Papers and Correspondence of the Fourteenth Earl of Derby, Box 125/5, Christ Church, Oxford); Edward Macarthur to James Macarthur, 1 October 1842 (Macarthur Papers, vol. 19); A. C. V. Melbourne, *Early Constitutional Development in Australia* (London, 1934), pt 3, ch. 12.

tution, because it combined the advantages of a powerful central government with protection of liberty by the division of legislative and executive powers, and the rights of property by in-built constitutional checks on radicalism; religious education so that citizens might know what was 'good and just'.

In the Colonial Office there were men who quickly became converts to the Tocqueville view. Viscount Howick, Under-Secretary for the Colonies, who was said to have enjoyed all his life a surfeit of that *gravitas* which Lord Stanley had lacked in his salad-days of the chase and the bottle, was a ready convert to a scheme which gave the elite a chance to go on 'practising on the lower orders', and delighted to find that it might be possible to devise political institutions for New South Wales in which the vicious levelling tendencies of convictism would receive little support. James Stephen, rudely known in Sydney and elsewhere as Mr Mother Country, who believed that only the few were elevated enough to see that joy in suffering was what was acceptable to God, was attracted to the idea of a Legislative Council for New South Wales in which the elite would have a majority.[31]

By contrast the other advice offered to the Colonial Office seemed to lack the high seriousness of these men who had sensed the religious terror de Tocqueville had felt about that irresistible revolution striding over the centuries and knocking down all obstacles in its way. Charles Buller, the London messenger boy for the leaders of the Australian Patriotic Association, cracked jokes and charmed the ladies and presented opinions from men who wanted to put the clock back in Sydney by retaining the old convict system. As for E. G. Wakefield, he had already blotted his copy-book in the past, and was doing it again, as such men always do, by holding up to public ridicule as incompetent dunderheads the very men whose minds he was trying to influence. The very handsome George Grote, the historian of Greece but not the wielder of a straight bat in cricket despite many attempts to acquire by practice the gift nature had denied him, spoke with a becoming moral passion in the House of Commons on the beauty of freedom and the ugliness of convict moral pollution. Like most men with a prodigious memory, a 'head-piece clever' and an eye for all the beauty in the world, he knew nothing of that 'religious terror' about the spread of equality over the face of the globe.[32]

When the news reached London that radicals such as Edward Flood and Henry Macdermott had spoken of the rights of man at a public meeting, and that chartists like Henry Parkes were already in the wings of the stage of public life waiting for the call to testify to the day when all men would live in dignity, Stanley had steered through the British parliament an Act for the Government of New South Wales and Van Diemen's Land which combined

[31] A. de Tocqueville, *De la Démocratie en Amérique* (3 vols, Paris, 1874), vol. 1, introduction; notes for a speech by Viscount Howick on Lytton Bulwer's motion on New South Wales, September 1831 (Papers on New South Wales, Grey Papers, Durham).

[32] Speech by C. Buller in House of Commons, 5 May 1840, *P.D.*, 3rd ser., vol. 53, pp. 1300-4; *Edinburgh Review*, vol. 75, 1842, pp. 140-62; ibid., vol. 71, 1840, pp. 88-98; M. L. Clarke, *George Grote* (London, 1962), ch. 8; speeches by G. Grote in House of Commons, 25 March, 22 April 1842, *P.D.*, 3rd ser., vol. 57, pp. 598-608, 974-87.

the ideas of the Macarthur brothers and the teachings of de Tocqueville. The Legislative Council was to consist of thirty-six members, twenty-four of whom were to be elected and twelve nominated. It enacted that the District of Port Phillip was to elect five members, the town of Melbourne one, and the town of Sydney two. So the two towns which contained 27 per cent of the population were to elect three members, and the country districts twenty-one. The boundary of the Port Phillip District in the north and north-east was to be a straight line drawn from Cape Howe to the nearest source of the River Murray and thence along the course of that river to the eastern boundary of the province of South Australia. The right to vote was given to all persons who possessed an estate of freehold of lands and tenements situated within the district of which such vote was to be given of the clear annual value of £200, or a householder within such district occupying a dwelling house of the clear annual value of £20 at least. No man could be elected a member of the Legislative Council unless he possessed an estate of freehold of the yearly value of £100 or of the value of £2000, above all charges and incumbrances affecting the same. By omission the holders of licences to depasture stock outside the boundaries were ineligible to vote or stand for election. Members were to be elected for a period of five years.

Of the twelve nominated members, six were to be chosen from senior government officers, and the other six to be nominated by the Governor for a term of five years. The elected and nominated members were to elect their own speaker. The Council was given power to make laws for the peace, order and good government of the colony provided such laws were not repugnant to the laws of England. The Council was expressly excluded from passing laws affecting the alienation of the Crown lands or the expenditure of the revenue derived from the sale, leasing and licensing of such lands. The Governor was empowered to assent, withold assent, or reserve bills for the signification of Her Majesty's pleasure. The Governor was expressly required to reserve all bills altering or affecting electoral districts, or altering the number to be chosen by a district, or increasing the number of members of Council, or altering the salaries of the Governor, the Superintendent of Port Phillip, or the judges, or altering certain duties. Three schedules were attached to the Act. Schedule A provided that £33 000 of the annual revenue of the colony was to be used to pay the salaries of the Governor, the Superintendent of Port Phillip, the Chief Justice, the three puisne judges, and the general expenses for the administration of justice. Schedule B set aside £15 000 each year for the cost of civil administration, and Schedule C set aside the annual sum of £30 000 for public worship. Out of an annual revenue of £325 000, £81 600 was outside the control of the Council.

This looked like a sharing of power between the property holders of New South Wales—both landed and mercantile—and the Imperial parliament, which had delegated part of its sovereignty, but not surrendered any of it. It looked like a constitution which the 'sons of Britain' men and the 'birthright of Englishmen' supporters could applaud, as well as all those who looked for the victory of conservatism in the politics of New South Wales. These groups at first welcomed the Act while the radicals, chartists and levellers called it a 'mockery of self-government' and a mockery of all those who were looking to 'a considerable extension of popular rights'. To strengthen the conservative forces in society the Act empowered the Governor to divide New South Wales into districts and create a district council in each district, the electors of which possessed the same property qualifications as electors for the Legislative Council. Each district council was to have power to make by-laws for the purposes of local government and to contribute towards the cost of the police establishment. Stanley believed, as did his admirers at the Colonial Office, that through participation in local government, and in what affected their daily lives, the men of property would acquire practice in and a taste for public life. By then the men of property were so incensed by the companion Act to the constitution—the Act for Regulating the Sale of Waste Land Belonging to the Crown in the Australian Colonies—that the split between conservatives and radicals in the response to the constitution Act was patched over and replaced by a union of all the political groups in New South Wales calling for self-government.[33]

Under the Waste Lands Act no waste land of the Crown was ever to be sold at less than 20s an acre. That news was enough to spread panic around Sydney and the country districts for if it meant anything, some said, it meant that no land whatsoever would be sold, and hence there would be no money to pay for the passages of immigrants. Immigration would cease and the sheep-walks of New South Wales would relapse to the natural state of lands wandered over by kangaroos, possums and aborigines. The Act prescribed that the proceeds from land sales were to be divided into two equal parts, one of which was to be used for migration, and the other in accordance with instructions issued by the Secretary of State. The application of only half the proceeds of land sales to migration was greeted with groans. The Act also prescribed that 15 per cent of the gross proceeds of the land sales was to be applied for the benefit, civilization and protection of the aborigines. There were more groans at this decision by the Mother Country to force the colonists to spend money so desperately needed for migration on the hopeless task of civilizing and protecting aborigines by paying salaries to 'swallow-tailed coated gentlemen'.

The Act contained no provisions for granting security of tenure to the holders of licences to depasture stock outside the boundaries of location. Again Broughton grieved. The great object he had in view, he said, was a moral one, for while the graziers were only squatters and had no title to the land they occupied, there would be very little religious or moral improvement.

---

[33] An Act for the Government of New South Wales and Van Diemen's Land, 5 & 6 Vic., c. 76, 30 July 1842, *Statutes at Large*, vol. 16; Stanley to Gipps, 5 September 1842, *H.R.A.*, I. xii. 238-43; *P.D.*, 3rd ser., vol. 63, p. 880; A. C. V. Melbourne, op. cit., pt 3, ch. 13; *S.M.H.*, 23 November, 27, 31 December 1842; *Sydney Gazette*, 13 October 1842; *Australian*, 18 November 1842.

He looked forward to the day when the patriarchs outside the boundaries became great men. Those plains over which the Old Testament patriarchs had driven their sheep had become the spot where Solomon had erected his temple. The licensees outside the boundaries reacted in a much more down-to-earth way. They said it was absurd for those Tory bumbureaucrats in London, those would-be Solons of the Adelphi and Downing Street theorists, to conceive of the sheep-walks of New South Wales as places where green grass and chocolate soil would sustain countless numbers of yeoman farmers. Once again, by withholding from such licensees the opportunity to purchase their land, or part of their land, men of the best blood of Old England, who might have become country gentlemen, magistrates, and heads of families had remained 'squatters' who had no home. Men who would have put down permanent roots in the country and become like those English oaks, not to be broken by those great winds of change and that destructive spirit of equality blowing over the civilized world, now joined with liberals and radicals in demanding a voice in their own affairs. Bourgeois, gentry, squatter and working man, Tory, Whig, liberal, radical and chartist, the Protestant and the Catholic joined hands to demand self-government for New South Wales.[34]

As the year drew to a close the commercial depression deepened. Sydney was dismal as the fashion centre moved from Government House to the insolvency court. 'Meetings of creditors this day' became an all too familiar headline in the local press. Up-country the price of stock fell so low that settlers had trouble paying the interest on their borrowed money. At Mudgee, Broughton found in December that the extreme pecuniary distress was making it next to impossible to collect the smallest donations to build churches. He had seen to his great regret churches only half finished. He went on believing that the Divine Power would in time provide them with means to accomplish their great design for the continuance of the Divine Kingdom upon earth.

The discontinuance of convict assignment and the almost complete cessation of immigration contributed to such a great and acknowledged want of labour throughout the colony and such a serious loss to flocks and herds that the landowners of the Middle District formed on 20 August 1842 an Association for Promotion of Immigration from India to Their Colony. In the remaining months of the year settlers from New England to the Monaro rushed to join the association. They believed coolies made excellent shepherds, herdsmen, ploughmen, garden labourers, field labourers, dairymen and mechanics and saved money for employers.

In Sydney Henry Parkes was losing heart. That September of 1842 his income was not sufficient for his support. Those days of ease and happiness, surrounded by all the luxuriant beauty of an Australian summer, were not to

[34] An Act for Regulating the Sale of Waste Land Belonging to the Crown in the Australian Colonies, 5 & 6 Vic., c. 36, 22 June 1842, *Statutes at Large*, vol. 34; Stanley to Gipps, 15 September 1842, *H.R.A.*, I. xxii. 279-84; A. C. V. Melbourne, op. cit., pp. 275-6; *S.M.H.*, 16 August, 10 September, 23 November 1842.

be his that year. Insolvency, he noted, 'like some fearful epidemic' was daily discovering itself in some new places. Wages were very low and employment was not plentiful in Sydney. When he heard that summer of the death of his mother, it was a comfort to him to know there was another and a better world where the weary were at rest and sorrow never troubled them. While he lived he would cling to the hope of returning to dear England. The man who had dreamed of achieving the brotherhood of man in the wilds of Australia was becoming faint of heart. Over in Norfolk Island another 'future of humanity' man, Alexander Maconochie, had the mortifying experience of discovering that music, which he had advocated as an instrument for the reformation of convicts, had provided the opportunity for a convict to seduce his own daughter.[35]

By contrast the faith of some of the native-born remained quite buoyant. On 27 October 1842 Charles Harpur published in the *Australasian Chronicle* his lyric 'To the Lyre of Australia' in which the glory of his native land was his theme. That summer he put down on paper his hopes for the future of man in 'This Southern Land of Ours'. As he saw it, if clowns continued to make their laws and knaves continued to rule them, their soil was rich in vain. But he did not despair. He was hopeful that the colonists would not go on chaining their enterprise and their thought to the service of a 'misguiding past'. He hoped they were about to have a 'braver system' and a 'nobler manhood' in this 'Southern Land of Ours'. Some warned their contemporaries that such Australianism nourished in the breasts of the native-born the viper of loathing for all other members of society. Harpur was confident that with the coming of industrial civilization to Australia, men would shed the shackles of colonialism and acquire the confidence and the power to make their own history. He believed that in time his fellow-countrymen would emancipate themselves from that terrible lie of squatterdom, that God and nature had decreed that New South Wales should be a sheep-walk, destined never to advance much beyond the stage reached by the two sons of Adam.[36]

[35] Georgiana Lowe to Mrs Sherbrooke, 28 May 1843 (Sherbrooke Papers), quoted in Ruth Knight, *Illiberal Liberal*, p. 38; S. J. Butlin, *Foundations of the Australian Monetary System*, pp. 322-3; extracts from report of W. G. Broughton in Report of Committee of Society in Aid of Propagating the Gospel, 6 December 1842 (Bonwick Transcripts, Missionary, vol. I, pp. 22-7); H. Parkes to his sister, 3 September 1842, 26 January 1843, H. Parkes, *An Emigrant's Home Letters*, pp. 128-35; private letter of Gipps to Stanley, 22 August 1842 (Papers of the Fourteenth Earl of Derby, Box 127/4); *Port Phillip Herald*, 18 November 1842; Report of Preliminary Meeting on Coolie Labour, 20 August 1842 (MS. in M.L.).

[36] *Australasian Chronicle*, 27 October, 6 December 1842; C. Harpur, 'This Southern Land of Ours' in Harpur's Poems in Early Life (Harpur Papers, MS. in M.L.); *S.M.H.*, 14 November, 31 December 1842.

9

EBB-TIDE IN VAN DIEMEN'S LAND

IN NEW SOUTH WALES the absence of inland water transport, the small extent of good land compared with the poor and the barren, and the dry seasons encouraged dispersion of settlement, the alienation of man from man, and the germ of a nation of men who were often strangers to the influences of women. By contrast in Van Diemen's Land in the settled districts of the Derwent River, in the Midlands around Campbelltown and in the northern districts around Longford, a benign and bounteous nature provided the grasses and the soil for a concentration of settlement, and a community of farmers in a countryside not unlike the country districts around Cork in Ireland or Dorchester in England. Agriculture flourished; the cultivated fields looked good. In New South Wales the lives of the settlers were bedevilled by the terror and abomination between white man and black man; in Van Diemen's Land ever since the round-up of the aborigines in 1830 the survivors were too few (probably not exceeding 250), and too broken in spirit to menace or disturb the life of the white man. In thirty years the aborigines had been banished from that land in what was probably the most striking instance of the comparative rate of increase of a civilized over a savage people in the history of mankind.[1]

In Van Diemen's Land nature was benign; history was malign. In New South Wales between 1837 and 1840 the great change from the use of semi-slave to free labour began; in Van Diemen's Land during the corresponding years no such change occurred. In New South Wales the sudden increase in the number of free immigrants and the decrease in the number of convicts arriving, so changed the composition of the population that by 1841 the convicts were becoming an insignificant fraction of the population. In Van Diemen's Land assisted immigration had not significantly affected the proportion of bond to free. In 1837 that proportion was 42 per cent and in 1840 it was still 40 per cent. In the latter year, out of a total population of 45 000 there were 17 763 convicts and 27 237 free persons. In that year one half of the population was of convict origin and one quarter was definitely not of convict origin. Possibly almost three-quarters of the population either were convicts or ex-convicts or had some convict ancestry. In New South Wales enlightened employers of labour were confident of their capacity to dispense with convict

---

[1] T. Walker, *A Month in the Bush of Australia* (London, 1838), pp. 52-3; C. Darwin, *Journal of Researches into the Geology and Natural History of the Various Countries Visited by H.M.S. Beagle* (London, 1839), pp. 533-5.

labour; in Van Diemen's Land enlightened employers and publicists doubted whether their society could take the leap forward and whether they could dispense with the £500 000 the British Government spent each year in the colony on convict administration. This expenditure, they said, flowed like a luxuriant current through the colony, enriching and irrigating it. The whole of society was tied to the convict system—the senior government officers, the military officers, the chaplains, the school-teachers and the employers of labour. No criticism of the effect of using convicts could be uttered without offending three-quarters of the population. In New South Wales the deadly animosity between the felonry and the free was gradually dying down with the great change in the proportion of the bond to the free; in Van Diemen's Land it smouldered on beneath the surface of life. In New South Wales the native-born and others celebrated with pride each year the anniversary of the foundation of their colony; in Van Diemen's Land the main public cere- monies were the levees at Government House to celebrate birthdays of the royal family. In New South Wales a grateful public had erected a statue to Governor Bourke for his contribution to the moral, religious and general improvement of all classes which had prepared them for the coming of free institutions; in Van Diemen's Land there were no monuments to their men of renown. In Van Diemen's Land it was that time in the history of a society when the swan's down feather stood upon the swell at full tide and was neither way inclined.[2]

By chance in 1836 the British Government chose as a successor to Lieuten- ant-Governor Arthur a man more suited by temperament to drift out to sea with the ebb-tide than to ride the waves of material progress which the raw industrial civilization of the United Kingdom was beginning to wash onto the shores of the New World. Nature had so fashioned the clay of Sir John Franklin that he seemed singled out by destiny to know failure. He was then in his fiftieth year. Short in height, he addressed his fellow-men with his head tilted backwards. His voice was sepulchral and other-worldly. His religion taught him to be indifferent to man's regard and to prefer the house of mourning to the house of feasting. Born in Spilsby in 1786 he had entered the navy at the age of fourteen and found that he trembled from head to foot whenever his duties required him to witness a flogging. Between 1818 and 1828 he had made three expeditions to the Arctic Circle in a vain search for the Northwest Passage, for which he had received a gold medal from the Royal Geographical Society, a knighthood from the Crown, and a D.C.L. from the University of Oxford on a day when the roof of the Sheldonian

[2] Minutes of the Legislative Council of Van Diemen's Land, 11 April 1837, C.O. 282/11; R. B. Madgwick, *Immigration into Eastern Australia* (London, 1937), pp. 167-8; Blue Book for 1838, Col. Sec.'s Office, T.S.A.; *Tasmanian and Austral-Asiatic Review*, 13 May 1842; Return of Emigration from the United Kingdom to Van Diemen's Land Since 1824, *P.P.*, 1851, xlvi, 684; Return of the Number of Convicts who Arrived in Van Diemen's Land, During Each Year, from the 1st Day of January 1823 to the 31st Day of December 1850, ibid.; for the text on the monument to Bourke see vol. 2, p. 254, fn. 26 of this history; C. Darwin, op. cit., p. 535.

Theatre rang in honour of his manly bearing and stout heart, and a poet read these words of recognition for his achievement:

> And in the proud memorials of her fame
> Lives, linked with deathless glory, Franklin's name.

He became the lion of London society, outwardly a hero but inwardly a man who was tormented by the worm of failure and the conviction that love of applause and quests for recognition were as dust and ashes beside the treasures of heavenly love and mercy.[3]

Chance and circumstance were reserving for Franklin a more cruel fate than this gap between his inner convictions and his outer glory. His first wife died, leaving behind a daughter Eleanor Isabella Franklin. In 1828 he married Jane Griffin, a woman through whom the gale of life blew so high that she was quite unfit to preside as the first lady in a convict society which promoted the backbiting, slander, and character assassination with which one of her temperament could not cope. She was born in 1791, the daughter of a wealthy silk weaver of Huguenot descent. Outwardly she had much to commend her: she shared the passion of her age for self-improvement, good works, Puritan morals, and a high sense of public duty. But there was a tempest deep inside her which caused her to lie on her bed in a wretched state of uncertainty and suffering for the greater part of many a day. Outwardly she was a person of many accomplishments: she had read voluminously and had filled shelves of notebooks with her thoughts; she had travelled widely; she had thought much, but her thinking had not taught her how to live or how to turn her knowledge into wisdom and understanding. By nature she was a proliferator and not a creator, for nature had robbed her of that one gift necessary to create art or literature out of her talents and knowledge. She believed she was marrying a hero, a manly and a generous man, someone who was worthy of a place at the top.[4]

Soon after the marriage the troll inside her whispered to her that the time

---

[3] For the early life of Franklin see Kathleen Fitzpatrick, *Sir John Franklin in Tasmania 1837-1843* (Melbourne, 1949); S. Osborn, *The Career, Last Voyage, and Fate of Captain Sir John Franklin* (London, 1860); H. D. Traill, *The Life of Sir John Franklin, R.N.* (London, 1896); E. Parry, *Memoirs of Rear-Admiral Sir W. Edward Parry* (4th ed., London, 1858), pp. 329-30; A. H. Beesly, *Sir John Franklin* (London, 1881), pp. 232-4; The poem, 'Voyages of Discovery to the Polar Regions' by T. L. Claughton, was recited by the author when the honorary degree of D.C.L. was conferred on W. Edward Parry, the director-elect of the Australian Agricultural Company, and J. Franklin as two brave seamen of Arctic exploration. See E. Parry, op. cit., pp. 215-17; J. Franklin to his sister Mrs Wright, winter of 1820, quoted in H. D. Traill, op. cit., pp. 77-8; Kathleen Fitzpatrick, op. cit., pp. 25-30.

[4] Private Journal of Jane Griffin 1823-4, and Private Journal of Jane Griffin 1825-6, 31 January 1825, 17 May 1826 (Franklin Papers, Scott Polar Research Institute); Jane Griffin to Captain Franklin, 26 July (1828), quoted in H. D. Traill, op. cit., pp. 145-7; Jane Franklin to John Franklin, 18 February 1831, and Jane Franklin to John Franklin, 8 December 1830 (Franklin Papers); F. J. Woodward, *Portrait of Jane: a life of Lady Franklin* (London, 1951).

had come to push her husband ahead. As the season of fogs and darkness descended on London in December 1830 she mapped out for her 'dearest love' a few years of hardship at the North Pole as a sure way of gaining preferment in the navy. She urged him to cure his 'sluggishness of feeling' by abandoning the London life of 'sanity, and trifling and idleness', and solicit some employment. Their life of idleness and vanity filled her with feelings of shame and remorse. She told him, 'not I only, but all the world knows what you can do' and went on to remind him that his name stood linked with deathless glory in the memorials of fame. So Franklin, at the age of forty-five, had to press on and look out for a position worthy of a hero of the Arctic, not knowing then, as she also did not and could not know, that in time she must ask for his life as the full, sufficient sacrifice, because he had nothing else to give that would satisfy her thirst for honour and glory. He put forward his name for more polar exploration and for the governorship of Antigua, but she dismissed that as quite unworthy of a man of his achievements. He rejected the offer to succeed his fellow-explorer Edward Parry as manager of the Australian Agricultural Company as being quite beneath him, for he had his pride, too. In 1836 Glenelg, who was looking for a man of authority cast in the evangelical mould, offered him the position of Lieutenant-Governor of Van Diemen's Land. So Sir John, his wife Jane, and Eleanor, his daughter by a former marriage (by then twelve years of age), his private secretary Alexander Maconochie, and the Archdeacon-elect of Hobart, William Hutchins, went on board the *Fairlie* at Portsmouth in August 1836. The man who trembled from head to foot whenever he had to witness a flogging was to preside over an island that had become a 'cage for the vultures of mankind'.[5]

On board ship Lady Jane pestered her 'dearest love' to do something about the quacking of the ducks which prevented her from getting a wink of sleep, to protect her ears from being offended by the 'anatomical frankness' of Maconochie, to protect her from the 'injudicious eloquence' of another lecturer on board who indulged in 'bad taste, illogical reasoning, exaggeration and tautology', and to protect her every Sunday evening from those vulgar Methodists who sang their hymns with a quite unbecoming gusto. Sir John, never a man to notice such things or to be put out by them, was enjoying the majesty of the sea and all the wondrous things God had made. With that decorous, solemn air with which he always confronted the public, he and his daughter went for a walk on the evening of their landing in Hobart Town on 6 January 1837 while the streets echoed with the joyful sounds of welcome. Father and daughter read together those pleasing words on many illumina-tions in houses and shop windows, 'John Franklin. Tasmania's Glory', and knew for a moment the ecstasy of love and recognition. The excitement of

[5] Jane Franklin to John Franklin, 8 December 1830. Quoted in W. F. Rawnsley, *The Life, Diaries, and Correspondence of Jane Lady Franklin 1792-1875* (London, 1923), pp. 68-9; Jane Franklin to Mrs Simpkinson, 4 March 1832 (Franklin Papers, Scott Polar Research Institute).

landing had been too much for Lady Jane: she had taken to her bed with one of those headaches which always laid her low when some excitement stirred up the madness in the blood. She lay prostrate while her 'dearest love' and her step-daughter enjoyed the role she believed to be his. With that strength she was always to display in such moments she rushed out to join them, but by the time she met them the moment had passed and they returned to Government House for family prayers. There all three joined together to recite the one prayer their Lord had taught them to say.

For weeks the inhabitants of Van Diemen's Land treated him as a hero, being quick to take the appointment of this 'lion of London', this man renowned for his courage, humanity and piety, as a compliment to themselves. In Hobart Town a list of 'good fellows' presented an address in which they expressed their confidence that Sir John's enlarged and philosophic views of government would be to the advantage of a 'freeborn and intelligent people'. Everywhere he went in the north he was attended with feasting, balls and public festivities. Three hundred horsemen and seventy carriages escorted him into Launceston where the streets were thronged and the windows crowded with spectators. Men noted with pleasure Sir John's warmth of heart and contrasted it with the coldness of his predecessor. They loved his candour: they loved it when he told them in the simplicity of his heart that he had come among them determined to 'see with his own eyes, hear with his own ears, and judge with his own judgment'. Their address of welcome took up the theme of his fame. 'Fame', the address said, 'has anticipated Your Excellency's arrival. The history of your life is before us.' Like their rivals down south in Hobart these men of the northern districts warmed to this candid, straightforward honest sailor, the warmth of whose heart breathed through all he said and did. They admired the steady eye with which he seemed to see into the heart of their situation. They saw him as a stranger to the wiles of his predecessor, that unctuous court-bred Machiavellian, who had been as cunning as a serpent.[6]

In those early months he became aware that he had come to live in a society that had a flavour all of its own. He felt that there was a general lack of neighbourly feeling and a deplorable deficiency in public spirit. He noted how each man sought his own individual advantage with little or no reference to his neighbours. He noted also an extraordinary degree of irritability in the insular temperament, an irritability fostered by a press that, in the hands of a few dedicated individuals, was exerting a degree of vicious power over the public mind and interfering in the privacy of domestic life by exposing the origins, habits and peculiarities of individuals with a malice he found difficult to account for. He had some gifts as an observer of the human scene, gifts

[6] Entries for whole of August, 22, 30 October 1836, in Jane Franklin's Journal of a Voyage to Van Diemen's Land (Franklin Papers, Scott Polar Research Institute); see also F. J. Woodward, op. cit., pp. 199-200; John Franklin to his sister, 6 January 1837 (Franklin Letters, Royal Geographical Society, London); entry for 9 January 1837 in Diaries of Eleanor Gell, vol. 1, (Gell and Franklin Papers, microfilm in NAT. L.); *Hobart Town Courier*, 6, 13 January 1837; *Cornwall Chronicle*, 14 January 1837.

which his wife had once urged him to bring to such perfection that he might put them into a book and so achieve what she longed for him. But his mind never went on to ask why 'as the birds that are taken in an evil net, and as the birds that are caught in the snare', so here in Van Diemen's Land were the sons of men snared.[7]

His religious convictions planted in him a vast indifference to any suggestion that a change in political institutions or social arrangements could add one jot to the sum of human happiness, let alone alter human behaviour. His experiences in the navy, and his hazy political convictions as an altar-and-throne Tory disposed him to carry out the command of his superiors. Unlike the Governor of New South Wales, the Lieutenant-Governor of Van Diemen's Land had not been instructed in 1837 to prepare for the change from convict to free labour. In April 1837 he accepted the recommendation of a committee of the Legislative Council that assisted immigration should be suspended altogether except for female domestic servants. At the end of the year he decided that the appointment of agents in the United Kingdom to select migrants would be a waste of public money. By then he was happy to hear from London that no immigrant ships would be sent to Van Diemen's Land for a considerable time, since there was no want of free labourers in that island. While 1837 was for New South Wales the year in which the transition from a bond to a free working class got under way, just over 1700 immigrants arrived in Van Diemen's Land, but only 571 arrived in the first year after assistance was suspended, 328 in 1839 and 299 in 1840.[8]

When Franklin first commented on the convict system in Van Diemen's Land he came down on the defenders of the old order rather than those who wanted to move forward to the light of freedom after the days of convict darkness. He was not blind to the evils of convictism. He was aware of the criticism that assignment was a form of employment 'in the lowest state of degradation', that it was a 'species of domestic slavery' injurious alike to both the bond and the free and that the ticket-of-leave system perpetuated those evils by so degrading the character of the prisoner as to unfit him to resume his place among free men. He was also aware of the praise for the convict system as the best school possible for moderate punishment and reform. For his part he accepted the three great objects of transportation: the expulsion of dangerous and mischievous subjects from the body of society at home, the reformation and ulterior moral and physical benefit of the prisoners, and the physical rather than moral interests of the colony to which they were sent to labour. He did not see the need to abolish the assignment system. In his eyes the advocates of total abolition were 'visionary' and supporters of untried experiments 'not free from danger'. Changes should be

[7] Diary of G. T. W. Boyes, March 1837; Franklin to Glenelg, 24 January, 4 March 1837, C.O. 280/77; J. West, *The History of Tasmania* (2 vols, Launceston, 1852), vol. 1, pp. 191-2.

[8] *Hobart Town Courier*, 31 March 1837; Franklin to Glenelg, 9 December 1837, C.O. 280/81; Franklin to Glenelg, 4 April 1838, C.O. 280/94.

introduced gradually. For if the number in assignment were reduced and the number in government gangs increased, the cost for the British Government would be increased. Besides he was certain the settlers of wealth and long standing were not keen on the abolition of assignment.[9]

By contrast, his private secretary Alexander Maconochie came to the conclusion that the fretfulness which so peculiarly characterized the intercourse of society in the penal colonies was to be attributed to the convict system. Degraded servants made suspicious masters: masters suspected their equals and superiors as well as their inferiors. The total disuse of moral motives in domestic relations, and the habit of enforcing obedience by mere compulsion gave a harsh and peremptory bearing to all transactions. Maconochie came to the conclusion that the colony was a sink of wickedness in which the inhabitants wallowed in profligacy, spite and ill will towards each other. He decided that the cause of such depravity was not that spot in the human heart planted there by Adam's fall, but the convict system under which over half of society were slaves to slave-holders. His mission in life was to slip the 'slave moorings' that tied the people to such viciousness. He put his ideas into his *Report on the State of Prison Discipline in Van Diemen's Land* which he forwarded on 20 May 1837 to Franklin who in turn enclosed it in his despatch of 7 October. It was not given to Sir John to accept Maconochie's hopes for the future. He shared the opinion of Dr Arnold of Rugby School that the convict stain would last for generations, that distinctions of moral breed were part of God's design for mankind, which no man could alter, and that the sins of the convict fathers would be visited upon the third and fourth generations of Vandemonions.[10]

When news reached Hobart Town in October 1838 that Captain Maconochie's report had become a public document, Sir John immediately asked for his resignation as private secretary for advocating publicly opinions inconsistent with the declared policy of government. By then he had reason to believe that Vandemonians were wounded by any criticism of the convict system. In September 1838 the inhabitants of Campbelltown told him they had read 'with serious and heart-felt grief, indeed with honest indignation the statements which [had been] propagated and afterwards disseminated throughout the press of the mother-country, calculated to inflict the deepest wounds on their own feelings, and also to be the cause of much uneasiness to those of their friends'. Sir John was pleased to tell them he knew that

[9] Franklin to Glenelg, 7 October 1837, C.O. 280/83.
[10] The development of Maconochie's attitude to the convict system can best be traced in his letters to Captain Washington (Maconochie Papers); see also A. Maconochie, statement with respect to his differences with Sir John Franklin, Hobart Town, 14 March 1839, ibid.; A. Maconochie, *Report on the State of Prison Discipline in Van Diemen's Land* (London, 1838); Franklin to Glenelg and encls, 7 October 1837, C.O. 280/83; J. Franklin to T. Arnold (written in 1837), quoted in H. D. Traill, *The Life of Sir John Franklin, R.N.*, pp. 250-4; J. Y. Barry, *Alexander Maconochie of Norfolk Island* (Melbourne, 1958), pp. 46-50; T. Arnold to John Franklin (Rugby, July 1836), quoted in H. D. Traill, op. cit., pp. 235-6.

several of the alleged causes of the moral corruption attributed to the penal colonies generally had no manner of existence in Van Diemen's Land: for in their island no members of the convict population occupied seats and discharged the functions of the colonial government, or sat upon and formed the majority in their juries, or wielded influence in the press, or acted as teachers in public schools, or monopolized the sale of spirits in public houses; nor had their ticket-of-leave men amassed fortunes or occupied the waste lands of the Crown. The members of the gallant regiment were not demoralized and their officers were distinguished by the usual characteristics of British officers—zeal in the public service and correct and honourable conduct. For his part he had complete confidence in the 'intellectual and moral respectability' of their community. He would tell the Secretary of State that in his view their 'free community need not shrink from a comparison with any corresponding population in Great Britain'. He proceeded to do just that with his usual candour and nobility of heart, for he shared their view that the truth would relieve them of the degradation that would have rendered the colonists unworthy of the privileges of Englishmen.

While Sir John in the goodness of his heart was finding everyone amicable and agreeable, Maconochie was telling his friends that Sir John was a man of quite childlike simplicity. G. T. W. Boyes, the Colonial Auditor, decided in October that Sir John was totally unfitted for his office. Sir John, never a man to suspect what was going on in the mind of another man, was wondering how he could promote Boyes for his years of distinguished and faithful public service. By then, too, in an endeavour to promote the harmony of parties Sir John had greatly increased the number of magistrates by adding a number of 'swallow tails' or gentlemen settlers to balance the pro-Arthur faction which still had such a stranglehold on the government service. The list was greeted with mockery and laughter, but Sir John seemed as deaf to the laughter of the mockers as he had been blind to what was going on in the hearts of Maconochie and Boyes.[11]

In the meantime Lady Jane was attempting to improve the minds of the ladies of Hobart Town. Although she had been warned that the young ladies of that town had a great fondness for dancing and singing popular songs, she began a series of evenings at Government House at which pretty young girls were placed in rooms full of books, pictures, shells, stones and other rubbish, with nothing to do but hear learned and solemn men talk. They sat quiet as mice as they listened to 'good music'. In their hearts they were waiting for the military band to strike up the one-two-three of the waltz and for the

[11] A. Maconochie to Captain Washington, 11 January, 18 March, 12 April 1839 (Maconochie Papers); A. Maconochie, statement with respect to his differences with Sir John Franklin, Hobart Town, 14 March 1839, ibid.; for Franklin's account of these events see John Franklin to Mary Simpkinson, 14 April 1839 (Franklin Papers, NAT. L.); Franklin to Glenelg and encls, 8 October 1838, C.O. 280/97; Jane Franklin to Sir John Franklin, 18 February 1831, quoted in F. J. Woodward, *Portrait of Jane: a life of Lady Franklin*, pp. 168-9; *Hobart Town Courier*, 1 June, 5 October 1838; J. West, *The History of Tasmania*, vol. 1, pp. 192-3; Government Notice, no. 191, 19 October 1837, published in *Hobart Town Courier*, 20 October 1837.

servants to roll up the carpets so that the voice of the moral improver reciting all the dreary facts of science and religion could be forgotten in the pleasures of the dance. Lady Jane also visited the Female Factory, for she was as solicitous for the salvation of 'this last' as she was for those born in high places, but the convict women greeted her by taking down their trousers and waggling their bare bottoms at her.[12]

Nor was she at ease with some of the senior members of Sir John's government. While Sir John met the elaborate courtesy of John Montagu with a flourish of the hands and the expression of his friendship and esteem, she, being born with a fatal tendency to suspect the motives of every human being, began to wonder why it was that this 'sprayer of courtesy' knew so much about everyone's business in Hobart Town, and to ask herself whether that boded good for any man. She began to wonder why it was that Montagu could mouth the principles of moral rectitude with the skill of a Tartuffe and enjoy the affection of his family and a reputation as an upright man and yet be so cold in his relations with other people. He wore such a cunning, shrewd look on his face that she thought of him, with alarm, as belonging to the clockwork types in the human family. She even began to wonder whether he was one of those cruel men who took pleasure in tormenting innocent men such as Sir John and crushing them without pity or remorse. Did not evil men always find that the discomfort and shame they experienced in the presence of the simple and the innocent only disappeared when they had destroyed them? For his part Montagu was not slow in detecting that behind the courtesy and the high-minded utterances of Sir John there was a little child who was tied to his wife's petticoat.

Nor was John Montagu the only one to give Lady Jane concern in those early days. She was worried whether her 'dearest love' had the force of personality to handle a man like John Gregory, the Colonial Treasurer. How could Sir John, a short man to whom words never came easily, assert his authority over a tall, long-legged creature such as Gregory who had that never-ending flow of a man who loved to hear himself talk? How could her Sir John, who had that blindness of the 'eternal husband', that failure to see what was before his very eyes, survive in a society in which those of quite different clay took a malicious delight in tittle-tattling about the number of morsels of meat their enemies put into their mouths? For in this society even the tradespeople had begun to exploit the presence of a non-noticer, a man with his head in the clouds, by boasting that they had one price for ordinary customers, and another for that gullible man at Government House.[13]

Nothing could disturb the even tenor of his life. He and his daughter

[12] Louisa Anne Meredith, *My Home in Tasmania during a Residence of Nine Years* (2 vols, London, 1852), vol. 1, pp. 29, 36.

[13] Jane Franklin to Mary Simpkinson, 7 October 1837 (Jane Franklin's Twenty Letters to Mary Simpkinson, 7 October 1837 to 19 April 1853, Scott Polar Research Institute); Eleanor Franklin to her aunt, Miss Franklin, 3 August 1837 (Franklin Papers, Royal Geographical Society); Jane Franklin to Mrs Simpkinson, 21 June 1838, printed in G. Mackaness (ed.), *Some Private Correspondence of Sir John and Lady Jane Franklin* (2 vols, Sydney, 1947), vol. 1, p. 36.

Eleanor rose at six, prepared their work for the day, walked together from eight to nine, he with hands clasped behind the back and head tilted backwards, always a pace or two apart from the one person he loved best in all the world. Then they took breakfast, followed by prayers in which they told their God they knew that in the world they would know tribulation and sorrow, but were nevertheless of good cheer because, thanks to their Saviour's teaching, they knew how to overcome the world.

Religion and education were Sir John's chief remedies for that taint of evil in the human heart. On first meeting the Legislative Council on 10 July 1837 he had spoken with warmth of the role of the Church of England in improving the morals of mankind. He shared the belief of the editor of the *Hobart Town Courier* that the doctrine taught by the 'special messenger . . . sent on earth' by God was as easily comprehended by men of the most humble capacity as by the wisest. Everyone could understand Christ's teaching on the immortality of the soul, a state of future rewards and punishments, the doctrine of redemption, and the resurrection of the dead. He agreed, too, that education of the lower classes in such doctrines would not tend to excite disaffection in their minds or provoke them to regard their superiors with envy. On the contrary, a sound education conducted on right principles would inculcate what he had found to be most precious in life—the strengthening of the will to endure, the seeking of refuge in higher contemplation, and the smiling at the vanities and empty glories of the world as transitory pleasures which were not in any way connected with human happiness. To achieve this he believed that all that was necessary was to give the children of Van Diemen's Land a 'true scriptural education' palatable to all the denominations of Christians. As he put it on 30 June 1838, despite the diversity of outward forms, there was a general concurrence of opinion among Presbyterians, Episcopalians, Wesleyans and Independents. He believed it might even be possible to persuade the Catholics to harmonize with the Protestants in a 'true scriptural education' which could be imparted to all children in schools built, financed, equipped and staffed by the government. When the Episcopalians jibbed at these proposals, and Archdeacon Hutchins took the view that the Church of England's monopoly of education could not and should not be usurped, Sir John at the end of 1838 published regulations which placed all schools supported by public funds 'under the immediate control of some ecclesiastical authority' and required them to be 'conducted in accordance with the principles of some Christian Church or congregation'.

His scheme for the education of the sons of the bourgeoisie and the professional classes bore fruit more quickly. While the parsons and priests tangled over his British and Foreign Bible Society type of proposals, Sir John suggested the foundation of a grammar school at Launceston under the charge of a clergyman of the Church of England at which the pupils would be given a grounding in a classical education, the Book of Common Prayer, the authorized version of the Bible, Shakespeare, Milton, the civilizations of Greece and Rome, and the contribution of the Protestant Reformation and the Glorious Revolution to the maintenance of true religion, virtue, material

BUSHMAN'S NIGHT CAMP

Drawing by S. T. Gill, Mitchell Library, Sydney

EMIGRATION of FEMALES to SIDNEY under SANCTION of GOVERNMENT

London Pub by J. Kendrick 54 Leicester Sq
Aug. 10, 1833.

EMIGRATION in SEARCH
of a
HUSBAND.

What are you going to Sidney for, pray m'am.
Vy they says as how theres lots of good husbands to be had cheap there whereas the brutes in England cant see no charms in a woman unless she's got plenty of money to keep 'em in idleness.

Broadsheet, Mitchell Library, Sydney

progress and ordered liberty. When Franklin came back to his British and Foreign Bible Society proposals on 6 May 1839 and announced that a fundamental condition for government aid was that the reading of portions of the Scriptures should be daily required in each, once again Archdeacon Hutchins donned the mantle of Bishop Broughton and prophesied that religion without doctrine would lead in time to a morality without a religion, and a secularization of life that would end at 'the entrance of . . . a temple of darkness'. Their age had to choose between teaching the children opinions that rested upon the unchanging and unmovable rock of truth, or the 'ever varying, vibrating quagmire of sophistry and scepticism'.[14]

It so happened that Lady Jane was absent from Van Diemen's Land when the education controversy began to warm up. In April 1839 she crossed Bass Strait in the brig *Tamar* for Melbourne from where, with that courage and resource she always displayed in the presence of adversity, she made the strenuous overland journey to Sydney. To her great delight, she took tea there with Bishop Broughton who charmed her by his digs at her husband's predecessor. Whether she knew that Broughton had his own reasons for denigrating Arthur—as Arthur seemed to have sensed that Broughton's word was not always to be relied on—must remain a mystery. As always, she beamed and glowed whenever people in high places testified to their esteem and regard for Sir John. While she sat there soaking up teacup flattery, sections of the press of Van Diemen's Land were telling their readers that it was very common 'for ladies to rule their husbands when their husbands were not able to rule them'. In Hobart Town, too, it had become part of the current gossip to pass on to those with ears to hear that if you wanted to know the 'measure of Sir John's foot', then try some bowings, knee-bendings, and 'Yes, Your Excellency' on him. The man purred, they said, like a cat after licking a saucer of cream. Unaware as ever of being weighed in such a balance and being found wanting, Sir John busied himself during the day by telling the members of the Legislative Council that the shouts of idle boys on the Sabbath could be the first steps to a dissolute and dishonest life, and at night by reciting with his daughter and the servants those words, 'The Lord shall preserve my going out, and my coming in from this time forth forever more.' Men with the eye of pity wondered how long it would be before the 'princes of the world' savaged this man with the saintly disposition and the harmlessness of a dove.[15]

Outwardly things seemed propitious. Observers described the agricul-

[14] Eleanor Franklin to her aunt, Mrs Booth, 8 October 1838 (Gell and Franklin Papers); *V. & P.* (L.C. V.D.L.), 10 July 1837; *Hobart Town Courier*, 6 April 1838; *V. & P.* (L.C. V.D.L.), 30 June 1838; *Hobart Town Gazette*, 14 December 1838; A. G. Austin, *Australian Education 1788-1900* (Melbourne, 1961), pp. 70-2; W. Hutchins, *A Letter on the School Question* (Hobart Town, 1839)

[15] Diary of Lady Jane Franklin's Journey from Port Phillip to Sydney, 1839 (typescript in NAT. L.); Lady Franklin to Sir John Franklin, 20 June 1839, in G. Mackaness, op. cit., pp. 92-3; Sir John Franklin to Lady Franklin, 23 April 1839, ibid.; J. West, *The History of Tasmania*, vol. I, p. 228; James Backhouse, *A Narrative of a Visit to the Australian Colonies* (London, 1843), p. 492; Miss J. B. G. Williamson, governess to Isabella Franklin, to J. Gould, 11 October 1839 (typescript in NAT. L.).

tural countryside as 'smiling', and added that the faces of those living in the country were both 'smiling' and 'prosperous'. The convict servants were 'well fed' and 'well dressed'. The people, too, had a capacity for gaiety and pleasure. At race meetings in the country there was quite a social whirl, with much gaiety under the tents, and lively drinking, followed by dancing in the evening as the houses of the country gentry resounded to all the revelry and pleasure. To those whose spirits had been depressed by the great dryness of the inland districts of New South Wales the cool moist greenness everywhere was most refreshing: the gardens in the town houses were filled with geraniums in bloom and sweet English flowers; the children looked happy and healthy, stout and rosy like children in the English countryside. Sir John and Lady Jane strove to arouse and foster a taste for literature, art and science. Yet some sensed an evil spirit in the land. It was not just those perpetual petty squabbles and quarrels which formed an unavoidable part of all small communities. Here the divisions between the convicts, their families and their descendants on the one hand and the free on the other were so bitter that some predicted that they would one day cause a bloody revolution, for the prejudices of the free against the rest were said to be as strong as those of the whites against the negroes in the southern states of the United States of America.[16]

On 5 March 1839 the settlers inhabiting the northern district petitioned Her Majesty not to adopt 'any measure having for its object the abolition of the System of Transportation, coupled with Assignment, as the National System of Secondary Punishment'. Their leaders were men such as Thomas Archer, whose mansion at Panshanger had been built by convict labour and who owed the splendour of his life in that delightful English parkland to convict labour, James Cox at Clarendon, and Edward Dumaresq at Mount Ireh, both of whom owed their wealth and standing in part to convict labour. They saw clearly that the penal system of Van Diemen's Land not only contributed to the punishment and reformation of British criminals but also happily answered their need for cheap, obedient labour. Sir John agreed with them, for in the two years in which he had been amongst them he had seen no reason to change his earlier opinion that if Great Britain abandoned the system of transportation without further trial, she would be relinquishing the best system known to mankind for the advantageous disposal and reform of criminals. He was also quite sure that the moral aspect of the community was far from being such that it should necessarily induce Her Majesty's Government to modify it materially. In a despatch of some thirty-five pages he never so much as glanced at the possibility that a prosperous and moral community could be poisoned by the differences between the convict and the free, and would go on being poisoned so long as convictism and its effects survived in Van Diemen's Land. No serious-minded or responsible person in a high place in London could possibly infer from the information supplied

---

[16] Dumont D'Urville, *Voyage au Pôle Sud* (23 vols, Paris, 1841), vol. 8, pp. 32-3, vol. 9, pp. 38-9, 59-62; Louisa Anne Meredith, *My Home in Tasmania*, pp. 22, 29.

by Sir John that there was any strong movement in favour of abolition. What Sir John and all those settlers who had waxed fat on the exploitation of cheap convict labour had lost sight of, or possibly did not want to face, was that official opinion in London was not prepared to go on doing what they wanted, namely to couple assignment with the system of secondary punishment. In London assignment was seen as a species of slavery which must be abolished forthwith. They were in danger of being left with a system of secondary punishment and a large convict community which was making no contribution to their material wealth.[17]

Nor did Sir John or all those whose worldly fortunes were tied to the existing convict system believe that the survival of transportation would delay the granting of free institutions. When Sir John forwarded to London early in 1839 a petition in which the influential inhabitants of the island prayed that Her Majesty would be graciously pleased to confer on the free inhabitants the privilege of electing their own representatives to the local legislature, he gladly added his support to their petition. He added that, even if Van Diemen's Land became the only depot for offenders transported from Great Britain, for his part he believed the right of election could still be conceded. All through 1839 he assured the convict users of Van Diemen's Land that they could retain their convicts and still receive the boon of free institutions.[18]

By the middle of 1840 the convict system of Van Diemen's Land seemed able to defang and render harmless those who had threatened to wreck it. Many members of the criminal classes in the United Kingdom were ending their days in this island of 'home-like English aspect' as members of an active, industrious and moral peasantry. That vagabond on the face of the earth, the convict novelist Henry Savery, was wandering around the penal settlement at Port Arthur, his lack-lustre eyes and his wasted face a reminder to all of that wreck to body and soul by which the transgressors of the laws of God and man were punished in this world before they appeared before the judgement seat of Almighty God.

Between April 1838 and February 1840 206 political prisoners arrived in Hobart Town after being sentenced to transportation for their part in the Canadian rebellion of 1837–8 and the subsequent attempt of Canadian refugees in the United States to take part in a piratical invasion of Upper Canada. Among them were men who had hoped to establish American freedom and republican government in Canada. Most of them insisted on being able to eat and sleep apart from the other convicts because they did not wish to 'associate with criminals from the lowest sinks of iniquity in England'. They knew Sir John as 'old Granny'. They complained of the indignities to which they were

---

[17] Franklin to Normanby, 31 May 1839, C.O. 280/108; Franklin to Normanby, 2 September 1839, C.O. 280/110; Franklin to Glenelg, 15 February 1839, C.O. 280/106; *Launceston Examiner*, 28 March 1839; Franklin to Glenelg, 11 March 1839, C.O. 280/107.

[18] Franklin to Glenelg, 3 January 1839, C.O. 280/104; Franklin to Normanby, 4 September 1839, C.O. 280/110.

subjected, not the least of which were the 'culinary delights offered by the Convict Department'. They also hated compulsory attendance at religious services on Sundays, when they were mustered and marched off to church to hear the detested ritual of the Church of England, the purgatory of two to three long doleful hours of rising, kneeling and sitting according to the rubrics in the Book of Common Prayer all the while 'holding [their faces] as grave as an owl'. One of them wrote later of the Reverend William Bedford: 'like the greater portion of Her Majesty's hirelings, Bedford loved the bottle more than the Lord'. They made no attempt to pass on to other convicts those hopes of better things for mankind which had inspired them to take up arms in the Canadas and to loathe the government of Little George, the late Lieutenant-Governor of Van Diemen's Land. Their one aim was to get out of Van Diemen's Land quickly. All of them, especially the French Canadians were 'a-hungered and a-thirst' for their home land and consumed with a desire to return to Canada. When they returned home in 1842 they wrote in their memoirs with love of the 'sweet, good customs' of their fore-fathers, and took no further interest in the people of Van Diemen's Land, where they left not a trace that men of their faith had once been there.[19]

The chartists John Frost, William Jones and Zephaniah Williams also left not a trace that they had been members of a society to promote the dignity of man. Williams, a free thinker and baiter of parsons, had been transported for participating in the raid on Newport in 1839. Frost was a strange member of a movement which had grown 'fierce and mad' after years of bitter dis-content. As early as 1822 he had advocated a simplistic solution to poverty and crime in the United Kingdom: every county should return members to parliament in proportion to its population, every man over the age of twenty-one being entitled to the vote. In this way, he believed, taxation would be reduced, and poverty and crime would disappear. His hope was that these changes could be achieved voluntarily, but that if there was resistance, force should be used. It was this latter conviction which led him to take part in the farcical invasion of Newport and brought him afterwards much suffering on board the convict hulk *York* where the appalling food and the brutality of officers wore him down so much that his friends believed he was 'evidently fast dropping into eternity'.

Before the departure of the convict ship Frost wrote his wife a letter full of Christian submission and humility, for there was inside him a double— a chartist with hopes of human dignity in this world, and a Christian who believed there was hope for God but not for man. He and his two fellow-chartists disembarked on 30 June 1840 and were sent to Port Arthur, where they were not called on to wear the distinctive yellow convict clothes but

---

[19] W. Gates, *Recollections of Life in Van Diemen's Land* (New York, 1850); M. G. Milne, North American Political Prisoners (thesis, Department of History, University of Tasmania); L. Ducharme, *Journal d'un Exilé Politique aux Terres Australes* (Montreal, 1845); F. X. Prieur, *Notes d'un Condamne Politique de 1838* (Montreal, 1884); S. Snow, *The Exile's Return* (Cleveland, 1846); B. Watt, *Letters from Van Diemen's Land* (Buffalo, 1843).

given junior civil service positions. Observers soon noted that these men, who had formerly not had civil tongues in their heads when speaking to their superiors, now seemed very mindful of their allotted place in society. The effect of exile and suffering on Frost was to drive him not to more desperate acts of defiance or to impart to others his vision of the disappearance of poverty and crime off the face of the earth after the introduction of manhood suffrage, but rather to turn to the world of the great unseen. He decided that continually looking at the dark side of life only left a man in a state of continual misery. Van Diemen's Land converted a one-time revolutionary into a spiritualist.[20]

In the meantime Sir John and Lady Jane continued their work for the promotion of art, science and learning. Ever since 1838 the distinguished ornithologist John Gould had been the recipient of such great kindness from both Sir John and Lady Jane that he was able to collect the material that became part of his *Birds of Australia*, the first part of which was published in 1841. In 1840 that 'wanderer without a nation or a home' Paul de Strzelecki turned up in Hobart Town looking, as ever, not so much for entertainment in the drawing-rooms of the gentry as for recognition from men in high places. Sir John responded with the warmth Sir George Gipps and 'Joey' La Trobe had so singularly failed to lavish on him and raised money for the publication of his book. Strzelecki replied by dedicating the book to Sir John with fulsome expressions of his regard, his esteem and his gratitude for all the courtesies and hospitality in Hobart Town. In the following year Sir John gave generous encouragement to the first publication of the *Tasmanian Journal of Natural Science* for the Tasmanian Society of Natural History. He shared the hopes of one of its founders, the Reverend John Lillee of the Presbyterian Church in Hobart, that the circulation of a journal of science would have beneficial effects on the morals and intellectual life and character of the inhabitants of their rising country. Sir John himself hoped the journal would help to withdraw their minds for a time from the engrossing calculations of traffic, and the contemplation of merely local interests which made so large a demand upon the time and attention of the colonists. As ever he was an enthusiastic supporter of any activity that would tend towards 'the general improvement and enlargement of the public mind'. He believed in the coming of the day when the aborigines on Flinders Island had advanced from the perception of simple truths to the acceptance of Christian society.

Under their joint patronage the arts flowered in Van Diemen's Land. In 1838 Benjamin Duterrau, a portrait painter and landscape artist of French descent, caught on the canvas a red-lipped aborigine, the eye reflecting the wild ecstasy of the killer as he pointed his sharp stick at the game. In 1841 he painted an aborigine on the sea-shore, dressed only in a loin cloth edged

[20] *Nenagh Guardian*, 21 April 1841; *Emigration Gazette*, 10 September 1842; J. Frost, *The Horrors of Convict Life* (London, 1856); *The Times*, 13 January 1841; *Launceston Advertiser*, 3 June 1841; *Hobart Town Courier*, 4 June 1841; D. Williams, *John Frost: a study in chartism* (Cardiff, 1939); J. Saville, *Ernest Jones: chartist* (London, 1952).

with fur, with that expressionless face of a people determined not to show their view to their eternal enemies. Thomas Bock, one-time choirboy at Lichfield who, when a married man with five children, was sentenced to transportation for fourteen years for administering drugs to a young woman, began to paint portraits in the late 1830s and early 1840s. He painted with such grace and serenity, such a celebration of life, that it was as though the suffering of penal servitude had stilled the madness in his heart. Earlier in his water-colour portraits of the aborigines he had uncovered in the sitters a beauty in the face and a light in the eye which had escaped all previous observers. Thomas Wainewright, one-time forger, painted portraits to express his gratitude to the men of quality in Van Diemen's Land for rescuing him from being a hounded man, but always found he transferred onto the face of his sitters all the anguish and torment and guilt in his own soul. John Glover, who had taken up land at Patterdale at the fort of Ben Lomond in 1832, was the first artist with an international reputation to settle in an Australian colony. A large heavy man with two clubbed feet, he became very friendly with his neighbour, John Batman, and, while presenting a placid exterior to casual observers, he was possibly a secret sharer of the Dionysian frenzy of Batman. There, and on his other estate by the River Ouse, he painted landscapes in which the gum-tree was given a shapeliness no other observer was ever to find in their random splendours of chaos. Some said his painting showed a lamentable lack of local characteristics, and some praised his 'hideous fidelity' to nature. Posterity honoured him by referring to the area he painted as 'Glover country'. Possibly in response to the enthusiasm and faith of Lady Jane in the spread of beauty and truth over the savage wilderness of Van Diemen's Land, he painted one huge landscape in which he planted the shells of three Greek temples in the midst of the sombre bush as a promise of that day when the spirit of Apollo lifted men from barbarism to civilization.[21]

In April 1840 Sir John believed that at long last Van Diemen's Land had a schoolmaster who could improve and enlarge the minds of the young. He was John Philip Gell, who was then just twenty-four years of age. Lord Stanley had described Gell as 'the noblest and most beloved' of all the pupils of Dr Arnold at Rugby School. Sir John had taken the liberty of asking Dr Arnold to recommend a 'Christian, a Gentleman, and a Scholar—a Member of one of our Universities—a man of Ability & of Vigour of Character—to become the Father of the Education of the whole Quarter of the Globe' to take up the position of first headmaster of a secondary school. In the early months Gell charmed and impressed all whom he met. Lady Jane loved him for his admirable natural spirits and his equanimity of temperament. Her one doubt

[21] A. H. Chisholm, *The Story of Elizabeth Gould* (Melbourne, 1944); Kathleen Fitzpatrick, *Sir John Franklin in Tasmania* (Melbourne, 1949), ch. 7; Franklin to Russell, 27 August 1841, C.O. 280/133; dedication to Captain Sir John Franklin in P. E. de Strzelecki, *Physical Description of New South Wales and Van Diemen's Land* (London, 1845); copies of etchings of Tasmanian aborigines by Benjamin Duterrau and Thomas Bock in Queen Victoria Museum, Launceston; Robert Travers, *The Tasmanians: the story of a doomed race* (Melbourne, 1968), pp. 208-14.

was whether the man could ever go into a passion and feel due indignation. Franklin applauded the young man's lofty aims which were to found Christ's College as a stronghold of learning and a school of Christian gentlemen. He wanted this institution for Christian learning to have some definite set of religious principles and practices. He believed these principles could best be taught by clergymen of the Church of England, not only because they represented the majority in the island but also because they were in that half-way house between Rome and Geneva, that incomparable piece of social machinery which Almighty God had printed on the minds of Englishmen to give them the secret of authority without despotism, and liberty without laxity.[22]

At the same time Sir John pressed on with his plans for the creation of a general scheme of education based on the British and Foreign Bible system. In the preceding December of 1839 he told the Legislative Council that to promote the moral and social welfare of the inhabitants of Van Diemen's Land, to initiate religious and civil distinctions and to prevent the domination of one religious sect over the rest (he meant the Church of England), a Board of Education would establish free day schools in which Christian principles would be taught. The textbooks of the British and Foreign Bible Society were to be reprinted in Hobart, for the children were to be brought up on these echoes from the Old World rather than proceed from their known world to the world at large. James Bonwick, a nonconformist schoolmaster and stout supporter of the temperance cause, a sabbatarian and advocate of evangelism, was selected to take charge of the main normal school in Hobart. To allay opposition from the Anglicans the Board of Education announced that the Anglican publication *The Faith and Duty of a Christian* would be a principal textbook in their schools. This work, supported by texts from the Scriptures, had many wholesome things to say on the duty of wives to obey their husbands, servants to obey their masters, and subjects to obey their rulers. It encouraged humility, diligence, temperance and contentment.

In an exuberant mood Sir John told the Legislative Council in August 1840 that such moral gardening, like material gardening, if carefully pursued, would bring forth its fruits even on their rugged soil and uncongenial clime, and that whatever unfavourable influences they had to contend with in Van Diemen's Land, they (he meant the evil influences of convictism) would eventually yield to that instrument of moral culture which had been put into their hands. A few days later he told the Legislative Council, in the solemn voice of a man who sounded as though he were addressing the Supreme Judge of the Universe, about the general prosperity, the increasing cultivation and flourishing trade of their colony. For all his eye could tell, their world went well.[23]

[22] Frances J. Woodward, *The Doctor's Disciples* (Oxford, 1954), pp. 74-98.

[23] G. Featherstone, Life and Times of James Bonwick (thesis in library of University of Melbourne); minute by Franklin to the Legislative Council of Van Diemen's Land, 15 August 1840, encl. in Franklin to Russell, 23 October 1840, C.O. 280/121; *Hobart Town Gazette*, 21 August 1840; R. M. Hartwell, *The Economic Development of Van Diemen's Land* (Melbourne, 1954), p. 220.

Seeing Christ's College as a symbol of the odious exclusiveness and insolence with which the privileged few in the free community regarded the
members of convict society, supporters and sympathizers of the latter over-
turned the foundation stone on the night it was laid. Some said these adventurous thieves had yielded only to the sordid temptation to steal the coins
placed under the foundation stone. Others said the delay caused to the
building should be used to change the site and to give some thought to the
teaching of useful subjects such as producing scholars of anatomy and future
medical students rather than young men whose heads were crammed with
dead languages and dead ideas about God. Some with a keen eye for the
significance of such an event whispered that there was more to it than just the
un-laying of a foundation stone, that it had some connection with the rift
between the Colonial Secretary, John Montagu, and Lady Jane on the best
site for the college. Gell took the incident as an example of the 'mistiest
ignorance and the iciest selfishness' of the convict community of Van
Diemen's Land. Sir John, optimistic as ever about the fruits of his own high-
minded endeavours for the well-being of his people, saw it as a vindication
of his view that in such a 'rugged soil' 'moral gardening' was urgently
required.[24]

In October 1840 news reached Hobart that the British Government had
abolished the transportation of convicts to New South Wales and would in
future send all convicts to Norfolk Island or Van Diemen's Land. Since the
end of 1838 they had been living under the fear that the days of assignment
were numbered. Officialdom in London was convinced that, instead of
reforming humanity, assignment degraded it and was in many instances
even the direct occasion of vice and crime. In July 1838 Glenelg instructed
Franklin to force all convicts into gangs under the control of government
before assigning them as workers, to discontinue assigning convicts for the
purposes of luxury or as domestic servants, and to oblige convicts in assignment to wear some distinguishing badge. In January 1839 Franklin announced
that assignment of convicts as domestic servants would end in July, when
assignment in Hobart and Launceston would also end. Now they were faced
with the prospect of a huge increase in the number of convicts in their society
and the prospect that in the not too distant future they could not be assigned
to settlers as workers. At year's end Franklin was instructed to work the
convicts in 'parties' after they had spent their prescribed time in the gangs.
This news that the settlers were gradually to be deprived of the main source
of their prosperity arrived just as gloom and despondency were beginning to
settle on the brows of members of the commercial world as one mercantile
establishment after another sank into ruin. Some prophesied that they had by
no means seen the end of these calamities.[25]

[24] *Hobart Town Courier*, 17 November 1840; Frances J. Woodward, op. cit., pp. 74-98.
[25] Glenelg to Franklin, 6 July 1838, encl. in Glenelg to Gipps, 6 July 1838, *H.R.A.*,
I. xix. 468-9; *Hobart Town Gazette*, 17 January 1839; Russell to Franklin, 10 September
1840, C.O. 408/19; *Murray's Review*, 4 February 1841; *Hobart Town Courier*, 8 January
1841; R. M. Hartwell, op. cit., p. 221.

While the men from the counting-houses were filled with dismay, and the settlers anticipated with foreboding the days when their labour costs would rise sharply, Sir John was strangely cheerful. In January 1841 he was feeling very pleased with himself. A few months earlier he had finally got rid of that thorn in his flesh, John Gregory, the Colonial Treasurer. Relations between the two had never been cordial since Sir John had passed Gregory over for the position of Acting Colonial Secretary in 1839. In September of that year Gregory had opposed Franklin during a debate on a government measure in the Legislative Council. Sir John, rather like Bourke in a similar situation in New South Wales, had asked the Colonial Office for a ruling on the duty of senior officers such as Gregory to support government measures in Council. When the reply came back in August 1840, Sir John promptly suspended Gregory, pending the approval of the Colonial Secretary. Gregory told his friends he would neither forget nor forgive the manner in which he was put out of office. For months after the episode Sir John continued to be pleased with himself for his firmness. In January 1841 he boasted to Boyes, the Colonial Auditor, 'Between ourselves my predecessor would never have been capable of it.' Boyes suspected Lady Jane had played a far too prominent role in the whole affair. So did the *Tasmanian and Austral-Asiatic Review* which published that January many innuendoes about petticoat government while Sir John was rather recklessly sharing some of the secrets of his heart with Boyes each night at Government House and even taking the risk of congratulating himself to such a man on the absence of any popular clamour or complaint against his administration.[26]

All the errors of the man were in the head rather than in the heart. In moments of grief, or moments in which men looked upwards to heaven for a sign that the promptings of their hearts did not go unnoticed, his heart was always bounteous and responsive. He loved it when his daughter Eleanor and Archdeacon Hutchins looked at him affectionately when he went through the motions of a dance, for lightness of foot eluded him all the days of his life. He was so overcome when the Archdeacon died in June 1841 that he had to go up-country for a few days to remind himself that that great gap in his life was as nothing beside the perfect felicity the Archdeacon was then enjoying in the presence of God. At the laying of the foundation stone of Trinity Church in October his face took on an air of exaltation as the band played the Halleluiah chorus from Handel's *Messiah*, for that contained the assurance that the teachings of his religion were true, that God's reign would be distinguished by a grandeur and a majesty so singularly lacking in man's life on earth. It never occurred to him that there were readers of the human face in Hobart who took such unguarded displays of emotion as evidence that the

---

[26] *Hobart Town Gazette*, 21 August 1840; R. M. Hartwell, op. cit., p. 220; Diary of G. T. W. Boyes, 8 August 1840, 28 January, 2 February 1841; Sir John Franklin to Richardson, 22 February 1841 (Gell and Franklin Papers); Franklin to Normanby, 25 September 1839, C.O. 280/110; Franklin to Normanby, 30 September, 15 October 1839, C.O. 280/110; Franklin to Russell, 19 February 1840, 19 March, 10, 31 August, 9 September, 23 October, 14 November 1840, C.O. 280/123; Russell to Franklin, 13 March 1840, C.O. 408/16; Russell to Franklin, 4 July 1840, 20 April 1841, C.O. 408/19.

man was vulnerable and that anyone capable of such excitement probably had the heart of a little child.[27]

All his life Sir John was concerned with those actions of a man which would enable him to pass the gate-keeper at the entrance to the Eternal City. One of these was what he called 'penitent reconciliation'. In August 1841 he had a chance himself to display the virtue. In that month the coroner of the Richmond district reported to the Colonial Secretary that the district surgeon, John Coverdale, had failed to attend a man who had been run over by a cart, and had later compounded the offence of neglect of duty by misinterpreting the cause of the man's death. Sir John concurred in dismissing Coverdale from office. When Coverdale pleaded for forgiveness Sir John exercised his prerogative of mercy to a penitent and restored Coverdale to his position. This intensely irritated John Montagu, the Colonial Secretary, because he took it as interference by the Lieutenant-Governor in the administration of his department. Behind Sir John's public displays of confidence in Coverdale he detected the hand of Lady Jane.

Relations between Lady Jane and the Colonial Secretary had been strained ever since Montagu had returned to Hobart early in 1841. Lady Jane resented Montagu's hostility to that 'baby-bubble called a College', the building for Christ's College where in her mind, and that of her husband, the much needed 'moral gardening' was to begin. Montagu, sound public servant that he was, thought of the building as one of those places without utility which Lady Jane put forward to waste the taxpayer's money. By then Lady Jane had lost the sympathy and regard of the members of the Government House circle. Ever since her arrival she had shown she cared little for dress or amusements, scarcely ever associated with ladies, and divided her time between science and politics. In her room in Government House snakes, toads, stuffed birds and animals, weapons of savages, specimens of wood and stone, and a lubra dress in bright scarlet greeted the eye of the visitor. In that *sanctum sanctorum* she had conducted the real business of the country. She never gave up. In 1839 she had bought 130 acres in the Lenah Valley near Hobart as a site for a botanical garden and a museum. In March 1842, in the middle of her row with Montagu, Sir John laid the foundation stone of this Greek Temple, a symbol of her faith in replacing barbarism with sweetness and light. She named it Ancanthe, or the vale of flowers. She, after all, had had the strength and the courage to be the first white woman to climb to the top of Mount Wellington.[28]

After the row she left Montagu so hurt by her behaviour that he decided not to visit Government House again socially and never to allow his wife to enter those doors again. As he saw it, Lady Jane now had the reins in her hand and, in collaboration with her husband, was about to make a 'pretty mess' of public

[27] Diary of G. T. W. Boyes, 4 June, 20 October 1841; entry for 9 June 1841 in Diaries of Eleanor Gell, vol. 2 (Gell and Franklin Papers).

[28] Based on J. Franklin, *Narrative of Some Passages in the History of Van Diemen's Land* (London, 1845), pp. 1-22; Franklin to Stanley, 27 January, 18 February 1842; C.O. 280/143; Diary of G. T. W. Boyes, August 1841 to 7 January 1842; *Van Diemen's Land Chronicle*, 28 January 1842; R. Crooke, *The Convict* (Hobart, 1958).

business. He saw her as 'a troublesome, interfering female', whose interference in government had driven him more and more into membership with those old Arthur hands—J. Pedder and Matthew Forster. Montagu waited upon Sir John and in a somewhat heated interview accused Lady Jane of organizing the movement in favour of Coverdale, and of besmirching his name in a conversation with Forster, the chief police magistrate and director of the probation system. From that day Montagu told his friends he would speedily bring Sir John to terms by using his office to obstruct the Lieutenant-Governor, while Lady Jane came to the conclusion that Montagu, Forster and the other members of the pro-Arthur clique were conspiring to destroy her 'dearest love'.[29]

In December 1841 the *Van Diemen's Land Chronicle* told its readers that the Lieutenant-Governor of their colony, Sir John Franklin, was a man of 'evident incapacity' and 'demonstrated feebleness' who had wantonly and disgracefully lavished immense sums of money upon 'ridiculous journeys and fantastical deviations from the beaten paths of men'. Early in the new year it accused him of making violent efforts to gain popularity at the expense of his station, and undermining every public officer who did not have a taste for 'carousals' of tea, muffins and lectures. Everyone in Hobart Town knew that the editor of the paper, Thomas Macdowell, had some scores to settle with Sir John. The gossips had egged him on by letting him know that Sir John did not really like him. Everyone also knew that Montagu was behind Macdowell. So Sir John asked Montagu to uphold the dignity of his government by a public disclaimer of his association with the articles, and an expression of regret for their offensive tone. Montagu refused to do either. On 17 January 1842 he added insult to injury in a letter to Sir John in which he accused the latter of being the possessor of a faulty memory. Though that left neither of them with room to manoeuvre, the cynics predicted that Sir John would snatch a suitable opportunity for one of those reconciliations he adored. They predicted that in the spirit of Christian forgiveness and penitence he would hold out the hand of friendship to Montagu and solicit oblivion for the past. Sir John really believed that no man should use the infirmity of his brother as his recreation, nor make sport of that which was heaven's sorrow. Others, including those who shared Sir John's view of the relevance of the divine command to forgive one's enemies, just did not believe Sir John was capable of being firm for more than a week unless he was kept in a constant state of excitement. To the astonishment of cynics, friends and foes, on 25 January he suspended Montagu as Colonial Secretary and sent for Boyes, and in a state of great excitement told him how he had always admired his high character and because of that wanted him to act as Colonial Secretary until such time as Her Majesty's pleasure could be known on the suspension of Montagu.[30]

[29] J. Montagu to Arthur, 12 December 1841, 10 January, 8 February 1842 (Arthur Papers, vol. 16); Kathleen Fitzpatrick, *Sir John Franklin in Tasmania*, pp. 259-62.
[30] *Van Diemen's Land Chronicle*, 24 December 1841, 7 January 1842; Diary of G. T. W. Boyes, 19, 21, 22, 25 January 1842; J. Franklin, op. cit., pp. 19-22.

Thomas Gregson, a wealthy settler, predicted that all the settlers would rejoice at Montagu's dismissal. Boyes, and others who had reason to be grateful for the turn of events, told Sir John that he had completely redeemed his character. Lady Jane, too, was full of praise for the 'sternness of his resolve' and for the equanimity of his mind. Gell told him that a frank and open-hearted man had triumphed over the selfishness and wickedness of Montagu. In her chamber at Government House Lady Jane gave Boyes examples of the selfish bitterness of Montagu's heart, and the paroxysms of anger with which he had assaulted all who had opposed him. Boyes gasped and made approving noises as she whispered to him story after story of that man's evil. Believing the people behind him in the blow he had struck at the overpowering influence of the Arthur faction, Sir John wrote to Lord Stanley like a man who had taken part in one of those encounters celebrated by the Psalmist in which all who worked wickedness were cast down and were not able to stand. He cherished confidently the hope that he would have His Lordship's support as a loyal servant of Her Majesty for his best endeavours to uphold a flourishing portion of her dominions. The source of his power, as he saw it, was his loyalty to ideals: to truth, justice and righteousness. Had they not all been assured that *Magna est veritas et praevalebit*.[31]

The source of Montagu's power was of quite a different order. A section of the press was on his side. The *Van Diemen's Land Chronicle* praised him as the man responsible for the survival of the convict system in Van Diemen's Land. They asked whether if Sir John could suspend the Colonial Secretary, any man was safe in his job. The *Tasmanian and Austral-Asiatic Review* declared the episode showed once again that the colony was governed by a 'lady'. The *Cornwall Chronicle* accused Sir John of blighting the last hopes of the colonists by suspending a man who had made manly endeavours to preserve the government from derision and 'blue stocking influence'. The *Colonial Times* also repeated the 'petticoat government' story. As for Montagu, he remained supremely confident. He knew that through his brother-in-law Forster, the convict department and 'the monied channels of the Derwent Bank' he had his hands on the three reins of power in that society—the police, the civil service, and the monied power. Add to that the man's own desire for revenge—'I'll *sweat* him', he threatened Lady Jane, 'I'll persecute him as long as I live'—and his influence in Downing Street, and the man ceased to be that wicked man in some fable about the triumph of good over evil and became a formidable opponent. With the energy and efficiency of the 'clock-work man', Montagu collected his notes for the indictment of Sir John, wound up his affairs and set sail in the *Derwent* for London in February 1842, his mind set on vengeance, while Sir John kept up the fun

---

[31] Diary of G. T. W. Boyes, 25 January, 15 February, 30 June 1842; J. P. Gell to his father, 17 March 1843 (Gell and Franklin Papers); Jane Franklin to James Clark Ross, 3 April 1842, and John Franklin to James Clark Ross, 31 March 1842, quoted in Kathleen Fitzpatrick, op. cit., p. 280; Franklin to Stanley, 18 February 1842, C.O. 280/143; Diaries of Eleanor Gell, 1, 6 January 1842 (Gell and Franklin Papers).

and gaiety with his wife and daughter at Government House and chatted to Boyes about his schemes for improving Her Majesty's loyal subjects by 'moral gardening' in the schoolroom and the church.[32]

While Sir John went down on his knees each morning and each night to ask God to graft in the hearts of the people of Van Diemen's Land the knowledge of His name, all the fruits of his endeavours in the five years in the island began to turn sour. Despite the instruction in the despatch of 6 July 1840 from Lord John Russell that assignment of convicts, when abolished, must in no shape be revived, both he and the settlers in the country districts hoped that common sense would ultimately prevail in Downing Street and that they would introduce a new system of convict discipline in which a properly regulated system of assignment would be combined with the new proposals for working men in parties in government service in the first years of their servitude. At the end of 1840 Sir John had been warned to prepare for the reception of a greater number of convicts, since transportation to New South Wales was at an end, and had been told by implication that convicts in Van Diemen's Land would not be assigned in the period between their forced labour for government and their working in parties as ticket-of-leave holders making roads, clearing lands, erecting buildings, making fences and in general improving Crown lands for sale.[33]

Hopes for the restoration of assignment were shattered by the news received in Hobart early in 1843 that henceforth all convicts sentenced to transportation were to pass through five stages—detention at Norfolk Island, the probation gang in Van Diemen's Land, the probation pass, ticket-of-leave and the pardon. The probation gangs were to be assembled in Van Diemen's Land. They were to be composed first of convicts who had passed through their detention at Norfolk Island and of convicts sentenced to transportation for less than life, who might be indicated by the Secretary of State for the Home Department as proper to be placed in that class. The probation gangs were to be employed in the service of the government in the unsettled districts of the colony. They were to be employed in hard labour under the general superintendence of the Comptroller of Convicts. These gangs of 250–300 men were to be hutted and quartered in situations where they could undertake work of public utility. Each gang was to have religious teachers, an overseer and subordinate officers. On receiving from the Comptroller a certificate of general good conduct, a man was entitled to his probation pass, any holder of which might with the consent of the government engage in any private service for wages. The fourth stage was the ticket-of-leave, and the fifth the conditional or absolute pardon. The duty of the Comptroller was to superintend the whole of the convict system acting in subordination to the

---

[32] *Van Diemen's Land Chronicle*, 26 January 1842; *Tasmanian and Austral-Asiatic Review*, 20 January, 4 February 1842; *Cornwall Chronicle*, 29 January 1842; *Hobart Town Courier*, 28 January 1842; *Hobart Town Advertiser*, 11 February 1842; Jane Franklin to Mrs Simpkinson, 7 February 1842 (Scott Polar Research Institute); Diaries of Eleanor Gell, 11 April 1842.

[33] Russell to Franklin, 6 July, 10 September 1840, C.O. 408/19.

Governor. In Hobart the news was greeted with dismay and alarm. Some said the transition from a wealthy to a pauperized country would speedily take place. Van Diemen's Land would become what Norfolk Island already was, a society in which the felons preponderated over the free, and the evils of older times—the abomination of sodomy and the eating of human flesh— would be renewed. They were stranded with convicts while the other colonies in Australia were enjoying or about to enjoy the privileges of the free.[34]

At the end of 1842 news reached Hobart that Her Majesty's Government had not felt justified in proposing to parliament the extension to Van Diemen's Land of a similar form of legislature to that introduced into New South Wales by the Act of 1842 because of the incompatibility between the grant of such a form of constitution and the continuance of transportation. They had also decided that, because of the animosity between persons origin- ally free and the emancipated, and the larger proportion of emancipists to the free in Van Diemen's Land in comparison with New South Wales, they were not prepared to recommend the establishment of municipal corporations in Van Diemen's Land. Some papers went into mourning for the generation that was not to be blessed with a free constitution. Sydney, Melbourne and Adelaide were electing their first Councils, while Hobart and Launceston were humiliated by the stigmas of convictism.[35]

To add to their consternation, the commercial depression became so serious early in 1843 that one banker had fears of a general bankruptcy. Unemploy- ment was increasing, aggravated as it was by the glut on the labour market by the increase in the number of convicts. The number of insolvencies increased among the retail traders and merchants; land-holders, pressed by the fall in prices for wool, wheat and their primary produce, began to haunt the bankruptcy court. Rumours flew around Hobart Town that not even the banks were safe from ruin. So economic failure was added to the political failure, while Sir John waited patiently for news from London, trusting that God would reward the righteous and abhor those who delighted in wicked- ness.[36]

In January 1843 Sir John received a despatch from London in which words were used that were to lie like lead on his heart until the day he died. Lord Stanley told him that reluctant as he was to employ a single expression that was likely to be unwelcome to him, he was compelled to say that Sir John's proceedings in the case of Mr Montagu did not appear to him to have been well judged and that his suspension of Montagu from office was not suf- ficiently justified. He also learned that that odious creature Montagu had been promoted to the position of Colonial Secretary at Cape Colony. Sir

---

[34] Stanley to Franklin, 25 November 1842, encl. in Stanley to Gipps, 26 January 1843, *H.R.A.*, I. xxii. 514-23; *True Colonist*, 5 August, 15 October 1842; *Hobart Town Adver- tiser*, 17 January 1843; *Colonial Times*, 7 February 1843.

[35] Stanley to Franklin, 5 September 1842, C.O. 408/21; *Tasmanian and Austral- Asiatic Review*, 27 January 1843.

[36] R. M. Hartwell, *The Economic Development of Van Diemen's Land*, pp. 227-8; Psalm XI: vi.

John never seemed to recover from the blow. His beloved daughter reminded him that such afflictions were often blessings in disguise. His wife assured him that he was still the object of universal respect and a flattering degree of outward consideration. Gell reminded him of God's promises to all his faithful children.

Nothing they could do eased the pain of such a humiliation. Sir John knew that, thanks to Montagu, a copy of this despatch with those wounding words was lying on the tables of all the partisans of Montagu in Hobart Town, Launceston and the country districts. He began to suspect everybody of trickery and disaffection, to refuse everything that was asked of him, to forget his promises and to shrink from every duty that required activity, vigour and decision. He wrote to Lord Stanley to tell him that he had read his despatch of 13 September with astonishment and much pain, but self-vindication could not and did not bring comfort or solace. His enemies in the press turned on him with the fury of wanton boys tormenting a wounded animal. The *Colonial Times* with studied cruelty told its readers that only a man who had suffered in the cold regions could be cool enough not to kick the beam at once and hand in his resignation, but poor Tasmania must wait and suffer with patience in the hope that sooner or later deliverance would arrive. The *Tasmanian and Austral-Asiatic Review* revived the charge of 'influences behind the throne' and accused Sir John of 'an undignified clinging to office' because of the extreme unwillingness to part with the honours and the pounds, shillings and pence consequent upon adherence thereto. Sir John would not stir one inch from Government House until his successor actually walked up the steps.[37]

When July came and Sir John sat down to read the dreaded words of recall he was not cheered by the dignified manner in which the instructions were conveyed. Lord Stanley told him, 'As the ordinary term of a Colonial Governor has expired since the date of your appointment to the administration of the Government of Van Diemen's Land, I have received the Queen's Command to intimate to you [that] such a change may be shortly anticipated.' The despatch contained no words of praise or gratitude. By then the press, hostile to him and his wife, were saying that Sir John was only fit to represent an old woman: the hero of the Arctic had degenerated into an imbecile. With his consciousness of the rectitude of his motives still unshaken Sir John asked Stanley for an investigation and another appointment to vindicate his name and honour, while the local press mocked him with the words that no Secretary of State would be so lunatic as to appoint him to another governorship. By the time his successor made his first public appearance at the end of August, Sir John was so broken that he walked into the reception room in

[37] Stanley to Franklin, 13 September 1842, C.O. 408/21; Jane Franklin to Mrs Simpkinson, 18 September 1843 (Scott Polar Research Institute); Eleanor Franklin to Catherine Rawnsley, 14 February 1843 (Gell and Franklin Papers); J. P. Gell to his father, 17 March 1843 (Gell and Franklin Papers); Diary of G. T. W. Boyes, 3 March 1843; *Tasmanian and Austral-Asiatic Review*, 12 May 1843; Franklin to Stanley, 20 January 1843, C.O. 280/153.

Government House, bowed to his successor, and retired before the doors were thrown open to the public. John Franklin, Tasmania's glory, was being told by the people for whom he had laboured for six years that he had had his full share of their loaves and fishes.[38]

His friends did not desert him in his days of great anguish. Over fifteen hundred signed an address calculated to restore his pride and confidence in the magnitude of his achievement. The friendly press professed their shame in belonging to a community that had indulged in such 'scurrilous vituperation' against him. Other addresses testified to his unbending rectitude of purpose, his high moral tone and his zeal for the public good, and expressed their gratitude for 'the benevolent and philanthropic exertions of [his] amiable and excellent lady'. When he finally left on 3 November 1843, over two thousand rent the air with expressions of their affection and regard. On arriving in London early in 1844 he asked Stanley to vindicate his name and person by appointing him to the government of another colony, but he declined. To win the battle for posterity he wrote *A Narrative of Some Passages in the History of Van Diemen's Land* and then turned to win the battle for the mind of his contemporaries. He thought of arctic exploration, that hazardous enterprise which had first put his name in the portals of fame. Lady Jane, dreading the effect on the mind of her 'dearest love' of being without honourable and immediate employment, encouraged him to pursue again the avenue of glory.

In May 1845, after a characteristic and moving appeal to Almighty God to watch over them all lest they fall, Sir John set out from Gravesend in charge of two ships. In the regions of eternal ice and snow where the paradox of his public life had begun, where fate or chance had apotheosized failure into glory, he experienced this time that final failure when death took him on 11 June 1847 as he lay in the *Erebus*, which was stuck fast in the ice-pack off the coast of King William's Land in sight of that Northwest Passage he had striven in vain five times to discover. The poet Tennyson believed that in death Sir John had won the prize he really wanted, that prize of passing on to a 'happier voyage toward no earthly pole'. The poet Swinburne prophesied that he would live on as part of 'the royal record of the sea'.[39]

His daughter felt no 'desire to have [her] stay on earth prolonged', and continued looking to Christ for spiritual growth and pardon for her 'many, many sins', and striving for 'spiritual good', as her father had done, until the day she died. In the days of adversity a mantle of tragic grandeur descended on Lady Jane. She lived on for another twenty-eight years, busy as ever with the reputation of the man she had pushed to reach beyond his strength. She circulated a ballad concerning Franklin and his gallant crew. She organized

[38] Draft despatch of Stanley to Franklin, 10 February 1843, C.O. 280/158; *Tasmanian and Austral-Asiatic Review*, 25 August 1843; *Colonial Times*, 1, 8, 15 August 1843; Diary of G. T. W. Boyes, 31 August 1843; Franklin to Stanley, 26 July, 21 August 1843, C.O. 280/158.

[39] *Hobart Town Advertiser*, 5 September 1843; *Hobart Town Courier*, 25 August 1843; Frances J. Woodward, *Portrait of Jane*, pp. 250-3.

expeditions to search for him. She did good work in schools, hospitals and institutions for the creatures whom God seemed to have forgotten. She travelled to Hawaii, India and North America, always accompanied by the woman she loved. When death finally took her on 18 July 1875 those present noticed the 'ghost of a pretty laugh on her face'. What that meant no one could tell, for who can know the human heart? As was said of old, only God knows what goes on in the heart of a woman. Well before this the inhabitants of Van Diemen's Land had put up a statue in Hobart in affectionate remembrance of their former governor.

It was as though in those years in which they became a stricken people some presence shaping human destiny let them hear the solemn, sepulchral voice of Sir John telling them of a place of refuge from failure in the life of the world to come. While the people of eastern and southern Australia shed the clothing of convictism and draped themselves in the moral philistinism of the immigrants, or the navitism of Australians, the people of Van Diemen's Land were left puzzled and bewildered about the future of their society. On the mainland the boiling down of sheep for tallow, and the discovery of copper mines and rich pastoral lands gave the colonists the confidence to shed their convict past just when the people of Van Diemen's Land seemed incapable of envisaging any life other than the one they had known. From that time the ghost of the past haunted the minds of the living: the people became embarrassed by their past and were not even able to tell themselves that the whole point of knowing the past is so that one can dispense with such ghosts.[40]

[40] Memorial to the memory of Sir John Franklin, Spilsby, Lincolnshire; memorial to Sir John Franklin, Franklin Square, Hobart; bust of Sir John Franklin, Westminster Abbey; statue of Franklin in Waterloo Place, London; bas-relief of Franklin in Royal Society of Tasmania, Hobart; Diaries of Eleanor Gell, January 1845 (Gell and Franklin Papers); A. C. Swinburne, *Complete Works of Algernon Charles Swinburne* (20 vols, New York, 1968), vol. 1, *The Death of Sir John Franklin*, pp. 1-8; Frances J. Woodward, op. cit., pp. 360-4; *Galway Vindicator*, 5 May 1852; J. West, *The History of Tasmania*, vol. 1, p. 224.

IO

A PLACE FOR A BELLY-FULL
BUT NOT A FULL-BLOWN CIVILIZATION

D URING THE convict era in New South Wales and Van Diemen's
Land it was said that whenever two or three convicts or their descendants gathered together the noise was like a menagerie at feeding
time. It was said that convictism had fashioned a distinctive human being who
spoke his own language with its own pronunciation and lively vocabulary and
had his own moral creed. The teacher of the convict was not Moses or Jesus
Christ but that mythical thief Charlie Wag who showed him how to avoid
work and go on lusting and thieving till the end of his days. But by 1840 the
decision-makers in London made up their minds that it would have been
better had the lands of New South Wales remained in their primitive wilderness till the end of time, better for the Mother Country, better for the aborigines
and better for the settlers had the whole region been swallowed up in the
ocean than continued as a stronghold for the corruption of mankind. The
Australian colonies must stop taking 'scum' with which to plant civilization,
and take a portion of the redundant population of the United Kingdom.[1]

There was no doubt that migration was the answer to the evils of both
the Old World and the New. In the Old World it would help to cure
pauperism, and provide an invaluable market for British manufactures, and
a happy British alternative to radicalism, chartism, socialism and all the other
'isms' that threatened the very foundations of society. In the New World it
would alleviate the chronic shortage of labour and provide a 'moral and
industrious' working class as a substitute for the 'convict polluters'. In the
United Kingdom 'haggard misery' was stalking abroad in the agricultural
and manufacturing districts, and the very elements of society were being
thrown into a state of hazardous confusion. By contrast, in all the Australian
colonies except Van Diemen's Land, labour was in intense demand, wages
were high, and there was comfort, abundance and happiness for the workers.

In the United Kingdom the system of cheap and rapid production, which
was essential to British supremacy in manufacturing meant the application
of more and more machinery to production, which added to the number of
redundant workers. The enthusiasts for migration argued that the sons of

[1] H. Mayhew, *London Labour and the London Poor* (4 vols, London, 1864), vol. 1,
pp. 466-7.

Britain would rot in their native land if they did not carry the steam-engine, the ploughshare, the halleluiahs of Christianity and all the other achievements of British civilization into the remotest parts of the Australian wilderness. Humanitarians and philanthropists asked whether the British wished to bear the guilt of driving the aborigine from the land of his birth and exterminating him. Patriots asked whether they wished to weaken their own power by draining away their 'pith and marrow'. Radicals warned the workers that migration was a smoke-screen used by their oppressors to prevent them from seeing that the only remedy for their misery lay in a radical change in the ownership and distribution of wealth. Enthusiasts for migration replied that it was unreasonable to expect men suffering from starvation to be swayed by high-minded or patriotic sentiments: it was inhumane to expect a man to prefer starvation at home to a full belly in a British colony.[2]

There was one other twist to the migration debate. The seekers after a belly-full were flocking to British North America and the United States rather than the Australian colonies. The passage was shorter—twenty to forty days to an Atlantic seaport compared with four to five months to Fremantle, Perth, Adelaide, Hobart, Melbourne or Sydney. The passage was cheaper—£5 to North America and £20 to an Australian colony. North America was the land of the free; the Australian colonies carried the stain of convictism, and authoritarian institutions were claimed appropriate for a gaol or the management of prisoners in a wilderness. In 1835 15 500 migrated from the United Kingdom to British North America, 26 250 to the United States, and about 1860 to the Australian colonies and New Zealand. The Atlantic passage was attended with great horrors. The intending migrant paid 12½ per cent above the fare to ships' brokers, who employed 'runners' at the ports of embarkation, who ran off with the luggage and extorted more money. The ships were dangerously overcrowded and the crew knocked down the passengers with buckets and knuckledusters. Typhus and other diseases decimated them. At the American ports the equivalent of the Liverpool 'runners' tormented them—brutes with fists like a sledge-hammer and muscle enough to overthrow a bull, and swindlers who sold false railway tickets.[3]

No man had a complete answer to the problem of distance and isolation. The solution adopted, the payment of the passages of migrants out of the revenue raised by the sale of waste lands had two unanticipated results. Introduced in part to overcome one of the great disadvantages of the Australian colonies in the competition for migrants, it had the paradoxical effect of

[2] *Emigration Gazette and Colonial Advocate*, 21 May 1835, 30 July 1842; *Australasian Record and Indian Observer*, 24 July, 11, 24 December 1841; *Edinburgh Review*, vol. 71, 1840, pp. 517-18.

[3] Statistical Tables Relating to Emigration to the U.S.A., British North America and the Australian Colonies and New Zealand, appendix 1 in S. C. Johnson, *A History of Emigration from the United Kingdom to North America, 1763-1912* (London, 1913); figures compiled by F. K. Crowley and published in C. M. H. Clark (ed.), *Select Documents in Australian History* (2 vols, Sydney, 1950 and 1955), vol. 1, pp. 406-8; *Emigrant*, 22 July 1848; T. Coleman, *Passage to America* (London, 1972).

replacing one disadvantage with two others. From 1832 onwards land, the prospective ownership of which was the great incentive to make such a hazardous journey, was cheaper in the United States than in Australia. The system also contributed to the material backwardness of the Australian colonies: the revenue which might have been used to build roads, public buildings, schools and churches, was earmarked to pay the passages of migrants and to civilize the aborigines. The dryness, the absence of inland rivers suitable for water transport, the dispersion of settlement, and the land laws all contributed to their being a half century behind the Old World and North America. There canals, railways, the electric telegraph and the application of machinery to production were creating not just a belly-full but untold riches for the few, and the incentive and conditions to encourage the migrants to participate in that great pulse of life.[4]

By contrast the benevolent intentions of British governments in drafting rules and regulations to protect migrants to the Australian colonies from wicked and designing men and to select only those with certificates of virtue, produced a race of men and women whose energies were smothered by such paternalism, and the pulse of life was enfeebled. The price of the molly-coddle and the encouragement to niceness and loving kindness was a great deep dullness from which it would take over a hundred years to recover. In the early years of assisted migration to the Australian colonies, as to the United States, confidence men tricked migrants to hand over their money by impersonating the local emigration agent. Runners at Liverpool, Gravesend, Plymouth, Queen's Town and Greenock stood over them and extorted their precious savings. Brokers charged exorbitant prices for lodging, till in 1840 a benevolent government through the Colonial Land and Emigration Commissioners drafted rules and regulations to shield them from such brutes. By 1842 every embarkation port for Australia had a depot capable of housing four to five hundred people, in which migrants were comfortably lodged free of charge till their ship sailed, and fully protected from the runners, the pea-and-thimble men and the spongers. A doctor visited them to watch over the health of their bodies, and parsons and priests attended to the health of their souls while, outside their sheltered existence, the unprotected migrants to the United States continued to be unfortunate victims of human roguery and swinishness.[5]

In the beginning there was the same rascality and exploitation on ships to Australia as on the ships crossing the Atlantic. In 1834 the *John Barry* had one bath-tub and two privies for four hundred migrants. In 1836 on the *Lady*

[4] S. C. Johnson, op. cit.; T. Coleman, op. cit.; W. Raymond, *A Few Brief Remarks on the Preliminary Arrangements for Collecting and the Conducting of Poor Emigrants* (London, 1848).

[5] Report of Select Committee on Immigration, *V. & P.* (L.C. N.S.W.), 1839; Report from the Select Committee on Passengers' Act, *P.P.*, 1851, xix, 632; *Galway Vindicator*, 1 December 1841; copies of Reports . . . by the Emigration Agents of Canada, New Brunswick, and New South Wales to the Governors and Councils of those Colonies, *P.P.*, 1843, xxxiv, 109.

McNaghten fifty bunks were provided for one hundred men and boys, 106 small berths and six hospital berths for 185 women. The women and children were driven to their bunks each day at 5 p.m. by sailors who used canes to hurry them along. They were not released again till 8 the following morning. On the voyage fifty-six children died of measles and whooping cough, fifty migrants and seamen died of typhus, and eighty more lay dying when the ship finally reached Sydney. On the *Layton* which sailed from Bristol on 27 September 1837 with three hundred on board, seventy of the 178 migrants died of measles. During that year 430 of the 6378 who embarked in ports in the United Kingdom died during the voyage of dysentery, scarlet fever, whooping cough, measles, wasting disease or bowel complaints.[6]

Again a benevolent government took steps to protect the sons of Britain from sinking into a watery grave or losing their dignity, so that the tales of horror might disappear off the pages of the story of migration to the Australian colonies. Regulations were gazetted to ensure a more effective check of the health of passengers before embarkation and to protect them against epidemics and the greed, lust or bloody-mindedness of ships' captains, officers, surgeons, and all in places of authority during the voyage. Migrants were reminded that reaching their destination in high health and spirits very much depended on the attention they paid to the rules provided for cleanliness and airiness. They were also reminded that on landing in the colony their conduct during the voyage was sure to become known, that persons who arrived in a happy and orderly ship might expect the best offers of employment, and those who bore the character of having been quarrelsome and refractory would naturally be avoided. In government ships, from 30 March 1839, migrants were to be out of bed by 7 a.m. By 8, when breakfast was to be served, the children were to be washed and dressed, the decks swept, the beds rolled and, weather permitting, carried on deck, after which the decks were to be cleaned and the berths well brushed out. No smoking was permitted between decks and spirits were not allowed to be brought on board. Dinner was served at 1 and tea at 6. Married men, in rotation, were to keep watch in their quarters to prevent irregularities. Monday and Friday were to be washing days. Every Sunday the surgeon superintendent was to muster the migrants at 10.30 and see whether they were personally clean and had on clean linen and clean and decent apparel, after which divine service was to be performed and the Lord's Day to be as religiously observed as circumstances would permit. The surgeon superintendent was to select one man to act as teacher to the children. There were similar regulations to ensure cleanliness, comfort and safety on board bounty ships.

[6] Evidence of J. Marshall to Select Committee on Immigration, 27 May 1835, *V. & P.* (L.C. N.S.W.), 1835; *Sydney Herald*, 14 August 1837; Report of Select Committee on Immigration, *V. & P.* (L.C. N.S.W.), 1839; Return of Immigrants sent from England to the Colony of New South Wales, in Vessels Chartered by Government, *V. & P.* (L.C. N.S.W.), 1839, p. 319; Journal of G. W. Walker, 3 September 1831 to 6 July 1832 (MS. in M.L.); M. Cannon, *Who's Master? Who's Man?* (Melbourne, 1971), pp. 128-9; *Fisher's Colonial Magazine*, September-December 1843, vol. 4, pp. 415-19.

In August 1842 the Carriage of Passengers in Merchant Vessels Act pre-scribed conditions to ensure the seaworthiness of the ship, the height between decks, the dimensions of sleeping berths, and the quantities of food and water to be issued to each passenger. By the 1840s the tales of horror which had stirred up consciences at both ends of the globe gave way to reports of passengers with cheerful looks and contented appearance being carried to the colonies in ships in which a benevolent government had taken precautions to protect the health, the physical comfort and the spiritual welfare of all on board. There was sago, arrowroot, oatmeal, Scotch barley, porter, wine and brandy to keep the body sound, and copies of the Bible, the Book of Common Prayer and religious tracts to cleanse the soul.[7]

At the same time a number of papers began to be published in London aiming to inform the labouring classes on the advantages of emigration in general and the superior attractions offered by the British colonies in Aus-tralia. The *South Australian Record*, which had been published in London since 8 November 1837, decided on 29 May 1841 to call itself the *Australasian Record and Emigration Journal* to advocate emigration to the Australian colonies. On 23 October 1841 the *Emigration Gazette and Colonial Settlers' Universal Guide* began publication with the slogan that emigration was as necessary in the economy of a state as a queen bee was to a beehive. On 22 July 1848 the *Emigrant and Colonial Advocate* was first published in London to provide information for the intending migrant to the Australian colonies. All these papers hammered at the simple point that the great dis-proportion between population and the means of subsistence in the United Kingdom could be easily relieved by virtuous and industrious migrants exploiting the opportunities and landed wealth at their disposal in the extensive unoccupied districts of the Australian colonies. All of them wanted to reduce the suffering and ruin occasioned by the injudicious direction given to the current of British emigration to the United States because that caused a great loss of labour for the colonies and a great loss of trade and commerce for the Mother Country.[8]

All through the decade of the forties the emigrant press in London, the provincial press in England, Scotland and Ireland—especially such papers as the *Cork Examiner*, the *Galway Vindicator*, the *Belfast Chronicle*, the *Inverness Courier*, the *Aberdeen Journal* and the *Glasgow Herald*—bom-barded their readers with the theme that the penniless and overcrowded people of the United Kingdom would find a plentiful home on the miserably

---

[7] Regulations to be Observed on Board Government Emigrant Ships, 30 March 1839, appendix 1 of Annual Report from T. Frederick Elliott, Agent General for Emigration, to the Marquess of Normanby, 15 August 1839, *P.P.*, 1839, xxxix, 536, pp. 390-1; An Act for Regulating the Carriage of Passengers in Merchant Vessels, 5 & 6 Vic., c. 107, 12 August 1842, *Statutes at Large*, vol. 82; *Galway Vindicator*, 3 August 1842; *Emigrant*, 10 February 1849.

[8] *Australasian Record and Emigration Journal*, 29 May 1841; *Emigration Gazette and Colonial Settlers' Universal Guide*, 23 October 1841; *Emigrant and Colonial Advocate*, 22 July 1848.

populated plains of Australia. They held out the prospect that the sober, the honest and the industrious in Australia were laying the foundation of independence and competence. They published 'success' stories—stories of bakers making fortunes of up to £10 000 in five years, and working men becoming landowners, or employers of labour in the space of three to five years. Readers were told that in Australia the able-bodied who were industrious enough to work hard for a season and steady enough to hoard instead of squandering their money would pass over in a few years from the ranks of the employed to those of the employer. They were told of the superabundance of food, the high wages, and the salubrious climate.

Some advocated life in Australian colonies as a way of escaping the corruption of industrial civilization, as one of the few places left in the world where a man could enjoy the domestic virtues, far removed from the dazzling sights and the tempting sounds of a city. Some assured their readers that not all the land of Australia was in a state of 'irreclaimable barrenness'. Others were pleased to inform migrants that the decencies of religion were observed in the large towns of Australia and that they should take no notice of stories to the contrary, for there were, in fact, three burying places in Sydney—one for free people, one for convicts and one for people who had been hanged. Others again told their readers that since they understood some were apprehensive that, were they to emigrate to Australia, they would expose themselves to destruction by savage natives, they would hope to assure them that their apprehensions were perfectly groundless.[9]

The shopkeepers of London, Edinburgh, Dublin and the ports of embarkation joined in the chorus of those who were taking the terrors and the hardships out of the long journey across the ocean. Actuated by a deep anxiety for the comfort of those who were about to quit their native land, Samuel Brothers of London respectfully begged to inform the public in August 1848 that they had added an important feature to their extensive and well-known establishment in Ludgate Hill, namely 'AN OUTFITTING DEPARTMENT FOR EMIGRANTS'. There government officers, clergymen, surgeons, surveyors, merchants, clerks, mechanics and labourers could rely on buying an outfit of the best materials and workmanship at much lower prices than in the Australian colonies. The more fastidious migrants were advised to buy their

[9] Advertisements in *Glasgow Herald*, 17, 21 February 1840; advertisements in *Ayr Advertiser*, 4 July 1839, and *Greenock Advertiser*, 27 September 1839; the emigrant press and the provincial press of the United Kingdom were studied in the Colindale branch of the British Museum in 1964 and 1968; Notice to Young Women Desirous of Bettering Their Condition by an Emigration to New South Wales (broadsheet in M.L.); S. C. Brees, *A Key to the Colonies* (London, 1849); Z. P. Pocock, *Emigration and the Position and Prospects of the Emigrant* (London, 1848); A. Andrews, *A Sketch of the Colony of Western Australia* (London, 1849); W. H. G. Kingston, *A Lecture on Colonization* (London, 1849); J. Brice, *South Australia As It Is* (Bristol, 1848); J. Stephens, *A Voice from Australia* (London, 1848); A. Hodgson, *Emigration to the Australian Settlements* (London, 1849); J. Russom, *Australia: a refuge for the destitute* (London, n.d.); broadsheet of Leeds and Yorkshire Australian Emigration Society (Leeds, n.d.); E. H. Mears, *On British Colonization: particularly in reference to South Australia* (London, 1839).

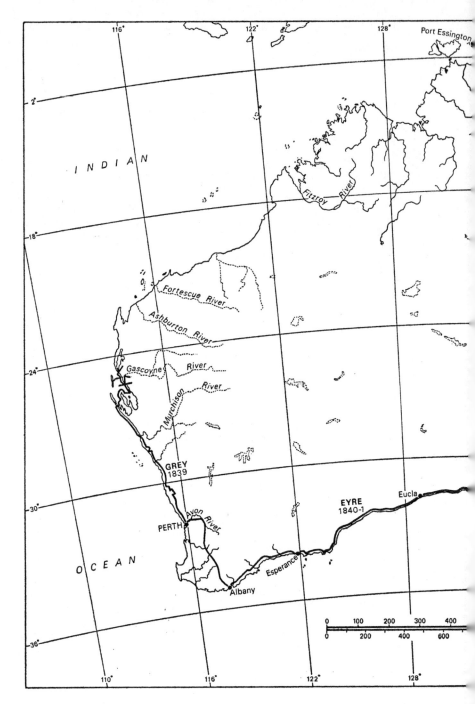

4   *The Expeditions of Mitchell, 1831–2, 1835, 1836; Grey, 1839; Eyre, 1840–1,*
1843; Leichhardt, 1844–5; Sturt, 1844–6; Kennedy, 1848

Based on maps in Mitchell, *Three Expeditions into the Interior of Eastern Australia* (2 vols,
London, 1839); Grey, *Journals of Two Expeditions of Discovery in Northwest and Western*

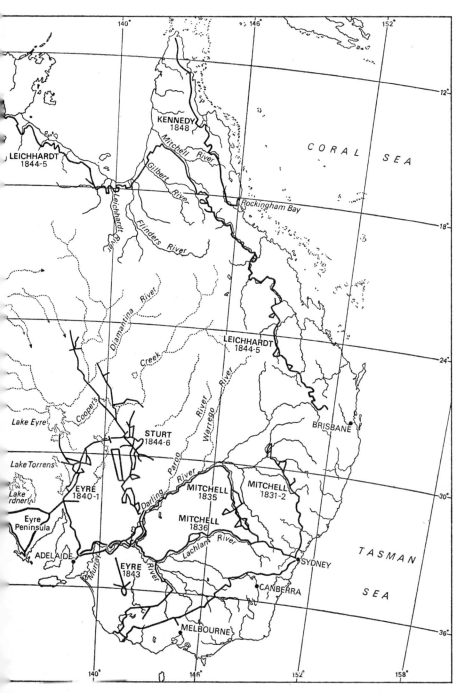

Australia (2 vols, London, 1841); Eyre, *Journals of Expeditions of Discovery into Central Australia and Overland from Adelaide to King George's Sound* (2 vols, London, 1845); Leichhardt, *Journal of an Overland Expedition in Australia from Moreton Bay to Essington* (London, 1847); Sturt, *Narrative of an Expedition into Central Australia* (2 vols, London, 1849); W. Carron, *Narrative of an Expedition* (Sydney, 1849)

perfumes, especially their eau-de-cologne, before departure since they would not find colonial products to be anywhere nearly as good.

Ironmongers and colonial implement makers begged to inform migrants to Australia and New Zealand that at their warehouses they could select for immediate shipment agricultural, mechanical and other tools, all kinds of articles for domestic and cooking purposes, carts, wagons, ploughs, barrows, timber carriages, thrashing and winnowing machines, mills and wood screws. Emigrants were invited to inspect a portable hand mill which ground and dressed in the most perfect manner in one operation coarse and fine flour from wheat, maize and oats. Some shops offered permanent houses for exportation, packed up and delivered at the docks ready for shipment. Others advertised tents and harnesses for sale. Others informed those inclined to seasickness that travellers might now enjoy the great blessing of health and comfort at sea by swallowing that delightful drink—Sir James Murray's Fluid Magnesia—the qualities of which had been testified to by people well known to Her Majesty and the nobility of England. A rival firm advised ladies and gentlemen who wished for comfort during the voyage to fit up their cabins with Joseph Brown's 'PATENT ANTI-SEA-SICK SOFA BEDS' which were constructed on the most simple and scientific principles, retaining their perpendicular in the most boisterous weather without subjecting persons to the least motion of the vessel. For infants they advised their 'SWINGING COT' since it was much superior to anything ever offered to any previous traveller by sea.[10]

Not free passages, nor the benevolence of government, nor the shielding of migrants from wicked men had the slightest effect on the numbers proceeding to Australia compared with those proceeding to North America. In 1850, nearly 30 000 migrated to British North America, just over 223 000 to the United States and just over 16 000 to the Australian colonies and New Zealand. Nor had the intervention of government been any more successful in attracting the more adventurous and the people of broader consciousness to the Australian colonies. As the half-century drew to a close observers were unanimous that those with the capacity to pay their own way, the 'pith and marrow', the 'bone and sinew' or the 'men of moral worth and intelligence' were thronging the quays in Ireland, Scotland and England for the United States, while those lower in the scale of human achievement were clamouring for free passages to Australia.

Believers in the British way of life drew odious comparisons between Yankee lawlessness and the British rule of law. In the United States the nativists talked of a war of extermination against the foreigners in their midst; in New South Wales and Van Diemen's Land the nativists nurtured in their breasts a sullen hostility towards all 'new chums' but did not speak of wars of extermination or draw a gun on intruders in their midst. In the United States the Irish were known as 'the boys who were sociable with

---

[10] Advertisements in *Australasian Record*, 24 July, 13 November 1841, and *Emigrant*, 2 August, 23 September, 7 October 1848.

paving stones'. They were known, too, for their lack of cleanliness, their addiction to the bottle, and their disgraceful conduct at their 'Paddy Funerals'. During riots against the Irish, the Yankee Protestants burned down convents and pronounced the negroes to be better citizens than the hordes of Catholic Irish. In the Australian colonies, by contrast, bitterness between the sects was a festering sore rather than an active volcano. Those who survived the jungle of free enterprise were different in kind from the products of British paternalism in Australia.[11]

What these migrants carried with them in their hearts contributed to the fashioning of an Australian way of life. The wilds of Australia were presented as offering salvation to those Scotsmen who might otherwise be dragged down from decent manhood to squalid apehood by Irish savages in their midst who had converted lodging rooms in Glasgow into lairs of fifteen or twenty shivering, wretched and hungry persons, littered the streets with fathers and children reeling about in a state of helpless drunkenness, and filled the air with the cries of women being beaten savagely by their husbands. Scottish migrants carried with them to Australia this dread of the Irish as superstitious savages who, if unchecked, would reproduce in the New World the squalor that seemed to accompany them wherever they settled. The streets of Glasgow sowed the seed of suspicion and fear of Irish Catholics in the mind of many a Scottish Presbyterian migrant to Sydney, Melbourne and Adelaide, and disposed their minds to listen with approval to the hatred the men of the Orange Lodge entertained for all Catholics.[12]

The Scots also brought with them two visions of life. One was the Goliard vision, according to which the tragedy in the human situation was smothered under gluttony, buffoonery, ribaldry, gay revelry, and wild dancing to the melodeon on the heather in summertime, preceded by enough huge draughts of whisky or 'mountain dew' to introduce the desired 'extra degree of elasticity in the men' and prepare the women to enjoy a fondle. The other was the Calvinist vision of God and man, according to which man's chief end was to glorify God and enjoy Him forever. God was omnipotent; man was impotent, insignificant and very wicked. Adam's fall brought mankind into an estate of sin and misery and left him so corrupt in his nature that his desires were ever at war with God's laws. Man must study the works of God and must treasure and develop the great gift God had planted in him—the ability to distinguish himself from the animal creation. He must therefore train and use his mind. Perfect obedience to the laws of God might require a man to perform an act offensive to his sense of humanity. Armed with a faith in the goodness of God, despite the evidence of human evil and misery, they

[11] Appendix I in S. C. Johnson, *A History of Emigration*; C. Wittke, *The Irish in America* (Baton Rouge, 1956), pp. 46-8, 114-19; R. T. Berthoff, *British Immigrants in Industrial America, 1790-1850* (Cambridge, Mass., 1953), p. 5.

[12] *Australasian Record*, 29 May 1841; *Inverness Courier*, 25 February 1846; *Glasgow Herald*, 24 February, 10 July, 21, 24 August 1840; *Aberdeen Herald*, 26 September 1846; *Aberdeen Journal*, 15 April 1846.

were taught that a whine against the fate of being a man was rebellion against their Creator. Good Calvinists were not likely to give way to despair on finding that the country that promised them a belly-full was cursed by Adam's fall to be barren and uncouth, or that merchants and landlords already controlled the landed wealth of the New World.[13]

By contrast the Irish believed a whine was the only way to express their feelings towards those hereditary enemies of their people who had oppressed and despised them ever since the English conquest of Ireland. In the eyes of their oppressors Ireland was crawled over by beggars, and her fields overgrown with weeds. Her people lived in mud hovels because the Irish themselves lacked those qualities of industry, frugality, sobriety and single-mindedness with which to use the railway, the steam-engine and the spinning jenny to raise them out of their material barbarism. Alcohol and ether drinking coarsened still further what their warm and excitable natures had begun, and fashioned a race of savage barbarians who threatened the very fabric of British society. Under the sway of brutal ignorance and hurried on by the violence of uncontrolled passion, the people practised the wild justice of revenge and committed deeds that made humanity shudder. To the barbarism of their poverty and their temperament, the priests had added that other pernicious barbarism of superstitiousness. In an age in which industrial civilization was holding out the promise of emancipating mankind from the curse of earning their living in the sweat of their brow, these wretches were crawling on their bare knees, sitting with heavy stones on their heads, lying down outside some miserable church while their compatriots trampled on them to expiate some trivial offence against the rules the priest had prescribed, or tossing the mite they could ill afford into the plate held by a priest who threatened to horsewhip all non-contributors. In Ireland this thraldom of peasant to priest, and the ignorance and the superstition of the peasants were perpetuating the servitude of a whole people.

The Irish had been taught for generations to view the English and the Scottish Presbyterians as those predatory oppressors of their people who had converted the most beautiful island on God's earth into a land of skulls and ghastly spectres. Why should they place the least confidence in such men? Why should they believe Irishmen would achieve justice in a British law court? Why should they observe the conventions of a civilized community in their behaviour towards a people who had done them such evil? Was it not understandable that priest and peasant should combine to terrorize those who ingratiated themselves to such monsters in return for some filthy material

---

[13] *Aberdeen Journal*, 23 December 1846; visit to Tongue and Scourie Bay, 29-30 May 1968; D. McLeod, 'Young memories: a series of letters to the Edinburgh Weekly Chronicle', reprinted in A. Mackenzie, *The History of the Highland Clearances* (Inverness, 1883), pp. 39-75, 119-24; *Inverness Courier*, 18 February, 25 November, 2 December 1846; *Aberdeen Herald*, 19, 26 September 1846; *Shorter Catechism of the Church of Scotland*; Walter Scott, *The Heart of Midlothian* (Australasian issue, Sydney, 1898), pp. 534, 540; P. L. Brown (ed.), *The Narrative of George Russell of Golf Hill* (London, 1935), pp. 36-7; Barron Field, *First Fruits of Australian Poetry* (Sydney, 1819), p. 7.

gain? Had they themselves not managed to preserve the image of Christ in the midst of revolting cruelty and degradation? Had they not Christ's promise that the meek would inherit the earth, that the hungry would be filled with good things and the rich sent away empty-handed? Were not their enemies men of such heartless brutality and so lacking in compassion for the poor that they had the effrontery to preach laissez-faire economics as the remedy for a starving people? Was it not typical of the satanic pride of those Anglo-Saxon barbarians to believe that they even enjoyed the divine favour for all the cruelty and suffering they were inflicting on the people of India?

There were great contrasts in the attitudes to fundamental questions. The loyalty of the English and the Scots was to the throne; the loyalty of the Irish was to Erin's green isle, Saint Patrick, the faith of their fathers, and the Pope. The English and the Scots viewed British institutions with an almost mystical awe and veneration; the Irish were trained in the virtues of lawlessness. The English and the Scots were favourably disposed to the Wentworth vision of Australia as a new Britannia in another world; the 'low Irish mob' was disposed to separation, indeed to any political move that would embarrass and humiliate their enemies. The English and the Scots were taught in the schoolroom, the pulpit and the press to believe that in the collision of truth with error in a rational civilized discussion, truth would prevail; the Irish nourished no such illusion. The English and the Scots held the opinion that the poverty, ignorance, superstition and erratic behaviour of the Irish disqualified them from holding positions of power in the community—that men who never looked you in the eye were unfit to run the affairs of state or to manage an estate—that they were the eternal publicans, bottle-washers, and boot-lickers of human society. The Irish on the other hand nourished the illusion that the cause of their inferior position in society lay not in themselves but in their melancholy past and in the hearts and minds of their oppressors.[14]

All the migrants carried in their hearts those parts of the English and Scottish puritan tradition and Irish Jansenism which taught them to be prudish about all things pertaining to the body and pessimistic about man's power to change the world without divine aid. All of them also carried with them the hope of inheriting the riches of the New World. They saw themselves as men and women who were fleeing from 'sorrow and crime' to 'meet amidst plenty' the 'good coming time'. They saw themselves as carriers of their liberty, their religion, their rights, their language and their laws to the Australian shores. Even though, as they put it in their song 'Emigration', the winds would waft them far away, 'Victoria's sceptre o'er us sway,/ For we are Britons still.' They were not inspired by a vision of men flying from

[14] *Quarterly Review*, no. 133, 1840, pp. 119-70, no. 31, 1841, pp. 350-60; *Cork Standard*, 4 February, 3 June 1839; *Cork Examiner*, 10 April, 17, 30 October 1846; *Tipperary Advocate*, 3 June 1848; *Galway Vindicator*, 15 December 1841, 11 June 1842; *Nenagh Guardian*, 31 March, 17 April 1841; *Fireside Journal*, 24 October 1839; *Galway Patriot*, 3 October 1835.

the evils of Europe to build a new society in the Australian wilderness, but rather of Australia providing an opportunity for them to become men of property. The Australian colonies which had begun as places for the punishment and reformation of British criminals were to become places where redundant workers from the British Isles would become both prosperous and respectable.[15]

From the day of their selection as migrants they were exposed to the full blast of propaganda to win them for the cause of bourgeois respectability in the New World. At the port of embarkation the women were told to spend their time on board reading the Bible, joining in family prayer, cultivating the habit of obedience, ridding their minds of extravagant notions, cultivating such purity of heart that nothing would induce them to flirt with the passengers or the crew. They were to be specially careful not to allow any exposure of any part of their bodies which might arouse desire in the men. The men were instructed to rise early, dress decently, discourage all idle words, indecent jests, and any remarks whatsoever on the physical appearance of the women on board. They were enjoined to cultivate the habits of temperance and moderation because the taking of spirituous liquors in excess was a plague, a pestilence and a poison. As a migrant ship weighed anchor at Plymouth, Scourie Bay, Greenock or Queen's Town those on board sang words of Christian resignation and humility, 'Asking Thy blessing and Thy love,/ We bow the knee', or chanted those simple words, 'The Lord is my shepherd. Therefore can I lack nothing.' There was little singing of chartist songs about the future of humanity, far less any Schilleresque professions of faith in the day when all men became brothers.[16]

On the journey a parson, a schoolmaster, the ship's captain or the surgeon pleaded with them each Sunday to observe frugality, industry, sobriety, purity, self-help and humility. Ordinary men presented to them a different vision of the world. They recommended the 'fresh heart', the 'light step', 'hopeful courage' and a willingness to 'go on cheerily', while the moral improvers urged them to acquire lowly hearts, bowed down by a sense of sin and a sense that only God's wondrous love could make such sinners clean. As the migrants sang in a doleful, monotonous tone their hymns and psalms of

[15] 'The poor British emigrants' Farewell, on leaving their country for the Australian colonies', *Colonial Magazine*, January-April 1842, vol. 7, p. 413; 'Emigration', a ballad by Agricola, *Emigrant*, 12 August 1848.

[16] 'A letter to young female emigrants proceeding to Australia', *Emigrant Tract No. 1* (London, 1850); K.E.F., 'Parting words to emigrant parents', *Emigrant Tract No. 2* (London, 1850); J.L.W., 'Hints for improvement during the outward voyage', *Emigrant Tract No. 8* (London, 1850); W. H. G. Kingston, *The Emigrants' Home* (London, 1856); W. H. G. Kingston, *Emigrant Manuals* (London, 1851); *Emigrants' Penny Magazine* (Plymouth), no. 1, May 1850; *Household Words*, no. 1, 30 March 1850, pp. 19-24; *Cork Examiner*, 5 November 1841, 3, 5, 22 January 1842, 1 February, 8, 22 March, 12 April 1843; *Tipperary Vindicator*, 17 May 1848; *Galway Vindicator*, 17 November 1841; 'The emigrants' morning hymn', *Emigrants' Penny Magazine*, no. 1, May 1850; 'Emigrants' evening hymn', *Emigrants' Penny Magazine*, no. 17, September 1851; *Inverness Courier*, 5 August 1852.

man's unworthiness to enter under God's roof, the sailors sang lustily that there was no drinking after death, down among the dead men.[17]

After landing in the Australian colonies the moral improvers fought anew for the hearts of the immigrants against the kingdom of darkness. In the first eight years of assisted immigration the behaviour of recent immigrants had fallen far short of the expectations of the pious and the profit-mongers of Sydney, Hobart, Adelaide and Perth. Boatloads of prostitutes, it was said, were let loose in the streets of Sydney and Hobart. Drunken Irishmen staggered around in the streets, kicking their wives and their children and replying to those who rebuked or despised them, 'I'm Colonial now'. Fancy men beguiled innocent girls with their talk about attending church on Sundays, followed by an invitation to the theatre, the gift of a flash dress, and the hint that they, too, had a gift to offer in return which would guarantee a life of idleness, if not of pleasure. But rescue was at hand.[18]

A woman short in stature, frail of body, but mighty of heart, with a lovely mouth and the sweetest smile this side of heaven, was already asking God to give her the strength never to rest until she had provided 'decent protection' for the morals of the migrant girls. Caroline Chisholm turned thirty-two in 1840. Born in England into a family steeped in the piety and preoccupation with sexual purity and prudery of the evangelical movement, at the age of twenty-two she had married an army officer on condition that he allow her to continue her good works in social philanthropy. She was also received into the Catholic Church. When her husband was posted to Madras in 1832 she began there a Female School of Industry to improve the morals of the women members of the European community. Shortly after she and her husband and three sons arrived in Sydney on leave in September 1838 she saw a gentleman taking liberties with a Highland girl and decided that the morals of the immigrant girls needed protection. In January 1841 she put forward to Lady Gipps her idea to raise money for a girls' home in which immigrant girls would receive 'decent protection' in the period between disembarkation and taking up their employment. By the end of that year she had accommodation for ninety in her Immigrants' Home. She herself was living with the girls in the home, where she spent part of her time compiling a register of employment. Hundreds of single girls were first protected by her and then placed in situations where they earned good wages and generally got married instead of going on the street. By the end of the

[17] W. Harbottle, Journal Kept During Voyage to Australia, 10, 14, 17 March, 26 April, 15 May 1849 (MS. in NAT. L.); E. Stamp, Daily Journals of the Voyage to Port Phillip per Ship *Tasman*, 24 August 1849 (MS. in NAT. L.); Female Servant to Mr. Milne, n.d., quoted in *Emigrants' Letters* (London, 1850), pp. 72-3; E. Stamp, op. cit., 29 August, 5, 27 September 1849; *Vindicator* (Belfast), 4 January 1842; Journal of A. W. Manning, 12, 14 November 1839 (photocopy in NAT. L.).

[18] *Sydney Gazette*, 18 February 1841; evidence of J. D. Pinnock to Select Committee on Immigration, *V. & P.* (L.C. N.S.W.), 1841; article on Caroline Chisholm in *Cork Examiner*, 26 April 1852; *Female Immigration Considered, in a Brief Account of the Sydney Immigrants' Home*, by the secretary, Caroline Chisholm (Sydney, 1842), pp. 19-22.

year the employment agency part of her work was extended to include married men, because they found Mrs Chisholm got them higher rates than those offered by the employers or their agents who came on board the migrant ships in Sydney Harbour.[19]

Despite all her efforts to persuade the young girls and the family men that country life was less corrupting than the city, migrants were still reluctant to face up to the dangers of aborigines and bushrangers. In 1841 she chartered a steamboat and took sixty females to the Hunter River district where they were snapped up by the settlers at double the wages they could obtain in the towns. For she believed in the moral benefits of providing families with female servants. She knew how much they were required as wives in a society in which men outnumbered the women so heavily, and knew, too, how much moral good they might do as wives. Within a year she conceived the idea of moving families into the interior where wages were high but employers could not afford the time or expense of a trip to Sydney to engage workers. She wrote to the newspapers to ask wealthy gentlemen and farmers to provide food on the road for the migrants. She put the women and children in wagons, made the strong men walk, and herself mounted a horse and rode out into the country at the head of a party seeking employment. They started at daylight each day and proceeded to the first place where servants were wanted. The farther they went the better the wages got. On some of these excursions she placed as many as two hundred people. In the middle of each day they halted, made a fire like gypsies, boiled their billies, made meat cakes and damper out of the meat and flour supplied by prospective employers, and at night camped out in the open, or dossed down in a deserted bush hut.

Hundreds of bachelors made applications to her for wives. 'Come now, Mrs. Chisholm', one desperate man wrote, 'do be a mother to me, and give me a wife; the smile of a woman has never welcomed me home after a hard day's work.' By 1846 hundreds of former bachelors were writing letters of gratitude to her for 'suiting' them. For women, she believed, were God's police to the men of New South Wales. Censorship and eternal vigilance, she believed, were God's protectors for the morals of the young. When she found children in the country reading a book that made what was morally bad look good she threw the book into the fire, feeling, she said, as though a venomous reptile had clung to her clothes. Between 1840 and 1846 she settled some eleven thousand people as servants or farmers in New South Wales, and taught many servants to succeed so well by exercising the virtues of sobriety and industry that they became independent farmers.[20]

In 1846 she left for England, where again she was never idle. She published a pamphlet on *Emigration and Transportation Relatively Considered.* She persuaded Earl Grey to grant free passages to the wives of emancipists in

[19] *Female Immigration Considered*, pp. 1-3; Margaret Kiddle, *Caroline Chisholm* (Melbourne, 1950).

[20] *What Has Mrs. Caroline Chisholm Done for the Colony of New South Wales?* (Sydney, 1862), p. 21; E. Mackenzie, *The Emigrant's Guide to Australia* (London, n.d.), p. 3.

New South Wales because all her experience in that colony had convinced her that those men, too, needed moral policing. She persuaded the emigration commissioners to protect the morals of young women on migrant ships in the way she had found so efficacious in her own Immigrants' Home in Sydney, which was simply to segregate the women from the men. She founded a Colonization Society in which migrants with families were encouraged to save two-thirds of the passage money and borrow the remaining third from the society. In this way she could contribute to those two things so close to her heart—the emancipation of suffering humanity from the thraldom of poverty, and the encouragement of industry and frugality in the working classes so that the proportion of the virtuous in the Australian colonies would be increased. Under her influence the emigrant press in London announced its intention to promote the formation of Mutual Assistance Emigrant Clubs so that the working man would no longer have to barter his labour for a free passage but might become a small landowner and so enjoy 'happy results and fair fortune' in the New World rather than remain an 'unhappy and almost destitute' operative in his native country.

She stamped up and down England and Scotland and crossed the sea to Ireland, preaching everywhere the doctrine of emigration and moral improvement as God's cures for the poverty, drunkenness, prostitution and cruelty which muddied the reputation of mankind. By 1852 she was answering 240 letters a day from people interested in emigration, writing pamphlets (*Comfort for the Poor!* had appeared in 1847 and *The A.B.C. of Colonization* in 1850), and still finding time to lecture. At Cork in May 1852, in the heart of that country where many pinned their hopes to the story of the miracle of the loaves and the fishes, the Irish paid homage to her as a great social reformer who had 'moralised emigration' by placing in the hands of the humble and the industrious the chance to move to lands where all honest labour might earn a just reward without detriment to their health, their self-respect or their morals. They thanked her especially for the arrangements she had made to secure 'a kindly and vigilant guardianship for the unprotected of [her own] sex, both during the voyage and after their arrival in the colony'. Mrs Chisholm then rose and proceeded to read in a low but clear voice her reply, in which she declared that the moral good of mankind had been her object.[21]

By then she had won the support of Charles Dickens who in the first issue of his new periodical *Household Words* on 30 March 1850 had supported her scheme. 'The best persons', he had written, 'to settle in a new country, [were] those whose morals were subject to the check of family responsibilities. A wife and children were precisely the encumbrances in a new country to chain a man to hard work and to probity . . . and confirm him in his place of service

---

[21] Caroline Chisholm, *Emigration and Transportation Relatively Considered* (London, 1847); Caroline Chisholm, *Comfort for the Poor!* (London, 1847); Caroline Chisholm, *The A.B.C. of Colonization* (London, 1850); E. Mackenzie, *The Emigrant's Guide to Australia*, pp. 13-15; *Cork Examiner*, 26 April, 10, 19 May 1852; *Liverpool Journal*, 24 April 1852; *The Story of the Life of Mrs. Caroline Chisholm, the Emigrant's Friend, and Her Adventures in Australia* (London, n.d.); *Emigrant*, 19 August 1848, 6 January 1849.

. . . and prevent him from making rash and fruitless changes!' The man who, on his own confession, did not know that year whether to laugh or cry at the madness in his own heart which had caused him to marry 'a child wife' recommended marriage as an estate for those who were to subdue the wilderness in Australia. That year Mrs Chisholm had uncovered part of the madness in her own heart. She had risked a meeting with Charles Dickens. From that day he was haunted by the bad dream of Mrs Chisholm and her poor housekeeping, and the dirty faces of her children became his continual companions. He satirized her in his novel *Bleak House* as Mrs Jellyby, the lady of remarkable strength of character who devoted herself to an extensive variety of public subjects, including the happy settlement on the banks of the African rivers of England's superabundant home population, and allowed her own children to be the 'dirtiest little unfortunates', while she, who never seemed to have any article of dress upon her, from a pin upwards, that was in its right condition or its right place, worked at her plans to settle families on the left bank of the Niger to cultivate coffee and educate the natives.[22]

In 1847 in his pamphlet *Popery in Australia and the Southern Hemisphere* Lang praised her humanity and her extraordinary spirit of devotion, but denounced her for attempting to 'Romanise that great Colony . . . [and] by means of a . . . land-flood of Irish Popery, under the guise of a great scheme of National Emigration, to present it in due time to God, the Virgin Mary, and the Pope'. He added that it was quite in accordance with the artful and insidious policy of the papacy to put forward 'an enthusiastic female for the promotion of its grand designs against the civil and religious liberties of men'. Broughton found her a 'lady-like person; and very prepossessing and interesting from the earnestness with which she had taken up a good cause'. Though he doubted whether a woman with such an air of openness and honesty could be an agent for others with ulterior purposes, he remained sufficiently suspicious about the uses the Roman clergy might make of her— for example, to say 'No' to her Immigrants' Home while remaining prepared to assist her in placing migrant girls in good and respectable places. When she went to Liverpool (England) in May 1852, the Orange brethren urged Protestants not to slumber at their posts lest Mrs Chisholm succeed in converting the Australian colonies into a province of the papacy, and print the image of the whore of Babylon where the convicts had already raised a 'dungheap'. Still others denounced her as an 'interfering old bitch' who wanted the pale Galilean to conquer the hearts of men and use women not as the ones who might take men on the walk through the paradise gardens but as moral police. Those who looked to emigration to distract the minds of the working classes from strikes, chartist mischief, and anarchy, and those who wanted the working classes to be taught the virtues of self-reliance, frugality, and industry and not waste their time listening to 'the incendiaries' jaw', named

[22] *Household Words*, no. 1, 30 March 1850; E. Johnson, *Charles Dickens* (2 vols, London, 1953), vol. 2, p. 768; Charles Dickens, *Bleak House* (New Oxford Illustrated Dickens, London, 1948), pp. 35-6, 640; C. Dickens to Miss Coutts, 3 April 1850, quoted in E. Johnson, op. cit., vol. 2, p. 65.

her 'a second Moses in bonnet and shawl' who, like Mary, had preserved the one thing needful in her heart and not allowed herself to be 'much cumbered' by the labours of the kitchen or the nursery.[23]

No other colony besides New South Wales produced a woman of the stature, single-mindedness or industry of Mrs Chisholm, but in all the others reception committees, immigration officers and philanthropists laboured for the protection of the immigrants' morals and encouraged the growth of those virtues of self-reliance, industry, purity and family affection so dear to the heart of Mrs Chisholm. In Melbourne there was a Ladies' Female Immigrant Society, presided over by the head of the Anglican Church, a fine example of benevolent usefulness, and a most necessary antidote to the rottenness, sloth and moral evils to which the migrants too often succumbed because of the monotony of their long journey. In South Australia, after Grey recommended its resumption in January 1843, assisted immigration resumed with such a bang that 35 per cent of all assisted migrants going to the Australian colonies were sent to South Australia. There a Benevolent and Strangers' Friend Society administered relief to the needy and promoted the moral and spiritual welfare of immigrants. Its secretary, a Mr Maguire, activated by much more exalted principles than gain, and a seasoner of all his work with true Christian humility, placed unmarried females in homes and found employment for the afflicted and disconsolate who were far from the land of their birth. There was also a Colonial Labour Committee which assumed the responsibility of finding employment for members of both sexes and of influencing both employers and workers to uphold agreements, taking care not to interfere with the price of labour but requiring master and man to make their own terms. In that colony the zeal to protect the morals of female immigrants reached such a pitch by the beginning of 1851 that the first mate on the *Joseph Soames* had £5 deducted from his gratuity for speaking to the female immigrants, notwithstanding the remonstrances of the surgeon on the ship not to do so, and despite testimony that in all other ways his conduct had been decorous and proper. In Hobart Town in Franklin's day the wife of the Lieutenant-Governor, the wife of the head of the Anglican Church and the wife of the Chief Justice appointed themselves guardians of the material and moral welfare of migrants.[24]

In the eyes of the recent migrants the Australian colonies were places where every man enjoyed that belly-full, the foundation of their 'good coming time' in the New World. They wrote back to their relatives and those who were

[23] J. D. Lang, *Popery in Australia and the Southern Hemisphere* (Edinburgh, 1847); A. Gilchrist, *John Dunmore Lang* (2 vols, Melbourne, 1951), vol. 2, pp. 423, 446, 448; W. G. Broughton to H. T. Stiles, 21 October 1841 (Stiles Papers, MS. in M.L.); *Liverpool Journal*, 24 April, 8 May 1852; *What Has Mrs. Caroline Chisholm Done for the Colony of New South Wales?*, p. 21; E. Mackenzie, *The Emigrant's Guide to Australia*, p. 3; *Household Words*, no. 1, 30 March 1850.

[24] D. H. Pike, *Paradise of Dissent* (London, 1957), pp. 186, 314-23; *South Australian Register*, 28 February 1849; *South Australian Government Gazette*, 12 July 1849, 16 January 1851; *Perth Gazette and West Australian Journal*, 14, 21 January, 18 March, 29 April 1843.

near and dear to them in the United Kingdom about Australia as a place
where no person was starving, where the dogs destroyed each year more beef
and bread than all the poor in Ireland could eat and where the poor man
could eat beef and mutton just like a rich man. There was

> plenty of everything that's good to eat. It was only five months ago we could not
> get enough to eat [i.e. when they were in England], and now we have a bag of
> flour, and as much meat as we can eat . . . Jane is as fat as a pig, we are happy as
> days be long, not forgetting all behind . . . Dear father, mother, brothers and
> sisters, *do come*, all if you can, give my love to all as ask after me, so good night,
> God bless you!

The letters took back to the United Kingdom the words of gratitude from
men and women who saw themselves as having said farewell to want, crime
and sorrow, and having found the secret of human happiness in a belly-full.
'Dear mother and father I ham very happy and comfortable, and shuld be
more so if you was all with us', wrote one migrant, 'I never was happy before
I came in this beautifule country as I ham now.' Migrants also liked the chance
of rising out of the working classes. 'Come, men, women, and children, for you
can do well here', wrote another migrant, 'I am getting good wages . . . plenty
here to eat and drink, and plenty of money. Next year I do intend, if please
God spare my life, to go on my own hands.'[25]

In the Old World where the earth was said to be soaked from its crust to
its core with the tears of humanity, the serious-minded were appalled at such
facile and superficial optimism. They warned migrants that Australia was a
very inferior part of the world, so lacking in water that the river-beds dried
up in seasons of drought. They solemnly reminded migrants that a society
composed of expatriated paupers and noisy, drunken and discontented idlers
could not be expected to find the secret of human happiness but would turn
instead into a social cesspool. How could ragged regiments of misery and
ignorance, who lacked leaders, respectability and intelligence, create anything
else except low life? Men who were condemned to spend their days cooking
dinners in log huts or feeding poultry and milking cows in the bush where
there was no British Museum, no National Gallery and no Covent Garden,
might enjoy a belly-full, but they would never enjoy a full-blown civilization
while they herded with cannibals and possums. But nothing they could say
or do could efface the great dream driving the migrant on to what he conceived to be his glory in Australia. Unlike the American dream, it was not a
dream of log cabin to White House, or a dream of a day when all men treated
each other as of equal significance, but simply a dream of becoming respectable
men of property. That was the 'good coming time' for an Australian.[26]

[25] *Emigrant*, 22 July, 19 August 1848, 24 February 1849; *Emigrants' Letters: being a
collection of recent communications from settlers in the British colonies* (London, 1850),
p. 73; S. Sidney (ed.), *Sidney's Emigrant's Journal and Traveller's Magazine* (2nd ser.,
London, 1850), p. 210.

[26] *Emigrant*, 9, 16 September 1830; *The Times*, 20 July 1848; for statistics on migra-
tion to eastern Australia 1839-51 see R. B. Madgwick, *Immigration into Eastern
Australia* (London, 1937), p. 234, and for immigration into South Australia 1836-51 see
D. H. Pike, op. cit., appendix A.

II

COUNTRY GENTLEMEN
AND BUSH BARBARIANS

B Y 1843 those who believed in the mission of the British people to spread their civilization over the Australian wilderness were pained to discover that barbarism was gaining the ascendancy in huge portions of the land. In the Darling Downs, Moreton Bay, New England, the Wellington Valley, the Bathurst Plains, the Monaro, Gippsland and Australia Felix a strange assemblage of human beings was glorying in lawlessness, and inflicting the most hideous cruelty on defenceless savages. The great dryness of the country, the increasing demand for fine Australian-grown wool in the United Kingdom, and the land laws and regulations were encouraging a dispersion of settlement into areas outside all the refining influences of civilization. Man was turning God's heritage into an abomination. In their greed for material gain, white men were prepared to lower themselves to the level of the beasts, and reduce the black men to a more miserable and degraded existence than the one they had known before the invasion of their country in 1788.[1]

The aspirations of the agents of civilization had been both noble and high-minded. In 1824 and 1825 the Australian Agricultural Company received its charter to introduce into New South Wales a large capital, agricultural skill, and the ultimate benefit of the increase of fine wool as a commodity for export. It was the hope of the directors that their servants should not only assist in the punishment and reformation of British criminals, but also diffuse useful knowledge throughout the colony, encourage the migration of useful settlers and female servants, and promote a system of rural industry. In their selection of a site for their operations the directors had the advantage of the services of Allan Cunningham. By profession a botanist, he came to Sydney in 1816 as a protegé of Joseph Banks, a one-time amoroso of Tahiti, who had become in that period of life when desire faded a patron of young men of promise. Cunningham had talent in abundance. He was also a fuss-pot who pestered the Colonial Secretary of New South Wales for a passport to travel outside the boundaries of location, and that blend of hero who also had the

[1] Report of Select Committee on Crown Land Grievances, *V & P*, (L.C. N.S.W.), 1844, vol. 2, pp. 10-11; H. W. Haygarth, *Recollections of Bush Life in Australia*, quoted in *Nenagh Guardian*, 24 June 1848; R. Howitt, *Impressions of Australia Felix* (London 1845), p. 165; 'Australian sketches by Mr. McCombie', quoted in *Port Phillip Patriot*, 15 January 1844; Gipps to Russell, 28 September 1840, *H.R.A.*, I. xx. 837-44; Book of Jeremiah, 2: 7.

soul of a lackey. In the spirit of the servant rather than the decision-maker he put down on paper the arguments for and against sites in the Bathurst district, the Monaro, the Liverpool Plains and the Hastings River. Robert Dawson, the first commissioner or manager for the company in New South Wales, persuaded the Sydney management committee, consisting of Hannibal Macarthur, James Macarthur and his brother-in-law James Bowman, to choose a site stretching from Port Stephens to the Hastings. This was their first piece of foolishness, for the narrow strip of land between the Great Dividing Range and the sea from Moreton Bay to the mouth of the Hunter River was not suitable for depasturing stock. With the young radical Wentworth raving about the company getting their 'filthy paws' on the best lands of the colony, Dawson occupied the site at Port Stephens.[2]

There the combination of Dawson's temperament and unsuitable land led to early failure and his own dismissal. In his place the directors appointed as manager Sir William Edward Parry, a man who had won 'deathless glory' in the Arctic and was a fervent believer in scriptural religion. He asked Henry Dangar, formerly a member of the Survey Department in Sydney, for advice on a site. Dangar was one of those men who was never certain all his life whether he thirsted for Christ or for the riches of this world, and ended up laying up for himself large landed treasures in New South Wales before he tried to enter by the narrow gate into the Eternal City. Driven at times by an evil spirit to wallow in the satisfaction of scoring off his enemies even at the expense of his career and his reputation, he was known as a 'wolf in the habit of a lamb'. Parry had chosen his man well for Dangar knew the Manning, the Hunter and the Liverpool Plains. He persuaded Parry to ask for a site on the latter. After tedious arguments with Governor Bourke and an appeal to London, Port Stephens, Stroud, Gloucester, the lower Hunter and an area at Warrah near Quirindi and Goonji-Goonji on the Red River near the present site of Tamworth became the property of the company.[3]

Under the commissionership of Parry and his successor Henry Dumaresq, brother-in-law of Governor Darling, the main lines of activity for the Australian Agricultural Company were laid down. They bred stud sheep, cattle and horses to raise the quality of stock in the colony, and for sale to other landholders in New South Wales and, after 1836, in South Australia. They

[2] For the foundation of the Australian Agricultural Company, see vol. 2, pp. 63-4 of this history; Bathurst to Brisbane, 13 July 1824, *H.R.A.*, I. xi. 305-6; Bathurst to Brisbane and encl., 18 May 1825, *H.R.A.*, I. xi. 591-4; R. Dawson, *The Present State of Australia* (London, 1830); W. G. McMinn, *Allan Cunningham* (Melbourne, 1970), ch. 4; Barron Field, *Geographical Memoirs of New South Wales* (London, 1825); A. Cunningham to H. Macarthur, J. Macarthur and J. Bowman, 30 November 1824, Australian Agricultural Company Despatches 78/1/1 (A.A. Co. Papers in A.N.U. Archives).

[3] Based on E. C. Rowland, 'The life and times of Henry Dangar', R.A.H.S., *J. & P.*, vol. 29, 1953; Agreement between the Australian Agricultural Company and Mr. Henry Dangar, 21 August 1829 (Dangar Papers, MS. in University of New England library); H. Dangar, *Index and Directory to Maps of the Country Bordering upon the River Hunter* (London, 1828); E. Parry to Bourke, 15 June 1832, encl. in Bourke to Goderich, 17 September 1832, *H.R.A.*, I. xvi. 733-41; Goderich to Bourke, 23 March 1833, *H.R.A.*, I. xvii. 57-8.

fattened sheep and cattle for the meat market and grew fine wool at Warrah and Goonji-Goonji which was carried by bullock-dray each year down to Newcastle for shipment to Sydney and the United Kingdom. The carriers refreshed themselves at the inns and stores that Henry Dangar had put up at strategic points on the route. When Dumaresq died in March 1838 the company was employing its entitled number of about five hundred convicts on its estates.[4]

Both Parry and Dumaresq were renowned for their sound evangelical conviction in trusting to obtain salvation not just through their own virtue but through the merits of their divine redeemer. The words on the tombstone of the convict woman Suzannah Craven at Stroud bore witness to the vision of the world taught to the servants of the company. She learned through divine grace of the vanity of the world and no longer looked to it for happiness but, convinced of her sinful and lost estate, eagerly sought to be saved through Jesus Christ. Those who lived on after the vicar's wife died on 21 October 1854 cut on her tombstone words of praise for her life of fervent piety in which her joyful hope of eternal life gave her the patience to endure the suffering and limitations of this life. By contrast most of the convict workers, their wives and their children barbarized their lives with their drinking, their promiscuity and their profane language. The carpenters at Stroud were more often drunk than sober; the two horse-shoers were always half tipsy and amused themselves by drinking instead of working on the horses. Parry did his best to impress on them the necessity of preparing for death: he distributed a great number of Bibles, Books of Common Prayer and tracts, but all to little avail. He tried a game of cricket with the indented servants of the company and felt that this induced a great relaxation as well as a reminder of 'dear old England'. After two years of trying to win the victory for civilization against all the barbarizing tendencies in the Australian bush, Parry asked in despair, 'What can be done with such people?' For nothing he or his successor Henry Dumaresq tried changed the behaviour of the convicts and the old hands who worked on the estates of the company.[5]

Nor was Dumaresq's successor, Phillip Parker King, who received his appointment as manager on 12 March 1839, any more successful than his two high-minded predecessors. Like them, King was always most anxious to persuade others to the prayer and self-denial he found so beneficial to his body as well as his soul. Shortly after he took over he wrote to the board of directors about the evil practice of the convicts and old hands at Warrah and Goonji-Goonji harbouring aboriginal women in their huts. He also complained that despite the kindness always shown to them and the protection afforded by the officers of the company the blacks were guilty of many acts of

[4] Employees of A.A. Co. to board of directors, 24 May 1838 (A.A. Co. Papers).

[5] Tomb of Henry Dumaresq, Church of England section of the Muswellbrook Cemetery; see also memorial tablet for Margaret Cowper on wall of St John's Church, Stroud, and headstone for Susannah Craven in the cemetery, personal visit, 24 August 1969; Journal of Sir Edward Parry, 17 January, 3 February, 10 June, 26 July 1831 (MS. in M.L.); W. E. Parry to board of directors, 13 January 1832 (Despatches and Letters from board of directors to Parry, 1829-34, A.A. Co. Papers).

hostility without the least cause or provocation. Shepherds at out-stations were murdered, bullocks speared and sheep slaughtered by these barbarous blacks even though the officers of the company took pains to see the blacks were never allowed to want, or to ask for protection in vain.[6]

The gradual change from convict to free labour between 1839 and 1843 at least raised the hope that the barbarism of the bond would give way to civilization under free men. But free workers refused to shepherd flocks of sheep and herds of cattle outside the boundaries of location. So King was forced to develop plans for a community of tenant farmers and workers on the company's land at Stroud, Gloucester, and Booral while using ticket-of-leave men and expirees as shepherds and rouseabouts on the estates at Warrah and Goonji-Goonji. Inside the boundaries there were the rudiments of civilization on the estates of the company; outside the boundaries there was barbarism. At Stroud, Gloucester and Booral the company proved that it was possible to colonize a part of New South Wales without degrading and brutalizing its servants. Tamworth and Quirindi by contrast were infected by low disorderly characters and bushrangers who did much mischief, by aborigines who inflicted the most barbarous cruelties on the white trespassers, and by those dregs of convictism, those monsters in human shape, who turned that part of God's heritage to the white man into an abomination. In the workers, it was said, all the fairer characters and qualities of human nature were obliterated by their isolation, their loneliness and their brutalizing labour, while the sensibilities of their masters and overseers were blunted by their sharing in an uncouth way of life.[7]

In all the pastoral districts of New South Wales the same pattern prevailed. Within the boundaries there were settlers on whom the title 'aristocrats of the soil' was not unjustly bestowed; outside the boundaries there were the 'outlandish settlers' and the 'monkeyfied men'. Some forty miles from Sydney on the great south road to Goulburn, Yass, Gundagai and Port Phillip there was the 25 000-acre estate of James and William Macarthur at Camden Park. The mansion, designed by the architect John Verge, was conceived on a grand scale for a family who believed they and their fellow landed proprietors should become powerful as an aristocracy to counter the democratic feeling in the colony spread by convicts, levellers and chartists. It was fashioned out of granite grained with marble. At the front entrance were four stone columns in the style of the plantation manors of Virginia and Maryland and the country houses of the nobility and gentry in Russia. They lacked the splendour and grandeur of their American and Russian counterparts, for not even the resources of the Macarthurs could command the labour and the wealth of

---

[6] P. P. King to board of directors, 15 March, 22 July 1839 (A.A. Co. Papers).

[7] J. E. Ebsworth to H. T. Ebsworth, 26 October 1838, J. E. Ebsworth to board of directors, 31 August 1838, 9 January 1839, P. P. King to board of directors, 10 October 1839, 1 February, 1 May 1841, 26 September 1846, encl. P. P. King to board of directors, 12 February 1840, P. P. King to board of directors, 1 January, 12 February 1840, 1 February, 5 November 1841, 1 September 1842, 11 April 1844, P. P. King to board of directors (A. A. Co. Papers); Charles Dickens, *American Notes and Pictures from Italy* (New Oxford Illustrated Dickens, London, 1957), pp. 135-7.

those Southern grandees whose houses were put up by negro or serf labour. Nor was the interior finished with such luxury and conspicuous waste as in the plantation houses of America or Russia, though the wood-panelled library, the piano, the Renaissance-style pendulum clock on the mantelpiece of the drawing-room, and the mahogany and cedar furniture testified to an interest in the graces and refinements of civilization over and above the crude struggle for survival. There was an air of order and opulence even in the dairy and the vineyard.[8]

As settlement spread along the river valleys and over the plains between the Hunter and the Darling Downs the same pattern was repeated in each district. The valley of the Hunter was won for the landed gentry well before the introduction of the sale of Crown land at a minimum upset price in 1832. At Illulaung at the head of the navigable waters of the Hunter, Edward Close, once lieutenant in the British army, took up his grant of 2560 acres and worked his estate in the English manorial tradition with the squire attending to the material needs of his tenants and workers and providing amusements on holidays. In politics a throne-and-altar man, he taught his tenants and his workers that those who claimed to be His Majesty's loyal subjects could not at the same time be members of an independent republic. He taught them, too, to say the Lord's Prayer, the creed and the ten commandments in the vulgar tongue so that they might renounce the pomps and vanities of this wicked world and all the sinful lusts of the flesh, and nurture their offspring in the ways of obedience, humility and acceptance.

In the great bend of the river at Patrick's Plains Henry Dangar put up his manor at Neotsfield on the land granted to him by Brisbane and Darling. A gentleman and his family took over from the convict flotsam and jetsam which had spilled into the area from Windsor in 1820. The manor at Neotsfield, with all the refinements of civilization introduced by Henry's wife Grace flourished in a district where the white man's society was pioneered by the flogging of Major Mudie and his brutal overseer John Larnach who had so enraged their assigned servants that they had threatened to chop Larnach's head off and stick it on the chimney of the hut. By 1840 Grace Dangar was dreaming of raising a 'Merry England' in that valley which had witnessed such evil, dreaming, too, of planting there the green lawns, the village church, the schoolhouse and the cultivated parkland with the gentleman's seat on the hill overlooking the village. She and her husband spent the summer on the estate, and went down to Sydney in the autumn to sell the wool clip, and enjoy race week, the agricultural show, the ball for the Queen's birthday, and dinners at Government House.[9]

---

[8] T. Walker, *A Month in the Bush of Australia* (London, 1838), p. 2; E. Delessert, *Souvenirs d'un Voyage à Sydney* (Paris, 1847), pp. 135-61.

[9] *Maitland Mercury*, 30 March 1844; J. H. Collinson Close, 'Edward Charles Close, pioneer of Morpeth, and "father of the Hunter"', R.A.H.S., *J. & P.*, vol. 8, 1927; E. C. Rowland, 'The life and times of Henry Dangar', R.A.H.S., *J. & P.*, vol. 39, 1953; *Maitland Mercury*, 18 February 1843; Grace Dangar to Henry Cary Dangar, 31 May 1846 (Dangar Papers, University of New England library); see also vol. 2, pp. 205-6, of this history.

Like so many of the landed gentry in the settled districts the squire of Neotsfield was also a squatter on the lands of the 'monkeyfied men'. He was consumed by the passion to acquire land on which to depasture his flocks. By 1842 Henry Dangar had taken out licences for the Gostwyck run of 48 000 acres, Paradise Creek of 32 000 acres, Bald Hills of 19 200 acres, Moonbi of 25 000 acres, Bulleroi of 64 000 acres, Karee of 64 000 acres and Myall Creek of 48 000 acres—each managed by an overseer and worked by teams of assigned servants, ticket-of-leave holders, emancipists and the odd free worker. While Henry and Grace Dangar were laying plans for the splendours of Neotsfield and plotting to use every inch of land they owned, leased, or held a licence for so that they and their children might live comfortably and appear as gentlemen and not have to cramp themselves too much, eleven convicts and ex-convicts and one free man were burning the bodies of twenty-eight aborigines they had slaughtered on Dangar's run at Myall Creek.[10]

In 1839 William Dangar, Henry's older brother, acquired Turanville near Scone, on those rich plains where W. B. Carlyle, the cousin of Thomas Carlyle, had begun the station at Invermien in 1825, and Peter McIntyre, the agent for T. P. Macqueen had begun Segenhoe. In private life William Dangar proclaimed all human beings except members of the landed gentry to be beyond the pale. Yet he and his brothers had heavy investments in shopkeeping which they denounced as soiling and degrading to gentlemen. Henry Dangar had a series of country stores on the track from Patrick's Plains to New England and Inverell. His younger brother Richard Cary Dangar was the first storekeeper at Muswellbrook and founder of the firm of Dangar, Gedye and Malloch. Another brother, Thomas Dangar, acquired an interest in Scone's first inn, the St Aubin's Arms, and later opened a store in that town. Through family ties a link was forged between the landed gentry, the squatters outside the boundaries, the country storekeepers and the licensees of the inns. This was the material foundation for the shibboleth of the age, that the prosperity of the pastoral industry was the key to the prosperity of New South Wales.

At Scone the gentry for a decade or more propagated the idea that God and nature had chosen them to sit on top of the social pyramid in New South Wales. Between the grandeur of this conception and its creation there fell the human shadow cast by its protagonists. That obese, dumpy and rather ill-natured Anglican clergyman, John Morse, with his 'dusty and deliquescent second-rate wife' went from door to door in the district warning people to have nothing to do with Methodists, those vile enthusiasts who deluded simple people with the promise of salvation while perverting their minds with schism, heresy and sedition. The local gentry took steps to keep chartists, democrats and socialists out of the district. It was even said in Scone that the Dangars took out a licence to sell fermented liquors, wines and spirits to entice the workers to spend their wages in riotous dissipation so that they

---

[10] Elizabeth Dangar, A Biography of William Dangar (typescript in Dangar Papers).

would lack the money with which to elevate themselves in the social scale. In the church and the schoolhouse, parson and schoolmaster in their own imperfect way put over their version of the message that just as the heavens themselves, the planets and the earth observed degree, priority and place, and just as when the planets in evil mixture to disorder wandered, there was mutiny, raging of the sea and shaking of the earth, so in human society. Take but degree and social rank away and men would become like wolves and eat each other up. In the court-house the squire magistrate enforced the laws devised by man for the protection of property and person, the magistrate and the police being as much the servants of the gentry's domination as the parsons and the schoolmasters.[11]

On 12 November 1834 Potter Macqueen welcomed Governor Bourke to Segenhoe in a bizarre ceremony. As the Governor's carriage entered the great avenue leading to the homestead and passed through a line of 144 working bullocks yoked up to eighteen iron ploughs, men in new suits of clothing, eighteen drays and eight pack-bullocks loaded for the distant out-stations, cannon were discharged and the British flag was raised. Farther on His Excellency passed the native chief of Segenhoe and his forty followers, all painted in the most grotesque manner and carrying spears 12–14 feet long, and eight black boys each holding a couple of kangaroo-dogs. His Excellency passed on through the inner gate amidst the roaring of the cannon and the deafening cheers of the whole establishment and told the manager of his unexpected pleasure in seeing such a pageant in the wild bush. To mark the occasion the manager presented the aborigines with two bullocks. The evening closed with a grand corroboree.[12]

By 1840 landed country gentlemen were also entrenched in the district around Muswellbrook. To the north of that area the character of life changed as men moved into areas free from magistrates, policemen, parsons, priests and schoolmasters. In the settled areas from Muswellbrook south to Windsor the free outnumbered the bond; in the districts outside the boundaries those in servitude and those who had once been in servitude far outnumbered the free. At Patrick's Plains in 1841 there were 1798 men and 861 women; 384 of the men were married and 357 of the women were married. A race of men was growing up who lived in concubinage with aboriginal women, without books of any description, and with their children growing up not only without the sacrament of baptism but without any acquaintance with the name of their Creator. Dirty, badly clothed, with heads and faces that had not come into contact with razor, scissors or comb for many a long year, they were rapidly reverting to the barbaric, nomadic life of the original tenants of the soil, the aborigines of New Holland. Other observers took the romantic

[11] Extract from papers of Dr John Goodwin (Papers in possession of A. J. and Nancy Gray, Scone); J. D. Lang, *An Historical and Statistical Account of New South Wales* (2 vols, 3rd ed., London, 1852), vol. 2, pp. 202-3; W. Shakespeare, *Troilus and Cressida*, I, iii, lines 101-37.

[12] *Sydney Herald*, 24 November 1834; *Sydney Gazette*, 25 November 1834.

view that many a noble heart preferred to beat away in the forests of Australia released from the burdens and constraints of civilization. The free wilderness promised future riches to those who were prepared to rough it so hard that 'townies' called them 'New South Wales orang outangs'. Men who concealed beneath their shaggy, grubby exterior their kinship with the gentry and nobility of old England, Scotland, or Erin's green isle roamed the bush with their stock, or dossed down at night in slab huts with one-time criminals whose consciences were not troubled by the number of lubras they had poxed or the number of 'black bastards' they had slaughtered.[13]

The way of life was just as various as the social origins of the men who were trying their luck in the bush of Australia. One man 'pigged it' on mutton, damper and tea, and slept on the floor under a kangaroo rug. Another lived off curries, soups, chickens, wild ducks, fish, mutton, beef and boiled puddings so well (though without green vegetables) that his New England hut became known as the 'fatting coop'. One man doted on horses, especially taking them at a gallop through a pleasant sapling scrub when the chances of getting a broken neck or a knee knocked out of joint seemed about equal. He spent his days breaking in wild horses, trying to domesticate the emu, attending corroborees, climbing trees in the native fashion (using notches in the tree trunk), and learning to throw spears. There were those days of never-ending boredom and low spirits when a man smoked away at his clay pipe, and had nothing to do, and everything around him—other men, horses, dogs, guns, spears, books and fishing-rods—became alike insufferable. On those days conversation dried up and gloom descended. Each man had to fill these intervals of boredom as best he could, since he might have to pass anything up to three weeks without seeing a human face, either white or black, except his own. At those times idleness filled a man's mind with feelings of self-reproach or unworthiness.

Others testified to no such boredom or loneliness. When John Everett occupied his run at Ollera near Guyra, some 400 miles north of Sydney and over 250 miles from the nearest church, school and police station, he brought enough furniture for body and mind to shield him from boredom and dryness of soul. By temperament he was not a man to punish himself for being born or to brood over his own folly and swinishness. He loaded onto the dray ten boxes, two iron bedsteads, one washing stand, one sofa, two gun cases, one gun, one box of garden seed, one barometer, one looking-glass, one bookshelf, two umbrellas, boxes containing personal clothing, two telescopes, eleven towels, twenty sheets, twenty pillowcases, four blankets, four counterpanes, two mattresses, two bolsters, two pillows, a box of glassware, a case of harness, a cask of powder, ironmongery, a pre-cut wooden house, building materials and tools, a stove, a bag of shot, kegs of linseed oil and turpentine,

[13] Abstract of the Population and Houses in the Different Police Districts, 23 August 1841, *V. & P.* (L.C. N.S.W.), 1841; *Report of Society for the Propagation of the Gospel, 1837* (Sydney, 1838), p. 49; 'Australian Sketches by Mr. McCombie', quoted in *Port Phillip Patriot*, 15 January 1844.

one paint brush, directions for erecting the house, two desks, one fishing-rod, one canteen, and one pit-saw. He also took a collection of books—practical manuals such as cook-books, books on stock, home medicine, and the management of the vine, some standard books of reference on the Australian colonies, such as James Macarthur's *New South Wales: its present state and future prospects*, and books such as a man might choose to have with him when marooned from civilization—the Bible, Shakespeare, Milton, Dr Johnson's Dictionary and the Odes of Pindar.[14]

Patrick Leslie thought of himself in 1842 as 'the most fortunate fellow in the world' because in that year he took the 'prettiest girl in the world' and her dowry of two thousand sheep as his comforters while he pioneered the white man's way of life on the banks of the Condamine at Canning Downs on the south-eastern edge of the Darling Downs. In 1840, impressed by the reports of the botanist and explorer, Allan Cunningham, of the open country he had discovered in 1827–8, he and six 'very nice gentlemen-like fellows' had examined the site. By then Gipps was maturing his plans to close down the penal settlement at Moreton Bay and throw the district open to free settlers. At the end of 1840 Walter Leslie (Patrick's brother) and Ernest Dalrymple overlanded the sheep and cattle, which had been raised on the Peel River estates of the Australian Agricultural Company, up to Canning Downs. They built that 'snug habitation' of a split timber hut, while in St John's Church, Parramatta, in the presence of the Macarthur family and all the representatives of the ancient nobility of New South Wales, Patrick Leslie was vowing that from that day he would forsake all others and love, honour and cherish Kate Macarthur until death did them part. He was thinking, too, during the marriage ceremony, how he could 'raise the wind' for more sheep, because then he and his brothers George and Walter could bring 'all the Scotch canny ways to bear' to make themselves into the Croesuses of the New World. In 1842 he brought his 'sweet Kate' to Canning Downs just as Gipps proclaimed that the district of Moreton Bay was no longer to be considered a penal settlement. In March of that year Gipps visited the area and gave the name Ipswich to a town site on the Brisbane River. The squatters on the Moreton Bay side of Cunningham's Gap and the squatters on the Downs were already using this site as a port to which to send their wool to be taken by barge down to Brisbane for shipment to Sydney and the United Kingdom.[15]

[14] T. Tourle to his sister Frances, 30 May 1842, and to his sister Caroline, 25 September 1842 (Tourle Letters, vol. 3, MS. in NAT. L.); E. M. Curr, *Recollections of Squatting in Victoria* (Melbourne, 1883), pp. 371-7; Inventory of G. & J. Everett's possessions . . . on their passage to Australia, part of Diary of John Everett, Trip to Ollera, 1838 (Everett Papers, University of New England library).

[15] Darling to Goderich, 12 November 1827, *H.R.A.*, I. xiii. 618-20. The important enclosure in the above despatch is in C.O. 201/184; Darling to Murray, 24 February 1829, *H.R.A.*, I. xiv. 668-9. The important enclosure in the above despatch is in C.O. 201/200; W. G. McMinn, *Allan Cunningham*, chs 5, 6; J. G. Steele, *The Explorers of the Moreton Bay District* (Brisbane, 1972); cairn at Cunningham's Gap, 'to the memory of Allan Cunningham who discovered the Darling Downs on 6th June 1827 and this mountain pass on 11th of the same month'; cairn in Ipswich Park 'To perpetuate the

By 1843 some of the squatters on the Downs and around Ipswich were flourishing. In 1841 David, William and Thomas Archer overlanded stock to Moreton Bay and occupied a £10 a year licence run at Durrundur. There they knocked up temporary huts from the bark the blacks stripped from the trees. They wondered whether they should teach savages not to harm trees, but for the most part they were anxious to disprove the prophecy Charles Darwin had made to them in 1836 at their station on the Bathurst Plains, that the white man's prosperity brought wickedness and degradation to the aborigine. One day early in 1842 Thomas Archer was mortified to discover one of his aboriginal workers dead drunk from drinking 'fire water'. In a rage he smashed every bottle of spirits in his dray and set out for the bush, hoping the pastoral life would shield the black man from decay. There he and his brothers heeded the teaching that marriage was ordained by God and took to themselves wives and begat families. Strengthened by Christ's assurance that since there was a special providence in the fall of a sparrow God would certainly bless and preserve His children in the Australian wilderness, they gathered their families and the station blacks each Sunday to hear God's holy word, while the blacks looked dumbly at yet another example of the queerness of the white man.[16]

As the Archers prospered, Patrick Leslie was so 'terribly pinched' to make ends meet by the catastrophic fall in prices for wool and the carcasses of sheep and cattle, and the demands for higher wages in this 'miserable democratic country' that his dream of founding a dynasty of gentlemen in the wilds of Australia vanished. He no longer wanted his body to lie after death under a gum-tree in 'this felonious land'. He decided to take his wife back to Scotland, having seen enough of the bush to make him wish never to come back. At the same time, those 'fine, stately well-formed people', so different from the wretched, degraded aborigines who hung around the outskirts of the towns in the settled districts, began to vanish from their hunting grounds on the Downs. In 1841 Christopher Eipper and his fellow Lutheran missionaries attempted to liberate the aboriginal women of Moreton Bay from their 'most deplorable slavery' to their men, and to prepare the latter to use their considerable intellectual faculties, the cunning, the skill and the enterprise they displayed as food gatherers and pathfinders in learning how to grow crops, domesticate animals, build permanent shelter, make clothes, and work regular

---

memory of the explorer Allan Cunningham who camped under these trees in the year 1828', personal visit to Darling Downs, Cunningham's Gap and Ipswich, 6 May 1971; memorial in the Royal Botanic Gardens, Sydney, beneath which his remains are interred; Gipps to Glenelg, 1 July 1839, *H.R.A.*, I. xx. 209; for some of the preceding correspondence, see Glenelg to Bourke, 26 December 1835, *H.R.A.*, I. xviii. 243-4, and Bourke to Glenelg, 5 November 1837, *H.R.A.*, I. xix. 150-5; Patrick Leslie to his parents, 13 February 1837, 29 April, 20 November 1839, 11 September 1840 (Leslie Letters, Oxley Library, Brisbane).

[16] Kate Leslie to all at Marthill, 4 April 1842, Patrick Leslie to his brother William, 26 August 1842, 1 April 1845 (Leslie Letters); Gipps to Russell, 1 February 1841, *H.R.A.*, I. xxi. 203; Russell to Gipps, 30 August 1841, *H.R.A.*, I. xxi. 496-7; Gipps to Stanley, 4 May 1842, *H.R.A.*, I. xxii. 35.

hours in return for a wage, as a preparation for preaching to them the gospel of everlasting life. There, too, as in the course of settlement in other areas, the aborigines looked on the white man not as the bearer of a precious gift but as an invader who had shattered the conditions of survival and the way of life their people had evolved since the beginning of time.[17]

In all the occupied districts of New South Wales the aspirants to gentility exploited the sheep, the grasses and the labour of convicts and ex-convicts to create the wealth that would enable their families to wear fine clothes, and adopt airs of superiority, leaving the missionaries to raise the aborigines from barbarism to civilization. On 29 April 1839 at St James's Church in Sydney the Lord Bishop of Australia William Grant Broughton pronounced Robert Venour Dulhunty and Eliza Julia Gibbes to be man and wife. Dulhunty, once a surgeon on a convict ship, had received a grant of two thousand acres at Cullen Bullen which was worked by cheap convict labour. In 1839 he took out a licence for a sheep-run at Dubbo; by the early 1840s he held licences for eighty thousand acres in that district. His wife was the eldest daughter of Major J. G. N. G. Gibbes, the Collector of Customs in New South Wales. They lived in style at Claremont, Emu Plains, gave parties attended by all the best people in Sydney, went to all the social occasions hosted by the best people in Sydney, and dined under the candelabra with a snowy white napkin on the lap, while the convicts on their runs at Dubbo shepherded their sheep and drove off aborigines and bushrangers, and slept at night in wattle-and-daub huts or spent the payments made to them at the Macquarie Inn, known as Bob's Pub, which Dulhunty had put up for run-searchers, itinerant workers, and station hands. The withdrawal of cheap convict labour and the fall in wool prices caused the hostess of Claremont to retrench a dish or two at her dinner parties. They drove the host to announce in the *Australian* that he was selling his breeding ewes and superior heifers with a station or run given away with each thousand sheep sold.[18]

The coming of the white man confronted the aborigines with a much greater disaster than settlers' battling against drought, labour problems and commercial depression. Believing that unrestrained intercourse between the natives and the lower class of settlers in a colony extinguished for ever all hope of the civilization of the former, the representative of the Church Missionary Society in London asked for a grant in perpetuity of the entire district of Wellington Valley to prevent any intrusion by the stockmen, to

[17] L. E. Slaughter, *Ipswich Municipal Centenary* (Ipswich, 1960), pp. 4-9; C. Eipper, *Statement of the Origin, Condition, and Prospects of the German Mission to the Aborigines at Moreton Bay* (Sydney, 1841); C. Darwin, *The Voyage of the Beagle* (Everyman ed., London, 1959), pp. 424-5; William Archer to William Archer II, 21 June 1839, David Archer to William Archer, n.d., John Archer to Julia Archer, 10 April 1842, Thomas Archer to William Archer, 10 September 1843, David Archer to William Archer, 7 January 1844 (Archer Papers); B. H. Crew, The History of the Walker and Archer Families (thesis, Australian National University library); V. Voss, 'Early pastoral settlement in the coastal district of central Queensland', R.A.H.S., *J. & P.*, vol. 39, 1953.

[18] Beryl Dulhunty, *The Dulhunty Papers* (Sydney, 1959); *Australian*, 5 May 1839, 30 November 1841.

provide security to the aborigines and to prepare the aborigines gradually to be members of the white man's society. From 1835 the missionaries William Watson, James Gunther and William Porter instructed the natives of the Wellington Valley in the knowledge of Jesus Christ and his salvation. By 1838 they regretted to record the gradual disappearance of the adult aborigines from the mission station. They were more sanguine about the young men and the children who were making progress in the reading of holy scriptures, and were very useful in the missionary garden. They expected the task of civilizing the aborigines to be a prolonged one, because they accepted the prevailing opinion that the aborigines of New Holland were more deeply sunk in moral degradation and possessed less intellectual capabilities than any other heathen.

When the aborigines perceived that the missionaries were unable to supply their wants during the great drought, they wandered away from the station. The arrival of more settlers and stockmen in the valley, and the indifference of the aborigines to the white man's version of salvation caused the mission to decline rapidly over the next three years. At the same time the Europeans asked the government of New South Wales to establish the instruments of civilization—a police force, public stores, and a township. They were aware of opposition to their project because of the aboriginal mission, but submitted that it would be a case of extreme hardship if the interests of the European population of the district were to be compromised in order to continue an experiment upon the natives which had proved a failure. By 1842 the missionaries were reporting in a tone of despondency that drunkenness was increasing among the aborigines, as were the other evils arising from their intermixture with Europeans, for the aborigine loved the liquors from the white man's tavern rather than all the other comforts of civilization. They reported also that the old men were succeeding in their schemes to keep the rising generation of aborigines in a savage state. At the end of 1842 Governor Gipps closed down the mission station at Wellington Valley, leaving the aborigines who hung around the taverns at Wellington or Bob's Pub at Dubbo in a state of degradation and decay, while Mr and Mrs Dulhunty went on with their gracious living at Emu Plains.[19]

Like the other members of the landed gentry with town houses, they gave dinner parties, followed by music and dancing, at which the quadrilles and the waltz were all the fashion. Those, like Alexander McLeay, who loved the old country dances, sometimes amused the young by dancing 'The Country

---

[19] D. Coates to Russell, 14 February 1840, colonial land and emigration commissioners to Stephen, 17 July 1840, encls 1 and 2 in Russell to Gipps, 5 August 1840, *H.R.A.*, I. xx. 735-43; Annual Report by W. Watson, J. Gunther and W. Porter of Aboriginal Mission Station, Wellington Valley, 1838, and W. Cowper to Col. Sec. of New South Wales, 17 April 1839, encls A1 and A2 to Minute no. 13 of 1839 in Gipps to Russell, 7 May 1840, *H.R.A.*, I. xx. 619-20; The Humble Petition of the Undersigned Magistrates, Landholders, Stockholders and Residents of the District of Wellington, encl. B4 to Minute no. 10 of 1839 in ibid., 613-14; Stanley to Gipps, 20 December 1842, *H.R.A.*, I. xxii. 436-9; Annual Report of the Aboriginal Mission at Wellington Valley by J. Gunther to Col. Sec. of New South Wales, 9 January 1843, encl. 1 in Gipps to Stanley, 3 April 1843, *H.R.A.*, I. xxii. 644-7; Gipps to Stanley, 21 March 1844, *H.R.A.*, I. xxiii. 484-5; C. D. Rowley, *The Destruction of Aboriginal Society* (Canberra, 1970), pp. 98-100.

Bumpkin', which was danced by six ladies and gentlemen, the gentlemen in the centre of the circle wearing a hat which he put on one of the others who then took his place, and so on till the music stopped. The dressing was of a high standard. The Highland lairds wore kilts. The most daring women wore black satin with a row of tiny aprons hanging from their waist, an assortment of large reticules, and a small flower garden flourishing in their hair. Some women wore their hair raised on a ball of plaits above their forehead in imitation of a laurel wreath. The talk of the women was of the frothiest. They seldom spoke of aught besides dress, and domestic events and troubles, 'bad servants' being the staple topic. Most gentlemen had their whole souls so 'felted up in wool, fleeces, flocks, and stock', that those with a thought for higher things sat through many a weary dinner and evening of incessant talking without hearing a single syllable on any other subject.[20]

The spread of settlement down the south coast from Sydney repeated the same pattern. Within the boundaries of location, down to and including the present site of Moruya, the white man put down permanent roots. Outside the boundaries, from Moruya southwards to Bermagui, Bega, Eden and Twofold Bay, the adventurers and the 'monster squatters' took out their licences for their hundred thousand-acre runs, worked feverishly for quick returns, and often vanished leaving only a wattle-and-daub hut, a ruined vegetable garden, and lichen-covered fruit trees as memorials of all their striving. In 1822 Alexander Berry and Edward Wollstonecraft were granted permission to select ten thousand acres on the north bank of the mouth of the Shoalhaven River on entering into an obligation to employ one hundred convicts on their estate. Captain Cook had seen the site in April 1770 when about three or four leagues from the shore but had not been willing to spare the time to beat inshore for a closer look. Lieutenant John Bowen had named the bay Jervis Bay in August 1791 after the victor of the battle of Cape St Vincent (Vincentia). George Bass had named the Shoalhaven (he called it Shoals' Haven) in 1797 on his way south to Bateman Bay, Twofold Bay and Western Port. Between 1812 and 1822 George Evans, Charles Throsby, John Oxley, James Meehan and Hamilton Hume had walked over the area from the Kangaroo Valley to the mouth of the Shoalhaven. The cedar cutters who had followed in their wake had loaded ships for Sydney from 1812 on at the mouth of the Shoalhaven.[21]

Berry was forty-one when he selected his grant in 1822. A one-time surgeon on an East Indiaman he had turned to trade to make his fortune, and had set up house at Crow's Nest in Sydney. His partner, Edward Wollstonecraft, the cousin of Mary Wollstonecraft, the second wife of Percy Bysshe Shelley and

[20] M. Herman (ed.), *Annabella Boswell's Journal* (Sydney, 1961), p. 61; Louisa Anne Meredith, *Notes and Sketches of New South Wales* (London, 1844), p. 161.

[21] Col. Sec. of New South Wales to A. Berry and E. Wollstonecraft, 5 March 1822, and A. Berry and E. Wollstonecraft to Brisbane, 30 July 1825 (Letter Book of Sir Thomas Brisbane, vol. I, MS. in M.L.); A. Berry, Diary of Expedition to Shoalhaven River, 21 June to 23 July 1822 (Berry Papers, MS. in M.L.); M. Flinders, *Voyage to Terra Australis* (2 vols, London, 1814), vol. I, p. 107; J. C. Beaglehole (ed.), *The Voyage of the Endeavour* (Cambridge, 1955), pp. 302-3.

the author of *Frankenstein*, arrived in Sydney in 1819 and built the warehouse of Berry and Wollstonecraft in George Street. Within a year of taking up the grant the one hundred convicts, including one of the heroes of Trafalgar who had been transported for striking an officer when in a state of intoxication, built the manor at Coolangatta for the laird of the Shoalhaven, sowed crops, grazed sheep and cattle and cut cedar. Berry was one of those romantics who set himself against the tendency of the age towards equality, urbanization and industrialism. He ordered his men to eat porridge for breakfast and to practice temperance though not abstinence. He encouraged the convicts to become tenant farmers on his estate at the end of their servitude, but refused to build a town or provide any of the amenities of a town, because he believed an industrious agricultural population was preferable to a crowd of starving town or village workers who were drawn to evil courses by herding together. In time John Dunmore Lang accused Alexander Berry of reducing his tenants to the status of serfs and of flogging the convict cedar cutters to within an inch of their lives. He saw Berry as one of those antediluvian oppressors of their fellow-men, for whose enormous wickedness and oppression God was pleased not only to shorten the duration of human life but to bring in a flood of water to destroy the world of the ungodly.

Berry was not a cruel man, but a man of 'singularly antiquated ideas'. He believed there was more common sense in the world before men of the Enlightenment muddied the waters for mankind and started movements which were taken up by the radicals and chartists of his own day. A pessimist on all attempts to change human nature, he thought it was a waste of time to assay the reformation of the incorrigible. He opposed the abolition of the land grant, because land sales stopped the 'influx of respectable immigrants as Settlers' and flooded the colony with the idle useless population of England who would spread disorder. He spent his days at Crow's Nest and Coolangatta between 1822 and 1850 fearful that the whole fabric of society was about to tumble down from want of principle in men in high places rather than the passions of the mob. While privately entertaining the nightmare that what he understood by civilization was doomed by men currying favour with the convict community, he also spent some of his time as secretary of the Agricultural Society, as a member of the Philosophical Society and as the author of a paper on the geology of New South Wales. He probably destroyed his chance to be heeded by the men of his day by the extravagance of his language. He warned the tenants of Coolangatta not to exchange the advantages of country life for the status of 'White Negroes or the Jews and publicans of Towns and Villages'. Yet he had the gift to prosper. By 1840 he had expanded the estate at Coolangatta from ten thousand to thirty-two thousand acres by purchases from the Crown and from private owners.[22]

[22] A. Berry to E. Wollstonecraft, 12 April 1838; A. Berry, Thoughts on the Present Crisis, 1839, Passages in the Life of a Nonagenarian (also published in *S.M.H.*, 24 December 1873), A. Berry to Mary Shelley, 20 April 1846, 1 August 1847, 3 October 1848, Some Aspects of the Berry Papers (Berry Papers); F. L. Jones, *The Letters of Mary Shelley* (2 vols, Oklahoma, 1944); *S.M.H.*, 18 December 1843.

By contrast, south of the limits of location in the country between Mount Dromedary, Bermagui, Lake Wapengo, Tathra, Bega and Twofold Bay, the nests of gentlefolk supported by convict labour, of eccentric squires with antiquated ideas and visions of the reign of Beelzebub, gave way to the life of adventurers and plunderers, who put down no roots and left no lasting memorial. Captain Cook had seen that stretch of the coast on a clear day in April and had found the 'view [of the country] had a very agreeable and promising aspect, the land is of a moderate height diversified with hills, ridges, planes and Vallies with some few small lawns'. The country was seen again by George Bass in December 1797 in a year when the water-holes were all dried up. Early in the 1830s three brothers, Peter, George and Alexander Imlay, the latter two being surgeons, took up runs in the Twofold Bay, Bega and Monaro districts, hoping for quick returns from depasturing stock, whaling, and trade with New Zealand and South Australia. Peter Imlay was a man of tremendous physical strength, who stood 6 feet 4 inches in his socks, and had an appetite for material gain to match his huge physique. By 1840 the three brothers had 18 600 acres at Kameruka, 20 000 acres at Bega, 6500 acres at Tarraganda, 1000 acres at Murrah, 6400 acres at Cobargo, 10 000 acres at Double Creek and 10 000 acres at Corridgeree. Their kingdom was not destined to endure. During the commercial depression they lost their runs in the Bega and Monaro districts to the Walker brothers, and Alexander and George died from attacks of the 'Botany Bay disease', the melancholy that afflicted those who failed to survive the ordeal of colonial backbiting, the raids of the savages and the hardships of subduing a harsh environment. Peter left for New Zealand. By 1847 all that remained of their kingdom was the Tarraganda homestead and the headstones on two graves.[23]

Nor did Benjamin Boyd leave much lasting memorial. Arriving in Sydney in July 1842 at a time when the commercial crisis created a buyer's market, he shone for a season like a meteor that was destined to consume itself and disappear almost without leaving a trace. He had a brief hour of glamour and glory. By buying sheep at 10d a head with the station thrown in, he held licences to depasture stock on two-and-a-half million acres of land, with runs as far down the Murray as the Riverina, on the Monaro and at Port Phillip. By 1843 he was employing over two hundred men as shepherds, or carpenters, joiners, bricklayers, stonemasons and blacksmiths at the whaling and coaling stations at Twofold Bay where his mechanics had built docks for his ships, a house for 'massa Boyd' and a church with a steeple reaching towards the heavens, for the hope lived in him, too, that he would lord it over the kingdom of heaven as he had lorded it over that kingdom of pygmies in New South Wales. Everything about the man had an air of extravagance and recklessness. When S. M. Mowle, an overseer in the Canberra district, called on him at Twofold Bay with Charles Cowper, the son of the Reverend William Cowper, Boyd dined them sumptuously in the *Wanderer* with un-

[23] J. C. Beaglehole (ed.), *The Voyage of the Endeavour*, p. 300; M. Flinders, *A Voyage to Terra Australis*, vol. 1, pp. 107-9; H. P. Wellings, 'The Brothers Imlay', R.A.H.S., *J. & P.*, vol. 17, 1931; H. P. Wellings, *The Imlay Brothers* (Sydney, n.d.).

limited champagne. Cowper knew, and so probably did the cautious Mowle, that the foundations of the man rested on that rapidly disappearing cheap convict labour, and the cheap squatter's licence, also vanishing with the advance of civilization into the bush.[24]

South-west from Camden in the open country suitable for grazing stock the same pattern was repeated. Within the boundaries there was the semblance of order, the trappings of civilization, and that confidence of men who believed they were starting family dynasties which would endure for generations to come. Outside the boundaries there was that rootless life which men of firm clay used to their advantage, while men whose sensibilities caused their clay to tremble and fragment were left sorrowing and wondering whether they were the victims of a hostile or malign environment, the sharp practices of colonial rogues or their own folly. From Camden to Picton, named after that irascible, fine soldier Sir Thomas Picton who was said by the Duke of Wellington to be as rough a foul-mouthed devil as ever lived, nests of gentlefolk had been built. South from that area over the Razorback to Mittagong, Bungonia, Sutton Forest, the Goulburn Plains and Yass the freeholders and leaseholders laboured to reproduce an English gentleman's establishment. They surrounded their huts or stone houses with rose-bushes, honeysuckle, and ivy and hawthorn hedges, and commissioned architects to design churches fashioned out of stone, with gothic arch and steeple towering over the countryside as a reminder of the faith by which they lived. There they sang songs about a God who cared for mankind in a land which breathed a vast indifference to all human endeavour. At Boorowa the three ladies on Broughton's sheep station and the menfolk did not let their souls get 'felted up in wool, fleeces, flocks, and stock' but kept a well-stocked library of books, the periodicals of the Mother Country and the latest Sydney newspapers. Hamilton Hume, the Australian who had made that long walk from Sydney to Corio Bay and back, took up his grant at Cooma Cottage where with the aid of convict labour he became one of the landed gentry. His neighbour at Douro, 'Black Harry' O'Brien, formerly holder of a land grant on the Bathurst Plains and later the holder of land at Yass and Jugiong, often gave a ball and supper for 'the rank, beauty and fashion of the neighbourhood', while on guest nights his wife sang about the wrongs of Ireland, woman's sadness, and what happened to a lassie's 'petticoatie' when she was 'comin' thro' the Rye'.[25]

[24] Evidence of B. Boyd to Select Committee on Immigration, *V. & P.* (L.C. N.S.W.), 1843; evidence of B. Boyd to Select Committee on Crown Land Grievances, *V. & P.* (L.C. N.S.W.), 1844, vol. 2; evidence of W. Bradley to Select Committee on Colonization from Ireland, *P.P.*, 1847, vi, 737; S. M. Mowle, Journal in Retrospect, p. 19 (typescript in NAT. L.).

[25] T. Walker, *A Month in the Bush of Australia*, pp. 2-14; E. Delessert, *Souvenirs d'un Voyage à Sydney*, pp. 135-61; L. F. Fitzhardinge, *St. John's Church and Canberra* (Canberra, 1941), pp. 12-26; Report of the Select Committee on Immigration, *V. & P.* (L.C. N.S.W.), 1841; Letters of W. J. Browne (MS. in M.L.); *Goulburn Herald*, 31 January, 3 February 1866, 10 July 1869.

On the Limestone Plains in the Canberra district there was another nest of gentlefolk, composed of families who had received grants in the period before 1832 or bought land from the original grantees. There was Robert Campbell at Duntroon, a Sydney merchant who hoped to raise his family into the ranks of the gentry by taking up land. In 1825 his overseer, James Ainslie, left Bathurst with a flock of sheep in search of land, on which Campbell conferred the name of Duntroon. In that year he took up 4000 acres, adding another 1000 in 1829. During the 1830s he increased this acreage to 8000 by judicious purchases on the Limestone Plains. Under the management of his son Charles, Duntroon was run like a manor. Opposed on moral grounds to the exploitation of convicts, Campbell imported Scottish Highlanders to work his estate. To give them a permanent interest in their work he built stone cottages for them in the neighbourhood of the manor and gave each family two acres on which to grow their own food and graze a dairy cow. While Campbell and his wife were putting on the airs of the country gentry, with their dinners, their hunts, their season in Sydney, and their appearance in the front pew of St John's at Canberra where the preacher reminded the congregation that the days of man were as grass which grew up and was cut down, the workers created by the labour of their hands the wealth which made all this display possible. By 1838 Charles Campbell was employing sixty-eight to seventy free workers on Duntroon. At sun-up on the Limestone Plains each shepherd took a flock of one thousand sheep to the pastures and brought them back at sunset with the aid of sheep-dogs to the home station where they were folded down for the night by the night-watchman. At lambing time the shepherd separated the ewes from the fold. At shearing time the shepherd earned extra wages assisting the itinerant shearers. They tried to heed the warning of Charles Campbell about the consequences of spending their wages at the 'grog' shop, because a frugal man could save enough from his £30 a year plus rations to buy a plot of land within five or ten years and become a peasant proprietor. After Campbell discovered that the cult of the Virgin encouraged humility and obedience in his workers, he became an advocate for the adoration of Our Lady by the shepherds in the wilds of Australia.[26]

In 1834 Edward John Eyre took up 1260 acres at Woodlands on the Molonglo Plains near Queanbeyan. He had spent the preceding two years learning the trade of growing fine wool under the good offices of Colonel H. Dumaresq, the commissioner of the Australian Agricultural Company. In 1834 he brought some four hundred of the company's sheep onto his run at Woodlands. Unlike Campbell at Duntroon or 'Black Harry' O'Brien at Douro, he had no family and so no incentive to join the social round of the gentry on the Limestone Plains. He used convicts as workers, an experience which convinced him of the beneficial effects of transportation. 'The fact is', he wrote later in his autobiography,

[26] L. F. Fitzhardinge, op. cit., pp. 12-26; Report of the Select Committee on Immigration, *V. & P.* (L.C. N.S.W.), 1841; Margaret Steven, *Merchant Campbell 1769-1846* (Melbourne, 1965); C. E. T. Newman, *The Spirit of Wharf House* (Sydney, 1961).

the men being removed from towns and from the influence of their associates in crime were leading a healthy useful life of labour on the country—well clothed and well fed, with the prospect of attaining their freedom and being soon able to set up for themselves if they conducted themselves . . . No wonder then that convicts behaved well and from being useful members of the community both gained the respect of others and learnt to respect themselves . . . This system was the making of Australia in its earlier career . . .

For the rest he spent his days on the Molonglo as one of those 'enthusiasts for wool' rather than the refinements of the drawing-room and wrote of his life there through the eyes of a man who had spent his days 'all among the wool, boys, all among the wool'. His life was taken up with anxiety about the bush-rangers, about his flocks catching the scab, falling prey to the wild dogs or wandering into the bush, and about the behaviour of his six convicts who shared the duties of day shepherds and night-watchmen.

Each spring he and his men selected a spot on the banks of the river where the sheep could be washed before shearing began. They made pens in the water by tying poles together on the surface to keep the sheep swimming within certain limits. A large table was constructed for rolling up the fleeces, the top consisting of narrow rounded bars about half an inch apart to let the dust and dirt fall through as the fleece was shaken over it. On the banks of the river, shearing booths and pens of rough poles and sheets of bark were rapidly put up, and a strong press was constructed for compressing the wool. The aborigines helped to strip the bark from the trees and were very skilful at it. Unlike Campbell and O'Brien, Eyre was only a sojourner on the Molonglo Plains, and, like all sojourners, he was an improver, who made do with equipment from season to season and behaved like a man who would one day push off without leaving a trace. Within three years he was overlanding stock from the Molonglo to Adelaide where he became an explorer who earned a lasting memorial of fame.[27]

By comparison with the retiring, introspective disposition of Eyre, everything in the life of Terence Aubrey Murray was on a grand scale or like a grand opera of many splendours, but ending in failure. He had come into the district to manage the land granted to his father at Collector. His appetites were gargantuan: he had known that magical moment of trying to 'preserve the centre of gravity' when walking home after a lively dinner. His energies were prodigious: in February 1841 he rode the eight hundred miles from the Limestone Plains to Melbourne and back in nineteen days. All his days his heart was hot within him: when he won the nomination for the electorate of Murray in the Legislative Council in 1843, proposed by his fellow-Irishman and co-religionist 'Black Harry' O'Brien and seconded by that fierce defender of the Protestant ascendancy 'Cast Iron' Faunce of Queanbeyan, he rolled out a hogshead of beer to celebrate the occasion with all and sundry. Baptized into the Catholic Church soon after his birth in Limerick in 1810 he gave

[27] E. J. Eyre, Autobiographical Narrative of Residence and Exploration in Australia, 1832-39, vol. I (MS. in M.L.).

generously to the fund for building St John's Church in Canberra and
entertained ideas of a Church which transcended differences of dogma and
concentrated on the worship of the Creator and the teaching of Jesus. For
though outwardly a member of that Church outside which he had been taught
as a child that there was no salvation, the sight of 'the vast abyss of [those]
desolate plains' in Australia stirred up doubts in his mind. Australia, he wrote
in his diary, was then seeing the life of man for the appointed period of
his mad career, but she would also witness the time when that period would
be past, and the place would know man no more. 'Alas,' he concluded, 'all
our contemplations come to this end and the burden of all is vanity.' He was
married in May 1843 to Mary, a daughter of Colonel Gibbes, the Collector of
Customs, thereby establishing one more link in the 'cousinhood' of the
country gentry. Mary's sister Eliza had married into the Dulhunty family,
which gave him interests in the Bathurst, Wellington Valley and Dubbo
districts, just as 'Black Harry' O'Brien had family ties with the land-holders
in the Richmond River district. Yet, passion's slave though he was, and a
stranger here, as all his people had been, and a petitioner to his God to spare
him a little before he went from hence and was seen no more, the one human
being he wore in his heart of hearts was S. M. Mowle, who, after Murray
died, wrote simply, 'Those who loved him well loved him with an unbounded
love.'[28]

While Murray was putting down in his diary at Yarralumla the confessions of a passionate heart, some forty miles away at Braidwood the world of
men was becoming more and more hateful and unbearable to a pioneer of
the district, Thomas Braidwood Wilson, once a surgeon of the navy who had
descended on the land in 1836 with seventy convicts, an unspecified number
of free workers, twelve to fifteen hundred sheep and great numbers of cattle
and horses. The iron had entered into his soul long before he grappled with a
dry country, scab and catarrh in the sheep, bushrangers, aborigines and
absconders. In his days in the navy he had never permitted the slightest slang,
flash songs or swearing. At Braidwood that war he had waged all his life as
an officer and a gentleman against the strongest passions in the human heart
broke out with renewed violence. The convicts on his estate bemoaned their
fate of being treated like 'bloody dogs' or 'bloody packhorses'. The drought
of 1838-9 during which Lake George dried up was followed by a fall in prices
for wool, beef and mutton, just as Wilson's expenses for running his estate
increased with the loss of convict labour. In the spring of 1843, with the
wattle in bloom and the sap rising again in the trees, Wilson set off with his
drays of wool from Braidwood down the old convict road to Jervis Bay where
he boarded the sailing ship for Sydney. He got such a low price for his wool
that he came back to Braidwood dejected and took to his bed where he

[28] Gwendoline Wilson, *Murray of Yarralumla* (Melbourne, 1968); T. Walker, op. cit.,
pp. 8-9, 140-1; Diary of T. A. Murray, 21 February 1841 (MS. in NAT. L.); advertisement in
S.M.H., 24 January 1843; S. M. Mowle, Journal in Retrospect, p. 17; *S.M.H.*, 9 June,
5 December 1846, 21 June, 16 September 1847, 6 June 1848.

remained till he died, with that nobility of countenance of a man who had looked on those around him as pygmies. His family, who had been left penniless, put his body in the ground of a country in which he had also felt like an intruder.[29]

While Edward Eyre was shocked by the sight of the bleeding back of a convict who had been 'kissing the three sisters', and Braidwood Wilson was muttering that though not a cruel man himself there ought to be more of that sort of thing if it would subdue the old Satan in the hearts of the rabble he had to use as workers, others were spending their days gossiping over leisurely lunches in the squatters' parlours at Duntroon or that other meeting place for the gentry, the Palmers' homestead at Gininderra. William Bunn, the nephew of Murray, spent a delightful morning at Yarralumla reading the most recent English literary periodicals, especially the *Quarterly Review* and the *Edinburgh Review*, after which he set out on his cob for a brisk trot to Gininderra for lunch with the Palmers. He loved it when Mrs Charles Campbell, despite her fervent requests each Sunday to live in love and fellowship with her neighbour, asked those present whether they thought a Mrs Gore was really pretty: she was not, of course, thinking that she was not pretty, she only wanted to know. Then she, Mrs Campbell, told them there was something else she would like to know, whether it was true that Sam Terry, ex-convict and father of Martha Foxlowe Hosking, the wife of the man who aspired to be the squire of Foxlowe on the Molonglo Plains, was known to have once kept geese, and when he was suspected of stealing the geese he used to make them look like his own, and that was why people always knew him as the 'Goose Doctor', because it was all very odd, all very queer seeing the man was not a 'clean potato'. Bunn loved it even more when Mrs Campbell told them another story of the early days in the colony when a man was looking over a book of the peerage when another asked him if he saw his name there, to which the first man replied that if it had been the Newgate Calendar he might have had a better chance.

Mrs Campbell asked them, had they heard that young Charles O'Connell, the son of *the* Sir Maurice O'Connell, if she might drop a name into the room, was the best dancer of the 'polka', because a young girl had once told her that for that lively dance 'The Country Bumpkin' give me George Macleay any time as a partner. Almost without pausing for breath Mrs Campbell went on to ask them whether they had heard that her Charles had discovered that the best way to keep the shearers in a happy frame of mind was to give them a keg of brandy when they arrived. When the Reverend G. E. Gregory, the vicar of St John's on the Limestone Plains and itinerant preacher at Gundaroo and down south on the Murrumbidgee, sat down to table with them he risked telling them how he loved the plains in the early spring, when the greening of the grass conveyed that promise of renewal and resurrection, but did not risk letting them know about the curious letters he was receiving

[29] Diary of John Rawson (MS. in NAT. L.); S. M. Mowle, Journal in Retrospect, p. 16; Braidwood Bench Book (MS. in M.L.).

from the Reverend James Hassall on the efficacy of infant baptism. Nor did he tell them that he was thinking of heeding the divine reminder that it was not good for a man to be alone, and setting out for Sydney to take unto himself a wife. He did not know then, and could not know that before he, a timid, vulnerable man, ever showed his view to a woman he would rashly strip off his outer clothing and plunge into a frothy, muddy Molonglo in flood and be drowned.[30]

Some fifteen to twenty miles south of Yarralumla and Duntroon the traveller crossed the boundary of the limits of location. On a foggy frosty day in June 1823 Lieutenant Mark John Currie of the royal navy passed through a chain of clear downs on his excursion to the south of Lake George, where he met a tribe of natives who fled at their approach, never having seen Europeans before. By tokens of kindness and offering them biscuits, together with the help of a domesticated native in their party they induced them to come nearer. Though they could not persuade the aborigines to go anywhere near the horses, they learned from the natives that the country was called 'Monaroo' and was very extensive. Currie wanted to call the country 'Brisbane Downs', but the name Monaro was to stick through all the vicissitudes of spelling that the white man inflicted on it. Currie found it much like the other plains of Australia, the soil being of various sorts, some good and some indifferent, the hills for the most part stony, and the country tolerably well watered. He found it had an 'interesting nature connected with the subject of sheep grazing'.

The idea caught on. Before 1836 pastoralists were illegally grazing stock outside the boundaries on the Monaro, it being found most economical to hut the convict workers, as the law required, inside the boundaries, and employ them as shepherds outside the boundaries on grass for which the stock-holder paid no fee. After 1836, the year of the introduction of the £10 licence fee for grazing stock outside the boundaries, the stock-holders, overseers and squatters drove their stock down the valley of the Murrumbidgee to the Cooma area, where they fanned out west to Adaminaby down Kosciusko way, and south to Nimmitabel and Bombala along the track first followed by McMillan. Their motives were as various as were the yearnings of those who drove sheep, cattle and horses into a district of such uplifting beauty. Some men were so deeply moved by the beauty of the scenery and the freshness and elasticity of its air that they could not imagine a man burying himself again in a town after experiencing the sublimities of the hills of the Monaro.[31]

Some let their hearts be troubled by those questions which have plagued men cursed with that passion to consume their days searching for answers

[30] Diary of William Bunn, 23 January 1848 (microfilm in NAT. L.); G. Gregory to J. Hassall, 23 May 1850 (Gregory Papers, MS. in NAT. L.); S. M. Mowle, Journal in Retrospect, pp. 45-6.

[31] M. J. Currie, 'Journal of an excursion to the southward of Lake George in New South Wales' in Barron Field (ed.), *Geographical Memoirs of New South Wales* (London, 1825), pp. 369-81; J. Lhotsky, *A Journey from Sydney to the Australian Alps* (Sydney, 1835), p. 94.

to unanswerable questions. On first appearances Farquhahr Mackenzie did
not look like a man to put the Hamlet questions in the wilds of Australia. He
arrived in Sydney in November 1836 with money in his purse (just over
£2000), letters of introduction to the heads of some of the 'best' families,
including that patriarch amongst the 'blue-bloods', old Alexander McLeay,
and a member of a Scottish family whose folk had covered themselves with
glory at Waterloo. His ambition was to purchase sheep and go with them into
the unappropriated lands outside the boundaries. In December 1836 he called
on that very pleasant and intelligent man Captain Charles Sturt at Mittagong
who accompanied him to Berrima, after which he came to Hanby's Inn at
Yass which he found a very miserable place since there was nothing but bread
and salt meat to eat and nothing but tea and rum to drink. His next call was
at Jackson's Inn at Gundaroo, one of the best inns on the road, and a source
of information, as the gallant Captain Sturt had been, about the runs in the
Monaro outside the boundaries of location. After a return to Sydney he was
back again early in 1837 looking for runs on the Monaro for 2450 sheep. He
ended pitching his tent in a beautiful little valley which he called Kerrisdale.

There he rose at six, ate breakfast and worked till ten or eleven, after which
he wrote for an hour or so, dined at twelve, and returned to his writing table
till two or three. He then worked out of doors till sunset, when he had his
supper or what he quaintly called 'a fashionable dinner', and then went to bed
at nine and was a little incommoded by the cold, the squeaking of possums
and the howling of native dogs. He and his men built a comfortable hut
and covered the wall slabs with bark. All in all he had nothing to complain
about, having plenty of all the necessaries and many of the comforts of life
and the prospect of doing well. He was badly off for books, however, and still
worse off for company. He kept longing to revisit his native land and dreamed
one night that he was dancing the quadrilles again with two pretty sisters he
had met during his brief stay in Sydney. The convict workers never stopped
their eternal threaten-threaten. One of the assigned servants threatened to
knock out the brains of anyone who tried to stop him leaving, just two nights
before he dreamed about dancing with a beautiful girl in his arms. Like
Job his soul was never quiet.[32]

Seven months later in October 1837 as the spring gales gave way to the clear
days of summer, he began to torment himself with a dark thought. If, as he
put it in his diary in that never-ending dialogue he conducted with himself,
there was a future state where eternal happiness was attendant upon actions
in this life, then every sacrifice ought certainly to be made during the short
time a man remained in this world to secure even a moderate degree of
enjoyment, for it would be foolish for a man to prefer a dutiful and interrupted state of happiness to external unmixed enjoyment. He decided to
impress upon his mind the truths of Christianity. He resolved to govern his
passions and to devote to this purpose a certain space out of every twenty-four

[32] Diary of F. Mackenzie, 5 October, 6, 13, 15 December 1836, 12 January, 19 February, 1, 17 March, 29 May 1837 (MS. in M.L.).

hours during which time he would endeavour to exclude worldly thoughts. He prayed to God to give him the strength not to become like the 'fool man' in the poem who interred celestial thoughts without one sigh. Like other men tormented by the eternal questions, he began to put other unanswerable questions to himself. He began to wonder how many minds were so constituted as to derive benefit from constant and long solitude; he began to derive comfort more and more from the hope of finding true joy in the life of the world to come:

> Dreams cannot picture a world so fair—
> Sorrow and death may not enter there;
> Time does not breathe on its fadeless bloom
> Far beyond the clouds and beyond the time,
> It is there, it is there my child.
> The Better Land by Mrs. Hemans

Inwardly indifferent to his worldly fortunes, he left the Monaro in December 1838 with his party of eleven men, two drays, his sheep and cattle and four months' supply and started run finding all over again on the Goulburn River. There again he became disturbed by the thought that in the future existence some were to enjoy inconceivable happiness and others to suffer the most acute anguish to which the sorrows and pains of this world were not to be compared. He had, he said, a constant sense of the impossibility of being saved from eternal woe otherwise than by faith in Christ's expiation for man's sins. 'I believe', he wrote in his diary while the Dick Drive Hards of the world around him went on with their never-ending small talk about rum, tobacco, cattle, brands, increase, and stockyards, always interlarded with abundance of oaths and imprecations. These men prided themselves on knowing all the ranges, creeks, gullies and swamps for one hundred miles around. On the other hand, he knew how to pass through the narrow gate into the kingdom of heaven. Whether he won that prize, no man can tell. He certainly won few prizes in the human lottery in this world: he tried marriage, descended in the social scale from run ownership to run management, but remained restless in that occupation. To the end of his days he kept his eye single-mindedly on what lay beyond the tomb.[33]

Benjamin Boyd's failure in Eden–Monaro was of quite a different order. By 1844 he held fourteen runs on the Monaro, including Bibbenluke near Bombala, totalling almost a quarter of a million acres, for which he was paying four licence fees or £40. Boyd's motive was that of the man in search of a 'quick quid', a man who believed he could buy and sell runs, stock and workers, just as he bought stocks and shares, commodities to further his aim to 'top a cloud'. He knew nothing about grass or stock and took little interest in the men working on his runs. By contrast William Bradley, the son of an army sergeant, who took out licences for 300 000 acres in the Cooma area on

[33] Ibid., 1 March 1837, 19 March 1838.

which he was running between 150 000 and 200 000 sheep by 1847, was one of those men who applied carefully the fruits of human knowledge to the problems of survival in a harsh country. He taught his men how to treat the sheep on his run with the medicine he had found effective for scab—to boil one pound of tobacco leaf in a gallon of water and dip the sheep in the mixture after they had been washed and curry-combed. He had ideas, too, on the maximum number of sheep per acre the grasses of the area could sustain without permanent harm to the soil.

So did William Whittakers who took up a run at Tambong and later at Tubbutt for £568 and had the good fortune to marry Louisa Grant who, despite her protests that the one thing she did not want to be in life was the lonely wife of a settler, gave him the strength to endure the despairs as well as enjoy the happy moments of the pioneering days on the Monaro. There were practical men such as Stewart Ryrie, and men of intellectual gifts such as W. A. Brodribb. There were also the inarticulate ones who left no record of what went on in their minds and hearts when they moved stock onto the Monaro high plains or down into the Bega valley. Army officers who lived on as a class in such places as Major's Creek and Captain's Flat became neighbours of illegitimate sons of convict women. Sometimes the settlers used descriptive names such as Eighteen Mile Creek, or Deep Creek, or Waterhole Creek; sometimes they preserved a beautiful aboriginal word such as Cuppa-cumbalong; sometimes they commemorated in a name an event without pausing to record it for posterity, such as Yankee Gap. When towns like Cooma, Queanbeyan and Bega were laid out they commemorated early governors, secretaries of state or English poets by naming the principal streets or the main street after them. Men of capital lived in the same valley or on the same plains as men who began with no capital but the labour of their hands. One penniless botanist drove a small herd of cattle to Bega to lay the foundations of a fortune. Another man was so upset by the cruelty of Hannibal Macarthur to his convict servants that he decided to start up on his own near Bombala where, thanks to advice from a convict, he landed a rich run and never looked back.[34]

For some there was a powerful charm in this free and wandering state beneath the sunny skies and the clear moonlight nights of Australia when the stars pricked the blackness with pin-points of light. Some loved the moment when they rolled themselves in a kangaroo skin cloak on a couch of grass or took shelter in a tent or a bark hut. Men then regained their innocence by shedding the constraints of civilization. The very appearance of

[34] W. A. Brodribb, *Recollections of an Australian Squatter* (Sydney, 1883), pp. 55-81; C. Macalister, *Old Pioneering Days in the Sunny South* (Goulburn, 1907), p. 6; evidence of Caroline Chisholm to Committee on Colonisation from Ireland, *P.P.*, 1847, vi, 737; evidence of W. Bradley, ibid., 347; C. Whittakers, The Whittakers Story (MS. in NAT. L.); William Whittakers Day Book (MS. in NAT. L.); S. Ryrie, Journal of a Certain Tour in 1840 (MS. in M.L.); A. Bruce, *Scab in Sheep and its Cure* (Sydney, 1864); W. K. Hancock, *Discovering Monaro* (Cambridge, 1972), pp. 40-4, 78-9; Lyndsay Gardiner, Eden-Monaro to 1850 (thesis in Australian National University library).

the aborigines in those areas outside the limits of location filled some with hope for the life of man when liberated from the chains of civilization and those stains left by herding together in towns. In the towns the white man was repelled by the sight of the aborigine, whose state of demoralization aroused in him either disgust or pity or shame that contact with civilization had served only to eradicate the aborigine's own good qualities and replace them with the vices of the white man. In the inland districts the pioneer white men again saw the aborigines of New Holland in their natural state and for a time entertained the same idea as the mighty Captain Cook that, though the aborigines might appear to be the most wretched people upon the earth, in reality they were far happier than Europeans, partly because they were wholly unacquainted with that pursuit of the superfluous and partly because they were not disturbed by inequality of condition. The earth and the sea furnished them with all things necessary for life: they wanted not magnificent houses, or household staff.

Again the mood of hope quickly gave way to horror, anger and despair. Down in Western Port on a pitch black night in March 1840 John Rawson, who had migrated to Sydney on an impulse and learnt all there was to know about sheep management from Dr Wilson at Braidwood, sat enthralled in the open air while the Assistant Protector of Aborigines for the district, William Thomas, read evensong to them from the Book of Common Prayer. The white men present then sang the Halleluiah chorus from Handel's *Messiah*, in parts of which the blacks participated with such fervour that Rawson was filled with a stronger religious feeling than he had ever felt in an English cathedral. Just over a week later the blacks came back to his tent bringing quantities of human flesh and began to eat it with much pleasure, and seemed hurt when Rawson refused to eat it, because they had joined in as best they could do in the white man's strange corroboree. Try as they would to make use of the aborigine, to make him part of the white man's society, and try as they did to use a language of a most ridiculous jargon, being a mixture of the blacks' language with their own language, the European soon despaired of persuading the aborigine to adopt his own settled mode of existence. As in the settled districts, here in the wilds the European concluded that there was something in the very constitution of an Australian aborigine that set at defiance all attempts at domestication. The savage might be reconciled to a temporary residence with the white man, he might laugh with him, smoke with him, and accompany him for a time on his excursions, but his stay would never be considered permanent. A settler who left his black man comfortably sleeping around the campfire with two sheets of bark above his head often awoke in the morning to find him gone. The aborigine might come back one day to pick up food, but soon he would go bush again for to him that had the superior attractions of freedom.

At the beginning of 1844 John Lambie, the Crown lands commissioner on the Monaro, told the Colonial Secretary in Sydney that although the aborigines of the district occasionally assisted the stock-holders in sheep washing, hoeing and reaping, unfortunately their habits of industry did not seem to increase. So far only one aborigine had separated himself from his tribe and enclosed a small block of land near the coast, but this was the only instance of any attempt being made to adopt a mode of civilized life. Other observers noted a steep decline in the number of aborigines since the settlement of the white man in the Monaro. Within ten years their number had been reduced to one-quarter of what it had been—a decline caused in the main not by loss of life in bloody encounters with the invader but by movement away in search of areas where the white man did not disturb their food gathering, and by the white man's diseases. The pox rather than the rifle was the main cause of their extermination as a people. The exhilaration of the first contact gave way to anger as the black man pilfered the white man's stores, speared his stock and murdered barbarously the shepherds on the lonely out-stations. The arrival of the blacks at a hut became the occasion for ringing the alarm bell, rather than the earlier gestures of welcome and the invitations to collaboration.[35]

As the squatter outside the boundaries proceeded farther and farther into the interior there was a gradual descent in the scale of civilization until scarcely a remnant was left. The means of transport declined from the royal mail coach on the Sydney–Liverpool stretch of the great south road to a market cart and then to a horse and saddle or bullock-dray; the stone or brick hotel gave way to the weatherboard cottage, which outside the boundaries dwindled down to the slab hut; the sumptuous meals available as far south as Jackson's Inn at Gundaroo gave way to the mutton, damper and tea of the interior. In the slab-hut days the only difference between a master and his men was that the master ate a loaf of bread and his men ate damper, an unleavened loaf baked in the hot ashes of the campfire. The number of women in proportion to the men in the Monaro was so low in 1836—probably not as high as 15 per cent—that one observer, after noting that in travelling over a hundred miles south of Michelago he saw no white females, commented that it all looked 'extremely masculine'. In the midst of such desolation, with little evidence of present or future luxury, the emphasis was on those allegedly male qualities of action and courage which Englishmen called 'pluck'.

The children of the few white women in the district were strangers to book learning. The sons of the Campbells at Duntroon were sent off to King's School, the sons of the Whittakers became boarders at the Melbourne Grammar School and the sons and daughters of others acquired the rudiments of knowledge from tutors or mothers. The illiterate knew about sheep, cattle, runs, dingoes, slab huts, stockyards, paddocks, and the ways of rivers. As for

---

[35] Journal of John Rawson, 1, 9 March 1840 (MS. in NAT. L.); H. W. Haygarth, *Recollections of Bush Life in Australia* (London, 1848), pp. 102-9; James Cook to John Walker, 13 September 1771, in J. C. Beaglehole (ed.), *The Voyage of the Endeavour*, appendix 1, pp. 508-9; Diary of Robert Hobler, vol. 4, 3 October 1846 (Hobler Papers, MS. in M.L.); J. Lambie to Col. Sec. of New South Wales, 9 January 1844 (N.S.W.S.A.); 'A few words on the aborigines of Australia', *New South Wales Magazine*, no. 2, February 1842; *Australasian Chronicle*, 4 February 1843.

their morality and their theology, they picked it up in the life around them. Mrs Whittakers gave her children homely advice: 'Whenever you are tempted, my dear boys, say to yourselves—What would Mama and God do?' It was a life in which a man learnt to endure privation and pain as best he could. Doctors were rare. In the early 1840s a Dr Reid served the whole of the Monaro, except for the Bombala district where the services of a Dr Campbell were available. In the Bega–Twofold Bay district there were the two Imlay brothers who sandwiched their medical practice in between coping with over a quarter million acres of land, the vagaries of prices, droughts, bushfires, bushrangers and aborigines. In addition to other human tribulations there was the fear of getting lost. Men were often lost on the plains because of their sameness. One man on the Monaro went in search of bullocks and was seen no more; another old hand was lost in a snow storm; another took his bullocks off the track to search for water in the Bathurst district and was found lying dead across a log with legs eaten away by the native dogs.[36]

For the few women who braved such hardships the great thing was to get over the first feeling of surprise and disgust on first contact with such a raw life. Early in 1839 a Mrs Thomson planted herself with her husband in a rude hut on a sheep-run some 120 miles west of Melbourne. At first she was astonished at the dirty and uncomfortable way in which the settlers lived, eating what was placed before them out of dirty tin plates, and only using a knife or fork if one could be found. Soon she found to her surprise that the bush was 'a bonny place' and her heart began to warm to it. Although they settled in a spot where no white woman had ever been before, time did not hang heavy on their hands. The men were always busy building huts or fences, and the women cooking and getting ready to dispense bush hospitality. When Mrs Thomson expected to be confined she set off for Melbourne in a dray covered by a tarpaulin, where she was as comfortable as in any covered wagon. Her husband, who travelled with her, read to her as the bullocks hauled them over the plains of Australia Felix. After she bore her child and had it christened in a basin which had formerly belonged to the Barony Church in Glasgow, she again set out in the dray, now loaded up with station provisions. On her return she found her servant Mary had been managing too long by herself to like being supervised again. Mary in fact led her a merry dance there in the bush. In addition there were occasional frights from the wild natives, who sometimes ran past their hut when the husband was away, all quite naked. They were troubled by native dogs, which set up a piteous howl, the signal to attack them before they made havoc with the livestock. Mrs Thomson spent over a year at that hut without seeing another white woman. When one eventually came her little daughter was so astonished to see a 'white lubra' that she dreamed about her for many nights afterwards. Some time after this her white visitor had occasion to go for a journey on horseback, accompanied by a native as a guide. When he tried to

[36] H. W. Haygarth, op. cit., pp. 6-7, 88-9; J. Lhotsky, *A Journey from Sydney to the Australian Alps*, pp. 87-8.

pull her off her horse to molest her, she drew a pistol. Her courage saved her and she arrived safely at journey's end.[37]

No wonder contemporaries coined the phrase that the bush was 'no place for a woman'. Yet, paradoxically, those who possessed the pluck and the will to endure acquired a prestige and a power in a society whose composition seemed designed to confer a power on the men even in excess of that on which Moses and the apostle Paul had conferred a divine sanction. Some of these bush heroines were fashioned from the most unlikely material. When William Whittakers proposed to Louisa Grant in Sydney in June 1841 she was a slip of a girl of some twenty-one summers, who weighed just under seven stone, and enjoyed a gay life in Sydney Town, which was then enlivened by the presence of the officers from the West Kent Regiment. She told him, 'You know, dearest William, I never wanted to be a settler's wife', but he was very persuasive and they were married at St Luke's Church, Liverpool, on 9 November 1841, she wearing brocaded satin, and he a new vest, black coat and trousers, new hat and gloves. Soon after the wedding they set out for the Monaro where, after an interval at Burnima, Whittakers took out a licence for thirteen thousand acres at Tambong. There they lived in a hut of slab walls, with two rooms and a skillion, spaces for windows but no glass, and a floor of hard trodden earth covered with mats of stringy-bark. There and at their next establishment she bore eleven children in twenty years, nine of whom survived, using the services of the bush midwife and sometimes the wives of assigned servants. She made the clothes for all the family by hand, cooked vast quantities of meat over an open fire-place (the standard practice being to cook two bullocks a week), ground wheat for flour, and fended off aborigines with a loaded gun when they attacked the hut during the absence of the menfolk. She washed the clothes in the river, and when the river rose suddenly at night she had to search downstream for the washing. When they moved from Tambong to Tubbutt in 1849 she had the great luxury of a hut with a wooden floor and glass windows. Her husband never addressed her as Louisa but always as Mrs Whittakers, for, despite its levelling and sentiment-stirring tendencies, bush life had its own courtesies. Out of such squalor and hardship, which drove the menfolk into erratic, unsteady ways in the primitive huts of the gentry, a matriarch quietly took over the central position in the family, and in the huts of the servants a 'Mum' came into her own.[38]

The bush workers struck observers as so uncouth that they were awarded with the unenviable distinction of being 'monkeyfied men'. Their manner of speech matched the ruggedness of their personal appearance. Only the 'inferior class' pushed off beyond the boundaries of location, where a 'steady couple' was as rare as hen's teeth. To the town dweller they spoke like men who had forgotten their mother tongue and adopted that of the devil in its stead. The

[37] A Lady (Mrs Thomson), *Life in the Bush* (Edinburgh, 1845).
[38] W. Whittakers, Correspondence, Journal, Account Book, and Other Records 1839-1910 (MS. in NAT. L.); C. Whittakers, *The Whittakers Story*.

native-born in the bush inherited the habit of talking in oaths and imprecations. Some said that the dryness and the hot winds of summer in the inland aggravated this habit by inducing a degree of irritability of temper which found relief in cursing and swearing, tormenting other human beings and mocking the whole of creation as a cruel joke. They likened their fellow-men to galahs or bloody jackasses or compared parts of their anatomy with those of the 'man kangaroo'.

The shepherd's task was to herd the sheep at out-stations some three or four miles from the head-station. They might be on their own or working with three or four men. Like their master or their overseer they lived in a hut, but generally of a more primitive kind than that at the head-station. Four corner posts were sunk into the ground to which walls of slats were fitted into grooves in the posts and finished off with an adze. The roof consisted of shingles or bark. The chimneys, attached to the outer wall, were built of wood, fortified on the inside with stone, and carried sufficiently high to prevent the flames from reaching the outer slabs. Pieces of salted meat hung from the roof. The furniture was sparse—a table and an armchair made from the local gum-tree, and a bed made of long sheets of bark. Since the huts were generally near water-holes, where humus and alluvial soil abounded, the men often cultivated fine gardens of water-melons, cabbages, and other vegetables. By day they shepherded the sheep very much like the shepherds inside the boundaries. Some assuaged the loneliness by improvising music on a gum-leaf, and some were sustained by the thought of what they would do when next they visited the grog shop; some became as mad as hatters, but few turned to God for consolation or were carried away by the ranting of a revivalist preacher, for there was no 'bible belt' in the bush of Australia.[39]

The monotony, the harshness and the loneliness were broken from time to time by a visit from the head-station, or the arrival of travelling stockmen, those adventurers who travelled the pathless wilds moving stock from station to station or to Sydney or Melbourne saleyards. Each traveller in the bush carried with him his tinder-box, and a quart-pot which dangled at the side of his saddle. Using the quart-pot as his teapot, he put it over an open fire, and cooked corned beef and damper for his evening meal, after which he rolled himself for the night in a blanket or 'possum's cloak', using his saddle as a pillow, and slept under the canopy of heaven. This sensation of absolute freedom, when united with the wonder and the mystery of the night, and that exhilaration of the body washed clean in some mountain stream, induced a sense of well-being, a sense of the majesty of life. It was as though life in the wilds of Australia cleansed a man from Adam's stain. Those men who had known this moment of renewed innocence, the moment of believing that from that day they would be strong and squander life no more, might find themselves a week or so later overwhelmed with shame and self-loathing

[39] Lyndsay Gardiner, Eden-Monaro to 1850, pp. 41-9; A. Harris, *Settlers and Convicts* (London, 1847), p. 241; Diary of F. Mackenzie, 1 March 1837; Haygarth, op. cit., pp. 18-21; Lhotsky, op. cit., p. 104.

at the end of a long spree in a bush shanty, grog shop, or inn. In such a grog shop a man often dissipated in a few days the whole earnings of the past year. In the Monaro in the early 1840s one man was such a slave to the habit that though he regularly set off to visit his relations in Sydney he did not succeed in reaching them despite many attempts over several years, being unable to 'guard his pockets', or control his thirst 'against the Siren influence of the road-side inns, from one of which he would constantly retrace his steps with exhausted means', to toil again for an end that he was never to attain.

At one of the inns on the Goulburn Plains, strategically placed to catch the traveller from the Murrumbidgee and Gundagai districts and the traveller from the Monaro, a party of free men arrived from up-country after taking pretty large sums at the sheep-shearing fully intending to have just a half-pint of rum and then go on, only to find that the first one spread such a sense of well-being over their whole body that they decided to try a second, which led to a third, and the third to a fourth, and so on 'till the count was lost in the unfathomable obscurities of a publican's conscience'. They went on drinking, singing, smoking, dancing (sometimes with each other and sometimes with a woman the publican kept around for the 'good time boys'), swearing, yelling, fighting. As an observer put it, 'to use the expressive simile of the class, after earning their money like horses they were spending it like asses'. One fellow hardly had trousers enough to retain a legal right to walk about; he spent there a £17 cheque in two days and a half without purchasing anything. As fast as one batch got soaked and went out, another batch walked in. The police, it was said, were the most notorious tosspots of the lot.[40]

The only other commercial centre was the country store, the proprietors of which boasted that they could supply the stock-holder or his men with anything they needed from a needle to a bullock-dray. There the settler obtained supplies for his men, slop clothing, rations of flour, salt beef, pork, tea, sugar, salt and soap. For the women there were dress materials, neat lace, gaudy ribbon, and more expensive silks. The storekeeper also acted as a general agent and banker on whom squatters, settlers and others drew money orders to pay wages. A storekeeper's cash box contained 'orders to pay' addressed to various mercantile houses in Sydney or Melbourne rather than coins or bank notes. Such orders passed as currency in the district. The social origins and motivations of the storekeepers were as various as those of the squatters and itinerant workers they served. One had spent his earlier days in the colony in a chain-gang and, like many another 'unclean potato', was not an enthusiast for research in early Australian history. Another at Goulburn was a Jew, and another was a one-time member of a theatre who took up the life of a country storekeeper because of the vast amusement he derived from the study of human character, and the pleasure in increasing his own 'happy knack of making himself perfectly at home either with a bullock-driver or an aristocrat of the first water'. Another was the younger brother of the squire of the

[40] H. W. Haygarth, op. cit., pp. 26-7; A. Harris, op. cit., pp. 235-6.

district, and yet another started a country store as the first step to raise his family into the social prominence and status bestowed by landed wealth and education.[41]

Despite the skill of the stockmen in the droving of sheep and cattle which enabled them to turn a horse 'upon a cabbage leaf' and cut out bullocks from a herd with consummate ease, these itinerant workers in the Australian bush were accused of being slothful. Their style of riding did not correspond with the English idea of excellence, for they rode in a generally loose seat, with long stirrups, and knees firmly dug into the withers of the horse, toes pointed out, and the reins held loosely. Yet they had a most astonishing capacity to stick in the saddle in broken, wild country, and to sit out a stumble, a pig-root, a buck or a shy with astonishing ease. In their private lives they behaved in ways which offended the self-appointed defenders and promoters of the faiths of the Old World. Unaware of what was beginning to take root in the minds of these men, unaware that in these men a new vision of the world was replacing the worn-out faiths of Europe, unaware of the powerful charm these men had found in their free and wandering state under the sunny skies and clear moonlight nights down on the Monaro or up on the Darling Downs or out on the plains of Australia Felix, the masters deplored the way of life of their itinerant workers. Down on the Murrumbidgee the righteous and peace-loving complained that shepherds, stock-keepers and bullock-drivers were creating near the numerous public houses the most appalling scenes of infamy and disorder even on the Sabbath day. Graziers who tried to prevent their stock being stolen by such marauders were insulted, punched and kicked. Scab and catarrh were spread among the local flocks by disease-carrying sheep. Bond and free servants were under little or no restraint.[42]

Some believed the cause of this lawlessness was the want of a resident police magistrate. Others believed the trouble was due to the absence of parsons and schoolmasters. Hundreds of British subjects, they said, might remain for years and years in the colony without hearing the consolatory or admonishing voice of a minister of religion; thousands of Christians were dying in this country like brutes and being buried like brutes. The 'galloping parson', the Reverend Thomas Hassall from Cobbitty, galloped over the Limestone Plains and gathered the faithful in the squatters' parlours at Duntroon or Gininderra, to hear the word of God. Father J. Therry rode over the Razor-back and through the dreary Bargo Brush to gather together the members of his flock and say those words, 'Ecco, Corpus Christi'. In the 1840s the Reverend E. G. Pryce, an Anglican clergyman on the Monaro, held religious services at intervals of six weeks at various stations, at which some twenty people generally gathered. But he was unhappy about the fruits of his ministry. 'The effects of an itinerating ministry', he wrote in a report to Bishop Broughton in January 1844, 'on the minds of the people are very

---

[41] H. W. Haygarth, op. cit., pp. 85-6; T. McCombie, *Australian Sketches* (Melbourne, 1847), pp. 35-8; *Heads of the People*, 6 November 1847.
[42] H. W. Haygarth, op. cit., pp. 61-2, 97; *Sydney Herald*, 21 April 1841.

desultory, especially a people who have been shut out for years from participation in the means of grace, and who consequently have in great measure
become careless about them.' Yet he believed it was urgent to do something:
the carelessness and ungodliness of the labouring classes in the bush were very
awful, the 'old hands' were in a deplorable state, and even the immigrants who
had been long in the bush without the means of grace were nearly as bad.
For his part he looked for improvement to the immigrant families, and the
increase in the number of married people, because that tended greatly to the
'amelioration of manners'. He was worried, too, by the difficulty of establishing schools for the children because the people lived so far apart that there
was no locality where the children could be brought together. Some families
were employing private tutors, but these men were incapable of any other
employment and generally unfit for teaching. The only solution he could
recommend was to get clergymen into the district quickly, so that the denizens of the bush of Australia might not continue 'so lax and dead to the
spiritual concerns of themselves and others'.[43]

When the parsons appeared on these frontiers of settlement to end this
'deadness and indifference', they spoke as upholders of a way of life and a
vision of the world to which the 'bush barbarian' hardly responded. At the
consecration of St Saviour's Church in Goulburn in February 1845 Bishop
Broughton told the congregation that Jesus Christ was the only way sinners
could be accepted in the sight of God, that His spiritual light alone could help
them to bear up against all the ills of life. All the hopes of man for salvation
from any other source were vain. He made the same point when he conse-
crated Christ Church in Queanbeyan, and St John's in Canberra, in March
1845, which both bore some of the appearance of an old English village
church. At both churches he told those who gathered to hear him how he
devoutly hoped that a clergyman would minister to the spiritual needs of a
people wandering in great darkness.[44]

What Broughton hoped was that through a knowledge of Christ's redeeming love for mankind a day would come when the countryside ceased to be
'infested with scoundrels', with men who slobbered at the mouth when they
spoke, and with aboriginal women who had been disfigured by the pox to
look like 'filthy animals'. In the bush some women, like Mrs Henry Zouch at
Bungendore, were renowned for their generous hospitality and their 'sweet
singing'. Others, like Eliza Smith of Queanbeyan, only knew shame, degradation and humiliation. In 1843 she was living with a ticket-of-leave holder,
James Nichols, who regularly gave her two 'lovely black eyes', and woke her
from her drunken stupors with a kick on the head and a nice cup of tea, just
to show he did not mean any real harm. She died from exposure to the cold
during one of her drinking bouts with Nichols which began on a Sunday and

[43] J. Lhotsky, *A Journey from Sydney to the Australian Alps*, p. 69; J. S. Hassall, *In
Old Australia* (Brisbane, 1902), pp. 87-92; E. G. Pryce, 'Account of the Mission of
Maneroo' in W. G. Broughton, *The Church in Australia* (London, 1845), pt 2, pp. 5-11.
[44] *S.M.H.*, 14 February, 15, 21 March 1845.

continued through the succeeding days as the two of them staggered after sheep in frosty weather on the Limestone Plains.

Broughton was working for the day when white men and women took on the appearance of being made in the image of God. It never occurred to him that a new faith was taking shape in the minds of the men on whom he believed God alone could work a great marvel. It never occurred to him that these men who drank all their earnings every fifteen or eighteen months and then came out of their spree penniless and 'suffering from the blue devils almost to madness' had uncovered something very precious. He never noticed that these men who were characterized by xenophobia, racism, an abominable attitude to the aborigine, absence of romantic love for women, derision of all who held out the prospect of better things for mankind and of people's misfortunes were bound by ties of affection and fellowship to each other.

Such a great deal of mutual regard and trust was engendered by two men working together in the solitary bush that habits of mutual helpfulness arose, which in turn led to gratitude and regard for each other. Under such circumstances men often stood by one another through thick and thin. In fact the feeling that a man ought to be able to trust his own mate in anything was universal. Men sustained by regard for their 'mates', strengthened by the discovery of their own pluck, courage and resource, and that self-confidence of men who looked down on the world from the saddle of a horse, no longer felt the need to turn to God for help, or the desire to wash away 'guilty stains' in Christ's redeeming blood. The mighty bush was planting in the hearts of these children of nature those beliefs in equality and the brotherhood of man which the teachers of the Enlightenment had put forward as alternatives to that infamy about man's sinful nature. But Broughton and men of like mind went on hoping that what that English village church at Canberra stood for—the Judaico-Christian belief that the hearts of men were filled with evil, and madness was in their hearts while they lived, after which they went to the dead—would one day have a great victory with the bush barbarians of Australia. The days of innocence when the bushmen were free from the ties of family and property were to end when they fell under the influence of that cult of respectability and a belly-full which the migrants brought with them as part of the baggage-train from the Old World. The iron rail was to bring British philistinism to the Australian bush.[45]

[45] E. Lea-Scarlett, 'Queanbeyan in distress. Some women who helped to shape local history', *Canberra Historical Journal*, no. 1, March 1973; A. Harris, *Settlers and Convicts*, pp. 12-13, 326.

12

SQUATTERDOM'S DOMINATION

O N 26 JANUARY 1843 on one of those summer days when not a cloud was visible in the sky, and the waters of Sydney Harbour were studded with golden fire-balls dancing in blue water, throngs of citizens flocked along the shores in their holiday clothes to celebrate the fifty-fifth anniversary of the foundation of the colony. At night there was a variety of entertainment. Government House and many private houses were illuminated to celebrate the successful planting of civilization in Australia and to greet their first year as a 'free and enfranchised' people. That year the property holders of New South Wales were to elect their own representatives to the Legislative Council of New South Wales. But when 150 gentlemen sat down that night to dinner at the Royal Hotel, Wentworth spoke to them like a prophet of lamentation rather than a conveyer of good cheer. The times, he said, were gloomy: labour was short, wages were high, prices were falling. Men would have to give up the habits of an age of plenty and learn the habits of an age of scarcity: they would have to turn their carriages into wheel-barrows or get rid of them, they would have to work to raise their country from a land of penury and starvation to one of plenty, and would have to settle more numerously in the country and less in the towns. In the churches the clergy pointed to the commercial depression as a sign of God's wrath at the wickedness of His people: woe, said the clergy in their comminations, unto those men whose wives in such times continued to display coats of armour on the doors of their carriages, and kept up their liveried servants and their champagne dinners while squatterdom faced its period of peril. The believers in the Dionysian frenzy, and the publicists of the Judaico-Christian infamy about man's depravity were at last speaking with one voice: squatterdom was in peril and, if squatterdom fell, the whole of society would be dragged down to ruin.[1]

That January the prophets of doom were also dwelling on the peril to the original inhabitants of Australia. The boot of the white man, they said, now stood on the grave of the aborigine. But the white men in general did not

---

[1] *Australasian Chronicle*, 28 January 1843; *Australian*, 27 January 1843; speech at election meeting by W. C. Wentworth, *S.M.H.*, 28 December 1842, 26, 27, 28 January 1843; J. D. Lang, *An Historical and Statistical Account of New South Wales* (2 vols, 3rd ed., London, 1852), vol. 1, pp. 306-17; J. Williams to Secretary of State of U.S.A., 1 January 1842, 1 July 1843, 1 January 1844. (Reports from United States Consul-General in Sydney, microfilm in NAT. L.).

view the aborigine's gradual and silent extermination as a subject calling for regret, still less as imperatively demanding a remedy. Who, it was argued, would attempt to claim that the 'factory' and the 'saw-mill', fields covered with grain, and waters cleft by the steamboat were not more to be desired than the rude but grand magnificence of nature? The extinction of un-improved humanity should not be regarded as a source of regret and certainly was no ground for blaming themselves as the agents of this improvement. These marks of the presence of civilized and enlightened man were wondrous examples of the infinite wisdom of his Creator. It could not be supposed that providence would wish to leave any country to be occupied by a few savages, who made no further use of it than wandering from place to place when at the same time millions of human beings in other places were crowded one upon another without means of subsistence. So why regret that in New England, Liverpool Plains, Bathurst Plains, Yass, the Monaro, Murrum-bidgee, Western Port, and Australia Felix the aborigines had been three or four times more numerous only ten or fifteen years ago? It was not necessary to accept the more pessimistic opinion that the aborigines were irreclaimable, or the view of some phrenologists that the black skull did not possess the faculties necessary for civilized life. Squatterdom's peril was redeemable, the extermination of the aborigines irreversible.[2]

Over in Western Australia there was the same sense of a society in a state of crisis. Stirling's successor, John Hutt, a man of that austere turn of mind and weariness of the flesh and vexation of spirit brought on by much study and solitude, warned Stanley in London that, unless some means were devised to procure farm labourers, house servants and artisans, society would come to a standstill, all progress would stop, and work on public works, on the farms, and in the houses of the people would cease. Since the original tenants of the land had a chronic aversion to labour, and neither a desire nor a capacity for that settled existence essential for the survival of civilization, and since the decision-makers of London had turned their backs on the use of coolie or Chinese labour, the only solution was to import convicts on an extensive scale. The question was whether the settlers, taught for a decade to view convicts as 'tainters' and 'polluters', would realize in time that their salvation depended on their willingness to adjust themselves to such 'filth'.[3]

By contrast, those children of the Solons of the Adelphi, the inhabitants of

[2] 'A few words on the aborigines of Australia', *New South Wales Magazine*, no. 2, February 1842; *Australasian Chronicle*, 4 February 1843; T. H. Braim, The Aborigines, pp. 3-4 (MS. in M.L.); W. R. Jacobs, *Dispossessing the American Indian* (New York, 1972), pp. 138-40.

[3] Hutt to Stanley, 31 October, 7 December 1843, C.O. 18/35; population figures for Western Australia are based on R. M. Martin, *The British Colonies: their history, extent, condition and resources*, pt 3 (London, 1850); Swan River Papers, *P.P.*, 1838, xi, 687; 'The humble memorial of the undersigned land owners, merchants and inhabitants of the colony of Western Australia', *Perth Gazette and Western Australian Journal*, 2 January 1847; Stanley to Hutt, 11 August 1843, 4 March 1844, C.O. 397/7; Hutt to Stanley, 15 August 1845, C.O. 18/39.

South Australia, were patting themselves on the back for the good sense they had displayed in having nothing to do with unplanned colonization as practised in Western Australia, or those social evils of convictism which disgraced the annals of New South Wales and Van Diemen's Land. Thanks to the wisdom of her government, the frugality of her people, their persevering industry and virtue, both government and people had weathered the storm of the commercial depression. At the beginning of 1843 public men were proud that that year the government finances were expected to show a slight credit balance for the first time since the foundation of the colony. The settlers had a similar story of progress to report: the quantity of land under cultivation increased that year from 18 940 to 26 570 acres; the number of sheep had increased from 241 000 in 1841 to 360 000 in 1843 and horned cattle from 16 696 to 20 000; the population had increased from 546 in 1836 to 17 196 in 1843, thanks, they believed, to their prudent migration system which was free from that disproportion between the sexes which had bedevilled the morals and coarsened the tone of life in eastern Australia. In politics there was a similar story of modest and judicious progress. In June of 1843 Governor Grey nominated T. S. O'Halloran, J. Morphett, G. F. Dashwood and T. Williams to be the unofficial members of the new Legislative Council created by the Imperial Act of July 1842 for the better government of South Australia. All four represented a combination of trade and landed wealth, and a habit of baiting radicals which distinguished the men at the top of society in colonial Adelaide. When announcing in June that he was prepared to admit the public to the debates in the Legislative Council and allow the press to report the proceedings, Grey made it quite clear that these councillors were to be humble obedient servants to His Excellency rather than spokesmen for a colonial bourgeoisie.[4]

Proud though they were of planting in the wilds of South Australia a civilization distinguished by the absence of those class privileges and restraints on the liberty of worship which still disgraced the societies of the Old World, a tyranny characteristic of the societies of the New World was already putting down tenacious roots in their soil. When Alexis de Tocqueville visited the United States of America in 1831 he noticed that a New World society did not persuade but forced men to adopt certain opinions, and infused them into the intellect by a sort of enormous pressure on the minds of all. Some eleven years later Charles Dickens wrote to his friend Forster that there was

<hr />

[4] Grey to Stanley, 20 February 1843, C.O. 13/31; Grey to Stanley, 20 September 1843, C.O. 13/34; *South Australian Register*, 7 January 1843; J. Boothby, *Statistical Sketch of South Australia* (Adelaide, 1876); South Australian Blue Books 1840-7; C. Sturt to W. Sturt, n.d. (probably late 1842 or early 1843), quoted in Mrs Napier George Sturt, *Life of Charles Sturt* (London, 1899), pp. 213-14; C. Sturt to private secretary to Governor of South Australia, 3 August 1844 (Sturt Papers, s.a.s.a.); Grey to Stanley, 7 December 1842, C.O. 13/27; *South Australian Register*, 7 January 1843; An Act to Provide for the Better Government of South Australia, 5 & 6 Vic., c. 61, 30 July 1842, *Statutes at Large*, vol. 82; Stanley to Grey, 6 September 1842, C.O. 397/5; Additional Instructions to Grey, 29 August 1842, encl. in Stanley to Grey, 6 September 1842, C.O. 397/5.

no country on earth in which there was less freedom of opinion than the United States, and he trembled for any radical who went there. There were signs that a similar tyranny of opinion was already being practised in South Australia. Early in 1843 W. W. Nicholls, who had been publishing the idea that only a socialist society could create the conditions in which all men would enjoy life, liberty and the pursuit of happiness, was dragged off his horse by a mob and beaten insensible. The believers in the bourgeois virtues of industry, frugality, knowledge and sobriety were not prepared to tolerate the dissemination of any other view of the world.[5]

Not long after this incident the *South Australian Magazine* in May and June of 1842 was proudly telling its readers that at long last, after the arduous pioneering days of providing food, clothing and shelter, men and women in South Australia had leisure to peep into nature's curiosities and a heart to sing out the peculiar joys and griefs of humanity without the 'help of feudal tenures, feudal aristocracy, or an orthodox State conscience'. The respectable matrons of North Terrace whispered behind their fans about the drunken abominations of the overlanders. The Reverend C. B. Howard proudly told his parishioners that the only rivalry he practised was that 'holy rivalry' of vying with his fellow-men in 'dispensing blessings to others'. The Reverend T. Q. Stow manfully told his people of their privilege in being born in a century characterized by great material and intellectual progress. As evidence of his faith, in November of 1843 one John Ridley, a miller by occupation and a preacher by inclination (the combination of industry and religious zeal being typical of the bourgeoisie of Adelaide), invented a reaping and thresh-ing machine, which solved the problem of how to farm successfully in a society short of labour.[6]

Some were troubled that the white man's invasion of South Australia had stripped the aborigines of all power except the power to 'sigh o'er loss of bygone pleasures' and to endure in sullen silence their bitterness that the only gift they had received from the white man for the loss of their land was those stories about a saviour of mankind called Jesus. The white man brutalized and degraded the aborigine, and then had the effrontery to expect the abo-rigine to look pleased when told the story of gentle Jesus meek and mild. As in New South Wales, others did not see why their hearts should be troubled just because useless savages were disappearing off the face of the earth before 'an immeasurably better and higher power than ever ran wild in any earthly woods'. At year's end, when all the respectable members of Adelaide society

[5] A. de Tocqueville, *De la Démocratie en Amérique* (3 vols, Paris, 1874); C. Dickens to W. Forster, 24 February 1842, quoted in A. Quiller-Couch, *Charles Dickens and Other Victorians* (Cambridge, 1925), p. 14; letter of W. W. Nicholls to *South Australian Register*, 11 March 1843.

[6] Catherine Helen Spence (Susan Eade ed.), *Clara Morison* (Adelaide, 1971), pp. xiv-xv; for the opinion of C. B. Howard see D. H. Pike, *Paradise of Dissent* (London, 1957), p. 252; *South Australian Register*, 15 November 1843, 11 February 1846; A. E. Ridley, *A Backward Glance* (London, 1904); G. L. Sutton, 'The invention of the stripper', *Western Australian Department of Agriculture Journal*, September 1937.

gathered for a concert and dance, an air of confidence and cheerfulness pervaded everyone. The Governor threw aside his dignity, the grave Chief Justice was all bows and smiles: they were all so happy, so gay, as they threw themselves into a harmless, exhilarating and improving evening. As they saw it, neither mankind in general nor their society in particular was in peril.[7]

Over in Van Diemen's Land foreboding about their future was temporarily lost to sight in the excitement, commotion and uproar of welcoming distinguished members to their society. The first to come, in April 1843, was James Bicheno, the Colonial Secretary. He was distinguished for his contribution to learning in philosophy, botany and zoology, but yet so unkindly treated by the gods in his personal appearance that within a few months the locals had christened him the 'Old Hen'—that fat smiling creature whose head was overflowing with Epicurean philanthropy and whose stomach was distended by a huge daily intake of food and drink.

In July Francis Russell Nixon stepped ashore at Hobart to take up his duties as the first Anglican bishop of Tasmania. A man whose vanity and love of display found satisfaction in wearing the gorgeous robes and performing the pantomimic gestures recommended by the Tractarians, he had also many of the attributes of the scholar, the artist and the bon viveur, of the squire parson of Jane Austen's England. He drew with distinction, he brewed his own lager, and could keep his end up very well in a wine tasters' conversation. He had a distinguished appearance and almost Byronic features, with his curly hair and his full, rather thick lips, as well as the manners of a man who had naturally taken a place in the salons and parsonages of Regency London. The press in Hobart hoped he would improve the disgraceful state of the schools, put an end to the slovenly manner in which divine service was performed in most of the churches, concentrate on his own vineyard, and lay aside all worldly titles and honours, thus setting an example of humility. On 31 October Nixon presented himself before the Legislative Council of Van Diemen's Land 'in all the theatrical frippery of white muslin . . . pudding-sleeves, and black silk apron' and told them to educate the children of the colony in a way that would make them 'wise unto salvation', and not to foster a sort of republicanism of religion—'I would rather see my children [he was to have three wives and thirteen children], one by one, die before my eyes, than that they should turn next door to infidels'. By then he had made it plain that the inhabitants of Van Diemen's Land must not look to literature and science to regenerate a fallen world, but to Christian faith. Like Broughton in New South Wales, he was to use all his vast energy and talents to stand up against the secular winds blowing over the civilized world. The new Lieutenant-Governor, Sir John Eardley-Wilmot, promptly made it plain that he was not going to be a party to any creation of privileges for the Anglican Church. The press applauded his stand. They were not to know and Eardley-Wilmot was

[7] *South Australian Register*, 11 November, 6 December 1843; Charles Dickens, 'The noble savage', reprinted in Charles Dickens, *The Uncommercial Traveller and Other Reprinted Pieces* (Oxford, 1958), pp. 467-73.

not to know that on that day he had ruffled a man who would one day help to bring him to his destruction.[8]

When Eardley-Wilmot arrived in Hobart on the night of 21 August 1843 bonfires lit up the neighbouring hills to celebrate the joyous event. The following day little children tumbled out of trees, and elegant ladies jostled on the balcony of the Waterloo Hotel to get a look at this man who had been selected by Lord Stanley to lead the men in the probation gangs into the paths of virtue and thwart that spirit of convictism which threatened to drag everyone down to the level of the gutter. That night a woman with a gift to see into the heart of the matter wrote that the reins of government in Van Diemen's Land had been placed in the hands of a 'battered old beau', and their society enlivened by the addition of a 'dandy' and a 'lady-like man', Eardley-Wilmot's son, Augustus Hillier. In those first few months neither she nor anyone else guessed at the fatal significance of those words. All the respectable people of Hobart, Launceston and the Midlands feted him as their gentleman governor who wore civilian clothes, a promise of the impending end of the 'iron age' in the history of their island.

He was then sixty. Born into the landed gentry, he had made enough of a mark at the Bar and in the House of Commons to win the patronage of Lord Stanley. At first glance he had an air of distinction, while his open and affable address warmed the people to him. Soon after his arrival Judge Montagu sentenced the bushranger Kavanagh to death for armed robbery, after one of those sermons from the Bench in which the learned judge remarked that he had seldom tried a culprit stained with so great an aggregate of crime. Eardley-Wilmot reprieved him ten minutes before the time set for the execution. The liberals and humanitarians believed one of their heroes now lived in Government House. The *Hobart Town Courier* was worried: 'Looking to the mixed and peculiar character of a considerable portion of our population, we fear the effect of this act of clemency will be misunderstood, or, at the least, give rise to a *calculation* of *chances* among those already too experienced in the lottery of criminal law, which will not tend to repress criminal actions'. What was to Eardley-Wilmot an act of compassion, a symbol of the passing of that elemental society of savage punishments to one of milder laws and a broader humanity, planted in the minds of the leaders and defenders of the old convict order a doubt whether this 'battered old beau' had the right sort of heart to preside over a gaol.

Soon some began to wonder whether the man's principles were as wishy-washy as his heart. In October he told the Legislative Council that religious

[8] Diary of G. T. W. Boyes, 2 August 1846; P. A. Howell, 'Bishop Nixon and public education in Tasmania', *Melbourne Studies in Education 1967* (Melbourne, 1968), pp. 168-75; W Hutchins, *A Letter on the School Question* (Hobart, 1839); *Colonial Times*, I, 15 August 1843; *Tasmanian*, 3 November 1843; *Hobart Town Advertiser*, 3 November 1843; N. Nixon, *The Pioneer Bishop in Van Diemen's Land* (Hobart, 1954); F. R. Nixon, *Lectures Historical, Doctrinal and Practical on the Catechism of the Church of England* (London, 1843); N. Batt, Bishop Nixon and Conflicts within the Church of England in Tasmania (thesis, History Department, University of Tasmania).

freedom was the right of all. He followed that up with a public despatch to Lord Stanley in which he explained that the Anglicans could not exercise a monopoly in education because they did not enjoy the same foundations of power as in England. All the liberals in Hobart and Launceston applauded him. But the conservatives who accepted the three propositions that the Bible was conservative, that the Book of Common Prayer was conservative and that the Anglican Church, the monarchy, and the aristocracy were the three pillars on which a British society rested, wondered whether a subverter of divine and natural law now held the highest office in the land. Gossips whispered that persons never before seen at Government House were boasting of their intimacy and influence with Eardley-Wilmot. When Bishop Nixon heard that the new lieutenant-governor was letting standards slip at Government House, the dark thought crossed his mind that there was a connection between his liberalism in education, the liberalism in etiquette, and a liberalism in morals. Other voices were prophesying doom and disaster. Charles Swanston, the banker, was issuing warnings that their society was heading for general bankruptcy. A section of the press was warning readers of 'the drivelling idiocy' of assuming that the colony could avoid great evils from the presence of a huge convict community which was making little contribution to the national wealth. Others with less insight into the signs of the times likened Eardley-Wilmot's presence to the vivifying rays of the sun after a long cheerless winter.[9]

At the same time over in New South Wales public men went on talking about those things which touched them most deeply. At the beginning of the year Bishop Broughton was stewing over the attitude of John Henry Newman to the teaching of the Catholic Church on purgatory, and was very fearful that the return of Polding to Sydney might mean that the Protestants would be absolutely overrun with Romanists whose schemes for the popish domination of New South Wales were 'bold, artful, and diversified beyond description'. He decided in March 1843 to make yet another public protest against Polding's calling himself a bishop:

> We, William Grant, by Divine Permission, Bishop and Ordinary Pastor of Australia, do protest publicly and explicitly . . . that the Bishop of Rome has not any right or authority, according to the laws of God, and the canonical order of the Church, to institute any episcopal or archiepiscopal see or sees, within the limits of the diocese of Australia and province of Canterbury aforesaid.

[9] *Hobart Town Advertiser*, 22 August 1843; *Colonial Times*, 22 August 1843; Journal of Marian Smith, 2 September 1843 (Papers of P. T. Smith, copies in library of University of Tasmania); *Launceston Examiner*, 19 September 1843; Eardley-Wilmot to Stanley, 2 March, 21 July 1843 (Correspondence of Stanley with Eardley-Wilmot, Stanley Papers, 135/6); *Launceston Examiner*, 12, 30 August, 9 September 1843; *Colonial Times*, 22 August, 19 September 1843; *V. & P.* (L.C. V.D.L.), 21 October 1843; *Colonial Times*, 28 November 1843; Eardley-Wilmot to Stanley, 4 November 1843, C.O. 280/160; J. West, *The History of Tasmania* (2 vols, Launceston, 1852), vol. 1, pp. 233-5; Eardley-Wilmot to Stanley, 28 September 1843, C.O. 280/160; *Hobart Town Courier*, 22 September 1843.

William Charles Wentworth was stewing over quite a different question. As he saw it, unless sufficient labour was made available quickly to the flock-masters of New South Wales, six million sheep must be turned into the wilds of the colony to be eaten by savages and native dogs. Down at Glenormiston in Australia Felix Niel Black was thinking of importing coolie labour, but was held back by the thought that government might not like that, and the rather quaint objection that he did not speak the same language as coolies. All over the sheep-walks of New South Wales stock-holders yarned over their quart-pots about handing back the country to the aborigines unless something was done quickly to lift squatterdom out of its depressed condition, for the great want of labour had roused the settlers to a sense of their impending ruin. The *Australian*, at that time a mouthpiece for the wool kings of New South Wales, ridiculed the opponents of the use of coolie workers for representing 'poor inoffensive Hindoos' as 'an immoral and blood-thirsty race likely to contaminate the pure breed of the colony'. The *Australian* reminded the employers of New South Wales of what the Chinese could accomplish under European direction, and how their acquaintance with various arts and manufactures was particularly valuable in a new country.[10]

By February 1843 the debate on the labour question became part of a wide-ranging debate on the election of twenty-four members to the new Legislative Council. Once again there was a great confusion of voices, all sound and fury signifying if not nothing, then very little, because the New South Wales Constitution Act of 1842 and the Electoral Districts Act of 1843 passed by the Legislative Council had already awarded the victory to the landed magnificoes of New South Wales and assured squatterdom's domination in the political life of the colony.

The Electoral Districts Act prescribed that the town of Parramatta in the county of Cumberland, the united towns of Windsor, Richmond, Campbelltown and Liverpool under the denomination of the Cumberland Boroughs, and the united towns of East Maitland, West Maitland and Newcastle under the denomination of the Northumberland Boroughs should respectively form electoral districts and return one member each. For the rest, the county of Cumberland, excluding the towns of Sydney, Parramatta, Liverpool, Campbelltown, Windsor and Richmond, was to return two members, and the counties of Camden, Argyle, Durham, Bathurst, the united counties of St Vincent and Auckland, the united south-western counties of Murray, King and Georgiana, and united Midland counties of Cook and Westmoreland, the united western counties of Roxburgh, Phillip and Wellington, the united northern counties of Gloucester, Macquarie and Stanley, and the united north-western counties of Hunter, Brisbane and Bligh should each form electoral districts and return one member each to the Legislative Council. The 'country

---

[10] W. G. Broughton to E. Coleridge, 14 February 1842, 27 March 1843 (microfilm in NAT. L.); N. Black to T. S. Gladstone, 30 December 1841, 20 January 1842 (Black Papers, LA TROBE L.); *Australian*, 30 January, 1 February 1843; W. A. Duncan, *A Letter to the Lord Bishop of Australia* (Sydney, 1843).

interest', the heart of squatterdom's domination, was to have eighteen members, and the 'town interest', the respectable bourgeoisie of Sydney, Melbourne, Parramatta, Windsor, Richmond, Campbelltown, Liverpool, East
Maitland, West Maitland and Newcastle, were to have six. Just over 47 000
town people were to have six members in the Council, and 66 500 country
dwellers were to have eighteen.[11]

In March the confusion of voices began. Gipps respectfully requested
support for candidates favourable to the government. The press slapped him
down and said that, on the contrary, it was the duty of the electors to stop the
executive government from having an undue preponderance in the new
legislature. Broughton and those close to him raised the cry, 'the Church is in
danger'; Catholics and non-Anglican Protestants retorted that he and his
party were using the election to promote an 'ecclesiastical dominancy' for
Anglicans. The *Australian* accused the candidates from the 'ancient nobility'
of New South Wales of encouraging the 'miserable affectation of exclusiveness' and attempting to establish a 'kind of cocktail aristocracy'; the *Sydney
Morning Herald* warned electors against vulgar convict upstarts. George
Robert Nichols, the native-born son of a convict, came before the electors as a
professed Australian. 'I am', he wrote in his letters to the electors, 'an Australian by birth.' Wentworth was proud to call himself a 'son of the soil'.
Some said they proposed to promote the good welfare of all classes in the
community: Robert Cooper, the emancipist, appeared before the electors as
a 'plain; blunt man . . . no wordy theorist, but a practical utilitarian' whose
aim was 'the public good of the working classes'. Some opposed the use of
coolie labour, some wanted to renew assisted immigration, some wanted to
renew transportation. Some said the electors had to decide whether political
power was to reside with 'clean potatoes' or the 'low Irish mob' and 'convict
levellers'. Some said three parties were contesting the election, a pro-govern-
ment party, a Macarthur–Wentworth landed gentry party, and a Sydney
radical party led by Robert Cooper; some said the election campaign, like all
the public life of the Australian colonies, was distinguished not by a clash of
groups or ideologies but by a performance in which Australians showed
themselves to be capital hands at blackguardism and gross personal abuse.[12]

[11] Section 2 of An Act for the Government of New South Wales and Van Diemen's
Land, 5 & 6 Vic., c. 76, 30 July 1842, *Statutes at Large*, vol. 16; sections 1, 2 of An Act
to Provide for the Division of the Colony of New South Wales into Electoral Districts,
and for the Election of Members to Serve in the Legislative Council, 6 Vic., no. 16,
23 February 1843, T. Callaghan, *Acts and Ordinances of the Governor and Council of
New South Wales*; census of 2 March 1841, Blue Book of Statistics, 1841; Blue Book of
Statistics, 1843; *Kerr's Melbourne Almanac and Port Phillip Directory* (Melbourne,
1841), p. 231; ibid. (Melbourne, 1842), p. 292; *V. & P.* (L.C. N.S.W.), 24 January, 14 February 1843; for a detailed description of these boundaries see the proclamations of
27 February and 24 March in *New South Wales Government Gazette*, 28 February,
28 March 1843; F. G. P. Neison, *Analysis of the Census of New South Wales* (Oxford,
1847).
[12] R. Howitt, *Impressions of Australia Felix* (London, 1845), p. 104; *S.M.H.*, 28
December 1842, 2 January, 24, 31 May 1843; *Australian*, 27 January, 1 February 1843;
letter of G. R. Nichols to *S.M.H.*, 27 December 1842; letter of W. C. Wentworth to

In the electorate of Sydney there was fighting between the supporters of the various candidates on nomination day, 13 June. Two days later on polling day a mob of four to five hundred tore down the colours of Wentworth and Bland and drove their supporters away. When Wentworth arrived at the hustings in Sydney, a fierce mob of ruffians howled at him 'Coolie' and 'No Convicts' and 'Norfolk Islander'. One man in the mob nearly strangled Bland. In one of the many scuffles during the day, one Daniel Fernie was so badly wounded that he died later. In the evening a ferocious mob wandered around the streets of Sydney breaking windows, threatening passers-by and drunkenly repeating the anti-Wentworth slogans of 'Coolie' and 'No Convicts', but all to no avail. For at the declaration of the poll on the following day the two defenders of the old order in New South Wales—Wentworth and Bland— were declared to be elected. The city of Sydney had chased away the 'wild boar' of radicalism which sought to fasten itself upon its new legislature.[13]

In the election for Camden, Cumberland and Melbourne, sectarian senti- ment rather than class or personality or the convict past came to the surface. For the election to the Camden seat Charles Cowper at first assured William Macarthur that he was not thinking of putting his name forward. Cowper was one of those deeply divided men, divided not between passion and reason, the traditional cause of self-division, but between God and Mammon. Born into a clergyman's family, he had learned in childhood from his father, the gentle Reverend William Cowper, about 'spiritual understanding', the 'evils of the human heart', of 'the plan of Salvation' and of 'the Grace and special providence of God'. When he came to man's estate he entered public life talking like a spokesman for the Church of England. He found it 'disgusting' to belong to a society without 'even one thought except for money & politics'. But Cowper was also a large landowner, with a sheep-run in the county of Argyle, a farm at Camden, and a huge squatting run on the Murray River. When he heard that Roger Therry, a Catholic and a salaried member of the government of New South Wales, proposed to stand for Camden, Cowper, influenced both by being a spokesman for the Church of England and by landowner antagonism to government influence, put his name for- ward for Camden. James Macarthur had decided to let Therry, who was a conservative, win Camden and stand himself for Cumberland so as to increase the number of conservatives in the Council. This whipped up sectarian bitter- ness in Camden, the very strife the Macarthurs were anxious to prevent. After the election of Therry, the Macarthurs looked on Cowper as a perpetrator of 'wilful falsehood', as a man with the 'daring of a habitual slanderer', and as a man who claimed to be 'pure in principle' but was wicked enough to do evil

S.M.H., 24 December 1842; letter of R. Cooper to *S.M.H.*, 27 December 1842, letters of H. Macdermott and M. C. O'Connell to *S.M.H.*, 27 December 1842; letter of John Hos- king to *S.M.H.*, 30 December 1842; Autobiography of W. A. Duncan (MS. in M.L.); *Australasian Chronicle*, 28 January 1843.
[13] *S.M.H.*, 14-17 June 1843; *V. & P.* (L.C. N.S.W.), 19 September 1843; *Australian*, 20 September 1843; *Weekly Register*, 2 September, 18 November 1843.

in order that good might come. By then Cowper announced his intention to oppose James Macarthur in Cumberland. Wentworth, who still had scores to settle with the Macarthurs persuaded old William Lawson, 'Iron Bark' Lawson, one of his mates on the historic journey over the Blue Mountains in 1813, to stand. At the poll Cowper and Lawson defeated James Macarthur and G. R. Nichols, the wealthy convict's son. The last-named, a native-born Australian, took his defeat with wit and urbanity. But James Macarthur spoke so bitterly at the declaration of the poll of the treachery of his one-time friend and the wickedness of his opponent that the by-standers called out 'Enough, go down' and even 'Shut up'.[14]

Until February it looked as though Edward Curr would be returned unopposed for the electorate of Melbourne. He was well known for his firm stand on the question of separation from New South Wales; he was also a supporter of squatterdom's domination, and was himself one of those squatters who lived in elegance in a town mansion. Endowed by nature with a commanding presence, he had the Wentworth gift of handling a mob like a demagogue, and reducing anyone in his presence to a state of vassalage. In time this tendency to reduce friend and foe alike to a position of servitude aroused resentment against the 'Father of Separation', but in 1843 the electors of Melbourne knew only the charisma and not the bitterness or the anger such men deposit in their train. Curr was also a Catholic. On 17 March 1843, after much liquoring-up and to the accompaniment of much cheering and boisterous merriment, there was a procession of the followers of Saint Patrick through the streets of Melbourne, preceded by banners bearing the emblem of the harp and a man swinging a cudgel covered in green wreaths, which he whirled like a fighting shillelagh in the hands of a drunken Irishman at Donnybrook Fair. The participants then entered the Church of St Francis for High Mass at which Father Patrick Geoghegan delivered a panegyric on the apostle of the 'Island of Saints' in a manner which confirmed his reputation as the best pulpit orator in the colony. The Catholics were sensing their strength.

Protestants were already anxious about a threat to the Protestant ascendancy. On 9 February the *Port Phillip Patriot* published a letter signed 'Homo' in which the writer remarked how odd it would be for Melbourne, a sound Protestant city, to be represented by a Roman Catholic. Everyone in Melbourne knew the letter had been written by John Dunmore Lang. For twenty years he had preached a harsh version of Calvinism. For twenty years he had been haunted by the nightmare of hordes of savages from Catholic Ireland barbarizing New South Wales as they had brutalized parts of his native Glasgow. He warned Protestants that a reckless Irish Catholic rabble

---

[14] Plaque to William Cowper in St Philip's Church, Sydney; *Weekly Register*, 27 January 1844; *S.M.H.*, 7 July 1843; W. Macarthur to James Macarthur, 28 December 1842, and W. Macarthur to G. Cox, 17 July 1843 (Macarthur Papers, vol. 39); postscript of Charles Cowper in William Cowper to Macquarie Cowper, 31 August 1828, and William Cowper to Macquarie Cowper, 29 September 1828 (Cowper Papers).

would lay Melbourne in ashes and crop the ears of all Protestants. In February he and William Kerr, newly appointed editor of the *Port Phillip Patriot*, a sound separation man, a sound liberal in politics, and an Orangeman in religion, called on Henry Condell, a merchant by profession and first mayor of the corporation of Melbourne. They persuaded him that it was his duty as a Protestant to keep a Catholic out of the Legislative Council of New South Wales. Condell's mother was a Catholic, but in the brief dog-fight that followed no one drew attention to that little irony. On 17 June the Catholic mob tore Condell's supporters from their horses, threatened to tar and feather J. P. Fawkner and other Protestants and tear out the hearts of all Orangemen in Melbourne, but, as in Sydney, the wild boars had no influence on the result. Condell was elected. The Protestants then hailed Condell as the champion of the British right of private judgement against Catholic despotism and superstition.[15]

On nomination day for the District of Port Phillip the Irish mob again hurled their slum slang at Lang, and hissed and groaned. On polling day in Melbourne, Geelong and Portland on 20 June, Catholics and Orangemen kept up their noisy exchanges, their brass bands beat out their respective professions of faith, and their drunken supporters hurled vile epithets at each other. When the returning officer declared the results of the poll on 24 June, it was clear that the conservatives, the supporters of squatterdom's domination, rather than the Orangemen or the followers of Saint Patrick had had a great victory. Charles Hotson Ebden, the squatter from Albury on the Murray, headed the poll. He was followed by Thomas Walker, a merchant who had fattened his purse in immigration and South Seas fisheries. Charles Nicholson, physician and landowner, with opinions as antediluvian as those of Alexander Berry but too shrewd to put them in such a way as to make people laugh at him, came next followed by Alexander Thomson of Kardinia Park, Geelong, another physician, a man with a deep interest in the treatment of the aborigines and a lofty disdain for the Melbourne mob but lacking the force of personality to cut a figure on the larger and stormier stage of Sydney. Lang sneaked into fifth position. That was no victory for the radicals, for at that time the day of Lang's vision of the colonies enjoying freedom and independence, the day when he became the darling of the radicals, was in the womb of time. The men who created the sound and fury on polling day were not qualified to vote. When the people hauled the Ebden carriage in triumph through the streets of Melbourne it was a symbol that the supporters of squatterdom rather than the bigots of the Protestant ascendancy or the benighted wearers of the green had won the day.[16]

[15] A. Gilchrist (ed.), *John Dunmore Lang* (2 vols, Melbourne, 1951), vol. I, pp. 335-7; *Port Phillip Patriot*, 9 February, 19, 23, 29 June 1843; *Port Phillip Herald*, 27 June 1843; *Weekly Register*, 9 December 1843.

[16] A. Gilchrist, op. cit., vol. I, p. 336; *Port Phillip Patriot*, 19 June 1843; *Port Phillip Herald*, 27 June 1843; Gipps to Stanley, 18 July 1843, *H.R.A.*, I. xxiii. 42-4; *Weekly Register*, 16 September, 28 October, 25 November 1843.

In all the other electorates squatterdom carried the day almost without opposition. Hannibal Macarthur was returned unopposed for Parramatta. Richard Windeyer, who held a high rank among the members of the legal profession in Sydney and so loved tormenting men in the witness box that he was a terror to witnesses cursed by any moral infirmity, was returned for the County of Durham. Up to that point he had professed himself to be an out-and-out radical in politics, but men of discernment were already predicting correctly that he would be found to be a staunch conservative. The electorate of Gloucester, Macquarie and Stanley returned Alexander McLeay, a staunch Tory of the old school, well known as a supporter of the arbitrary measures of General Darling and an opponent of the enlightened policy of Sir Richard Bourke. All the other country electorates returned sheep men to the Council. William Bradley, who had risen from comparative obscurity as the son of a sergeant in the 102nd Regiment to become a successful wool grower in the Monaro, was returned for Argyle. He had married Emily, the only daughter of William Hovell, another Tory of the old school, and so joined the 'cousin-hood' of squatterdom. In addition J. Coghill for St Vincent and Auckland, W. Bowman for Cumberland Boroughs, Terence Murray for Georgiana, King and Murray, D'Arcy Wentworth for Northumberland Boroughs, F. Lord for Bathurst, W. H. Suttor for Roxburgh, Phillip and Wellington, and W. Dumaresq for Hunter, Brisbane and Bligh were all solid for squatterdom's domination. The only exceptions were W. Foster, the member for the county of Northumberland, a lawyer who wanted to stand up to Wentworth's bullying and bluster about the sheep men but lacked the force for such an encounter, and John Panton, the member for the counties of Cook and Westmoreland, a Sydney merchant of some discernment who shared Charles Darwin's view that industry and trade would one day drag Australia into the nineteenth century, but nature had made him a silent man.[17]

Squatterdom also had supporters among the unofficial nominees. There was John Blaxland with pretensions to independence, but no pretensions to oratory, having never ventured beyond the enunciation of a detached sentence. Like McLeay, he was old, being then in his seventy-fifth year, a patriarch who was played out, who had given up 'leading the van of the Anglo-Saxon race in the onward march of civilization, Christianity and all the blessings that follow in their train'. He was waiting for day to break in the life of the world to come, rather than dreaming any great dream of what man could achieve in New South Wales. There was Thomas Icely, a landowner at Coombing and one of the finest gentlemen in the colony, who thought it was the duty of a legislator to preserve that sheep-walk which he believed God and nature had decreed for man in Australia. Then there was Hastings Elwin who was descended from a good country gentleman's family in Norfolk and was determined to 'keep it up' in New South Wales. So was

[17] *Weekly Register*, 19 August, 16, 23, 30 September, 25 November 1843; *S.M.H.*, 5 July 1843.

Edward Hamilton. Last but not least there was Alexander Berry, the man of retired habits and singularly antiquated ideas who was to go on telling the new Council what he had often told the old—namely, that there was common sense in the world before the birth of the present century.[18]

Of the official nominees—Lieutenant-General M. O'Donnell as Commander of the Forces, Deas Thomson as Colonial Secretary, C. D. Riddell as Colonial Treasurer, Lieutenant-Colonel John George Nathaniel Gibbes as Collector of Customs, W. Lithgow as Auditor-General, and Lieutenant-General George Barney as proxy for J. H. Plunkett, the Attorney-General, until the latter returned from England—Thomson and Plunkett were the only two with any pretence to a liberal position in politics. Colonel Gibbes was tied by marriage to that great 'cousinhood', the pastoral families of New South Wales. Riddell and Lithgow belonged to the old order. Plunkett was an enigma. Decidedly liberal in his political opinions, he was still somewhat diffident in letting himself go in public, except on subjects like equality before the law, on which he always spoke with energy and firmness. This well-known support for equality before the law suggested that he would not fall in with any demand from squatterdom that they should be endowed with the privileges and titles of the landed aristocracy of the Old Country. Deas Thomson was a man who had already won praise for his active business habits and urbane deportment. Up to that point fate had cast him in the role of a server, first to his father-in-law Sir Richard Bourke and then to Sir George Gipps. Under the new constitution with the Governor no longer to sit in Council, the Colonial Secretary became the government leader in the house. Just as Wentworth and James Macarthur flowered on the death of their fathers, so Thomson, with the Governor no longer looking over his shoulder, began to display the judgement and tact that were to win him the respect of all shades of opinion, and even conceal from radicals and liberals his melancholy foreboding that those 'wild boars' of Sydney would one day bring everything he believed in to ruin.[19]

At the first meeting of the new Legislative Council on 1 August the members elected that staunch Tory of the old school Alexander McLeay to the office of Speaker. Wentworth marked his membership of the Legislative Council as he marked every event in his life by offending grossly against good taste in a savage, coarse attack on McLeay as an octogenarian who could neither hear nor understand anything except how to accumulate wealth and 'place'. The press accused Wentworth of coveting the position. 'Demosthenes himself', the *Weekly Register* wrote, 'having attained the object of his ambition, wishes to pocket the people's money, and to recline [on] a woolsack!' By then Wentworth expected abuse from the scribblers of Botany Bay. McLeay had the benevolence and unaffected kindliness as well as the love of recognition and 'showing off' to commend him for the position, for he had

---

[18] *Weekly Register*, 4 November 1843; plaque for John Blaxland on interior wall of St John's Church, Parramatta; *Weekly Register*, 7 October, 11 December 1843.
[19] *Weekly Register*, 10 February 1844, 23 September, 13 January 1843.

devoted his life to science and the promotion of charity, education and religion. For this he had already won the praise, respect and regard of his fellow-citizens. It was his aim and his end, looking humbly to the anchor of his faith, to obtain the testimony that, in Christ, 'he pleased God'. His wife, Eliza, the honoured mother of seventeen children, had a face of surpassing beauty, and that still laughter women who have known tenderness with a man wear in their eyes.[20]

While all this tumult and shouting were going on in Sydney and Melbourne, William Grant Broughton was finding the insensibility towards religion of the country people of New South Wales very distressing to contemplate. At Cam-ya-Allyn in the county of Durham on 24 June he told the squatters, shepherds and itinerant workers, 'Your riches are corrupted, or have rotted away'. In June, July and August he visited Singleton, Scone, Mudgee, Cullen Bullen and Bathurst to tell those who gathered to listen to him, 'one thing is needful'. In September he embarked on the *Rajah* for Port Phillip. With a gale blowing the ship far out to sea he preached to all on board on the text, 'He talked with them, and said unto them, Be of good cheer: it is I: be not afraid'. Though he suffered extremely from seasickness, he continued to exhort the crew with sermons on texts such as, 'Are not two sparrows sold for a farthing?' In the Port Phillip District he offered consolation to the sick and the dying, and provided an opportunity for the faithful to partake of the holy sacraments so that they should not lack those means of grace which would guard them from damnation in this world and from being sent to Hell in the next world.

He found that Melbourne was still debating the Willis question. In the preceding May, La Trobe decided reluctantly that because of the judge's excitability, wielding a power close to despotism in his court and allowing his private passions to collide with his public duty, he should ask Gipps to remove him from office since he had lost the confidence and esteem of the colonial government and his continuance in office was incompatible with the real well-being of the community. Gipps submitted all the relative papers to the Executive Council which resolved on 17 June to issue a Writ of Amotion to remove Willis from office. By the time Broughton arrived in Melbourne all the very best people had put their signatures to a petition approving the action, and over a thousand had signed a counter-petition but they were said to be people of no substance, importance or influence. One woman wrote in her diary, 'Poor man! . . . he was never considered quite sane in his conduct both public and private'. Another dismissed him as 'a disreputable old rip who, I think, was in consort with the devil'. So Port Phillip lost a man with a scurrilous tongue and was to get in his place a judge whose family was to leave its mark on the intellectual and artistic life of the whole society. But Gipps and La Trobe were not to know then what was to flow from an action

---

[20] *S.M.H.*, 2 August 1843; plaque to Alexander McLeay on interior wall of St James's Church, Sydney; *Weekly Register*, 29 July, 5 August 1843; portraits of Alexander and Elizabeth McLeay in Dixson Gallery, Mitchell Library.

which left the 'not-very-much-sought-after position of resident judge of Port Phillip going begging.'[21]

By then public confidence was at an end in New South Wales. The money market was rocking as if the ground were moved by an earthquake. Formerly men were anxious to become owners of sheep, and those who had them were anxious to enlarge their flocks. In the first half of 1843 those who were asked to purchase a flock, even at their own price, shrugged their shoulders, and replied that they would not accept them as a gift. All sections of the population were affected. In 1842, as the *Sydney Morning Herald* put it in January 1843, the commercial aspect had been dismal enough: 'commerce, agriculture, and even the great staple in which they once exulted, as their golden fleece, were alike laid waste by the blasts of a pitiless adversity'. In 1842 there had been six hundred insolvencies in a free population of little more than a hundred thousand souls. In April 1842 the firm of R. Duke and Company collapsed; in June 1842 the affairs of T. Gore and Company were in the insolvency court; joint stock companies such as the General Steam Navigation Company and the Sydney and Hunter's River Auction Company were in difficulties in 1842; in March 1843 the firm of Hughes and Hosking collapsed, bringing down with it the Bank of Australia. John Terry Hughes and John Hosking, who carried on business as merchants, brokers, and general agents at Market Wharf, Sydney, had married co-heiresses of Samuel Terry. Hosking had been first mayor of Sydney. The very foundations of successful, bourgeois, emancipist Sydney society were rocking.

In November Richard Jones, a member of the Legislative Council from 1828 to 1843, a magistrate and a prominent figure in the public and social life of Sydney, with interests in deep-sea whaling, sandalwood and huge pastoral holdings, was declared insolvent. Prices for primary produce on the Sydney market tumbled. At the end of December 1841 the price of beef and mutton was 4¾–5d per pound; by January 1843 it was 2½–3¼d per pound, and by December of the same year 1–2d per pound. Wheat prices also tumbled from 5–6s a bushel in December 1841 to about 3s 6d in December 1843. Wool which had sold for 25d a pound in 1836 was down to 12–13d in 1843. Prime wethers which were selling for 6s to 7s 6d in December 1842 were going for half that price by the middle of 1843. Fat cattle dropped from £7 in March 1841 to under £3 in June 1843. Working bullocks, valued at £8 each early in 1841 were being sold at seven for £14 by the second half of 1843. The prices for horses almost halved.

By the second half of 1843, 1243 mechanics or labourers were unemployed

[21] W. G. Broughton, *The Church in Australia* (London, 1843), pp. 6-33; La Trobe to Col. Sec. of New South Wales, 20 February 1843 (Gipps-La Trobe Correspondence); La Trobe to Gipps, 29 May 1843; Gipps to La Trobe, 13, 15 May 1843; Gipps to Stanley, 26 June 1843, *H.R.A.*, I. xxii. 796-7; Gipps to Stanley, 19 July 1843, *H.R.A.*, I. xxiii. 48-52; *Port Phillip Herald*, 27, 30 June 1843; *Port Phillip Patriot*, 27 June 1843; *Port Phillip Gazette*, 28 June 1843; H. McCrae (ed.), *Georgiana's Journal* (2nd ed., Sydney, 1934), entry for 28 June 1843, p. 101; Jillian Raven, John Walpole Willis in Port Phillip (thesis, History Department, Australian National University).

in Sydney. After adding the number of wives and children dependent on these persons 3750 out of a population of approximately 37000 were facing destitution. Henry Parkes was finding his income was not sufficient to support his family because of the 'fearful epidemic' of insolvency which had broken out in Sydney. Mechanics and labourers were taking employment at 40–50 per cent lower wages. Mechanics in desperation were taking the tools of their trade to the pawnbroker or the auction market. Edward Mullens, a painter by trade, had brought his wife and seven children to Sydney to enjoy that 'bellyful and sunshine' promised by the emigrant agents in the United Kingdom only to be unemployed for seven months. John Drummond Crawford got drunk one night as the commercial aspect began to be 'fearfully dismal' and was dismissed from his position of clerk in Sydney Gaol, and suffered want, as did his family, for seven months because his act of folly happened to coincide with this other crisis in society of which he was not guilty.[22]

Those in authority and the publicists detected a moral lesson in what was happening. Gipps believed nearly all the evils of the commercial crisis were to be ascribed to the reckless rapidity with which capital of all sorts, but especially banking capital, was poured into the colony to seek greedy gains at usurious interest between the years 1834 and 1840. The lenders of money in New South Wales had lent largely to parties who never ought to have been trusted. The *Weekly Register* and its adversary the *Sydney Morning Herald* heartily agreed that the distress was the natural and inevitable consequence of gambling, folly and extravagance. The people had 'played with the dice'; in future they must wield the spade. The *Sydney Record*, a fine flower of the Anglican pharisees in Sydney said the people had allowed the charms of social life and its moderate enjoyments to give way to vulgar profusion and wasteful expenditure. Men had left their counters to dissipate over the table. The clerk, the mechanic, and the bullock-driver had rioted away their time. Up-country squatters had deserted their estates to frequent the town and its distracting pleasures. When the extravagance of private life had failed, they had indulged themselves in the excitement of public balls and dinners. A deluded people had been seduced into universal folly. Now they must suffer

[22] Letter of A. Berry to *S.M.H.*, 14 April 1843; *S.M.H.*, 2 January 1843; Return of the Quantity and Value of Wool Exported from the Colony of New South Wales (including the District of Port Phillip), from the Year 1836 to 1845, Inclusive, *V. & P.* (L.C. N.S.W.), 1846, vol. 2; market prices for livestock in *S.M.H.*, seriatim from December 1841 to December 1843; on the number of insolvencies see Return to Address of Mr. Lamb on Number of Estates Sequestrated, 19 June 1849, *V. & P.* (L.C. N.S.W.), 1849, vol. 1; Gipps to Stanley, 31 March 1843, *H.R.A.*, I. xxii. 611-14; Gipps to Stanley, 7 October 1843, *H.R.A.*, I. xxiii. 180-2; Gipps to Stanley, 1 January 1845, *H.R.A.*, I. xxiv. 164-7; S. J. Butlin, *Foundations of the Australian Monetary System 1788-1851* (Melbourne 1953), pp. 346-50; H. Parkes to his sister, 3 September 1842, H. Parkes, *An Emigrant's Home Letters* (Sydney, 1896), pp. 129-30; Report from the Select Committee on the Petition from Distressed Mechanics and Labourers, *V. & P.* (L.C. N.S.W.), 1843; Evidence of E. Mullens and J. D. Crawford, ibid.; Gipps to Stanley, 19 August 1843, *H.R.A.*, I. xxiii. 86.

the just punishment for their sin of wanton extravagance. Down in Melbourne the *Port Phillip Patriot* also wrote of the depression as a just retribution for human wickedness and folly.[23]

In January 1842 the Consul-General for the United States of America in Sydney attributed the depression of the commercial and agricultural interests of the colony to the decline in the demand for English woollen manufactures which had almost entirely prostrated the wool-growing interest of New South Wales. By mid-1843 he was telling his superiors in Washington that only a revival of trade in Great Britain and the United States would give that increased value to the wool on which the prosperity of the colony mainly depended. The *Port Phillip Patriot* agreed that the fall in the price of wool 'at home' had proved very unfavourable to the clips of 1841 and 1842, but they hastened to add that this empirical cause was not as powerful as that greed which had fed the speculation mania. Some blamed the banks for making credit easily available to feed the speculation mania at excessive rates of interest, the colonial government for aggravating the situation by first making funds available to banks, then withdrawing them in 1840–1 to pay for immigration, and so causing contraction of credit. Others blamed the increasing cost of labour due to the cessation of transportation in 1840, the drought and the increased price of land.[24]

When the wattle blossomed in August 1843 the merchants of Sydney, Melbourne, Hobart and Adelaide were still gloomy. By contrast the flock-masters of New South Wales were cheerful. In July 'Black Harry' O'Brien of Yass slaughtered his unprofitable sheep, boiled them in large iron vats, extracted the fat as tallow, which he packed in wooden casks and shipped to England where it raised about £3 a hundredweight. O'Brien's brother-in-law, William Wilson, introduced boiling down to the squatters in the Clarence and Richmond river districts. Edward Hamilton, a member of the Legislative Council, boiled down his sheep at Wooroowoolgen on the Richmond. George Russell at Golf Hill in Australia Felix learnt about boiling down from reading a letter the explorer Hamilton Hume had inserted in a Sydney newspaper. In September Terence Aubrey Murray boiled down one thousand wethers to pay his small debts to the merchants and outfitters of Sydney Town. In October W. C. Wentworth, having engaged a competent superin-

---

[23] Gipps to Stanley, 6 May 1843, *H.R.A.*, I. xxii. 707-9; *S.M.H.*, 16 May, 18 July 1843; *Weekly Register*, 5 August 1843; *Sydney Record*, 7 October 1843; 'An enquiry into the causes of the present commercial depression in the Australian colonies, Part II', *Port Phillip Patriot*, 1 June 1843.

[24] Consul-General to Secretary of State of U.S.A., 1 January 1842, 1 July 1843, 1 January 1844 (Reports from United States Consul-General in Sydney); *S.M.H.*, 16 May, 18 July 1843; *Colonial Observer*, 16 September 1843; *New South Wales Monthly Magazine*, vol. 1, July 1843; Report from Select Committee on Monetary Confusion, *V. & P.* (L.C. N.S.W.), 1843; *Port Phillip Patriot*, 29 May, 1, 5, 8, 22 June 1843; S. J. Butlin, *Foundations of the Australian Monetary System*; T. A. Coghlan, *Labour and Industry in Australia* (4 vols, Oxford, 1918), vol. 1; B. Fitzpatrick, *The British Empire in Australia* (Melbourne, 1941); S. H. Roberts, *The Squatting Age in Australia, 1835-1847* (Melbourne, 1937).

tendent to boil down his own surplus stock on his station at Windermere
near Maitland offered to accommodate the settlers in the districts of the
Hunter, Wellington, Liverpool Plains and New England at 9d for slaughtering, skinning, cutting up and boiling down each sheep, and 3d per sheep for
washing skins, taking off the whole of the wool, drying and putting it into
packs, the grass to be gratis and the shepherds to be supplied with rations at
moderate charges. Sheep which were selling at 3–4s a head in June were
selling for 9–10s a head between August and November. The moralizers
urged the sheep men not to squander their wealth in return for quick profits:
'A sheep shorn may live to be shorn again; but a sheep boiled down may be
gone forever.' Ben Boyd thought of boiling down as 'a melancholy expedient',
which must ultimately ruin the colony by greatly reducing the number of
sheep. Migrants from Ireland gasped at the wantonness and folly of allowing
the heads of sheep slaughtered for boiling down to rot on the plains of New
South Wales while their fellow-countrymen starved.[25]

While the fires were being stoked to rescue squatterdom from disaster,
the spokesmen for the sheep men in the Legislative Council were using the
institutions of the state to give them the financial security with which to
weather any future trough. On 10 August Wentworth moved in the Legislative Council to bring in a bill enabling the proprietors of sheep and cattle
to give a preferable lien on their clips of wool and to grant mortgage securities on cattle, sheep and horses without delivery of the same to the mortgagees.
At the second reading stage on 31 August he explained that the object of the
bill was two-fold: first, to give parties who were in possession of money, and
were disposed to advance it upon wool, a security upon that wool, even while
it was upon the back of the sheep and, secondly, to give the owners of sheep
and cattle an opportunity of raising money upon them by means of a valid
mortgage. By the end of September the Council had passed the bill and
Gipps had added the Governor's assent to this Act to provide squatterdom
with a happy issue out of its financial afflictions.

When Bland presented a petition to the Legislative Council that the rate
of interest charged by banks be restrained by law to a fair and reasonable
amount, they threw out the proposal by voting twenty-one votes to thirteen
that a bill embodying such a proposal be read a second time this day one
month. On 21 September there was some amusing clowning by Alexander
Berry who, like his fellow sheep man, Charles Campbell, felt it was a bit steep
for banks to get away with lending money upon landed property at the rate
of 15 per cent. But the sheep men who had just used the state to put money in
their purse solemnly resolved that any interference by the state with the

---

[25] *Port Phillip Herald*, 11 August 1843; *S.M.H.*, 21 September 1843; Gwendoline
Wilson, *Murray of Yarralumla* (Melbourne, 1968), pp. 151-3; Margaret Kiddle, *Men of
Yesterday* (Melbourne, 1961), p. 136; P. L. Brown (ed.), *The Narrative of George Russell
of Golf Hill* (London, 1935), pp. 204-5; Richmond River Historical Society, *A History
of the Richmond River* (Lismore, n.d.), p. 3; advertisement in *Sydney Record*, 21
October 1843; evidence of Benjamin Boyd to Select Committee on Immigration, 27
September 1843, *V. & P.* (L.C. N.S.W.), 1843.

operations of the law of supply and demand was foreign to the object of legitimate government.[26]

The men who sniffed danger in the use of the institutions of the state to regulate the economy shouted a loud 'Amen' to the proposals by Gipps to slash salaries in the government service and reduce the number of government employees. Some three thousand of the working classes met at the racecourse on 7 August to discuss how the state could best relieve their several necessities. One man asked government to introduce the American system of free grants of land to industrious members of the working classes, the working class of Sydney being an early convert to the petit-bourgeois ambition of property ownership. Other speakers urged government to withdraw convicts from Sydney to create employment for the starving artisans. When representatives from the meeting asked Gipps to give such an undertaking on 8 August, he told them he had no power to withdraw assigned servants from Sydney.

The members of the Australian Mutual Protection Society drew up a petition in which they urged government to withdraw assigned servants from Sydney and force them to work in the interior rather than offer inducements to free workers to go up-country. The former habits of the working men disqualified them for agricultural labour or pastoral pursuits, to say nothing of their being thus deprived of the comforts of civilized life, and their children debarred the advantages of that education and religious instruction so indispensable to the formation of a virtuous population. The members of the Council insisted that it was not a legitimate function of government to 'tinker' with the economy. Moved though they were by compassion at the suffering of the workers in their state of utter destitution and want, the mysterious laws of political economy rendered them powerless to come to the assistance of the workers. The *Weekly Register* tersely pointed out that the wool men in Council had engineered financial schemes for the benefit of the 'silly squatters', but hid behind the laws of political economy when it came to helping men who were perishing in the streets.[27]

The other field in which Gipps and his government deemed it judicious to economize was state aid for the civilization and protection of the aborigines. The climate of opinion in Sydney was favourable to a substantial chop in such government expenditure. In mid-year when all the high-minded men of Sydney were busy ferreting out examples of extravagance or useless expen-

[26] *Australian*, 11, 23, 25, 28, 30 August, 1, 4, 6 September 1843; *Australasian Chronicle*, 6 September 1843; *Australian*, 22 September 1843; *Weekly Register*, 12 August, 9 September 1843; memorandum by Sir George Gipps on state aid during the depression, 1843 in *Economic Record*, vol. 39, 1963, pp. 371-6.

[27] See, for example, report of debate in the Legislative Council on 16 October 1843 on proposal to reduce the estimate for the judicial establishments, *Sydney Record*, 21 October 1843; *Weekly Register*, 5, 12 August, 1843; The Humble Petition of the Members of the Australian Mutual Protection Association, and Others, *V. & P.* (L.C. N.S.W.), 1843; Report from Select Committee on the Petition from Distressed Mechanics and Labourers, *V. & P.* (L.C. N.S.W.), 1843.

diture of public money, Gipps opened a despatch from Stanley in which the
latter informed him that he had decided that the aborigines showed little
desire for instruction, that in their relations with the white man they displayed a 'thoughtlessness, a spirit of independence, ingratitude and want of
straightforward dealing' which often tried Europeans 'in the extreme'. He
had come to the conclusion that aborigines were being gradually swept away
by debauchery and other evils arising from their intermixture with Europeans. The same June the press in Sydney and Melbourne was insisting that
the aborigine would never become civilized. He was too degraded to marry
a European or to be of any service in the white man's society. The aborigine
would always be in the way while British enterprise spread over the continent
of New Holland. All experience pointed to the conclusion that they must
die off in the 'unwholesome atmosphere of civilization'. With government
revenue shrinking rapidly with the decline in land rates, it was fatuous to
spend what little they had on attempting to civilize the uncivilizable. In 1841
government spent £1629 16s 2d on the missions, and in 1842 £1046 0s 5d; in
1843 government spent £125, and in 1844 nothing. By March 1844 Gipps was
writing to Stanley that there were no longer any missions receiving aid from
his government. The last of them, the Wesleyan mission, had been closed at
the end of 1843 because of its want of success. As for the protectorate, he did
not think it was right entirely to break up that establishment, but instructed
La Trobe to reduce expenditure from £7967 5s 1d in 1842 to £3000 in 1843. In
the latter year La Trobe spent nearly £4000, but after a polite reminder from
Gipps on the need for rigid economy he managed to keep the figure just
below £3000 in 1844, where it remained each year till the protectorate was
wound up in 1850.[28]

It was a grim year for the aborigines. At Maitland in October two aborigines, known to the white men as Harry and Melville, were found guilty
of the murder of a white man at Stanhope and sentenced to death. On the
morning of the execution the two condemned men talked with some black
gins from the town and bade them an emotional farewell. After they ascended
the scaffold and the ropes were adjusted around their necks, the Reverend Mr
Wilton told the crowd which had gathered to witness the execution that both
Harry and Melville acknowledged that the Governor was doing right to take
their lives, because they had committed the crime for which they were about
to die. The clergyman then left the unhappy men. The bolt was drawn and
Harry and Melville were launched into eternity, or nothingness, while their
own people sobbed piteously.[29]

By then those with eyes to see in Maitland as in other centres of Australia
were familiar with the sorry aspects of the story of the coming of the white

[28] Gipps to La Trobe, 15 May, 28 July 1843 (Gipps-La Trobe Correspondence); Stanley
to Gipps, 20 December 1842, *H.R.A.*, I. xxii. 436-9; 'Enquiry into the causes of the
present commercial depression in the Australian colonies, Part III', *Port Phillip Patriot*,
8 June 1843; Gipps to Stanley, 21 March 1844, *H.R.A.*, I. xxii. 484-97; E. J. B. Foxcroft,
Australian Native Policy (Melbourne, 1941), pp. 83-5; Papers on Aborigines, *P.P.*, 1844,
xxxiv, 627, pp. 315-771.
[29] *Weekly Register*, 28 October 1843.

man. They had seen the bodies of aborigines dangling in the hangman's noose; they had seen the decay of the aborigine from the noble savage to the degraded 'cadger of booze and baccy'; they had seen the abomination of flogging; they had seen the drays pass through bearing men and their goods up-country and had seen the same men years later broken by drought, the catastrophic fall in prices, diseases in their stock and marauding aborigines and bushrangers; they had seen what years of work trying to exact a living from a hard country with only the labour of their hands did to a man's face, especially the expression in the eyes and the shape of the mouth. That August in the very trough of the commercial depression, before the boiling down establishments lifted the gloom in the pastoral industry, the people of Maitland gathered in the Northumberland Hotel for a concert. One man recited a ballad about a success story: the new chum just landed on Australian shores cursed his luck, deplored his weary lot, and sighed for the joys of old England, but in six months he became a squatter roaming merrily, content to take his pipe and pot of tea by the bushfire:

> . . . Ask him, and, lo! he'll ring
> It's praise and say he's happy as a king
> This is the true philosophy.

That touched those present very little, not just because the words were lacking in memorability but because the sentiments set up no resonance deep inside them.

Then another entertainer sang a song which he called 'Billy Barlow in Australia'. It was a song about a man who had been 'down on his luck' at home in the Old Country. That was something with which this audience of migrants and expirees and descendants of convicts were very familiar. The song went on to tell how his old aunt had died and left him a thousand. So off to Australia came Billy Barlow. Here he met one misfortune after another. In Sydney a merchant 'gammoned' all his cash out of him for stock and a station past the colony's bounds. In New England bushrangers, police, disease, and drought killed off all his stock and robbed him of all he possessed.

> Then once more I got free, but in poverty's toil;
> I've no 'cattle for salting', no 'sheep for to boil';
> I can't get a job—tho' to any I'd stoop,
> It 'twas only the making of 'portable soup'.
> Oh dear, lackaday, oh,
> Pray give some employment to Billy Barlow.

The song ended not with a whine or any playing for self pity or any promise of things ever being any different; it ended with a sardonic joke:

> So if any lass here has 'ten thousand' or so,
> She can just drop a line addressed 'Mr. Barlow'.
> Oh dear, lackaday, oh,
> The dear angel shall be 'Mrs. William Barlow'.

The audience gave him three hearty cheers. He had touched on one thing they knew in life—failure. In time the only public monuments Australians (from tiny hamlets on the Darling to the capital cities) would erect would be to commemorate great failures. The folk heroes would be men who had displayed the qualities of the hero when defeated by overwhelming odds—explorers such as Sturt, Leichhardt, Burke and Wills, and bushrangers such as Ned Kelly.[30]

When they came to speak about themselves and their response to the harsh, weird beauty of their country they fumbled like men who accepted the proposition that the price of exile from Europe was to be robbed of the charm of life. When they fronted up to all that was missing in their world—the storied tombs, the sculptured shrines, the fretted roofs, the princely halls, and the 'mournful scenes of guilt', since their 'new regions' were so far free from that long drip of human tears 'which peoples old in tragedy' had 'left upon the centuried years'—they could only manage a rather solemn, humourless prophesy that

> Apollo will ere long erect a throne,
> The Muses with them bring their varied lore;
> Knowledge be prized, and useful arts atone
> For that neglect so many now deplore.[31]

Their political life, too, was characterized by the timidity and obsequiousness of colonials, rather than the rumbustious arrogance of men in charge of their own destiny. In the Legislative Council Wentworth and Lang tangled with their colonial masters. On 27 October 1843 Wentworth accused Gipps of interfering with that perfect freedom of debate which was the inherent privilege of every branch of a free legislature. On 21 December Lang asked the members of the Legislative Council to resolve that the right of Her Majesty's Government under the Constitution Act of 1842 to nominate one-third of their members was, in the opinion of Council, contrary to the Bill of Rights and the fundamental principles of the British constitution, subversive of the constitutional privileges of the free inhabitants of the colony, unjustifiable in any principle of expediency or necessity, and irreconcilable with the establishment of a system of government professedly based on the recognition of popular rights in the territory. Except for Wentworth and Windeyer the other councillors shrank from that. If, it was argued, the colony was really prepared to assert its independence, if its grievances were so great that the yoke of Downing Street was too heavy to be borne by free men, if it was desirable that the colony should govern itself, that the patronage of the Crown

[30] *Maitland Mercury*, 2 September 1843.
[31] W.H.B., *Headlong Rhymes by a Policeman* (Launceston, 1843); *The Annual Report of the Commercial Reading Rooms and Library for the Year 1843* (Sydney, 1843); James Curr, 'Stanzas, Written on the Heads by Moonlight', *Weekly Register*, 9 December 1843; T. Hardy, 'On an Invitation to the United States', *Collected Poems of Thomas Hardy* (London, 1919), p. 99.

should be forthwith abolished, that the filling up of appointments from 'home' was an 'unmixed evil', then the sooner they selected their Washingtons, Jeffersons, Hamiltons and Franklins the better. But if their separation from the British Empire was to be postponed for at least another century, as they presumed all wise men would wish it to be, it was the height of folly to stir up rancorous and interminable hostility between the colony and those in authority. Surely it was possible for members of the legislature to examine minutely every item of public expenditure without indulging in such a 'heartless, misanthropic, and disloyal spirit'.[32]

That November all those in favour of the British connection congratulated Gipps on having at long last in Council a defender of the government who could speak as well as anyone who had ever been heard within the walls of the Council chamber. By December this new apologist for the government of New South Wales was holding up Wentworth to ridicule as a 'darling dodo' who wanted to preserve their country as an asylum for all the exploded fallacies of the rest of the world. Robert Lowe had arrived in Sydney with his wife in October of the preceding year, hoping that New South Wales could cure the weaknesses his flesh was heir to. Nature had endowed him with great intelligence but had given him the weak eyes of an albino and such a vulnerable look on the face that men averted their gaze when he approached. Neither Gipps nor anyone else who rejoiced that Wentworth had met his match noticed that nature had not been lavish with Lowe in gifts of the heart, but had given him the constitution of a 'psychological monster', who was so hollow inside that he was quite capable of presenting a brilliant argument while remaining quite untouched by any generous or noble impulse. He was a man who had no principles but was driven by some subterranean desire to punish humanity at large for the cruel jokes nature had played on him.[33]

At the dinner to commemorate the fifty-sixth anniversary of the foundation of New South Wales on 26 January 1844 an air of great cordiality prevailed between the leaders of squatterdom and the Governor of New South Wales. It was one of those days in Sydney when the sky presented one beautiful expanse of unvaried loveliness. This January the dinner was held on the naval ship *General Hewett*, with the Royal Standard flying at the masthead. The chair was taken by Ben Boyd, supported on his right by the Governor and on his left by Lady Gipps. At speech time Boyd reminded those present that there was no part of the world in which there were more loyal subjects of the Queen than in New South Wales. After flattering Gipps as 'a

---

[32] *V. & P.* (L.C. N.S.W.), 27 October, 21 December 1843; article on retrenchment in *Weekly Register*, 21 October 1843.

[33] Gipps to Stanley, 10 November 1843, *H.R.A.*, I. xxiii. 216; Ruth Knight, *Illiberal Liberal: Robert Lowe in New South Wales 1842-1850* (Melbourne, 1966), pp. 1-64; Gipps to La Trobe, 25 November 1843 (Gipps-La Trobe Correspondence); S. C. McCulloch, 'Unguarded comments on the administration of New South Wales, 1839-46', *Hist. Studies*, vol. 9, 1959; Gipps to Stanley, 1 January 1844, *H.R.A.*, I. xxiii. 309-11; C. Nicholson to A. Cunningham, 4 March 1849 (Cunningham Papers, vol. 3); *Weekly Register*, 16 December 1843.

brilliant ornament of the profession to which he belonged', Boyd turned to him and said, 'give us immigration, give us population for the interior'. Gipps was deeply pleased. After they had drunk his health he told them he shared Mr Boyd's belief that the colony would one day become one of the fairest gems in the British Crown. After dinner the dancing began, and as the magic moment of darkness came down over Sydney Harbour no one present sensed that the Governor of New South Wales was about to raise the whole question of squatterdom's domination in New South Wales.[34]

Gipps had already decided that the time had come to tackle the problem of the way of life of the squatters beyond the limits of location. He realized that it was a problem of great complexity. Outside the limits of location there was a population of 9885 people stretched over an area of 1100 square miles, the inhabitants of which were beyond the influence of civilization, without a minister of religion and destitute of all means of instruction. In those areas a race of Englishmen was springing up in 'a state of untutored barbarism' because the occupiers of that vast wilderness had no inducement to make permanent improvements in it simply because they had no property of any sort in the soil they occupied. Great numbers of young men who were in every way entitled to be called gentlemen, men who would make excellent magistrates, were treating with disrespect the very government they would be the stoutest defenders of once they achieved security of tenure. So long as there was a high minimum price for land, it was not economic for the sheep men in the inland to purchase a freehold in their runs. So long as the squatters' only title to their runs was the annual £10 licence fee and the stock tax, they had no incentive to make improvements. So long as the squatters outside the boundaries had no security of tenure, the sheep lobby in the Legislative Council—Wentworth, Berry, Hamilton, Icely, Dumaresq and company— were not prepared to use their power to vote the necessary supplies to take civilization into the Australian bush. Gipps wanted to devise a scheme for improving the conditions of the squatters by giving to the occupier of a run or station a 'property in his own improvements'. He also believed the 'monster squatters', men such as Ben Boyd, W. C. Wentworth, William Bradley, the Van Diemen's Land Company, the Henty brothers and Pratt Winter should pay more than £10 a year for the right to depasture their stock over two hundred to five hundred thousand acres of land.[35]

Honourable and upright as ever, Gipps asked for the advice of two men who had no vested interest in the squatting system, but a high-minded desire to end barbarism in the Australian bush and to cement the alliance between gentlemen squatters and the government of New South Wales—the Lord Bishop of Australia, William Grant Broughton, and the commander of the forces, Lieutenant-General Maurice O'Connell. The three of them agreed on proposals which were submitted to the Executive Council which modified

[34] *Weekly Register*, 13 January 1844; *S.M.H.*, 27 January 1844.
[35] Gipps to Stanley, 17 January 1844, *H.R.A.*, I. xxiii, 336-46; Gipps to Stanley, 3 April 1844, *H.R.A.*, I. xxiii. 507-15.

them and prepared them for publication in the *New South Wales Government Gazette* on 2 April. Under these regulations His Excellency the Governor directed that parties occupying stations in separate districts would in
future be required to take out a separate licence for each such district and
pay the established fee of £10 for the same. In future no person would be
allowed to take up a new station either in the same district in which his stock
might be depastured or in any other without having first obtained a separate
licence for the same under the recommendation of the Commissioner of
Crown Lands in the relevant district and paid the fee of £10 thereon. From
and after 1 July 1845 a separate licence must be taken out and the fee of £10
paid thereon for each separate station or run occupied, even though situated
in the same district; no one station was to consist of more than twenty square
miles; every station at a greater distance than seven miles from another would
be deemed a separate station; no one licence would cover a station capable of
depasturing more than 4000 sheep or 500 head of cattle, or a mixed herd of
sheep and cattle equal to either 500 head of cattle or 4000 sheep.

To give the squatters an incentive to make improvements in their runs
the Governor proposed that any person who had occupied a station for not
less than five years might demand to purchase as a homestead any part of his
run at £1 per acre provided he did not purchase less than 320 acres. On the
same day the courier from Government House placed a copy of the new
squatting regulations and the accompanying despatch for transmission to
London on board the *General Hewett*, that ship on which only two months
earlier Sir George and Ben Boyd had drunk those toasts of undying friendship between the sheep men and the government of New South Wales. Four
days later a steamship towed the *General Hewett* to the Heads, which she
cleared with a favourable wind, and the party which had gone for the trip
returned to Sydney much pleased with their outing. They came back to a
fierce hurricane brewing over the public life of New South Wales.[36]

On 9 April some 350 gentlemen assembled in the saloon of the Royal Hotel.
Bland took the chair. Wentworth, who had many scores to settle against
Sir George, being not the least thwarted in his attempt to lay his hands on the
South Island of New Zealand, asked them what the value was of electing
representatives of the people if an autocrat could, on his own authority, make
an imposition of this kind. After reminding them that 'these wilds belong
to us, and not to the British Government', he called for a 'reverberating yell'
against Gipps which would 'speak plainly the feelings and curses of those
whom he had oppressed'. He asked them to resolve that in the opinion of the
meeting the regulations were unconstitutional in their application and character, oppressive in their influence, and calculated to add materially to the
existing distresses of the colony. He ended by calling on them not to take up
arms but to use passive and constitutional resistance. A great change had come

[36] *New South Wales Government Gazette*, 2 April 1844; encls in Gipps to Stanley,
3 April 1844, C.O. 201/345; encls nos 2 and 3 in Gipps to Stanley, 1 May 1844, C.O.
201/346; *S.M.H.*, 5, 8, 10 April 1844.

over Wentworth since those days in the 1820s when he had urged his fellow-countrymen to 'shake off the yoke'. The behaviour of those 'wild boars' of Sydney during the election of the Legislative Council had convinced him of the role of the British connection in preserving squatterdom's domination.

Ben Boyd, the 'aggrandizer' who held a licence to depasture stock on 426 000 acres of land in return for paying a fee of £10 and was now expected to pay over a hundred pounds in a year when squatters lacked cash, understandably spoke of Gipps as an agent of 'grinding oppression' rather than as one of the 'fairest ornaments' in the British Crown. He asked them to resolve that un-certain occupancy and increase in charges had a most ruinous tendency upon the most valuable property in the colony and would continue to do so until fixity of tenure was granted to the occupier. Henry Macdermott, known to be a bit of a leveller and a chartist, asked for leave to speak on behalf of the small land-holders, who were being hounded by the large proprietors, but the 'mustachioed and long-spurred' stock-holders shouted him down. Francis Kemble, who had arrived in Sydney the previous year with sundry steam-engines and machinery, then asked the meeting to agree that the commercial and trading classes of the community were most intimately connected with and dependent upon the prosperity of the great pastoral interests of the colony, and that the members of those classes most cordially supported the objects of the meeting. After George Mackay solemnly reminded them that an extra £10 burden might be the straw that broke the camel's back and destroyed the squatter, and so dragged all the other classes to ruin, they agreed to form the Pastoral Association of New South Wales to protect the pastoral interests of the colony.[37]

Outside the public meeting the ancient nobility of New South Wales dis-owned the squatters. At Camden Park the Macarthur brothers had nothing but contempt for the grasping nature of Boyd and Wentworth and their hollow pretensions for the public welfare. The *Weekly Register* disputed the claim of the squatters that the lands were their inheritance and should be handed over to them as a reward for pioneering civilization in the bush. If these immense runs were handed over to the squatters, all those who came to these shores would be slaves of an oligarchy, which would speedily become powerful and irresponsible.[38]

All through April in the pastoral districts of New South Wales British gentlemen of old and honourable families, country storekeepers, publicans, shanty-keepers, itinerant bushmen, and old lags rolled up to meetings con-vened in their centres to pass resolutions in which they testified to their belief

[37] *S.M.H.*, 10 April 1844; for Wentworth and 'shaking off the yoke' see vol. 2, pp. 71-2 of this history; Ruth Knight, *Illiberal Liberal*, pp. 169-71; S. Sidney, *The Three Colonies of Australia* (London, 1853), pp. 130-3; M. Boyd, *Reminiscences of Fifty Years* (London, 1871), p. 465; H. McCrae (ed.), *Georgiana's Journal*, p. 57; *Arden's Sydney Magazine*, October 1843, pp. 118-20; Gipps to Stanley, 12 February 1846, *H.R.A.*, I. xxiv. 768.
[38] S. Forster to James Macarthur, 1 November 1844 (Macarthur Papers, vol. 31); *Weekly Register*, 13, 20 April 1844.

TWO GALE-OF-LIFE MEN AND A
MEASURER

John Eardley-Wilmot
*Copy of portrait by an unknown artist, in private
possession*

Charles Augustus FitzRoy
*Engraving of portrait by G. Buckner, Rex Nan Kivell
collection, National Library, Canberra*

George Gipps
*Portrait attributed to H. W. Pickersgill, Mitchell Library,
Sydney*

A CHRISTIAN KNIGHT WITH A SORROWFUL COUNTENANCE

Rosendo Salvado

Photograph of part of portrait by an unknown artist,
Benedictine Monastery, New Norcia

in the connection between the prosperity of the pastoral industry and the general prosperity of New South Wales, and to profess their loyalty to the Queen, and their love of the institutions of the Mother Country. Like Wentworth, the country squatters looked to the throne and the British connection to rescue them from their oppressors in Sydney. When the *Sydney Morning Herald* bluntly asked them whether they proposed to be like Russian serfs and quietly look on while their taskmasters prepared new fetters for their limbs or whether they would show the courage of the lion-hearted race from which they had sprung, they baulked. Like Wentworth they were afraid that any such stand might lead to revolution in New South Wales.[39]

This vociferous insistence on their rights to the pastoral lands of New South Wales, accompanied by assurances of their loyalty and their moderation in politics, characterized both the petition of the Pastoral Association and the contribution of the squatters to the debate in the Legislative Council. In the petition they traversed the ground covered by the speakers at the public meeting. They argued that they could not in fairness be called upon to contribute to the peopling and improvement of lands from which they were liable to be driven by a single arbitrary proclamation. They repeated again the 'pioneers of civilization' argument. They reiterated how ungracious and impolitic it was to raise charges just when they had scarcely begun to recover from the great commercial disaster. They repeated that their economic position would force them to increase boiling down so that a great portion of the stock of the colony would be annihilated. They repeated that no man could be expected to effect improvements on land from which he might be ejected without notice or compensation, and that so long as this continued the European population would be demoralized and the aborigines would remain uncivilized. The only remedy for these evils was to repeal the Waste Lands Act of 1842 and to transfer all power and authority over the said lands and the revenues arising therefrom to the Governor and Legislative Council of New South Wales.[40]

Wentworth wanted them to go a stage further. He believed the time was ripe for the colonists to take over the highest offices of the local government. He believed that if the whole career of public service were open to the colonists, if their available talents were drawn upon, it would give renewed vigour to the administration and strengthen the attachment of the native-born to the Mother Country. The local aristocracies of rank, wealth and talent would then aspire to the offices now filled by men who had no fixed interest in the soil and whose sympathies were exclusively directed to their Downing Street masters. But the Legislative Council was not prepared to go as far as this. The select committee which they appointed to inquire into Crown lands grievances came to precisely the same conclusion as the members of the Pastoral Association, namely that the management of the Crown lands and

the revenue arising therefrom should be vested in the Governor and Legislative Council of New South Wales. They looked to London to rescue the
landed interest from the oppression from which it suffered in New South
Wales.[41]

By an odd irony the critics of the Pastoral Association also looked to
London rather than to the people of New South Wales for their economic
salvation. In the eyes of the editor of the *Weekly Register* the squatters' protest
was a 'rude, ungrammatical, rash and inconsiderate production, unworthy of
honest, sensible and well-bred men'. In June they denounced the pretence of
the 'patriots' that they were fighting against the government in a battle of the
constitution—an attempt to cover their design of appropriating to their own
use the public lands of the colony and reducing its inhabitants to slavery. The
truth was that the 'patriots' were 'aspirants to oligarchic domination': the
'patriots' were the men who stood between the people and what God and
nature obviously intended Australia to be—the paradise of the world. The real
question, as they saw it, was: Should the Queen or the squatters reign? So
both sides looked to London and government rather than Sydney and themselves to rescue them from the follies and evils of the land laws of New South
Wales.[42]

By June the excitement on the squatting question was dying down. When
the Legislative Council began its winter session only Wentworth and Robinson declined to accept Gipps's invitation to attend a ceremonial dinner. By
then some were saying that the financial difficulties of the squatters were
caused by their own gross mismanagement, inattention to their duties as
flock-masters, and rash speculation rather than the 'screw measures' of
Governor Gipps. Down in Melbourne on Batman's Hill a gathering of squatters on horseback thanked the Governor for his efforts to win for them a legal
proprietorship in the soil. By then there were other sources of public and
private excitement. Robert Lowe had blotted his copybook by a piece of social
arrogance: 'Do you think', he had asked, 'that I, a man of family, should
explain to Mr. Macdermott, who came here a sergeant of a marching regiment?' Henry Parkes was having a prolonged fit of melancholy, for he could
not get his mind that winter off the 'leperous [sic] horror' of death. Broughton
was in a state of much despondency, too, but for a different reason. He could
not get the people of New South Wales to subscribe to the building of
'edifices of religion'. Then the miracle happened: his friend Edward Coleridge
sent him a few thousand pounds of English money with which to raise
temples to God in the Australian wilderness.[43]

---

[41] *Australian*, 12 April 1844; Report of Select Committee on Crown Lands Grievances,
V. & P. (L.C. N.S.W.), 1844, vol. 2.

[42] *Weekly Register*, 27 April, 4 May, 28 June, 2 November, 14 December 1844.

[43] Gipps to La Trobe, 15 May, 1 June 1844 (Gipps-La Trobe Correspondence); *Weekly
Register*, 25 May 1844; P. L. Brown (ed.), *The Narrative of George Russell of Golf Hill*,
pp. 239-42; *S.M.H.*, 2 July, 23 October 1844; *Weekly Register*, 20 July 1844; Ruth
Knight, *Illiberal Liberal*, pp. 97-101; Gipps to La Trobe, 16 May 1844 (Gipps-La Trobe
Correspondence); W. G. Broughton, *A Journal of Visitation by the Lord Bishop of
Australia, 1845* (London, 1846), pp. 3-4.

While Wentworth was telling the squatters in Sydney that the Gipps imposition was one such as a lord put upon his serf—fit for Tunis and Tripoli, worthy of the Bey of Algiers (he was fond of sprinkling his speeches with references to bar-room ballads)—'God's fool', G. A. Robinson, was preparing to set out from Melbourne to investigate the murder of a Mr McAlister by aborigines near Alberton (Port Albert) in Gippsland. He set out from Melbourne on 13 April. At Alberton he heard the old story of how some drunken and depraved white men had killed some friendly natives and how the other members of the tribe had murdered Mr McAlister in retaliation. Robinson hoped the arrival of Charles James Tyers as first Crown lands commissioner for Gippsland would put an end to the mischief inflicted on the aborigines by lawless Vandemonians. From Alberton he and his party proceeded to Omeo where he saw blanched human bones marking the spot where the mountain tribes had wiped out the natives of the coast. He saw, too, how the loathsome disease syphilis, imparted by Europeans, was causing ravages among the aborigines. From Omeo he crossed the mountains into the Monaro where he turned east to Nimmitabel, then down the mountain to Twofold Bay and Cape Howe, after which he returned to Alberton.

From there he turned north again to Cann River, Pambula, and Twofold Bay where he was delighted to find that the Imlay brothers were encouraging the aborigines in habits of industry by employing them in whaling, stock-keeping, shepherding, bullock-driving and other useful pursuits. From Twofold Bay he turned inland to Bega and Nimmitabel, Michelago, Queanbeyan, Yass, Gundagai, Albury, Seymour and Melbourne which he reached on 20 October after an absence of six months and seven days. He had travelled across 32 000 square miles. He had not found one solitary clergyman engaged in the sacred duties of his office, or one schoolmaster. He had concluded that the situation of emigrant families without the means of instruction for their children was very distressing. He had also been distressed to find the aborigines decaying, their diminution being caused by petty feuds and intestine strife and European diseases such as smallpox, influenza, febrile syphilis, ophthalmia and cutaneous infections. He had been happy to note the spread of temperance among the peasantry, and especially happy to find among the settlers a sympathy for the aborigines.[44]

While Robinson contemplated the wondrous ways of God in planting sympathy for aborigines in the breasts of the settlers, the Governor communicated by message to the Legislative Council on 5 June the text of a bill to allow the aboriginal natives of New South Wales to be received as competent witnesses in criminal proceedings in the law courts of New South Wales. In the debate on the second reading of the bill on 20 June Plunkett said the purpose of the bill was to put an end to bloodshed and murder which escaped detection because the aboriginal natives were excluded from the witness box. Lang urged his fellow-councillors to do justice to their sable brethren by supporting the bill. Lowe was not prepared to trust the fate of

[44] G. Mackaness, 'George Augustus Robinson's journey in south-eastern Australia, 1844', R.A.H.S., *J. & P.*, vol. 27, 1941, pp. 318-49.

a man to untutored savages or allow a prisoner to gather his future state from 'the stolid apathy, or malignant scowl of those scarce human lineaments'. Why trust the life of a human being to men of such savage waywardness, such puerile petulance and such susceptibility to paltry bribes, that they would hurry a fellow-creature into the presence of that God who was a stranger to them? Wentworth told them that it would be just as defensible to receive as evidence in a court of justice the chatterings of the orang-outang as the evidence of members of this savage race. The *Sydney Morning Herald* and the *Australian* asked in indignation why the government of New South Wales should confer on savages the opportunity to trample on human beings of whose unspeakable importance in the mind of God they had never heard. So Council threw out the bill by fourteen votes to ten—the end of yet another attempt by Gipps and Plunkett to achieve equality before the law between white men and aborigines.[45]

At the same time as Robinson was struggling through the bush of Gipps-land to rescue the 'least of the little ones' from decay and extermination, two men in Sydney, James Beading and Francis Sandoe published on 27 June the first number of the *Colonial Literary Journal*, which was dedicated to the high-minded task of upholding the Christian faith in New South Wales. In their journal they proposed to publish miscellanies, essays, articles on literary and other topics, and extracts from the works of historians because they believed a study of history led to an improvement in private virtue and all those qualities which rendered man useful in society. History, they reminded their readers, was philosophy teaching by examples. As a supplement to the beneficent influence exerted on the morals of mankind by a knowledge of the past, they published in each issue a series of moral maxims such as:

A bad style is better than a lewd story

A chaste eye exiles licentious looks
A clean glove often hides a dirty hand

Acquire honesty : seek humility : practice economy : love fidelity.

They also recommended their readers to attend the courses of lectures on mind-improving and moral-improving subjects at the Commercial Reading Room, the Mechanics' Institute, the City Theatre and the School of Arts where a great array of talent had been engaged to spread 'moral enlightenment'.[46]

As the moral improvers trained their big guns on the battlefield of the

45 Stanley to Gipps, 20 December 1842, *H.R.A.*, I. xxii. 439; *V. & P.* (L.C. N.S.W.), 5, 20 June 1844; *S.M.H.*, 21 June 1844; *Australian*, 21 June 1844; Stanley to Gipps, 6 July 1843, *H.R.A.*, I. xxiii. 9; Normanby to Gipps, 17 July 1839, *H.R.A.*, I. xx. 242-3; Normanby to Gipps, 31 August 1839, ibid., 302-3; Gipps to Russell, 14 October 1839, ibid., 368; Russell to Gipps, 11 August 1840, ibid., 756.
46 *Colonial Literary Journal*, 27 June, 4 July 1844.

human heart, squatterdom was quickly winning its victories in the struggle for political power. In the middle months of 1844 they captured the separation movement in Port Phillip. At the separation meeting in Geelong on 28 May eighty of the three hundred present were squatters. Their spokesmen told the meeting how unjust it was for the sheep men of Port Phillip to pay 20s an acre for Crown land when in the Middle District of New South Wales land had either been given away or sold for 5s an acre. Again they presented the argument that an alliance of landowners, merchants, townspeople, and working class working together to obtain separation would make Port Phillip the brightest star in the Southern Cross. Ten days earlier at Port Fairy the spokesmen for the squatters asked those present why their money should be used to build government houses in Sydney and lay out pleasure grounds for the gentry of the Middle District. They told them, too, that the government in Sydney would not be influenced by any clamour about equality and the rights of man, for squatterdom was always anxious lest nativism or local chauvinism should turn into radicalism.

On the eve of the Melbourne meetings for separation early in June the squatters gave a grand ball and supper to the ladies of Melbourne in the long room of the Mechanics' Institute. All the rank, beauty and fashion of the province were there—two hundred all told by 10 p.m.—to join in the quadrilles, waltzes, and gallopades which were kept up with the greatest spirit till midnight. When the musicians retired for refreshment, a Highland piper in full costume struck up some Scottish reels which acted like magic on those sons and daughters of Scotland who for good or evil had come to a position of prominence in the squatting society of Port Phillip. At the meeting those present agreed on the text of a petition for separation in which they repeated the arguments of the 1840 petition, in that flat language of a document from which the wells of life and spontaneity had been dried up by over-use. They begged leave to approach Her Majesty with the assurance of their cordial attachment to Her Majesty's Royal Person and Government. They asserted that the southern portion of the colony of New South Wales was peculiarly fitted as well from its superficial extent, its geographical position and its other physical characteristics as from the respectability and intelligence of its population, from its entire isolation from all other colonial communities and from the comparatively high state of general advancement which it had so speedily attained, for being a separate and independent colony. They referred again to the great practical grievance of which the inhabitants of Port Phillip universally and justly complained—namely, the annual abstraction of a large portion of the proper revenue of the District, and its appropriation under the authority of the Legislative Council for purposes and objects in which the inhabitants of Port Phillip could have no interest or concern, thereby retarding indefinitely the general advancement of the District. They pointed out that it had been found impracticable to obtain the services of a single resident proprietor or inhabitant of the District to represent them in the Legislative Council. So the Acts of legislation as far as the interests of the District were concerned were constructed in great measures in the dark. They therefore asked Her Majesty to take the requisite steps to effect the entire separation of the District of Port Phillip from New South Wales, and to erect it into a separate and independent colony. Similar petitions were also drafted to Her Gracious Majesty from the warden and council of the district of Bourke and the merchants, settlers and other inhabitants of the town of Geelong praying that the District of Port Phillip might be erected into a 'Separate and Independent Colony'. For the inhabitants of Port Phillip, like their counterparts in the Middle District of New South Wales, suffered from the colonial disease of looking to the Mother Country rather than to themselves for relief from their afflictions. They were all beneficiaries and prisoners of their veneration of the law.[47]

Those who believed enlightenment would contribute to the moral well-being and happiness of mankind again turned their attention to the problem of providing a universal system of education in New South Wales. The need was urgent. Of the 25 626 children between the ages of four and fourteen, at least 13 000 were receiving no instruction in school. If moral enlightenment were to win the battle against city vice and bush barbarism, educational opportunities should be provided for all in schools teaching subjects relevant to the needs of colonial youth. On 21 June Lowe asked the Legislative Council to appoint a select committee to inquire into and report upon the state of education in the colony and to devise the means of placing the education of youth upon a basis suited to the wants and wishes of the community. In their report to Council on 28 August the committee pronounced the state of education to be extremely deficient, partly because of the ignorance, dissolute habits and avarice of too many of the parents and partly because of the want of good schoolmasters and school-books, but mainly because of the denominational character of the public schools. As they saw it, the effect of the denominational system was to leave the majority uneducated, in order thoroughly to imbue the minority with peculiar tenets. Wherever one school was founded, two or three others arose, not because they were wanted, but because it was feared that proselytes would be made. Besides, the denominational system was far too costly.[48]

Having agreed to recommend the abolition of the denominational system the committee had to decide which system of general education it favoured. They rejected the British and Foreign Bible system, because it required portions of

[47] *Port Phillip Herald*, 24, 31 May, 7 June 1844; Address to the Queen's Most Excellent Majesty, encl. in Gipps to Stanley, 12 January 1845, *H.R.A.*, I. xxiv, 190-5; The Humble Petition of the Warden and Council of the District of Port Phillip, in the Colony of New South Wales, 24 June, *V. & P.* (L.C. N.S.W.), 25 July 1844; The Humble Petition of the Merchants, Settlers and Other Inhabitants of the Town of Geelong, and District of Grant, in Public Meeting Assembled, *V. & P.* (L.C. N.S.W.), 20 August 1844; *S.M.H.*, 21 August 1844; A. Gilchrist (ed.), *John Dunmore Lang*, vol. 1, pp. 356-8; Gipps to Stanley, 12 January 1845, *H.R.A.*, I. xxiv. 190-5; Gipps to Stanley, 6 March 1845, *H.R.A.*, I. xxiv. 284.
[48] *Weekly Register*, 14 September 1844; Report from Select Committee on Education, *V. & P.* (L.C. N.S.W.), 1844, vol. 2, pp. 1-2.

Holy Scripture to be read each day in the schools without note or comment. Since the reading of the Holy Scriptures by children without note or comment was particularly obnoxious to the Catholic Church, the committee believed the Catholics would insist on a separate system for their own members. This would perpetuate the denominational system of public education. They there- fore recommended Lord Stanley's system of national education, which they believed to be capable of being so far adapted to the views of different religious persuasions as to render it in truth a system of national education for the lower classes of the community. Under this system extracts from the Holy Scriptures prepared by the Board of Education might be used for instruction in literary and moral education. In addition on one day of each week pastors or other persons approved by parents or guardians would be permitted to teach the children of their own denominations. The committee trusted that Christians of all denominations would feel that the adoption of this system would tend to soften down sectarian feelings and to promote union, toleration and charity. They recommended that a board should be appointed by the Governor of persons who were favourable to the proposed plan and who possessed the confidence of the different denominations. They also expressed the wish that no parents would ever be compelled to send a child to school, because that would infringe on their liberty. They were also not prepared to recommend the establishment of local boards of education, conceiving that a central board, with an efficient system of inspection would produce results more uniform and satisfactory. Sectarianism had prepared the way for administrative centralization and a system of education in which the teachers ducked the great questions of life, because neither the members of the Christian denominations nor the secular humanists could agree on what the children were to be told about the creation of the world and the problem of human evil.[49]

Once again the quest for universal education was bedevilled by squabbles and backbiting between the various religious sects. William Grant Broughton made the same point to the committee that he had made in all the public discussion of the appropriate education for the children of New South Wales, that education without doctrine would lead to a permissiveness in moral behaviour, and a republicanism in politics, which would bring ship-wreck to Christian civilization. He told the committee he was not prepared to teach Christianity without a creed. He would rather not teach at all than be guilty of encouraging the belief that all forms of religion were equally entitled to support, because under such a system there was a danger that truth would ultimately be almost driven from the world. Polding told the committee he thought it was just as important to adopt a system that would curb the 'animal propensities' in children as to teach them to read and write. He was too cunning to be trapped, as Broughton had been, into saying that he would prefer ignorance to error, while insisting that the most educated countries

[49] Report from Select Committee on Education, ibid., pp. 1-4.

such as Sweden and Prussia were the most depraved. By then the Protestants in New South Wales had stripped off the mask of saintliness Polding wore on his face, and were describing him as just another one of those zealots of the Roman persuasion who was busy taking measures for the speedy reduction of the whole Southern Hemisphere 'under the degrading yoke of the Man of Sin'. Polding was being described as a 'very weak, and . . . very vain, and exceedingly superstitious man'. Peter Robertson, speaking for the secular humanists, told the committee that the time had come to rescue the minds of children from being tainted and poisoned with the infamous concept of the total depravity of mankind, and that men who had been liberated from the Judaico-Christian slander might become as gods and eat of the tree of knowledge. He begged the committee not to hand over the minds of the children to those priests and parsons who misspent the time of the pupils in expounding theological punctilios when they ought to be instructing them in the useful arts of reading, writing and arithmetic.[50]

When the report of the committee was debated in the Legislative Council in September and October, Cowper spoke like a member of the Church of England, and Wentworth growled and snarled at the malevolent influences of priests and parsons on the minds of the young. Squatterdom made it plain that they were not prepared to spend a penny of public money on civilizing 'bush barbarians' until they got their fixity of tenure at a price they could afford to pay. The opponents of the recommendations of the committee laid on the table of the Legislative Council fifty petitions bearing over fifteen thousand signatures. On 10 October the Council adopted the recommendations by only one vote. Since by then it was clear that all the clergy of the Church of England and the priests of the Catholic Church were decidedly opposed to the recommendations, Gipps informed the Council on 27 November that he had given up the attempt to introduce a general system. Religious differences, he said, had once again induced government to abandon proposals in respect of education. The opposition to a government system had in no way diminished. Squatterdom and the bigoted clamour of parsons and priests compelled half of the children of New South Wales to come to man's estate not only ignorant of how to read and write, but with their animal propensities untamed by the teacher's birch or the parson's list of 'Thou shalt nots'.[51]

In the meantime the squatters went on repeating the first article in their creed—God and nature had decreed that New South Wales should be a sheep-walk for centuries to come. It was their task to assist the Mighty Disposer by proving that wool could be produced and sold at a profit, and that there was land farther out with enough grass for stock. During the debate on the

---

[50] Evidence of W. G. Broughton, J. B. Polding and P. Robertson to Select Committee on Education, ibid.; J. D. Lang, *Popery in Australia and the Southern Hemisphere* (Edinburgh, 1847), pp. 6-7.

[51] *V. & P.* (L.C. N.S.W.), 27 November 1844; *S.M.H.*, 28 November 1844; Gipps to Stanley, 1 February 1845, *H.R.A.*, I. xxiv. 232-3; A. G. Austin, *Australian Education 1788-1900* (Melbourne, 1961), pp. 41-4.

regulations of 2 April some had raised this question of whether wool could be produced at a profit. As passions cooled down after the curses and the mud-slinging that followed the publication of those regulations, the leaders of the squattocracy turned their minds to ways and means of reducing costs. Some suggested the costs of transport could be reduced by the introduction of steam communication between the Australian colonies and the United Kingdom. They suggested that the quickest steam communication would be from Port Essington to London via India, a journey of some sixty days.

In October 1838 the British Government had established a settlement in Victoria at Port Essington to act as a great commercial entrepôt for British trade with India, China, the southern parts of Asia and the islands of the eastern archipelago. By 1843 the sheep men in the Legislative Council believed they had an interest in Port Essington as a possible terminus for steam communication between London and Australia, provided a satisfactory land route were opened up between Sydney and Port Essington. Some said any exploring party in search of such a route would confirm John Oxley's prophecy of 30 August 1817 that the interior was uninhabitable and useless for all the purposes of civilized man. Others prophesied that they would find an inland river emptying its waters into an inland sea, which could be used to convert the vast and mournful wilderness into a smiling seat of industry, with the hills covered with bleating flocks, lowing herds and waving corn. They prophesied, as had Wentworth in 1819, that the enlivening cries of the husbandmen, instead of the appalling yell of the savage and the plaintive howl of the wolf, would be heard in the centre of their dark, mysterious continent. Then mankind would look on Australia as that country which nature had designed as her masterpiece and not that 'perfect desolation' that had made some people think of it as a country which had emerged at man's first sinning, when God had cursed the ground and created their 'barren wood'.[52]

In January of 1843 Charles Sturt offered to roll back those 'mists of un-certainty' which had hung over the centre by crossing the continent from east to west and from north to south. Governor Grey had left him with nothing to do. He had taken him away from the position in the Survey Department and left him as Registrar-General, where he had no employment that was congenial to him, suffered a reduction of £200 in salary, and lost his seat in the Legislative Council. The only enjoyment he had left in life was to wander over his garden with his two beautiful boys. He told his friend Charles Campbell of Duntroon, 'I had not the means of acting up to the impulse of my own heart. I could not indulge my wife, or do anything for my own children. I was unhappy, Campbell, very unhappy and I sought this

---

[52] Report from the Select Committee on the Proposed Overland Route to Port Essing-ton, *V. & P.* (L.C. N.S.W.), 1843; article on route to Port Essington in *Weekly Register*, 28 October 1843; J. Oxley to Macquarie, 30 August 1817, encl. in Macquarie to Bathurst, 5 September 1817, *H.R.A.*, I. ix. 479-84; for Oxley see vol. 1, pp. 298-300 of this history; W. C. Wentworth, *A Statistical, Historical and Political Description of the Colony of New South Wales, and Its Dependent Settlements in Van Diemen's Land* (London, 1819), pp. 64-5; Barron Field, *First Fruits of Australian Poetry* (Sydney, 1819), p. 7.

service in despair'. By then he knew the terrible despair of a man who had found he was never able so to please his wife that she as little as nodded her approval, or to do anything for his children. He also knew that terrible despair of a man who had wanted to leave his mark on the world, but now that, too, was slipping away from him. The hero of the great journey of 1829–30 now knew neither love nor glory. So he put forward his name in 1843 to put himself square with the world and win the battle for the heart of his wife. In December of 1843 Stanley instructed Grey to commission Sturt to proceed to the centre of the continent and examine the course of any rivers that rose west of the Darling. Two women of Adelaide to whom he risked showing his heart sewed a Union Jack for him to erect in the Centre, for that faith in the beneficent influence of British civilization had not died in him. As travelling companions he chose James Poole, John McDouall Stuart, John Harris Browne, Louis Piesse, Daniel Brock, Robert Flood and David Morgan. They took along two servants, five bullock-drivers, a shepherd, eleven horses, thirty bullocks, a boat, four drays, a cart, two hundred sheep, four kangaroo-dogs, two sheep-dogs, and provisions for the journey.

Early in August Sturt puzzled and worried some of his friends by imploring them to tell him frankly whether they had been laughing at him, and to tell him what they knew about his wife. On the morning of 10 August at the farewell breakfast given in his honour by the Governor and all the respectable people of Adelaide, he told them with a catch in his voice that glory always attended the death of a hero. He and the other fine fellows of the expedition were cheered as they made their way down King William Street, while women in bonnets and shawls, swallow-tailed gentlemen sporting top hats, workers in knee-breeches, shirt sleeves and wide-awakes, and scantily clad aborigines stood idly by. He dashed off for a last farewell with his wife, but either there or at that breakfast something happened to cause again 'pangs of recollection' as he made his way to Moorundie on the Murray and wondered how many of those who were leaving in such exuberant spirits would be permitted by the Mighty Disposer to return to their homes.[53]

After they reached Moorundie on 18 August he assembled all the members of his party one majestic evening after the bright winter sunshine had spent its force on the gaunt river cliffs and barren plains and told them that as they were now about to begin a journey from which none of them could tell who would return, it was a duty they owed themselves to ask the blessing and

[53] C. Sturt to Stanley, 25 January 1843, C.O. 13/35; C. Sturt to C. Campbell, 3 July 1840, 18 June 1845 (Sturt Papers, Rhodes House, Oxford); Stanley to Grey, 6 December 1843, C.O. 396/2; C. Sturt to R. Darling, 25 January 1843 (Sturt Papers, Rhodes House); C. Sturt to G. Macleay, 4 May 1841 (Sturt Papers, Rhodes House); D. Sturt to Miss Cooper, 7 August 1844 (Sturt Papers, s.a.s.a.); *Southern Australian*, 13 August 1844; *Adelaide Observer*, 17 August 1844; Diary of C. W. Davies, 23 November 1844 (ms. in s.a.s.a.); Diary of G. F. Dashwood, 10, 12 August 1844 (ms. in s.a.s.a.); C. Sturt, *Narrative of an Expedition into Central Australia* (2 vols, London, 1849), vol. 1, p. 46; S. T. Gill, 'Sturt's Overland Expedition Leaving Adelaide, August 10th, 1844' (water-colour in National Gallery of South Australia).

protection of that Power which alone could conduct them in safety through it. Within a few months he and the other 'fine fellows of the expedition' were beginning to wonder whether God ever sent signs from Heaven in the interior of Australia in response to what their hearts yearned for. After proceeding from Moorundie to the Darling, and moving north up the west bank of that stream to Menindee he still looked forward to that joyous day when they would be launched on an unknown sea and run happily towards the tropics. Instead they came to a desert where he and his immediate companion were the only living things in a 'death-like solitude'. A feeling of awe came over him as he cast his eye all around the horizon and saw no change in that terrible desert. It appeared to him that he and his companion were the last of the human race left on the earth to witness the destruction of the planet, as his eye roved over the chilling and repulsive aspect of a wilderness he hoped never to cross again.[54]

By 27 January 1845 they arrived at Depot Glen on Preservation Creek, where the thermometer registered 131° F. in the shade. To Sturt's great grief Poole died. Sturt then set out for the interior on 18 July. Again the appearance of the country mocked him. As he and Dr John Browne surveyed the miles and miles of red sand country stretching to the horizon whichever way they looked on that desert, littered with stones and spotted with the forbidding spinifex, the latter expressed all that a man could say: 'Good Heavens, did ever man see such a country.' Sturt was confident that the country had no parallel on the earth's surface. He gave up all hope of finding any body of water or making any discovery of use to civilized man. He had failed. After he returned to Fort Grey he made one more attempt to find country suitable for the white man. He set out once more for the north and followed the bed of a creek, but finding nothing to cheer him except vast accumulations of sand and rocks, he turned back to Fort Grey after conferring the name of Cooper on that dried-up creek-bed in honour of the woman who had sewn his flag in Adelaide. Having concluded that the centre of the vast continent was a desert of boundless extent, and accepted the melancholy fact that the aborigines of Australia had no idea of a superintending providence, he and the remainder of his party set out for Adelaide. Sturt expressed his fervent thanks to Almighty God for the mercies vouchsafed to him during the trying and doubtful service in which he had been employed. He reached his home in Adelaide at midnight on 19 January 1846. On crossing the threshold, his wife fell on the floor in a faint.[55]

When he rose to his feet to return thanks for the kind words expressed at a dinner in his honour on 20 February, he began to tell about what he had seen in that 'fearful desert', but the memory of it was too much and he broke down

[54] C. Sturt, op. cit., passim.; C. Sturt to C. Campbell, 18 June 1845 (Sturt Papers, Rhodes House); Journal of J. H. Browne, 4 May, 1 June 1845 (MS. in S.A.S.A.); Diary of D. Brock, 11, 13, 27 September, 7, 30 December 1844 (MS. in S.A.S.A.).

[55] Based on C. Sturt, op. cit.; Journal of J. H. Browne, passim.; *Adelaide Observer*, 17 January 1846; M. Langley, *Sturt of the Murray* (London, 1969), chs 14, 15.

and wept. For even though Earl Grey, in his capacity of Secretary of State for the Colonies, asked the Governor of South Australia to convey to Captain Sturt his high sense of the courage and perseverance displayed by him and his companions in the arduous service they had performed, Sturt knew that for the rest of his life he would have to find the strength to live with the horror of what he had seen and his failure to discover anything that would entitle him to substantial credit or reward. Squatterdom and the people of Australia in general had also to learn to live with the knowledge that the heart of their dark and mysterious continent was as dry as the soul of the gallant Captain Charles Sturt.[56]

[56] M. Langley, ibid., pp. 214-19; J. H. L. Cumpston, *Charles Sturt* (Melbourne, 1951); C. Sturt, op. cit., vol. 2, p. 2; *South Australian Gazette*, 21 February 1846; M. R. Casson, *The Story of 'Grange', the House of Capt. Charles Sturt* (Adelaide, 1966).

13

SELF-GOVERNMENT FOR PLUTOCRATS

O N THE NIGHT of 7 October 1844 fifty of the plutocrats of New
South Wales gave a dinner for Ben Boyd to celebrate his election to
the Legislative Council in place of Sir Thomas Mitchell who had
resigned because of the difficulty of reconciling his conception of the independence of elected members with pressure from Gipps that as Surveyor-
General he would be expected to support government measures. After the
table-cloth had been removed Windeyer toasted Boyd as a hero in the struggle
for self-government. In reply Boyd presented squatterdom's view of their
situation: 'I care not', he told them, 'whether he be banker, merchant, shipowner, or tradesman, we only have our existence through our pastoral
resources—our wool, our tallow, and our hides. We are all squatters to a man;
and I glory in the name.' If the squatter were left to the exercise of his own
industry and enterprise then at no distant day the pastoral lands of Australia
might be regarded as the sheep-walk for the world. To achieve this they could
put no trust or confidence in Sir George Gipps and the members of his
government. They could turn with confidence only to their beloved Queen,
not just to redress their grievances but to give them what British subjects in
Canada already enjoyed—responsible self-government.[1]

All through 1844 Wentworth was making the same point. He was still a
bundle of contradictions. All questions affecting the future greatness and glory
of Australia still moved him so deeply that he had earned from his contemporaries the title of 'great son of the soil'. As a man he was more at ease in
the company of Bob Nichols and other native-born Australians even though
he was divided from them on all political questions. He still loved men's jokes
—the bawdier the better—and collected paintings of the Magdalene, not so
much in the hope that those who had loved much would one day be forgiven,
but rather that they would be understood. He was then fifty-four. He was
sufficiently tall and athletic to lend a commanding weight to what he had
to say. His ability in debate was greater than that of any other member of the
Council except for Robert Lowe. Yet at times contemporaries and admirers
deplored the inexcusable slovenliness and disrespectful bearing which he often
adopted during his speeches in Council and at public meetings. His voice was

[1] *Port Phillip Herald*, 15 November 1844; *S.M.H.*, 10 October 1844. Sir Thomas
Mitchell was elected to the Legislative Council in April 1844 at a by-election. Finding it
difficult to reconcile his independence in Council because of his position as Surveyor-
General, he resigned his seat. Boyd replaced him in September.

discordant and grating and degenerated into a harsh drawl. By the end of 1844 there was about him the air of a man who had known greater days and was beginning to find it an effort to give youth a picture of what that grandeur was and what he might have been had he not squandered his great gifts in vulgar vendettas against his enemies and all who had despitefully used him. His air of faded grandeur seemed to have had its root in no common soul. At times he looked like a tamed tiger about to sidle from one end of his cage to the other for a chance to claw those who teased or enraged him. On such occasions his face became quite florid and was marked by a look of wildness which often comes over the face of a man for whom destroying enemies is the great sport of life.[2]

The public campaign for self-government provided just the spur he needed to discard his indolence and slovenliness, because it enabled him to play once again the role he had always hoped to play as the acclaimed champion of Australian liberty. It gave him also the chance to claw Sir George Gipps. Ever since Sir George had foiled his attempt to purchase the South Island of New Zealand from the Maori chiefs, he had been looking for an opportunity to get even with him. He had started his new campaign early in April when he spoke of self-government as providing careers for the 'sons of the soil', who could then replace the present incumbents who had no fixed interest in the soil of Australia and no passionate concern for its future glory. When on 21 June he moved in the Legislative Council for the appointment of a select committee to report on general grievances, he spoke with such rancour and calumny against Sir George that it was said anyone not living in the colony might well have been persuaded that their government was the most oppressive and they themselves the most oppressed people on the face of the earth.

This high-minded vision of the future greatness of Australia, and the mad drive to deride and gloat over the discomfiture of his enemies, lived uneasily side by side in the report he wrote as chairman of the committee. 'Nothing', he wrote, 'can more clearly evince the evil tendencies of that entire separation of the Legislative and Executive powers, which exists here at present, than the perfect indifference, if not contempt, with which the most important decisions and resolutions of your Honourable House have been treated by the head of the government during the course of this Session.' The one way to prevent such collisions was to give the Legislative Council the necessary privileges of a representative body, which implied the control over the ministers and administration of the colony which belonged to responsible government.

Wentworth wanted a satisfaction beyond that of being hailed as the champion of liberty or the founding father of the constitution. He still wanted to spill the blood of his enemies, just as he had wanted to spill the blood of John Thomas Bigge in 1822 to show the world that he had a 'dire sense' of

---

[2] 'William Charles Wentworth', *People's Advocate*, 18 August 1849; for the patriotism of the young Wentworth, see vol. 2, pp. 48-9 of this history; paintings of La Magdalena at Vaucluse House.

what was 'due from a child to an affectionate father'. He therefore demanded that the Legislative Council be empowered to draw up bills of impeachment against ministers of the Crown. This dip into the dark side of his heart came between the remarks of that other Wentworth who had once dreamed a great dream of the future of British civilization in his own 'dear Australasia'. After this subterranean aside he went on to describe the 'utter state of pupillage' in which governors of colonies were held by that necessity for constant reference to Downing Street, and how the remedy for that evil was the same as the remedy for the collisions between the legislature and the executive—namely, responsible government and an absence of all interference on the part of the home authorities, except on questions purely imperial or on matters referred to them by way of appeal when the executive and legislative bodies happened to differ.[3]

When he presented this report of the Select Committee on General Grievances to the Legislative Council on 19 December, again he spoke like a man to whom had been vouchsafed a great gift, and like a man who had been cursed with an evil passion. He took his fellow-members up on a high mountain and showed them that responsible government was the only antidote to all the evils and mischiefs from which they suffered. He also took them down into that hell where men mock and deride each other: he sneered at the 'transcendental abilities of the highly elevated Gipps' whom he, a mere colonial, would not dare to approach without first taking off his shoes. For in him lived also that readiness to protest his own unworthiness as a 'mere colonial', side by side with the determination not to suffer himself to be outstripped by any competitor. The man had a self-destroying fatality. At that very moment when he showed he had 'no common soul', he rushed into some mad deed which caused people to wonder whether he could govern himself, let alone create the conditions in which society at large could govern itself.[4]

By the second half of 1844 Wentworth, Lang, Windeyer and others had recruited a powerful ally in the person of Robert Lowe to the opposition party in Council against Gipps. By the end of July Gipps was complaining to London that although Lowe had pledged himself to resign whenever he found he could not conscientiously support government measures, he had recently joined the Pastoral Association and voted against government measures. 'Mr. Lowe's appointment to the Council', he told Stanley on 27 July, 'is one of the acts of my Government, which I have had most reason to be sorry for.' On 30 November 1844 Lowe compounded his offence by bringing out the first issue of the *Atlas*, a paper which described itself as a weekly journal of politics, commerce and literature. It quickly became a mirror in which each week Lowe and other contributors held Gipps and the actions of his government up

[3] *Australian*, 12 April 1844; *S.M.H.*, 10 April 1844; *Weekly Register*, 22 June 1844; Report from the Select Committee on General Grievances, *V. & P.* (L.C. N.S.W.), 1844, vol. 2.
[4] *S.M.H.*, 19, 20, 21 December 1844.

to public ridicule and abuse. They told their readers that the Legislative Council of New South Wales had only to form a wish in order to inspire His Excellency the Governor with a morbid desire of thwarting it. They asserted that Sir George was following the advice of Machiavelli to all tyrants: keeping his people in ignorance, drunkenness, poverty and slavery to ensure that they would fawn on him. They accused him of swallowing the 'clap trap' and the 'maudlin sentiment' of the 'little mad men' of Exeter Hall, those 'bum-boys' who had foisted those protectors of aborigines on the overburdened taxpayers of New South Wales. They warned their readers that Gipps and Plunkett were playing with fire, because once the savages of New Zealand and Australia learned of their rights from these 'bum-boys', the whole of Australia would be burnt in a huge fire of destruction.

Like Wentworth they wanted to put an end to their existing system of government which permitted, as they put it, 'an utterly unknown and obscure clerk' to tamper with the interests of their great colony. They were fighting not for those 'fanciful and metaphysical rights of man' advocated by democratic chartists, radicals and levellers, but for 'the unquestionable and undeniable rights of property'. Nature and the laws of political economy had conspired to make New South Wales a sheep-walk in which wool was grown most profitably by a few men. Those 'ignorant clerks' in London wanted to act both against nature and the laws of political economy. Their power to decree who should and should not possess the landed wealth of New South Wales should be taken away from them and handed to the men of property in the colony. If anyone's conscience was troubled by this perpetuation of a monopoly of land or if anyone wanted to know why some were rich and some were poor, he should be told that that was a question no man could answer until he had discovered why there was evil in the world. He should also be told to look at nature:

> Ask of thy mother earth why oaks are made
> Taller or weaker than the weeds they shade.[5]

Boyd and most of the members of the Pastoral Association were most anxious that all their tirades against Gipps and the members of his government should not be construed as the start of a campaign to 'shake off the yoke'. They were caught up in a movement to win self-government for the plutocrats of New South Wales, and not touched by any enthusiasm for the achievements of Australians. There was the unbridgeable gulf between Lowe and Wentworth: Lowe was an English exile, Wentworth a native-born Australian. Lowe believed that Australian literature could be crammed into a nutshell, that the only science the locals practised or knew anything about was sheep-shearing, that the fine arts were in a state of stagnation, that for

---

[5] Gipps to Stanley, 27 July 1844, *H.R.A.*, I. xxiii. 704-5; Gipps to Stanley, 27 July 1844, ibid., 709; Ruth Knight, *Illiberal Liberal: Robert Lowe in New South Wales 1842-1850* (Melbourne, 1966), pp. 85-7; *Atlas*, 30 November, 14 December 1844, 15, 22 February, 8 March, 25 April, 11 October 1845.

TWO MELBOURNE MEN OF RECTITUDE

James Goold

Portrait by an unknown artist, Convent of Mercy,
Fitzroy

Charles La Trobe

Part of portrait by Francis Grant, La Trobe Cottage,
Melbourne

TWO IMPROVERS OF MANKIND

Henry Parkes

Drawing by Charles Rodius, Mitchell Library,
Sydney

John West

Portrait by John Glover, Tasmanian Museum and
Art Gallery, Hobart

AUSTRALIA'S GREATEST NATIVE SON

William Charles Wentworth

Copy of portrait by J. Anderson, Mitchell Library, Sydney

Australians philosophy was a drug and belles-lettres something that was 'most popular on ginger-bread'. Lowe looked to Europe for the main content of the literary *Atlas*. He was graciously prepared to offer a quiet niche in the *Atlas* for the offerings of such of his colonial friends as might occasionally wander from the cold realms of utilitarianism to the warm regions of the emotional and the imaginative. Like the members of the Pastoral Association, he and his colleagues of the *Atlas* looked to Archibald Boyd, the lobbyist for the squatters, to persuade those 'ignorant clerks' in Downing Street of the errors of their ways, so that they, too, might at long last realize that in New South Wales banker, merchant, farmer, shipowner or tradesman were all, in the words of his cousin, Ben Boyd, 'squatters to a man'.[6]

The mortal blow to this fixed, immutable, organic 'decree of God and nature' view of their society came from one of the main creators of their prosperity, cheap convict labour. The convict question was about to become one of the grave-diggers of squatterdom's domination in the Australian colonies. On 16 November 1844, 'something extraordinary' happened in Melbourne: twenty probation men landed from the *Royal George*. As they blackened each other's eyes during drinking bouts in the low dives of Melbourne Town, the press asked the people of Port Phillip whether they wanted to have the canaille of the London streets. On 17 December about 165 squatters and their sympathizers gathered in the Royal Hotel in Melbourne to hear men such as E. Curr and A. Cunningham argue that unless they accepted probation labour, wages would soon be as high as five years ago and the squatters would be ruined.

On 22 December townspeople and members of the working classes crowded into the long room of the Royal Exchange Hotel in Melbourne to applaud wildly speakers who asked them whether they wanted to be put on a level with felons and whether they wanted to put in jeopardy the hope of able-bodied, sober and industrious immigrants being able to rise in the social scale. Speakers reminded them that three-quarters of the population of Port Phillip believed they were becoming inhabitants of a settlement free from the taint of convict origins. This freedom from the convict stain was an inseparable part of their case for separation, indeed an argument for giving them self-government forthwith. The squatters, they said, were prepared to sacrifice the whole community, all their aspirations for freedom, morality and happiness at the shrine of Mammon. La Trobe was distressed that at a meeting for a free discussion the poor squatters were hustled and not even allowed to record their dissent from a set of resolutions passed mainly by the labouring classes. In the eyes of the bourgeoisie the community had dealt a death-blow to the squatters' attempt to convert the fair, free and fertile province of Port Phillip into a den of thieves.[7]

On Christmas Day those 'unsophisticated children of the forest', the abori-

---

[6] *Atlas*, 28 December 1844.

[7] *Port Phillip Herald*, 19, 22 November, 22, 27 December 1844; *Port Phillip Patriot*, 21 November, 19, 26 December 1844; La Trobe to Gipps, 25 December 1844 (Gipps-La Trobe Correspondence).

gines of Wooloomooloo and Shoalhaven, sat down to dinner under an awning in the yard of Mr Charles Smith, a merchant and benevolent bourgeois of Sydney Town. The men were all washed and shaved before the dinner, and the women were specially cleaned up for the occasion. Mr Smith and his friends waited at table, mindful of their Saviour's words about the blessedness of those who showed loving kindness to the least of the little men. A number of respectable people stood round the tables to watch the aborigines eat roast beef, roast mutton and plum pudding in the 'most abundant liberality' and wash it down with 'a moderate and judicious supply of ale, porter and wine'. Some said such gestures were all 'humbug and mawkish sentimentality', since the only thing the white man could do for the aborigines of New Holland was to soften their disappearance off the face of the earth as an 'immeasurably superior power' spread over the land. The inevitability of their disappearance off the face of the earth mattered little when compared with this blatant move by the squatters of New South Wales to solve their labour problem by sacrificing morality and material progress at the shrine of Mammon.[8]

Down in Van Diemen's Land, too, the convict question was beginning to create a great stir. The abolition of transportation to New South Wales in 1840 increased the number of convicts arriving in the island to two or three times the number that had arrived in preceding years. The cost of the convict department trebled at a time when commercial crisis and monetary confusion forced the government to reduce government expenditure. The end of assignment revolutionized the attitude of the settlers to the presence of convicts from an acceptance of 'contamination' as a 'regrettable necessity' to denunciations of the 'stain'. In December 1843 Eardley-Wilmot asked Stanley to relax the regulations requiring all convicts under the new probation system to be employed on public works, so that settlers might reap the advantages of the flood of labour in the island under this new system of penal discipline. If Stanley was not prepared to consider that, Eardley-Wilmot would ask the British Government to bear a greater proportion of the cost of maintaining convicts. Stanley rejected the first request because, as he saw it, any such change could only lead to a return of the bad old days, characterized by the evils of the road parties and the semi-slavery of assignment. He went on to remind Eardley-Wilmot that all the free inhabitants of Van Diemen's Land accepted the financial burdens and restrictions on freedom when they decided to cast their lot in a penal society. This left Eardley-Wilmot with the task of administering a system of penal discipline which had ceased to contribute to the production of wealth for the settlers of Van Diemen's Land.[9]

During 1844, as talk of moral pollution began to spread all over the island, Eardley-Wilmot's actions planted in the minds of some the suspicion that he lacked either the tact or the conviction to shield the inhabitants from the evils

---

    [8] *Australian*, 27 December 1844.
    [9] Eardley-Wilmot to Stanley, 2, 5 December 1843, C.O. 280/161; Stanley to Eardley-Wilmot, 31 August 1844, C.O. 408/23; Earl Grey, *The Colonial Policy of Lord John Russell's Administration* (2 vols, London, 1853), vol. 2, pp. 1-6.

of moral corruption. Early in that year F. R. Nixon withdrew the licences of two chaplains for 'unbecoming behaviour'; Eardley-Wilmot continued to pay their salaries. By then Nixon was convinced that since the probation system was converting the colony into 'the lazar house of the British dominions', only men of proven moral rectitude should be entrusted with the task of instructing the convicts in their duties to God and man. In his eyes Eardley-Wilmot was indifferent to their moral welfare. During the year Nixon also wrangled with the Catholic Bishop, Dr R. W. Willson, about the latter's use of the title 'Bishop of Hobart Town'. When Willson rebuked him for engaging in religious strife and allowing the religion of Christ to degenerate into a 'tinkling cymbal' at a time when thousands of their respective flocks were festering in misery, and crying for spiritual aid and consolation, Nixon replied with a series of sermons in St David's Church on the errors of the Catholic Church. He noted with much injury to his pride and his vanity that the Lieutenant-Governor was always absent.

Nixon was already convinced by Eardley-Wilmot's support for national education and by his policy in the appointment of convict chaplains that he was no friend of the Church, when the events of 1845 planted in his mind even more monstrous suspicions about the morals of the Lieutenant-Governor. Early in the year Eardley-Wilmot invited Nixon to dinner at Government House. Nixon replied that it would be indecorous of him as the spiritual head of the Church of England in the colony if he were to break her rules by giving or accepting invitations to parties during the holy season of Lent, a season which from the earliest days of Christianity had been set aside as one of abstinence and, as far as possible, of retirement. By then it was the common theme of conversation at Bishop's Court that Sir Eardley was no friend of the Church.

That year tongues began to wag about 'goings on' at Government House. Those walls, which in previous decades had heard the moving petitions by Lieutenant-Governor Arthur and his wife to make them worthy of entering into the kingdom of heaven, and the lectures by Lady Franklin for the moral improvement of mankind were now the silent witnesses of unbecoming scandal and impropriety. It was said that Sir Eardley had a very peculiar way of establishing a friendly understanding with girls—that he sat on the sofa with them and passed his arm around their necks. It was said that the girls seemed to enjoy those little innocent familiarities amazingly. Several persons, including J. P. Gell, refused to attend the levee for the Queen's birthday at Government House because Sir Eardley, by making no provision to exclude 'improper persons', turned the levee into a curious farce. One evening in October 1845 at a Government House dinner party Miss Kemp, one of the daughters of that old veteran of the people's rights, A. F. Kemp, told those present that if she were a man, she would never marry but would take as many lovers as she liked. Sir Eardley told her what a devil she was, to which she replied 'you are another'. That exchange soon went the rounds of Hobart Town, Launceston and the Midlands, and was destined to live on, not because of any intrinsic memorability in the words, but because it illustrated the point his enemies were making—that he was polluting the morals of Government House society at a time when the convicts were spreading their deadly moral pollution over the lower orders. Some said Sir Eardley was seeing far too much of Julia Sorell, a strikingly handsome girl of nineteen, with delicate features, small beautifully shaped hands and feet, and a French vivacity and quickness likely to stir up the madness in a battered old Regency beau.[10]

At the same time Eardley-Wilmot clashed with the leaders of opinion in Van Diemen's Land. By mid-1845 landowners, merchants and bankers were grumbling that money was being filched from their pockets each year to pay the costs of a 'moral sewer' from which they derived no material benefits. Eardley-Wilmot blandly assured them that the solution to the corrupting influences of the probation gangs was to move them to unoccupied districts. To improve the morals of the members of the gangs he provided teachers for their moral and religious instruction. He did not know of any country in the world which had a more virtuous peasantry and working class than Van Diemen's Land. In mid-1845 he saw no reason to change his mind about their progress towards material and moral well-being.

On 31 July a great gathering of cabmen and cabs collected outside the theatre in Hobart and watched an angry crowd pour into the building. They attended to draw up a remonstrance against unconstitutional taxation. That old veteran of their rights, A. F. Kemp, told them that he was devoted heart and soul to the colony, that he was no unprincipled opponent of government, but that if they wanted to respect themselves, they must transmit to the rising generation the privileges and feelings of true-born Britons. A Dr Rowe denounced the drivelling idiocy of trusting the Legislative Council who, as then constituted, were like schoolboys doing in silence their master's bidding or like spaniels crouching at the feet of their master at the least sign of his displeasure. To tremendous cheers he urged them not to continue as 'the taxed gaol of the British Empire', for then they would neither walk, ride, sail nor drink, nor do any of those things which were the breath of life to a Vandemonian without having to pay for the privilege. For his part he was sorry the women were not present, because he believed they would never consent to be the wives and mothers of spiritless slaves. T. Macdowell accused Eardley-Wilmot of forwarding 'immature representations . . . as to the actual state of the colony' to Lord Stanley. M. Allport demanded that the revenue of the colony be placed under the control of the representatives of the people. Other speakers complained of having to pay taxes to pay huge salaries to officers

---

[10] *Launceston Examiner*, 16 November 1844; Nixon to Stanley, 29 May 1844, encl. in Eardley-Wilmot to Stanley, 3 June 1844, C.O. 280/169; F. R. Nixon to R. W. Willson, 8 October 1844, and R. W. Willson to F. R. Nixon, 14 October 1844, 14 February 1845, quoted in F. R. Nixon, *A Charge Delivered to the Clergy of the Diocese of Tasmania* (London, 1848), pp. 62-70; *Hobart Town Courier*, 12 November 1844; Diary of G. T. W. Boyes, 17 May 1844, 23 October 1845; J. P. Gell to J. Franklin, 10 June 1845 (Gell and Franklin Papers).

who did nothing, or for the support of prisoners whose labour was not being applied to any works of public utility.[11]

By October the cry of no taxation without representation was raised in the Legislative Council. When Eardley-Wilmot moved in Council on 29 October 1845 the second reading of the Estimates Bill, Richard Dry asked that it be read again that day six months. He was supported by Thomas George Gregson. Dry was a native-born Vandemonian, born near Launceston in 1815 and the inheritor of the Quamby estate which was a social gathering place for the landed gentry of the northern district. He was a lovable man, known to his contemporaries by the affectionate name of 'Dicky'. By contrast, Gregson was always known as Gregson. He was an odd man to lead any movement either for the winning of rights by the people or for the liberation of the convicts from their gaolers. Like Dry, Gregson was one of the largest employers of convict labour on his estate Northumbria at Jericho and his town establishment at Risdon. Unlike Dry he had conducted his public life with a violence and an extravagance which caused him to be feared by friend and foe alike, but never loved. In 1836 he had fought a duel with one of his political opponents and horsewhipped another. Indeed his whole public career was one uninterrupted story of libelling, horsewhipping and pistolling. As for his attitude to the convicts, he was known as the man who expressed hatred and indigation against the whole prisoner population, in taverns, at private parties, in the Council and at public meetings. The gentry adored him for his genial and kindly bearing in private circles, and for his lively social life, great lover that he was of horseflesh and a pack of hounds. For them he was an 'embodiment of John Bull-ism in the antipodes'. The convicts and their descendants looked on him as an 'imperious, self-willed' man who held 'the most numerous class of the community in something worse than contempt'.

On 29 October 1845 Gregson spoke not as the tribune of the people, but as a country gentleman who believed the probation system had ruined the free settler and spread Sodom and Gomorrah throughout the land. The Comptroller-General asked him to produce facts and stop making assertions. Tempers ran high till Gregson stormed out of the room followed by Michael Fenton, once an army captain but now a large employer of convict labour on his estate at New Norfolk, and by 'Dicky' Dry. When Council met again on 1 November, Gregson asked leave to explain the differences between the six unofficial members and the Lieutenant-Governor. Eardley-Wilmot replied by giving the absentees half an hour in which to enter the chamber. When they failed to appear he bowed and retired.

When Dry returned to Launceston on 6 December, he was greeted with wild cheers. A number of horsemen and tradesmen escorted him into town behind two banners on which was inscribed 'The Patriotic Six' and 'Dry for Ever'. Every street through which the procession passed was thronged with

[11] *Colonial Times*, 1 August 1845; *Hobart Town Courier*, 2 August 1845; Eardley-Wilmot to Stanley, 29 May 1844, C.O. 280/169; Eardley-Wilmot to Stanley, 15 October 1844, C.O. 280/172; Stanley to Eardley-Wilmot, 10 February 1845, C.O. 280/180.

spectators. Flags and banners streamed from the windows in honour of 'Dry and independence', the 'native patriot', 'non-official, independent legislation'. In a becoming speech Dry told them that Eardley-Wilmot had accused the Patriotic Six of 'factious, unconstitutional and disloyal' opposition to his government, but he urged his hearers to hurl back the charges with indignation. Between Eardley-Wilmot and the creative forces of his day a great gap was beginning to open up. Gregson was given a public dinner in Hobart Town. As in New South Wales, the plutocrats of the colony became the warmest advocates for self-government and captured local patriotism by calling their spokesmen the 'Patriotic Six'.[12]

At the same time in Van Diemen's Land the complaints about the convict taint were swelling into a great howl of moral indignation. The men in the probation gangs were said to be practising the horrid, debasing, disgusting and detestable sin of the 'cities of the plain': the lash was being used too often; the superintendents were not able to supply adequate vigilance. This confronted the plutocrats in the self-government movement with a difficult dilemma. Dependent as they were on the use of convict labour on their own estates, they could not join in any movement for abolition without endangering their own interests or exposing themselves to the charge of hypocrisy. Nor could they engage in any attack on the convict system at large without offending most of their fellow-inhabitants of the island. They could ask what Eardley-Wilmot was doing to end the 'disgusting pollution'. They could and did ask whether the 'battered old beau' who enjoyed sitting on the sofa in the drawing-room of Government House with pretty girls was morally fit to take a stand against the evils of the probation system. In the meantime Eardley-Wilmot, a man of appetites but with an inadequate consciousness of what others thought of those appetites, told his friends he proposed to endure all such calumnies in silence and with resignation, since he believed there was nothing really permanent but truth.[13]

By then the settlers were using more and more gloomy language to describe their way of life. Because of the probation gangs, robbery and violence were stalking through the land. The few labourers who had the means to do so were leaving the colony in droves, while those who could not get away were obliged to compete with the convicts, and thus earned a miserable subsistence in a degraded colony. They had been happy, prosperous and flourishing before Lord Stanley inundated them with an overwhelming flood of crime. They also insisted that the probation system was so polluting the whole of society that, as they put it in the petition of 1846, 'the worst days of Sodom and Gomorrah were not so bad as the present days of Van Diemen's Land', and

[12] *V. & P.* (L.C. V.D.L.), 21, 29 October 1845; *Launceston Examiner*, 6 January 1874; *Mercury*, 6 January 1874; *Hobarton Guardian*, 16 April 1851, 29 January 1853; *Tasmanian Tribune*, 23 August 1872; *Cornwall Chronicle*, 27 September 1854; *Colonial Times*, 4, 7 November 1845; Diary of G. T. W. Boyes, 1 November 1845; Eardley-Wilmot to Stanley, 5 November 1845, C.O. 280/185; *Launceston Examiner*, 8 December 1845.

[13] *Spectator*, 24 October 1846; J. Syme, *Nine Years in Van Diemen's Land* (Dundee, 1848), p. 200; Eardley-Wilmot to Stanley, 17 March 1846, C.O. 280/193; Eardley-Wilmot to Gladstone, 10 July 1864, C.O. 280/194.

that such was the inevitable result of large aggregations of vicious men debarred from access to female society and composed as they were of the very dregs of society. This was a 'disastrous experiment' on which many millions were spent without any material benefits and without preventing crime in the Mother Country or reforming the convicts themselves.[14]

Some of the convicts experienced little pain at the hands of their gaolers and passed from penury to a material well-being to which they had been strangers in the United Kingdom; others were ravaged and scarred for life. There was Patrick Kehoe, tried at Wexford in April 1842 for receiving stolen sheep, who arrived on the *Navarino* on 10 January 1843. Kehoe was a quiet man who was only charged with one offence during his days of servitude. By contrast, there was Timothy Kidney, tried in Cork on 12 August 1842 for stealing lead. Within two months of his arrival on the *Navarino* he was up before the magistrate for disobedience of orders. From then on at intervals of a month to two months he came before the magistrate on charges of idleness, insolence to his overseer, absenteeism, pilfering flour, making away with a government knife, misconduct in being at a campfire in the bush where some stolen potatoes were roasted, and insubordination. On 5 November 1850 he was emancipated, but he was back in court again on 26 June 1851 charged with stealing a goat and other articles, after which the courts of Van Diemen's Land saw him no more, not because he had learnt to 'cleanse his ways' but because death took him to a place where his tormentors and improvers could not reach him.

There was William Linneen, a likeness to Shakespeare's Michael Cassio, in the probation gangs of Van Diemen's Land, who believed that some men were to be saved and some were not to be saved. He wanted to be saved himself but his potter had planted in him a 'riot of passion' to madden His handiwork. One day in 1842 in the green fields near Waterford when his blood had been stirred by strong drink he forced a pretty girl to lie with him. For this he was sentenced to transportation and so joined Kehoe and Kidney and some 250 others on the *Navarino*, and arrived in Hobart in January 1843. There the moments of madness never left him. He was up before the magistrate for defacing a government spelling book and, being drunk at the time, for disturbing the congregation at the Catholic church at Richmond. From the year he arrived until he received his conditional pardon in February 1856 he appeared regularly before the magistrate charged with drunkenness and its attendant frolics, a story of the terrible punishment a man exposed himself to if he lacked the will or the power to restrain the 'riot of passion' in his heart.[15]

[14] Extract from a letter from Van Diemen's Land dated 30 April 1845, *Galway Mercury*, 20 September 1845; Report of Select Committee on the Renewal of Transportation, *V, & P.* (L.C. N.S.W.), 1846, vol. 2; J. Syme, op. cit., pp. 183-245; H. P. Fry, *A System of Penal Discipline* (London, 1850), pp. 153-203; A. G. L. Shaw, 'Sir John Eardley-Wilmot and the probation system in Tasmania', *Tasmanian Historical Research Association Proceedings*, vol. 11, 1963, pp. 5-19; A. G. L. Shaw, *Convicts and the Colonies* (London, 1966).
[15] Record Book of Convicts Arriving in Van Diemen's Land per *Navarino*, 10 January 1843 (Principal Superintendent of Convicts, T.S.A.),

There were those wild asses of men, those Ishmaels of the probation gangs, whom neither the fear of human punishment nor the threat of God's wrath through all eternity could keep out of the clutches of their gaolers. There was John Taylor, a man of ruddy complexion, small black whiskers and dark blue eyes who went on being drunk and violent and being found in disorderly houses on a Sunday from the day he arrived in the *Duchess of Northumberland* in January 1843 until he was freed from his servitude in August 1851. There was George Mills, another quarrelsome man on the same ship, who was driven all his life to discharge the great rage inside him on his fellow-men. Every month or so he appeared before the magistrate for offences such as making a noise in the men's room, for destroying a fellow-prisoner's plate, for having the trousers of a fellow-prisoner in his possession, for insolence, or for being absent from his work without permission.[16]

With the women, too, there was the same variety of behaviour. Among those who arrived in 1844 was Matilda Duncan, a housemaid just five feet high, with a yellow complexion, who had broken the commandment 'Thou shalt not steal' so many times that she was known in her native Yorkshire as a 'travelling thief'. In prison in England and on the convict ship *Emma Eugenia* she was often drunk and disorderly. Yet Van Diemen's Land seemed to work a great marvel in her, for she only appeared once before the magistrate in the ten years between her arrival in April 1844 and her emancipation in September 1854. She did not escape, however, into the bright light of the sun, but into the darkness of the Hobart Lunatic Asylum. By contrast, there was Caroline Hopkins, a Londoner just over five feet high whose wayward-ness, like Matilda Duncan's, consisted of stealing. During her early years in Hobart she was regularly convicted for drinking in a public house on the Lord's Day or obtaining a gallon of wine by telling a lie. After two years of such aberrations she vanished off the pages of human history in Van Diemen's Land where only crimes, follies and passions were recorded.

There was Mary Latham, a housemaid in Cheshire, just five feet high, twenty-two years of age, with pock-pitted skin, an alarmingly snub nose, and an unhappily large chin, and a temper to match the cruel joke nature committed when fashioning her, for she was much given to drunkenness and human swinishness, which led her one day to steal clothes from her own mother. In Van Diemen's Land she continued on the same mad path, assaulting those placed in authority over her when in a drunken rage, and destroying the property of government regularly until October 1849 when she married, but that holy estate, blessed by her Saviour at Cana in Galilea, could do little for her. Within a month she was back in the cells for misconduct.[17]

While the agents of the criminal law went on from day to day imposing penalties on those who either could not or would not resist following the

---

[16] Record Book of Convicts Arriving in Van Diemen's Land per *Duchess of Northumberland*, 18 January 1843 (T.S.A.).

[17] Record Book of Female Convicts Arriving in Van Diemen's Land per *Emma Eugenia*, 7 April 1844 (Comptroller-General of Convicts, T.S.A.).

devices and desires of their own hearts, society at large was about to exact a more terrible penalty from the Lieutenant-Governor. An unnamed person in Melbourne had published a comment on the morals of Eardley-Wilmot in the *Naval and Military Gazette* in London on 11 October 1845. 'Van Diemen's Land', he wrote, 'is in a bad state. The men in the bush are almost their own masters, and crimes the most horrible are of daily occurrence. All the females have left the bush and have taken refuge in the towns, and even [there] are subject to every kind of insult. Sir Eardley sets a bad example himself. No people of any standing will now enter Government House except on business. No ladies can.' Visitors to London were telling the men in black at Downing Street about strange 'goings on' at Government House and hinting at a connection between the looseness of Government House and looseness in society at large. A Mr George Dayman gave Lord Stanley a 'dreadful account' of these things. Eardley-Wilmot had set free three thousand convicts in the streets of Hobart as a Christmas Day treat. Early in 1846 George Dayman gave James Stephen a picture of vice and degradation in Van Diemen's Land such as he had never contemplated in any human society. In this way a picture of Eardley-Wilmot as a hoary debaucher, who had converted the seat of government into a den of infamy, took shape in the mind of James Stephen. Well before these stories of moral infamy reached his ears, he had come to the conclusion that Eardley-Wilmot was a hopeless administrator. He was there-fore defective in the two qualities Stephen esteemed most highly—moral rectitude and efficiency. In April Stephen learnt of yet another way in which Eardley-Wilmot had offended against the principles of all good government: he had lost the respect of the men nominated to the Legislative Council. He therefore decided to recommend to the new Secretary of State for the Colonies, William Ewart Gladstone, that Eardley-Wilmot be recalled.

Gladstone had a peculiar horror of the vices of the 'cities of the plain'. He was also inclined to lend an unguarded ear to bishops, priests and deacons when they passed on stories about breaches of the seventh commandment by colonial governors. Nixon, who had his own reasons for doubt about the morals of the Lieutenant-Governor, told Gladstone that the conduct of Eardley-Wilmot in regard to women constituted a notorious scandal in the colony, and urged him to take some step to abate the same. When 'Gladdy' asked for proof, Nixon assured him there was no more need of evidence about such a man as Eardley-Wilmot than there was for establishing the existence of the sun on a bright noon-day. As far as Gladstone was concerned, that was that.[18]

---

[18] *Naval and Military Gazette*, 11 October 1845; Adelaide Lubbock, *Owen Stanley, R.N.* (Melbourne, 1968), p. 177; Journal of James Stephen, 3 May 1846 (MS. in Trinity College, Cambridge); W. E. Gladstone (J. Brooke and M. Sorenson, eds), *Autobiographica* (London, 1971), appendix 7; *Launceston Examiner*, 27 October 1847; *S.M.H.*, 10 November 1847; Kathleen Fitzpatrick, 'Mr. Gladstone and the Governor', *Hist. Studies*, vol. 1, 1940, pp. 31-45; M. Roe, *Quest for Authority in Eastern Australia* (Melbourne, 1965), p. 20.

On 30 April Gladstone told Eardley-Wilmot, in that prose which seemed fashioned to serve the punishers of mankind, that since he had failed in his duty to amend the horrible and revolting state of the morals of the convicts in Van Diemen's Land Her Majesty's Government had decided he could no longer exercise his present function with advantage or justice to the public. He went on to say that Her Majesty's Government had instructed C. J. La Trobe, the Superintendent of Port Phillip, to proceed to Hobart to take over the administration of the colony until such time as Her Majesty was graciously pleased to announce the name of his successor. In a private despatch on the same day Gladstone told Eardley-Wilmot that certain rumours had reached him from a variety of quarters relating to Eardley-Wilmot's private life to the nature of which it was perhaps unnecessary that he should particularly refer. He did not disclose what those rumours were or the names of his informants. Years later, looking back on these events in the autumn of his life, he referred to them as one of the 'undoubted errors' of his life. But the damage had been done. With Stephen telling him posterity would pay homage to him for this display of 'high courage' in dismissing a sinner, the two despatches were on their way to Van Diemen's Land early in May 1846.[19]

In the meantime Eardley-Wilmot saw no reason to doubt the rectitude either of his own behaviour or his conduct in high office. All through 1845 Stanley had rebuked him for faults in his administration. He had accused him of sending answers to enquiries which were 'both defective in substance and obscure in style', forwarding returns on new appointments which were 'imperfectly drawn up' and allowing reports to 'escape his recollection'. But neither the rebukes of Stanley nor the demands of the Patriotic Six to see their country free from the moral pollution of the concentrated crime of the Empire nor their hope that the country which had spent millions to emancipate the negro would soon ransom the colonists from a position worse than slavery, touched him at all. He carried on unaware of the seas that were about to engulf him.[20]

Eardley-Wilmot was about to pay a terrible price for complacency, and a consciousness inadequate for his high office. Like Lepidus in *Antony and Cleopatra* he was as a man called into a huge sphere but was not seen to move in it. In August 1846 William Race Allison, a large employer of convict labour who had been nominated to the Council to replace one of the Patriotic Six, asked His Excellency to recommend to the Secretary of State the propriety of leaving open to colonial youth the higher and more valuable government offices instead of appointing persons from 'home'. Roderic O'Connor, another large landed proprietor with a huge retinue of convict servants,

---

[19] Gladstone to Eardley-Wilmot (public), 30 April 1846, and Gladstone to Eardley-Wilmot (private), 30 April 1846, C.O. 408/25; W. E. Gladstone, op. cit., appendix 7; Journal of James Stephen, 28 June 1846.

[20] Stanley to Eardley-Wilmot, 30 June, 11 August, 20 September, 3 October 1845, C.O. 408/25; Eardley-Wilmot to Stanley, 1 August 1845, C.O. 280/184; Eardley-Wilmot to Stanley, 9 January 1846, C.O. 280/191.

thought such a move would stop both young men of talent and enterprise drifting over the water to Melbourne, and able youths idling away their time with pipes in their mouths in public houses. It looked as though that dead hand of the past which had condemned them to the fate of a stricken people while New South Wales was shedding convictism was about to be removed. It looked as though Van Diemen's Land was about to rejoin the great river of life in Australia.

Eardley-Wilmot made no contribution to that debate. In the spring of 1846 he wept as he read to members of the Council those words of Gladstone in which the latter told him Her Majesty's Government had decided that he could no longer exercise his present functions with advantage or justice to the public. He went on to tell them in a voice broken by anguish that his recall had been brought about not by the dispute between himself and the late members of the Council but by the conviction forced upon Her Majesty's Government that he had not paid sufficient attention to the moral and religious welfare of the convicts. Some said he was only paying a just penalty for his conceit and his self-confidence; others claimed he was another victim of 'that stiletto system' and the 'holy autocracy', which stifled all human striving in their society; others with an eye for the deeper causes bringing a man to destruction detected a 'retributive justice' in the removal of Sir Eardley, since he had voluntarily identified himself with a system which he should have condemned, and had become the patron and defender of a scheme he should have denounced in the most emphatic language. He had been held responsible for its failure, and fallen beneath its ruins.[21]

With great dignity Eardley-Wilmot protested his innocence. He asked Gladstone to rescue him from the double loss of character and office occasioned by these 'grossest falsehoods that ever oppressed an English gentleman', by conferring on him a personal mark of distinction so that the world might see that Her Gracious Majesty would not suffer the lowest of her subjects to be treated with injustice. He still had his faith that in the end the truth would prevail. Before those in high places could make amends for judging him so harshly and so hastily 'poor old Sir Eardley' began to waste away in Hobart till death liberated him on 4 February 1847 from the sufferings the character assassins had inflicted on him. At his funeral on 10 February, as the band struck up the 'Dead March' from Handel's *Saul*, irrepressible grief swept over the huge crowd that turned up to atone to the dead. As the body of Sir Eardley rotted in the soil of St David's Park, the survivors took up the struggle for self-government and the end of the convict taint. Another survivor, Lady Eardley-Wilmot, went on living quietly at the shores of the Mediterranean. The one woman who probably knew what went on in the heart of Sir Eardley kept her silence about those years when what came up from

---

[21] *Colonial Times*, 22 August 1846; Diary of G. T. W. Boyes, 25 September 1846; *Tasmanian*, 29 September 1846; *Colonial Times*, 6, 20, 27 October 1846; *Hobart Town Courier*, 26 October 1846; *Launceston Examiner*, 26 September 1846; *Hobart Town Advertiser*, 15, 29 September, 6 October 1846; *Atlas*, 17 October 1846.

inside him, or the 'holy autocracy' or both, or chance nailed her husband to the tree.[22]

Four months later a Dr W. R. Pugh in Launceston used the agent sulphuric ether to render two people in a surgical operation unconscious and insensible to pain. This resulted in a trial. He had copied the idea from surgeons at Boston in the United States. The result of the trial was so satisfactory as to lead him to hope that, in future, surgery would cease to be looked upon with that dread which had been from the earliest times associated with its proceedings. The epoch of material progress, begun with the application of machinery to production, and the use of steam communication on both sea and land, was to be accompanied by a diminution in one great area of human suffering. That tear duct of humanity was about to be dried up.[23]

At the same time the inhabitants of South Australia were quite determined that their worldly prospects and the proper moral tone with which they had so diligently fertilized their spiritual soil not be blighted by the 'loathsome putridity' that preyed on the vitals of Van Diemen's Land. When news reached Adelaide that the British Government was proposing to introduce convicts from Parkhurst Prison in London as free immigrants, a public meeting was held on 21 January 1845 at which the respectable bourgeoisie voiced their claim that convicts would put an end to the days of 'profitable returns' and 'virtuous, happy and permanent homes'. They knew that the garment of respectability they so proudly wore had some grubby spots. From time to time there were reports of white men committing barbarous deeds against aborigines in revenge for the latter stealing sheep or disturbing the white man's occupation of the land. From time to time some uncouth creatures intruded on one of the ceremonies of their respectability cult. In January 1845 a drunken fellow reeled into St John's Church on a Sunday evening during the reading of prayers, placed himself next to His Excellency the Governor and began to talk loudly in between imbibing copious draughts from a bottle of a well-known inflaming fluid.[24]

From the Bible they drew the lesson that man's punishment for Adam's fall was to earn his living in the sweat of his brow. A week's cessation of business, or any abandonment to mere pleasure, plagued them with feelings of guilt. All the outward and visible signs illustrated their superiority over the penal colonies, and the wisdom of having nothing to do with convict labour. Their population had increased from 14 884 in 1841 to 17 196 in 1843 and 22 460 in 1845. Unlike the penal colony of New South Wales, they had preserved an equal proportion between the sexes and so avoided the moral

---

[22] Eardley-Wilmot to Gladstone, 26 September, 5 October 1846, C.O. 280/196 and copies of correspondence between the Secretary of State and Sir Eardley-Wilmot, *P.P.*, 1847, xxxviii, 262, pp. 527-37; *Colonial Times*, 5, 9, 10 February 1847; Diary of G. T. W. Boyes, 1, 4, 10 February 1847; memorial to Sir John Eardley-Wilmot in St David's Park, Hobart, erected in 1850.
[23] *Launceston Examiner*, 9 June 1847.
[24] *South Australian Register*, 1, 6, 7, 25 January, 6, 10 September 1845; J. Boothby, *A Statistical Sketch of South Australia* (Adelaide, 1876).

evils of prostitution and sodomy which were the price New South Wales paid for the gross disproportion between the sexes. In the city of Adelaide the proportion between the sexes was approximately equal. Even in the country districts the proportion of men to women was five to four, and not that disastrous five, six, seven, or eight to one which was the rule in the districts in New South Wales outside the limits of location. Nor were they blighted with bush barbarism and the other evils attendant on dispersion of settlement. In 1841 there were just over six thousand people in the town of Adelaide and nearly fifteen thousand in the country districts. The aborigines were dwindling. By that year there were just over six hundred in Adelaide and a similar number in the country districts out of the ten thousand believed to be in the province when John Hindmarsh held out the hand of friendship to them on foundation day in December 1836.[25]

Their production of wealth illustrated the same superiority: New South Wales imported wheat; South Australia exported its surplus to England, New South Wales and Western Australia. New South Wales, Van Diemen's Land and Western Australia were dependent on hand labour to till the soil and depasture their stock; South Australia was beginning to use the Ridley agricultural machine which reaped, threshed and winnowed wheat simultaneously, and promised to relieve the farmers from their dependence on cheap migrant labour. The frontiers of settlement in New South Wales were characterized by barbarism and desolation; in South Australia an extraordinary throw of chance changed part of the frontier imposed by nature to the north of Adelaide from desolation to a land of unsuspected riches.

On a day of drenching rain late in 1842 Francis Stacker Dutton, the gentleman proprietor of Anlaby, pulled his horse up at Kapunda beside a large mass of protruding clay slate, which he found on examination to be impregnated with copper. In the same months the son of Captain Bagot found more evidence of copper in the area. Dutton and Bagot marked out eighty acres around the site which they bought at £1 an acre. Dutton then recruited Cornish miners, housed them in bluestone cottages, built a school for their children and a chapel for Sunday observance, and proceeded to make a fortune out of copper mining. In 1845 even richer deposits were discovered at Burra on the very fringe of those deserts of desolation which had plunged Eyre and Sturt into despair.[26]

By the middle of 1845 these adventurers in South Australia were looking to the railway to introduce the next step in the story of subduing a harsh, uncouth land, and to bring an even higher level of prosperity. Men of sensibility were beginning to have qualms that the railway would destroy the romance of country life and begrime the cottages and the leafy nooks. 'Where

[25] *South Australian Parliamentary Papers*, 1857-8, paper no. 47; Blue Books of the Colony of South Australia, 1841, 1843 and 1845, C.O. 17/13; F. Lancaster Jones, *The Structure and Growth of Australia: aboriginal population* (Canberra, 1970), p. 4.
[26] *South Australian Register*, 15 January, 7 February 1845; F. Dutton, *South Australia and Its Mines* (London, 1846), pp. 77-8, 266-91.

the cow once lowed', they wistfully said, 'the engine now screams, and the pipe of the gentle Corybon is completely put out by the funnel of the loco-motive.' Some prophesied that the railway would level all distinctions in society by ending the unique dignity and style in which persons of conse-quence were wont to travel. Such a prospect did not disquiet the benevolent bourgeoisie of Adelaide or the settlers in the Mount Barker district, the Barossa Valley, Anlaby and Port Lincoln. Life in the bush was a more power-ful leveller of social distinctions than any machine invented in the Old World. Besides, the Australian bush had rarely provided the setting for any pastoral idyll but rather the setting for the dusky savage and the white barbarian. Surrounded by a society of men who found no need to put between themselves and death the myths with which men had consoled themselves through the ages, they were interested in the problems of utilitarian book-keepers, such as how much it would cost to build a railway and who was going to pay for it.[27]

They had no reason to resent the Mother Country. The plutocrats of New South Wales might denounce the rule by 'ignorant clerks' in Downing Street; the apologists for the plutocrats of South Australia mouthed sentiments of gratitude and benevolence towards the land of their fathers. If England drooped, they drooped; when she lifted up her head, they exulted. Nor did they entertain any sustained ill will towards their governor or the members of his government. Grey had smoothed the way for the adventurers and plutocrats to get their hands on the mineral wealth of the colony. He had played his part in the establishment of prosperous tenant farmers at Mount Barker and the Barossa Valley, renting land from the South Australian Company and large landowners such as the Dutton brothers and J. Morphett. While Wentworth was teaching his fellow-countrymen not to forget that the wilds of Australia belonged to them, and not to the British Government, it never occurred to any public men to stake such a claim. In the same year as Wentworth was whipping up hatred against Gipps, Dutton was praising Grey as a man who, though young in years, was old enough in wisdom and the knowledge of finance to make a most excellent governor. When the time came to farewell Grey in October 1845 on the eve of his departure to take up his new post as Governor of New Zealand, the people of Adelaide and the surrounding districts congratulated the home government for selecting such 'an indefatigable and truly excellent Governor' for the important post.[28]

No such praise from a prominent public figure in New South Wales ever warmed the heart of Sir George Gipps. From London there had been pleasing words of commendation. For his behaviour in the controversy over the regu-lations of 2 April, Stanley complimented him highly on the exercise of 'that sense of public duty' which had led him to incur odium. Stanley also con-

---

[27] *Punch* (London), vol. 9, July-December 1845, p. 26, vol. 12, January-June 1847, p. 151; *South Australian Register*, 8 October 1845.

[28] *South Australian Register*, 1, 15, 18, 22 January 1845; F. Dutton, op. cit., pp. 77-8; speech by W. C. Wentworth, *S.M.H.*, 10 April 1844.

gratulated him on acting with justice and propriety in not sacrificing the interests of the colony and the Empire at large, as well as the universally admitted rights of the Crown, for the purpose of disarming opposition. So, despite the vigorous opposition from Ben Boyd and the Pastoral Association, Stanley gave his approval to the regulations of 2 April. By the end of 1845 Stanley dismissed sharply the Wentworth demand for responsible government in the Report of the Select Committee on General Grievances. 'Her Majesty', he wrote, 'must decline to enter into any stipulation at once so abstract and so vague . . . nor is Her Majesty advised that to discuss such Theories, or to propound such abstract principles, forms any branch of the duties which the Laws and Constitution of the British Empire call on her to discharge.' As for the proposal for a tribunal of impeachment, Stanley dismissed that too with the curt remark that 'it exists in no one of the Colonies subject to the British Crown'. When Stanley told him in a despatch of 16 March 1845 that towards the close of the year he might expect his successor to reach New South Wales, his term of office having expired on 23 February 1844 he went on to tell him that he (Gipps) would quit New South Wales in possession of the approbation of the Queen, of the confidence of Her Majesty's Government, and of the attachment of the great body of the people whom he had been called to govern.[29]

By contrast, in New South Wales there was naught for his comfort. Estranged from Broughton during the education controversy in 1844, and still not finding it easy to share the secrets of his heart with any man, Gipps became more and more isolated with the passage of time. None of the policies with which he was associated seemed to produce results. After Windeyer persuaded the Legislative Council on 19 August 1845 to appoint a select committee to consider the condition of the aborigines and the best means of promoting their welfare, Mahroot, one of the few aborigines left in Sydney, told them it would not do blackfellows any good to be made like white-fellows. He also told them that the only good the members of the Legislative Council could do for blackfellows was to keep them away from whitefellows. Polding told them that some white men believed there was no more evil in shooting a blackfellow than in shooting a dingo.

The political comments in the public press were just as depressing. The *Sydney Morning Herald* warned its readers not to expect too much from the exercise of political power, it being the duty of all God's children to submit to the powers that be and to God's immutable decrees. The *Atlas* hurt Gipps by asking the *Herald* to give an example of a nation that had been liberated by submission and prayer or of a tyrant who had been persuaded to break the bonds of his slaves for humility's sake. The *Southern Queen*, an altar-and-throne sheet of the old school, which published its first number on 1 January 1845, expressed sentiments that were a caricature of Broughton's

[29] Stanley to Gipps, 30 January 1845, *H.R.A.*, I. xxiv. 218-19; Stanley to Gipps, 20 August 1845, *H.R.A.*, I. xxiv. 479; Stanley to Gipps, 16 March 1845, C.O. 202/5; Gipps to Stanley, 16 August 1845, *H.R.A.*, I. xxiv. 475.

impressive stand against the forces of his age. It opposed those persons who in their short-sighted foolishness would substitute a universal education and general culture, at the expense of the state, for the universal culture of the church. It warned its contemporaries not to put asunder what the constitution of England had joined together—namely, Church and State. The life of man without God would be a moral Babel which would not only confound its founders but crush and grind them into the very dust. The true conservative, it reminded its readers in a later number of the paper, denounced democratic principles because they led to unrestricted liberty and equality.[30]

Gipps knew that the proposals of 2 April had caused a permanent estrangement between him and many of the most educated, the most intelligent and the most wealthy inhabitants of the colony. He knew that in the homes of the best families in the colony the cry had gone up, 'Gipps must go.' He knew they called him a 'despotic radical' who was doing all in his power to ruin the colony. He knew that even amongst the ancient nobility of New South Wales the only family making a show for him was the Macarthur family at Camden. Week in week out through 1845 he had to endure as best he could the vulgar abuse in the *Atlas*. That paper had not only taken its stand on the proposition that the 'present absurd system of governing' the dependencies ought not to be continued by the Mother Country, but had the effrontery to paint Gipps as a monster who wanted to cheat them of the boon of responsible government. Week after week they insisted that until the lands of the colony were placed under the control of the government and the Legislative Council they were 'nothing more than the serfs of Lord Stanley and Sir George Gipps', and did not enjoy 'the benefits of the British Constitution'. In July 1845 they argued that a British governor who attempted to regulate by his own will the most important affairs of the people over whom he ruled, and studiously endeavoured to prevent the representatives of the people from interfering in any way with what most concerned them, was no better than a public enemy and should be treated accordingly. Sir George had most abundantly shown himself to be such a public enemy. They therefore echoed the call of the squatters: 'Gipps must go.'[31]

Soon rumours began to fly around Sydney Town and the inland that all was not well with the Captain-General and Governor-in-Chief of the colony of New South Wales. Sir George was no longer able to walk up the stairs of Government House in Sydney or Parramatta without pausing several times for breath. Doctors were consulted; they shook their heads and murmured sagely words such as 'asthma' and 'bilious headache'. But Gipps knew, and so did Lady Gipps know, that these bodily disorders were but the symptoms of a deeper malaise. The Captain-General and Governor-in-Chief was done. In the days of his great anguish he looked more and more to God to console him for being cheated of that recognition which the world either would not or could

[30] Evidence of Mahroot and J. B. Polding to the Select Committee on the Aborigines, *V. & P.* (L.C. N.S.W.), 1845; *S.M.H.*, 30 December 1844, 1 January 1845; *Atlas*, 4 January 1845; *Southern Queen*, 1, 23 January 1845.
[31] *Atlas*, 30 November 1844, 12 July, 24, 31 May, 26 July 1845.

not give, while Lowe, that great mistake of his life, tormented him for boring the world with his sorrows.[32]

To aggravate this wound to his heart, the opposition used Anniversary Day on 26 January 1846 as an occasion to give a dinner to honour Wentworth for his deep and fervent desire to benefit his native land and to endow it with those noble institutions which had been the glory and the fame of their fatherland. It was not one of those occasions when Wentworth distinguished himself either by the brilliance of his oratory or his taste for clawing his opponents. His speech was long, rambling and often incoherent. He did manage a few wounding words about the regulations of 2 April: he was happy to say that, though the Secretary of State had sanctioned them, the Governor of New South Wales had not dared to act on them. Lowe was the hero of the evening. To immense cheering, he told them that if they were given a fair participation in the rights enjoyed by other British subjects, there would be no conceivable reason for divorcing themselves from the parent state. If the Colonial Office persevered in its present policy, the bloody and expensive lesson of America would have to be read again in every quarter of the globe. It was as though Gipps would go down in history as an enemy of human freedom. To add insult to injury, Lowe asked those present the simple question: whom would they choose for their political ruler? He answered that question for them: the man to whom they had been doing honour that evening—William Charles Wentworth. This implied that Gipps was not wanted, that for eight years he had reduced himself to a nervous wreck only to live on in the minds of those over whom he had presided as a man who had stood between them and their enjoyment of the rights of Englishmen.[33]

Humanity was on the march in New South Wales. A month after James Norton escorted Wentworth home from that dinner in his honour, at which he had babbled on about being 'too much of a squatter', the *Sydney Morning Herald* was prophesying that the introduction of the railway would diffuse blessings over the whole community. The traveller who had to mount a horse and by dint of whip and spur urge his way over rugged roads, the rough dust and dirt, and under the scorching glare of the Australian sun, would then just have to step into a comfortable saloon, stretch his legs upon its carpeted floor, compose himself into a brown study and presently find himself at his journey's end. The settler who had to send his produce to Sydney and to bring back his supplies by the tedious, expensive and hazardous means of bullock-drays would then have nothing to do but place his commodities in the train at one end of the journey and take them out at the other without a moment's anxiety about drays breaking down, bullocks knocking up, drivers getting drunk, or bushrangers laying violent hands upon his property.[34]

[32] S. C. McCulloch, 'Unguarded comments on the administration of New South Wales, 1839-46', *Hist. Studies*, vol. 9, 1859, p. 42.
[33] *S.M.H.*, 28 January 1846; E. H. Statham to James Macarthur, 27 January 1846 (Macarthur Papers, vol. 31); Ruth Knight, *Illiberal Liberal*, pp. 115-17.
[34] *S.M.H.*, 7 February 1846.

Just one month after the *Sydney Morning Herald* was predicting that the iron rail would begin a new era in the history of mankind, a man came back to Sydney with news that promised squatterdom a new lease of life. On 29 March Ludwig Leichhardt came back from Port Essington not only with news that he had beaten the bush, but with stories of having seen land on which stock-holders could graze thousands and thousands of sheep and cattle. He was one of those giants in the land in the days before the levelling flood of industrial civilization, one of those mighty spirits with a vision of the grandeur of the human spirit to match the vision of grandeur entertained by Wentworth, the Dutton brothers, Phillip Parker King, James, William and Hannibal Macarthur, Thomas George Gregson, Samuel Pratt Winter, the Henty brothers, Charles Hotson Ebden and the other plutocrats of the Australian colonies. Born in Trebatsch, Prussia, in 1813, the gods had planted in him both the mind of a scientist and the creative imagination of an artist. His appetites for life and his own achievements were on a scale to match such talents. He wanted to find the answer to Faust's question: what held the world together in its innermost parts. He wanted to achieve 'something exceptional on a grand scale'; he wanted an 'heroic friendship' with another man; he wanted to play the piano well; he wanted to purify his soul and to bring it to perfection. He wanted also to study all the lechery and beastliness in man, because, like Schiller, he was puzzled why God should plant in the heart of the same creature both a vision of His throne, and the insect of sensual lust.

Nature certainly so mixed up the two elements in Leichhardt that in the eyes of his admirers he was a godlike creature, who talked of how the great souls perfected themselves through pain and suffering, and of his faith in his own 'higher development' in an endless hereafter. He knew himself to be one of those elect of God who were being prepared for an even higher destiny in the life of the world to come. In the eyes of his critics he was a sponger, a *poseur*, and a human fraud with disgusting personal habits—he tore into his food with the savagery of the beasts of the field; he spoke much of that love between man and man which surpassed that of woman, as though it were a love between two souls, but was much given to 'brotherly kissing'. Those who were uneasy in his presence or rejected the spirituality he spoke of as humbug and twaddle, noted that he spent his life either fawning on the men of substance such as James and William Macarthur, or talking to the aborigines. Others who did not respond to the magic and charisma dismissed him as a bad-tempered, ill-mannered brute who was pitting against the egalitarian tendencies of his age the mystical nonsense about God's elect. He had the appearance of a man who was singled out from the vast majority of mankind: he had a high intellectual forehead, the eye of a man whose vision was single, and the body of a man who was full of light; he had delicate, girlish hands which he was wont to hold clasped as a symbol of that harmony and serenity which settled deep in the heart of a man who had that love of things as they are, that *amor fati* of God's elect, that desire to say to the Mighty Disposer, 'Thy will be done on earth as it is in heaven'. After spending his youth in

Prussia he had studied in London and Paris and had then turned his mind to Australia, telling the man he loved in the mystical language with which he described all the actions of his life: 'The interior, the heart of this dark continent, is my goal, and I will never relinquish the quest for it until I get there'.

With the help of £200 from William Nicholson, who also paid his fare and provided an outfit of clothes, Leichhardt reached Sydney in February 1842. Between that year and 1844 he began his mystical communion with the Australian bush, sensing in those plains of desolation what he was seeking in life, that occasion when life and death united in love's embrace. He tried to interest Sir George Gipps in an expedition to Port Essington, but the latter was not swayed by his charm and charisma. So he turned to the sheep-walk men, who equipped him and put up the money to pay for a team of five. In August 1844 he and his party left Sydney by steamboat for Moreton Bay where they were joined by four others before setting out for Jimba, the most northerly squatting run on the Darling Downs. In October he and his party set out from Jimba to walk across the continent to Port Essington. They travelled down the Condamine River and over to Peak Downs which Leich-hardt believed could be used to graze cattle by the thousands. From there they travelled north to a river which he named the 'Burdekin' after one of his financial backers. In May in the Gulf country John Gilbert, like Grey and Mitchell, prophesied that so fine a country would soon be peopled with an industrious and persevering British population. Three weeks later the aborigines sneaked up behind him and plunged many spears in his back to avenge molestation of their women by two aborigines in Leichhardt's party.

The other members of the expedition begged Leichhardt to return at once to civilization but, believing the terror, the pain and the suffering they were experiencing were part of God's training to bring a great soul to perfection, he feasted his eyes instead on the beauty of the star-studded sky, which led his mind round to contemplating the greater beauty of God's world in the life of the world to come. His men, fashioned, as he saw it, of baser clay, pined for their liquor and their women. He told them sternly that they must endure to the end. They pushed on around the south-west corner of the Gulf and turned for Port Essington which they reached on 17 December 1845, when Leichhardt's heart was visited with a sense of gratitude to Almighty God for His infinite kindness to him. The commandant at Port Essington, Captain John Macarthur, found Leichhardt to be 'bitter, virulent, malicious, dishonest, shifting and mean'. Leichhardt's mind was, as ever, on higher things. He was told that one man from the marines had come to Port Essington solely to find John Gilbert and take revenge on him for seducing his sister, only to find Gilbert had been killed. He then asked Leichhardt in great emotion, 'Gilbert—is he gone then?' Life is immense. After a month's recuperation they boarded the steamer *Heroine* and reached Sydney on 29 March 1846.[35]

[35] F. W. L. Leichhardt, Tagebücher, 27, 29 September, 7 October 1832 (MS. in M.L.); M. Aurousseau (ed.), *The Letters of F. W. Ludwig Leichhardt* (3 vols, Cambridge, 1968), vol. I, pp. 29-31, 154, 166, 227-8, 375, 392; portrait of Leichhardt by William Nicholas;

Sydney gave him a hero's welcome. A song was composed in his honour. 'Mr. Leichhardt', wrote the *Sydney Morning Herald* on 28 March,

> has established the broad fact, that our continent possesses an Australia Felix to the north as well as to the south . . . a land of mingled sublimity and beauty; a land of majestic rivers and graceful streams . . . a land . . . of wheat and barley, and vines and fig-trees, and pomegranates; a land of oil-olive, and honey; a land wherein thou shalt eat bread without scarceness; a land whose stones are iron, and out of whose hills thou mayest dig brass!

Here indeed was a huge stretch of country in which the Ben Boyds, the Duttons, the Wentworths, the Macarthurs, and all those other giants in the land—those men who saw Australia as a country where eagles flew in the sky, and the *grands coeurs* lorded it on earth—could carve out landed empires for themselves. Or so they hoped, and dreamed and schemed while their benefactor, Ludwig Leichhardt, in those golden days in May when the waters of Sydney Harbour were stippled with silver, and such radiance hung in the air that the desire to send up a hymn of praise to the creator of such loveliness was bringing tears of joy to his eyes, retired to Camden Park as the guest of James Macarthur. He began to work on his journal for publication, choosing a text from Goethe's *Iphigenie auf Tauris* for his title-page: 'the gods make use of many good men to serve them on this wide earth'. He dedicated the book to William Alleyne Nicholson of Bristol, England, to Robert Lynd of Sydney and to the generous people of New South Wales. While he was penning these words about God's elect, he also wrote off a catty letter to a friend complaining that the Macarthur family did not provide him with free writing paper.[36]

Wentworth, too, had his hopes during the autumn of 1846. Everyone in public life knew that the octogenarian McLeay had at last decided to give up the position of Speaker of the Legislative Council. Wentworth promptly proposed that the next Speaker should have what he called a 'dinner salary' so that he could entertain fellow-members and distinguished guests at dinners, where a forest of glasses beside each setting gave a promise of a wine with each course, champagne with the pudding, and brandy and water over the cigars. Members of Council laughed in his face, for they knew Wentworth had his eyes on the job. On 19 May, on the motion of Charles Cowper,

---

J. F. Mann, *Eight Months with Dr. Leichhardt in the Years 1846-47* (Sydney, 1888); Leichhardt to W. J. Little, 12 November 1842, M. Aurousseau (ed.), op. cit., vol. 2, p. 590; Leichhardt to John Murphy, 3 December 1842, ibid., vol. 2, p. 600; Leichhardt to William Nicholson, 26 October 1842, ibid., p. 552; Leichhardt to T. L. Mitchell, 24 July 1844, ibid., p. 780; Diary of John Gilbert, 10 May 1845 (MS. in M.L.); Journal of L. Leichhardt, 1845, p. 431 (MS. in M.L.); P. G. Spillett, *Forsaken Settlement* (Melbourne, 1972), p. 128.

[36] *S.M.H.*, 28 March 1846; F. W. L. Leichhardt, *Journal of an Overland Expedition in Australia from Moreton Bay to Port Essington* (London, 1847); Leichhardt to R. Lynd, 20 April 1846, M. Aurousseau (ed.), op. cit., vol. 3, p. 863; Leichhardt to Gaetano Durando, 27 September 1846, ibid., pp. 906-8.

seconded by Terence Murray, the Council called Charles Nicholson to the chair.

In May Gipps had the severest paroxysm of asthma he had ever experienced, and found after his recovery that he could not bear rapid motion of any sort. He even had to abandon horseback riding, one of his few pleasures in life. The doctors pressed him not to wait for the arrival of his successor, but to book his passage back to England immediately. At the very moment that Wentworth was on the prowl for a victim to relieve the humiliation he had exposed himself to during the election of the new Speaker, the Captain-General and Governor-in-Chief of the colony of New South Wales took the risk of appearing in person at the bar of the Legislative Council where he took the still more enormous risk of singing an aria, as it were, on his achievements during his eight years in office. The members thanked him in words which fell far short of what Sir George expected. Within a few weeks they again rubbed salt in the wounds by sending a message to the Governor that Council could not uphold the Crown's right to tax by use of the pre-rogative powers of the executive. Gipps snapped back that since this was an address to which no reply was required, no reply would be given, and pro-rogued the Council until such time as his successor arrived. He told his friend La Trobe how delighted he was at having got rid of the Legislative Council, for he knew that they had hoped to annoy him but now could not. He had booked his passage for dear old England, and hoped to be quite well before the ship rounded Cape Horn.[37]

His friends vainly tried to soften the agony of his last days in Australia. La Trobe told him he had found the hand of Sir George to be a 'kind, agree-able & steady one'. Broughton reminded him of his Saviour's warning that in the world all God's children must expect tribulation and sorrow. Edward Deas Thomson and John Hubert Plunkett let him know he would live on in their hearts and minds. The Total Abstinence Societies of New South Wales presented him with an address of thanks for his sturdy and liberal support of the temperance cause during his administration. But nothing they did stopped the voices of his enemies ringing in his ears. The *Sydney Morning Herald* accused him of converting a people heretofore glorying in the name of Britons into a community of 'fretful, angry, discontented spirits'. They accused him of being the worst governor New South Wales had ever had. They reminded him cruelly that out of a population of 180 000 only 205 were prepared to put their names on a testimonial in his honour, despite the importunity of the testimonial beggars. The *Atlas* said he was leaving the colony with a constitution almost as much disorganized as the government which he had embroiled by his mismanagement. When he left Sydney on 11 July they described how seventeen hundred unwashed low fellows flourished their dirty handkerchiefs in the face of Sir George and begged to

[37] *S.M.H.*, 15, 20 May 1846; *V. & P.* (L.C. N.S.W.), 14, 19 May 1846; Gipps to La Trobe, 9, 19 June 1846 (Gipps-La Trobe Correspondence); Ruth Knight, *Illiberal Liberal*, pp. 136-8.

assure him that the people of New South Wales would not mourn when he died.[38]

After he arrived in London from Portsmouth by rail on 21 December 1846 the doctors placed him under the most arbitrary commands not to engage in any kind of business, not to write to or see anybody and not to take exercise of any sort. Neither doctors nor his own great strength of character could avail him. He died suddenly of a heart attack on 28 February 1847 in his fifty-seventh year. A month later Elizabeth Gipps wrote to Thomson, 'the Friend with whom you were so intimately associated for so long a period is no more. His [so] sudden removal was as unlooked for by me as it was bitter . . . how wretched I am . . .' She ended with a human cry: '[do] not forget me'. Those who had loved him erected a memorial in Canterbury Cathedral to Lieutenant-Colonel Sir George Gipps, late Governor of New South Wales and its dependencies who had expired beloved, honoured and regretted by all who knew him. They chose as the text to sum up his life the words: 'the memory of the just is blessed'.

When the news reached Sydney, some said the time had come for the generous foe to mourn, and frankly say, 'The man indeed was great', and leave his 'wounded soul to God'. Some said he had fallen, a sacrifice to his 'indefatigable and unrelaxed endeavours to promote the interests' of New South Wales. Some said those cares and vexations of his office which had broken his health had been caused by his own wilful and wrong-headed policy. Some said his period of government was an unhappy one because Sir George, though a man of great intellect, knowledge and integrity, had a somewhat proud and peremptory disposition, and an infirmity of temper that had aggravated the unpleasant collision between him and the Legislative Council. Yet whatever complaint there might be against his prudence, he had retired with his honour unsullied and the purity of his motives acknowledged. That was the difference between Sir George and Sir Eardley, though both of them had fallen victims to the same historical situation. Both had found themselves the unwitting defenders of a political order that was passing away. Gipps was condemned in his lifetime by supporters of the old order in society and praised in posterity by those people who benefited from his support for the creative forces of his time.[39]

One month after Gipps set out on that journey which was to end with his body being laid to its eternal rest beside the marble angels, the martyrs and

[38] La Trobe to Gipps, 31 October 1845 (Gipps-La Trobe Correspondence); *Maitland Mercury*, 1 July 1846, W. Macarthur to Bidwill, 7 August 1846 (Macarthur Papers, vol. 37); *S.M.H.*, 4, 6, 8, 11 July 1846; *Atlas*, 4, 11 July 1846.

[39] G. Gipps to E. D. Thomson, 30 December 1846 (Deas Thomson Papers, vol. 3); Gipps to La Trobe, 30 December 1846 (Gipps-La Trobe Correspondence); Elizabeth Gipps to E. D. Thomson, 29 March 1847 (Deas Thomson Papers, vol. 3); *Bell's Life in Sydney*, 10 July 1847; monody on the death of Sir George Gipps by Samuel Prout Hill, *Heads of the People*, 31 July 1847; William Macarthur to — Bidwill, 7 August 1846 (Macarthur Papers, vol. 37); bust of Sir George Gipps in Canterbury Cathedral, personal visit, 5 May 1968.

the prophets, a huge concourse of people assembled at Circular Quay to welcome Sir Charles FitzRoy as the Governor-elect of New South Wales. Robert Lowe moved around that vast crowd dressed in a flowered waistcoat and a bright claret-coloured overcoat as a sign or portent of the new spirit abroad. After landing, His Excellency mounted an horse and rode slowly towards Government House amidst the immense cheers of the crowd, which he heartily acknowledged, for his manly and dignified person and deportment seemed golden auguries of his popularity. Sir Charles had all the distinguishing marks of a high-born Englishman. Born in 1796, he was the grandson of that third duke of Grafton whose illustrious ancestress was one of the many women whose charms were said to be the boast and whose vices the disgrace of three nations during the reign of Charles II. He had fought at Waterloo, held a seat in the unreformed House of Commons, and revelled in the gaiety and pleasure of life in the great houses during the Regency period. In manner he was cordial, good-humoured, jolly and warm, all qualities his predecessor had patently lacked.

His wife, Lady Mary FitzRoy, was a woman of great beauty. She was the eldest daughter of the fourth duke of Richmond and his wife Charlotte, who was the eldest daughter of the fourth duke of Gordon. As a child she had romped with Arthur Wellesley, the future Duke of Wellington, and enjoyed riding with him in Phoenix Park, Dublin. As a young girl she had spent the night upstairs in that rented house in Brussels in which her parents gave a ball on the eve of Waterloo—that night of many splendours when 'There was a sound of revelry by night'. Her mother had told her the Iron Duke's laconic reply to her question whether he had taken lovers during his year as ambassador in Paris: 'There was plenty of that.' Her mother had told her, too, of the Duke's comment on Waterloo: 'The finger of Providence was upon me, and I escaped unhurt.'

According to the local scribblers, the upstart in his mushroom arrogance, who had been as difficult of access as the icy regions of the north, had been replaced by a plain, simple, unaffected, high-souled Christian gentleman, descended, like his charming and beautiful wife, from a line of nobility. Unlike Sir George, FitzRoy soon mixed cordially in all the convivialities of Sydney. He gave a series of dinner parties to members of the Legislative Council and their wives: invitation cards poured out of Government House. He went to the Five Dock Races and experienced a hearty welcome from the gentlemen present. The sport was exceedingly good and Sir Charles seemed fully to enjoy it. He delighted the people of Sydney and Parramatta with displays of his skill in driving a four-in-hand through the streets, and caught the eye of the ladies with his elegant dress. Sir George had ruled from his 'closet' and those communions with his Maker in the bedchamber. Sir Charles soon toured the country districts. Grace Dangar of Neotsfield was bowled over by his charm and his warmth, as were other hostesses in the mansions of the country gentry. Sir Charles soon showed the members of the government as well as the members of the Legislative Council that good statesmanship was compatible with a cheerful enjoyment of life. By September observers noted that Wentworth's greeting to the new governor was rough and warm. Her Gracious Majesty had chosen a friend of the plutocrats to be the captain-general and governor-in-chief in and over the colony of New South Wales.[40]

Sir Charles believed that his first duty was to restore harmony between the executive and the legislature and replace those coarse and disrespectful exchanges during the period of his predecessor by a more wholesome relationship which would improve the feelings of the leading and most influential members of the community towards the Home Government. Sir George had gone to England impressed with the conviction that he had nothing to retract or modify. Sir Charles would not make the mistake of trying to overbear single-handed all opposition, because as things stood the representative body, the Legislative Council, was fully aware of its own power to thwart every government measure whenever it was so inclined.

When the replies came in from the clergy in Sydney and the outlying districts to the questionnaire of a committee of the Legislative Council on the best means of promoting the welfare of aborigines, Sir Charles had not the slightest difficulty in passing by on the other side of the road. The Reverend William Cowper reported that the diminution and final disappearance of the tribes in the neighbourhood of Sydney had been caused by adopting the vicious habits of immoral Europeans. From Brisbane Water the Reverend John Gregory reported that the Europeans in his district attributed the total failure of every attempt to ameliorate their barbarous state to the fact that these untutored savages were decreed by their creator to be permanently an inferior race of beings. Sir Charles did not even believe that their gradual disappearance off the face of the earth, which caused such pain to all those who believed God might judge them by what they had not done for 'the least of the little ones', was worthy of comment.[41]

Much of life in New South Wales struck Sir Charles as coarse, loud-mouthed and vulgar. In Melbourne and Sydney hooligans regularly desecrated the Sabbath by brawling in the streets. In Melbourne the celebration of St Patrick's Day in March by the Catholics and the Battle of the Boyne day on 12 July by the Orangemen often ended in riot and bloodshed. The latter gave the Orangemen the opportunity to taunt the Irish Catholics as that 'mob of cowstealers who had run like sheep when the English soldiers crossed the Boyne river in July 1690'. There was more to it than this beating on the drums of the past. As in the United States the increase in the number of Irish Catholic migrants in the early 1840s had threatened the traditional Protestant ascendancy both in wealth and employment opportunities. In the

United States the know-nothing and nativist movements, the raising of the cry 'America for the Americans', heralded two decades of excitement, lawlessness and mob rule. In New South Wales the news that the British Government had begun to subsidize the training of priests at Maynooth, and the arrival of the French, a Catholic power, at Tahiti fanned the flames of Protestant hostility to Catholics. In New South Wales, as in the United Kingdom and the United States, the members of the Orange Lodge exploited such fears.

Orange Clubs had existed in Ireland since 1690 to save the country from 'popery, slavery, arbitrary power, brass money and wooden shoes'. In 1795 they had united to form the Orange Lodge, the members of which took an oath to preserve the Protestant ascendancy. By that year they had also committed their members to the defence of the existing order against revolution or social change. The Orange Lodge was active both in Sydney and Melbourne by 1840. By 1844 both in Sydney and Melbourne Irish Catholics were accusing the Orangemen of swearing to write their names in papist blood. The Orangemen countered by accusing the Irish Catholics of treasonable practices, of cherishing Irish patriotism and of educating their children to be loyal to 'dear old mother Ireland' while remaining silent on loyalty to Her Majesty and the United Kingdom. The Irish Catholics threatened wild acts to avenge the ancient wrong against their people. They preserved in the hearts of their people that picture of the Protestant as an ogre driven by some diabolical passion to impoverish and degrade the Irish people. The Orange Lodge maintained that the Irish Catholics wanted to convert New South Wales into a 'replica of Tipperary' where superstition-ridden, priest-ridden semi-savages roamed the countryside threatening Protestant landlords to 'bespeak a coffin and get the death of Barrabas the Jew'. The Irish Catholics wore a shamrock in their hats and carried a shillelagh in one hand and a bottle in the other. The only happiness they knew was when they were fighting. Some Protestants saw them as a dirty, disgusting people who insulted the dead with their drunken Irish wakes.

On 13 July 1846 the Orangemen hung banners portraying their version of the abominations of popish superstition from the windows of the Pastoral Hotel in Melbourne. That afternoon several bands of 'ruffian looking fellows', some armed with muskets and fowling-pieces, and others with bludgeons of all sorts and descriptions, gathered outside the hotel to demand that the banners be removed. When that demand was rejected with indignation, the 'croppies' broke down the door of the hotel and charged up the staircase, from where the Orangemen drove them back into the street. Shots were exchanged. Two 'croppies' fell. The mayor ordered the landlord of the Pastoral Hotel to close his doors against the admission of all parties that night.

All that night in Melbourne members of both sides discharged fire-arms. One Orangeman, quietly proceeding homewards, was assailed in the streets and seriously maltreated. The following day eighty to one hundred armed 'croppies' gathered at a public house in Elizabeth Street kept by one Collins, while sixty-odd Orangemen gathered at the Bird-in-Hand Hotel in Flinders Street as rumours flew around Melbourne of the vengeance the Orangemen were plotting against the authorities for arresting only Orangemen the preceding day. Later that day a mob of 'croppies' shouted abuse at His Honour the Superintendent's coachman and uttered threats of what they would do to His Honour if he fell into their hands. Some days later the defenders of the Protestant ascendancy were still praising the Orangemen for their efforts to prevent the transformation of Port Phillip into 'a province of Popedom' by standing 'shoulder to shoulder' in the streets of Melbourne for the preservation of the Protestant religion, the maintenance of the British constitution, and the observance of 'peace and order' against a 'furious Popish rabble'.

Fearing such riots might damage the reputation of Port Phillip and even cause a delay in the granting of separation from New South Wales, the solid bourgeoisie of Melbourne asked their absentee government in Sydney to ban all processions that perpetuated national animosities, political feuds and religious embroilments. The members of the Executive Council in Sydney agreed that the time had come to put a stop to such sectarian excesses. In Sydney that July, despite a request by Father McEnroe to Irish Catholics to conduct themselves in an orderly and peaceable manner and to attend a meeting of St Patrick's Teetotal Society, great numbers of 'hurlers' gathered outside the Orange Lodge in King Street, where the members had assembled in convivial conclave to manifest their devotion to the Queen and the British constitution. Soon a riotous and blood-thirsty mob threatened to murder 'all b----y Orangemen' and 'all b----y Protestant dogs' with their hurling-sticks. They also threatened the life of the proprietor of the weekly paper, the *Sentinel*, the avowed and uncompromising defender of Orange Protestantism, and the implacable foe of popery, who had pledged himself to carry on despite 'the rabid ravings', 'turbulent bluster' and 'bragadocia [sic] threats' of the popish mob.

In October the government introduced into the Legislative Council the Party Processions Bill which declared it an offence punishable by law for any body of persons to meet and parade together, join in procession, or assemble in any public house, tavern or other place within the colony for the purpose of commemorating any festival, anniversary or political event related to or connected with any religion or other distinctions or differences, and who should bear, wear or have among them any fire-arms or other offensive weapons, or should have publicly exhibited any banner, emblem, flag or symbol calculated to provoke animosity between Her Majesty's subjects of different religious persuasions, or who should be accompanied by any music of a like nature or tendency. Some members of Council had misgivings about restrictions on the liberty of the subject, but the 'calm down conformists' had their way, and the bill became an Act. Sir Charles made light of the whole affair. For him it was a riot between the 'lower orders of the Catholic and Protestant Inhabitants', and he was glad to say that the Party Processions Act had had the effect of preventing a repetition of such unseemly and vulgar behaviour on the occasion of Guy Fawkes day that year.[42]

The men with an eye on the way forward believed such sectarianism to be part of the dead past, one of those echoes of ancient wrongs in the Old World. The men in the New World ought to go forward into the new era of industrial civilization and tether the mighty bush to the world with an iron rail rather than keep it as a sheep-walk. Thanks to the iron rail, Europe and North America were taking a great leap forward while Australia was at least a century behind them. On 6 May 1846 a public meeting was held in Sydney of all those friendly to the building of a railway from Sydney to Goulburn. Speakers argued that such a development would provide a field of investment for British capital, reduce the cost of transport for goods going up-country, and make New South Wales the example of the most rapid advancement to prosperity the world had ever seen. Some drew attention to the moral benefits to be gained from dispensing with those bullock-drivers whose 'horrid oaths and blasphemy' debased their community. Some predicted the iron rail would increase their creature comforts. This prompted the Cassandras in their midst to prophesy that creature comforts would destroy the moral fibre of the people by conveying the delusion that a man might become rich by speculation, fraud and bribery rather than by honest labour. No revivalist preacher warned them that the railway was being sent by a 'tireless Satan to try all Christian men'. Nor were they bothered by the Old World fears that the railway would put their country in iron chains, end the pastoral of country life, begrime the countryside, and level all social distinctions. New South Wales had known no 'Philemon and Bauchis', no idyll of country life, but only the bush barbarians. New South Wales was not put out by the threat of the railway as a leveller of social distinctions, because their own past and their harsh, uncouth environment had already levelled out what the iron rail was about to level in the Old World. They were looking to the steam-engine to drag them out of their material backwardness and to contribute to the reduction in the cost of production of their staple wool. The same men looked to the introduction of steam communication between the Australian colonies and the United Kingdom as another means of reducing costs.[43]

---

[42] T. B. Macaulay, *The History of England* (2 vols, London, 1889), vol. 2, p. 191; R. A. Billington, *The Protestant Ascendancy* (2 vols, New York, 1960), vol. 1, pp. 256-8; C. Wittke, *The Irish in America* (Baton Rouge, 1956), pp. 46-8, 114-20; N. Longmate, *The Water Drinkers: a history of temperance* (London, 1968); H. Senior, *Orangeism in Ireland and Britain* (London, 1966), pp. 1-21, 284; *Port Phillip Herald*, 14, 16, 23 July 1846; *S.M.H.*, 22 October 1846; An Act to Prevent for a Time, Party Processions, and Certain Other Public Exhibitions, in the Colony of New South Wales, 10 Vic., no. 1, 27 October 1846, T. Callaghan, *Supplement to Acts and Ordinances of the Governor and Council of New South Wales* (Sydney, 1846); FitzRoy to Grey, 9 January 1847, *H.R.A.*, I. xxv. 308; *Argus*, 14, 17, 21 July 1846; *Sentinel*, 16 July 1846.

[43] *S.M.H.*, 5 April 1845, 7 February, 9, 12, 14 May 1846; *Atlas*, 22 August 1846; *Argus*, 11 September 1846; S. H. Holbrook, *The Story of American Railroads* (New York, 1847), pp. 24-5; *Punch* (London), vol. 10, January-June 1846, p. 163, vol. 9, July-December 1845, p. 214; Report from Select Committee on Steam Communication with England, 3 October 1846, *V. & P.* (L.C. N.S.W.), 1846, vol. 2.

The names of Ben Boyd, William Charles Wentworth, James Macarthur, William Lawson, Alexander Berry, the Henty brothers, Samuel Pratt Winter, the Dangar brothers and all the other rabid supporters of squatterdom's domination were conspicuously absent from the list of prominent supporters of the railway and the steamship. They still believed that hands rather than machines were the answer to the problems of the production, distribution and exchange of wealth in the Australian colonies. When Gladstone told FitzRoy in the spring of 1846 that Her Majesty's Government was aware that the supply of free labour in the Australian colonies was below the demand, and asked him to ascertain the disposition of the colonists to the introduction of 'bondsmen to enlarge its permanent supply', squatterdom was jubilant. On 13 October Wentworth, backed up by the sheep lobby in the Legislative Council, persuaded the Council to appoint a select committee to report on the proposal to renew transportation to New South Wales.[44]

A carefully stacked committee, supported by the evidence of hand-picked witnesses such as Ben Boyd, came to the conclusion that the renewal of transportation would be 'conducive to the interests and agreeable to the inclinations of those whom it would most directly and intimately concern'. They pointed out that the colony was already inundated on the south with the outpourings of the probation system in Van Diemen's Land. They also pointed out that New South Wales was soon to have poured into it from the north the exiles from the penitentiaries of the Mother Country. While they were collecting evidence, Gladstone had informed FitzRoy that North Australia was to be established as a separate colony as a receptacle for convicts in the Australian colonies who, by pardon or by lapse of time, had regained their freedom, but who might be unable to find elsewhere an effective demand for their services. This confirmed the information conveyed to Eardley-Wilmot in the preceding year that a new colony, to be called North Australia, was to be founded north of 26° S., to which would be sent all the liberated convicts of Van Diemen's Land who might throw themselves on the government of that colony. New South Wales, they argued, was entitled to 'counteracting advantages' in the shape of 'a modified and carefully regulated introduction of convict labourers'.

They did not want the probation gangs of Van Diemen's Land to be introduced into New South Wales. Such gangs were notorious cradles of vileness, vice and hypocrisy, where nothing beneficial to society had been accomplished, and the last lingering principles of rectitude were merged in the immense mass of surrounding villainy. Societies constituted of such men became a mass of festering infamy and the hotbeds of a nameless and abominable crime too deeply rooted and too widespread for the repressive powers of the criminal judicature of the land. They believed imprisonment in one's native land could not be so effectual by way of punishment as the solitude of the distant wilds of Australia. As a reformation, too, they did not believe there was anything equally effectual as the life of an assigned convict

[44] Gladstone to FitzRoy, 30 April 1846, *H.R.A.*, I. xxv. 34-7.

servant in the Australian bush. If anything could restore a fallen being, it must be the constant opportunities for reflection which such a life presented, the remorse it sometimes awakened in the most obdurate natures, the gradual estrangement from former tastes and pursuits, and the constant contemplation of the 'power and beneficence of the Great Author of the Universe'. They therefore asked for a quota of five thousand male convicts annually, provided it was accompanied by free immigration of both sexes to double that extent. They, too, were anxious to avoid a repetition of those vices that had disgraced the old convict system and the probation gangs. They painted a picture of the 'immense gains and mighty influences for good' which would flow from such a renewal of transportation. The seeds of a great community would be sown on this continent, which would shoot up with a vigour and rapidity unexampled in the history of their race. A 'mighty Colony' would arise linked to the Mother Country by strong ties of common origin and mutual interest. Australia would be a faithful subject and never-failing customer and would be attached to the Mother Country in time of peace and would not desert her in time of war.[45]

On 22 October the stage, the pit, the boxes and the galleries of the City Theatre in Sydney were filled to capacity by a huge audience which gathered to protest against this proposal to renew the abomination of assignment. Speaker after speaker expressed indignation that the colony had been sacri-ficed to the private aggrandizement of certain of its chosen guardians, who in the cause of that 'griping selfishness' were putting money into their own pockets. That blustering one-time champion of the people, William Charles Wentworth, with his iron tongue and his face of brass, had audaciously asserted that the convict system was the most reformatory, the most inexpensive and the most humane that had ever been devised. But the speakers shouted to immense cheering that the days of these defenders of the old order were numbered: their senatorial race was well-nigh run. They would be scattered like chaff before the wind. The *Australian* maintained that the popular clamour had uncovered a difference of opinion between the upper classes and the working classes. For their part they were not prepared to take it for granted that the workers were right. They argued with Went-worth that if the Home Government undertook to send out at its own expense a hundred free women for every hundred male convicts, then the drunkenness, the thievery, and all the evils predicted by the opponents of renewal would be demolished. The *Sydney Chronicle* hoped the Secretary of State would ignore this invitation from the mercenary few, and not outrage the feelings and undermine the affectionate loyalty of the many by renewing transportation.[46]

---

[45] Report from Select Committee on Renewal of Transportation, 31 October 1846, *V. & P.* (L.C. N.S.W.), 1846, vol. 2; Gladstone to FitzRoy, 7 May 1846, C.O. 395/1; Stanley's proposed despatch to Eardley-Wilmot, September 1845, encl. no. 1 in J. Stephen to S. M. Phillips, 8 September 1845, C.O. 201/370.
[46] *S.M.H.*, 24, 26 October 1846; *Australian*, 24 October 1846; *Sydney Chronicle*, 24 October 1846.

In all the country towns of New South Wales the people gathered to express this sense of outrage and indignation. At Maitland on 28 October the Catholic priest, Dean Lynch, roused those present to a frenzy with his simple words of denunciation: the lash, he said, 'might keep men in order, but a land watered with blood could never prosper'. At meetings at Murrurundi, Scone, Muswellbrook, Singleton, Paterson, Dungog and Newcastle speakers expressed their horror that a few mercenary stock-jobbers and stock-holders should dare to imperil the lives and property, the moral and social well-being, and the civil and political rights of the colonists for the sake of an extra 5 or 10 per cent per annum. Australian children would grow up like all children in slave countries, using the whip to make others work because they would not work themselves. Convicts would revive distinctions which were fast fading away, and revive the old system of 'legalized slavery'. It was better to be poor, but free and virtuous, than become opulent from a system of such evils. At Singleton a native-born son of convict parents, Joseph Jehoshaphat Harpur, the older brother of Charles Harpur, after expressing the fervent hope that those painful recollections of his childhood, those damning scenes and those cruelties had perished from the face of the earth, drew their attention to one terrible consequence of the renewal of transportation: convicts were men of such violent passions that they would finally exterminate the aborigines.[47]

The question men had to face was whether they wanted to enrich graziers at the moral expense of the whole community. On 22 December three thousand of the operative classes gathered in Sydney to testify that they preferred goodness and virtue to baseness and avariciousness. All the speakers played on the double threat to wages and to morals. A Mr Gould told them to deafening applause that he would rather slave and work the flesh off his bones to obtain a bare subsistence than wallow in wealth derived from convict labour, if he felt that his wife and family were exposed to its baleful and contaminating influences. For above all things the 'Missus' and the kids must be kept pure: she must be both a madonna and a domestic slave, both a 'Mother Machree' and a 'dish-washer'. When a Mr Tracy stated that he did not believe one in a hundred convicts ever became good and useful members of society, many called on him to shut up because many of those present had strong family ties with convicts. Then a Mr Hamilton asked them whether they wanted to have anything to do with reforming a convict by sending him into the wilderness to be eaten by the blacks or tortured into madness by unbearable solitude. He reminded them that in a convict society there would always be a system of police espionage. Mr J. Raphael was highly indignant at the proposal to introduce thousands of females to become the wives or concubines of convicts. He found this an 'infamous suggestion' and 'worthy

[47] *V. & P.* (L.C. N.S.W.), 30, 31 October 1846; *S.M.H.*, 11 November, 4 December 1846; FitzRoy to Gladstone, 6 November 1846, *H.R.A.*, I. xxv. 249-50 and encls in above; encl. in FitzRoy to Grey, 22 February 1847, ibid., 367-8; *Maitland Mercury*, 25, 28 November, 2, 9 December 1846.

of him who first drew his breath in that cess-pool of vice and infamy—Norfolk Island'. There were loud and prolonged cheers for that, not only because a dig at Wentworth's early associations with the convict community always pleased the opponents of Botany Bay Whigs and Tories, but because the working classes took pride in the contrast between their own purity, and the muddy morals of the supporters of renewal.

A Mr Geoghegan, an Irish working man, wound up proceedings with a clarion call: 'I call upon you, natives of Australia', he said, 'to record your opposition—will you tamely submit to behold your fair native land again being made the depôt of degradation? to hear in your streets the clank of the chain, and from yonder building [the Sydney Gaol] . . . hear the hissing of the scourge and the outcry of agony from the triangle?' He asked the Englishmen present, whose proud boast it was to belong to the land of the free, the Scotsmen whose ancestors had dyed the heather with their blood in the cause of freedom, and the sons of Erin, who had their own past to influence them against the use of the chain and the scourge, whether they would allow their adopted country to suffer such a fate. They all cried out 'Never!' He called on the citizens of Sydney to elect their own representatives to the Legislative Council and to establish a trades union for the protection of the citizen and labourer against the encroachments of monopoly and tyranny. There were loud and continued cheers for that. Geoghegan, who was one of what Wentworth called 'the low Irish mob', linked the campaign against renewal with the campaign for political power for the working classes. Those unruly fellows in the streets of Sydney, those youths who dressed in a loud colonial tweed and wore cabbage-tree hats on their heads, those loud-mouthed vulgarians who murdered the English language by speaking it with their nauseating and inane nasal twang and who delighted in picking on anyone in the streets wearing an imported beaver hat, and pulling it down over his eyes, proposed that the one way to rescue New South Wales from the moral pollution of convictism was for the people to seize the government and govern themselves.[48]

The native-born had already added their support to this opposition to a renewal of the 'shame of bondage'. As Charles Harpur saw it, the pastoralists of New South Wales, driven on by that passion 'to puff their windy shows of aristocracy', had shown themselves prepared to horde into New South Wales those who would 'perpetuate the shameful brand'. He was beginning to regret his lot of being born into a society of worldly men who declared that gain was good and fair. Outraged and disgusted by the drift of events in New South Wales, he decided at the close of 1846 to write a satire to expose and root up the thousand and one infamies that were everywhere depraving the

[48] *Citizen*, 26 December 1846; The Memorial of the Anti-Transportation Committee of Sydney and The Humble Petition of the Undersigned Operatives of the City of Sydney . . . to Her Most Gracious Majesty the Queen, encls 1 and 2 in FitzRoy to Grey, 1 February 1847, *H.R.A.*, I. xxv. 348-50; G. C. Mundy, *Our Antipodes* (London, 1855), pp. 15-17; Ruth Knight, *Illiberal Liberal*, p. 166.

morals and debasing the intellect of the rising generation of the colonial public, for he believed that the 'directest means of permanently establishing the righteous' arose 'out of the signal overthrow of the wicked'. He called his poem 'The Temple of Infamy'. He peopled it with the plutocrats of New South Wales. Of Ben Boyd he wrote:

> Of Benjamin say naught, 'All flesh is grass!'
> And thence his grazing passion—let him pass.

Of Wentworth he wrote that the one-time champion of the people had degenerated into

> The bullying, bellowing champion of the Few!
> A Patriot?—he who hath nor sense nor heed
> Of public ends beyond his *own* mere need!
> Whose Country's ruin, to his public fear,
> Means only this—the love of Windermere!
> And by the same self legislature rule,
> Australia's growth the growth of W—tw—th's wool!
> Her rights—her liberties, for number *one*
> A *Patriot*! He from whose statistic care
> All that his Country's general homes should bear
> Of mind and happiness, is thrust by that
> Which by some process may be turned to fat,
> And, duly barrelled and exported, then
> Return in *wine* for grazier *gentlemen*!

> Such is yon Man! and not a whit belied!
> A Patriot? Let him 'doff that lion's Hide'!
> Well may those Landsharks call him their pure Gem
> For bound thus to *himself*, he's bound to *them*.

By the end of 1846 Harpur was so weary of life when he saw how infamy waxed strong in his native land, how those who pretended to fear God were secretly worshipping Mammon, and how the people were tarnished with intellectual grossness, though a republican in politics, he decided it would be best for his country to continue during the present century at least a part of the British Monarchy. In his mind, even the 'state-botchers' of Downing Street were fully fifty years in advance of the half-educated wool kings of New South Wales, and infinitely preferable to anything of the kind which the latter could or would tinker up in the event of a premature separation. He still believed in God's goodness as the fountain-head of all true religion and still held a large faith in the capacity of human nature for good. To believe men radically incapable was to live with a degrading estimate of one's fellow-man. What pulled him up short from proclaiming a faith in man's powers to do something worthwhile in Australia was the dreadful society he had been compelled to herd with during the best years of his life and their perverse delight in dragging him down to their own miry level. Like the squatters and the patriarchs of the Council, this young Australian looked to London to save society from being run by men with an appetite for a belly-full but no interest in a full-blown civilization. Convictism, British philistinism and the spirit of the place had not bred cowards, crawlers or timid souls, but men with the limited vision that characterizes those who worship the gods of material well-being and happiness.[49]

[49] C. Harpur, 'The Proposed Recurrence to Transportation', 'To the Spirit of Poesie', 'The Tree of Liberty', 'Have Faith' and 'The Temple of Infamy', Miscellaneous Poems, 1847-8 (Harpur Papers, MS. in M.L.); *Citizen*, 26 December 1846.

14

THE IN-BETWEEN YEARS

ON CHRISTMAS DAY 1846 the Lord Bishop of Australia, William Grant Broughton, was mortified to see the Speaker of the Legislative Council, Dr Charles Nicholson, lolling in a carriage while reading a newspaper, and obviously having not the slightest intention of attending church on that day. The scene reminded Broughton of the number of men in public life who were either irreligious or not friends of the Church of England. There were Wentworth, Lowe, Windeyer, McLeay and that sybarite Nicholson, whose indifference contributed to the spread of unbelief in the Australian towns. The atheism of the town dwellers was the 'unlovely fruit' of that 'careless liberalism' of men in high places. In the interior the squatters' energies were fully absorbed in one intense effort to grasp 'unbounded acres and uncountable flocks', and they displayed an 'appalling remissness' and indifference to introducing the worship of God to the 'unhappy dwellers in those solitary places'. The Lord Bishop grew quite sad that day as he walked into the darkness of St James's Church while Nicholson stayed in the bright light of the sun.[1]

Humanity was on the long march away from the Judaico-Christian view of the world. The sublime hopes of humanity were about to disappear. God was about to be divested of his grace, and man of his divinely conferred dignity, of his special place in the scale of creation—lower than the angels but higher than the beasts. The tie between earth and heaven was about to be cut; the great idea of immortality was about to vanish. Heaven and Hell were about to be dropped as priests' inventions, to be replaced by a trust in the brotherhood of man, as men substituted love of each other for the hopes of the resurrection morning. At mid-century the men of imagination turned their minds to the life of man without God. Melville had his quarrel with God and made up his mind it was the fate of man to be annihilated, only to find he could neither believe nor be comfortable in unbelief; Hawthorne wrote his *Scarlet Letter*; Emily Brontë still cast her anchor of desire deep in unknown eternity; Dostoevsky wrote of his thirst to believe; Tennyson wrote of his anguish in 'In Memoriam':

> Man, her last work, who seem'd so fair,
> Such splendid purpose in his eyes,
> Who roll'd the psalm to wintry skies,
> Who built him fanes of fruitless prayer.

[1] W. G. Broughton to E. Coleridge, 9 January, 6 March 1847 (microfilm in NAT. L.).

Who trusted God was love indeed
And love, Creation's final law—
Tho' Nature, red in tooth and claw
With ravine, shriek'd against his creed—

Who loved, who suffer'd countless ills,
Who battled for the True, the Just,
Be blown about the desert dust,
Or real'd within the iron hills?

He decided he could not live by such a faith. He proposed to 'faintly trust the larger hope', that 'one far-off divine event/ To which the whole creation moves'. So did Charles Harpur in Australia in his own more anaemic discussion of the same agony. In his poem 'To the Spirit of Poesie', written in 1847, he put into words the grief of a man deprived of the hope of meeting beyond the grave and of belief in a God who cared for a man who had been compelled to herd in this world with a people who gloried in their 'intellectual grossness'.

But can it be that all we see,
Feel, think, is but a Panorama
Made up of past and present dreams?
That Heaven is vacant as it seems;
And life a breath exhaled, by death,
Which ends the drama?

Then is Man's great and rich Estate
But such as worldlings deem it ever!
Earth and sky, with naught between
Of spiritual life unseen!
And if so, fly! for those and I
At once should sever.

While Charles Harpur was taking the enormous risk of showing his heart to that 'sordid generation' or, as he called them, the 'present men of Australia', Charles Darwin, who had seen the dead bark swaying from the gum-trees in 1836, was thinking his way towards the bleak conclusions he was to put in *The Origin of Species*. Besides, Harpur and all the men of sensibility in Australia had to endure as best they could a second twist of the screw. They had to live not only in a country where most men gloried in their 'intellectual grossness', but where the uncouth environment, the weird animals, the sense of nature's vast indifference and man's insignificance and impotence, tended to mock the idea that the world was the creation of some benevolent being. In Australia the man who went on rolling 'psalms to wintry skies' and faintly trusting 'the larger hope' became like the 'knight of the sorrowful countenance'.[2]

In 1845 the Catholic bishop-elect of Western Australia John Brady, persuaded two Spanish Benedictines, Rosendo Salvado and Joseph Serra in Rome, that it was the duty of men to whom God had given 'heroic souls' to 'assay the infinite labour of bringing God's infinite light to the aborigines of New Holland, and save them from disappearing off the face of the earth.' Salvado, who was born into a hidalgo family in Spain, was just thirty-one. He was one of those men who believed the whole human race was the victim of that 'aboriginal calamity' in the Garden of Eden: he saw natural man as a criminal whose only chance of peace and happiness was to look to God for redemption. For him God and his 'sweet sacrament' of the mass alone could rescue men from the consequences of the evil imaginations of their hearts. Salvado and Serra hoped that just as their illustrious predecessors in the Benedictine Order had converted a great portion of the people of Europe to the Christian faith and provided for them the blessings of civilization, so by their preaching and labours they might transform the savage peoples of Western Australia into cultured nations.

On 8 January 1846 Salvado and his party of missionaries came ashore at Fremantle and knelt on the sand while they chanted a Te Deum to Almighty God for preserving them during their perilous journey half way round the world. Tears of joy flowed down Salvado's cheeks as he sang those words which had been part of the 'aliment of humanity' for the thousand years and more of the Christian epoch, the solemn majesty of the plain-song seeming a happy medium for the profession of faith in God's world with all those hardships and the difficulties weighing men down. The temperature rose to nearly 108° F. in the shade, the flies and mosquitoes pestered them, frogs croaked loudly, and the aborigines made plain their excessive distrust for all Europeans. They decided to split into three parties. One set off for Albany where, to their mortification, the aborigines displayed a vast indifference to God's 'sweet sacrament'. Another party which set out for Port Essington was shipwrecked. The sole survivor, Father Angelo Gonfalonieri, struggled to the settlement at Victoria where he died lonely and defeated in June 1848 as the workers of Paris began their 'mighty explosion'.

In the meantime Salvado and his party planned to establish a mission to the north-east of Perth. On 16 February he received the kiss of peace from Bishop John Brady in one of those epiphanies in which the cheek of a man with the stamp both of the larrikin and the saint brushed up against the cheek of a man whose face bore the stamp of aristocratic disdain. Then their party of five set out by moonlight to begin their task of winning the aborigines of New Holland for Christ and civilization. Some eighty miles

---

[2] A. Tennyson, 'In Memoriam', lvi and cxxxi; C. Harpur, 'To the Spirit of Poesie', Miscellaneous Poems, 1847-8 (Harpur Papers, MS. in M.L.); Dr David Friedrich Strauss, *The Life of Jesus*, trans. from the fourth German edition by George Eliot (London, 1906), p. 757.

from Perth they came on the valley of the Moore River. They offered presents to the aborigines, who so loved licking sugar that Salvado prematurely thanked God for giving him the victory.

After an arduous trip to Perth, during which he raised funds by giving a concert, Salvado decided to found a monastery which was to be a centre at which the aborigines would be won for Christ. They built a spacious house of stone, a chapel, a stable and a barn and began to change the appearance of the Moore River district from one of wild solitude to that of a well-kept English manor farm. They named the place Nova Nursia (now New Norcia) after the birth-place of Saint Benedict in Italy. The aborigines came to gape at the white man's odd behaviour. To the Europeans as well as to the aborigines Salvado seemed to possess superhuman or charismatic powers. At the concert in Perth a poor Irish woman was so moved by his very presence that she gave him all she had—a pair of shoes. Back at New Norcia when the monks rescued a woman who was being savagely beaten by her husband (for the Australian bush at mid-century was peopled by many a Peter Grimes fond of the 'exercise' of thrashing wife or children), the enraged man set fire to the bush. A strong wind fanned the flames. Salvado ran to the chapel, took the picture of the Madonna from the altar and rushed back to the scene, whereupon the wind changed, leaving the natives amazed and awe-stricken.

Salvado had novel ideas for the civilization of the aborigines. He encouraged the men to take up small plots of land on which they could learn the art of husbandry and acquire a taste for a settled, as distinct from a nomadic, mode of existence. He started a school for the children at which the boys learnt useful trades and the girls domestic crafts. He issued an order that no aborigine was to receive a bowl of soup from the monastery kitchen unless he covered the 'unmentionables' with a kangaroo skin, for he believed that wearing clothes was part of the price men had to pay since they became 'ashamed'. He met the aborigines half way on their love of going walkabout by allowing them one day a week in the bush. He encouraged them to hold corroborees and to practise their methods of appeasing the spirits of the dead in the hope that this awareness of things unseen might be a starting point for their journey towards Christ's Holy Catholic Church. In 1849 he took some aborigines to Rome to study for the priesthood, only to find to his mortification that the Eternal City was no more effective than the wilds of Australia to win aborigines for Christ and civilization. When he returned to New Norcia in 1850, he found to his dark, undying pain that between him and Bishop Brady a great gulf had been set. He found, too, that although he watered the ground of New Norcia with his blood and sweat, he still was not sure whether the aborigines under his care had any idea of God. He began to wonder whether perhaps Florence Nightingale was right to ask the question: Can Europeans civilize aborigines without destroying them? And as he peered into the heart of that great mystery, his face acquired the majestic splendour of a man who knew both horror and beauty, a man who had Christ's assurance about the tares and the wheat, and a man who knew that the story of the Prodigal Son was not so much the story of a penitent sinner but a reminder that God's idea of desert was not the same as man's. As he lay dying in Rome on 29 December 1900, unlike Falstaff he did not babble of green fields, or cry out to God three or four times, or cry out for sack and complain that women were devils incarnate, but held forth his hands as though to signify that in death as in life he glorified his God in all things.[3]

In April 1841 John Ramsden Wollaston arrived in Fremantle just as determined as Salvado to glorify God in all things, but in his version God's glory could best be manifested by building a rural society of squire, parson and yeomen farmers in the Australian bush. In May he and his wife and children, their sheep, goats, pigs, dogs, and pre-cut house sailed on a ship from Fremantle to Port Leschenault to join the Australind settlement at Picton. In 1839 the Western Australian Company was founded in London to colonize the Bunbury district by selling 100-acre lots at £1 an acre. The proceeds of the land sales were to be used to pay the passages of the required workers. The directors of the company chose Leschenault Inlet as their site. From this scheme Western Australia netted over a thousand migrants in the years 1841-2 and the bitter lesson that her country was not suited to the purposes of intensive farming.

Like the other 'new chums' the Reverend Mr Wollaston found much at Leschenault that disquieted him. The leaves of the trees were of the same sombre hue from one season to another, so different from the great variety of colours in an English forest, and not subject to the change from the 'bare choirs' of winter to those delicate greens of an English June. He was tempted to shed tears whenever his eye roamed over the desolation of the scene, and his ear waited for some friendly sound to break the silence. Here the mysterious silence of the bush was broken only by the jabber of the aborigines, the weird howl of the native dog or the disturbing kah-kah of the crow. The absence of servants forced him and his wife to omit from their life all civilized forms and to be so oppressed with the weight of labour that they had little time or opportunity to manifest the outward and visible signs of the civilization they had come to plant. With the labour of their hands he and his sons built the church at Picton by September 1842. They also put up their

---

[3] Epitaph on tomb of Bishop Salvado, Benedictine Monastery, New Norcia, W.A.; H. N. Birt, *Benedictine Pioneers in Australia* (2 vols, London, 1911), vol. 2, pp. 469-72; P. F. Moran, *History of the Catholic Church in Australia* (2 vols, Sydney, 1896), vol. 2, ch. 14; P. McCarthy, *The Foundations of Catholicism in Western Australia, 1829-1911*; T. Bérangier, *La Nouvelle Nursie: histoire d'une colonie Bénédictine dans l'Australie occidentale 1846-1878* (Paris, n.d.); R. Salvado, *Mémoires Historiques sur d'Australie . . . Traduits de l'Italien en Francais par l'Abbé J. J. Falcimagne* (Paris, 1854); J. McMahon, *Bishop Salvado* (Perth, 1943); E. Perez, New Norcia (MS. at Benedictine Monastery, New Norcia); G. H. Russo, Bishop Salvado: plan to civilize and christianize aborigines (thesis in library of University of Western Australia); J. Stokes, *The Western State* (Perth, 1962), p. 33; *West Australian*, 31 December 1900; W. Shakespeare, *Henry V*, III, iii, lines 20-35; Gospel according to St John, XXI: xviii-xix; personal visit to grave of Father Gonfalonieri at Smith Point, Port Essington, 3 June 1969; personal visit to New Norcia, 9 June 1970; portrait of R. Salvado by Graner in Benedictine Monastery, New Norcia.

house, planted a garden and cleared some acres of land on which to sow crops. He wanted every man to share his belief that after death the body rested in peace in the earth until the resurrection morning when soul and body met once more and God wiped away all tears from men's eyes. He found to his dismay that his fellow-colonists were indifferent to this life of the world to come, and were so involved in finding 'hands' to work their land in the 'here and now' that this promise of a day in some distant future when the trumpet would sound and the dead would be raised incorruptible touched them not at all.[4]

The great want of labour in country districts dominated public life in the Australian colonies in the years after the recovery from the commercial crisis of 1840-3 until the discovery of gold early in 1851. In Western Australia some suggested importing Germans and some suggested importing Chinese, but all such proposals lapsed. At the end of 1846 some landowners decided that the only way to prevent their colony from becoming an encumbrance upon the Empire, and ruinous to those individuals who had been led to settle there was to persuade Her Majesty's Government to send sufficient numbers of convicts to build the required roads, bridges, wharves, lighthouses and other public works, and to provide the settlers with sufficient labour to produce a surplus for sale in the markets of Perth, York, Picton and Albany. F. C. Irwin, the Acting Governor after Hutt left for England early in 1847, told the Legislative Council of his grief that settlers could be so deluded by the dearth of labour as to risk the convict pestilence which might bring them wealth at the high price of 'moral pollution' and that 'stain' which had dirtied the societies of New South Wales and Van Diemen's Land. But the 'humble memorial of the land owners, merchants, and inhabitants of the colony of Western Australia to make and declare their Colony a Penal Settlement Upon An Extensive Scale' fell onto the desks of the men in Downing Street just when they were looking for places in the British Empire suitable for the punishment and reformation of British criminals.[5]

Down in Van Diemen's Land the convict question was so acute that it quickly took the place of gossip about the private life of Sir John Eardley-Wilmot, or remorse and contrition over his cruel fate. Everyone knew that the administrator, Charles Joseph La Trobe, had been asked to tell London

---

[4] *Journals and Diaries of the Rev. J. R. Wollaston* (Perth, 1948), pp. 1-9, 70-1, 131, 310; *Western Australia, Containing a Statement of the Conditions and Prospects of that Colony and Some Account of the Western Australian Company's Settlement of Australind* (London, 1842); E. L. Burgess, 'Australind' in *Report of Meeting of Australasian Association for the Advancement of Science* (Perth, 1926); F. K. Crowley, *Australia's Western Third* (London, 1960), pp. 15-16.

[5] Hutt to Stanley, 31 October 1843, C.O. 18/35; Stanley to Hutt, 4 March 1844, C.O. 397/7; *Proceedings of Legislative Council of Western Australia*, 3 June 1847; *Perth Gazette*, 3 June, 10, 15 July, 6 November 1847; Hutt to Stanley, 15 August 1845, C.O. 18/39; J. S. Battye, *Western Australia: a history from its discovery to the inauguration of the Commonwealth* (Oxford, 1924), pp. 185-7; 'The humble memorial of the undersigned land owners, merchants, and inhabitants of the colony of Western Australia, February 1846', *Perth Gazette*, 2 January 1847.

how far the probation system had succeeded in improving the morals of the convicts. In May 1847 he damned it in words similar to the sweeping condemnation by the Molesworth Committee of the old convict system, charging it with corrupting still further those who were undergoing the punishment, and, worse, with bringing into being nations or the germs of nations most thoroughly depraved in their vicious propensities. The convict sank into moral degradation in the very country in which he was to be a future inhabitant. He became idle, insolent and insubordinate, manifesting in his person those same stains which had disgraced the convicts in the early days. The system encouraged no bond of respect between employer and employed but rather, as in all slave or semi-slave societies, promoted the tendency of the slave-holder to laugh at and make light of the sufferings and behaviour of the convict, and the tendency of convict to loathe and despise the bond-holder or those placed in authority over him in the probation gangs.

The pass-holders spent much of their time in drunken brawls in taverns where they stunned the ears of the free with their shameless and disgusting language. The herding together of men in the probation gangs, and their isolation from the society of women, encouraged so much the practice of 'unnatural crime' that neither individuals nor communities could escape from the knowledge and contemplation of such abomination without moral injury. The public mind had been tainted by over-familiarity with the idea. One of the entertainments open to the public was to roll up to the court-room whenever the 'calendar contained such a blot upon its columns' and laugh shamelessly. The lower classes of society were becoming hopelessly corrupted by this incitement and encouragement not to feel shame in the presence of such evil, but to glory and revel in it. For the credit of the government and of the Mother Country and the future welfare of both the convict and the free, the evil of the probation system must go.[6]

The rapid increase in the convict population in the years after the abolition of transportation to New South Wales created alarm in Van Diemen's Land. Crimes reached a proportion exceeding that of any other civilized community. The townsmen and settlers, who had been the beneficiaries under the old assignment system, now found themselves forced to guard their families and their houses as though the convicts were a foreign enemy, or a foe more powerful and more dangerous than the aborigines on the island in those days when almost every country house had its 'enfilado' entrance to ensure that no savage could get into the house. As early as August 1845 the press in Launceston was reporting that numbers of probationers were roaming about that town on Saturday afternoons under the pretence of seeking employment. They were becoming complete pests and did not hesitate to beg in the streets for pence and tobacco. The petty robberies by these probationers were causing an anxiety, the *Launceston Examiner* said, 'anything but

<hr/>

[6] La Trobe to Grey, 31 May 1847 (General Correspondence of La Trobe, La Trobe Papers); Earl Grey, *The Colonial Policy of Lord John Russell's Administration* (2 vols, London, 1853), vol. 2, pp. 70-2.

favourable to domestic comfort or mental repose'. There were stories of respectable inhabitants being subject to all sorts of annoyances in the streets of Launceston and Hobart. One Saturday in September 1845 two ladies were walking down Charles Street in Launceston when one of those probationer fellows snatched at a brooch one of the ladies was wearing.

From the country came similar stories of outrages by probationers against the settlers and their families. In October 1845 in the Westbury district twenty-five absconders stripped a farm-house of everything that could be moved, and took liberties with the farmer's wife. In that district fifteen men were in charge of a thousand desperate and dangerous men. There were complaints against the loose manner in which the probationers travelled about the country in mobs of up to sixty or seventy apparently without being under the smallest surveillance. Woe betide the luckless traveller found by them on any unfrequented part of the road. There were also reports of the destitution of probation pass-holders and ticket-of-leave men who could not obtain employment because of the inundation of the island since 1840 with convicts and the consequent glutting of the labour market. Men were reduced to such straits that they depended on the charity of their neighbours for a little bread to eat, a rug, a blanket and a little straw to sleep on. Men condemned to semi-starvation and a brutish concern for their daily bread were driven to petty theft to remain alive. The press in both Hobart and Launceston was sprinkled in almost every issue with reports of probationers knocking down respectable people and robbing them of their money and their clothes. The convicts were both polluting and terrorizing society.[7]

The settler was inclined to reply to all the arguments about the convicts as polluters, not by chewing over the problem whether it was possible to make straight that which God had made crooked, but by asking whether he could afford to dispense with cheap convict labour. Van Diemen's Land was an agricultural country whose buoyancy could only be maintained by cheap rents for land and cheap labour. For that reason the inhabitants should endeavour to prevail upon England to keep the island the great unwalled gaol of the offenders of the Empire, for they faced certain ruin the moment the nourishment afforded them by British expenditure ceased to bestow its vital influence upon them. The problem was to restore a system of prison discipline in which government assigned convicts to work that was useful to the settlers.[8]

That was the task Her Majesty's Government had asked Eardley-Wilmot's successor, William Thomas Denison, to perform. He was then forty-three years of age. He was born in London on 3 May 1804 into a family of Leeds

[7] J. West, *The History of Tasmania* (2 vols, Launceston, 1852), vol. 2, pp. 211-12; H. P. Fry, *A System of Penal Discipline, with a Report on the Treatment of Prisoners in Great Britain and Van Diemen's Land* (London, 1850); *Launceston Examiner*, 26 July, 27 August, 24 September, 8 October 1845, 17 January 1846; *Hobart Town Courier*, 29 March, 20 August, 11 October 1845, 14 February, 6 May, 9 September, 14 November 1846.

[8] *Colonial Times*, 5 January 1847.

patricians who were clamouring to share political power with the landed aristocracy. After a period at Eton, he had entered the navy and had won some distinction for his work as an engineer in the dockyards, only to find promotion devilishly slow in the long period of peace, after Waterloo granted a reprieve to aristocratic privilege in England. The abilities he had displayed in the control of the prisoners in the dockyards probably persuaded Gladstone that he was the man to administer the convict system successfully. Gladstone offered him the position of Lieutenant-Governor, and Grey honoured that offer. When Grey transmitted to him on 30 September 1846 the royal sign manual appointing him Lieutenant-Governor of Van Diemen's Land and its dependencies, he warned him that the great interests confided to his care had become the subject of no common solicitude. Grey went on to explain that he was thinking of that large assemblage of thirty thousand convicts in a colony of some sixty-six thousand people.

Grey told Denison of the difficulties that had been encountered in making Stanley's probation system work. It had been found impossible to maintain discipline in the gangs because the numbers of officers or overseers were inadequate. It had not been practicable to provide proper work for the convicts in the probation gangs since there had not been sufficient demand for the labour of the convicts either as pass-holders or as holders of tickets-of-leave, with the result that the ticket-of-leave men were suffering great distress. Grey told him that there had existed a fearful propensity among the convicts to commit unnatural crimes. To remedy these defects Her Majesty's Government had decided to stop altogether the transportation of convicts to Van Diemen's Land, male convicts at all events, for the space of two years. Grey added that since he did not believe that any scheme would absorb all the available convict labour, he did not propose that the United Kingdom should resume at any time the plan of pouring into Van Diemen's Land such an annual flood of transported convicts as had recently been sent to the island. These vague words, tossed off in the middle of a long despatch, were pregnant with misunderstanding and future differences between the people of Van Diemen's Land and Her Majesty's Government.

Grey went on to outline for Denison proposals for the future administration of the convict system. A pass-holder was to be allowed to hire himself out to private individuals or public bodies and, if not so hired, to be required to work for government by task work. Ticket-of-leave men unable to find employment were to be placed by the Governor in the hiring gangs, and pass-holders to be employed by government in erecting villages. To prevent unnatural crimes, the men in their present dormitories were to be separated by partitions made of strong bars of wood from floor to ceiling, leaving a passage through which the air could circulate. The number of officers and overseers was to be supplemented by employing non-commissioned officers of the sappers, miners and the royal artillery. He also proposed to send in future all female convicts to Van Diemen's Land. The most assiduous attention must be given to their moral and religious instruction so that they might in some measure be fitted to become wives and mothers of families. He also proposed to encourage wives and families of hardened convicts to join them. For Grey was most anxious, and so were all the men in high places in Downing Street, to prove it was possible to use convicts without suffering 'moral pollution'.

The question was whether Denison and his wife had the gifts of head and heart to preside over a scheme for the restitution of men from criminality to respectability. As a man, it was said, he lacked the discretion, the caution and the judgement with which to preside over a society in its in-between years. It was said that he and his wife made no attempt to disguise their lack of sympathy for the democratic tendencies of their age. They set out in the last quarter of 1846 with instructions to discover the most effective use of convicts at a time when the existing convict system had so corrupted society that fathers were said to tremble for the future of their children, the country-born youth was no longer able to live in his native land, the tone of public morals had sunk so low that crime was spoken of merely as a fault or a misfortune, and the press 'teemed with vicious sentimentalism'. People scanned the censuses of past years to discover the origins of their neighbours, for their society had inherited some of the evils of the use of slaves, without deriving any countervailing material benefits. As the ship bearing him and his family headed south from Madeira towards the end of 1846, a melancholy feeling began to descend on Denison, just as it had descended on one of his predecessors, David Collins, when the ship on which he was sailing left civilization behind in 1787 and sailed on towards the land of savages and barbarians. Denison felt he was leaving the history of the world behind, leaving the full-blown civilization of Europe which had known all the great and noble deeds in sacred and profane history of which the people in the Antipodes knew nothing. His wife then asked him: what if he should show them some?[9]

On his arrival in Hobart on 25 January 1847 he was delighted to find the people proud of their 'loyal hearts and British affections'. He and his secretary, Charles Stanley, found that the best people were nearly all English, all having come from 'home' so recently that they had kept up their interest in it. As for the colonials, they seemed very rough and coarse with very few subjects to talk about: the men were noisy and the women awkward and silent. They looked as though they had never been in a room in polite society before, and were much given to the shyness colonials often display in the presence of their masters. Everyone that counted spoke of England as 'home' and of Van Diemen's Land as a place of banishment. Hobart looked like an English country town, except for the convicts in the streets and the cries of the fish-mongers. Society ladies had just as sharp an eye for rank and standing and

---

[9] W. Denison, *Varieties of Vice-Regal Life* (2 vols, London, 1870), vol. 1, p. 27; J. West, op. cit., vol. 2, pp. 334-5, vol. 1, pp. 265-6; Grey to Denison, 30 September 1846, C.O. 408/28; C. Nicholson to James Macarthur, 15 September 1855 (Macarthur Papers, vol. 27), James Macarthur to Edward Macarthur, 14 September 1855 (Macarthur Papers, vol. 35); for later opinions of Denison see W. Denison, *A Church: a social institution* (Sydney, 1858) and *Two Lectures on Colonization* (Richmond, 1870).

comme il faut behaviour as the hostesses of the London season. Not even the handicap of the primitive means of transport from a country mansion to Hobart prevented ladies from appearing at the balls in that town in all the splendours of crinolines, ribbons, fans, shawls and lace handkerchiefs. At the ball to celebrate the Queen's Birthday in May of that year gentlewomen arrived in Hobart with their finery for the ball slung from the pommels of their saddles. Gentlemen slung their swallow-tails, fancy waistcoats, dancing pumps, and hip-flasks in knapsacks on their backs as they rode down to town for the delights of a local ball.[10]

In politics there was a lull. The Patriotic Six were still outside the Council. Denison wrote off to London to ask whether he was to ask them to resume their seats as nominee members or sound out six other men to replace them. That, at least, gave him some breathing space. On the convict question there was now the same uproar and anger and division as in New South Wales. In the mother colony the support of the landed grandees for the renewal of transportation triggered off a lively debate during which radicals and colonial chauvinists pushed the conservatives into defending the imperial connection. In Van Diemen's Land Grey's proposal to break up the convict establishments on Norfolk Island and New South Wales and transfer all the incorrigibles to whom tickets-of-leave or conditional pardons could not safely be granted to Van Diemen's Land roused great moral indignation. At a public meeting in Hobart on 21 October 1847, men testified, as had the solid bourgeoisie and virtuous workers of New South Wales, to their horror at being expected to live with such 'irreclaimable guilt'. At Launceston on 2 November some four to five thousand crowded into the Assembly Room to hear the clergy and all the believers in moral enlightenment urge them to enlist under the banners of truth, morality and religion. As in New South Wales, speakers with tears running down their cheeks stated that, though there had been a time when they believed convict labour was indispensable, they now could not bear to think of their wives and their children being corrupted by convicts. As in New South Wales, they wanted the 'Missus' to be a madonna and the Mother Machree of the kitchen sink and bedroom of Van Diemen's Land. They believed they could look with confidence to His Excellency and the Queen to rid them of this 'scum and refuse of the convict population'. At Richmond a few days later some of the inhabitants drafted a petition against infusing the 'noxious poison of twice and thrice convicted felons in their midst'. Denison, too, spoke publicly against the incorrigibles from Norfolk Island and New South Wales, a stand which caused the abolitionists to assume His Excellency was on their side. They were not to know then that, while condemning the Grey proposal, he was telling the men in power in London of the valuable contribution convicts made to preserving subordination in a colonial society.

---

[10] W. Denison, *Varieties of Vice-Regal Life*, vol. 1, pp. 9-11, 19-21, 44-6; *Hobart Town Courier*, 27 January, 6 February 1847; *Launceston Examiner*, 30 January 1847; Eliza Stanley to Catherine Stanley, 24 March 1847 (Letters of Charles Stanley, microfilm in NAT. L.); Denison to Grey, 27 January 1847, C.O. 280/207.

By then those close to Government House society were beginning to have second thoughts about Denison and his wife. His private secretary, Charles Stanley, was finding Sir William's temper to be so violent that he was sure he would one day get himself into a mess. He viewed things *en militaire* and tried to enforce the same strict discipline and obedience among his civil officers as he would among the soldiers of a regiment. He was a dreadful man to travel with for he simply could not be still for one moment. He was also a fearful slave-driver. As for Lady Denison, her social ineptitude was astonishing: she behaved like a girl out of school and never knew what to do on the simplest occasion. Her manner was so cold and stiff that nobody in high or low society got on with her for she neither received nor made advances. By the end of 1847 it was said she had not a person to speak to in Van Diemen's Land. God alone knew whether she and Sir William had anything to say to each other when they were alone together.[11]

Down in Port Phillip the squatters' want of labour, and the fear of bourgeois and worker that convicts would debauch their morals and postpone their enjoyment of all the birthrights of Englishmen also dominated public life. On 29 December 1846 employers of convict labour and their sympathizers gathered at the Royal Hotel to draft a petition for the renewal of convict labour under certain conditions. This petition repeated all the arguments used by the sheep men in the Middle District. The great want of labour, they wrote, was causing crops to be left on the ground for want of reapers. Graziers were compelled to keep their stock in flocks that were injuriously large. Employers had been obliged to perform manual work, their wives had been obliged to wash dishes and mend clothes, and their children had been taken from school prematurely to be put to work in the fields. They therefore asked for a supply of convicts who had reached the stage at which they were entitled to tickets-of-leave, provided the use of such convicts did not delay their separation from New South Wales. They also wanted the British Government to bear one-third of the expense of police and gaols, to agree that free emigration would be carried on simultaneously, and to promise to pay for the emigration of the wives and families of convicts and such other females as would be necessary to preserve equality of numbers between the sexes. They believed passionately that their pockets could be filled without endangering the wants of the solid bourgeoisie and virtuous hungry workers of Australia Felix. They also believed convicts could be used to build tracks

---

[11] Grey to FitzRoy, 4 May 1847, *H.R.A.*, I. xxv. 535-6; Grey to FitzRoy, 27 February 1847, ibid., 375-6; *Hobart Town Courier*, 23 October, 3, 6 November 1847; 'Memorial of the clergy, magistrates, landholders and other inhabitants of the district of Richmond, 6 November 1847', *Hobart Town Courier*, 10 November 1847; Denison to Grey, 5 February 1848, C.O. 280/20; Eliza Stanley to Catherine Stanley, 24 March 1847, Charles Stanley to Catherine Stanley, 26 April 1847, Charles Stanley to his mother, 13 July 1847, Charles Stanley to Catherine Stanley, 22 February 1849 (Letters of Charles Stanley); Adelaide Lubbock, *Owen Stanley, R.N.* (Melbourne, 1967), pp. 191-3; J. Bertram (ed.), *New Zealand Letters of Thomas Arnold the Younger with Further Letters from Van Diemen's Land and Letters of Arthur Hugh Clough, 1847-1851* (Wellington, 1966).

for the iron rail, and then withdrawn before they polluted the population.[12]

The bourgeoisie and workers of Melbourne and Geelong were not impressed. Some fifteen hundred people crowded into Queen's Theatre in Melbourne on 1 March 1847 to draft a petition which repeated all the arguments of the abolitionists in the Middle District and in Van Diemen's Land on the effects of convicts on the morals of the good citizens of Port Phillip. They added a point that had been sketched in the first petitions for separation. The old convict society of New South Wales, they wrote, consisted of masters and servants. They wanted a society with a strong middle class. They insisted that their free workers had left behind the civilization of the Mother Country on the understanding that in Port Phillip they would live not in a penal but in a free society in which they would enjoy material well-being and have the chance to rise out of the working into the middle class.[13]

In the meantime over in South Australia pastoralists and tenant farmers were still proving it was possible to accumulate wealth without exploiting the labour of those who had practised iniquity. In March 1847 J. F. Hayward, a gentleman of some twenty-four years, of that modest fortune which generally characterized the sons of the British gentry who sought their fortunes in the Australian colonies, arrived in Adelaide with £40 in his pocket, and in his heart the hope that by displaying the prevailing virtues of frugality, industry and clean living he would become 'disgustingly rich'. Before going up-country he was much taken with the huge quantities of food and drink the colonists swallowed, the mammoth steaks, the juicy water-melons and the quantity of peas, lettuces, cabbages, tomatoes and potatoes, as well as pint-pots of tea or beer. Life seemed more spacious. The climate allowed a man to camp anywhere. The habit of roughing it in the bush had stripped away most of the Old World distinctions between master and servant, for here rich men drove drays and took their turn with the spade or the hoe.

At the end of April Hayward set out for Pekina, some seventy miles to the north-east of Burra, where he had been offered the position of overseer on a run depasturing some three thousand sheep in dry country on the very frontier of the plains of desolation. At Burra he was struck again by the coarse, elemental life of the miners and their families and yet intrigued to sense a great pulse of life beating away in such a crude setting. Some of the copper miners and their families were living in holes dug into the banks of the creek. After a thunderstorm rolled over those arid plains, they were flooded out and had to dry out their possessions and start life again. The men rocked with laughter when their neighbours were discomfited, especially when a brick landed in the pot in which the evening meal was being cooked. At the weatherboard inn the proprietor did a roaring trade every Saturday

[12] N. Black to W. E. Gladstone, 30 September 1846 (Black Papers, LA TROBE L.); 'The humble petition of the undersigned inhabitants of the District of Port Phillip, employers of rural labour', *Port Phillip Patriot*, 8, 11 January 1847.

[13] 'The humble petition of the undersigned inhabitants of the town of Melbourne and District of Port Phillip', *Argus*, 2 March 1847; H. G. Turner, *A History of the Colony of Victoria* (2 vols, London, 1904), vol. 1, pp. 325-8.

night selling pannikins of malt liquor or spirits to the miners who, when sufficiently elevated, broke windows, sang and fought, or fondled the women present till the landlord cleared them all out with a cricket bat. On Sunday morning some gathered again in the yard behind the inn for a 'hair of the dog' and a settling of scores of the previous evening in bare-knuckle fights with a kick by the victor to finish off his victim. Over at the chapel a sprinkling of some twenty-five lugubrious penitents and seekers after the means of grace, hoping for the glory that was to come rather than the frenzy of the tap-room and the dance floor, gathered each Sunday to hear the Reverend Mr Bagshaw's reminder that drunkards, fornicators and liars would not enter the Kingdom of Heaven.[14]

Hayward lived at Pekina in a small ill-thatched hut with no chimney or door, an earthen floor and no stove, all the cooking and boiling of water being done on an open campfire. He was disgusted that his only companions were the offscourings of the colony, for only old lags from the penal colonies and eccentrics and 'fringe' men chose life on an out-station, out of reach of police, wives, and all the tormentors who either would not or could not leave the weak to follow the desires of their own hearts. Like many another overseer or stock-holder in the Australian bush, he had to learn to endure watching the 'scum of humanity' hack and tomahawk the sheep at shearing time. He had to learn also, as had the settlers in the interior of New South Wales, that it was wisest not to capture the aboriginal sheep-stealers and cart them the seventy miles to Burra where the nearest magistrate administered the colonial version of English law: the sentimentalists of Exeter Hall had so poisoned the minds of those charged with the punishment of wickedness and vice that the plaintiff generally got a lecture on his duties to the 'least of the little ones' and the responsibility of ensuring that the black thief had transport back to his own people. It was far better to go in for the sport of 'nigger tracking' and turn the wild dogs on them. That at least gave him a feeling of exhilaration. So, strangely enough, did standing on those plains under that immense sky, when he experienced the delight of being free from all the restraints that men imposed on each other in society. Besides, by using his savings to acquire stock of his own he found that within five years he was becoming a man of substance, a man who by frugality and the labour of his own hands was ready to make the move from bush barbarism to the civilization of a provincial town such as Adelaide.[15]

At the same time, at Anlaby near Kapunda, Francis Dutton was also coming into his kingdom. The profits from the copper mines at Kapunda and Burra, the income from the annual wool clip, the income from leasing land to industrious German farmers, and the profits from trading ventures to Singapore had made him something more than a man of substance. When death took his son-in-law early in 1847, his aged mother urged him to be resigned to the will of Him who did everything well, as everything that came from the Almighty's hand was right, and they must submit to His Holy

[14] Diary of J. F. Hayward (MS. in S.A.S.A.).
[15] Ibid.

Will. Paradoxically, Francis Dutton, who had laid up for himself such treasures from the grasses and minerals of South Australia, welcomed death as a boon sent by the 'wise disposer of wants' who in his infinite mercy rescued men from the afflictions of this life.

In South Australia they had no need of ticket-of-leave men, pass-holders, exiles, Chinese coolies, or sisyphean attempts to train the aborigines to be the bottle-washers and ploughboys, shepherds and messenger boys of their society. The renewal of assisted immigration in 1847 was supplying them with workers who did not pollute the respectable bourgeoisie of Adelaide or contaminate the settlers and their families. The one menace threatening them came from the old lags and bolters from the penal colonies who muddied their pure waters. Their presence heightened interest in attempts in New South Wales and Van Diemen's Land to renew the transportation of convicts. It also prompted them to ask for self-government so that they might be in charge of their own affairs and not expose themselves to the risk of all their achievements being brought to ruin by convict 'putridity'. On this convict question they were beginning to discover a bond with all those bourgeois immigrants and workers in Port Phillip, the Middle District of New South Wales and Van Diemen's Land who looked on renewal as a threat to their virtue, their happiness and their liberty.[16]

In Sydney, too, the middle and working class were equally determined to have nothing to do with the 'pottage of tainted wealth' and not to exchange the 'birth-right of rejoicing in [their] own fair fame' for wealth gained either by convict or coloured labour. The leaders of these classes were determined to take their stand against what in their eyes was one of the most formidable evils that ever menaced a community rapidly rising to distinction, importance and respect. The priests and the parsons, too, spoke of the 'formidable dangers' in renewing transportation to remedy the want of a sufficient supply of labour, since renewal would lower the repute of the colony and close the door to the hope of receiving more free immigrants. Broughton and his fellow-clergymen warned the members of the Church of England and Ireland in the colony of New South Wales that no supposed benefits could compensate for the moral, social and political evils of renewal. But Broughton had other things on his mind in 1847. He warned the clergy to be on guard against attempts by agents of the Church of Rome to further their organized design of winning converts to Rome. These designs were addressed to the uninformed who knew not the principles of scriptural truth, or to the vicious who were naturally disposed to fly to what promised them an easier assurance of absolution and forgiveness. 'Watch, therefore', he exhorted his brother clergy, 'lest coming suddenly it find you sleeping'.[17]

[16] Maryanne Dutton to Francis Dutton, 4 October 1847, 13, 16, 28 April 1850 (Dutton Papers, Anlaby, S.A.).
[17] *S.M.H.*, 27 January, 25 February 1847; Memorial of the Bishop of Australia and of the Undersigned Clergymen of the United Church of England and Ireland in the Colony of New South Wales . . . , 1847 (MS. in M.L.); W. G. Broughton, Circular to the Reverend the Clergy of the United Church of England and Ireland within the Diocese of Australia, 17 April 1847 (Russell Correspondence, vol. 2, pp. 1051-3, MS. in M.L.).

By contrast, the employers of rural labour were keeping out a watch for a source of useful and cheap labour. Some contemplated the advantages of using Indian labour in the Australian colonies. At Moreton Bay there was a society to promote the use of such labour. Late in March 1846 fifty-one coolies from India arrived on the *Orwell* under indenture to Robert Towns, William Charles Wentworth and Charles Campbell. Some of these went to work with Ben Boyd for five rupees a month, but their overseers reported that they were quite unfit for work in the bush. The *Sydney Morning Herald* commented in April 1847 that the mere fact of graziers having recourse to such experiments ought to impress upon the government the necessity of the revival of British immigration. The colonists, they wrote, would never think of importing foreigners, much less savages and heathens, if their demands could be adequately supplied from their own countrymen. They could have no wish to people their sheep-walk with strange races. The mere idea of their doing so was repugnant to all their national predilections. Much rather would they see Australia replenished and subdued by the unmixed, undeteriorated progeny of their own Anglo-Saxon fathers. The *Atlas* expressed the opinion that coolies were far more objectionable than convicts: imagine, it warned its readers, Buddhist temples rising beside churches! or, worse still, imagine cannibals, fresh from their last disgusting banquet of human flesh, landing in New South Wales.[18]

That was precisely what that would-be cloud-topper Ben Boyd was doing that April: he was submitting to a harsh and cruel necessity by using the barbarous islanders of Polynesia on his sheep-walks on the Monaro and the Riverina. To him, as ever, the problem was quite simple: the employers of rural labour wanted workers; the poor creatures of Polynesia wanted food. It seemed, therefore, a dispensation of Divine Providence that the labourers required by this vast continent should be taken from the overpeopled lands. Besides, their emigration would be the surest means of Christianizing them and so abolishing forever the dreadful crimes of cannibalism and infanticide from Polynesia. Believing that in the green year of 1847 the grass would grow high and sheep would die for want of shepherds, he despatched his ship, the *Velocity*, under Captain Kirsopp on 31 January 1847 to recruit labourers in the islands of Polynesia. On 9 April that ship sailed into the majestic waters of Twofold Bay with sixty-five young men from the Loyalty Islands who had all agreed to work as shepherds or labourers for five years on stations run by Ben Boyd. None of them could speak English, all were naked, the hair of many of them being dressed in an extraordinary manner. They all seemed wild and restless.[19]

On 14 April sixty-two of them set off from Boyd Town to walk over the

[18] *S.M.H.*, 30 March, 4, 6, 9 April 1846, 23 April 1847; *Atlas*, 27 March, 24 April 1847.
[19] *Heads of the People*, 1 May 1847; *S.M.H.*, 1 November 1847; *Bell's Life in Sydney*, 20 November 1847; *Port Phillip Gazette*, 20 October 1847; H. P. Wellings, 'Ben Boyd's labour supplies', R.A.H.S., *J. & P.*, vol. 19, 1933; J. H. Watson, 'Benjamin Boyd, merchant', R.A.H.S., *J. & P.*, vol. 2, 1907; J. H. Heaton, *Australian Dictionary of Dates and Men of the Time* (London, 1879), p. 23.

Brown Mountain to the Monaro and then down the Murray to the Boyd squatting run at Deniliquin. The other three were taken to Sydney to show what manner of men they were. Some of the Monaro and Riverina party bolted back to Boyd Town before they had got very far and demanded a return passage. Others got as far as Deniliquin but found the conditions so strange that they swore that if they got their hands on Catpain Kirsopp, who was then on a second recruiting voyage, they would eat him for bringing them to a country where they froze and suffered terrible homesickness. They set out on the long walk of some four hundred miles to Sydney via Wagga Wagga, Gundagai, Yass and Goulburn. Early in November a group of a dozen or more of these 'creatures', as the press called them, strode down George Street, only three of them being encumbered with the article of clothing generally considered the most indispensable of male attire. Within a week inhabitants of Sydney were complaining that 'these fiendish looking cannibals' had become a nuisance in that city. They entered without ceremony at every door and demanded food, clothing and money in a tone and manner at once impudent and threatening. It was plain that the object for which they had been seduced from their native land had failed, that they were now mercilessly left to their fate by their self-created masters, and that the citizens were subjected to insult and outrage from a mob of starving and desperate intruders. Ben Boyd was held up to ridicule in some doggerel verse in *Bell's Life in Sydney*:

Cannibalania

Benny Boyd when he found out that shepherds were scarce,
    Looked anxiously round for to see
From whence he could get them, but—none could be found—
    Says the Quaker, 'let's try the Fegee.

From what I have heard they're as hungry as rats,
    And often they go without dinner,
In fact I have heard that they eat their own brats,
    It's true, as I feel I'm a sinner.

So let's start off a craft, and we'll try a new spec,
    It aint *slaving*, whatever Lowe calls it,
The beggars you know can all live upon deck,
    And appetite—sea-sickness palls it'.

So he sent off his ship for a cargo of blacks,
    And finding they came off like winking,
He started another, the Quaker went snacks,
    Always ready the tin to be chinking.

To Maneroo, to Boyd Town, and every where else,
    He sent these poor man-eating wretches,
But though with good promises he did abound,
    He forgot to provide them with breeches.

Maneroo they found was so d–m–y cold,
  And they'd no cocoa nuts for to patter,
Being perfectly sure as they'd nothing to eat,
  'Twas impossible they could get fatter.

So they bolted, as many have done before,
  Nor took a long time on their journey,
Having nothing to eat, why they robb'd their way down,
  'Twas a logic well worthy of 'Gurney'.*

As with beggars our city already abounds,
  I trust Mr. Boyd will be willing
To send those poor devils all back to their homes,
  And himself save a shirt and a shilling.

* Necessity knows no law.

As loud voices of protest were raised, a writer in the *Sydney Morning Herald* wrote a spirited defence of the Hebrideans, asserting *inter alia* that they would not eat human flesh when beef and mutton were in abundance, and appealing to his fellow-countrymen to rejoice that the providence of God had given them an opportunity to convert savages. He went on to ask the leading question: 'Are we not all brothers?' He ended with a high-minded exhortation to the people of Sydney to rid their minds of the silly notion that the mind of the savage differed in any respect from that of their own race, in historical background. Ben Boyd mocked the opponents of the Hebrideans, calling Lowe the 'mock patriot and puppet' and Cowper 'that weak and silly place hunter'. But neither high-minded sentiments nor mockery could change the antipathy of both government and public to what opponents of cannibals called the introduction of degenerate elements into their population. In September and October, government, Legislative Council and the people at large insisted that the population of New South Wales was to be supplemented not by convicts or cannibals or coolies but by free men of their own race and colour who would obtain their livelihood by honest industry.[20]

On 14 September Charles Cowper asked the Legislative Council to record its opinion that 'a return to the system of Transportation and Assignment would be opposed to the wishes of this Community, and would also be most injurious to the moral, social and political advancement of the Colony'. He took his stand on the principle that colonization by the free was preferable to colonization by convicts, because he shrank in horror from New South Wales being known as one of the most contaminated places in the world. W. Bland, loyal as ever to the emancipists, protested that convicts were not the irreclaimable monsters described by the abolitionists, but men capable of regeneration. They had pioneered civilization in a country which for thou-

[20] *Bell's Life in Sydney*, 20 November 1847; article on the New Hebrideans in *S.M.H.*, 5 November 1847; letter by W. in *S.M.H.*, 15 December 1847; FitzRoy to Grey, 24 December 1847, C.O. 201/386.

sands of years had only known savagery and barbarism. Wentworth declared himself a quite unrepentant believer in convict labour and went on to say that, unlike 'Slippery Charlie', he did not propose to be influenced by every popular breeze, or pander for favours by advocating measures he believed to be fatal to the prosperity of the colony. If he was in error then he must insist that it was an error of conviction and not, as his enemies wickedly maintained, an error of interest. The Council voted him down. The voting figures were eleven for Cowper's motion and seven for the opposition.

Outside Council the *Sydney Morning Herald* jubilantly told its readers the vote would convince Her Majesty's Government that the inhabitants of New South Wales were worthy of their virtuous ancestry and fit to be entrusted with the free institutions of their fatherland. No longer now would the people of England be able to say that in Australia the scum of the earth represented the splendours of the British character and race, nor that Australia was more vulgar than the meanest suburb in London. Down in Melbourne at a huge public meeting on 21 September Alderman William Kerr, proprietor of the *Argus*, a fanatical 'No Pollution' paper, harangued them on the need to keep Port Phillip free from people with the taint of convict origin and its attendant 'hideous mass of deformity'. From Moreton Bay to Melbourne bourgeoisie, workers and even sheep-walk men such as Terence Murray, Alexander Berry, Charles Cowper and William Bowman took up the cry, 'No more convicts in New South Wales.'[21]

On 1 October Robert Lowe moved a motion in the Legislative Council against the importation of savages from the islands of the Pacific. Mr Parker moved as an amendment that an address be presented to His Excellency drawing the serious attention of the executive government to the evils likely to arise from the introduction of natives of barbarous tribes, which might, if not checked, develop into a traffic in slaves. To much laughter from members, Lowe ridiculed Boyd's claim that he had brought savages to New South Wales 'in the greatness of his love'. The truth was the savages were not getting enough 'tomahawking and scalping' in their own country. Boyd decided to give them such exercise on 'the breezy plains of Maneroo'. Lowe proposed to redress the wrongs of an outraged community exposed to the indecency and obscenity of hordes of cannibals by insisting that they not be allowed in as immigrants, and to protect the aborigines whom the introduction of this slave labour might expose to a war of extermination. Otherwise this remote corner of the earth would be the first to renew a system which poets, sages and orators had held up to the detestation of mankind. As he saw it, a 'grasping monopoly', a 'griping, overreaching, and tyrannous oppression' threatened to turn a garden into a wilderness and accomplish ruin for the sons of the soil. Besides, Boyd's great dream had ended. He had hoped to rescue the islanders from scenes of carnage and terror on their islands, and send them out to the far interior, where peace and innocence were said to reign and

[21] *V. & P.* (L.C. N.S.W.), 14 September 1847; supplement to *S.M.H.*, 16 September 1847; *The Times*, 4 June 1847, quoted in *S.M.H.*, 9 October 1847; *Argus*, 23 September 1847.

guileless flocks lay down on green pastures and merry lambkins disported without fear. These 'children of nature' had proved that their nature was not exactly the patient, plodding nature of shepherds. It was the nature of a disgusting man-eater.[22]

In sections of the press the anti-transportation, anti-coolie and anti-savages men were exposed to quite unfair rubbishing and vulgar abuse:

> Hear Campbell with his squeaking voice,
> Fret and fume with feeble noise
> 'Gainst transportation plans;
> So does a magpie make a noise,
> And we but wonder that this noise
> Is so much like a man's.

But the high-minded opponents of convicts, coolies and cannibals were not to be silenced by the character assassins of Sydney's Grub Street. Members of the government were on their side. Edward Deas Thomson and John Hubert Plunkett also agreed that a coloured population would introduce terrible evils into society. By October to the cry 'No more convicts' was added 'No black, brown, yellow or brindle people' and 'Preserve Australia for the white man by sending us men of our own colour, men of our own race'. While this public debate was warming up, Thomas Sutcliffe Mort drew up a scheme to import five thousand immigrants straight away by raising a loan on the security of the land fund. Mort was a man behind the organization of the first wool sales in Sydney, a shareholder in the Hunter River Steamship Navigation Company, a vigorous advocate of steamship communication with England and the introduction of the railway in New South Wales. Like Cowper, he saw that the sheep-walk and industrialized towns could flourish together in the future. Over in England Grey was so impressed by the demand for labour in New South Wales that he proposed in August 1847 to supply the want by sending out without delay five thousand adults. Australia must belong to the white man.[23]

It was just sixty years since the first Captain-General and Governor-in-Chief in and over the territory of New South Wales and its dependencies, the trusty and well-beloved Arthur Phillip received the instruction,

> You are to endeavour by every possible means to open an intercourse with the natives, and to conciliate their affections, enjoining all our subjects to live in amity and kindness with them. And if any of our subjects shall wantonly destroy them, or give them any unnecessary interruption in the exercise of their several occupations, it is our will and pleasure that you do cause such offenders to be brought to punishment according to the degree of the offence. You will . . . report your opinion to one of our Secretaries of State in what manner our intercourse with these people may be turned to the advantage of this Colony.

[22] *V. & P.* (L.C. N.S.W.), 1 October 1847; *S.M.H.*, 2 October, 3 November 1847.
[23] *Heads of the People*, 8 May 1847; *V. & P.* (L.C. N.S.W.), 21 September 1847; *S.M.H.*, 24 September 1847; Grey to FitzRoy, 30 August 1847, *H.R.A.*, I. xxv. 728-31; FitzRoy to Grey, 14 December 1847, *H.R.A.*, I. xxvi. 70-2; Grey to FitzRoy, 18 December 1847, ibid., 104-8.

After sixty years of this official policy, several of the commissioners of Crown lands in New South Wales in 1846 sent in melancholy reports on the condition of the aborigine in their area. From the Lachlan district Edgar Beckham reported that the condition of the aborigines was in no way improving, and no moral improvement could ever take place so long as they adhered to their present love of a wandering life. He deemed it impossible to induce them to forget and resign their natural savage habits. From the Wellington district W. H. Wright regretted that he could not have the satisfaction of reporting any improvement in their social or moral condition. Nor could he suggest in what way such improvement might be effected with the unmixed race.

From the districts of Bligh and New England there were more hopeful reports of aborigines being found useful to the squatters as shepherds, stock-men and house servants. There were reports, too, of a Christian missionary in the Wellington district who was zealously teaching aboriginal children to read and write, and telling them, too, the 'truth of Christian religion'. But he was said to be succeeding only as well as could be expected in trying to preserve the 'unfortunate race of New Holland'. From the Portland Bay district H. Smythe regretted that he had not seen any improvement for the better in his ten years in the district and added his candid opinion that no such change was to be expected, for the aborigines' habits were so directly opposed to any settled way of living, their roaming propensity being so strong that they could not be expected to remain long in any place. From Gippsland C. Tyers wrote of his despair of ever discovering how to civilize or improve a people who were inseparably attached to a 'vagabond Gipsy-like life'. From the Macleay River in New South Wales Robert George Massie reported that the aborigines in his area had the same characteristics of all savages—apathy, insensibility and stupidity. They looked with indifference upon any kindness done them; the white man could not expect them even to display 'the bare remembrance of it'. They were gluttons when they got anything to satisfy their appetites, lazy and improvident, occupied entirely by the task at hand and determined by it alone. They had no solicitude about the future. It was most hopeless and dispiriting to any one taking a lively interest in the social improvement of the aborigines to see how little they benefited from their intercourse with white people. They had only acquired an intimate acquaintance with every vice and profligacy that could be instilled into their ears by stockmen and shepherds: the savage character was spoiled and the civilized man was not formed.[24]

It was because the protectors in Port Phillip and the government-supported mission stations at Lake Macquarie, Wellington Valley and Buntingdale near Geelong had so signally failed to form the civilized man out of the aborigine that FitzRoy in May 1847 concluded that the time had come to wind up the

[24] Instructions for our Trusty and Well-Beloved Arthur Phillip . . . 25th Day of April, 1787, *H.R.A.*, I. i. 13-14; encls 1-12 in FitzRoy to Grey, 17 May 1847, *H.R.A.*, I. xxv. 559-73; for the reports from the commissioners for Crown lands for Western Port, Portland Bay, Murray, Grant and Bourke see the encls in FitzRoy to Grey, 17 May 1847, C.O. 201-382,

protectorate. From the reply he had received from La Trobe to his question whether he (La Trobe) would recommend continuance, FitzRoy decided the protectorate had failed in all the higher and more important objects expected from it. For the moment he proposed to postpone making any firm recommendation until he heard again from La Trobe. But the writing was on the wall. The white man was about to give up the aim of forming the civilized man out of the savage, to abandon the policy of integrating the aborigine into the white man's society. He was about to substitute a policy of segregation as the one way to prevent the extermination of the aborigine, to prevent his greater degradation by white stockmen and shepherds, and to protect the white man's life and property from his savage attempts to resist the invasion of his own country. From 1847 onwards the white man ceased attempting to 'open an intercourse', hoping that at least the black man might survive and the white man not be molested.[25]

What stuck in the gullets of the graziers was that in 1846 government had spent more money on this hopeless venture of forming civilized men out of black men than on immigration. Yet when news reached Sydney in the middle of the year that the British Government had stuck to the principle of a minimum upset price of £1 per acre for the waste lands of the Crown, squatterdom uttered words of praise and thanksgiving. Grey had argued in his despatch of 29 November 1846 that a high price both checked dispersion of settlement and the attendant evils of bush barbarism, and created a large fund which might be applied to the increase of the population by migration and to the improvement of the territory. He had also insisted that to encourage the great staple products of New South Wales it was essential that the sheep and cattle farmers of Australia have the right to depasture their stock over far wider tracts than they could possibly afford to purchase. They should not be given permanent property in these vast tracts of land, because that would mean that there would be no land for future settlers. The Act of 1846 empowered the Crown to issue an Order in Council giving the licence holders of such runs security of tenure for periods of up to fourteen years.[26]

On 9 March 1847 Her Majesty's Government in London published an Order in Council designed to make concessions to the squatters and to secure proper accommodation for other classes of the community who might desire to occupy land. The Order divided the colony into three districts. In the settled districts, the Governor was empowered to grant leases of land exclusively for pastoral purposes for terms not exceeding one year and to make general rules under which holders of pastoral land in the said settled districts might be permitted to depasture free of charge any adjacent Crown lands. In the intermediate districts, the Governor was empowered to grant leases for squatting runs for periods of not more than eight years, the Governor having

---

[25] FitzRoy to Grey, 17 May 1847, *H.R.A.*, I. xxv. 558.

[26] FitzRoy to Grey, 27 May, *H.R.A.*, I. xxv. 597; An Act to Amend An Act for Regulating the Sale of Waste Land Belonging to the Crown in the Australian Colonies, 9 & 10 Vic., c. 104, 28 August 1846, *Statutes at Large*, vol. 86; Grey to FitzRoy, 29 November 1846, *H.R.A.*, I. xxv. 271-8.

the power every year to offer such lands for sale provided he gave sixty days notice to the lessee. In the unsettled districts, the Governor was empowered to lease land for pastoral purposes for any term up to fourteen years, the rent to be paid to be proportionate to the number of sheep or equivalent number of cattle, each run to be capable of carrying at least four thousand sheep or equivalent numbers of cattle, and not let at a lower rent than £10 per annum. During the continuance of the lease the land could only be sold to the occupant. Upon the expiration of a lease the government could put up all or any part of the run for sale, provided the previous lessee had the option of purchasing the land for its fair value in an unimproved state at never less than £1 per acre.[27]

In June 1847 the text of the Order in Council arrived in Sydney. While the lawyers were making up their minds on the precise meaning of the Order, the public at large had no such doubts about what it meant. On the big runs from the Darling Downs to Portland Bay there was great rejoicing and jubilation that the large squatters had got their security of tenure at a price they could afford to pay. But on 18 June Robert Lowe told the Council that the interests of the public at large had been sacrificed for the benefit of one class, that the civilization of the country had been overlooked for the purposes of providing facilities for the depasturing of sheep. Now that the squatters had had their way there would be no money in the land fund with which to import free labour. Instead there would be an increase of slaves, because squatters insisted on cheap labour. Cannibals would again be imported to serve the squatters' aggression on the lands of New South Wales. The native-born would not be prepared to live the 'degraded and inanimate life of a shepherd'. Railways would not be built if all the land was locked up in squatting leases. On 1 August Lowe predicted that the small squatters with less than five thousand sheep would be ruined by the regulations but that five hundred large squatters would benefit from 'this monstrous confiscation, this gross injustice . . . perpetrated to glut the avarice, to gorge the ambition of from four to five hundred persons'. When Wentworth asked him why he did not join the squatters, for, after all, paraphrasing Louis XIV, the squatters were the colony, Lowe snapped back that he did not propose to join the company of highwaymen with plenty of money. The tone of the debate was turning nasty. The *Atlas* accused Wentworth of sacrificing 'patriotism at the shrine of avarice'. W. Bland deplored the sacrifice of this brightest gem of the Empire to the most paltry pursuit that ever afflicted a country—the growing of wool. On 26 August W. Foster proposed the appointment of a select committee under the chairmanship of Lowe on the minimum upset price of Crown land.[28]

[27] Grey to FitzRoy, 30 March 1847, *H.R.A.*, I. xxv. 427-30; Order in Council for rules and regulations for occupation of pastoral lands, 9 March 1847, encl. in ibid. 430-8.
[28] Minutes of Executive Council of N.S.W., vol. 7, 15, 28 June, 28 July, 2 August 1847 (n.s.w.s.a.); *V. & P.* (L.C. N.S.W.), 23 July, 1, 12, 23, 26 August 1847; *S.M.H.*, 24 July 12, 13, 27, 28 August 1847; *Atlas*, 21 August 1847.

On 27 September Lowe tabled the report of the committee in the Legis-lative Council. The minimum upset price of £1 per acre, he wrote, was in effect a declaration that land should not be sold at all. By thus virtually pro-hibiting the sale of land, government had not only given an undue stimulus to pastoral pursuits at the expense of agricultural and settled industry but, in conjunction with the system of leases under the Order in Council, govern-ment was appropriating 180 million acres of land to about eighteen hundred persons. In other words, they were endowing a most favoured class at the rate of one hundred thousand acres for every large run-holder in New South Wales. In a decade in which the steamship and the railway were drawing mankind together for the great march into the future, the Order in Council was mummifying New South Wales as a sheep-walk and unnecessarily pro-longing the material backwardness of the Australian colonies. Up-country, cattle-duffing, sly-grog selling, bushranging, all the abominations the white shepherds and stockmen practised on black gins, and the horrible outrages by the aborigines against both black and white, lent weight to the townsmen's case against squatterdom's domination.[29]

Nevertheless, the bourgeoisie were busy conferring the benefits of material progress on the towns. On 21 October 1847 the *Juno* began regular steamship communication between Sydney and Adelaide. Gas lighting was already shedding a dazzling radiance over the streets of Sydney, Melbourne, Adelaide, Hobart and Launceston. Behaviour still lagged far behind the changes in the material setting. The cabbage-tree-hatted mob still gestured lewdly at all who were distinguished by elegance of speech and dress. In Sydney and Hobart prostitutes were just as high in proportion to population as they had been in the old convict days. In Adelaide harlots pleasured the bourgeoisie and workers as well as overlanders and bushmen on a spree after enforced celibacy in the bush. The vulgarians from convict society still caught the eye at all social occasions in Sydney and Hobart. At the Mayor's fancy-dress ball in Sydney on 13 July 1847 the emancipist Robert Cooper staggered drunkenly around the room all night, while another emancipist, Sam Lyons, boasted to the ladies about how many peas he proposed to stuff down at supper time.

Entertainment was on a lavish scale. At Camperdown the Mayor of Sydney often entertained up to eighty guests at dinner. They sat down to a roast goose, a ham and a huge pie, and enough strong drink to 'connublify' the company, and to cause some guests to make 'good night' such a certainty that they had to be led away from the table. At Brisbane, Sydney and Melbourne squatters down from the country were treated as 'arch-lions' by the hotel-keepers. They forced everyone in the hotel to drink with them as their guests, and sang and roistered till three or four in the morning. In Sydney, Melbourne, Hobart and Adelaide men gathered at night in their favourite tavern for drinking, gambling, swapping stories about sportsmen, horses and bets, and 'male conversation', followed by a late night visit to the brothel, as the believers in

[29] Report from Select Committee on the Minimum Upset Price of Land, *V. & P.* (L.C. N.S.W.), 1847, vol. 2; *S.M.H.*, 14, 15, 16 October 1847.

moral enlightenment lectured and preached of the rocks and shoals surrounding the entrance to the harbour of human happiness.

On their attitude to the afflictions of mankind there was as much variety as in attitudes to any public question. Some frowned on drunkenness; others found drunkards amusing or used them as an occasion for a display of their wit. After St Patrick's Day each year the magistrates of Sydney accepted the plea of 'once a year' and 'St Patrick', while the press wrote with relish of the victims of 'excessive attachment to nobblers', and those who were overcome by the 'united strength of Messrs. Wright, Tooth and Cooper'. Some thought the lame and the blind were such a nuisance on the streets of Sydney, Melbourne, Hobart and Adelaide that they ought to be confined in a place where they would not incommode respectable people, and others argued that as there was no moral guilt attached to either, both being 'severe visitations of Providence', people should not be severe on the lame or on the blind, who had the great moral use of teaching those more fortunate gratitude and benevolence. There was a similar variety of opinion in attitudes to insanity. In Sydney and Hobart until 1846 asylums for the insane were highly inefficient, disgusting, harsh and brutal. The inmates were condemned to live ill-fed, ill-lodged lives which were worse than those of common felons. In both colonies between the years 1848 and 1850, under the influence of men like Charles Cowper with a Christ-like compassion for all creatures whom God seemed to have forgotten, policies of non-coercion and humanity were introduced into the treatment of inmates. Ever since 1821 there had been a Benevolent Asylum in Sydney to relieve the poor, the distressed and the aged, and thereby to discountenance, as much as possible, mendicancy and vagrancy and to encourage industrious habits among the indigent as well as afford them religious instruction and consolation in their distress. In 1851, out of an estimated population of 44 240 in Sydney, there were 302 inmates in the Benevolent Asylum of whom over four-fifths were ex-convicts. Then, by mid-century, the committee was pleased to come to the aid of those 'claiming no relationship, indeed, but a common Father, presenting no claim but a common humanity, having no recommendation but the cry of distress!'[30]

From time to time the chill hand of death silenced the human uproar in Sydney and the surrounding districts. On 7 December the phaeton with Sir Charles FitzRoy in the driver's seat, and Lady Mary and Lieutenant G. C. Master as passengers, capsized at the entrance to the drive of Government House in Parramatta, throwing all three passengers to the ground. When the son of Sir Charles rushed to the scene of the disaster, Sir Charles took hold of his hand, kissed it with passion, and sobbed the words, 'Oh George, I've killed Lady Mary, I've killed your mother.' Lieutenant Master never again gave a sign of life. The inhabitants of Sydney and Parramatta promptly put on one of those acts of public grief which underlined the importance they attached both to death and to events in the lives of the high-born. Shops were

---

[30] *S.M.H.*, 16, 21, 23, 29 October, 2, 8 November 1847; *Bell's Life in Sydney*, 17 July, 7 August, 18 September, 2, 16 October 1847; J. E. Sweetman, Journal of a Surveying Voyage to the N.E. Coast of Australia & Torres Sts. . . . 1842-47 (MS. in M.L.).

closed, business was at a standstill for days, and newspapers were printed with black borders on every page as a portentous sadness descended on the city whose inhabitants prepared solemnly for the emotional bath for which such a death provided the occasion.

On 9 December mourning carriages lined the dusty road from Sydney to Parramatta, and men dressed in sombre black crowded the decks of steamships plying between those towns. People gathered inside and outside the church of St John's at Parramatta to hear the Reverend J. Vincent recite the moving words, the breathless silence of the large congregation being broken only by the hysterical sobbing of those unable to restrain their emotion. After the service in the church the funeral carriage, bearing the remains of Lady Mary and the young lieutenant, the two chief mourners, and all who had gathered to pay their last respects, proceeded slowly to the neighbouring burial ground to hear the Reverend Vincent recite solemnly, 'Man that is born of woman hath but a short time to live, and is full of misery. He commeth up, and is cut down, like a flower.' Then the two coffins were lowered into the 'drear abode' appointed for all the dead.[31]

From time to time God visited men, they believed, with lesser chastisings and smitings for their sins. On 21 February 1848 Robert Knox Sconce and Thomas Cooper Makinson, two Church of England clergymen who had been troubled, as had that mighty spirit John Henry Newman, by the claims of their Church to historical continuity with the Holy Catholic and Apostolic Church, resigned their orders and were received into the Catholic Church. Broughton was shocked. Only two years previously he had referred to Sconce and himself as the only two sound and reliable clerks in holy orders in the whole of New South Wales. His first reaction to the blow was to ask God to give all Anglicans the grace and resolution to remain firm in the defence of that inheritance of truth which their forefathers had purchased for them at such a cost. God was sifting them in a day of trouble, rebuke and humiliation for their own vices and negligences. This was a warning to them all to humble themselves before Almighty God. He therefore summoned all Anglicans to a day of public contrition on which they would ask God to forgive them for those sins which had led to the apostasy of Sconce and Makinson. While clergy and laity in Sydney, Parramatta, Goulburn, Yass, Canberra, Queanbeyan, Scone, Maitland, Melbourne, Geelong and Portland asked their God to bring into the way of truth all such as had erred and were deceived, the Very Reverend John Bede Polding, the Catholic Bishop of Sydney, offered a special prayer of praise to Almighty God for the great joy of heart he had experienced in receiving Sconce and Makinson and their families into the bosom of the Church.

The *Atlas* saw the whole episode as a warning to the members of the Church of England against the charms of Puseyism. There was no rest, they

---

[31] *Australian*, 10 December 1847; *S.M.H.*, 10, 13 December 1847; *Bell's Life in Sydney*, 11 December 1847; *Heads of the People*, 11 December 1847; J. Morley, *Death, Heaven and the Victorians* (London, 1971), ch. 2; description of funeral in *Hobart Town Courier*, 12 April 1848.

argued, for the sole of their foot in the bogs and morasses of Puseyism until they had struck into the high road to Rome. The spacious allurements of the new tenets, like those of popery itself, were particularly qualified to deceive the superficial and gratify vanity, self-love and the love of ostentation. Beautiful architecture, painted windows, ornamental carvings and decorations and all that gorgeous pomp and circumstance so characteristic of medieval Christianity appealed to a natural love of the beautiful and the sublime and invested the exercise of religion with a charm. But in those forms the substance of religion was lost, and its exercise became a mere formal ceremony, and an enthusiastic furore wherein reason was clouded by fanatical zeal.[32]

The publication of the despatch of 31 July 1847 by Earl Grey on the future constitutions of the colonies soon pushed the Sconce and Makinson affair off the pages of the public prints. In Grey there was both a spiritual bully and the values of 'grocerdom'. Like Jeremy Bentham, he was tempted to apply the methods of the counting-house to the problem of human happiness. Resembling in some ways the cartoon John Bull of the mid-century, he suffered from the incurable disease of members of his class who regarded colonials as sham Britons, lacking the redeeming graces of the lower orders in the United Kingdom. Colonials were stricken with some defect in their being which made them politically unreliable and far too inclined to bellow without cause or provocation that the Mother Country was ill-using them. Like his predecessor Lord Stanley, he was looking for political institutions for the Australian colonies which would safeguard their society against destruction by radicals, chartists and convict levellers, all of whom had a depraved taste for equality and were driven by an evil spirit to take down the mighty from their seat and send the rich away empty-handed. He had read de Tocqueville and had come away from that experience more determined than ever to find a check to the democratic revolution which was sweeping over the whole civilized world. From de Tocqueville he had picked up the idea that indirect election protected the interests of the men of property and the men of intelligence against egalitarianism and the tyranny of the majority. He had also picked up the idea that participation in local government was the best school for those who were about to govern the affairs of their own society and that a federal constitution provided both strength for the purpose of defence, and protection of liberty against the evil of administrative centralization that characterized the governments of France, Russia and the South American republics.[33]

[32] *S.M.H.*, 24, 29 February, 4 March 1848; W. G. Broughton to E. Coleridge, 4 July 1848 (microfilm in NAT. L.); J. B. Polding to Father Heptonstall, 1 November 1848, quoted in H. N. Birt, *Benedictine Pioneers in Australia* (2 vols, London, 1911), vol. 2, pp. 142-3; *Atlas*, 26 February 1848; W. B. Clarke, *The Claims and Supremacy of the Scriptures as the Rule of Faith and Practice . . . a sermon . . . 27th February, 1848* (Sydney, 1848); R. K. Sconce, *Reasons for Submitting to the Catholic Church* (Sydney, 1848).

[33] G. F. Hursthouse to Messrs Youl, Sewell and Blaine, n.d. (Papers of Third Earl Grey, Box 139, File 3, Durham, England); A. de Tocqueville, *De la Démocratie en Amérique* (3 vols, Paris, 1874), vol. 1, pp. 1-24; for other aspects of Grey see Grey to FitzRoy, 31 July 1847, *H.R.A.*, I. xxv. 698-703; J. M. Ward, *Earl Grey and the Australian Colonies 1846-1857* (Melbourne, 1958), ch. 2.

In a prayer-book prose drained of some of the passion which enlivened that great statement of an English view of man's fate, Grey charged the colonists to hear what comfortable words he had to say to all those who accepted the principle that affairs of local concern should be left to the regulation of the local authorities. Her Majesty's Government hoped to introduce a bill in the next session of parliament for the division of New South Wales into two colonies, the northern of which would retain its present name while the southern colony would, by Her Majesty's gracious permission, receive the name of the Province of Victoria. After the petition for separation of June 1844 was studied in London, Stanley asked Sir George Gipps for a full report of his views on the proposed separation of Port Phillip, outlining the probable advantages and disadvantages of the measure. He asked him to request the Executive Council for advice on the question. On 30 March 1846 Gipps asked the Executive Council whether they recommended the separation of Port Phillip from the rest of New South Wales and the erection of the district so constituted into a distinct colony. After investigating whether the opinions of the inhabitants of the district and the opinions of the inhabitants of the Middle District were truly represented in the separation petitions, two members of the Executive Council, the Colonial Secretary Deas Thomson and the Commander of the Forces Sir Maurice O'Connell voted affirmatively, and the Treasurer C. D. Riddell and Bishop Broughton opposed the motion. Gipps gave his casting vote in favour of separation. He was influenced, he said, by the very general desire for separation that existed in the district, by the geographical position of the district which rendered it already in a great degree distinct from the rest of the colony, by the ability of the district to bear the expense of a separate government, and by the intention since 1836 to form it into a distinct colony. He did not believe there had been any administrative evil of sufficient magnitude to call for so important a change. He did however agree with the petitioners for separation about the difficulty of finding suitable persons to represent the district in Sydney, and on the strength of opinion for separation in the district.[34]

For the future constitution of the Australian colonies Her Majesty's Government proposed to create two distinct Houses to replace the existing legislature of New South Wales which was composed partly of nominees of the Crown and partly of the representatives of the people. It proposed to devolve the management of local affairs upon the inhabitants of districts of moderate size, and to consider whether such local bodies might not be made to bear to the House of Assembly the relation of constituents and representatives. He added that some method would also be devised for enabling the various legislatures of the several Australian colonies to co-operate with each other in the enactment of such laws as might be necessary for regulating the interests common to those possessions collectively, such as the imposition

[34] Grey to FitzRoy, 31 July 1847, *H.R.A.* I. xxv. 698-703; Stanley to Gipps, 12 June 1845, *H.R.A.*, I. xxiv. 370; Stanley to Gipps, 22 August 1845, ibid., 482-3; Gipps to Stanley, 29 April 1846, *H.R.A.*, I. xxv. 26-33; Minutes of Executive Council of N.S.W. on separation of Port Phillip, encls in ibid.

of duties of import and export, the conveyance of letters, and the formation of roads, railways or other internal communications traversing any two or more of the colonies. To implement that part of the plan it had in mind the creation of a central authority, a system of representative legislation through-out the whole of the Australian colonies, including Van Diemen's Land, South Australia and Western Australia. Grey wound up by asking FitzRoy to put him in possession of the opinions of the most eminent local authorities on these proposals, and by saying that it would be a source of highest gratifica-tion to him if, under the authority of parliament, the colonial government of Australia could be settled on a basis on which the colonists might, under the blessing of Divine Providence, themselves erect institutions worthy of the Empire to which they belonged and worthy of the people from whom they were descended. But on such questions the wool gatherers and the men of the counting-house in Australia had neither opinions nor ideas.[35]

In Port Phillip the news that the District was to become a separate colony bearing the name of Victoria was greeted with wild enthusiasm. The very name fed their own much vaunted sense of moral superiority over the old penal colonies, as well as their satisfaction in taking this first step in the march towards freedom. The differences between the anti-transportationist and respectable burgher of Melbourne, William Kerr, and the pro-transportationist and Melbourne spokesman for squatterdom's domination, Edward Curr, were buried away in the celebration of their impending liberation from the rich men of Sydney. In congratulating themselves on their coming deliverance from the thraldom of New South Wales, William Kerr paused to express his warm indignation at Broughton's opposition. 'Oh! that we had the ducking of the Right Rev. Prelate in the deepest pool of the Yarra Yarra; we should so cool his courage that we dare venture to say he would never again attempt to interpose his flash prelacy as a hindrance to civil rights!' In Adelaide the press and the public at large welcomed the proposed concession of represen-tative government as a wise, liberal and comprehensive measure, but baulked at the formation of a general assembly of the colonies as unconstitutional, morally opposed to the social constitution of the colony, and endangering their colonial independence. Perth was silent, for they had opted for convict labour rather than the birthrights of Englishmen. In Hobart and Launceston, people were more concerned with the pressing problem of how to prevent their society from being inundated with irreclaimable guilt than with any vague promise that they were about to receive a constitution similar to that of New South Wales.[36]

On 19 January 1848 a vast assembly filled the Victoria Theatre in Sydney for a noble display of true British feeling by a people who did not propose to be

[35] Grey to FitzRoy, 31 July 1847, *H.R.A.*, I. xxv. 698-703; R. Gurry, Never Say Die—Our Cause is a Righteous One (thesis in History Department, Australian National Uni-versity).
[36] *Argus*, 21, 31 December 1847; *South Australian Register*, 19 January 1848; *Hobart Town Courier*, 15 January 1848.

robbed of their rights by a despotic minister or hoodwinked by the parliament in London. Wentworth stood it very bravely when the 'Pittites' interrupted his remarks with cries of 'No Coolies', 'No Himmigrants', 'No Hexiles' and 'No Nuffin'. The 'Pittites' cheered ironically when James Macarthur apologized for not being able to read to them because of the poor light, for the people were weary of all the bores from the Old Guard. They loved it when Robert Lowe ridiculed the constitutions of crack-brained philosophers, and urged them to demand an intelligible scheme of representation such as existed in their parent land, and not the degraded, absurd, nonsensical scheme proposed by Earl Grey which would only lead to their own slavery and ruin. If the Colonial Office persisted with its mad scheme of indirect election, they might have to consider whether the time had come for them to declare their independence. There was tremendous cheering for that. But neither Lowe nor Wentworth had any constructive ideas on their future constitution. The administrative centralization and paternalism from the convict era, and the dispersion of settlement caused by the sterility of the land, the land laws and the use of eastern Australia as a sheep-walk had left them inexperienced in any participation in politics except the public meeting. So they fell back on the platitude of aspiring to copy the institutions of the Mother Country, when they well knew that their problem arose in part because of their failure to transplant the society of the Old World.[37]

At meetings at Camden, Penrith, Patrick's Plains and Goulburn the country gentry insisted that it was just because they were so English at heart that they asked Grey to drop the shameful mockery of indirect election and give them the British constitution as quickly as possible. Then neither the threats of independence nor the full-throated roar of the workers of Sydney Town would strike terror in the hearts of the men of property and education. Faced with such opposition from both town and country, Grey wrote to FitzRoy in July 1848 that since he could have no wish to impose upon the inhabitants of the colony a form of government they judged to be not suited to their wants, he would advise against carrying the proposal into action.[38]

At the same time the British Government took another step to strengthen and comfort those who wanted Australia to remain English at heart. In 1847, in response to the suggestions of Bishop Broughton, they decided to subdivide the diocese of Australia into the dioceses of Sydney, Newcastle, Melbourne and Adelaide. Believing with Lord Macaulay that it was the genius of the Church of England to hold a middle course between the Churches of Rome and Geneva, Earl Grey was careful to select men who were not tainted with too much Puseyism or so much of the evangelical tradition as to cause them to discard the vestments, the liturgy and the ceremonial which propped up

[37] *S.M.H.*, 19, 21 January 1848; *Bell's Life in Sydney*, 29 January 1848.
[38] *S.M.H.*, 8, 9, 16, 19, 21 February, 13 March 1848; *Bell's Life in Sydney*, 15 January 1848; Petition against Changes in the Constitution from the Residents of Singleton, Port Phillip, Windsor, Picton, and Queanbeyan, encls in FitzRoy to Grey, 27 March 1848, *H.R.A.*, I. xxvi. 294-9; Grey to FitzRoy, 31 July 1848, *H.R.A.*, I. xxvi. 530.

authority and order in society. For the diocese of Melbourne he chose Charles Perry, then a rather spare, muscular Christian of some forty-one years. Perry was an able and cultured graduate of Cambridge University who had, it was believed, the right degree of horror of Rome as a centre of superstition and arbitrary power, and of Puseyites as men who seduced the weak and the unwary into embracing the whore of Babylon. Though leaning towards the evangelical wing of the Church, he was thoroughly reliable on the question of prelacy, on the monarchy and on the established order in society. He arrived in Melbourne early in February 1848 to take up his office as bishop. The *Port Phillip Gazette* declared that the arrival of a bishop made Melbourne a city; it was the first instalment of 'Separation', and would give a higher tone to their society. In deference to the susceptibilities of His Grace, Puseyite observances were swept away from the services of the Church of England in Melbourne; a paintbrush obliterated the crosses on the windows of St James's Church and the crucifix at St Peter's, Eastern Hill, was discreetly removed.

Father Patrick Bonaventure Geoghegan, the Franciscan who had celebrated the first mass in Melbourne at a temporary open-air altar on 19 May 1838 and had laid the foundation stone of the church of St Francis on 4 October 1841, called at the Bishop's residence, but, not finding him at home, left his card. Perry wrote to Geoghegan to acknowledge the receipt of the card, but took the opportunity to express his surprise at receiving a visit from a Romish priest, because, although for his part he was willing that every man should be allowed to worship God according to the dictates of his conscience, as a prelate of the Church of England he must decline intercourse with the Reverend Father because his infallible guide to conduct, holy scripture, taught him that if any man taught any gospel other than the one he received that man should be accursed. The Romanists were incensed. The evangelicals, the Presbyterians, the Methodists, the Congregationalists and others hailed the advent of Perry in the province as 'a blessing to the cause of genuine Protestantism'.[39]

As first Church of England Bishop of Newcastle Grey selected William Tyrrell, who was then forty-one years of age. In January 1848 Tyrrell arrived in Sydney with a retinue of twenty. Like Perry he was a distinguished graduate of the University of Cambridge. Like Perry he believed in episcopacy, but did not accept the teaching of the Church of Rome that supernatural graces of a high order descended on bishops through the ceremony of the laying on of hands. Like Perry he looked to God rather than the Sacraments of the Church for the means of grace and the hope of glory. Like Perry and Charles Kingsley, Tyrrell was a man who believed in the cultivation of the body rather than that effeminate Mariolatry which degraded the Puseyites. At Cambridge he was known for his great love of athletic sports, especially cricket and boating, which toughened his body which he kept well

[39] *Port Phillip Gazette*, 2 February 1848; *Argus*, 8, 18 February 1848; A. de Q. Robin, *Charles Perry Bishop of Melbourne* (Nedlands, 1967), chs 1-3.

under control by prudent and regular habits. Like Perry he had the evangelical's attitude to hard work. He generally rose at four in the morning and was to be seen on summer mornings walking in his garden reading his Greek Testament. Like Perry he had a great love of Shakespeare. Both of them hoped to plant in the minds of the rising generation a love of the great products of the English genius—the Bible, the Book of Common Prayer, Shakespeare and Milton. So did Augustus Short, the bishop-elect of Adelaide, who came later on in that year in which these three men tried to graft the love of God's name and English things on the hearts of Australians.[40]

While Perry, Tyrrell and Short made their bow on the colonial scene, and Polding announced that plans were maturing in Rome to erect Melbourne into a Catholic see, the people of Europe threatened to demolish the entire fabric of society. In Sydney, too, the people were on the march. On 27 June writs were issued for the election of the twenty-four members of the Legislative Council. On 17 July a public meeting was held in the School of Arts to hear Wentworth and Bland present the case for their re-election as the two representatives for the electorate of Sydney. Bob Nichols strained his voice trying to be heard. The heroic Stuart Donaldson, uncompromising advocate for squatterdom's domination, one-time back-stabber of Patrick Leslie at whose wedding he was best man, stood there swelling with indignation because his voice could not be heard above the storm of voices. The frantic Edward Flood told them he was a son of the soil, but the people there would not hear him either, although he became frightfully red in the face while screaming for silence at the top of his very shrill voice.

The people would not be silent. Wentworth and Bland had to leave by a side door and the chairman closed the meeting. The conservatives and all the members of the Old Guard were disgusted that the men from the radical and popish parties who were all but identical with the supporters of the chartist petition for universal suffrage, vote by ballot and all the other incendiary and revolutionary rubbish, had established themselves in the building with a full determination to interrupt the proceedings. The people were determined that the electorate of Sydney should not be represented by these men who were supporters of a high property qualification, the introduction of cannibals, convicts and coolies and, indeed, any device that would keep down the price of labour.[41]

Those who wanted to protest against the wicked endeavour by Wentworth to introduce 'men of colour and heathens' and so create for the ends of private aggrandizement an inferior class in the community, were urged to vote for Robert Lowe. Early in July a group of electors, led by such 'universal palaver' men as Henry Parkes, requested Lowe to stand for election. At the first

---

[40] R. G. Boodle, *The Life and Labours of the Right Rev. William Tyrrell, D.D.* (London, 1881); A. P. Elkin, *The Diocese of Newcastle* (Sydney, 1955), p. 135.

[41] *S.M.H.*, 24 June 1848; *South Australian Register*, 14 June 1848; *Elector* (a magazine of politics and literature), 27 July 1848; *Atlas*, 22 July 1848; *Australasian Chronicle*, 15 July 1848; *Sentinel*, 20, 27 July 1848.

courting Lowe was coy and bashful. At the second he answered 'Yes' after making it quite clear that he would never be a hireling of the people. The supporters of the people's voice in politics then told the electors that all who wanted to strike at the unjust enormities of class legislation would vote for Robert Lowe. The alternative was summed up in a quatrain:

> Monopolist of Sugar;
> Monopolist of Land;
> Monopolist of Nonsense;
> Lamb, Wentworth, and poor Bland!

After the declaration on 28 July that Wentworth and Lowe had been elected and Lamb and Bland defeated, the supporters of the people's cause carried Lowe in triumph in a carriage through the streets of Sydney to his house.[42]

Three days before the declaration of the Sydney poll large numbers gathered in St James's Church to hear the Lord Bishop of Australia recite the words for the burial of the dead over the coffin of the octogenarian Alexander McLeay, who had just 'gone to his reward' for his 'consistent Christian character'. In the minds of the people, McLeay had been their arch enemy from the days of Governor Darling to the present day. The scythe of time was cutting down all such grass: Braidwood Wilson had gone in 1843; Dr George Imlay, adventurer, land monopolist, an eagle in the sky, had shot himself in October 1846. Now Broughton and Allwood were committing another Old Guard man to the dust from whence he came.[43]

Yet when the results of the election were announced in July, it was clear that Botany Bay Whigs and Tories, and supporters of the sheep-walk economy were as strongly entrenched as ever in the Legislative Council of New South Wales. There were exceptions. Bob Nichols, that tall, well-made, handsome 'son of the soil' of some forty summers, with the hint of 'I don't care' in his face, which was said to distinguish the native-born from the 'himmigrants', was returned for Northumberland Boroughs. There was a hint about him of that grace which portrays an inner kindness of heart. He was known to go for all the points of the People's Charter, for a thorough reform of the land system, and was sound as a bell—a 'dinkum Aussie'—on the questions of cannibals, coolies and convicts. The bond which drew all the 'sons of the soil' together made him behave in a kindly and friendly way towards those two 'bellowing champions of the few', Wentworth and James

[42] H. Parkes, 'The friends of free election and their opponents', *Elector*, 27 July 1848; R. Lowe, To the Electors Signing the Requisition to Become a Candidate for the City of Sydney, 6 July 1848, and To the Committee who have been Appointed to take Measures for my Return, 10 July 1848 (Autographed Letters to H. Parkes, MS. in M.L.); *Bell's Life in Sydney*, 15, 29 July 1848; *S.M.H.*, 21, 28, 29, 31 July, 1 August 1848; *Australian*, 6, 13 July 1848.

[43] *S.M.H.*, 26 July 1848; plaque for Alexander McLeay in St James's Church, Sydney; J. J. Fletcher, 'The society's heritage from the Macleays', *Proceedings of the Linnean Society of New South Wales*, 1920, vol. 45.

Martin. The latter, who had first taken his bow in public at the age of eighteen as the author of *The Australian Sketch Book* was returned for Cook and Westmoreland. He was already known in public as a political friend of 'that evil genius of Australia—that arch hater of the British poor—Mr. Wentworth'. Indeed it was said during the election campaign that Martin would be another 'tool' for Wentworth in the Council, that when 'the true liberties of this country [were] to be kept back, the growl of the great dung-hill aristocrat [would] find its obsequious echo in James Martin'.

James Macarthur, Charles Nicholson, Stuart Donaldson, Terence Murray, Donald McIntyre, Charles Cowper, Nelson Lawson, J. B. Darvall, W. H. Suttor and Henry Dangar who had never once in their lives been suspected of radicalism but were sound 'South-Sea Solons' were all returned to take that large view of things, which meant, in effect, championing the pastoral patriarchs of New South Wales. Alexander Berry, the white-haired country squire of seventy, who was known in Sydney as 'the last of the ancient nominees . . . [and] a part of human antiquity in our midst', remained a nominated member. He was joined by men of like mind such as George Allen, the late mayor of Sydney and host at Camperdown to the country gentry, Edward Hamilton, Thomas Icely, Phillip Parker King and John Lamb. Among the official nominees Edward Deas Thomson and John Hubert Plunkett were blithe of heart and young in love of justice and hate of wrong. They were both prepared to battle at least for equality before the law. Plunkett was said to hide beneath his official countenance the same Dionysian passions which swept through Henry Parkes. Behind the reserved and urbane exterior he presented to the world, Thomson was already fearful lest those winds of revolution which had begun to blow in Europe would one day level all social distinctions in Australia.[44]

When the time came to elect a member for Melbourne and five for the District of Port Phillip, the burgher wing of the separation movement used the occasion to make a histrionic gesture to force the British Government to consider separation without delay. On nomination day on 25 July, Thomas McCombie, after comparing Sydney to a churlish old father, and Port Phillip to a spirited young son who did not receive sufficient pocket-money from the old miser, formally nominated Earl Grey, Secretary of State for the Colonies, as a fit and proper person to represent the city of Melbourne. Alderman Greeves, after arguing cheekily that a Melbourne man in Sydney would be reduced to the position of a slave and a tool, seconded the nomination. The squatter or 'aristocratic' wing of the separation movement then nominated J. F. L. Foster. John Pascoe Fawkner warned the burgesses that Foster was a representative of the squatting interests, who regarded the working classes as the rabble of society. A. F. Mollison, another man identified with squatter-dom's domination, warned them that if they elected Grey the whole of their

[44] *People's Advocate*, 14, 21 July, 18 August, 1, 8, 22, 29 September 1849; *Bell's Life in Sydney*, 29 July 1848; *Sentinel*, 3 August 1848; *S.M.H.*, 29, 31 July 1848; H. Parkes, 'Gone over to the Majority' in H. Parkes, *Studies in Rhyme* (Sydney, 1870).

society might fall to pieces. At the poll on 26 July 295 votes were cast for Grey and 102 for Foster. The aristocratic party accused the bourgeoisie of committing an act of constitutional suicide, of disfranchising themselves and actually demonstrating to the world that they were unfit for free institutions. Three-fourths of those who had voted for Grey, they argued, had done so for a 'lark', but they would find that it was too dearly purchased. The price for such 'an exquisite bit of Tomfoolery' would furnish a 'glorious anti-separation argument' for their hereditary enemies in Sydney and substantiate the force of La Trobe's celebrated and much condemned admission that '*Port Phillip was not ripe for Self-Government*'. Since only 397 persons had voted out of a constituency of 935, some said the electors obviously looked upon the affair as 'downright humbug'. By contrast the bourgeoisie and the workers patted themselves on the back for yet another one of their 'wise and righteous' acts which, they believed, could not fail to arrest the attention of the Home Government and the British public.[45]

On 21 September the bourgeois party, known to their opponents as the 'Melbourne mob', and the squatter party, known to their opponents as the 'brute force savages', confronted each other again at Geelong for the election of five representatives for the District of Port Phillip. The rain poured down in buckets as two to three hundred people, mostly consisting of the squattocracy of Geelong and its neighbourhood, with their usual retinue of hangers-on, gathered at the hustings to give expression to their version of public opinion. Dr Thomson pleaded with them not to elect British peers because that would defeat all their hopes of separation merely for the purpose of gratifying the wishes and administering to the vanity of a set of Melbourne agitators. A Mr Lloyd also spoke of 'their foolish Melbourne brethren'. Fawkner, who had spent his years denouncing aristocratic privilege, nominated five peers of the United Kingdom. The so-called aristocratic party or squatter party promptly put forward the names of five colonial commoners. Captain Foster Fyans, the hero of the Norfolk Island meeting of 1834 but now a magistrate and squatter near Geelong, and Dr Robert Hope, one-time prize winner in the Edinburgh Medical School and now the holder of a squatting run at Darriwil, near Geelong, recommended the local boys. At the poll on 3 October at Melbourne, Geelong, Belfast (Port Fairy) and Portland the squatting or pro-representation party won a resounding victory. At long last Edward Curr, the father of the separation movement, won his seat in the Legislative Council just as a mortal illness intimated that he would be lucky to enjoy the fruits of all his striving and his humiliations. La Trobe stuck to his point that the people of Port Phillip were not fit for self-government, but by then the brawny pioneers of civilization in Port Phillip almost expected treachery from the

[45] *Port Phillip Herald*, 27 June, 6, 27 July, 1, 3 August 1848; The Humble Memorial of Certain Inhabitants of the Districts of Port Phillip in the Colony of New South Wales, in Public Meeting Assembled, encl. in FitzRoy to Grey, 23 September 1848, C.O. 201/399; La Trobe to Col. Sec. of New South Wales, 10 August 1848, C.O. 201/399; *Argus*, 25, 28 July 1848; *Port Phillip Patriot*, 21, 26 July, 2 August 1848.

man they thought of as a sanctimonious fop. Some people in Sydney said with a maddening condescension that the remnants of the dispersed and scattered aboriginal tribes south of the Murrumbidgee might lay more reasonable claims to an independent legislature and self-government than their white brothers, but Melburnians expected that sort of thing from Sydneysiders. FitzRoy, who was gradually coming back into public life after his self-lacerations after the death of Lady Mary, told Grey that a community in which such acts of folly were committed was scarcely fitted to be trusted with the rights of a free representative system of government. It was the first intimation that Sir Charles would not be joining the people in their march to power.[46]

Like Sir Charles, Sir William Denison, the Lieutenant-Governor of Van Diemen's Land, and his cold, tongue-tied wife believed the cultivation of a strong landed gentry was the most effective antidote to all those forces in the colonies making for a Yankee-type democratic republic. As on the mainland, the differences in the response of people to life were enormous. Some believed the best benefit the rich could confer on the poor was to minister to their spiritual needs rather than give them food and drink. Some believed they could best serve their Lord by dwelling at inordinate length on the enormity of keeping common brothels in Hobart Town. Some believed God would be pleased if they used their talents to prove that no Protestant could enter the Kingdom of Heaven, and some with equal fervour believed God's pleasure would be increased if they used their verbal gifts to persuade mankind that no Catholic could enter the Kingdom of Heaven. Some enjoyed the 'high order' and the great solemnity of Handel's oratorio *The Messiah*, while others preferred to spend their evenings in a continuous roar of laughter at the variety and dancing show at the Royal Albert Theatre where the disagreeable habit of smoking had been entirely put down.[47]

Others again were caught up in the hope that the white man in Van Diemen's Land had been given yet another opportunity that year to convert to Christian civilization the fifty-two survivors of the five thousand-odd savages who had inhabited the island before the white man's invasion in 1804. Since 'God's fool', G. A. Robinson, had left for Port Phillip in 1838, things had not gone well at Wybalenna. The Reverend Thomas Dove, an M.A. of Glasgow University, quarrelled with the commandant, Captain Malcolm Laing Smith. He also told the Lieutenant-Governor that his own occupation was worse than useless respecting the aborigines. Indeed he could regard his attempts to teach the aborigines the truths of Christianity as anything but an elevation in his clerical calling! The white man thought of Dove as a man who ministered faithfully and unremittingly to the spiritual wants of his people until God took him to his rest. In August 1846 Eardley-Wilmot suggested to Gladstone that the time had come to break up the aboriginal

---

[46] *Argus*, 12, 26 September 1848; *Port Phillip Herald*, 28 September 1848; FitzRoy to Grey, 4 December 1848, *H.R.A.*, I. xxvi. 729-30; *Bell's Life in Sydney*, 5 August 1848.
[47] *Colonial Times*, 14 January, 21 April, 23, 30 May, 6 June 1848.

establishment on Flinders Island, partly because the aborigines had been made unhappy in a row between Dr Henry Jeanneret and Dr Joseph Milligan. Dr Jeanneret accused Dr Milligan of turning the dormitory of the aborigines into a pigsty, of underfeeding them and beating them unmercifully when tied naked to a table. Their numbers did not much exceed fifty and the people themselves were so broken in spirit that they were in no position to use force on the white man. The one hundred graves at Wybalenna were silent testimony that European civilization destroyed the will to live in the Tasmanian aborigine. In April 1847 Grey ordered Denison to break up the establishment and settle the survivors in Van Diemen's Land. On 18 October 1847 Truganini and the other fifty-one survivors were moved to Oyster Cove in D'Entrecasteaux Channel and placed under the charge of Dr Milligan. Denison was delighted to provide catechists to teach them to read and write in case they wanted to submit to the restraints of civilization. Privately he thought of them as little children who were doomed to die. By mid-1848 he was pleased they had made such progress that they were able to sing to him unaided that hymn he had loved at matins in England, 'Awake my soul, and with the sun'.

By contrast the press in Hobart and Launceston published accounts of the disgusting behaviour of the aborigines of the Port Phillip District, brought on by over-indulgence in 'strong waters', to warn the people of Van Diemen's Land against mistaken deeds of kindness. The Hobart press quoted with approval the way the Melbourne press wrote up the reports of trials of aborigines. They gloated over the expression 'snaky locks of Stygian blackness'. They enjoyed the accounts of the magistrate and the servants of the court treating savages as figures of fun. They loved to read how Billy was 'plenty drunk'. They thought it was very funny when Billy explained that he would not be able to pay the fine, and the magistrate ordered him to spend forty-eight hours in the cells on bread and water. They found that both funny and a warning of what to expect if those men who wore on their faces 'the livery of the burnish'd sun' prowled around Van Diemen's Land again.[48]

The arrival of convicts in May touched the colonists much more deeply than any twinges of conscience about whether they were still capable of showing amity and kindness to wrecks of savages. In May the *John Calvin* arrived in the River Derwent with 140 female convicts from Ireland, and the *Mount Stuart Elphinstone* with 240 male convicts from England. The antitransportationists talked of a 'manifest breach of faith towards the colonists'. The Lord Bishop of Tasmania told the clergy and laity that penal discipline schemes had already inflicted 'grievous wrong' upon the colonists of Tasmania. The *Hobart Town Advertiser* predicted that the mechanics and the

[48] Report of Committee of Enquiry on Thomas Dove (Col. Sec.'s Office, 8 ii 266, T.S.A.); epitaph on tomb of T. Dove at Swansea, Tasmania; Wilmot to Gladstone, 13 August 1846, C.O. 280/195; Grey to Denison, 1 April 1847, C.O. 408/28; Denison to Grey, 7 December 1847, C.O. 280/215; H. Jeanneret, *A Letter to the Right Hon. Earl Grey* (London, 1851); W. Denison, *Varieties of Vice-Regal Life*, vol. 1, pp. 78-9; *Colonial Times*, 29 August 1848.

rising generation, both male and female, would feel the evil most of all. For whereas the 'mere laborer' could find work in the neighbouring colonies, the mechanic would be faced with the choice of work at lower wages or up-rooting himself from his family. As for the youths of the rising generation they could not hope to compete with prison labour and so must break the ties of home, parents, friends and companions and seek a living on the main-land. The fate of the daughters was even worse. They were bound to the place where their parents lived. They could not leave the protection of a parent's roof without danger to their morals. The men who might have been their partners for life would leave the island or, if they stayed, would not be able to support families. Cheap labour was about to injure 'every tie of social and moral relationship'.[49]

The members of the Legislative Council were more equivocal. They resolved on 14 October that renewal of transportation would be in the highest degree injurious to the colony, detrimental to the convicts themselves and productive of no advantage whatever to the Mother Country. They went on to say that a plan by which the convicts, if sent out to these colonies after having undergone their punishment in England, might be distributed over the whole surface of the Australian continent would to a certain extent neutralize the evil effects consequent upon the influx of a felon population, more especially if combined with an immigration of well-selected free persons to an equivalent amount. If this principle of part felon, part free immigration were acted on, they had no doubt that the moral and social conditions of the convicts would be improved and the interest both of England and the Australian colonies promoted.[50]

In Western Australia most of the inhabitants were convinced by 1848 that the arrival of convicts was the one way to ensure that the 'colours of Western Australia' would not for an instant be pulled down. By October 1848 there were still only 4622 Europeans, and an estimated 1960 aborigines over an area of one-third of Australia. It was over four hundred years since the Chinese had abandoned their journeys of exploration in the South Seas, over four hundred years since the Japanese ships sailed in the waters to the north of Arnhem Land and Timor Island. It was over three hundred years since the Dutch seamen had described the west coast of New Holland as a coast of iron, inhabited by exceedingly black, barbarian savages. The American whalers had used the south-west coast as a base of operations but had never intimated an intention to stay. The fear of the French had evaporated almost as soon as Captain Stirling had christened the colony in June 1829. The confidence of the colonists had not been shaken. They remained strangely unaware of what their harsh environment had done to both man and beast. When the

[49] *Hobart Town Courier*, 20, 24 May 1848; *Hobart Town Advertiser*, 30 May 1848.

[50] Resolutions of the Legislative Council of Van Diemen's Land on the proposal contained in Earl Grey's despatch of the 27th April 1848 to send all convicts to Van Diemen's Land, encl. in Denison to Grey, 17 November 1848, C.O. 280/233; Grey to Denison, 27 April 1848, C.O. 408/30; *Hobart Town Courier*, 10 June 1848.

'very ugly misshapen kangaroo' fled away in long bounds, they felt no sense of horror or anxiety lest nature here had perpetrated some mistake, or forms and shapes that everywhere else had been supplanted by more viable species had survived here. They were not alarmed that nature in New Holland had been left behind other parts of the world, nor did they believe for one moment that the aborigines had stayed at the cultural level of the Stone Age because that was the human culture appropriate for such a continent, or that there was a connection between petrifaction of the mind and their stony environment. On the contrary, the effect of the environment, isolation and the sight of this primitive people drove them to profess all the more belligerently their allegiance and loyalty to the throne, to cultivate the habits, feelings and prejudices of Englishmen and to take pride in such transplanted English institutions and habits as trial by jury, the independence of the magistracy, private property, an unfettered press, freedom of discussion, a gentlemanly tone and a scrupulous delicacy in veiling the privacy of domestic life.[51]

Confident that they would not continue the ghastly mistakes into which nature had stumbled in that part of the world, they brazenly professed their superiority over all the other Australian colonies. They boasted of the 'crushing superiority of their position', ridiculed Port Phillip as 'that pert dependency of a dependency', mocked the 'laudable purpose' men of South Australia and congratulated themselves on their escape from the 'bush barbarism' of New South Wales and the absence in their vast territory of those human monsters of Van Diemen's Land. Their one great lack was an adequate supply of labour. Influenced by favourable accounts of the character of the German people—their patience, steadiness, sobriety, perseverance, and readiness to work for low wages—they had tried in 1847 to import them by shiploads. They had also tried without success to import Chinese. By 1848 the majority of settlers were convinced that the convicts were their one chance to make roads, build bridges, harvest crops and provide a steady demand for their wheat and other agricultural produce. The Jeremiahs warned them in vain to take care lest they attained material well-being at the dreadful price of contamination and vice. In 1848 they repeated their 'plain, unvarnished statement' of their wants and wishes: they wanted convicts.[52]

By contrast in South Australia country settlers, merchants and shopkeepers in towns, and mechanics, shepherds and general labourers were quite determined that their morals not be polluted or their pockets adversely affected by the competition of cheap convict labour. By the beginning of 1848 they believed they had proved their point that it was possible to plant civilization in the wilds of Australia without the use of slave or semi-slave labour. By that year the European population had increased to 38 666. On all the

[51] 'Statistics of population, live stock and agriculture, Western Australia', *Perth Government Gazette*, 19 December 1848; *Inquirer* (Perth), 29 July 1846; A. Lommel, *Fortschritt ins Nichts* (Zurich, 1969), pp. 14-15; *Report on the Statistics of Western Australia* (Perth, 1841), p. 44.

[52] *Inquirer*, 3 June, 8 September, 1 December 1847; *Perth Gazette*, 2 January, 17 April, 10, 17 July 1847.

available evidence it appeared that the aborigines were fortunately disappearing off the face of the earth or retiring to places where they could no longer destroy the white man's stock, burn his crops, or practise those abominations on each other which were so offensive to the eyes and ears of civilized men. In Adelaide, Kapunda, Burra, Gawler, the Barossa Valley, the Mount Barker district, Mount Gambier, Port Lincoln and west to the boundaries of European settlement at Streaky Bay the clergy, schoolmasters and public press went on recommending the virtues of industry, frugality, temperance, godliness and quietness.

At the end of 1847 the forces working for the victory of British philistinism in a land distinguished for its garish days and its majestic nights were greatly strengthened by the arrival of Augustus Short to take up his position as the Church of England Bishop of Adelaide. He was then forty-six years old. Educated at Westminster School and Christ Church, Oxford, where he took a first-class honour in classics, he came to man's estate retaining all the warmth of manner and the impetuosity of a boy. In conversation he had the same boyish playfulness and the generosity of spirit not to put on black looks with those who were 'wanting in heart'. He had been toughened in his school days at Westminster by savage initiations and fagging against showing his view to the measurers or the women with hard hearts. He had the appearance of a man who believed God had chosen him as His advocate for all those sober virtues which would qualify a man to enter at the narrow gate.

Soon after his arrival in Adelaide on 28 December 1847, he told a delegation from the South Australian Church Society that he hoped to start a Collegiate School which would provide a superior English classical and mathematical education for sons of gentlemen. Ever since 15 July 1847 there had been such a school for the sons of respectable parents in the School House near Trinity Church. Two years later, on Her Majesty's birthday, Short had the honour to lay the foundation stone, to the glory of the 'triune God' and the advancement of religious and useful learning, of the Catholic School of St Peter. On that occasion Francis Dutton, large landowner, Anglican and political conservative, stood on the ground near David McLaren, the manager of the South Australian Company, a dissenter, a man much given to improving the morals of his fellow-men, and Thomas Stow, the Congregational minister, who believed God had chosen South Australia as a place where science and religion would work harmoniously together to man's comfort and God's glory. In South Australia, government, the Church of England and dissent found themselves allies.[53]

While the boys at St Peter's began to learn the rudiments of Latin and Greek to equip them to contribute to the victory of civilization over bar-

---

[53] J. Boothby, *A Statistical Sketch of South Australia* (Adelaide 1876); South Australian Blue Book, 1848; F. T. Whitington (ed.), *Augustus Short: first bishop of Adelaide* (Adelaide, 1887), pp. 6-7, 143, 262-3; *South Australian Register*, 1, 7 July 1847, 1 January 1848, 14, 26 April 1849; A. G. Price, *The Collegiate School of St. Peter, 1847-1947* (Adelaide, 1947).

barism in South Australia, the citizens of Adelaide cordially bade adieu to Governor Robe, who had won their esteem by the very inflexibility of his character and his high sense of duty. On 2 August 1848 Sir Henry Edward Fox Young arrived in Adelaide to take office as Governor of the Province of South Australia. He was just forty. He had already had some twenty years as a government servant administering British colonies. By temperament and conviction he was one of those men of 'heroic ingredients' who believed moral enlightenment would usher in an age of benevolence and material well-being for mankind. Like Macaulay and Carlyle he thought of history as the true stoic poem and universal divine scripture which no man should bring in question, for history was philosophy teaching by experience. Like Macaulay he looked forward with confidence to that time when 'men would be in the habit of sailing without wind, and would ride without horses', and machines as yet undiscovered would be in every house. Before he left London he had professed his faith at a dinner to honour the colony of South Australia. England, he said, stood unshaken by the political and social convulsions that were heaving the society of Europe because she occupied the foremost rank of those who professed to serve under the banners of truth, liberty and justice, while other nations continued to live by mediaeval precepts. England therefore could not and would not treat her colonies as conquered provinces to be kept in subordination, ruled by incompetent and domineering governors acting under orders from uninformed or misinformed and obstinate officials in the Mother Country. The ties of brotherhood must not become a yoke of bondage. He wanted the colonists to have the same rights and privileges as they would have had had they remained in the Mother Country. He also proposed not to neglect his blessed Saviour's divine command to his followers to love one another. He proposed to observe the principle that all sects and parties of Christians in South Australia should be granted such liberty of conscience and equality of treatment that charity and goodwill between the religious sects should distinguish their society from the other societies in Australia.[54]

In South Australia the ministers of religion not only fussed over morals but also had a very special role in establishing harmony between masters and men. In September 1848 three hundred miners at Burra, aggrieved by the proprietors' behaviour, went on strike, took absolute possession of the mine and would not allow a ton of ore to be removed. No sooner was this dispute settled by negotiation between the miners' representatives and the directors than the latter announced their decision to reduce the wages of miners from 25s to 21s per week. The workers, convinced as they were of the absolute necessity of raising rather than lowering wages if they were to maintain their

[54] T. Carlyle, 'On history', *Fraser's Magazine*, no. 10, 1830; T. Carlyle, 'On history again', *Fraser's Magazine*, no. 41, 1833; T. B. Macaulay, 'The Constitutional History of England . . . by Henry Hallam', *Edinburgh Review*, September 1828; T. B. Macaulay, 'Sir Thomas More; or colloquies on the progress and prospects of society by Robert Southey', *Edinburgh Review*, January 1830; *South Australian Register*, 26 July, 9, 12, 16 August 1848.

standard of living, went on strike again. Once again the directors agreed to talk with the men. The gentlemen of the press awarded the highest praise to the pastoral efforts of those reverend gentlemen in South Australia who had trained their flocks in so admirable a manner that they viewed mob rule or lynch law with horror and there was no quarrelling, rioting or violation of the law throughout the proceedings. The only two men at Burra who were drunk as fiddlers all through the strikes were not miners. The clergy had taught the workers not only be mindful of Saint Paul's command to be sober and vigilant in the presence of man's adversary, the Devil, but also to remember his command to servants to obey their masters.[55]

At the same time the cause of respectability and social quietness was also being reinforced in Melbourne. On 4 October 1848 a large contingent of Catholics, some in gorgeous carriages and some on horseback, met James Alipius Goold some fifteen miles from Melbourne and escorted him in regal state into Melbourne. Four days later he was installed as Bishop of the See of Melbourne. He was not quite thirty-six years old when Pius IX called him from his work as a missionary priest in Sydney to take the office of Bishop on the recommendation of Archbishop Polding. Goold had the round, good-humoured face that the painters of Europe once used as a model for their cherubs. It was the face of an innocent child on the shoulders of a man. He had already won a reputation in New South Wales for piety, learning and humility. Born into a prosperous merchant family in Cork, he had entered the Augustinian order and studied for the priesthood at Rome and Perugia. Mother Ireland had already stamped him indelibly with the Jansenism that branded all the passions of the flesh as sinful and taught men to look to God, Christ, the Holy Mother of God, the saints and the Sacraments of the Church to rescue them both from their sinful nature and their own impotence to save themselves from their follies.

In Melbourne James Goold taught his flock to equate evil with the sinful lusts of the flesh, and to abhor laziness and drunkenness lest they convert Melbourne into a great centre of Egyptian filth. He taught his people that the good life could only be realized by resort to a life of prayer, fasting, participation in the Sacraments of the Eucharist and the confession, and attendance at spiritual retreats. In Van Diemen's Land the Catholic Bishop, Robert Willson, also condemned 'the debasing and hideous sin of drunkenness' and told his fellow-Catholics, 'Beloved . . . avoid the company of any one who drinks, or would allure you to drink, even in private'. Every Lent he upbraided the faithful servants of Christ's Church for preferring horse-races and public amusements to retirement, prayer and fasting, and was saddened by his people going on pleasure trips and parties for merry-making on Good Friday. In Sydney Father McEncroe told the faithful that the Total Abstinence Society was the stepping-stone to religion. At Maitland Dean Lynch warned the faithful that the drunkard had no prospects in this world and no hopes for

[55] *South Australian Register*, 20, 23, 30 September, 14 October 1848.

the next, because he defiled the image of his creator; he was lost to the precepts of religion, lost to society and lost to himself.

The Protestant clergy took up the same themes. A generation in Australia was implored to mortify the flesh, to avoid the sensual feast, to let the ape and the tiger die in them, and to cultivate instead the domestic virtues. In Australia the first half of the century was noted for the solitude of the bush barbarian; the second half was to be characterized by the solitude of the city dweller cultivating the domestic virtues in his own home, isolated from his fellow-man, a victim of the extravagances of bourgeois individualism and British philistinism.[56]

Just as bishops, priests, deacons and laity were busy printing the stamp of British philistinism on the minds of the rising generation in the Australian colonies, reports arrived in Sydney and the other capitals that the old order in Europe was doomed. St Peter's Chair, the *Argus* reported on 6 October 1848, would soon be a relic! The winds of revolution were blowing through the musty palaces of Europe. Some said their echo was already being heard in Australia. On 14 November a letter writer in the *Argus* urged the denizens of their heaven-favoured country to follow the patriotic example of America and rend the chain asunder. At the election for the municipal corporation in Melbourne in November, candidates were careful to speak of themselves as working men who had earned their living in the sweat of their brow, and not aristocratic loafers who lived off unearned increment by exploiting the labour of the working men. A new era was about to dawn for the people.[57]

On 2 December 1848 F. Cunninghame, C. St Julian and E. J. Hawksley published in Sydney the first number of 'a *peculiarly* Working Man's Paper', the *People's Advocate*, which aspired to help the working man thrash out the solution to the great social problems of the day. Old virtues, they said, were breaking up. On every side the publishers perceived the 'up-heavings of the new birth of a fresh and happy state of civilization'. The downtrodden citizens of Australia could not be kept any longer from that fair share of political power to which their intelligence, their worth, their perseverance and their continuous industry entitled them. They wrote in the first issue, 'All power springs from the people'. In Australia the wealthy had secured all the power; the rich were supposed to possess all the intelligence while the poor and hardy sons of labour, the really honest intelligent mechanic, the patient, much-enduring and robust labourer, had been utterly disregarded. They had been looked upon by the colonial aristocrats as mere 'hewers of wood and drawers of water', incapable of appreciating or exercising the rights of free men. With

[56] F. P. Moran, *History of the Catholic Church in Australasia*, vol. 2, ch. 17; J. F. Hogan, *A Biographical Sketch of the Late Most Rev. James Alipius Goold* (Melbourne, 1886); *Freeman's Journal*, 19 June, 3 July 1886; H. Nicholson, *Tennyson* (London, 1923), pp. 246-8; W. H. Southerwood, *Planting a Faith* (Hobart, n.d.), pp. 34-7; *Australasian Chronicle*, 2 June 1842, 11 July 1843; H. N. Birt, *Benedictine Pioneers in Australia*, vol. 2, p. 47; Diary of J. A. Goold, 3 September 1848 to 20 November 1850 (MS. in Catholic Archives, Diocese of Melbourne).
[57] *Argus*, 6 October, 3, 7, 10, 14 November 1848.

God's help the people would do something to crush this many-headed monster which had been spawned amongst them.[58]

Hawksley was just forty-one. By birth and conviction he belonged to that broad group in the Australian colonies who were believers in evolution rather than bloody revolution, believers in extending the creature comforts and values of the bourgeoisie to the workers rather than destroying the institution of private property and creating a new society. He was born in Nottingham into a Unitarian family and converted to the Catholic Church, probably by the example of Ullathorne who persuaded him to offer his services as a teacher in Catholic schools in New South Wales. After his arrival in Sydney in July 1838 he taught at Maitland until he caught the eye of Polding with his pamphlet *The Worship of the Catholic Church Not Idolatrous* and his popular hymn on the Holy Church of Rome which Hawksley found sublime and pure and safe as a rock. In July 1846 he became the editor of the *Australasian Chronicle* and at the end of 1848 the principal publisher of the *People's Advocate*. No man who thought of Rome as 'the rock of ages' was likely to advocate the teachings of either the utopians or the scientific socialists. Before Marx had written that the proletarians had nothing to lose but their chains, and a world to win, Pius IX denounced those greatly deceived people who set up a utopia of their own and taught the false and dangerous doctrine that man would create a heaven on earth before passing on to God's heaven.[59]

Late in November men like Henry Parkes, Richard Hipkiss, B. Sutherland, G. Lloyd and E. Macdonald, who were influenced by chartist ideas, joined with Catholic visionaries such as E. J. Hawksley, E. McEncroe (the brother of the priest) and J. K. Heydon to form the Constitutional Association. Their statement of objects published on 13 December stressed moral improvement rather than the sentiments or principles of social revolutionaries. They sought to elevate the masses without doing injury to any class in the community. They declared their intention to oppose wrong, to dispel ignorance, to abridge human misery, to support order, to disseminate truth, to achieve liberty, to maintain justice and to establish national prosperity. They spoke the language of the visionary. They had espoused, they declared, the cause of the human race. The end they had in view was the true greatness and independence of the country in which their common lot was cast, and its fullest participation in the benefits and glory of the British constitution.

When they put down on paper their ideas on how these objectives were to be achieved, again they spoke as men who proposed to tinker with the existing society rather than creators of a new one. They called for an immediate extension of the elective franchise, and a just and equitable representative principle, to be achieved by increasing the number of representatives of

[58] *People's Advocate*, 2 December 1848.

[59] E. J. Hawksley, *The Worship of the Catholic Church Not Idolatrous* (Sydney, 1838); entry under E. J. Hawksley in ms. catalogue of M.L.; J. M. O'Brien, Catholics and Politics in New South Wales, 1835-1870, (thesis in library of University of Newcastle); K. Marx and F. Engels, *Manifesto of the Communist Party*; E. F. Y. Hales, *Pio Nono* (New York, 1962), ch. 2.

Sydney and other constituencies in proportion to the amount of population. They wanted a complete change in the administration of the public lands so as to throw open a field for the introduction and prosperous growth of an industrious, permanent class of agriculturists, thereby counteracting the barbarous effects of the present iniquitous system of land occupancy in the interior. They proposed to replace squatterdom's landed aristocracy with a society of peasant proprietors. 'Give a man a foot of land to call his own', they said, 'if you want to make him patriotic, good and useful.'[60]

They wanted a society in the Australian colonies in which the working man could become a respectable man of property. As the *People's Advocate* put it on 30 December, the immigrant mechanic had the same object in view as the capitalist—to better his condition. They believed the worker had a right by honest industry to raise himself in the social scale and not to work for a bare livelihood. The whole aim of the worker was to rise above the 'necessity to labour' and not to be 'always in drudgery'. They were not dewy-eyed about country life. They had no desire to bury themselves in a vast wilderness. They denounced the abominations of their day in the bush and in the town with all the moral fervour of the prophets of the Old Testament. They wrote stories in their paper to illustrate the brutality of working-class husbands to their wives, and the depravity of their women. They denounced drunkenness and riots as states that disgraced a man, impaired his faculties and injured his health. They recommended Sabbath observance to the worker as a time when he could meditate on how to amend his life. They recommended the celebration of Christmas because it generated the sentiments they wanted to encourage—cheerfulness and loving kindness.[61]

They opposed the introduction of convicts, because they would bring all the attendant horrors of the lash and the chain and would degrade their colony in the eyes of the world. Familiarity with scenes of horror hardened hearts, stifled all the emotions of patriotism and all the high and noble aspirations after freedom. Convicts, they added, also drove mechanics from their work to starve. As for the coolies, their very lack of the bourgeois virtues made them quite unsuitable, it being notorious that coolies were adroit swindlers, professed cheats, men unrestrained by any moral feeling, unacquainted with Christianity, and erecters of heathenish temples in which they practised their devilish rites and gave full and unrestrained sway to their own evil passions. It would not be possible for any white man, however small a sense of morality or knowledge of Christianity he might possess, to live in the midst of such companionship. The white man would think himself superior and the coolie or the Chinaman would think it most meritorious to cut the white man's throat. As for the white woman, the *People's Advocate* shuddered at the bare contemplation of what their fate would be. Like the bourgeoisie, the leaders of the workers had their ideal of woman as a

---

[60] *Objects and Laws and Regulations of the Constitutional Association and Address of the Provisional Council* (Sydney, 1848); *People's Advocate*, 16 December 1848.
[61] *People's Advocate*, 9, 23, 30 December 1848, 17, 24 February 1849.

madonna who slaved in the kitchen. In their eyes the cause of the human race was to be served by men cultivating virtue in the home rather than following any apocalyptic vision of man stealing fire from heaven.[62]

A whole world away from this petit-bourgeois ideal, one of the giants in the land vanished off the face of the earth without so much as leaving a trace of where he had ended his days. In December 1846 the renowned explorer of the trackless regions of Australia, Ludwig Leichhardt and seven others had set out from the Darling Downs to cross to the west coast of New Holland. Again the grandees were his providers. Hannibal Macarthur, for example, promised two mules, and Ben Boyd promised one. Again the men were puzzled and angered by the contradictions in the behaviour of their leader. He spoke to them of his forthcoming fulfilment in death's embrace but alarmed them at night by screaming that he was going 'down, down, down'. He asked them to explain to him why he had offended providence. He spoke to them about spiritual love and self-denial, but made the dirty-minded snigger by kissing passionately the better-looking members of the party, and offended all of them by greedy licking of the sugar bowl. The heavens also seemed malign. They poured down buckets of water over the plains and Leichhardt returned to the Downs in June 1847 to rest for a fortnight. He then set out again down the Condamine for some six hundred miles. The men still proving refractory, he decided to let them have their liquor and their women and take them back quickly to the 'fleshpots of Egypt in Sydney', which they reached in August of that year.[63]

In Sydney he began to wonder whether perhaps he had been forsaken by providence. He was troubled by Goethe's remark that every extraordinary man had a mission to fulfil, after which, being no longer required on earth, providence destroyed him. He began to wonder whether providence took the giants early in their lives, as it had taken Mozart and Byron, so that there would be things left for other men to do. He was irritated, too, by reports in Sydney that surgeons were using ether to deaden the pain suffered by a patient during an operation. He believed this in time would turn men into delicate pain-shy creatures incapable of bearing the least hurt with manly patience. A generation of Australians not toughened by pain and other hardships would not be capable of resisting any invader of their country from the north. Australians, he predicted, would become effeminate like the Romans. As an antidote to all these corrupting creature comforts of the new industrial civilization he yearned for a 'lonely bed in [an] everlasting camp'.

In February 1848 he and six others assembled again on the Darling Downs to take on a task worthy of one of those *gute Männer* God chose for his elect.

[62] *People's Advocate*, 10 March 1849; see also the poem 'Labour, Wisdom, Unity' by Henry Parkes in *People's Advocate*, 23 December 1848.
[63] *S.M.H.*, 30 October 1846; *Heads of the People*, 16 October 1847; F. W. L. Leichhardt to his brother-in-law, 20 October 1847, in M. Aurousseau (ed.), *The Letters of F. W. L. Leichhardt* (3 vols, Cambridge, 1968), vol. 3, p. 953; J. F. Mann, *Eight Months with Dr. Leichhardt in the Years 1846-47* (Sydney, 1888), pp. 11-13, 32, 44; L. Leichhardt to P. P. King, 19 September 1846 (King Papers, vol. 2).

On 4 April he and his party set off from Macpherson's station at Cogoon to cross to the west coast of the continent. As ever, he was full of hope that his Mighty Protector would bring his darling scheme to a successful termination. The party was never heard of again. No one was to know whether Leichhardt welcomed the 'great doom's image' with dignity or with terror. No one was to know whether they were slaughtered by the aborigines, died of thirst, were swept away by floods, sank in a quicksand or butchered each other. Leichhardt was to live on in the poetry and prose of those who were aware that in 1848 somewhere on that vast continent there was a great going of a mighty spirit.[64]

Over the same years other men had walked over those stony plains of desolation. In December of 1845 Sir Thomas Mitchell set out from Sydney to prove Port Essington could be used as a port of entry for the products and people of Asia. By June 1846 he established a depot on the Maranoa, from where he searched for a river flowing to the north coast. Believing he had found such a river, he conferred on it the name of Victoria and returned to Sydney confident that the creator of the universe had singled out the land in the hinterland of the Gulf of Carpentaria for British colonization, just as in 1836 he had prophesied that Australia Felix would be English for thousands of years. He suggested that this part of Australia be known as Capricornia, and added with pleasure that at long last he had found two aborigines who actually expressed a desire to live like white men. Then he left for London to press his claims for recognition of his achievement, while the two aborigines became vagabonds again.[65]

A man who had been with him when he had discovered the Victoria River proved that he was in error in believing the river ran into the Gulf of Carpentaria and that it was in fact a stretch of Cooper's Creek which had caused poor Dr Brown and the gallant Captain Charles Sturt to stop in their tracks in 1846 and ask each other whether any man had ever seen such a country before. Sydney society knew Edmund Besley Court Kennedy as a

[64] J. P. Eckermann, *Gespräche mit Goethe, 11 März 1828* (2 vols, Berlin, n.d.), vol. 2, p. 17; F. W. L. Leichhardt to C. Schmalfuss, 21 October 1847, in M. Aurousseau, op. cit., vol. 3, pp. 962-6; Leichhardt to C. Schmalfuss, 22 February 1848, ibid., p. 992; Leichhardt to J. Mackay, 6 February 1848, ibid., pp. 983-4; Leichhardt to D. Archer, 10 March 1848, ibid., pp. 1004-6; Leichhardt to J. Mackay, 3 April 1848, ibid., pp. 1007-8; Leichhardt to P. P. King, 3 April 1848, ibid., pp. 1008-9; Leichhardt to the editors of *S.M.H.*, 4 April 1848, ibid., pp. 1009-13; A. H. Chisholm, *Strange New World* (Sydney, 1941); C. D. C. Cotton, *Ludwig Leichhardt and the Great South Land* (Sydney 1938); D. Bunce, *Travels with Dr. Leichhardt in Australia* (Melbourne, 1859); Patrick White, *Voss* (London, 1957); Francis Webb, *Leichhardt in Theatre* (Sydney, 1952); Henry Kendall, 'Leichhardt' in T. T. Reed (ed.), *The Poetical Works of Henry Kendall* (Adelaide, 1966), pp. 228-30; R. Erdos, *Ludwig Leichhardt* (Melbourne, 1963); *S.M.H.*, 6 March 1848; F. von Mueller, 'The Fate of Dr. Leichhardt', *Australian*, 18 February 1865; E. Favenc, *The History of Australian Exploration from 1788 to 1888* (Sydney, 1888), p. 168; A. Vickers, *Voyage en Australie et en Nouvelle Zelande* (Paris, 1883), pp. 239-41; A. Grenfell Price, *Island Continent* (Sydney, 1972), ch. 6.

[65] T. L. Mitchell, *Journal of an Expedition into the Interior of Tropical Australia* (London, 1848), pp. 429-30; FitzRoy to Grey, 3 January 1847, *H.R.A.*, I. xxv. 299; FitzRoy to Grey, 9 January 1847, *H.R.A.*, I. xxv. 316; *New South Wales Government Gazette*, 7, 31 December 1846.

young man who sang and danced with such gaiety that some women were said to gaze on him with a wild ecstasy in the heart. He was also a man of some accomplishment as a painter of water-colours. Some women whispered to each other behind their fans that this handsome, lovable man had had a 'wee lapse' from the path of rectitude in his first years in the colony, that not only was he the father of a bastard but, horror of horrors, the mother was one of those low Irish Catholic women. He had come to the colony in 1840 at the age of twenty-two, yet another son of Britain who hoped Australia would guarantee what seemed remote and quite out of reach in England—permanent membership in the society of the gentry. In March 1847 he offered to find out whether Mitchell's Victoria River really did flow into the Gulf and, finding it to be in fact part of Cooper's Creek, he renamed that stretch the Barcoo before returning to Sydney in February 1848. In that month FitzRoy asked him to lead an expedition to explore the north-eastern coast of New South Wales between Rockingham Bay and Cape York, and the country between the head of the Gulf of Carpentaria and the rivers discovered by Sir Thomas Mitchell in 1846.[66]

On 28 April 1848 Kennedy and twelve others, including Jackey Jackey, an aboriginal native of a Patrick's Plains tribe, who was known to his people as Galmahra, or song man, set out by ship from Sydney for Rockingham Bay where they arrived on 21 May. Every Sunday Kennedy read prayers to the men at eleven o'clock and halted for the day. From Rockingham Bay the whole party made their way to Weymouth Bay despite the dense vegetation, the infuriating insects and the menacing aborigines. In that stern school the attractive, lovable Kennedy learnt that terrible lesson: how much it sometimes cost to make a name even in the Australian colonies. On 13 November Kennedy, Jackey Jackey and three others left Weymouth Bay for Cape York, not knowing that only the aborigine would survive to tell the story of their sufferings in his own deeply moving narrative.

Kennedy left the three white men at Shelburne Bay. Then Jackey Jackey and Kennedy hacked their way through thick scrub until they reached the mouth of the Escape River. All the time the blackfellows followed them like a flock of sheep. In the second week of December the blackfellows came behind in the scrub and threw many spears, and Jackey took the white man's gun and fired at his own people and was pleased to hit one blackfellow all over the face with buckshot, and Mr Kennedy tried to fire at them but his gun would not go off, and the blackfellows sneaked back and speared Mr Kennedy again in the knee and the side, and he told Jackey Jackey 'I am bad inside' and added 'I am out of wind, Jackey', and asked for paper and he

[66] E. Beale, 'Edmund Besley Court Kennedy', R.A.H.S., *J. & P.*, vol. 35, 1949; Marnie Bassett, *Behind the Picture* (Melbourne, 1966), p. 23; F. Beale, *Kennedy of Cape York* (Adelaide, 1970), pp. 49-50; Surveyor-General to Col. Sec. of New South Wales, 5 September 1843 (Col. Sec. In Letters 43/6494, N.S.W.S.A.), see esp. the minute by Sir George Gipps in the margin of this letter; FitzRoy to Grey, 18 March 1848, H.R.A., I. xxvi. 281-2; instructions by Sir Charles Augustus FitzRoy to Edmund Besley Court Kennedy, 7 April 1848, encl. in FitzRoy to Grey, 2 June 1848, H.R.A., I. xxvi. 440-3.

tried to write, and he then fell back and died, and Jackey caught him as he fell
back and held him, and then turned round and cried for a good while until he
got well, when he buried Mr Kennedy in a shallow grave, and then made for
Port Albany, being frightened all the way of the black men, and 'murry
murry glad' that when he cooeed from a rock, the men in the boat at Port
Albany, who had come to pick up Mr Kennedy and his party, answered his
call. On 6 March 1849 the only survivors, Jackey Jackey and two white men,
reduced to skeletons by what they had gone through, arrived back in Sydney
on the *Ariel*.[67]

The wild men of Sydney asked Plunkett to prosecute the aborigines
who had speared Kennedy. Tributes were paid to Kennedy as such a great
pioneer of the wilderness and such a true developer of nature's vast resources
that the spot where he had fallen would be a prouder cenotaph than the
mausoleum of the warrior. All the respectable people in Sydney gathered in
St James's Church for the unveiling of a plaque to the man who had served
the cause of science, the advancement of the colony, and the interests of
humanity, and to Jackey Jackey, Mr Kennedy's sole companion in the conflict
with the savages, who had tended his leader with a courage and devotion
worthy of remembrance. There was talk of a more tangible reward for Jackey
Jackey. Charles Rodius did a lithograph of him, but there it ended. In January
1854 he spent a blowzy summer's day droving cattle some thirty miles from
Albury. As night descended on the plains, Jackey Jackey drank himself into a
stupor, fell into the campfire and was burnt to death. Jackey Jackey paid
his terrible price almost six years after Mr Kennedy had paid his.[68]

In the year in which Kennedy began to run out of wind, Ben Boyd also
paid his price for all his *folie de la grandeur humaine*. In March of 1848 *Bell's
Life in Sydney* stated that Bibbenluke, Boyd's great station in the Monaro,
was nothing but a barren waste with volumes of dust whirling in every
direction. Rotting carcasses and well-picked bones had usurped the place of
the living. Boyd Town on Twofold Bay was deserted. Silence had again
descended on those blue-green waters from Cape Everard to Bateman Bay,
from where the mighty Captain Cook had first seen the 'smook of fire' on one
of those clear days on the far south coast when the breeze was gentle, when
the beauty of sea and sky brought a leap of joy to the heart. The kingdom of
Boyd was on the way out: its palaces were rapidly falling into decay. 'The
sceptre of the tribe of Benjamin is shaken as a reed by the whirlwind.' The
time was not far distant when the whales would again spout unscared by

[67] W. Carron, *Narrative of an Expedition, Undertaken under the Direction of the Late
Mr. Assistant Surveyor E. B. Kennedy* (Sydney, 1849); statement of Jackey Jackey, ibid.,
appendix 1; statement of Dr Vallack, ibid.; *S.M.H.*, 6, 7 March 1849; 'Two Sides of a
Story: I. Kennedy, II. Jacky Jacky' in Judith Wright, *Collected Poems* (Sydney 1971), pp.
259-62; Marnie Bassett, *Behind the Picture*, pp. 22-6.
[68] Plaque in St James's Church, Sydney; copy of lithograph of Jackey Jackey in M.L.;
FitzRoy to Grey, 25 April 1849, C.O. 201/412; minute by J. H. Plunkett, 22 March 1849
(Archival estrays, list 15, Dixson Library); *Empire*, 28 January 1854; *Argus*, 4 February
1854.

the harpoon of Tiger Davis in the waters of that most lovely Twofold Bay.

By October and November the Sydney press was carrying notices of the sales of the properties of Ben Boyd in the Wellington Valley and in the Monaro. Archibald Boyd left the colony, having been obliged to part with his property to meet his debts there. To evade the suit of creditors, Archibald was obliged to embark on his ship on a Sunday morning near Sydney Heads. In November the elegant mansion of Darlinghurst had a visit from Ben Boyd. But 'that illustrious stranger' only stayed for a brief period. Those who believed it was madness for men to chase such greatness rubbed their hands that a man of such pretension and hectoring was now in a common gaol. Hannibal Macarthur, who had often strutted on the stage of life as the squire of Subiaco, while in private preparing himself daily for what he called that 'great change' after death when all men would be changed, also had to bend to the storm and go through the insolvency court. A generation was passing away.[69]

That year Charles Kemp had many talks with Charles Cowper about the proposal to send 'exiles' to New South Wales to solve the labour shortage. Kemp had many reasons to be pleased with himself that year. He had come to Sydney in 1831 as a poor lad of eighteen. By 1842, thanks to his industry, frugality and high-mindedness, he became joint owner with John Fairfax of the *Sydney Morning Herald*. By 1847 he was worth £10 000 and had, as he put it in the diary which he began on 2 June of that year, 'the social advantage arising from my being Editor and joint proprietor of the *Sydney Morning Herald* which places one on a much higher grade than I had any right to expect to reach when in 1831 I came up to Sydney and worked in a carpenter's shop for 14/- a week and my board!' There were other pleasing things in his life in 1847. He became a landed proprietor at Darlinghurst. He was elected a director of the Sydney Fire Insurance Company. He had some teeth extracted after the inhalation of ether vapours which allowed his dentist to perform the operation without torturing him. He reproached himself for being idle and not spending more time in private prayer. Happily on this and other questions he found Broughton's sermons most helpful. That year he heard one admirable sermon on the text 'We have lived in pleasure on the earth and been wanton.' The Lord Bishop had been very helpful on the proneness to frivolity and dissipation which was too generally the characteristic of the age.

On this and allied matters he saw eye to eye with his partner on the *Herald*, John Fairfax, a gentleman of clear discernment and strong character, a deacon of the Congregational Church in Sydney, a director of commercial companies, prime mover for the formation of an Australian Mutual Provident Society, and strong advocate for the introduction of railway and steam communication

[69] *Bell's Life in Sydney*, 4 March, 4 November 1848; *S.M.H.*, 6, 27, 30 September, 18 December 1848; C. Nicholson to A. Cunningham, 4 March 1849 (Cunningham Papers, vol. 3); Francis Webb, *A Drum for Ben Boyd* (Sydney, 1948); P. P. King to Stilwell, 8 July 1848 (King Papers, vol. 2); P. P. King to James Macarthur, 17 January 1862 (Macarthur Papers, vol. 29).

between England and Australia. Like Kemp he was sustained through life by such a strong Christian faith that when he died those who had loved him testified that 'He was a good man, full of faith and of the Holy Spirit'. Both Kemp and Fairfax were models of the bourgeois virtues. They were affectionate in their family lives, promoted the domestic virtues, were upright in business, incapable of anything tortuous or mean, liberal in the use of their wealth, firm in friendship and active promoters of benevolence to the poor, with charity of heart towards all those who were in any way afflicted in mind, body or estate. When Kemp died in August 1864 they said of him, as they were to say of Fairfax, 'A good man has fallen.'

In Melbourne on 6 November 1848 Edward Wilson took over the editorial chair of the *Argus*. Known to his enemies as 'Edward the Black Prince', he was a large, sombre, silent but striking figure wherever he appeared in public. Like Kemp and Fairfax, he was a strong supporter of the Protestant ascendancy. He had three beliefs: his belief in himself, his belief in the *Argus*, and his belief that Port Phillip would become one of the most flourishing colonial dominions over which the flag of Britain waved. In clubs and around the dinner tables of Melbourne he joined those country gentlemen who were identifying that city with the Presbyterian spirit. In Sydney there were many men of like mind. There was Robert Tooth, the brewer, who had given £500 towards the building of a church in Redfern. There was Thomas Mort, the wool broker, who also invested some of his profits in those activities of the Anglican Church which he shrewdly intuited would contribute towards the creation of bourgeois Australia. Another generation was coming into being just as the pastoral patriarchs seemed to be passing away.[70]

[70] Diary of C. Kemp, 2, 9 June, 22 August, 16 October 1847, 8 February 1848 (MS. in M.L.); *S.M.H.*, 26 August 1864; H. Parkes, *Fifty Years in the Making of Australian History* (London, 1892), p. 934; J. F. Fairfax, *The Story of John Fairfax* (Sydney, 1941); *The Sydney Morning Herald, 1831-1931* (Sydney, 1931); plaque 'In Loving Remembrance of John Fairfax', Pitt Street Congregational Church, Sydney; Charles Gavan Duffy, *My Life in Two Hemispheres* (2 vols, London, 1898), vol. 2, pp. 147-8; A. G. Gresford, The *Argus* under Its First Three Editors, 1846-1859 (thesis, Department of History, Australian National University; 'Garryowen' (E. Finn), *The Chronicles of Early Melbourne* (2 vols, Melbourne, 1888), vol. 2, pp. 835-7.

15

TETHERING THE MIGHTY BUSH
TO THE WORLD

O N 16 September 1849 Sarah Broughton, the wife of William Grant
Broughton, died in Sydney. For a short period Broughton was
broken, for he had loved his wife. But God gave him the strength to
endure the cruel fate of being left alone in a country in which he had always
felt a stranger ever since that chill in the heart on first seeing the forbidding
and inhospitable coast of New South Wales in September 1829. His God had
promised His faithful children that on the resurrection morning, the trumpet
would sound and the dead would be raised and they would see again those
whom they had loved. With that majestic dignity with which he surrounded
himself as the shadows of the evening stole across the sky, he sang with all
the fervour of a man with a great thirst in his soul the last two lines of John
Henry Newman's 'Lead Kindly Light':

> And with the morn those Angel faces smile,
> Which I have loved long since, and lost awhile.[1]

The age was characterized by a strange paradox. The intellectuals of
Europe, North America and Australia were discussing how much of the Old
and New Testaments could be believed after the onslaughts of German biblical criticism, the geologists and the logicians, and arguing about the life of
man without God, the origin of the world and the immortality of the soul.
But ordinary British people, both in the United Kingdom and in their overseas
possessions seemed to be passing through a religious revival. It was like the
point made about love and its corruption by the King in *Hamlet*:

> Time qualifies the spark and fire of it.
> There lives within the very flame of love
> A kind of wick or snuff that will abate it.[2]

---

[1] *S.M.H.*, 21 September 1849; W. G. Broughton to E. Coleridge, 2 April 1850
(Broughton Letters, microfilm in NAT. L.).
[2] C. Lyell, *Principles of Geology* (2 vols, London, 1830-3); J. S. Mill, *Logic* (London,
1833); D. F. Strauss, *The Life of Jesus*, trans. from the fourth German edition by George
Eliot (London, 1848), p. 757; D. Magarshack (ed.), *Ivan Turgenev: literary reminiscences* (New York, 1958), p. 128; W. Shakespeare, *Hamlet*, IV, vii, lines 111-13.

For a time the flame of Christianity and its attendant morality burned brightly. Men clung passionately to the great hope:

> Ah Christ, that it were possible
> For one short hour to see
> The souls we loved, that they might tell us
> What and where they be.

Men who could not endure the pain of being deprived of a meeting beyond the grave faintly trusted the larger hope. On the tombstones in Sydney, Parramatta, Melbourne, Hobart, Launceston, Adelaide and Perth, and in the inland districts, the relatives of the dead carved words to convey to posterity their hope that they would all see each other again in a land where God wiped away all tears from their eyes. They wrote that though they walked through the valley of the shadow of death, they would fear no evil, because their God was with them. They wrote of this life as one of pain:

> Affliction sore long time I bore:
> All human aids were vain;
> Till death gave ease when God did please
> To take away my pain.

They wrote that 'to die was gain'. They wrote of those they had loved as people who had practised 'every Christian and womanly virtue and died in the full assurance of a better life beyond the grave'. While the men of stern countenance were teaching that after death the remains were blown about as desert dust, men in the autumn of Christianity in the Australian colonies prepared themselves for what they called 'the great change'.[3]

The parsons and the priests preached the Pauline doctrine that if Christ be not risen, all their preaching was vain, their faith was vain, and they were of all men the most miserable. The Reverend W. B. Clarke, a geologist of some distinction who had arrived in Sydney in May 1839 and had been a rector at Campbelltown and headmaster of the King's School before taking up duty at St Thomas's Church in North Sydney in 1846, found no difficulty in reconciling the account in Genesis with the writings of his learned colleagues in geology. His luxuriant patriarchal beard, his decorous black suit and his white starched shirt fronts, cuffs and collars lent an air of authority to what for others was surrounded with doubt, uncertainty and difficulty. J. D. Lang in a breezy confident tone told his congregation he still believed in the story of Noah and the great flood, the confusion of tongues at Babel, the loquacity of

[3] A. Tennyson, 'Maud', part IV, 3-6; A. Tennyson, 'In Memoriam', XXV, v. 1, and LV, v. 5; P. P. King to James Macarthur, 17 January 1862 (Macarthur Papers, vol. 29); tombstones in the cemeteries of St Matthew's, Windsor, St John's, Parramatta, and St David's Park, Hobart; epitaphs in Kirklands Churchyard, near Campbelltown, Tasmania; epitaph on tomb of Amelia Penelope Dumaresq, churchyard of Christ Church, Illawarra, Tasmania; epitaph on tomb of Eliza Milligan, Wybalenna Cemetery, Flinders Island.

Balaam's beast, and all the other miraculous and supernatural events described in the Bible just as he believed in the coming of that day when the blind would see and the lame would walk. Broughton prophesied that if certain scientists persuaded men that they had no immortal souls, the order God had imposed on the universe in the beginning would disappear and men would kill each other down to the last two men on earth.[4]

The churches seemed to flourish. In the country districts the days of unleavened bread for the apostles of revealed religion seemed to have come to an end. The Reverend Thomas Hassall galloped from out-station to out-station preaching the truths of the Gospel and forcing the morals of Paul of Tarsus on the prisoner population and the itinerant workers. After the service he generally stayed for a pot of tea, some beef and damper and a profitable chat with the shepherd or hut-keeper. Sometimes he spent the night and shared blankets and bed with the hut dwellers. Father Joseph Therry carried in his saddle-bags the bread and the wine of eternal life to minister to members of his flock. By the end of the 1840s parsons, priests and schoolmasters were lending the weight of divine authority to the bourgeois virtues of industry, frugality, humility, and the obedience of servants to masters, and wives to their husbands. They were telling the Australian bushmen of the superiority of the citizen of heaven over the barbarian in the earthly temples and striving manfully to plant in the solitary wastes the memorials of the Judaico-Christian view of the world.

By 1850 itinerant Wesleyan preachers were winning souls for Christ in the Australian colonies. At services held either in some public hall, in a room in a convert's house or in the open air, J. Watsford so worked on his congregations that there were showers of blessing, glorious revivals, and wonderful displays of the Holy Spirit's power in convincing and saving men. At Windsor in 1841 huge numbers flocked to the meetings to take part in remarkable cases of conversion, in which the best customers of the publicans were plucked from the burning, and the power of God so worked on them that they fell to the floor where they sighed, and sobbed and groaned, and cried loudly for mercy until they experienced God's saving grace.[5]

[4] J. Lillie, *Opening Lecture . . . upon the Subserviency of the Works of Nature to Religion* (Hobart, 1841); J. West, *The Hope of Life Eternal* (Launceston, 1850); A. Gilchrist (ed.), *John Dunmore Lang* (2 vols, Melbourne, 1951), vol. 2, p. 393; W. G. Broughton, *The Present Position and Duties of the Church of England* (Canterbury, n.d.); *Cork Examiner*, 26 April 1852, on evil influences of the novels of George Sand; W. B. Clarke, *The Anniversary Sermon Preached in the Church of St. James, Sydney . . . 24th June 1840* (Sydney, 1840); J. D. Lang, *The Mosaic Account of the Creation* (Sydney, 1846).

[5] J. S. Hassall, *In Old Australia* (Brisbane, 1902), pp. 188-9; W. P. Wilmot, *The Natural & Spiritual Mind* (Melbourne, 1850); Diary of J. J. Therry, 23 October 1830 to 4 October 1835 (MS. in Archives of St Mary's Cathedral, Sydney); J. Watsford, *Glorious Gospel Triumphs* (London, 1900); J. Barrett, *That Better Country* (Melbourne, 1966), pp. 4, 11, 12, 13; D. Mackenzie, *Ten Years in Australia* (London, 1852), pp. 45-6; T. H. Braim, *A History of New South Wales* (2 vols, London, 1846), vol. 2, pp. 168-9; A. Marjoribanks, *Travels in New South Wales* (London, 1847), pp. 44-6.

In the towns of the Australian colonies at the end of the 1840s observers noted a visible increase of religious consciousness and the growth of a sentiment of fidelity towards the church. The church became a social centre, a gathering place for those interested in the dress fashions of the day, and a place where people were seated strictly according to their rank in society. The sermon was like a leading article in a newspaper or a pamphlet rather than an injunction to charity and the love of God, or an exposition of Christian doctrine. Parsons lent the weight of divine authority to the bourgeois vision of the world. Even though in Sydney, a town of some forty-five thousand people, no more than five thousand ever put a foot inside a church except for a christening, a marriage or a burial, the influence of the churches pervaded the whole community. Their morality was taught to the children in the schools; the Mosaic law provided the foundations of the criminal law; the teaching of Moses and that ambiguous remark by Christ about marriage meant that for all practical purposes marriage was an indissoluble union between a husband and a wife.

Outside the churches the parsons and the priests were the self-appointed patrons of all the nostrums of the age for the moral improvement of mankind. They joined forces with the temperance movements in a war on the 'debasing and hideous sin of drunkenness'. The Temperance Society of New South Wales was founded in September 1832 by the Reverend W. P. Crook. Firmly convinced that the overwhelming cause of the crime and misery of this otherwise happy land was the use of ardent spirits, they campaigned for temperance at public meetings and in their publications. In 1842 the Hobart Town Total Abstinence Society was founded. By 1849 there were Total Abstinence Societies in South Australia and Western Australia. At their meetings priest, parson and reformed drunkard became the leaders of the 'Cold Water Army'.[6]

The parsons of the Protestant community took their stand on God's command to mankind to remember the Sabbath day and to keep it holy. In this weekly return of the Lord's Day men were given a foretaste of that ultimate rest which God in his infinite love and mercy had promised to all those who kept His commandments. They devoted much of their energy to the task of ensuring that Sunday was observed as a day of rest and prayer and meditation in a country where the climate and the tastes of the people clamoured for a day of pleasure on the one day in the week when they were freed from the slavery of earning their daily bread. The currency lads and

---

[6] *Australian Temperance Magazine* (Sydney), vol. 1, 1838; *Fourth Report of the New South Wales Temperance Society* (Sydney, 1839); B. Carvosso, *Drunkenness, the Enemy of Britain, Arrested by the Hand of God in the Recent Temperance Movement* (Hobart, 1840); *First Annual Report of the Hobart Town Total Abstinence Society* (Hobart Town, 1843); A. Barnes, *General Views and Practical Deductions of the Principle of Temperance* (Hobart Town, 1847); *Annual Report of the South Australian Total Abstinence Society for the Year 1848* (Adelaide, 1848); *Annual Report of the Western Australian Total Abstinence Society* (Perth, 1849); *Inquirer* (Perth), 2 May, 28 November 1849; W. T. Poyser, *Cold Water Army: or suggestions for the formation of juvenile societies* (Hobarton, 1850).

new chums thought of Sunday as a day on which they could shoot parrots in the bush. The Protestant leaders tried to make Sunday shooting a mis-demeanour punishable by imprisonment.

Some Sabbatarians even frowned on cooking on Sunday as a sin. But no picture they painted of the future torments God had in store for Sabbath breakers deterred the working classes of Sydney, Melbourne, Hobart, Adelaide and Perth from making Sunday the great day of feasting. On that day huge quantities of pies and roasted meats of all descriptions were carried through the streets for sale to those who wanted to be saved from the trouble of cooking on Sundays, not because it was a sin, but rather for the luxury of freedom from kitchen drudgery. In the afternoon the gentry travelled in their carriages and gigs along the Parramatta Road, while others went for a ride on horseback, and those who lacked the means for such a display splashed away in the water in defiance of the parsons' lugubrious demand that on the Lord's Day a holy quiet should descend on their city and all over the wilds of New Holland. The evangelical wing of the Church of England and the Methodists also opposed dancing and gambling on any day of the week.

Catholic priests and laymen, influenced by the Jansenist movement in Ireland, also lent their support to Sabbatarianism and puritan morality. E. J. Hawksley, the part-owner of the *People's Advocate*, stated in that paper his hope that Australia would not copy the drinking usages of England because they were the implacable enemies of the Sabbath and made an escape from the bewitching snares of alcohol an impossibility. He believed that order, morality and religion would soon be banished from the land unless Sunday were kept as a day of rest. Not only would the Sabbath day be spent in drinking, but the effects of the Saturday evening debauch would quite incapacitate the mind for any religious exercises on the following day. The day of rest would become 'the festival of sensuality and disorder', and the next step would be its sacrifice to the grasp of commercial cupidity, whereby its beneficent social, political and moral influences would be entirely lost.[7]

In every colony the Anglicans, Presbyterians, Methodists, Congregationalists and Baptists were firmly behind the local branch of the Auxiliary Bible Society. The virtue of Bible reading was that it softened the heart, convinced a man of sin and exhibited to the sinner a crucified Saviour waiting to be gracious. Bible reading also Protestantized mankind and so rescued minds enslaved by the priests of Rome from the worship of idols and other disgusting practices such as ladies divulging the secrets of their sex life to lascivious bachelors. Bible reading contributed to the spread of the virtues of quietness, resignation, sobriety and high seriousness. Bible reading promoted a good 'common human brotherhood'.[8]

In all the colonies, save Western Australia, the strength of those striving to

[7] *Voice in the Wilderness*, 15 May, 2 July 1849; A. Marjoribanks, *Travels in New South Wales*, p. 44; *People's Advocate*, 30 June 1849; *S.M.H.*, 12 December 1848, 22 March 1850.

[8] *Sentinel*, 3 August 1848; *Launceston Examiner*, 19 June 1850, for a report of a meeting of the Cornwall Auxiliary Bible Society at the Temperance Hall on 18 June.

improve the morals of mankind was increased by the arrival between 1847 and 1851 of batches of assisted and unassisted migrants who had grown up in an atmosphere pervaded by kindred sentiments. In *A Christmas Carol*, first published in book form in 1843, Charles Dickens recommended the man Christ to mankind. He was a cheerful, tender, compassionate and loving Christ, the man who had delivered the Sermon on the Mount and told the story of the Good Samaritan. Martin Tupper, a composer of ballads for those seeking the way, the truth and the light, preached the teaching of the man Jesus as the daystar of England and her colonies. In his *Proverbial Philosophy*, published in 1835, he recommended the 'cheerful countenance' and the 'innocent life'. For him there was no cosmetic anywhere nearly so beautiful as 'a holy countenance'.

Just as the Wesleyan preachers saved England from bloody revolution and the tyranny of any would-be conqueror at the turn of the century, so in the 1840s the gospel of acceptance, patience under suffering, mildness of disposition, frugality and industry was used to shield the minds of the workers in the United Kingdom and the Australian colonies against the atheistic libertinism and bohemianism of socialists and revolutionaries. The advice was wholesome: keep the Sabbath day holy, shun evil company, avoid public houses and intoxicating liquors, never give utterance to a profane or sinful word, unite in family worship, permit no laughing or talking after children have gone to bed, and encourage every member of the family to be modest. Wives and mothers would make their homes happy by careful attention to their husbands' comforts and commands. By observing such precepts a man would rise from poverty to affluence.[9]

Outwardly the difference between Protestant and Catholic seemed plain enough for all to see. The Protestant rejoiced on the Queen's birthday; the Catholic celebrated St Patrick's Day. The Protestant celebrated at Christmas and New Year; the Catholic stressed Easter. The Protestant placed neither intercessor nor aids between himself and his God; the Catholic placed statues in his churches and conducted his services in a way that looked like a series of pantomimic gestures or a ballet of men dressed in gorgeous white robes. The Protestant sang 'Abide with Me' and 'Rock of Ages' (the one a counsel of resignation and the other a profession of man's foulness); the Catholic had 'Faith of Our Fathers' in which he was assured of the help of Erin's saints in his struggle to keep undimmed the light of the faith in Australia. The Protestant prayed for the Queen; the Catholic put his trust in the 'panting heart of Rome' and 'Glorious St. Patrick'. In Sydney, Melbourne, Hobart, Adelaide and Perth the Catholic layman grew up in an atmosphere of incense,

---

[9] Charles Dickens, *A Christmas Carol* (London, 1843) and *The Cricket on the Hearth* (London, 1845); M. Tupper, *Proverbial Philosophy* (London, 1838); D. Hudson, *Martin Tupper: his rise and fall* (London, 1949); 'A word in season', 'A word of caution to everybody', 'A short letter to the servants of Great Britain', 'The emigrant's friend', 'The Sunday school boy in Australia', 'Parting works to emigrant parents', 'Hints to matrons of emigrant ships', 'The young emigrants', *Emigrant Tracts* (London, 1850-2).

plain-song and Mozart masses; in the country districts he relied on the rosary, pious prayers and full-throated singing of 'Faith of Our Fathers' whenever he joined in public worship. Yet these outward and visible signs of difference concealed the underlying bond of a common morality and agreement on what to prize in life. Both were firm believers in 'the good coming time', both grew up in the hope of a belly-full, both believed that the Australian colonies would provide the opportunity for the working man to become a respectable bourgeois.[10]

In the last three years of the decade renewed attempts were made to provide schools for all in which the children of Australia were to be trained to compete in the race of life according to the rules prescribed by the bourgeoisie. On 21 March 1848 Sir Charles FitzRoy, now recovered from his grief and ready once again to show people good statesmanship, informed the Legislative Council of his government's plans to remove the reproach about the gross ignorance and barbarism of over half the children of the colony by creating a dual system of education. The denominational schools would continue under the supervision of the Denominational Education Board, which would be supported in whole or in part by public funds. In these schools the religious instruction of the children would be left entirely under the control of the clergymen of the different denominations to which the children belonged. The national schools would be under the supervision of the National Education Board. The times seemed favourable. A year earlier Broughton had informed him that the Anglicans were now perfectly prepared to admit the right of government to determine what branches of secular knowledge should be taught in national schools provided their religious education were left under the exclusive direction of the clergy of their own denomination without interference from other quarters. With the coming of security of tenure in the lands outside the boundaries of location, squatterdom dropped opposition to the use of public funds for the war by parson, priest and schoolmaster on barbarism in the Australian bush.

It was only four years since the priests and the parsons had defeated Gipps's proposal for a comprehensive system of education, but during that time the support for a system unencumbered by the dogmas of every obsolete and obscure theology had increased. When it was made clear that in these national schools the teachings of Christ rather than the doctrines of any religious sect were to provide the moral education of the young, that a pure and undefiled religion was to be imparted to the children, that feelings of brotherly love were to be encouraged amongst the children of the different sects, binding them all and preparing them to belong to that one great family of enlightened mankind, only those who held that a morality without dogma was like a house built on sand demurred or took fright. Christ was stripped of his

---

[10] W. Gahan, *The Christian's Guide to Heaven; or, a Complete Manual of Catholic Piety* (Dublin, 1823); *Catholic Hymns* (Sydney, 1859); J. Barrett, *That Better Country*, ch. 12.

divinity and became a teacher of benevolence, moral enlightenment and brotherhood.[11]

In the other colonies similar changes were made to introduce a dual system of education. In Van Diemen's Land, Denison took steps to provide education for all. He was influenced by the gap between the number of children receiving any kind of instruction (3707 at the beginning of 1848) and the number who ought to be receiving instruction (9767 in the same year). He was influenced, too, by his conviction that in a society in which at least three-quarters of the people had some connection with convicts, moral feeling was fearfully low and no value but a monetary one was attached to education. He was fearful of the state of the next generation, because while the present generation acknowledged their inferiority and retained some respect for the great body of the upper and middle class 'at home', the next generation, unless it was exposed to a sound moral education, would lose this feeling of respect altogether and be imbued instead with a presumptuous self-confidence arising out of their ignorance of their intellectual and moral inferiority, and become so ignorant and vain that they would not even feel the need to be rescued from such evils. In March 1848 he introduced an education bill to the Legislative Council under which each child attending school would pay a levy of 4s per annum. Council rejected the proposal by a majority of two, partly because colonists could not afford to pay the tax and partly because it was believed government should provide free education for the poor.[12]

In May 1846 Gladstone instructed Governor Robe of South Australia to offer financial assistance to the four principal denominations of Christians. In June of the same year the Legislative Council of South Australia resolved to give financial assistance to all denominations and in September resolved that aid for religion and education be divided amongst the different denominations in proportion to the respective numbers of their membership. In August 1847 the government created a Board of Education to supervise the schools receiving aid. They also decided to pay teachers and give aid according to numbers. It was not till 1851 that the Legislative Council established a Central Board of Education charged with the duty of giving all children secular instruction based on the Christian religion, free from all theological and controversial differences of doctrine but calculated very much to plant sentiments of benevolence, moral enlightenment and brotherhood in the minds of the children.[13]

[11] FitzRoy to Grey, 24 April 1848, *H.R.A.*, I. xxvi. 376-7; *New South Wales Government Gazette*, 7 January 1848; *V. & P.* (L.C. N.S.W.), 21 March, 10 May 1848; *S.M.H.*, 12 May 1848; W. G. Broughton to FitzRoy, 3 May 1847 (N.S.W.S.A. 47/4786); Second Report of the Board of National Education in New South Wales, *V. & P.* (L.C. N.S.W.), 1850, vol. 1.
[12] Denison to Grey, 25 April 1848, C.O. 280/227; *Hobart Town Gazette*, 14 March 1848; *Hobart Town Courier*, 22 March 1848.
[13] Gladstone to Robe, 15 May 1846, C.O. 396/6; Ordinance no. 14, 2 September 1846, and Ordinance no. 11, 17 August 1847, *South Australian Government Gazette*; Report of Select Committee of Legislative Council on a General Education Measure, *V. & P.* (L.C. S.A.), 1851; An Act to Promote Education in South Australia by Aids Towards the Erection of Schools, and the Payment of Stipends to Teachers, no. 20, 29 December 1851.

In Western Australia in mid-1847 a committee of the Legislative Council recommended that schools built and financed by government should be open to all denominations of Christians and teach the general principles of Christianity. After the Catholics objected to this suggestion, Governor Fitzgerald early in 1849 placed on the Estimates a grant for the maintenance of Catholic schools in proportion to their numbers. At mid-century in that colony the government schools were Protestant, and Catholic schools received a special grant.[14]

On the surface there was great variety between the schools. At private schools for girls in the towns of all the colonies girls were offered for a fee an education under teachers whose object was to exhibit knowledge in an attractive way and to accompany its infusion with the soundest principles of morality and religion. The private schools for boys professed strong attachment to the same principles. In the denominational schools pupils were sharply reminded of the pernicious errors subscribed to by all the denominations save the one in which that lesson was being conducted. Methods differed from school to school. All of them practised corporal punishment, since experience had proved that certain characters must be held *in terrorem*, but differed in the manner of inflicting it. In Catholic schools in New South Wales any child knowingly putting out the right hand for punishment received two slaps; in some schools a piece of harness was used freely on the right hand; at the King's School, Hutchins School and St Peter's College the boys were smacked on the bottom. In Catholic schools in all the colonies the day's instruction began and ended with the recitation in unison of the Lord's Prayer, Hail Mary, Apostle's Creed, Acts of Faith, and Prayers for the Archbishop or Bishop, Queen, and the Faithful Departed. In the schools of other denominations the day began with prayer. In the national schools the day began with the reading of one of those edifying pieces designed to rouse benevolence and kindness in the hearts of the children. In Catholic schools children absent from mass on Sunday lost their play time for three days. In other denominational schools there was much talk of the first duty of a Christian on Sunday to attend church. In Church of England schools the parsons were said to be uniformly on the side of wealth, rank and power, and to teach the children to be on their guard against universal suffrage, vote by ballot and the rights of men. In Catholic schools the children were taught much about the wrongs done to the Irish.[15]

At the same time the children in all the schools were exposed to a common vision of the world. They were all encouraged to mortify the flesh, to be prudish and reticent in their references to certain parts of the body, and to treat sex as a dirty little secret. In co-educational national and denominational schools no boy was to approach the water-closets while the girls were in the

[14] *Perth Gazette*, 5 June 1847; Fitzgerald to Grey, 26 April 1849, C.O. 18/50.

[15] Advertisements in *Sydney Herald*, 3, 14 January 1842; R. Fogarty, *Catholic Education in Australia 1806-1850* (2 vols, Melbourne, 1957), vol. 2, appendix 6, pp. 490-1; J. D. Lang, *Freedom and Independence for the Golden Lands of Australia* (Sydney, 1857), pp. 365-6.

playground. As a general rule only one pupil at a time was allowed to be absent for what was euphemistically described as 'necessary purposes'. In general retiring from school during study hours was considered to be an idle habit which ought not to be encouraged. All the children were taught to believe that British civilization enjoyed some special place in the divine plan for the amelioration of mankind. In their readers there was much praise for the industry and genius of the British people, much praise for their strengths, and side-swipes at the weaknesses of other peoples which rightly robbed them of that first rank enjoyed by the British people. Russians and Swedes, for example, were peoples of great ability flawed by the vice of drunkenness.

Their readers, substitutes for the Bible in the national schools, and supplements to doctrine in the denominational schools, inculcated the bourgeois values of industry, frugality, sobriety and resignation. Pupils were warned of the folly of thinking it unjust that one man should be wealthier than another. They were told that the only way a man could improve his lot was by acquiring the habits of forethought, temperance and economy. They were told to avoid profane swearing, observe the Sabbath, avoid bad company and observe the law since that was essential for the happiness of the poor as well as the rich. They were taught certain simple laws of behaviour: to yield to temptation, for instance, was the characteristic of a weak mind. The minds of children in the Australian colonies were tethered to the tenets of British philistinism in the decade before the iron rail tethered the mighty bush to the world.[16]

The authorities hoped this clear stream of moral enlightenment would prevent the continued fouling of the waters of Australian life by the convict past, ecclesiastical bigotry and strife, class antagonism and the flaws in human nature. They knew how much they had to overcome. They knew that in the manufacturing districts of England children were still 'drugged to a death-like sleep' by being given laudanum disguised as Godfrey's Cordial. They knew that a week never passed in Sydney without a woman dropping her child on a doorstep with a note attached to the dress of the infant, addressed to the alleged father. They knew that every day women's faces were becoming quite unrecognizable because of the 'rough usage' inflicted by drunken husbands. They believed that the tendency of their age was upwards towards the light, rather than towards darkness. They believed a generation taught to believe in loving kindness, benevolence and 'God Save the Queen' would take humanity along that road at the end of which men would neither hurt nor destroy. They believed it was possible for mankind to dispense with all the abominations practised under the sun.[17]

[16] H. Dunn and J. T. Crossley (eds), *Daily Lesson Book for the Use of Schools and Families* (Hobart Town, 1849); *Scripture Lessons for the Use of Schools, New Testament No. 1* (Sydney, 1849); J. Bonwick, *Geography for the Use of Australian Youth* (Hobart, 1845); J. Ferguson, *Book of Lessons for the Use of Schools* (Sydney, n.d.); W. Westgarth, *Lecture at the Mechanics' Institution* (Melbourne, 1842); A. G. Austin, *Australian Education 1788-1900* (Melbourne, 1961), chs 2, 3; J. Barrett, *That Better Country*, chs 7-10.
[17] *People's Advocate*, 13 January, 12, 24 March 1849.

Early in 1849, as the schoolchildren were learning of the 'good coming time', their parents were put to the test. At the end of February the press in Sydney published a despatch written by Grey on 8 September 1848 in which he announced that because of the information that had reached him from various sources as to the urgent want of labour in the colony of New South Wales, and the great usefulness of convicts who had been previously trained in the United Kingdom, he had been led to the conclusion that the colonists would prefer a moderate number of convicts, even unaccompanied by an equal number of free emigrants, sent to the colony without charge. He intended, he said, to send to New South Wales only those convicts who were considered to be deserving of tickets-of-leave on their arrival and calculated to become useful as labourers in the colony. He also proposed at once to advise Her Majesty to revoke the Order in Council of 22 May 1840 by which New South Wales was no longer to receive convicts under sentence of transportation. By an Order in Council of 4 September 1848 New South Wales was once again named as a place to which felons or other offenders in the United Kingdom under sentence or order of transportation should be conveyed.[18]

In Sydney, howls of moral indignation greeted the news. The *Sydney Morning Herald* called the decision 'Our Country's Degradation'. 'A man', they wrote, 'cannot touch pitch without being defiled.' At a public meeting on 1 March, convened to consider what steps should be taken about the intention of Her Majesty's Government to make New South Wales a penal settlement, Charles Cowper spluttered about a 'gross breach of faith'. Robert Lowe squeaked he hoped the colonists would have nothing to do with convicts at all. Bob Nichols trusted that the Legislative Council would repeal all the laws relating to convicts so as to render it impossible to carry out penal discipline in the colony. At the second public meeting of protest on 9 March those present roared their applause when Charles Cowper told them that the small amount of labour the convicts would provide would never replace the 'stream of free and virtuous immigration'. A Mr Wilshire thought the best thing they could do would be to go down to the Circular Quay on the arrival of the first ship and refuse to allow the convicts to land. The bourgeoisie of Sydney, encouraged and supported by the working classes, had started the cry of 'no convicts on any terms' and 'away with the convicts and all that pertains to them'.[19]

Down in Melbourne the bourgeoisie and workers beat their breasts and asked why the British Government should doom their beauteous province to be converted into another 'hell upon earth' to gratify the insatiable cupidity of a few of the more greedy squatters, rather than promote the welfare of virtuous immigrants. They also wanted to keep their womenfolk pure: for them the idea of a convict cohabiting with a free woman was 'repulsive to the

---

[18] Grey to FitzRoy, 8 September 1848, *H.R.A.*, I. xxvi. 587-90; the Order in Council of 4 September 1848 was enclosed in Grey to FitzRoy, 4 December 1848. That despatch is in *H.R.A.*, I. xxvi. 723-4 and C.O. 202/54, but neither includes the enclosure. The text is published in *P.P.*, 1849, xliii, 1022, pp. 22-3.
[19] *S.M.H.*, 2, 10, 12 March 1849; *People's Advocate*, 14 April 1849.

feelings' and 'disgusting to every well-regulated mind'. At a public meeting on 6 March those present resolved to protest against the 'contamination and vice inseparable from any Penal system'. They predicted that renewal of transportation would stop the present abundant supply of virtuous and industrious immigrants and substitute a degraded labouring population for the respectable citizens and yeomen the province was in the process of acquiring. They insisted that the importation of convicts would be a violation of faith with the great majority of the inhabitants who emigrated from the Mother Country on the direct assurance of both the home and colonial governments that the District of Port Phillip was never to be regarded as a penal settlement. They would tell the captain of any convict ship to take his cargo of moral filth away and, if he refused, capsize the ship.[20]

Frightened by such militant rhetoric about independence, and mindful of how blood had recently flowed in the streets of Europe when the people tried to seize power, the Legislative Council on 15 May agreed on the text of a petition to the Queen's Most Excellent Majesty in which the members respectfully declined to accede to the proposal to renew transportation. They also respectfully but strongly protested against any measure by which the colony would be degraded into a penal settlement, and earnestly entreated Her Majesty that she might be graciously pleased to revoke the Order in Council by which the colony had been again made a place to which British offenders might be transported.[21]

Amongst society at large the use of convicts still had supporters. Sheep men still said there was no other country in the world that could furnish such an effectual penitentiary as the sheep-walks of eastern Australia. In the back country at Moreton Bay, Ipswich, Warwick on the Darling Downs, in New England, the Wellington Valley, the Riverina, and at Coleraine, Belfast (Port Fairy) and Portland Bay some squatters saw no alternative to convicts as a solution to the labour shortage. They were preferable to coolies and cannibals because they were white and were at least nominally Christian. The two main spokesmen for such squatters—Wentworth and James Martin—were in especially bad odour with the bourgeoisie and working classes of Sydney that year. Early in the year Wentworth had blotted his copy-book once again by the outrageous suggestion that people should subscribe to a fund to relieve him from the drudgery of earning his living and allow him to devote all his time and energy to public life. A one-time giant was reeling, and only Jimmy Martin, himself the butt of all men's ridicule, was prepared to say a word in his defence. Besides, the cabbage-tree-hatted youth of Sydney were no longer in awe of fine old squatter gentlemen and were beginning to

[20] *Argus*, 20 February, 13 March 1849; Report of Public General Meeting in Melbourne of the Inhabitants of Port Phillip, 6 March 1849, encl. in FitzRoy to Grey, 21 March 1849, C.O. 201/412.

[21] *V. & P.* (L.C. N.S.W.), 15 May 1849; Petition of the Legislative Council of New South Wales to the Queen's Most Excellent Majesty, 15 May 1849, encl. in FitzRoy to Grey, 1 June 1849, C.O. 201/414.

laugh at them as men who charged their servants double prices for their rations and oppressed them in the magistrates' courts in the bush of Australia.[22]

On 9 and 10 June 1849 great excitement prevailed in Sydney as the people awaited the arrival in Sydney Harbour of the convict ship *Hashemy*. On Monday 11 June when the ship cast anchor at Circular Quay the shopkeepers closed their premises as five thousand people gathered at the Quay for a great protest meeting with the rain pouring down so heavily that the area was quickly converted into a sea of mud. On orders from Sir Charles FitzRoy the gates of the Domain were locked against the people, soldiers with fixed bayonets stood guard at the entrance to Government House, and extra squads of police were seen parading the grounds at Government House. The army and the police, it was rumoured, were being used to awe the people. It was said that Sir Charles had dropped the mask of impartiality and identified himself with the gaolers and oppressors of mankind. In the meantime down at the Quay the people awaited the arrival of Robert Lowe, but when he failed to turn up they put Robert Campbell, the nephew of Robert Campbell the merchant, into the chair. They cheered him when he told them:

> Convicts had been the source of wealth to many: many hoped again to amass riches from their services; but Australia now wanted them not—she could very well do without them. They—the men of Australia [another male gathering to protect the virtue of the women and children of Australia] had wives, and children, and they would be content to subdue the land and replenish it without the introduction of British crime and its attendant British misery (Cheers).

They were asked to receive an importation which they should look on with abhorrence. John Lamb, a nominee member of the Legislative Council and, like Campbell, no longer a new chum, moved the adoption of the following protest:

> We, the free and loyal subjects of Her Most Gracious Majesty, inhabitants of the city of Sydney and its immediate neighbourhood, in public meeting assembled, do hereby enter our most deliberate and solemn Protest against the transportation of British criminals to the colony of New South Wales.
>
> FIRSTLY—Because it is in violation of the will of the majority of the colonists, as is clearly evidenced by their expressed opinions on this question at all times.
>
> SECONDLY—Because numbers among us have emigrated on the faith of the British Government, that transportation to this colony had ceased for ever.
>
> THIRDLY—Because it is incompatible with our existence as a free colony, desiring self-government, to be the receptacle of another country's felons.
>
> FOURTHLY—Because it is in the highest degree unjust, to sacrifice the great social and political interests of the colony at large to the pecuniary profit of a fraction of its inhabitants.

[22] *People's Advocate*, 10, 17, 24 February 1849; *S.M.H.*, 5 February 1849; (Pick-Up) 'The old squatter gentleman' in *People's Advocate*, 1 September 1849; *S.M.H.*, 12 June 1849; *People's Advocate*, 16 June 1849.

FIFTHLY—Because being firmly and devotedly attached to the British Crown, we greatly fear that the perpetration of so stupendous an act of injustice by Her Majesty's Government, will go far towards alienating the affections of the people of this colony from the mother country.

For these and many kindred reasons, in the exercise of our duty to our country,—for the love we bear our families,—in the strength of our loyalty to Great Britain—and from the depth of our reverence for Almighty God—we protest against the landing again of British convicts on these shores.

Lowe, yet another new chum and, like Lamb, a great believer in the 'British character' of their community and in the spirit of loyalty to the Queen, then climbed on top of the omnibus used by the speakers and harangued them:

The threat of degradation had been fulfilled. The stately presence of their city, the beautiful waters of their harbour, were this day again polluted with the presence of that floating hell—a convict ship (Immense cheers). They had lived again to behold the cargo of crime borne across the waves to them. In their port they behold a ship freighted not with the comforts of life, not with luxuries of civilised nations, not with the commodities of commerce, in exchange for our produce; but with the moral degradation of a community—the picked and selected criminals of Great Britain . . . New South Wales must be the university at which these scholars in vice and iniquity must finish their course of instruction . . . Here it was where the rubbish—the moral filth of Great Britain—must be shot . . . He viewed this attempt to inflict the worst and most degrading slavery on the colony only as sequence [sic] of that oppressive tyranny which had confiscated the lands of the colony—for the benefit of a class. That class had felt their power—they were not content to get the lands alone, without labour they were worthless, and therefore they must enrich them with slaves (Great cheers).

Carried away by the loud applause that interrupted his speech, Lowe ended with a very emotional peroration:

Let them send across the Pacific their emphatic declaration that they would not be slaves—that they would be free. Let them exercise the right that every English subject had—to assert his freedom (Cheers). He could see from the meeting the time was not far distant when they would assert their freedom not by words alone. As in America, oppression was the parent of independence, so would it be in the colony. The tea which the Americans flung into the water rather than pay the tax upon it, was not the cause of the revolt of the American States; it was the unrighteousness of the tax—it was the degradation of submission to an unrighteous demand. And so sure as the seed will grow into the plant, and the plant to the tree, in all times, and in all nations, so will injustice and tyranny ripen into rebellion, and rebellion into independence.

There was immense cheering for that.

Although he and other speakers called on those present to send that cargo of moral filth back to where it came from, things never got out of hand. The meeting dispersed without any noise or tumult, and the conduct of those present was 'grave, decorous and becoming'. Nor were their decisions couched in the revolutionary language Lowe and others had used. Many speakers had stressed their fear lest such a stupendous act of injustice should go far towards alienating the affection of the people of the colony from the Mother Country. The only speaker for the working classes on that day was Henry Parkes, who spoke on behalf of the migrant working man and his right to be protected from the degradation of working with convicts. Not one of the native-born spoke that day. They had an understandable reluctance to join with those new chums in branding their fathers, their mothers, their grandfathers, their grandmothers, or even their great grandparents as 'moral filth' and 'rubbish'. Grave, decorous, solemn British migrants, rather than the sons of the soil or the men of the 'cabbage-tree mob', agreed that day to send a delegation from the meeting to Sir Charles to present him with the text of the protest and the resolutions, and to request him to tell the captain to take his ship and his cargo back to England.[23]

The *People's Advocate* believed the first blow had been struck for the freedom of the people of Australia. The *Sydney Morning Herald* was confident that the demonstration would persuade the British Government that they could no longer think of making New South Wales a receptacle for British felons without doing violence to the feelings of the vast majority of the inhabitants. Charles Cowper and his fellow-moderates in Council prayed fervently that the British Government would revoke the hateful Order in Council quickly because otherwise those angry men who shouted to high heaven when Lowe worked on their passions might press for independence and a Yankee-style republic. There was a danger that if the cabbage-tree mob joined with the chartists and universal suffrage men amongst the new chums, blood would flow in the streets of Sydney.

The supporters of convictism seemed to be spoiling for a fight. With the popular press circulating stories that government was planning to dragoon the people with the use of the police and the army, the delegation from the great protest meeting were told at Government House on that memorable Monday 11 June that if they wanted to see the Governor they would have to make an appointment. When this took place at 2 p.m. on the following day, FitzRoy assured them he would lose no time in forwarding the protest and the resolutions. Lowe then asked him to send the prisoners back. Sir Charles told him curtly that that was quite impossible. Robert Campbell attempted to express his regret that His Excellency was unable to return a more satisfactory answer, but His Excellency became angry and cut him short and said he was not prepared to enter into any discussion of the matter.

The members of the delegation decided to summon another public meeting on 18 June to which they proposed to submit three resolutions: first, to censure the Governor for his discourtesy to the delegation; second, to petition for the dismissal of Earl Grey; and third, to demand responsible government for the

[23] *People's Advocate*, 16 June 1849; *S.M.H.*, 12, 13, 16, 18 June 1849.

colony of New South Wales. When Monday came the proposers decided to drop the censure of His Excellency. In another display of mob oratory Lowe called on those present to agree to two resolutions: first, 'That considering the arbitrary and faithless manner in which this colony has been treated by the Right Honourable Grey, this Meeting most humbly prays Her Majesty to remove that Nobleman from Her Majesty's counsels'; second, that it was indispensable 'to the well-being of this colony, and to the satisfactory conduct of its affairs, that its Government should no longer be administered by the remote, ill-informed, and irresponsible Colonial Office, but by Ministers chosen from, and responsible to the colonists themselves, in accordance with the principles of the British Constitution'. Lowe called on those present to brave death for the rights of their country and their kind, and free their necks from the odious domination to which they had been subjected. This convinced Cowper and all the moderates that they must persuade the British Government to abolish transportation before the people changed their umbrellas into arms and established a people's republic. Unless the British Government acted quickly, the people would soon stop calling themselves 'loyal subjects' who did not propose to make use of 'the intimidations of powder and shot'.[24]

The *People's Advocate* boasted that the supporters of the old order could not go on much longer propping up the rotten system upon which they had become bloated and fattened. The defenders of transportation were just as intransigent and insolent. They called the proceedings of 18 June the work of the idlers of the city who could not be taken to represent the real views of the community. Sir Charles told Grey that the question of the resumption of transportation had been seized by a small faction whose influence only extended to the mob of Sydney. He went on to assure His Lordship that the present plan of sending out convicts could not possibly be construed as a breach of faith. He went on to say that in view of the attempts to inflame the minds of the lower classes in Sydney and to instigate them to a demonstration of physical force he had thought it wise to have on hand a sufficient number of troops to assist the police in putting a stop to acts of violence.[25]

Down in Melbourne the attempt to land convicts also brought some men to the edge of that abyss of rebellion into which they peered, took fright, recoiled in horror and begged Her Majesty's Government, in the name of God, to rescue them from that fate by ending the transportation of convicts. On 9 August the *Argus* informed its readers that the convicts on the *Randolph* were already in their bay. They must see to it that convicts obtained no footing there, and so avert the moral plague. La Trobe, somewhat unwontedly, acted promptly and told the captain to unload his cargo of filth in Sydney. The ship sailed out of Port Phillip. To guard themselves against a repetition, the people of Melbourne crammed into the Queen's Theatre on 20 August to express the determination of the whole community not to submit to the intro-

[24] *S.M.H.*, 19, 20 June 1849; *People's Advocate*, 23 June 1849.
[25] *People's Advocate*, 23 June, 7, 21 July 1849; Address to His Excellency Sir Charles Augustus FitzRoy, *S.M.H.*, 29 June 1849; FitzRoy to Grey, 30 June 1849, C.O. 201/414.

duction of convicts. Speaker after speaker professed their loyalty to Her Majesty's throne and Her Majesty's person. They solemnly and emphatically protested against the right asserted by Her Majesty's Government of sending convicts to any British colony contrary to the express wish of its inhabitants, and claimed the protection of the great constitutional principle that the Mother Country had no right to tax free British colonies for imperial pur-poses. They maintained that Australia Felix was now prepared to undergo any extremity rather than submit to the degradation both of the name and the reality of a penal settlement.

If remonstrance after remonstrance proved unavailing, some speakers proclaimed, they would have no choice but to declare themselves a free and independent people. Let them, as one speaker put it, have a council of their own and a senate of their own. A voice in the audience added, 'yes, and an army of our own', and was loudly applauded. If they wished to preserve a proper tone in society to keep their children free from pollution so that they might continue virtuous and happy, they must be prepared to fight for it. To great roars of laughter John Pascoe Fawkner went down on his knees on the speaker's platform to tell them that Johnny Fawkner was prepared to shoulder a rifle, as a voice called out, 'Good on you, Johnny', for there was a devil inside him which drove him to use the most solemn moments of life for the purposes of his own vulgar buffoonery. Councillor Thomas McCombie, to cries of 'Bravo Tommy', denounced the scheme of marrying the fair province of Port Phillip to a hideous monster. Sound product of his day and age that he was, he believed in the efficacy of moral force to shield men from this greatest curse that could ever be inflicted on their province. When Alderman Grieves, another man who loathed the hideous mien of vice, asked them whether in an emergency they were prepared to resist to the death, some called out in alarm at the drift of events, 'Not they.' So he asked them, failing that, were they prepared to adopt the means used at Cape Colony and refuse to employ, or associate or do business with those who employed prisoners. There was much applause from one section of the audience. L. Mackinnon, a squatter, leapt to his feet and said he could not let such a 'windy and humbugging speech' pass without a reply. He was not prepared to make a clean break with the use of convicts. Then the chairman restored unity to the meeting by repeating the slogans on which they could all agree. 'Let them all be united then, and exclaim', he said, 'the die is cast, Victoria will be free; hoist the banner of liberty, and repudiate convictism in every form.' They cheered because they were expecting to hear from London soon of their liberation from Sydney. When they read at the end of the month that the supine people of Sydney had allowed the convicts on the *Randolph* to land and proceed by boat to Parra-matta where they had become beastly drunk and rolled about the streets, they gave themselves a hearty pat on the back and went in for one of those colonial bouts of self-congratulation in which they raised their eyes to heaven and said, 'If only the people of Sydney had not been content with empty bombast, and become like the people of Melbourne, then they would have been spared from witnessing such degradation.' That was a very Melbourne thing to do.[26]

Melbourne was a migrant community. Adelaide was also a migrant community and much given to the same rhetoric, self-praise and rebellion on paper. By contrast, Hobart, Launceston and the country districts of Van Diemen's Land were communities in which four-fifths of the population were convicts, relatives of convicts or descendants of convicts. They were also communities in which the employers still used convict labour extensively. In such a society talk of moral pollution was offensive to four-fifths of the people. Swearing never to use convict labour was unthinkable for employers in the country districts. That left the bourgeoisie in the towns and those clergymen who had no connection with the convict system and were not dependent on government for their stipend. In Launceston this brought Henry Dowling into prominence in the agitation against transportation. The son of a Baptist minister who dedicated his life to the moral elevation of the people of Van Diemen's Land, and thought of death as the ejectment of the soul from its mud tenement, he believed, with his father, that men were perfect helplessness, but that Christ was perfect ability. He was active in every movement to improve the morals of his contemporaries. He started his own circulating library, opened a savings bank and supported schemes to select only the virtuous for free passages from the United Kingdom to Van Diemen's Land. He refused to allow liquor in the office of his paper the *Launceston Advertiser*, first published in 1831. 'Ah,' he would exclaim in his jolly, cheerful voice, 'I can smell rum.' In 1839 he published in Launceston the *Pickwick Papers* of Charles Dickens to inspire men, with God's help, to work for the day when sunshine flooded the whole world.[27]

Another agitator was John West, minister of St John's Congregational Church in Milton Hall, Launceston. Born in England in 1809, he was inducted into the ministry at the tender age of twenty and arrived in Launceston in 1839. There he won a reputation for large wisdom, a gentle heart and a great public spirit. He always seemed so lost in thought that he would pass well-known persons without noticing them. In the pulpit he did strange things like tying his handkerchief into knots, as in his musical voice he uttered the sentiments of evangelical piety in grandiloquent Johnsonian periods of language. All his life he was sustained by the hope of eternal life. His favourite text from the New Testament was the passage in the Epistle to the Hebrews, 'To die is gain'. Like Henry Dowling, he looked forward to the day when God stripped him of his house of clay and converted that great loss into gain. He was fond of leaning over the huge pulpit in Milton Hall and

26 *Argus*, 9, 10, 13, 21 August, 8, 10 September 1849.

27 H. Button, *Flotsam and Jetsam* (London, 1909), pp. 80, 103-4; Eardley-Wilmot to Stanley, 7 June 1844, duplicate despatches of Lieutenant-Governor of Van Diemen's Land, vol. 48, pp. 478-81 (T.S.A.); H. Dowling to Col. Sec. of Van Diemen's Land, 18 June 1840, ibid., vol. 44, pp. 584-8; S. Cozens, *A Tribute of Affection to the Memory of the Late Rev. Henry Dowling* (Launceston, 1869).

putting that question of questions, 'If a man die, shall he live again?' and replying to his own question, 'I say confidently, yes.'

As a young man he had adopted enough of the radical sentiments in non-conformist circles to be known to some as a rabid radical. His public life in the colonies was the story of a man so swayed by success that the one-time radical turned his coat inside out and embraced a mawkish conservatism when he became the editor of the *Sydney Morning Herald* in 1854. In all his public life he never identified himself with those who taught that man's behaviour could be changed by tinkering with political institutions. Like Henry Dowling, he was an active supporter of the temperance movement, the mechanics' institute and the savings bank, all designed to instil the virtues of industry, frugality, sobriety and purity. For him everything that gave men a fuller consciousness of their dignity should be encouraged, because then dissipation would be resisted and men would sow a moral harvest for the future. In 1848 he was preoccupied with the problem of how to preserve primitive virtues in societies threatened with opulence. He told the members of his congregation in Launceston not to envy the gilded couch of decaying nations or to sigh for the works of art created in more opulent societies. The vigorous intellect, the robust constitution and the industrious habits of her children would be the best presages in Van Diemen's Land that their country should be great. 'The plough,' he insisted, 'not the pencil—must be the crest of infant empires.[28]

When he first took up the convict question in the pamphlet *Common Sense: an enquiry into the influence of transportation on the colony of Van Diemen's Land* in 1847, he signed it significantly Jacob Lackland, for he had at that time the visionary tendencies of an Old Testament prophet and the enthusiasm of the social reformer. He foresaw a society of petty bourgeois peasant proprietors replacing the landed gentry who had waxed fat by the exploitation of semi-slave convict labour. In the pamphlet, he called on Britons, Christians and parents to show that they prized their rights and loved their children. That land, he wrote, which the supporters of transportation predicted would become desert, when the clank of chains, the cries of torture, the noise of riot and the groans of despair were no longer heard, would not become a desert; it would blossom abundantly and rejoice with singing when their sons and daughters would go forth, the free among the free. He appealed to them not to cause the eyes of mankind to look upon them with abhorrence. 'Make not your name a scorn, and a hissing! Perform your duty! And save your adopted country.'

When he replied a few weeks later to the arguments of a Mr Williamson

---

[28] Plaque in Loving Memory of the Rev. John West, Milton Hall, Launceston; H. Button, op. cit., pp. 56-60; J. Reynolds, 'John West 1809-1873', *Service*, December 1952; J. West, *The Hope of Life Eternal* (Launceston, 1850); J. West, *The Fine Arts: a lecture* (Launceston, 1848); documents in libel of J. West by J. D. Lang, printed by J. West for private circulation (T.S.A.); John West, *The History of Tasmania* (2 vols, Launceston, 1852); E. Morris Miller, 'John West: man of letters', *Proceedings of the Tasmanian Historical Research Association*, vol. 2, 1952.

for the continuance of transportation, he argued that continuation implied a further debasement of morals, that a man must have sunk very low in his own estimation if he preferred the society of the degraded felon to that of the lowest upright emigrant. He went on to paint a visionary picture of a Van Diemen's Land after transportation had ended, telling his readers that abolition would release an energy hitherto unknown in Van Diemen's Land and that their minds would be divested of a burden which had haunted every thinking family man in the island and pressed on him like a nightmare. Above all, abolition would be the means of creating what was to him a great good—a class of small farmers. For in him there was a blend of the apocalyptic view of man's destiny—the fruit of much reading of the prophets of the Old Testament and the Book of Revelations—and the pastoral sentiment that small farmers cultivated the desirable domestic virtues and the town and the tavern corrupted a man's immortal soul.[29]

In 1847 and 1848 all this talk about transportation and pollution seemed like tilting at windmills. Soon after the suspension of transportation to Van Diemen's Land in 1846 the press in Hobart and Launceston stopped reporting stories of packs of convicts roving the streets in those towns to the great terror of bejewelled old women. They stopped reporting stories of hordes of convicts roaming the countryside slitting the throats of travellers and threatening defenceless country women with that fate worse than death. Gone, too, was the talk of a glutted labour market, of the sons of Van Diemen's Land being driven out of their native land, and the daughters rotting away in some lonely hamlet into the 'dried up creek-bed' years of spinsterhood because their childhood sweetheart could find no gainful employment in their stricken land.

At the beginning of 1849 the whole question of transportation leapt out of the pulpit into the market-place. Despite the assurance given by Grey to Denison in the despatch of 5 February 1847 that it was not the intention of Her Majesty's Government that transportation to Van Diemen's Land should be resumed at the expiration of the two years for which it had already been decided that it should be discontinued, in April 1848 Grey wrote to Denison that Her Majesty's Government proposed to transport ticket-of-leave holders to Van Diemen's Land. He had been influenced in part by reports of the success of sending convicts to the colonies in once more making them useful members of society, and in part by evidence in the United Kingdom that the deterrent effect of the sentence of transportation would be impaired if it came to be understood that the punishment would not in future involve the actual removal of the offender from his native country. On 6 September 1848 Grey confirmed the decision to send ticket-of-leave holders to Van Diemen's Land, and enclosed a copy of the Order in Council of 4 September in which

---

[29] Jacob Lackland, *Common Sense: an enquiry into the influence of transportation on the Colony of Van Diemen's Land* (Launceston, 1847); extract of above with comment in *Launceston Examiner*, 17 April 1847; Reply to Thirty-Nine Reasons for the Continuance of Transportation, as Set Forth by Mr. Williamson, *Launceston Examiner*, 1 May 1847.

Van Diemen's Land was once again named as a place to which felons under-going the punishment of transportation might be sent.[30]

In October 1848 the Legislative Council resolved decorously that the pro-posal to send convicts to Van Diemen's Land was in the highest degree injurious to the colony. They then ducked the whole issue by going on to say that transportation if combined with an immigration of selected free persons of an equivalent amount would help to develop the resources of Australia. The news that Van Diemen's Land was in fact once more a penal colony drove such caution to the winds. By the beginning of 1849 the lovers of the chase, gaiety and hilarity, like Dicky Dry, a landed gentleman near Launces-ton, were beating their breasts in public and joining with the parsons in public recitations of that oft-quoted, oft-ignored remark by Christ, 'Ye cannot serve both God and Mammon.' At Launceston on 24 January 1849 the opponents of transportation summoned people to a public meeting at the Cornwall Assembly Room for the purpose of forming an Anti-Transportation League, the only condition of membership to be a written obligation not to engage any convict, whether probationer or ticket-of-leave holder, who had arrived in the colony since 1 January 1849.

At the meeting all the rhetoric and bombast that had characterized the anti-transportation meetings on the mainland poured out. Speakers professed anger about the 'breach of faith', and love for the British constitution and their native country. Since their requests had been disregarded, now was the time for them to act for themselves. They deplored that their society was again to become a byword and a reproach on account of its convict character. They vowed that if they continued to employ the prisoners sent them they merited the scorn, contempt and abhorrence of the civilized world. 'Will you have any of this opium?' Theodore Bartley asked them. They cried out 'No, no.' 'The other colonies have refused it', he continued, 'will you swallow it all?' 'No! no! no!' they shouted. Despite all their high-minded protestations that they were unable to serve both God and Mammon, they had no intention of dispensing with the use of convicts. They accepted the moderate policy of gradual extinction rather than follow the advice of the hot-heads at the meeting to 'Strike a death blow at once'. They agreed with W. P. Weston, a pastoralist and friend of John West, that it was quite impracticable to make 'short work and return all the convicts to the government', because free labour had been driven out of the colony and they could not dispense with what was available. They ended up saying that convictism was destructive of the best interests of the colony but, since free labour was not available, that

[30] Grey to Denison, 5 February 1847, C.O. 408/28; Grey to Denison, 6 September 1848, C.O. 408/30; *Bell's Life in Sydney*, 23 March 1850; *Colonial Times*, 23 July 1850; J. Bos-tock, *The Dawn of Australian Psychiatry* (Sydney, 1968), pp. 17 134; Report of Select Committee on Lunatic Asylum, *V. & P.* (L.C. N.S.W.), 1846, vol. 2; *S.M.H.*, 4 September 1846; *Report of the Benevolent Society of New South Wales for Year Ended 30th June 1849* (Sydney, 1849); Dora Peyser, 'A study of the history of welfare work in Sydney from 1788 till about 1900', R.A.H.S., *J. & P.*, vol. 25, 1939, pp. 89-128, 169-212; T. H. Braim, *A History of New South Wales*, vol. 2, pp. 302-5.

the colony could not dispense with what was already in the country. This was merely to add to all those humiliating contradictions with which men encumber themselves when they try to reconcile the claims of God and Mammon.[31]

It was a time when men with a conscience experienced great anguish. Bishop Willson was deeply troubled. When he reflected on all the abominations practised by convicts, he wondered whether any Christian nation was morally justified in inflicting such punishment. He knew that convict life had encouraged men to commit the most detestable deeds. Men convicts actually boasted of being married to each other. But he also believed Van Diemen's Land could not dispense with the labour of convicts. The only possible solution was for the British Government only to transport reformed convicts. From one end of Van Diemen's Land to the other, pious congregations of Baptists, Congregationalists, Wesleyans and Presbyterians also expressed their horror at being exposed any longer to the convict polluters. But the time for such agonizing was coming to an end. The great increase in the migration of the free in 1849 swelled the ranks of those who felt either 'patriotic indignation' or 'prudish virtue' about the presence of convicts.[32]

In October 1849 the patriots were beside themselves with rage and indignation. In that month William Smith O'Brien, Thomas Francis Meagher, Patrick O'Donohoe and Terence Bellew McManus, who had been sentenced to transportation for life at Clonmel Assizes the preceding October for sedition, arrived on the *Swift* in Hobart Town. They had been preceded by two other political prisoners from Ireland, John Martin and Kevin Izod O'Doherty, who had arrived on the *Dublin City* in August 1848. Van Diemen's Land acquired the stigma of the place of punishment for men who, in the eyes of the civilized world, were victims of a brutal and repulsive penal code befitting a degraded and barbarous nation. At Clonmel in October 1848 an English judge had sentenced O'Brien to be drawn on a hurdle to a place of execution, where he was to be hanged by the neck until he was dead, after which his head was to be severed from his body, which was then to be carved into four quarters. O'Brien claimed descent from Brien Boru, the greatest of Ireland's monarchs. He was educated at Harrow and Cambridge, where he acquired skill in the most varied attainments. He was the crack horseman of the Clare hunt, a man who had defended his honour at least three times by challenging opponents to duels with pistols. He had had a distinguished career in the British House of Commons and enjoyed a reputation for being

---

[31] *Launceston Examiner*, 27 January 1849; Denison to Grey, 11 February 1849, C.O. 280/243; *Colonial Times*, 2 February 1849; *Hobart Town Courier*, 14 April 1849.

[32] *Hobart Town Courier*, 14 April 1849; evidence of Robert Willson to Select Committee of the House of Lords on the Execution of the Criminal Law, *P.P.*, 1847, vii, 533. Petitions of the congregations of the churches of St Andrew's, Perth, and St Andrew's, Evandale; Church of Bothwell adhering to the communion of the Church of Scotland; Wesleyan Chapel, Oatlands; St John's Square Chapel, Launceston; Baptist Chapel, Launceston, Independent Chapel, Green Ponds and St John's Church, Launceston, encls in Denison to Grey, 31 August 1849, C.O. 280/246.

as upright and prudish in his private life as he was honourable in his public life. The barbarous death sentence was commuted to transportation for life. Van Diemen's Land suffered the infamy of being the gaol in which a man of his talent and moral excellence was degraded to the wearing of a felon's garb, and forced to mingle with common criminals because he rejected with contempt the suggestion of his gaolers that he should petition Her Majesty graciously to grant him a ticket-of-leave. His five companions were all men of honour, talent and integrity who were forced to live with felons on an island which had once had the unenviable reputation of being a cage for the vultures of mankind.[33]

In the meantime employers of labour on the frontiers of settlement in New South Wales still complained of the great want of labour in their districts and prayed Her Majesty please to send convicts quickly. Patrick Leslie, pioneer squatter on the Darling Downs, told a meeting in Ipswich on 10 January 1850 that the best servants he had ever had were convicts, that up on the Downs they were not supplied with one fourth of the labour they required and that they required a continuous influx of free hands to keep pace with the demands of the flock-masters. Up on the Downs the cry of 'No emigrants' had already been raised because they did not take to shepherding. That left a choice between the Chinese and convicts. On that Leslie and his fellow-squatters were of one mind. As Leslie told that meeting in Ipswich, 'What they wanted was men of their own country and colour', and the crowd called out loudly, 'No Chinese.'[34]

As for the aborigines, employers had given up all hope of making them like 'the men of their own country'. In all the districts of Australia that had been exposed to colonial enterprise the numbers of aborigines were diminishing. The aborigine Mahroot told a select committee of the Legislative Council of New South Wales in 1845 that out of the four hundred of his tribe which occupied the southern coast of Port Jackson in the time of Governor Macquarie there were now only four left. The Chief Protector of the Aborigines, George Augustus Robinson, estimated that between 1840 and 1846 the aboriginal population of the District of Port Phillip decreased by 20 per cent. In 1846 Robinson reported to FitzRoy that every acre of their native soil was either leased out or occupied by the white man's flocks. The aborigines had 'no place for the sole of their feet'. The causes of their diminution in population were said to be the wars of destruction between tribes, the hostile encounters with the whites, the diseases and vices of European society, aggravated by the irregularity in their own mode of life and the absence of proper medical

[33] *Galway Vindicator*, 7 August 1852; *Hobart Town Courier*, 31 October 1849; *Punch* (London), vol. 10, January-June 1846, p. 247; *Tipperary Vindicator*, 11, 18 October, 30 September, 28 October 1848; W. S. O'Brien, *Principles of Government: or, meditations in exile* (2 vols, Dublin, 1856); T. J. Kiernan, Irish Exiles of 1848 in Australia (MS. in possession of author).

[34] *S.M.H.*, 28 November, 10 December 1849; *People's Advocate*, 23 June 1849; *Bell's Life in Sydney*, 2 February 1850; FitzRoy to Grey, 17 November 1849 and encls, C.O. 201/417.

treatment, the practice of infanticide, and the gradual disappearance of various animals used as food, and other sources of sustaining life.[35]

The reports from the commissioners of Crown lands for 1849 confirmed this solid decrease in the race, as well as the little progress in improving the way of life of 'this helpless portion of mankind'. The commissioners wrote of the prostration of the native—the consequence, it was believed, of being deprived of their pursuit of hunting, and the introduction among them of the habit of drinking ardent spirits. The crime of infanticide was increasing, especially the killing of half-caste children, there being few instances of such children coming to maturity. Sexual intercourse between aboriginal females and colonists, chiefly of the working classes, was already a great cause of misery to the aborigines, partly from the diseases it introduced among them and partly from the hostile feeling of male blacks towards the white men who stole their women. In some districts it was becoming common to hear the natives remark that the ground on which settlers had formed their stations belonged to a tribe or an individual member of that tribe. The comments on the failure to convert the aborigines to a civilized way of life were universal.[36]

The criminal law on the aborigines reflected the gap between the white man's professed aspiration and the actual steps he had taken to protect his life and property against a hostile people. From the beginning of settlement in all the Australian colonies the aborigines had been declared subjects of the British Crown—an honour, it was said, that had been conferred without either their knowledge or consent. As Assistant Protector Dredge put it, 'it is verily believed that they have never yet been able to comprehend' that honour. They had been made accountable to British law for offences not only against the colonists but also for those actions they committed amongst themselves which might not contravene their own code of behaviour but were crimes under the white man's law. For the white man since the mid-1830s had been committed to the principle of their equality before the law, partly in deference to the metaphysical doctrine that all men, whatever their colour, are equal in the sight of God and partly as a consequence of the injunction from London to integrate the aborigine as quickly as possible into the white man's civilization. In obedience to this policy the colonies of South Australia and Western Australia had placed on their statute books a series of Acts to allow the aborigines to appear as competent witnesses in the law courts of their colonies.

Every attempt to put such an Act on the statute book of New South Wales had been thwarted by the conviction of some white men that the aborigine was not a proper human being, that he was an incomplete biped, closer in the scale of creation to the brutes than to man. When the patient J. H. Plunkett

---

[35] W. Westgarth, *A Report on the Condition, Capabilities, and Prospects of the Australian Aborigines* (Melbourne, 1846), pp. 5-7; Grey to FitzRoy, 11 February 1848, *H.R.A.*, I. xxvi. 223-4.

[36] Reports of commissioners of Crown lands for 1849, encls in FitzRoy to Grey, 18 July 1850, C.O. 201/430.

introduced into the Legislative Council of New South Wales in June 1849 yet another bill to render the evidence of aboriginal witnesses admissible if corroborated by other testimony, Lowe ridiculed this attempt to put on a footing of equality with Europeans men whose minds could only be controlled by fear. He believed the wisest step to take was to have the blacks and the settlers fight it out between themselves so that these benighted people might be taught how immeasurably inferior they were in every respect to civilized man. Wentworth had no time for what he called such 'morbid and ill-directed sympathy with the aborigines', or any steps to put a stop to the spread of the white man's way of life over the interior. Other speakers scarcely concealed their wish that government should connive at the extermination of the aborigine. Once again the Legislative Council rejected the bill. Sections of the press accused speakers in the Council of using language which would have been more seemly in a barbarian camp than in the hall of civilized legislation.[37]

The white man was ready to drop all his hopes and his friendly gestures towards the 'helpless people'. Collisions between Europeans and aborigines leading to loss of life in the colonies of New South Wales, South Australia and Western Australia prepared the way for such a change. The aborigines in Sydney, Melbourne, Adelaide, Perth and the tiny country towns disgusted the white man by misconduct, typical not of ordinary human beings, it was said, but of 'poor wretches'. They drank and insulted respectable females in the streets and staggered back to their camps in the outskirts of the town, where they sometimes murdered helpless fellow-members of their tribes in sordid drunken fights or fell into a campfire in an alcoholic stupor. Some flock-masters shot down aborigines like kangaroos, or dosed them with arsenic as though they were dingoes. The voice of those urging the white man to take pity on such helpless creatures and win them for Christ and His Church was dropping to a whisper.

In the preceding ten years the bounty and charity the white man had bestowed on the aborigine had been withdrawn. Ever since the days of Macquarie the white man had given annual feasts for the aborigines at Parramatta. This practice was stopped by Governor Bourke in April 1835. Each year the government of New South Wales distributed blankets gratis to the aborigines in the towns. Believing a free distribution of blankets only rewarded their natural habits of indolence, Gipps in May 1838 ordered rigid economies and stopped the practice in 1844. It was revived in a modest way

---

[37] W. Westgarth, op. cit., pp. 32-3; An Ordinance to Allow the Aboriginal Inhabitants of South Australia and the Parts Adjacent, to Give Information and Evidence without the Sanction of an Oath, 7 & 8 Vic., no. 8, 12 August 1844 (amended by Ordinance no. 5, 23 July 1846, no. 3, 21 July 1848 and no. 4, 25 July 1849); An Act to Allow the Aboriginal Natives of Western Australia to Give Information and Evidence without the Sanction of an Oath, 4 & 5 Vic., no. 22, 26 November 1841 (amended by no. 7, 3 August 1843 and no. 14, 9 May 1849); A Bill to Allow the Aboriginal Natives of New South Wales to be Received as Competent Witnesses in Criminal Proceedings, *V. & P.* (L.C. N.S.W.), 1849, vol. 1, pp. 43, 58, 89; *S.M.H.*, 29, 30 June 1849.

by FitzRoy in 1848. Ever since the days of Macquarie the government of New South Wales had given badges of distinction to the chiefs of the aborigines on which were engraved their names, such as 'King Bungaree, Chief of Broken Bay Tribe' and 'Cora Gooseberry Freeman Bungaree, Queen of Sydney and Botany'. But by 1849 the days of feasts, free blankets and 'badges of merit' belonged to the past.[38]

As for the law, it was riddled with contradictions. The law solemnly pronounced the equality of white man and aborigine, but those who enforced the law always distinguished between white man and black man on such offences as vagrancy and indecent exposure. The law pronounced the aborigines to be subjects of the Queen; the officers of the law often treated them as agents of some hostile power. Some laws treated them as adults; others treated them as little children. In 1838, when Gipps was getting ready to publish that proclamation on the significance of the aborigines in the eye of the Christian God, he rushed through the Legislative Council a bill to prohibit the licensees of the inns of New South Wales serving ardent spirits to the aborigines of New South Wales. In 1840 the Legislative Council of New South Wales passed an Act to prohibit the aboriginal natives of New South Wales from having fire-arms or ammunition in their possession without the permission of a magistrate. In 1844 the Legislative Council of South Australia passed an ordinance to provide protection for half-caste and orphan children of the aborigines left destitute and without proper means of support.[39]

Faced with the evidence that the aborigines were fast diminishing in number and that the cause of this decrease and their progressive degradation was to be attributed to their partial assumption of a civilized way of life, the Chief Protector of the Aborigines in Port Phillip came up with the suggestion that one way of ensuring that there was at least some land for them 'under the soles of their feet' was to form suitable reserves for the protection of the natives in the midst of an advancing population of European settlers.

[38] *S.M.H.*, 30 June 1849; Grey to FitzRoy, 11 February 1848, *H.R.A.*, I. xxvi. 223-8; J. B. Polding to Grey, 20 November 1846, encl. in Grey to FitzRoy, 4 December 1846, *H.R.A.*, I. xxv. 281-2; Proceedings of Executive Council of New South Wales, 28 June, 8 July 1847, encl. in FitzRoy to Grey, 16 July 1847, *H.R.A.*, I. xxv. 669-70; R. H. W. Reece, 'Feasts and blankets: the history of some early attempts to establish relations with the aborigines of New South Wales, 1814-1846', *Archaeology & Physical Anthropology in Oceania*, vol. 2, 1967; W. R. Jacobs, *Diplomacy and Indian Gifts* (Stanford, 1950), p. 52; *Sydney Gazette*, 4 January 1817; Gipps to Glenelg, 31 January 1838, *H.R.A.*, I. xix. 252-8; C. Rodius, Portrait of King Bungaree (copy in M.L.); see also vol. 1, pp. 315-17, of this history.

[39] An Act for Consolidating and Amending the Laws Relating to the Licensing of Public-Houses, and for Further Regulating the Sale and Consumption of Fermented and Spirituous Liquors in New South Wales, 2 Vic., no. 18, sec. 49, 26 September 1838; An Act to Prohibit the Aboriginal Natives of New South Wales from having Fire Arms or Ammunition in their Possession, without the Permission of a Magistrate, 4 Vic., no. 8, 11 August 1840; An Ordinance to Provide for the Protection, Maintenance, and Upbringing of Orphans and other Destitute Children of the Aborigines, 7 & 8 Vic., no. 12, 28 August 1844 (S.A.); Grey to Young, 27 February, 27 November 1849, C.O. 396/7.

Grey was sceptical partly because of the necessity the settlers felt of extending their own occupation of land, partly because of the barren and inhospitable character of large tracts of the Australian soil and partly because the migratory habits of the scanty survivors of the aborigines in search of sustenance made it impracticable to confine them within a reserve. Besides, he was reluctant at the beginning of 1848 to accept the melancholy conclusion that nothing else could be done to improve the lot of 'this helpless portion of our fellow subjects'. It was of the highest importance, he told FitzRoy, that no one in power should suffer himself to be discouraged by the failure of the experiments hitherto tried. He hoped that some inducement would be found to persuade them so forcefully to remain in a state of civilization that it would tend to destroy their hitherto ineffaceable preference for the wild and roving life over the settled mode of existence of the white man.[40]

No one in public life in the Australian colonies shared his hope. At the end of 1848 La Trobe told the Colonial Secretary of New South Wales that the protectorate had totally failed to effect any of the higher and more important objects aimed at in its formation. It had exercised no good influence upon the condition of the aboriginal native, and if no such establishment had existed, the state of the aborigines would not have differed very greatly from what it was when the protectorate was established. In response to such criticism and the prevailing opinion that money spent on civilizing aborigines was a wicked waste, the Legislative Council of New South Wales appointed a select committee on 29 June 1849 to inquire into the state of the aboriginal inhabitants of the colony and more especially the success or failure of the protectorate system in Port Phillip. Relying on written replies from magistrates and some teachers at aboriginal schools, the committee came to the conclusion that the present system of protection of the aborigines had totally failed in its object. It therefore recommended the abolition of the protectorate. They were unable to recommend any other measures as a substitute. They drew attention to the great expense of £61 000 in thirteen years—£42 000 on the protectorate, £11 000 on native police, £6900 on missions and £800 on the Merri Creek School—all failures. They therefore hoped no lasting steps would be taken towards a new system until it was given mature consideration. This report strengthened FitzRoy's own decision to close the protectorate at the end of 1849. He therefore instructed La Trobe to give notice to the Chief Protector and his assistants that their offices would be abolished as from 31 December 1849.

In the other colonies the hope of civilizing the aborigines had been replaced by the more limited aims of protecting them against the European and protecting the European against them. In Van Diemen's Land, Denison still conceived it as his duty to induce the fifty-odd survivors at Oyster Cove to accept the restraints of civilization, but if they still longed for their original state of unrestricted freedom, he thought they might be allowed to resume their old habits of life without any risk to the colonists. In South Australia

[40] Grey to FitzRoy, 11 February 1848, *H.R.A.*, I. xxvi. 223-8.

the Protector, M. Moorhouse, had long given up hope of domesticating the aborigines, partly because their elders threatened them with death by sorcery if they adopted the white man's ways and partly because the aborigines preferred their own erratic liberty to what the white man offered. As a symbol of the new order in Western Australia, Governor Fitzgerald in April 1849 changed the office of Protector to Guardian of Aborigines and Protector of Settlers. In succeeding years the guardian was able to report a gradual change in the aboriginal character and disposition which led to a most welcome general freedom from aggression. Guardianship was comparatively easy; civilizing was onerous and discouraging and ended in failure.

The white man was at last resigned to the idea that 'the cumberer of the ground', the 'barbarous, unreflecting and superstitious black fellow' must be left to his primitive way of life and his own restless habits. As for his decline and the degradation and suffering inflicted on him by the invasion of his country, the white man was at times visited by anger, regret, and disgust, but not by guilt. The white man's confidence in his own righteousness was based on two propositions: the aborigine had never owned the land and it was part of the divine plan that a primitive people should disappear off the face of the earth before the onward march of an immeasurably superior power. The white man came not as a robber and a destroyer but in order that all people on this continent might have life and have it more abundantly. Those who either could not or would not share this higher phase of life must decay and die.[41]

At the same time as the white man abandoned the idea of sharing his great civilization with the aborigines of New Holland, that great son of the soil William Charles Wentworth conceived the grandiose idea of providing the native-born with an education that would equip them to run the affairs of their country. His idea was to found a university in Sydney at which the native youth of the country would obtain the education that would fit them for high places in government. These Australians and not men from abroad —the foreigners in their midst—would run their country. He wanted the gates of the university to be open to all, whether they were the disciples of Moses, Jesus, Brahmin, Mohammed, Vishnu or Buddha. He wanted the institution to cause the light of civilization to shine in every cottage. He wanted the better aspirations of the patriot and the philanthropist to glow in every heart. He saw in this measure the path opened to the child of the poor man to the highest position the country could afford him. He hoped above all that the members of the Council would cast their minds forward to that time

[41] La Trobe to Col. Sec. of New South Wales, 18 November 1848, *V. & P.* (L.C. N.S.W.), 1849, vol. 2, pp. 423-30; Report of Select Committee to Enquire into the State of the Aboriginal Inhabitants of this Colony, *V. & P.* (L.C. N.S.W.), 1849, vol. 2; FitzRoy to Grey, 12 November 1849, C.O. 201/416; minute of Executive Council of New South Wales 49/25, 11 June 1849, encl. in ibid.; E. J. B. Foxcroft, *Australian Native Policy* (Melbourne, 1940), pp. 73-8; *Western Australian Government Gazette*, 3 April 1849; speech by Denison, 20 June 1847, in *Hobart Town Courier*, 21 July 1847; C. D. Rowley, *The Destruction of Aboriginal Society* (Canberra, 1970), pp. 55-62; P. Hasluck, *Black Australians* (Melbourne, 1942), pp. 75-9.

when they ceased to be a dependency and stood amongst the nations of the world, enlightened and refined. When the hour of their deliverance drew nigh, he hoped the university would help to ensure that their nation was unstained by the torrents of blood that had marked the severance of the American colonies from the Empire. He hoped their glorious ensign of freedom would not be washed in the blood of free men, that British bayonets would never again be directed to the hearts of British subjects to compel them to a slavery that their hearts disdained. He hoped that through the means of such institutions as he was advocating a more peaceful regeneration of the liberties of mankind could be effected, that there would be no national feuds, no separation of friends, no betrayal of trusts, no breaking of hearts, no reciprocation of animosities and differences, but a multiplication of benefits and blessings. He wanted this university to enlighten the mind, to refine the understanding and to elevate the soul of their fellow-men. He hoped that from the womb of this institution there would arise a long line of illustrious names of statesmen, patriots, philanthropists, philosophers, poets and heroes, who would shed a deathless halo, not only on their country, but on the university which called them into being.

He wanted the clergy of all denominations to be excluded from the management of the institution, he wanted the university to be confined to secular instruction. He added his private belief that the higher the extent to which education was carried, the more elevated the state of morality of the colony would become. He believed too that the best mode of proving the divinity of the great Christian code was to advance the intellect of those who trusted and relied upon it. In the golden autumn of his life the one-time Byronic mocker moved towards acceptance of God's world. Other speakers on Wentworth's bill, such as James Macarthur, believed the measure would be effectually carried out by the co-operation of the various great religious communities of the colony, which would establish institutions of their own in the university in which their own peculiar doctrines would be inculcated. Outside the Council men predicted that professors who taught their students that man was descended from the monkey would disseminate atheism, which was the parent of that 'red republicanism' which was still devastating the ancient cities of Europe and threatening to destroy the foundations of European civilization.[42]

No sooner was the ink dry in FitzRoy's assent to the bill to create the University of Sydney than one of the great adventurers of the convict era left the country. On 25 October the yacht *Wanderer* with Benjamin Boyd Esq. on board went down Sydney Harbour and sailed majestically through the Heads bound for Cali-forni-a, where, as the song put it, the grass was green, and gold was to be had in such abundance that one man was said to have dug up $3000-worth in twenty-nine days. The man who had hoped to 'top a cloud' in Australia threw in his luck with a country where there were said to be

[42] *V. & P.* (L.C. N.S.W.), 4, 10, 11 October 1849; *S.M.H.*, 5, 11, 12, 20 October 1849.

huge nets to snare the unwary. There were warnings galore in the Sydney press of men dying in California of dysentery, fever and ague, and warnings that hundreds and thousands would perish there cursing the gold which seduced them into such an inhospitable country, away from their homes and friends, to die unknown amongst strangers. But the lure of glory still drove Ben Boyd out into that very vast sea where the swell coming up from the south tossed his ship as he had been tossed in life. In the eyes of the unwise it seemed then that he had left in Australia no memorial of his brief stay there except a few wattle-and-daub huts which tumbled down and became part of the dust that engulfed all men's strivings in Australia. Something lingered on: there was that eye for grandeur and that eye for beauty which led him to choose Twofold Bay, the majesty of Bibbenluke on the Bombala River, and the gaunt, eerie loveliness of Deniliquin out on the plains where the Murray glides forever towards that relentless southern sea. There was the beauty of the man which caused some to liken him to a painting by Rubens. There was that church at Twofold Bay, with its hint that this greedy slave of Mammon also drew strength from lifting up his eyes unto the hills. That October no one played a drum for Ben Boyd as the bow of the *Wanderer* dipped into one of those curlers which had cracked and boomed and tossed their spray on the rocks at South Head since the beginning of time.[43]

Nor did many grieve when ill-health persuaded that other 'migratory bird' Robert Lowe that the time had come for him to return to his native land. Lowe was one of those men who had never shared the Wentworth or the Harpur vision of a day of glory for the sons of Australia. Only a few friends accompanied the former tribune of the people and his wife to the landing barge on 27 January 1850. As the 'white haired boy' moved off towards the ship, which would carry him back to the land of a full-blown civilization and away from the 'belly-full' vulgarians, no one even managed a cheer or a cry of 'God bless you'. As the cabbage-tree boys and Wentworth and Bob Nichols were not slow to point out, the man's handshake was as cold as a fish, and the man himself composed of so much head and so little heart that he was never motivated by a single generous or noble impulse.

One generation was passing away. On 9 February 1850 Elizabeth Macarthur died at Camden Park. She was then in her eighty-third year. Her sons William and James, who had a deep admiration and affection for her, bore her body to that hill where her husband John had been buried. Unlike her husband, who had lived and died in the faith of an old Roman stoic, she believed all her life that when she died she would be 'gathered into the fold'. For she had loved God's world. She had loved men like Sam Marsden because he, like her husband, though wayward and vagrant and not always

[43] *People's Advocate*, 27 October 1849; *S.M.H.*, 28 June, 16 November 1849; C. Nicholson to A. Cunningham, 12 February 1851 (Cunningham Papers, vol. 3, MS. in M.L.); *S.M.H.*, 10, 12, 27 November 1849; *Bell's Life in Sydney*, 26 January, 2 February 1850; Ruth Knight, *Illiberal Liberal: Robert Lowe in New South Wales 1842-1850* (Melbourne, 1966), pp. 249-51.

in his right mind, was warm of heart. It was sixteen years since the fountain of her eyes had flowed so freely when her husband had died. Just before she died, there were signs that the democracy that her beloved husband had so dreaded, and against which her sons James, William and Edward, the one-time hero of Waterloo, her son-in-law William Bowman, dear old Alexander McLeay, Charles Sturt, and Ludwig Leichhardt, had pitted their strength, was raising its ugly head in the town of Sydney.

Between the last hour of the old year 1849 and the dawn of the new year in Sydney many of the citizens were startled from their slumber by the yells of a set of demons in human form, and the pelting of stones and brick-bats through their windows. These were not mobs goaded to madness by starvation, nor were they mobs fired with political disaffection, but rather mobs of giddy boys rioting for rioting's sake, for whom midnight violence was an amusing pastime. Wentworth was convinced that such riot sprang from the inflammatory rubbish published each week in the *People's Advocate*, but others said sixty summers were beginning to take such a toll on the son of the soil that the river of life was beginning to pass him by. Large parties of boys, all strangers to the fear of God and lacking any reverence for the mystery at the heart of things, gathered outside the churches of Sydney on Sunday evenings and blew smoke into the eyes of the worshippers as they left the church. In Newcastle, Sydney, Hobart, Launceston and Brisbane ticket-of-leave men lay about in the streets in the evening in a beastly state of intoxication, vomiting in the gutters, putting their hands up ladies' dresses and boasting all too loudly that Australia was a convict's country on which they and those who came after them would impose the way of life beloved of the thieves of the United Kingdom—a life of riot, debauchery and idleness.[44]

Squatters were threatening separation and a plantation-style republic if they did not get convicts: the petty bourgeois radicals like Parkes, Hawksley and Charles Harpur behind the *People's Advocate* were threatening independence and a Yankee-type republic if the British Government sent any more convicts or did not give the 'elective franchise', as they called it, at least to all male householders or, better still, to all males, excluding, of course, aborigines, of the age of twenty-one years and over. The 'cabbage-tree mob' in Sydney, Parramatta and Newcastle, and all the 'old hands' and the itinerant workers, who hung around Lazy Harry's down at Gundagai, Brown's Pub at Sleepy Hollow (Albury) or Bob's Pub at Dubbo, or gathered for a yarn in a bush hut in the wilds of Australia, sometimes dreamed of what the natives of Erin's Isle and the natives of Scotland and of England's green and pleasant land would make of this southern land of theirs.

All through 1849 a bewildering variety of opinion flowed onto the desk of Earl Grey in London as he tried to make up his mind on the future constitu-

[44] On death of Elizabeth Macarthur see *S.M.H.*, 16 February 1850; Elizabeth Macarthur to William Macarthur, 18 March 1841 (Macarthur Papers, vol. 21); M. H. Ellis, *John Macarthur* (Sydney, 1955), p. 531; tombstone of Elizabeth Macarthur at Camden Park; *S.M.H.*, 17, 19, 20, 22 December 1849, 12, 15, 16 January 1850.

tion of the Australian colonies. The writers in the *People's Advocate* urged
an extension of the elective franchise: Sir Charles FitzRoy felt it was his duty
to tell Grey that in the present social state of the colony he was not prepared
to recommend any extension of the elective franchise. Sir William Denison told
Grey that when he considered the elements of which society in Van Diemen's
Land was composed, when he saw the low estimate that was placed upon
everything that could distinguish a man from his fellows, with the sole
exception of wealth, it would hardly be a subject of surprise that so few were
found who rose above the general level, or that those few owed more to the
possession of a certain oratorical facility than to their powers of mind or
the justness of the opinions they advocated. As in America, he told Grey that
the broad plain of equality pervaded the whole of the community. Although
there were many who would gladly avail themselves of any opportunity of
raising themselves above the general level, here, as in America, any attempt to
do so would be frustrated by the jealousy of the remainder of the community.
An essentially democratic spirit activated the large mass of the community.
To check the development of this spirit he suggested the formation of an
Upper Chamber. Alexander Cunningham, the spokesman for the Port
Phillip separation movement in London, put the case for a colonial aristocracy
as a counter to the egalitarian materialism of the colonists of Australia Felix.
The press of Hobart Town said an aristocracy was all poppycock. What they
wanted was their constitutional freedom and not any constitutional device
that might lead to their slavery.

In South Australia J. H. Morphett also suggested an aristocracy as the one
way to preserve the two essential features of government—liberty and stability.
When the local egalitarians howled him down, he withdrew the suggestion,
taking the opportunity to stress that he had not met people in South Australia
worthy of being dukes or marquises. Others in that colony argued that as
such a high proportion of the population had a stake in the colony, either as
freeholders or leaseholders, that manhood suffrage could be conceded in the
new constitution without the slightest threat to the rights of private property.
Others again pleaded with Grey not to create an elective general assembly
since the physical features of the different colonies of Australia were totally
dissimilar, and the habits, views, and feelings of the people were opposed to
each other. They would also object to such an Assembly, because the relative
proportions of inhabitants were such that their colony would practically have
no effective voice in deciding the questions brought under the consideration
of the Assembly. They were quite confident that those revolutions in Europe
in which the institution of private property had been attacked would be most
unlikely to erupt in South Australia because they did not have a propertyless
class of ex-convicts, but a strong middle class, and a working class who could
see the chance of becoming property owners. The European revolutionaries
had denied God, and so taken away that best part of man and reduced him to
the level of the beasts that perished. Men imbued with these principles must
regard all who stood in their way as noxious vermin, to be exterminated by

the speediest method. Those scenes of horror such as happened in Paris would never occur in South Australia, because their belief in God stood between them and the law of the jungle.[45]

Grey also had before him an expression of loyalty to Her Most Excellent Majesty from her most dutiful and loyal subjects at Port Phillip, and an expression of gratitude that they were about to receive a liberal form of constitution which accorded with the enlightened spirit of the age and was worthy of the great nation from which they were proud to claim descent. He also had a most respectful request to grant them speedy separation from New South Wales so that they might have roads, bridges, wharves, improved harbours, and better-formed and better-drained streets. He had a humble prayer to Her Majesty to command her ministers to prepare and lay before parliament a bill for the separation of Port Phillip from the province of New South Wales, and its erection into a separate colony to be called Victoria, to be governed according to the constitution now in force in New South Wales.[46]

The Governor, the members of the Executive and Legislative Councils and the settlers of Western Australia told him that if they had to choose between free institutions and convicts, they wanted convicts. Early in 1849 Governor Fitzgerald informed Grey that if Her Majesty's Government wished to establish another penal settlement in Australia, the majority of the inhabitants of his colony would gladly learn that Western Australia had been chosen as the site. When Grey wrote on 5 January 1850 to say that approximately 150 convicts would be sent off in the first ship available, Fitzgerald greeted the news as a promise that the day was not far distant when civilization would win the victory over barbarism in Western Australia.[47]

By contrast, from Van Diemen's Land came news that more and more influential people were coming around to the view that it was better to have the institutions of the free than the material benefits of cheap convict labour. On 20 December 1849, at a large and highly respectable meeting in the Cornwall Hotel in Launceston, speaker after speaker warned against the great calamity of resuming transportation, and the vile and unfounded calumnies to which the colonists were exposed so long as they were deprived

---

[45] *People's Advocate*, 16 June 1849; *Freeman's Journal*, 26 September 1850; FitzRoy to Grey, 27 February 1849, C.O. 201/411; Denison to Grey, 15 March 1848, C.O. 280/226; *Hobart Town Courier*, 30 January 1850; *South Australian Register*, 15 December 1849; Resolutions of the Legislative Council of South Australia, 14 November 1849; *South Australian Government Gazette*, 15 November 1849; A. Boyd to Grey, 27 June 1849, C.O. 201/424; Grey to Denison, 15 March 1848, C.O. 408/30; Denison to Grey, 25 September 1849, C.O. 280/247; Denison to Grey, 28 December 1849, C.O. 280/249; *South Australian Register*, 9 May 1849.

[46] The Humble Petition of the Burgesses of Geelong, and the Petition of the Colonists of the District of Port Phillip, Colony of New South Wales, encls in FitzRoy to Grey, 14 February 1850, and FitzRoy to Grey, 22 February 1850, C.O. 201/426; FitzRoy to Grey, 8 January 1850, C.O. 201/426.

[47] Fitzgerald to Grey, 3 March 1849, C.O. 18/50; Grey to Fitzgerald, 12 July 1849, C.O. 397/9; Grey to Fitzgerald, 5 January 1850, C.O. 397/9.

of free institutions. On 30 January 1850 the hall of the mechanics' institute in Hobart Town was filled to suffocation as T. F. Gregson repeated the point made in Launceston about the heavy calamity of not having the institutions of the free, and their deepest anxiety lest their rights as British subjects should be again sacrificed to the schemes of the Colonial Office for the disposal of convicts. One-time supporters of convict labour now stood on public platforms with tears rolling down their cheeks as an expiation for past offences and vowed they would never again let one of those human monsters put his filthy paws on their wives or their children.[48]

When the *Neptune* arrived in the River Derwent on 5 April with 282 male prisoners on board, these convicts brazenly asked the highest figure for their labour. Once again the 'rejected of the whole universe' were being poured into Van Diemen's Land. Cape Colony had rejected them, so had New South Wales, New Zealand, South Australia and Port Phillip. Yet Van Diemen's Land had to put up with men of such sordid spirit, such gross immorality and such social worthlessness who debased labour, robbed the poor man's child of his bread, filled the towns with thieves and prostitutes and prepared a scourge and a curse for future years. To add insult to such grave moral injury the *Neptune* had on board one convict who was certain to strengthen that colony's reputation for infamy in the eyes of all men of good will in the civilized world. The man was John Mitchel who had been arraigned before the Queen's Bench in Dublin on 17 May 1848 for writing articles in the *United Irishman* of 6 and 13 May 1848, the object of which was to devise the deposing of our Most Gracious Sovereign Lady the Queen from the high honour and royal name of the Imperial Crown of the United Kingdom, and was sentenced to transportation for fourteen years. He saw himself as a man who had promulgated doctrines of a democratic and revolutionary kind on the rights of tenant farmers, labourers and artisans. Born in County Derry on 3 November 1815, the son of a Presbyterian minister, in the eyes of the world he was a cultivated, high-minded, passionate man, who believed in God and looked for the resurrection of the dead and the life of the world to come. He was treated as a common convict, obliged to sleep with every species of scoundrel and to work in a gang from six o'clock in the morning to six o'clock in the evening. Being all the while next to starved, he was kept alive by the strength he derived from reading the words of Thomas à Kempis, and the thought that the example of his sufferings might help others to keep out of the clutches of such demons. One of the truest and noblest of mankind, he was exposed to the petty malignity and vindictiveness of an English Lieutenant-Governor who was not renowned for generosity of spirit, and prison officials who seemed to take a fiendish delight in rubbing salt in the wounds of a man who was great of heart.[49]

[48] *Hobart Town Courier*, 29 December 1849, 1, 2 February 1850.
[49] *Hobart Town Courier*, 6, 10, 17 April 1850; *Cork Examiner*, 24 October, 29 December 1851; *Tipperary Vindicator*, 20, 24-27 May, 2, 3, 7, 14, 21 June 1848; *Irish Tribune*, 10 June 1848; J. H. Cullen, *Young Ireland in Exile* (Dublin, 1928), pp. 78,

At the same time as the press of Melbourne and Adelaide screamed, 'Didn't I tell you so?' the press in Perth was reporting an increase in crime since the arrival of the first convicts in the *Scindian*. The ticket-of-leave men were also corrupting free men and women and congregating at dusk on street corners, much like the cabbage-tree men of Sydney, asking respectable maidens such suggestive questions as whether they had the time and, if so, whether they had the inclination, and generally behaving in that overbearing, threatening way of the Australian when offended or incensed at being treated as a social inferior. The respectable matrons of Perth were beginning to understand why their counterparts in Hobart, Launceston, Melbourne, Adelaide and Sydney had petitioned Her Gracious Majesty to instruct the ministers to protect the morals of Australian women by sending no more convicts to Australia. The men of Western Australia who had sent for convicts to save them from the humiliation of handing one-third of Australia back to the aborigines stead-fastly refused to join the 'liberty and morality' men in the eastern colonies. They were only too happy to allow convicts to mummify their society into one distinguished for its 'gentility' and 'loyalty', while the eastern colonies prepared for the great change when the machine gave men the power to print their mark on a land of iron.[50]

In London, Grey, whose attitudes still combined the principles of grocer-dom and the arrogance of superior knowledge, was not yet sure that the Australian colonies did not want convicts. By the beginning of 1850 he doubted very much whether the opinion of the colonists was so much against trans-portation as was supposed. Real public opinion, as he put it, using one of his favourite elitist phrases, was not always to be gathered from clamour and the newspaper press. What he had in mind was an item of information he had received from Sir Charles FitzRoy. After the abolitionists had insulted FitzRoy at the second protest meeting on 18 June 1849, over fifteen hundred names were inserted in the visiting book at Government House by 'Ladies and Gentlemen of the society received as guests at the Government house, in token of their respect' for FitzRoy and their disapprobation of the insulting behaviour by the abolitionists. Archibald Boyd, who was in London as a spokesman for the Pastoral Association, had told him in October 1849 that the arrival of convicts from England was in the highest degree grateful and beneficial to 'the most important portion of the Australian community'.

From Ipswich and the Darling Downs, F. Bigge informed him that all the northern districts urgently required labour; their flocks and herds were increasing and it was impossible to get labour to tend them. Bigge also told

130-1; C. G. Duffy, *Four Years of Irish History, 1845-1849* (London, 1883); J. Mitchel, *Jail Journal* (New York, 1854), pp. 279, 342; epitaph on tombstone of John Mitchel (Sen.), Newry; epitaph on tombstone in memory of John Mitchel (Jun,), 'After twenty seven years spent in exile for the sake of Ireland he returned in honour to die among his own people, and he rests with his father and mother in the adjoining tomb', died 20 March 1875; private visit to Newry, 24 May 1964; T. J. Kiernan, A Convict Newspaper in Tasmania (MS. in author's possession).
[50] *Inquirer* (Perth), 18 September, 9 October, 25 December 1850.

him that he would rather have the pick of the gaols than the refuse of the work-houses, and begged him not to take any notice of those 'dirty Brisbane-ites' with all their moral twaddle about pollution. Others from the same district were telling him that if they could not get convicts they would send for Chinese, but they wanted him to know that, like that grand old gentleman, Patrick Leslie, they all wanted 'men of their own colour'. From Portland the squatters were crying out for convict labour, though it was true that Edward Henty through his business connections in Launceston had been converted to the abolitionist cause by such 'holier than thou' moral prigs as John West and Henry Dowling. Like most squatters in the district, Samuel Pratt Winter, who went in for all the bizarre trappings of a gentleman, with liveried ser-vants, groomsmen and thoroughbred horses, desperately wanted convicts to keep his show going at The Grange (Hamilton).

In Van Diemen's Land there was a formidable list of 'the best people' in favour of transportation. There was the Lieutenant-Governor for a start, loyally supported by his wife; there was Chief Justice Pedder who was quite incapable of seeing Van Diemen's Land as anything but a terror to the evil-doers of the United Kingdom; there were prominent men like W. R. Allison and the Bishop of the Catholic Church Robert Willson. Then there was that great army of dependants on the convict system—all the civil and military officers and non-commissioned officers and privates and commissariat officials, and businessmen with contracts to supply goods to the convict department, and chaplains (civil servants in gaolers' cassocks), and the wives and the children of all these men. In April 1850 Grey rose in the House of Lords and told their lordships that Her Majesty's Government had come to the conclusion that opposition to transportation was calming down and, come what may, both Van Diemen's Land and New South Wales must continue to receive convicts.[51]

When the news of this speech reached Van Diemen's Land at the beginning of August 1850 the liberty and morality men flew into a great rage. At a public meeting in the Cornwall Hotel on 9 August, called to ensure the abolition of transportation to the island at once and forever, everyone agreed that the only way to ensure this was for people to pledge themselves solemnly never to employ convicts, never to work with convicts and in general never to have anything to do with convicts. Henry Dowling was pretty confident that tradesmen would participate without treachery, backsliding, or resort to any of those subterfuges by which the sanctimonious attempt to conceal their enslavement to Mammon. He was by no means certain that abolitionists could count on those squires of Clarendon, Woolmers, Panshanger, Mount

[51] Earl Grey, *The Colonial Policy of Lord John Russell's Administration* (2 vols, London, 1853), vol. 2, pp. 80-3; Speech by Earl Grey in House of Lords, 22 March 1850, *P.D.*, 1850, vol. 109, cols 852-80; FitzRoy to Grey, 30 September 1850, C.O. 201/431; A. Boyd to Grey, 29 October 1849, C.O. 201/424; report of meeting of squatters at Ipswich, 10 January 1850, *S.M.H.*, 23 January 1850; Grey to FitzRoy, 16 November 1849, C.O. 202/56.

Ireh, or the pleasure-lovers like Dicky Dry. John West, looking fierce as had the prophets of old when they threatened drunkards that they would be drowned in their own vomit, and tying the ends of his handkerchief into knots, called on them to end once and for all this 'servile bondage', to renounce all questions of present gain and to join with him and others of like mind in rescuing their country from ruin and their children from destruction. They all resolved that from that day on no person would employ prison labour, that after 10 September every prisoner would be returned to government, that anyone who refused to comply with these decisions was to be considered to be an enemy of the public weal, that banks, insurance companies and other public institutions should pledge themselves not to transact business with any persons employing convicts, that butchers, bakers and other tradesmen should refuse to contract with the government to supply their goods to convicts, and that no minister of religion should hold communion with any convict.[52]

As the catty, witty, scurrilous editor of the *Cornwall Chronicle* put it on 17 August, it was all very well for this Anti-Transportation League to 'vomit forth their puny splutterings of armed resistance' and recommend to the people to resist the landing of convicts, but everyone knew that the men who shed tears of remorse about having once exploited convict labour were still busy hiring convicts as fast as they could. If they meant what they said, let them publish lists of the numbers of convicts they were employing and then return them to government. Let the Lieutenant-Governor publish in the *Government Gazette* the names of probation employers, and the numbers in their employ. Besides, these anti-transportationists were guilty of a great crime against their country: the crime of proclaiming to the civilized world that their colony was unfit for the habitation of man.[53]

On 12 September the liberty and morality men crowded into the Victoria Theatre in Hobart Town to petition against transportation and to form a league against the employment of prisoners. Again and again all the high-minded men present, led by the clergymen, thundered against the evils of transportation. But, as the *Hobarton Guardian* pointed out with heavy sarcasm, to cry down transportation and still go on employing its victims was humbug. Immaculate biblical gentlemen who spoke the patois of the self-elected upper classes of Van Diemen's Land had the brazen effrontery to ask, through tears, 'who among you would leave his children with a prisoner female', when everyone was aware that the man who had put the question knew full well that at that very moment his own children were being looked after by one of those unfortunates against whom he was then raising his mighty voice. In using such language as 'scum', 'pollution', 'trash' and 'depravity' these biblical gentlemen and their strange partners—the fox-hunters and one-time convict baiters such as Thomas Gregson—were besmirching and degrading four-fifths of the population of the island.

It was high time that someone ripped the mask of moral indignation from

[52] *Hobarton Guardian*, 15 August 1850.
[53] *Cornwall Chronicle*, 10, 14, 17, 21 August 1850.

the face of the abolitionists and exposed their sordid selfishness and their loathing for the prisoner population. That unctuous John West, with his ridiculous countenance and all his spirituality, his Protestant cheerfulness and his buffoonery, should be shown up for what he was—a gentleman in the lying line who was prostituting the image of Christ to help the men from 'the swell mob' to go on doing what they had always been doing, namely, filling their pockets. Since the publication of the first number of the *Irish Exile and Freedom's Advocate* on 26 January 1850 the editor, Patrick O'Donohoe, one of those Irish political prisoners who had been sentenced to be hanged, drawn and quartered for wanting to end the wrongs and sufferings of the Irish people, had been having a go at the 'leering eyes' of the Protestant ascendancy in Van Diemen's Land. Since August 1850 the Reverend William Bailey, an Anglican convert to Rome and editor of the *Hobarton Guardian*, had been warning the convict and ex-convict working classes of Van Diemen's Land that an attempt was being made by the once heartless traders in human flesh and blood to disenfranchise them as citizens. He reminded them that the country by right was theirs alone and did not belong to those who had 'but too frequently dipped their hands in their pockets and in their blood'. He called on the working classes not to allow 'the swell mob' to give their country a name for infamy which it would take centuries to wash away. He told them to stop listening to these hypocrites who swore they would not have an abandoned woman in their home when everyone in Hobart knew no human beings loved 'horizontal refreshment' with abandoned women more than preachers. If these abolitionists were allowed to go on calling their fellow-men 'wolves, and tigers, crocodiles and bears', who were destitute of all feeling except a loyalty to their own class, a terrible hatred would be stirred up in Van Diemen's Land that would last down the ages, and kindle on both sides the basest passions of human nature. As the *Irish Exile* put it, 'in the fresh scenes of a young democratic nation's germing hopes, it is miserable to see . . . ghosts of old distinctions . . . stalking about in all the frippery of ruffles and point-lace, the faded ideas of lackey reminiscences'. The drums of social revolution were beating faintly in Hobart Town. The working classes and their sympathizers formed the Tasmanian Union to see that when the colonists won their free institutions there were equal laws and equal rights for all. The transportation question threatened to develop into a class war. Radicals were talking of all men being created equal and of the capacity of the people to deliver a death blow to invidious distinctions. They were warning the 'swells' of Van Diemen's Land that they were no longer to call the working classes the 'scum of the earth' or 'putrid manure'. The working classes were beginning to talk of the island as belonging to them, and of their destiny to raise its people from infamy to manhood.[54]

---

[54] *Hobarton Guardian*, 7 September 1850; *Irish Exile and Freedom's Advocate*, 26 January 1850; *Hobarton Guardian*, 14, 28 September, 19 October 1850, 15 January 1851; *Cornwall Chronicle*, 14 September 1850; *Irish Exile*, 5 October 1850.

In Sydney, Grey's words in the House of Lords provoked similar threats and tensions. Early in September 1850, the *People's Advocate* threatened that the miserable squatters who were waxing fat on felon blood would drive the colony to rebellion. Since 27 June 1850 the *Freeman's Journal*, which was modelled on its namesake in Dublin, its pages filled with much of the prudery and puritanism of Catholic Ireland and slogans about the love of God and one's neighbour, called on the colonists to mop up the remnants of their penal condition and extend the franchise. Behind the *Freeman's Journal* was Father John McEncroe, a Tipperary man who believed that the Anglo-Saxon barbarians were now about to commit another unlovely and ungracious thing and reconvert New South Wales into a human sewer. He had come to New South Wales in 1832 and had served on Norfolk Island from 1838 to 1842. God had given him a great cross to bear. From time to time he was overwhelmed with a sense of being abandoned by God, a terrible melancholy, a peculiar twitching of the corners of the mouth, and such an uncontrollable longing for drink that he would implore his friends for the love of God to pour light wine down his throat until he lost consciousness in a drunken stupor. Then, overwhelmed with remorse, he asked the Holy Mother of God to give him the strength not to fall again. He stood up regularly at meetings of the Total Abstinence Society in Sydney with the busts of Robert Emmett and Daniel O'Connell on each side of him, and a banner with the emblem of a harp behind him, and told side-splitting jokes, and sang 'Oft in the Stilly Night', and talked as though if he were God he would forgive everyone. He had the face of a man ravaged by a terrible infirmity and the haunted look of a man who had fought a long hard fight with his adversary the Devil. Despite the fears of the Botany Bay Tories, McEncroe was after no earthly prize.[55]

Nor was Jabez King Heydon. He arrived in Sydney in 1838 as a free migrant, a family man and a staunch Wesleyan. In 1845 he was received into the Catholic Church. In the eyes of Polding and the Botany Bay Tories he was a man of low origin and social position who was threatening the foundation of society. In fact he was closely associated with movements such as temperance, mechanics' institute and a people's library which were designed to promote peace and order rather than riot and turbulence. He wanted to abolish caste rather than class. He shared with the men of goodwill in the Constitutional Association the opinion that the time had come to stop gazing on the serpent of caste which threatened to hold him and other ambitious men in subjection forever. Like Parkes, Hipkiss, Macdermott and others he saw that caste stood between them and their advancement in New South

[55] Speech by Grey on 3rd Reading of Convict Prisons Bill, House of Lords, 12 April 1850, *P.D.*, 1850, vol. 110, cols 205-18; *People's Advocate*, 7 September 1850; *Freeman's Journal*, 27 June 1850; J. McEncroe, *The Wanderings of the Human Mind* (Sydney, 1841); McEncroe Papers, St Mary's Archives, Sydney; J. G. O'Connor, *An Account of the Life & Missionary Labours of the Late Venerable Archdeacon McEncroe* (Sydney, 1868); *People's Advocate*, 30 December 1848; *Australasian Chronicle*, 2 June 1842; Diary of Andrew Byrne (MS. in S.A.S.A.).

Wales. He believed that convict labour was being used to preserve caste. That was why he shouted himself hoarse on 11 June 1849 when Robert Lowe called on them to capsize the cargo of human filth on the *Hashemy* into Sydney Harbour. He also believed that an extension of the franchise would end the domination of caste in the Legislative Council. Although as a businessman, he put his name to an advertisement for Holloway's Pills which promised a 'cure for ague, asthma, bilious complaints, blotches on the skin, bowel complaints, constipation, debility, female irregularities, fevers of all kinds, fits, gout, rheumatism, retention of urine, tumours, turn of life, ulcers, venereal affections, worms of all kinds, weaknesses from whatever causes &c &c', he was too much under the influence of the Judaico-Christian persuasion to believe any such nonsense about human society. But transportation was a different thing: that stood between him and what he wanted. So when he heard about the Grey speech he was ready to join with his colleagues in the Constitutional Association in what was for them the great cause of the human race.[56]

There was also John Dunmore Lang, who had returned to Sydney at the end of 1849. Before 1847 Lang was known as a man of unfathomable malevolence towards his enemies, a man who spewed out the politics of the Orange Lodge and engaged in monstrous attacks on saintly women such as Caroline Chisholm. He was just as severe on his fellow-ministers as on Catholic priests and Episcopalians whom he referred to as 'four Judas Iscariots and eight full-grown specimens of contemptible shuffling and drivelling'. In politics he had always been thought of as a crack-pot millenarian who did not stand on any entrenched ground, held no firm opinions and got only a subterranean, fiendish satisfaction out of denouncing anyone who stood in his way. The one redeeming human quality he had displayed, over and above his courage, his superhuman energy and his great verbal gift, was his love for his wife. He seemed to have prostituted the great gifts God had lavished on him in frenzied denunciations of the wickedness of mankind.

Now Lang had found a new theme. In April 1850 he gave a course of lectures in Sydney in which he advocated a republic for Australia. During his last trip to England and Scotland he had become a convert to the six points of the Charter and had announced his new faith in a series of letters to the *British Banner*. After his return to Sydney there were two Langs. There was the old Lang who accused a devotee of the papacy of selecting Catholics from the most thoroughly romish and bigoted parts of Ireland as free emigrants for Australia expressly with the view of their becoming the wives of the English and Scottish Protestant shepherds and stockmen of New South Wales, and thereby silently subverting the Protestantism and extending the Romanism of the colony through the vile, Jesuitical, diabolical system of

---

[56] Papers of J. K. Heydon (in private possession of Lady Heydon, Canberra); J. B. Polding to Cardinal Prefect of Propaganda, probably written in 1859 (Polding Papers, Catholic Archives, Sydney); T. L. Suttor, *Hierarchy and Democracy in Australia* (Melbourne, 1965), pp. 171-85; advertisement for Holloway's Pills by J. K. Heydon in *People's Advocate*, 20 July 1850.

'mixed marriages'. And there was the new Lang who uttered the 'menacing monition' that by his convict policy Earl Grey had prepared the way for the 'United States of Australia'.[57]

He was not the only one to use the language of 'menacing monition'. The *People's Advocate* said the question now was whether New South Wales was to remain a colony of Great Britain. Wentworth warned the people of Sydney against 'mobs' and 'tumult'. The *People's Advocate* countered by warning the people against Wentworth's 'besottedness', and jeered at him as the 'Norfolk Island Patriot . . . this same William Crawley Wentworth' (an unkind dig at his convict mother) who spoke like a drunken maniac for 'dunghill oligarchs' in the days of his 'contemptible dotage'. It looked as though there was to be a show-down between the 'dunghill oligarchs' and the petty bourgeois radicals of Sydney.

With tension mounting and tempers rising, over six thousand persons gathered in the Barrack Square on 16 September to demand the revocation of the Order in Council naming New South Wales as a place to which convicts could be sent. Charles Cowper was in the chair. He and the Reverend Mr Ross opened the meeting by using the language of the moralizers to denounce the sordid-minded men who worshipped golden idols. Father McEncroe asked them whether they wanted to be free men or slaves. Lang told them that if they did not want to be lickspittles and slaves, they must strike for their freedom and independence. England was in no position to retake the colony by force of arms. If England persisted in transporting convicts, he would haul down the glorious flag of England and unfurl the flag of an Australian republic. There were no cries of horror, no cries of protest, only immense cheering. A revolutionary fire was flicking around the edges of the meeting.

Then the moderates moved in to save the day. Thomas Mort, a wool broker and, like Cowper, a great believer in all that the venerable Church of England had to say about order, obedience and hierarchy, moved that they agree to form the New South Wales Association for Preventing the Revival of Transportation. He also moved that such an association be not dissolved until the transportation question was finally settled, for he feared, and so did Cowper, John Lamb and all the other moderates, that unless the British Government abolished transportation and extended the franchise the chairman's table at public meetings would be draped not with the Union Jack but with the flag of the Southern Cross. Those sons of the soil who had so far kept quiet on the convict question because they were not going to insult or defame their families, would say once again that the country was *theirs*, and all British philistines could go to 'bloody Hell'.[58]

On 27 September John Lamb asked the Legislative Council to resolve that

[57] Letters of J. D. Lang to *British Banner*, 12 July 1848 to 13 November 1849, and letter by J. D. Lang to *Lloyd's Weekly Newspaper*, 25 November 1849, copies presented to author by Margaret Kiddle in token of a long friendship.

[58] *People's Advocate*, 7, 21 September 1850; *Freeman's Journal*, 19, 26 September 1850; *S.M.H.*, 18 September 1850.

no more convicts, under any conditions, be sent to any part of New South Wales, that Her Majesty be asked to revoke the Order in Council naming New South Wales as a place to which offenders might be sent, and that His Excellency the Governor be asked to forward these requests to London with the recommendation that the prayer of this Council might be acceded to with the least possible delay. James Martin and James Macarthur pushed their chests out and said that they were not men to bow before any popular clamour. They had their pride. Henry Dangar could not understand why parsons had so forgotten their station in life as to take part in politics. Australia's greatest native son, William Charles Wentworth, his face bearing the signs of that majesty which descends on a man when he knows that all he had ever stood for was doomed, rose to his feet. No one knew whether he would use the occasion for yet another magnificent display of his invective against sanctimonious parsons, or some brilliant Rabelaisian witticism about what my lord Hamlet called 'country matters'. He walked out of the Council chamber without saying a word and set out for Vaucluse House where he was surrounded with all those examples of the great civilization he believed was about to be inundated by the levelling flood of bourgeois civilization. On 1 October the Legislative Council passed the resolution calling on the British Government to revoke the Order in Council. There was no need now to tear down the Union Jack and unfurl the Australian flag. In great haste FitzRoy wrote off to Grey to implore him to do something quickly about the convict question, or designing and disaffected persons would instil sentiments of disloyalty into the minds of the people and turn them against their Mother Country. But by then as the *Sydney Morning Herald* realized, that nightmare had disappeared. The Legislative Council of New South Wales had set a seal on the Magna Carta of the moral and political liberties of New South Wales.[59]

On the same day as the Legislative Council dealt its death blow to convictism in New South Wales the five bishops of the Church of England in Australia and the Bishop of New Zealand gathered in Sydney to discuss matters of common concern. Their lordships offered their unfeigned thankfulness to Almighty God for the gift and preservation of the faith of the Church of England, and reminded each other that personal repentance and faith were the only sure evidence men had that they were indeed the children of God. They had much to say about education: they were not prepared to incur the responsibility of seeming to countenance any system of erroneous, defective or indefinite religious instruction. Bishop Perry told them that if the Gospel of Jesus Christ was true, it must be a heinous crime for government to pay money to a synagogue where the people called Christ 'that deceiver'. He also said, as he was to say many times again, that if popery was a soul-ruining delusion, and the Pope a man of sin, the endowment of the priests of this system with monies, houses or lands must be a heinously guilty deed.

[59] *People's Advocate*, 28 September, 5 October 1850; *V. & P.* (L.C. N.S.W.), 27 September, 1 October 1850.

Their lordships also spoke of their hopes for the conversion and civilization of the aborigines and of the heathen races of all the islands of the southern Pacific, but they were troubled by the low state of barbarism and the unsettled habits of the race, and thought perhaps the only thing to do was to civilize a select number and then keep them at a distance from the members of their own tribe.[60]

While Broughton was warning his fellow-bishops to be on their guard against the 'zealots of a wild excess of private judgment' and the dagger the Church of Rome pointed at the throat of the Church of England, the men who took an interest in the things of this world had a great load lifted off their hearts. Fears of an imminent clash between the petty bourgeois radicals and the dunghill oligarchs suddenly evaporated. On 3 October, just two days after the Legislative Council had settled the great and important question of transportation, there was again glorious and most important news to gladden the heart of every friend of British freedom and the British connection. Under the Australian Colonies Government Act of 1850 the elective franchise had been granted to the £10 householder. The aristocratic legislators in the Imperial Parliament had realized in the nick of time that the only safeguard against 'democratic' turbulence and 'red republicanism' was to be found in the admission of the populous masses to a fair and well-regulated share in making the laws. Once again a 'prolific source' of revolution had been dried up by the English genius for compromise, or the policy of the embrace of moderates and the isolation of revolutionaries by the established order.[61]

In January 1849 Grey asked a committee of Her Majesty's Privy Council for Trade and Plantations to report on what should be in the future bill for the government of the Australian colonies. They said the time had not yet arrived for conferring the franchise on the colonists of Western Australia because they were unable to sustain the expense of their own civil government by means of local revenue. The colonies of South Australia and Van Diemen's Land being at once willing and able to provide by local resources for the public expenditure of each, or at least so much of that expenditure as was incurred by local objects, the time had arrived when those two colonies could have a legislature in which the representatives of the people at large should enjoy and exercise their constitutional authority. They went on to advise that parliament be authorized to divide New South Wales into a northern and a southern province, Sydney to be the capital of the northern which was to retain the name of New South Wales, and Melbourne to be the capital of the southern division on which they humbly advised that Her Majesty should be graciously pleased to confer the name of Victoria. The

[60] *Minutes of Proceedings at a Meeting of the Metropolitan and Suffragan Bishops of the Province of Australasia* (Sydney, 1850); C. Perry, Journal of the Meeting of Bishops at Sydney 1 October 1850 (Melbourne Diocesan Archives); for another example of Broughton's obsession with the 'dagger' pointing from Rome, see W. G. Broughton, *A Letter to the Right Rev. Nicholas Wiseman, D.D.* (Sydney, 1850).

[61] J. Bonwick, *Curious Facts of Old Colonial Days* (London, 1870), p. 55; *Freeman's Journal*, 3 October 1850.

boundary between the two should commence at Cape Howe, pursue a straight line to the nearest source of the River Murray, and follow the course of that river as far as the boundary between New South Wales and South Australia. If unfettered in their judgement, they would have recommended a constitution in each of the four colonies of a governor, a council and an assembly, but the past in Australia forced them to build on what existed. They therefore recommended a single house of legislature in each of the four, one-third of which was to be nominated by Her Majesty and the remaining two-thirds elected by the colonists. For the rest they recommended another attempt to establish district councils, the vesting in the new legislative councils of a power to change their own constitutions, a schedule to the Act providing for a sum of money for the support of public worship by the four Churches in each colony, the legislative councils not to be subjected to any other restriction on their public expenditure, and the adoption of a uniform tariff by all four colonies based on the existing tariff of New South Wales.

They recommended the appointment of one of the governors of the Australian colonies as a governor-general. He would be authorized to convene a general assembly of between twenty and thirty delegates elected by the legislatures of the different colonies, with legislative authority over the following: duties upon imports and exports; the conveyance of letters; the formation of roads, canals or railways traversing any two or more of such colonies; the erection and maintenance of beacons and lighthouses; the imposition of dues or other charges on shipping in every port or harbour; the establishment of a general supreme court to be a court of original jurisdiction or a court of appeal for any of the 'inferior courts of the separate provinces'; the determining of the extent of the jurisdiction and the forms and manner of proceeding of such a court; the regulation of weights and measures; the enactment of laws affecting all the colonies represented in the general assembly on any subject not specifically mentioned in the preceding list but on which the general assembly should desire to legislate by address for that purpose presented to them from the legislatures of all those colonies; and the appropriation to any of the preceding objects of such sums as may be necessary, by an equal percentage from the revenue received in all the Australian colonies, in virtue of any enactments of the general assembly of Australia. They had the impression, they said, that the necessity of creating some such general authority for the Australian colonies had begun to be seriously felt.

On 30 August 1850 Grey wrote to FitzRoy that the Act had at long last received the royal assent on 5 August. He explained that Her Majesty's Government had had no other object in view but that of establishing in the Australian colonies a system of government founded on those British principles of well-regulated freedom under which the British Empire had risen to so high a pitch of greatness and power. Under this Act the territories then comprised within the District of Port Phillip should be separated from the colony of New South Wales and erected into and henceforth formed a separate colony, to be known and designated as the 'Colony of Victoria'. The governor and legislative council of New South Wales were to determine the number of members of the legislative councils of both New South Wales and Victoria, provided one-third was appointed by Her Majesty and two-thirds elected by the inhabitants of each colony. The governor and council of New South Wales was to divide both colonies into suitable electoral districts. The qualifications for voting were that a man be twenty-one years old and a natural-born or naturalized subject of Her Majesty, and that he have freehold estate of £100 situated within the district for which the vote was to be given, or be the occupier of a dwelling house of the clear annual value of £10 per annum. The authority of the governor and legislative council of New South Wales over Victoria was to cease on the issuing of writs for the elections. Legislative councils were to be created in Van Diemen's Land and South Australia not exceeding twenty-four members each, of whom one-third were to be nominated by Her Majesty and two-thirds elected by the inhabitants of the colony concerned, the existing councils in those two colonies to cease to exist on the issuing of writs for the first elections. A legislative council of a similar composition might be established in Western Australia as soon as they were in a position to defray the expenses of the civil establishment from the revenues of the colony. The governors and legislative councils of New South Wales, Victoria, Van Diemen's Land and South Australia were empowered to establish new electoral districts, alter existing electoral districts, and increase the number of members, provided they did not upset the one-third nominated/ two-thirds elected proportion.

The governors of Victoria, Van Diemen's Land, South Australia and Western Australia, with the advice and consent of their legislative councils, were to have power to make laws for the peace, order and good government of their respective colonies, and appropriate to the public service all revenues from taxes, duties, rates and imposts, provided no such law was repugnant to the laws of England, or interfered with the sale or appropriation of lands belonging to the Crown or with the revenue arising therefrom. Each legislative council was empowered to create district councils, as provided in the Act of 1842 for the better government of New South Wales and Van Diemen's Land. The governors and legislative councils of the four colonies were empowered to alter the constitutions of their legislative councils, provided that all such proposed amendments were to be reserved for the signification of Her Majesty's pleasure. On petition from the inhabitant householders of the district northward of the 13° S. those districts might be detached from New South Wales and formed into a separate colony or colonies. Under the schedules to the Act the salaries of the governors, the chief justices, the judges, the senior civil officers and public worship were permanently provided for, there being no sum provided for public worship in the schedule for the colony of South Australia.[62]

---

[62] Report of Select Committee of Trade and Plantations on Future Constitution of the Australian Colonies. Papers Relative to the Proposed Alterations in the Constitutions of the Australian Colonies, pp. 36-7, *P.P.*, 1849, xxxv, 1074; An Act for the Better Government of Her Majesty's Australian Colonies, 13 & 14 Vic., vol. 159, 5 August 1850, *Statutes at Large*, vol. 20; Grey to FitzRoy, 30 August 1850, C.O. 202/58.

In Perth there was the pain of sensing that they had been left behind in the race for material progress and free institutions. In Adelaide the good bourgeoisie were delighted that their susceptibilities on government aid to religion had been respected by not including any sum for public worship in the schedule to the Act. That gave them something of what they were after—a society in which liberty of conscience lived side by side with dunghill oligarchs. The conservatives feared that the local Political Association in Adelaide might ask for universal franchise as the only possible way to salvation. They also feared that since the British Government had not so far abolished transportation those fire-brands in Sydney might again talk about independence and a republic for the Australian colonies.[63]

In Hobart Town the bells of Trinity Church rang out a merry peal, ships' sirens hooted in the harbour, houses were illuminated at night, the inmates of the Orphan Schools and the local alms-house were given liberal extra rations of food. Five hundred sat down to dinner in the Government Paddock at which the food was 'exclusively colonial'. After the celebrations, doubts began to gnaw in the minds of the colonists. They wondered whether they would ever be free from the curse of their past. They had all been so contaminated by the habits acquired in the convict era that they might not be capable of bearing the burden of freedom. Both electors and elected might be open to bribery, and political liberty might only exacerbate the antagonism between the descendants of the bond and the descendants of the free. In Hobart, Launceston and the Midlands convictism had left this terrible legacy of doubt in its descendants of their own powers: convictism had lamed them for generations to come.[64]

By contrast in Port Phillip both joy and confidence knew no bounds. The Geelongites set their town in a blaze of light on the night of 11 November. The following day at noon the guns boomed from Flagstaff Hill in Melbourne and two attempts were made to launch a balloon, but the spring winds proved too strong. November 14 was set aside as a day of thanksgiving in the churches. Four to five hundred strong gathered in St James's, St Peter's, St Francis', Scots Church and the Wesleyan Chapel to hear the priests and deacons assure them that the glad tidings were another proof of how 'a Lord God omnipotent' reigned over all of them. The following day was a public holiday. Shops were closed. A huge crowd gathered to watch La Trobe open the new bridge over the Yarra. The 'hat and feathers', as the press called him, declared the bridge open to all the people of—what should he say—Port Phillip or Victoria, for he went on making these effeminate jokes even in the moment of their manhood. Then they dispersed, the freemasons to the Rainbow Inn for a cold collation, convivial harmony and toasts to friendship, love and truth; the Teetotallers to a tea meeting and some excellent songs; the

[63] *South Australian Register*, 2, 6, 13, 15, 19, 23, 27, 28, 29 November 1850, 2 December 1850; Young to Grey, 25 February 1851, C.O. 13/72.
[64] *Hobart Town Courier*, 6, 16, 20, 23, 27 November 1850; Denison to Grey, 17 February 1851, C.O. 280/274.

Germans to their club where British and German flags were displayed side by side; and the native police to much meat and grog provided by whitefellows who wanted blackfellows to celebrate the arrival of 'big one separation'.

Up-country, too, the whitefellow went mad for a season. At Kilmore, with fires blazing all around the town, the proprietor of the local inn, Mr Reay Clarke, provided 'sober tack' free for the teetotallers, followed by a dinner. Up at Horsham there were scenes of riot and excess among the shearers. One drunkard perched on a stump and began to howl in imitation of a wild dog much to the amusement of a group of drunken whites and a tribe of blacks. Down at Portland there were scenes of mirth and gaiety as the people lit bonfires and danced on the bluff beside that huge sea to celebrate their liberation from 'the great Australian shark'. By the beginning of December the madness had passed. On 5 December the *Argus* thanked a Mr Wilkie for relieving the monotony of their somewhat prosaic city with a concert. By then they had heard that Sydneysiders were maliciously dubbing Melbourne 'only a provincial town', to which the *Argus* retorted to those 'drivelling old washerwomen in Sydney' that they begged to say Melbourne was no longer a provincial town, that it now had perfect equality in all political matters with their 'most greedy and unworthy sister'.[65]

In Sydney the radical press, led by the *People's Advocate* and *Freeman's Journal*, hailed the Act as their saviour from those French revolutionaries and 'Red Republicans' who proposed to use the bodies of their enemies to manure the soil for some future human harmony in Australia. A new radical newspaper, the *Empire*, which began weekly publication on 28 December 1850 under the editorship of Henry Parkes, wrote of their good fortune on entering the field at a time when enlarged franchises and powers of government were about to be worked out by the native talent and energy of the country. Liberals and radicals were warned to be on their guard when the Legislative Council determined the electoral districts because then the 'Norfolk Island Patriot' and his two hangers-on, Martin and Dangar, were certain to move for acres rather than men. The Tories of New South Wales were not like the old-fashioned Tories of England with their 'broadcloth without and their warm heart within'. Nor were they distinguished by the enlightenment of modern liberalism. They had all the qualities of Australian newness and might be styled, said the *Empire*, 'the platypus of our stagnant political pool'.[66]

One of the themes for the celebrations of Anniversary Day on 26 January 1851 was the future greatness of New South Wales as a commercial country replacing the old plantation convict labour society. Another was their pride in creating a society in which the working classes were indistinguishable from their superiors in society, and looked as proud and happy and as well dressed and handsome as the best amongst any gay crowd of Sydneyside

[65] *Argus*, 12, 14, 19, 22, 23, 28, 30 November 1850, 2, 5, 6, 24 December 1850.
[66] *People's Advocate*, 2 November 1850; *Freeman's Journal*, 3 October 1850; *Empire*, 28 December 1850, 11 January 1851.

Saxons. Over in England hopes were being entertained that industrial civilization would achieve what no other society, religious creed or political ideology had been able to achieve, namely, to unite humanity into one fold. Men were contrasting humanity's march forward in an industrial society with civilizations such as the Chinese in which a people had come to a dead stop. Some predicted that the material well-being that industrial society would provide for every man would make revolution there as likely as the falling of the moon.[67]

The important thing was to abolish transportation quickly lest revolution come to the Australian colonies before industrial civilization spread its beneficent, calming influence. In Melbourne on 1 February 1851 the opponents of transportation held a public meeting at which those present agreed to form the Australian League, the members of which would accept the League and Solemn Engagement of the Australian Colonies. They vowed not to employ any persons hereafter arriving under sentence of transportation for crime committed in Europe. They vowed to use all the powers they possessed, official, electoral and legislative, to prevent the establishment of English prisons or penal settlements within their bounds, to refuse assent to any projects to facilitate the administration of such penal systems and to seek the repeal of all regulations and the removal of all establishments for such purposes. They vowed that from 1 January 1852 they would refuse all dealings, intercourse and fellowship (so far as might be consistent with religious or natural obligations) with any and all colonists who might be found advocating or endeavouring to procure the transportation of British convicts to the Australian colonies. They vowed solemnly to engage with each other to support by their advice and their money all who might suffer in the lawful promotion of this cause, and never to dissolve their league until the transportation of convicts to the Australian colonies finally ceased.

They saw themselves as men who wanted to unite Australia into one moral confederation against social degradation so that they might raise in the Pacific a civilization worthy of and similar to the name, the language and the institutions of their fatherland. They called on Australia's greatest son, William Charles Wentworth, to join their noble cause, but he would have nothing to do with these men who wanted to plant British philistinism in the ancient, barbaric land of his birth. In Hobart the self-appointed spokesmen for the convict community asked what was going to be the fate of four-fifths of the population if these British philistines were allowed to leave an eternal brand of infamy on the soul of a people, and convict-haters and one-time white nigger-drivers to take over the government of the colony. The Tasmanians should copy the splendid example of America and declare that

[67] *S.M.H.*, 28 January 1851; Journal of T. B. Macaulay, 1 May 1851 (MS. in library of Trinity College, Cambridge); Charles Dickens, 'The Chinese junk', *Examiner*, 24 June 1848; *Household Words*, 7 June, 5 July 1851; C. Hobhouse, *1851 and the Crystal Palace* (London, 1937); Y. French, *The Great Exhibition* (London, 1951); Asa Briggs, *Victorian People* (London, 1965), ch. 2.

all men were created equal and endowed by their creator with certain inalienable rights—life, liberty and the pursuit of happiness.[68]

In the meantime people in the Australian colonies went about the trivial round and the common task oblivious of what was in store. The convicts of Van Diemen's Land continued to be punished by their overseers for idleness, insolence, negligence, drunkenness, indecently passing water in a public street, lifting the dresses of young girls, being found in the beds of women who were not their wives, drinking in a public house during divine service, not having proper control of their horse in a public street, and continuing to talk when ordered to be silent. In Melbourne the Irish held meetings to refute charges against their immorality and incapacity as servants, Bishop Goold praised Catholic orphan girls for refusing to become 'perverts' (his word for an apostate), and asked God to reward them for their attachment to the faith. In South Australia men continued to boast of their pride and satisfaction in the material prosperity of their province, and the steady advance in their moral condition. They continued to behave like goldfish who never doubted that the particular walls of their aquarium—British institutions, liberty of conscience and private property—would always protect such wonderful creatures while they feasted with a proper decorum at the banquet of life. In Sydney, Henry Parkes was deploring the contrast between the great pulse of life in the Old World and their own stagnant pool.[69]

Out in the Never Never things seemed as though they would never change. The great dryness, the dearth of inland water transport and the precarious, slow means of land transport by coach over the few made roads, on horseback, or by bullock-dray forcing its way through mud and dust over the trackless wastes and miles of solitude, had imposed a never-changing pattern of life. At distances of forty to sixty miles from each other small numbers of people clustered in towns: in Gundagai there were 234 men and 163 women in 1851, in Albury 263 men and 179 women, in Yass 370 men and 283 women, in Ipswich 530 men and 402 women, and in Braidwood 116 men and 96 women. Not even Christmas brought relief from the monotony of these dull country towns. In the hilarious season the only relief men found from the heat, the flies and drudgery was in the local temples dedicated to Bacchus. People in towns like Mudgee, Bathurst or Albury had to wait at least fourteen days for a reply to any correspondence they might have about the things that matter in life—love, money or physic.

[68] *Argus*, 3, 4 February 1851; *S.M.H.*, 13 February 1851; *Cornwall Chronicle*, 18, 25 January 1851; *Irish Exile*, 12 October, 2 November 1850; *Hobarton Guardian*, 26 February 1851, 21, 28 September 1850; W. Denison to E. D. Thomson, 29 October 1850 (Denison Papers, vol. 2, microfilm in M.L.).

[69] Example taken from Record Books of Male Convicts and Record Books of Female Convicts Arriving in Van Diemen's Land, 1848, 1849 and 1850 (T.S.A.); *Argus*, 22 November, 24 December 1850; extracts from minutes of the proceedings of the Legislative Council of South Australia, 21 February 1851, encl. in Young to Grey, 25 February 1851, C.O. 13/72; *S.M.H.*, 8 February 1851; *Empire*, 11 January 1851; Diary of J. Goold, April and 18 October 1850 (MS. in Catholic Archives, Archdiocese of Melbourne).

In those towns the convicts had practically disappeared. Ipswich had thirty convicts, Gundagai one and Braidwood two. Each town had its own flour mill, its school, its court-house and gaol and its churches. For by mid-century in the Australian bush two buildings in a tiny hamlet testified to the memory of that day over three hundred years earlier when the single monk led astray by private judgement had set himself against a body which had been held as the repository of absolute truth for a thousand years and more. Outside each church two tiny out-houses testified eloquently to the truth of the proposition in the Book of Genesis, 'Male and female created He them.' The very names in common usage symbolized the way of life. Albury was known as 'Sleepy Hollow'; Gundagai was known as the town of 'Lazy Harrys'. In these country towns those weighed down by the curse of earning their living with the labour of their hands amused themselves on holidays with games such as climbing the greasy pole, horse-racing and chasing the pig.[70]

Already there were signs that a great change was coming. In March 1850 Sir Charles FitzRoy made a flying visit to an iron foundry at Mittagong. At Berrima and other centres people were talking about how they would be able to market their goods once a railway was built. On 3 July ten thousand people gathered at Redfern in Sydney to watch Mrs Keith Stewart, the daughter of Sir Charles FitzRoy, cut the first turf for the first railway in Australia with a spade manufactured from materials indigenous to Australia. Charles Cowper, the chairman of the Sydney Railway Company, spoke briefly on the influence of the railway on the social and moral advancement of the colony. The English ensign was hoisted at the spot where the turf was turned. After the ceremony John Lamb, one of the few merchants in Sydney's Squatting Club, the Legislative Council of New South Wales, proposed the loyal toast to the Queen, and spoke of the effect the electric telegraph would soon have on isolation and distance. Cowper spoke again some affectionate words about Prince Albert and how, if he had his way, a railway would girdle the earth. Sir Charles FitzRoy cheered them by predicting that the railway would be especially beneficial to a country that was wholly destitute of internal water communication and in which a scattered population prevented the formation of good roads. Over the viands and wines of a first-rate description those present were given a vision of an Australia in which bush barbarism, material backwardness, isolation, alienation and solitude would gradually disappear.

While men were dreaming dreams of the future of humanity in Australia, Edward Hargraves left Guyong near Bathurst on 12 February 1851 with a companion and moved down the course of the Lewes Pond Creek searching for gold. He scratched the gravel, filled a pan with the earth, and washed the

[70] Grey to FitzRoy, 27 January 1849, C.O. 202/56; *Argus*, 30 November 1850; Census of the Colony of N.S.W. taken on the 1st of March 1851, *V. & P.* (L.C. N.S.W.), 1851, vol. 2; W. A. Bayley, *Border City* (Albury, 1954), pp. 23-5; A. C. Butcher, *Gundagai: its history, verse and song* (Gundagai, 1956), pp. 5-7; *S.M.H.*, 7 January 1850; *Cornwall Chronicle*, 21 August 1850; *Heads of the People*, 1 January 1848; *Household Words*, 6 April 1850, p. 43; *Bell's Life in Sydney*, 5 January 1850; Barron Field, *Geographical Memoirs of New South Wales* (London, 1825), p. 497.

dirt away till he saw that speck he was looking for. 'There it is!' he exclaimed. 'This is a memorable day in the history of New South Wales. I shall be a baronet, you will be knighted, and my old horse will be stuffed, and put into a glass-case, and sent to the British Museum.' That did not happen to Hargraves, or his man, or his horse, for they were not destined to gain prizes in the great lottery of life. But something was about to happen to the land about which men of renown in China, India, Indonesia, Catholic Christendom, Protestant England, and Europe of the Enlightenment had dreamed their own great dreams. An iron rail was about to tether the mighty bush to the world of British industrial civilization.[71]

[71] *S.M.H.*, 22 March 1850; E. H. Hargraves, *Australia and Its Gold Fields* (London, 1855), pp. 114-16; G. Blainey, *The Rush That Never Ended* (Melbourne, 1963), ch. 2; *People's Advocate*, 6, 13 July 1850; *S.M.H.*, 4 July 1850.

16

EPILOGUE

FOR THE MIGHTY MEN of renown who had their moments of glory in the days before the levelling flood of industrial civilization flowed over the land the mysterious powers in charge of the universe administered some cruel blows. Ben Boyd was seen with a pick and pannikin working the auriferous sand in California. That proving just as gigantic a failure for him as all his schemes in Australia, in June 1851 he sailed again in the *Wanderer* from San Francisco for the islands of the Pacific, still with greed in the heart, and heaven having no part in his dream of grandeur. At the island of Guadalcanal on 15 October he went on shore with a native of Panapa. He was never seen again. Those people he had once wanted to recruit for his plantations in New South Wales ate 'Massa Boyd'.[1]

The hero of the epic voyage down the Murrumbidgee and the Murray in 1829–30 and the voyage to central Australia in 1844–6, Captain Charles Sturt, decided to take his family back to England in 1853 because his wife was not able to get domestic servants in Adelaide. He retired to Cheltenham where over tea and cakes he had many helpful conversations with Lady Eliza Darling, wife of the one-time Governor of New South Wales, about what life would be like in the world to come. Twice he asked to be appointed a governor of a colony in recognition of his meritorious services in Australia, but each time he was told 'Her Majesty regrets . . .' In 1869 he asked to be given one of the new knighthoods specially created for men with a distinguished record in any of Her Majesty's colonies, but when the letter saying 'Yes' was on its way to Cheltenham, the kingdom of perpetual night took him. Her Majesty graciously allowed his wife to use the title he had coveted. Lady Sturt lived on with that droop of disappointment at the corners of the mouth as a hint of what she and the Captain had done to each other, and what life had done to both of them.[2]

William Grant Broughton hastened down to the gold-fields at Bathurst and urged the diggers to help him build a church. Seizing a pick-axe the old man dug a hole himself. When the building was finished he put on his

[1] M. Boyd, *Reminiscences of Fifty Years* (London, 1871), pp. 104-8; J. Webster, *The Last Cruise of the Wanderer* (Sydney, n.d.), pp. 111-23; C. Nicholson to A. Cunningham, 12 February 1851 (Cunningham Papers, vol. 3, MS. in M.L.).

[2] C. Sturt to A. Sturt, August or September 1856 (S.A.S.A.); J. H. L. Cumpston, *Charles Sturt* (Melbourne, 1951), ch. 12; C. Sturt to Sir George Grey, 20 April 1869 (Sturt Papers, Rhodes House, Oxford); daguerrotype of Lady Sturt at 'The Grange', the last home of Captain Sturt in Adelaide, personal visit, 5 August 1970.

episcopal robes and solemnly proclaimed, 'I set apart this building to the worship of God the Father, Son, and Holy Ghost'. He told the diggers to beware of the Church of Rome, to beware of those 'zealots of a wild excess of private judgment, and the advocates of a contumacious self-will' and to follow the middle way of truth. Worn out by years of hardship, and witness to his majestic vision of man's destiny, he set out for England in August 1852. The members of his faith farewelled him on 14 August in the school-room attached to St Andrew's Cathedral. They listened with 'tearful atten-tion' as he told them of the 'largeness' of that vision that had sustained him during his days in New South Wales, and his exhortation to them to live in brotherly love and forbearance. There was about the gathering that solemnity of being present at a great moment. He had been like that 'good bishop' described by Saint Paul in the Epistle to Titus: 'a steward of God; not self-willed, not soon angry, not given to wine, no striker, nor given to filthy lucre. But a lover of hospitality, a lover of good men, sober, just, holy, tem-perate. Holding fast the faithful word.'

Like Saint Paul's 'good bishop' he had believed there were 'many unruly and vain talkers and deceivers . . . whose mouths must be stopped', and he had followed the advice of the apostle and 'rebuked them sharply'. His tragedy was that those 'unruly and vain talkers and deceivers' came from the creative forces of his day, while his own voice belonged to those forces which, once heard as a great roar, were destined to drop to a whisper. As he was obliged to travel via South America he decided to use his days there trying to convert people from the excesses and extremes of Rome and the darkness of barbarism. As he sailed up the Thames he heard the guns boom for the death of the Duke of Wellington. In the land of his birth one generation was passing away and another was coming into being. Worn out by his long life in God's service, he declined rapidly after arriving in England, and died in the home of Lady Gipps on 20 February 1853. Those who had loved him arranged for a marble likeness to be placed in Canterbury Cathedral next to the bust of Sir George Gipps. With great wisdom they had Broughton lying down. After the great fever of his life he deserved to sleep well.[3]

On 10 June 1868 Charles Harpur, by then a noble ruin, his giant frame having been scorched and wasted as by a fire, died at Eurobodalla and was buried on the top of a steep hill overlooking the beautiful valley of the Tuross River. On his tombstone his family carved none of those words of hope, but just the simple statement: 'Sacred to the memory of Charles Harpur. Poet. Died June 10th 1868.' As in the days of his youth he was still reluctant to mix with Australians as they were such a bloody lot of fellows, they made him hang his head to call himself a man. For that ghost of the intellectuals lived

[3] J. Bonwick, *Curious Facts of Old Colonial Days* (London, 1870), pp. 49-50; *The Farewell Address of William Grant Broughton . . . Delivered in the School Room, Adjoining the Cathedral Church of St. Andrew in Sydney . . . 14 August 1852* (Sydney, 1853); memorial to W. G. Broughton, Canterbury Cathedral; memorial to W. G. Broughton, St Andrew's Cathedral, Sydney; Epistle of Paul to Titus, 1:7-13.

on—that ghost which alienated them from their fellow-men. So did the 'ghost' of dependence on God live on in other families. Not long after the discovery of gold, Catherine Hope, the daughter of the Reverend Thomas Hassall and granddaughter of the Reverend Samuel Marsden, had a baby which died soon after its birth. She behaved like all the members of her family in their hour of need. When her grandmother died in 1835 dear Grandpapa, Sam Marsden, prayed to God for Christ's sake to take her soul to that happy place God had prepared for all his dear children. So she prayed to God believing He would arrange for her to see her baby again, and allow her to hold her baby in her arms. In all families 'what we have inherited from our fathers and mothers . . . walks in us . . . all sorts of dead ideas and lifeless old beliefs . . . cling to us all the same . . . we are, one and all, so pitifully afraid of the light'.[4]

Taking less and less kindly to the rabid abuse to which every act of his public life was subjected, in 1854 Wentworth sought refuge from the rabble of Australia in the aristocratic society of Dorsetshire. He lived at Wimborne not far from where Thomas Hardy took shelter from the wound that pierced him through. There the ghosts of the past plagued him. A son brought him pain. In the autumn of his life he began to take interest in his destiny in the countless ages which lay before him. He began to find belief in survival after death a source of hope and consolation and to look forward to meeting again in futurity those from whom he was separated in this world. He found comfort in the knowledge that he had an affectionate daughter who was praying for the salvation of her father. The one-time Macbeth of Botany Bay ended his days a lonely, Lear-like exile from his kingdom. He died at Wimborne on 20 March 1872. When his body was brought back from England and placed in the sarcophagus at Vaucluse on 6 May 1873, a clergyman recited those words about the fire that kindles inside a man whose heart is hot within him, what grief and agony it is for such a man to hold his tongue, and how man walks in a vain shadow and disquiets himself in vain. Australia's great Promethean figure was conquered in death by a pale version of the Galilean.[5]

By then the buildings at Wybalenna to house the remainder of the aborigines of Van Diemen's Land were in ruins. The brick chapel in which the great reconciler, George Augustus Robinson, had hoped to dispel the darkness in the hearts of the aborigines and cheer them with a dawn of hope, freedom and happiness, was being used as a shearing shed. Robinson, despairing of ever guiding the aborigines either of New Holland or Van Diemen's Land into the habits of the civilized, and the enjoyment of security

[4] J. Normington-Rawling, *Charles Harpur, an Australian* (Sydney, 1962), pp. 302-9; personal visit to grave of Charles Harpur at Eurobodalla, 2 January 1973; T. Hassall to his children, 3 October 1835 (Hassall Correspondence, vol. 4, MS. in M.L.); C. Hope to J. Hassall, 28 November 1851 (Hassall Correspondence, vol. 1); H. Ibsen, *Ghosts*, act 2.

[5] W. C. Wentworth to T. Wentworth, n.d. (Parkes Correspondence, vol. 18); *Public Funeral of the Late W. C. Wentworth* (Sydney, 1873); A. C. V. Melbourne, *William Charles Wentworth* (Brisbane, 1934), ch. 4; Thomas Hardy, 'The Wound' in *Collected Poems of Thomas Hardy* (London, 1919) p. 436; Florence Emily Hardy, *The Life of Thomas Hardy* (London, 1962), p. 149.

from the oppression of bad men, left for England in 1853. He died in 1866 at Bath where Arthur Phillip, the first captain-general and governor-in-chief to be enjoined in solemn words to conciliate the affections of the black men by treating them with amity and kindness, had also died. The forty-four aborigines who were moved from Wybalenna to the convict barracks at Oyster Cove in 1847 wasted away from neglect, disease, association with poor whites, and that insidious apathy and drunkenness of a people who had been forcefully separated from all that gave meaning and purpose to their lives. In 1863 the high-minded were still saying that sin would lie heavily at the doors of the white men if those who were blessed with civilization and Christianity neglected to perform the simplest duties laid upon them by the requirements of Christian charity for the six surviving aborigines at Oyster Cove. But the aborigines continued to live in the 'profoundly dirty' penal establishment which was swarming with fleas.

By 3 March 1869 only Truganini was left. In her childhood she had hunted on Bruny Island where in June 1777 the mighty Captain Cook had given each of her ancestors a string of beads and a medal which they had received with great satisfaction. In her halcyon years her beauty of appearance had caught the eye of the painter Thomas Bock. Between 1830 and 1833 she had worked with Robinson to persuade her people to surrender to the white man. In her middle years she only just escaped being hanged for a murder in the Port Phillip District. Later she had pined away on Flinders Island, soaking the earth there with her tears as she yearned for the old life on the island of her birth. In old age she lived at Lalla Rookh in Macquarie Street, Hobart, where she enjoyed her glass of beer and tobacco by day, and a nightcap of hot ale spiced with ginger and sugar. By then her face expressed the horror of what had happened to the people. The occasional gusts of ferociousness which still swept over her face were the sole sign of the suffering of her people. As the intimations of death became unmistakable she was seized with the terror that the white man would again use her body for the advancement of his science and his learning. On 3 May 1876 she called her housekeeper, Mrs Dandridge, to tell her of yet another terror: the devil was on her hand and would not go away. She asked Mrs Dandridge to catch him. In the middle of that great torment she fell into unconsciousness, the power of speech was lost to her, and she passed away to her eternal rest as peacefully as a child on 9 May. She was said to be the last of the aborigines in Van Diemen's Land. The Cape Barren Islanders, a mixture of Tasmanian aborigine, Australian aborigine, Polynesian, American whaler, convict bolter and British seaman, lived on as the sole survivors of the coming of the white man into the South Seas. Rock carvings such as at the Mersey Bluff near Devonport, some place names, and the paintings of Duterrau, Bock, Glover, Prout and de Wesselow, were also left behind as a sign to posterity that they had been here.[6]

---

[6] J. Bonwick, *The Last of the Tasmanians* (London, 1870), pp. 274-94, 391-400; C. Turnbull, *Black War* (Melbourne, 1965), pp. 226-36; R. Travers, *The Tasmanians: the story of a doomed race* (Melbourne, 1968), pp. 226-30; *Mercury* (Hobart), 9 May, 6 June 1876; Report of Ven. Archdeacon Reibey of Half-Caste Islanders in Bass's Strait,

While the aborigines of Van Diemen's Land were disappearing from the face of the earth, the white man was rapidly putting into effect the counsel of Abel Tasman to leave such a mark on all the land of New Holland and Van Diemen's Land that those who came after them might become aware that they had been here. In August 1852 the first steamship arrived in Sydney from England. On 12 September 1854 the electric telegraph was first used in Sydney. Between 1851 and 1861 the number of white men increased from 437 665 to 1 168 149. As British philistinism and industrial civilization began to leave their mark on the ancient barbaric land, another voice was added to the conversation of mankind in Australia. Since time immemorial there had been the cry of the crow and the melancholy chant of the aborigine. After 1788 the men in black taught their fellow-men that the hearts of the sons of men were filled with evil, and that madness was in their hearts while they lived. The bush barbarians added their sardonic comment that Australians were certain to be down on their luck. But as industrial civilization provided the machines with which to subdue the mighty bush, some Australians began to dream a great dream: that they could banish the Old World errors and wrongs and lies, that Heaven and Hell were priests' inventions and that they could build a paradise in the land that belonged to them.[7]

---

26 August 1863, paper no. 48 of Legislative Council of Tasmania, 1863; personal visit to Oyster Cove, Adventure Bay on Bruny Island, and site of *Lalla Rookh*, 12-13 May 1973; J. Bonwick, *Daily Life and Origin of the Tasmanians* (London, 1870); J. E. Calder, *Some Account of the Wars, Extirpation, Habits, &c., of the Native Tribes of Tasmania* (Hobart Town, 1875), pp. 104-15; H. Ling Roth, *The Aborigines of Tasmania* (Halifax, 1899).

[7] Deas Thomson Papers, vol. 1; Pakington to Denison, 14 December 1852, C.O. 408/37; Pakington to FitzRoy, 15 December 1852, C.O. 202/60; *Argus*, 12 September 1854; these events will be described in the final volume of this history; Henry Lawson, 'Song of the Republic' in *Bulletin*, 1 October 1887; see also Henry Lawson (C. Roderick, ed.), *Collected Verse* (3 vols, Sydney, 1967-9), vol. 1, p. 1.

APPENDIX

THE COUNTIES OF NEW SOUTH WALES

1. Definition of limits of settlement, *Sydney Gazette*, 6 September 1826.
2. Definition of the Nineteen Counties, *Sydney Gazette*, 17 October 1829.
3. Sir Thomas Mitchell's map of the Nineteen Counties, 1831.
4. Proclamation of the Nineteen Counties, 26 November 1835.
5. Definition of the boundaries of the Counties of Macquarie and Auckland. *New South Wales Government Gazette*, 28 February 1843.
6. County of Bourke, 13 September 1838. *New South Wales Government Gazette*, 30 May 1838.
7. County of Grant, 3 October 1839. *New South Wales Government Gazette*, 6 July 1839.
8. County of Normanby, 15 October 1840. *New South Wales Government Gazette*, 22 July 1840.
9. County of Stanley (Brisbane, Ipswich area), 27 February 1843. *New South Wales Government Gazette*, 28 February 1843.

THE DISTRICTS OF NEW SOUTH WALES

1. Proclamation of the Nine Districts of New South Wales, 21 May 1839. *New South Wales Government Gazette*, 22 May 1839.
2. District of Port Macquarie divided into Macleay River District and Clarence River District, 1 March 1842. *New South Wales Government Gazette*, 4 March 1842.
3. District of New England divided into New England District and Darling Downs District, 11 May 1843. *New South Wales Government Gazette*, 12 May 1843.
4. Proclamation of Lower Darling District and change of boundaries of Liverpool Plains, Bligh and Wellington, and extension of western districts to the River Darling, 4 December 1847. *New South Wales Government Gazette*, 7 December 1847.
5. Proclamation of District of Port Phillip, 21 May 1839. *New South Wales Government Gazette*, 22 May 1839.
6. Division of Port Phillip District into Western Port District and Portland Bay District, 1 July 1840. *New South Wales Government Gazette*, 8 July 1840.
7. Division of Port Phillip District into Gipps Land District, Murray District, Western Port District and Portland Bay District, 13 September 1843. *New South Wales Government Gazette*, 15 September 1843.

8. Division of Port Phillip into Gipps Land District, Murray District, Western Port District and Wimmera District, 9 November 1846. *New South Wales Government Gazette*, 10 November 1846.

9. Proclamation of District of Moreton Bay, 5 May 1842. *New South Wales Government Gazette*, 10 May 1842.

10. Proclamation of District of Darling Downs, 11 May 1843. *New South Wales Government Gazette*, 12 May 1843.

11. Division of Liverpool Plains District into Liverpool Plains District and Gwydir District, 4 December 1847. *New South Wales Government Gazette*, 7 December 1847.

12. Boundaries of Moreton Bay, Darling Downs and Gwydir Districts amended to create Moreton District, Darling Downs District, Gwydir District, Wide Bay District, Burnett District and Maranoa District, 7 November 1848. *New South Wales Government Gazette*, 7 November 1848.

LIVERPOOL PLAINS

Tamworth

Kempsey

Hastings River

Port Macquarie

MACQUARIE

BLIGH   BRISBANE

Hunter River

Manning River

GLOUCESTER

Goulburn River

DURHAM

Dungog

Stroud

Booral

PHILLIP

Mudgee

Clarence Town

Sedham

Port Stephens

WELLINGTON   HUNTER

Maitland

NEWCASTLE

ROXBURGH

Colo River

NORTHUMBERLAND

BATHURST   COOK

Rydal

Nepean River

Hawkesbury River

BATHURST

WESTMORE-

LAND

Emu

CUMBERLAND

Cox R.

SYDNEY

Lachlan

GEORGIANA

Wollondilly River

Appin

Botany Bay

Berrima

WOLLONGONG

River

KING   ARGYLE

CAMDEN

Lake Illawarra

Goulburn

River

Kiama

Yass

Shoalhaven

Shoalhaven

Murrumbidgee

Jervis Bay

River

MURRAY   ST VINCENT

Bateman Bay

0   10   20   30   40 MILES

0   20   40   60 KM

Settled districts when sales started
22. 7. 1826

Australian Agricultural Co. land

Nineteen counties, 14. 10. 1829

5 *The Counties of the Middle District of New South Wales*
Based on *Map of the Colony of New South Wales*, R. Dixon, London, 1837

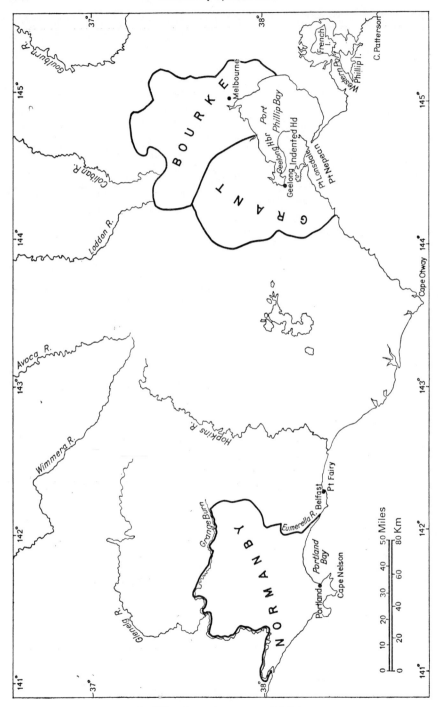

6   *The Counties of Port Phillip*
Based on *A Map of Australia Felix*, T. Ham, Melbourne, 1847

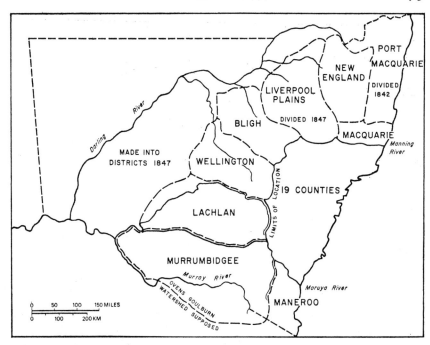

7   *The Districts of the Middle District of New South Wales*
Based on *Map of a Portion of Australia*, W. Baker, Sydney, 1841

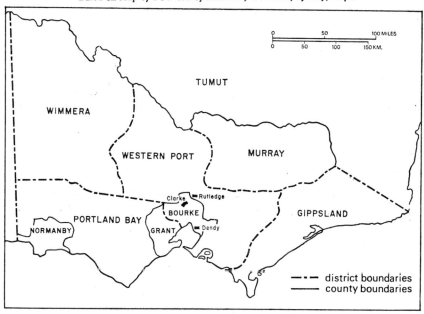

8   *The Districts of Port Phillip*
Based on *A Map of Australia Felix*, T. Ham, Melbourne, 1847

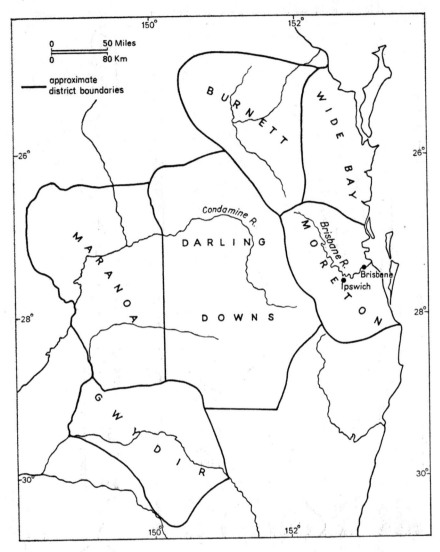

9 *The Districts of the Northern District of New South Wales*
Based on *Map of the Eastern Provinces of Australia*, J. Arrowsmith, London, 1852

SOURCES

A general bibliography for the period 1822 to the present is planned in the fourth and final volume.

I GUIDES, INDEXES AND BIBLIOGRAPHIES

Adam, M. I., Ewing, J. and Munro, J. *Guide to the Principal Parliamentary Papers relating to the Dominions 1812-1911*. Edinburgh, 1913.

Cambridge History of the British Empire, vol. 7, pt 1, Australia. Cambridge, 1933, pp. 645-718.

Concise Guide to the State Archives of New South Wales. Sydney, 1970.

Crowley, F. K. *A Guide to the Principal Documents and Publications relating to the History of Western Australia*. Perth, 1949.

———*South Australian History: a survey for research students*. Adelaide, 1966.

Department of History, University of Melbourne. *An Outline List of Documents Mainly in the Public Library of Victoria and relating to the History of Victoria*. Melbourne, 1949.

Dillon, J. L. and McFarlane, G. C. *An Australian Bibliography of Agricultural Economics 1788-1960*. Sydney, 1967.

Dixon, W., Dennis, J., Musgrave, A. and Whitley, G. (eds). *Index to Titles of Articles, Authors and Illustrations contained in Volumes 1-43 of the Journal and Proceedings of the R.A.H.S.* Sydney, 1958.

Ferguson, J. A. *Bibliography of Australia*, 4 vols, 1784-1850. Sydney, 1941-55.

Fuller, G. H. (ed.). *A Selected List of References on Australia in the Library of United States Congress*. Washington, 1942.

General Index to the Accounts and Papers, Reports of Commissioners, Estimates etc. 1801-1852, *P.P.* 1854, LXVIII, 159.

General Index to the Reports of Select Committees 1801-1852, *P.P.* 1854, LXX, 509.

Greenwood, G. (ed.). *Australia: a social and political history*. Sydney, 1955, pp. 418-27.

Guide to Collections of Manuscripts relating to Australia. National Library, Canberra, 1965- .

Hewitt, A. R. *Guide to Resources for Commonwealth Studies in London, Oxford and Cambridge*. London, 1957.

———*Union List of Commonwealth Newspapers in London*. London, 1960.

Higher Degree Theses in Australian University Libraries: a union list. Hobart, 1967.

Jeffrey, W. J. *The Edinburgh Review (Index to) Extracts relating to Australasia, the South Pacific and the Malay Archipelago, 1801-1884.* Sydney, 1911.

———*The Quarterly Review (Index to) Extracts relating to Australasia, the South Pacific and the Malay Archipelago.* Sydney, n.d.

Mander-Jones, Phyllis (ed.). *Manuscripts in the British Isles relating to Australia, New Zealand and the Pacific.* Canberra, 1972.

Mozley, Ann. *A Guide to the Manuscript Records of Australian Science.* Canberra, 1966.

Newspapers in Australian Libraries: a union list. 2nd ed., Canberra. 1966.

Politzer, L. L. *Bibliography of German Literature on Australia 1770-1947.* Melbourne, 1952.

Roe, M. *Quest for Authority in Eastern Australia 1835-1851.* Melbourne, 1965, pp. 234-48.

Simpson, D. H. *Biography Catalogue of the Library of the Royal Commonwealth Society.* London, 1961.

Ward, J. M. *Earl Grey and the Australian Colonies, 1846-1857.* Melbourne, 1958, pp. 471-90.

II MANUSCRIPT MATERIAL

The author has found the following collections of manuscripts most useful for his purposes:

Mitchell Library, Sydney

Archer Papers	Logan Papers
Arthur Papers	Macarthur Papers
Broughton Papers	Mackenzie Papers
Close Papers	Marsden Papers
Cowper Papers	Mitchell Papers
Cunningham Papers	Port Phillip Association Papers
Currie Papers	Stephen Papers
Denison Papers	Stirling Papers
Hassall Papers	Therry Papers
Henty Papers	Thomson (Deas) Papers
King Papers	Towns Papers
Lang Papers	Wentworth Papers
Leichhardt Papers	

National Library of Australia, Canberra

Broughton Papers	Mowle Papers
Collie Papers	Murray Papers

La Trobe Library, Melbourne

Batman Papers	Henty Papers
Fawkner Papers	La Trobe Papers
Gipps–La Trobe Correspondence	Todd Papers

Royal Historical Society of Victoria
  Willis Papers

Tasmanian State Archives
  Franklin Papers
  Gregson Papers

Northern Region Library, Launceston
  Papers on John West and Anti-Transportation Movement

Royal Society of Tasmania Library, Hobart
  Boyes Diary

Oxley Library, Brisbane
  Leslie Letters

South Australian State Archives
  Angas Papers
  Hayward Papers
  Sturt Papers

Battye Library, Perth
  Molloy Letters
  Spencer Papers
  Stirling Papers

University of New England Library, Armidale
  Dangar Papers
  Everett Papers

Old Farm, Strawberry Hill, Albany
  Spencer Papers

Benedictine Monastery, New Norcia
  Salvado Papers

Royal Geographical Society, London
  Franklin Papers
  Maconochie Papers

Rhodes House, Oxford
  Sturt Papers

Scott Polar Research Institute, Cambridge
  Franklin Papers

Australian National University Archives
  Australian Agricultural Company Papers

Private Collections
  Dumaresq Papers, Mt Ireh, Longford, Tasmania
  Dutton Papers, Anlaby, South Australia
  Historical Collection of A. J. and Nancy Gray, Scone, N.S.W.

III PRINTED MATERIAL

See the guides and bibliographies above and the footnote references in this and preceding volumes.

IV PORTRAITS, LANDSCAPES, LITHOGRAPHS, ETC.

There are valuable collections in the public libraries and art galleries of the six states, and in the National Library in Canberra. For a guide to this material, and some valuable comments on it, see Eve Buscombe, Artists and Their Sitters: a colonial portrait (thesis in Chifley Library, Australian National University, Canberra), and N. J. B. Plomley, *Thomas Bock's Portraits of the Tasmanian Aborigines* (Launceston, 1965). See also the valuable pictorial catalogue of the Mitchell Library in Sydney.

V CEMETERIES AND OTHER BURIAL PLACES

The inscriptions on the tombstones in the following cemeteries were found useful:

Norfolk Island Cemetery	Christ Church, Illawarra
St John's, Parramatta	Kirklands, near Campbelltown
St Mary's Cathedral, Sydney	St David's Park, Hobart
St Matthew's, Windsor	St Peter's, Richmond
Wentworth Mausoleum, Vaucluse	Wybalenna Cemetery
Koroit Cemetery	Benedictine Monastery, New Norcia
Melbourne General Cemetery	Busselton Cemetery
Phillip Island Cemetery	Old Farm, Strawberry Hill, Albany

In country districts such as Bega, Menangle, Chiltern and Eurobodalla those looking for a sign of where it all started may find a hint scratched on what remains of the stone erected over those who lie below.

Seekers may also find much written on memorial plaques in such churches as St James's, St Andrew's, St Mary's, Pitt Street Congregational Church in Sydney, St James's, St Francis and St Paul's in Melbourne, Trinity Church in Adelaide, St George's in Perth, Monastic Church at New Norcia, Church of England at Albany, St John's in Brisbane and St John's in Canberra.

One other source was to go to the site where the event occurred. These are listed in the footnotes. The only two not listed there were perhaps the most fruitful of all. One was to stand at the South Head of Sydney Harbour and gaze at what Magellan called that 'very vast sea', and then gaze at Sydney Harbour. That was always exhilarating and always rewarding because it turned the mind towards what this country did to those who made the long journey over the oceans. A regular visit to the Henry Lawson statue in the Sydney Domain, on the other hand, turned the mind towards what men have done to each other in Australia.

INDEX

by Dorothy F. Prescott

Place names have been qualified by the current state name in order to facilitate identification in current locational guides, e.g. Melbourne (Victoria) rather than Melbourne (Port Phillip). Entries relating to individual churches, newspapers, journals, magazines, and ships are grouped under the collective headings 'churches', 'newspapers, journals and magazines' and 'ships'. Abbreviations are as follows: G.B., Great Britain; P.Ph., Port Phillip; L.C., Legislative Council; N.S.W., New South Wales; N.T., Northern Territory; N.Z., New Zealand; Q., Queensland; S.A., South Australia; Tas., Tasmania; V.D.L., Van Diemen's Land; Vic., Victoria; W.A., Western Australia.